Theorizing the Moving Image brings together a selection of essays written by one of the leading theorists of film over the last two decades. In this volume, Noël Carroll examines theoretical aspects of film and television through penetrating analyses of such genres as soap opera, documentary, and comedy, and such topics as sight gags, film metaphor, point-of-view editing, and movie music. Throughout, individual films are considered in depth. Carroll's essays, moreover, represent the cognitivist turn in film studies, containing in-depth criticism of existing approaches to film theory, and heralding a new approach to film theory.

D1344515

THEORIZING THE MOVING IMAGE

Cambridge Studies in Film

GENERAL EDITORS
Henry Breitrose, *Stanford University*
William Rothman, *University of Miami*

ADVISORY BOARD
Dudley Andrew, *University of Iowa*
Anthony Smith, *Magdalen College, Oxford*
Colin Young, *National Film School*

OTHER BOOKS IN THE SERIES

Film and Phenomenology, by Allan Casebier
Metaphor and Film, by Trevor Whittock
The Gorgon's Gaze: German Cinema, Expressionism, and the Image of Horror, by Paul Coates
Renoir on Renoir: Interviews, Essays, and Remarks, by Jean Renoir (translated by Carol Volk)
The Taste for Beauty, by Eric Rohmer (translated by Carol Volk)
The British Documentary Film Movement, 1926–1946, by Paul Swann
Chinese Cinema: Culture and Politics Since 1949, by Paul Clark
The "I" of the Camera: Essays in Film Criticism, History, and Aesthetics, by William Rothman
Nonindifferent Nature: Film and the Structure of Things, by Sergei Eisenstein (translated by Herbert Marshall)
Constructivism in Film: The Man with the Movie Camera, by Vlada Petrić
Inside Soviet Film Satire: Laughter with a Lash, Andrew Horton, editor
Melodrama and Asian Cinema, by Wimal Dissanayake
Film at the Intersection of High and Mass Culture, by Paul Coates
Another Frank Capra, by Leland Poague
Russian Critics on the Cinema of Glasnost, Michael Brashinsky and Andrew Horton, editors
Projecting Illusion: Film Spectatorship and the Impression of Reality, by Richard Allen

THEORIZING THE
MOVING IMAGE

NOËL CARROLL
University of Wisconsin, Madison

CAMBRIDGE
UNIVERSITY PRESS

Published by the Press Syndicate of the University of Cambridge
The Pitt Building, Trumpington Street, Cambridge CB2 1RP
40 West 20th Street, New York, NY 10011-4211, USA
10 Stamford Road, Oakleigh, Melbourne 3166, Australia

First published 1996

Library of Congress Cataloging-in-Publication Data
Carroll, Noël (Noël E.)
    Theorizing the moving image / Noël Carroll.
      p. cm. – (Cambridge studies in film)
    ISBN 0-521-46049-2. – ISBN 0-521-46607-5 (pbk.)
    1. Motion pictures – Philosophy. 2. Television – Philosophy.
    3. Television broadcasting – Philosophy. I. Title. II. Series.
    PN1995.C358 1996
    791.43′01 – dc20   95-21558
                                                CIP

A catalog record for this book is available from the British Library.

ISBN   0-521-46049-2 Hardback
         0-521-46607-5 Paperback

Acknowledgments

The original places and dates of publication of articles in this anthology are as follows: "Medium Specificity Arguments and the Self-Consciously Invented Arts," *Millennium Film Journal*, nos. 14/15 (Fall/Winter 1984–5), pp. 127–53; "The Specificity of Media in the Arts," *Journal of Aesthetic Education*, 19, no. 4 (Winter 1985), pp. 5–20; "Concerning Uniqueness Claims for Photographic and Cinematographic Representation," *Dialectics and Humanism*, no. 2 (1987), pp. 29–43; "The Power of Movies," *Daedalus* (Fall 1985), pp. 79–103; "Toward a Theory of Film Suspense," *Persistence of Vision*, no. 1 (Summer 1984), pp. 65–89; "As the Dial Turns," *Boston Review*, XIII, no. 1 (February 1988), pp. 5–6, 20–1; "Toward a Theory of Point-of-View Editing," *Poetics Today*, 14, no. 1 (Spring 1993), pp. 123–42; "Notes on Movie Music," *Studies in the Literary Imagination*, XIX, no. 1 (Spring 1986), pp. 73–81; "Notes on the Sight Gag," *comedy/cinema/theory*, edited by Andrew Horton (Berkeley: University of California Press, 1991), pp. 25–42; "Avant-Garde Film and Film Theory," *Millennium Film Journal*, nos. 4/5 (Summer/Fall 1979), pp. 135–44; "Causation, the Ampliation of Movement and Avant-Garde Film," *Millennium Film Journal*, nos. 10/11 (Fall/Winter 1981–2), pp. 61–82; "Language and Cinema," *Millennium Film Journal*, nos. 7/8/9 (Fall/Winter 1980–1), pp. 186–217; "A Note on Film Metaphor," *Journal of Pragmatics* forthcoming; "From Real to Reel," *Philosophic Exchange*, (1983), pp. 5–46; "Reply to Carol Brownson and Jack C. Wolf," *Philosophic Exchange*, (1983), pp. 59–64; "The Image of Women in Film," *Journal of Aesthetics and Art Criticism*, 48 no. 4 (Fall 1990), pp. 349–60; "Film, Rhetoric and Ideology," *Explanation and Value in the Arts*, edited by Salim Kemal and I. Gaskell (Cambridge University Press, 1993), pp. 215–37; "Film/Mind Analogies," *Journal of Aesthetics and Art Criticism*, XLV, no. 4 (Summer 1988), pp. 489–99; "Hans Richter's *Struggle for Film*," *Millennium Film Journal*, no. 19 (Fall/Winter 1987–8), pp. 104–12; "A Brief Comment on Frampton's Notion of Metahistory," *Millennium Film Journal*, (Fall/Winter 1986–7), pp. 200–05; "Cognitivism, Contemporary Film Theory and Method," *Journal of Dramatic Theory and Criticism*," VI, no. 2 (Spring 1992), pp. 199–219; "A Reply to Heath," *October* (Winter 1983), pp. 81–102; "Film History and Film Theory," *Film Reader*, no. 4 (1979), pp. 81–96; "Art, Film and Ideology," *Millennium Film Journal*," (Winter/Fall 1983–4) no. 15, pp. 120–32; "Toward a Theory of Film Editing," *Millennium Film Journal*, no. 3 (Winter/Spring 1979), pp. 79–99.

Transferred to digital printing 2001

Dedicated to My Brothers
Hugh Felix Carroll III
and
Patrick Joseph Carroll

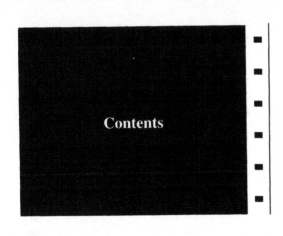

Contents

Contents

FOREWORD

by David Bordwell

"Classical" film theory, usually taken as spanning the fifty years or so before the rise of semiology in the mid-1960s, was often concerned to define film as an art. Theorists such as André Bazin, Rudolf Arnheim, and the Soviet Montage directors sought to isolate distinctively cinematic principles of representation and expression. These were investigated with an eye to the artistic qualities of films and the aesthetic experience of audiences.

Yet in recent years, the film-as-art approach has seemed to many a dead end. Semiologists often saw no reason to distinguish between aesthetic and nonaesthetic sign systems; psychoanalytically-inclined theorists treated the art/non-art distinction as irrelevant to the study of cinema's relation to the unconscious, and theorists pursuing ideological critique often charged that the very concept of aesthetics was a heritage of "bourgeois idealism."

Today much of this reaction looks shortsighted. Many objectors understood aesthetics as a batch of ahistorical speculations on art and beauty, and this notion, quaint even then, can no longer be seriously sustained. It has become clear that aesthetics, conceived as an open-ended inquiry into the problems surrounding the arts and art criticism, has much to teach film studies – not least in serving as a model for what energetic, enlightening theorizing might look like.

Over some twenty years, Noël Carroll's work has displayed many of the benefits which the aesthetic mode of inquiry offers to scholars in the humanities. What we have in this first collection of his essays is a positive, wholly up-to-date effort to make progress in some problems around cinema.

This progress is marked, initially, by a position of skepticism. Contemporary film scholars often want to believe in some theory or another, with the consequence that they accept many theoretical claims uncritically. Carroll starts with the assumption that any theory, from the most intuitively obvious to the most flagrantly uncommonsensical, should be able to summon rational arguments on its behalf. Most famously, Carroll's skepticism has led to the scrutiny of 1970s and 1980s film theory carried out in *Mystifying Movies* (1988). Here, through painstakingly close reading and analysis, Carroll shows that much of contemporary film theory rides on equivocation, overgeneralization, misplaced analogies, and sheer appeal to authority. If the influence of this strand of contemporary theory is waning now, Carroll's book is one major cause.

Carroll's skepticism toward current developments is not a conservative reflex. He displays no nostalgia for the good old days. *Philosophical Problems of Classical Film Theory* (1988) scrutinizes three major traditional thinkers (Arnheim, Bazin, and V. F. Perkins), and it finds each position problematic. "We must start again": The last line of *Mystifying Movies* is no less appropriate as Carroll's verdict on these classical theories.

For this reason, perhaps the strongest initial impression left by Carroll's first two books is his skeptical rejection of major positions. But his third book, *The Philosophy of Horror* (1990), examined a cluster of problems around the structure, effect, and social functions of "art-horror" fictions. Here the critique of alternative theories throws into relief his own solution to the problem of the design and appeal of such tales. In the course of his investigations of the horror genre, he also confronts and makes progress on such general matters as suspense and character identification.

The collection you now hold is similarly balanced between criticism and theory-building. Although some pieces undertake demolition jobs, most are devoted to constructive theorizing. And the breadth of inquiry is striking. Carroll takes on several issues that crop up in the traditional literature – medium specificity, visual metaphor, the realism of documentary. But he also addresses issues which post-1980s film theory put on the agenda. He asks how films function ideologically, whether an avant-garde film can proffer a theory, how film theorists can engage with feminism, how a political theory of cinema might become viable.

As we might expect, Carroll sets forth some fairly unorthodox views. He argues that ideology, rather than involving depth-psychological processes such as "subject-positioning" and "identification," is better considered in the light of the folk wisdom of maxims and the practical reasoning mobilized by informal rhetoric. He proposes that the "images-of-women" research tradition rejected by some feminists is in many ways more tenable than the view that patriarchal power is exercised through the look. He suggests that a promising model for politics-based theorizing can be found in Hans Richter's work. He argues for the view that documentary films can, in significant respects, be objective and yield knowledge.

Many of these arguments will be attractive to readers beyond the narrow precincts of media studies. Yet insiders who may instinctively resist Carroll's claims must reckon with the fact that he cannot be caricatured as the hidebound advocate of theory as it once was. He argues, for instance, that there is no "nature" or onto-logical essence of an art medium – that indeed the very existence of art media is radically contingent. Instead of essentialism,

Carroll advocates sensitivity to historical context. But his conception of history harbors no "grand narratives." There are only norms, styles, and practices, each with a fine-grained causal history. And this historical sensitivity is required for all theorizing: any film theory, classic or modern, which ignores the history of the medium is likely to blind itself to counterexamples and plausible alternatives. Moreover, history is conceived not as "the facts" or sheer data. Carroll insists on the theory-governed quality of research programs.

This project, then, squarely faces the challenges flung down by contemporary theorists. If it often displays skepticism toward those theorists' conclusions, it does so on the basis of a sophisticated conception of research and theoretical disputation. "Empiricism," "positivism," "scientism," and other labels freely plastered up nowadays will not stick to Carroll's account. (They are all due for discard anyhow.) If you doubt this, turn immediately to the essay "Cognitivism, Contemporary Film Theory and Method," wherein Carroll spells out a subtle version of "fallibilism," the belief in approximate, comparatively reliable knowledge as a realistic goal of scholarly inquiry. If *Theorizing the Moving Image* does nothing else, I hope it makes it impossible for film theorists to claim that a position proposing such a goal is inevitably vitiated by a faith in "certainty," "absolute truth," or "disinterested knowledge."

Carroll's conclusions, whether or not they chime with the dominant opinion of the moment, arise from a very different process of reasoning than is common in the humanities today. Much of contemporary theory in literature, art, and film consists of assembling received doctrines of vast generality, recasting them to fit one's interests, yoking them to other (often incommensurate) doctrines, and then applying the result to a task at hand (typically, interpreting a particular art work). If the theorist undertakes analysis of a theory, the process usually focuses on rhetorical argument rather than logical inference. The reasoning routines of contemporary film theory warrant a separate study, but it seems fair to say that few writers engage in an activity of advancing, *for criticism and rebuttal,* reasonably well-justified conceptual analyses and inferences. There is something called Theory, to be quoted or mimicked, but not much theorizing.

Carroll does theory differently. He identifies a problem area – say, medium specificity, or analogies between film and mind, or sight gags. Instead of immediately dragging onstage a big theory on loan from elsewhere (Derrida on Kant, Freud on jokes), Carroll tries to focus on a medium-level question, such as what features of mainstream movies might lend themselves to cross-cultural comprehension.

This inquiry is not staged in a vacuum. Few theorists in any academic specialty command as wide a range of knowledge as does Carroll. He mobilizes the literature of the visual arts, theater, dance, music, and the philosophy of mind and history in order to canvass theoretical answers to the target question. He thereby surveys a wider range of opinions than one normally finds in a film essay. And there is usually a surprise. (Who else found Löker on suspense?)

Out of this survey there crystallize some alternative positions. Carroll holds the view, common enough in domains of philosophy I believe, that if knowledge is approximate and only relatively reliable, our best theories will be those which emerge as most plausible from a competitive field. Put another way, there is no perfect theory; there is only a theory which is, right now, to be reasonably preferred to its rivals.

In order to compare theories, they may need some sympathetic clarification or restructuring. It is not noted frequently enough that, before the talk turns critical, Carroll is at pains to provide quite plausible versions of some of the positions he eventually rejects. Some contemporary theorists might even owe him thanks for making their positions more intelligible and appealing than they have managed to do.

Now comes the analysis. How informative, consistent, and cogent are the concepts informing the view under discussion? How wide is the evidence base? (Carroll makes diabolical use of counterexamples.) What distinctions need making, for example, in the concepts of "point of view" or "objectivity?" What is presupposed or implied by the theory, and is that presupposition absurd? The ideas must be *worked through,* and there are no shortcuts or free rides. This is not Theory but theorizing, and in Carroll's hands it is exhilarating.

Part of the pleasure is that the activity stands open to all. Carroll refreshingly avoids the appeal to authority, the tactic of "My source can lick your argument," the belief that quoting Bakhtin somehow counts as a criticism of Chomsky. (Recall the old complaint: when confronted with an objection, a Structuralist would answer with a bibliography.) Appeal to authority intimidates the interlocutor (maybe I haven't read your source) and encourages either uncritical acceptance or unreasoning rejection. Carroll operates on a level playing field; anyone with an argument can get into the game, but then skill will be required to keep up.

Having examined the competitors, Carroll lays out their difficulties. (If he didn't, he wouldn't have undertaken the task of theorizing in the first place.) He then proposes a more plausible alternative. Whatever its virtues, it will at least seek to avoid the faults already diagnosed. More often, it will have a few extra values – clarity, cogency, coverage. But faithful to his fallibilism, Carroll will acknowledge the partial, approximative nature of his results. What matters is that some progress has been made, not that some new dogma has been established. Open-ended and corrigible, theories can only be provisional pausepoints, moments in the activity of doing theory.

Significantly, the result will not have to mesh with all our other beliefs about things cinematic. Carroll's account of ampliation in editing will not be drafted to reinforce his attack on medium specificity. A theory of "verbal images" will not necessarily shore up a conception of why psychoanalytic conceptions of "the look" are weak justifications for ideological critique. One of Carroll's theories might be better justified than another; they come in separate packages. Thus no one theory stands or falls by the fate of its mates.

The result is rather unexpected. If your theory consists largely of applications of one Big Theory (or an amalgam of several), then every question you pick out will have similar answers. If you have only a hammer, every problem looks like a nail. But if your theoretical work is driven by intriguing questions and nagging problems, there is no guarantee that all your conclusions will hook up into something called a theory of film. Carroll welcomes the upshot: unlike his predecessors, both classical and contemporary, he does not offer us a system.

This "piecemeal" theorizing has startling implications. What could be more unnerving, even to the most self-consciously radical media theorist of today, than the cheerful acknowledgment that if there is no Big Theory of Everything, there is no Big Theory of Everything about Motion Pictures? But it is a natural consequence of treating film aesthetics as a mode of philosophical inquiry and debate. And the reward is that, in cultivating unorthodox views and pursuing a rigorous method of reasoning, Carroll simply risks being original.

All this is set forth in a direct, often amusing prose. The style cultivated by many contemporary theorists offers evidence for Nietzsche's remark that readers often consider something deep just because they cannot see to the bottom. Carroll's style, by contrast, lives by one precept: Let each sentence be impossible to misunderstand. Not the smallest pleasure of this book is its effort to be the most lucid, unshowoffish piece of academic film writing of recent years.

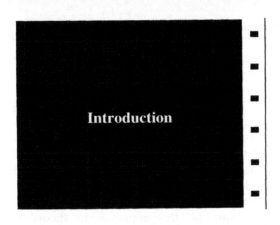

Introduction

This book is a collection of my essays – mostly old, but some new. They are all concerned with theorizing moving images. The term "theorizing moving images" is perhaps obscure and warrants some immediate comment. It is not just a fancy way of saying film theory. I prefer the idiom of *moving images* rather than *film* because I predict that what we call film and, for that matter, film history will, in generations to come, be seen as part of a larger continuous history that will not be restricted to things made only in the so-called medium of film but, as well, will apply to things made in the media of video, TV, computer-generated imagery, and we know not what. It will be a history of motion pictures or moving pictures, as we now say in ordinary language, or, as I recommend we call it, a history of "moving images," of which the age of film, strictly speaking, is likely to be only a phase.

Moreover, I prefer "moving images" to "moving pictures," since *pictures* imply recognizable representations, whereas by "images" I mean to signal that much of the art that concerns us has been and will be nonrepresentational and abstract. Many of the essays in this book were written in terms of film. But, in retrospect, it seems to me that none of the theories I advance in this book need be taken to be film-specific; they all pertain to the aesthetics of moving images. For although the artform was born in film and although when I started writing about it I thought I was merely a film theorist, I now believe that it is more accurate for us to be thinking in terms of the broader concept of moving images.

In naming my domain of inquiry, not only have I substituted "moving images" for "film," but I have replaced "theory" with "theorizing." By doing this, I intend to lay emphasis on theorizing as an activity – an ongoing process rather than a product. Many of the essays in this volume bear titles like "Toward a Theory of This or That," or "Notes on Such and Such," or "An Outline of. . . ." These titles are meant to acknowledge the provisional nature of my hypotheses. I present them to other theorists for criticism and for comment; I admit that they can sustain refinement and expansion, perhaps by theorists other than myself. And, of course, some of my hypotheses will probably have to be abandoned once they are subjected to rigorous scrutiny. I regard these articles as contributions to a continuing dialogue, not the last word on the subject.

To say "a theory of film" or "the theory of film" has a ring of finality about it. It makes it sound as though our research is finished and the topic closed. But I would not want to leave the impression that I think that film theory has been completed between the covers of this book. Indeed, I think it's hardly begun.

Another problem that I have with calling what I've been doing "a theory of film" is that it suggests a singular, unified enterprise. But I do not believe that there is *a* theory of film, or *the* theory of film. Rather, there are film theor*ies,* or, as I say, "theories of the moving image." There are theories of film narration and of metaphor, of editing and acting. I, at least, do not proceed on the presumption that these will all add up to one theory, organized by a single set of principles or laws. Rather, my own work has been piecemeal, theorizing one mechanism of cinematic articulation or confronting one problem at a time.[1]

Thus, this volume is a collection of theories, not a theory of film, nor even a theory of the moving image. Many of the theories are involved in isolating and explaining specific devices or structures or mechanisms of cinematic signification including erotetic narration, variable framing, modifying music, sight gags, point-of-view editing, suspense, weak and strong ampliation, verbal images, film metaphors, and so on. Some of these small-scale or piecemeal theories can be connected into larger constellations, such as my conception of the power of movies, but others are autonomous. For example, neither my account of sight gags nor my account of film metaphor is connected to a larger theoretical framework that pertains uniquely to cinema.

Moreover, the activity of theorizing herein is not simply restricted to explaining cinematic devices. I also address some long-standing theoretical questions that arise out of film practice, such as whether nonfiction films can be objective, and whether avant-garde films are theoretical. Conjectures are also offered on the way in which to talk about the ontology of film, about the film medium, and about cinematic representation. In short, there are a lot of different things discussed in this book, and they don't add up to a single, unified theory of film, or of anything else, for that matter.

This, I believe, is as it should be. Sociology is not reducible to a single unified theory. It is comprised of many different theories of different levels of generality – theories of the homeless in America, of the caste system in India, of modernization in developing countries, of socialization, and so on. My conception of film theory is similar. It is not a matter of producing a grand theory that will answer every question in our area of study by reference to a foundational set of laws or principles. Rather, it is the activity of answering a gamut of general questions about the practice of making and receiving moving images. And since these questions can be raised at different levels of generality – how do films make metaphors? what is a documentary? – we should expect to find a range of different

kinds of answers, many of which may not segue into one neat story of the sort previously called a theory of film.

For me, film theorizing involves posing general questions – such as how does point-of-view editing work? – and then attempting to answer them. I have called this piecemeal theorizing, and this book is a collection of the piecemeal theorizing I've done for nearly twenty years. It is my opinion that this approach to theory is rather different than the kind of work done by the classical film theorists, like Arnheim, Kracauer, and Bazin, on the one hand, and by contemporary film theorists, like Heath and Silverman, on the other hand. Both classical film theory and contemporary film theory strike me as grand theory, the attempt to ground a comprehensive perspective of film on certain foundational principles, whether those concern the ontology of the cinematic image or subject positioning.

Classical film theory, of course, focused more on the analysis of the so-called film medium, whereas contemporary film theory has been preoccupied with questions of ideology. And yet both approach the subject as a unified field. Both try to isolate either an essence or a function of film. And having isolated that essence or function to their own satisfaction, these theorists go on to refer every question of cinema back to it. My own suspicion has been that film cannot be reduced to a single essence or function, and, correspondingly, I do not presume that our theories will result in a tidy package. Rather than an essence or a function of film, what we have are a lot of questions about film. Answering them will not yield a single theory, but a collection of piecemeal theories. I hope that this book will provide a fruitful approximation of some of them.

I also would like to add that I think that the piecemeal approach to theorizing is, in many ways, liberating. It is a very intimidating prospect to imagine that what a film theorist must do is to erect a totalizing theory that has something informative to say about every aspect of cinematic practice. It is far more practicable to proceed by posing well-defined questions about cinema. More people are likely to engage in original theorizing when the sights are lowered. More progress is likely to ensue if prospective theorists work on solving precise problems that can be answered manageably. Of course, I do not recommend piecemeal theorizing for its heuristic value; I think that the likelihood of a grand theory of film is slim. But one mustn't overlook the fact that a piecemeal approach makes theorizing more accessible at the same time that it brings theory down to earth.

Many of the theories in this volume are apt to be rebuked as formalist, insofar as they concentrate on the communicative operation of certain devices – like variable framing – without commenting on their political or ideological significance. The reason for this is that I do not believe that such cinematic devices are inherently ideological. This, of course, is an issue that sets me apart from most contemporary film theorists. However, it is important to stress that in spite of the fact that some of my analyses are what they call formalist, my overall position is not formalist, since, given my piecemeal disposition, along with the fact that I agree that some films are ideological (sexist and racist), I think that we can ask about the ways in which film and TV disseminate ideology and sexism. Indeed, these are theoretical questions that I attempt to answer in some of the essays in this volume. Thus, there is no reason to suppose that an approach to film theory like mine is antithetical to the sort of ideological research that preeminently interests film scholars in the United States and Britain today.

I do not think that all of our questions about film are political, nor do I think that all of our questions are reducible to gender. But I agree that some are of this sort, and I have even tried to begin to answer some of them. Thus, I am not a formalist; I do not think that questions of politics and gender

are irrelevant to film studies. At the same time, I do think that certain questions about the workings of moving images do not entail questions of politics. But that cannot be misconstrued as formalism, since I also believe that the ideological operation of cinema raises legitimate questions for theory.

This volume is divided into seven parts. Part I deals with questions about the nature of the film medium and the nature of cinematic representation. Much of this section is critical. It is directed against the notion that film can be analyzed in terms of its possession of a unique, determinate medium that has directive implications about what artists should and should not do. Indeed, the arguments in this section travel farther afield than film and mount a general attack of the doctrine of medium specificity across the arts. Throughout, I try to encourage a general skepticism about the theoretical usefulness of the ideas of *the medium* for aesthetic theorizing in general and for film theorizing in particular.

In this section, I also consider the case for photographic realism, the view that there is something ontologically unique about photographic and cinematic images, and I reject it. However, Part I is not completely negative. It concludes by attempting to construct an account of the moving image, although the ontological framework that I propose is neither medium-specific nor essentialist.

In a manner of speaking, Part I represents my brief against the notion of film theory that dominates the classical tradition. That tradition attempted to organize its accounts of film around foundational conceptions of the essence of cinema, typically thought of in terms of the putative medium of film. That is, a conception of the medium/essence of film that provided theorists like Kuleshov and Bazin with the keystone that held their unified theories together. But I have eschewed an essence, a medium, and a keystone, and, with them, the promise of a unified theory. Instead, I proceed by answering questions, loosely organized under headings that pretend to neither exhaustiveness nor exclusiveness.

That is, for organizational purposes, I begin by accepting the traditional, rough-and-ready distinction of film into different modes: the movies, avant-garde film, and the documentary. Part II is a group of essays concerned with movies, under which rubric I include not only mainstream fiction film, but also commercial, narrative TV fiction. In this section, I offer theories of movie suspense, point-of-view editing, movie music and sight gags. Each of these is a piecemeal theory. At the same time, in Part II, I also offer an overarching theory about what makes certain devices appropriate to the movies, given the intention of movie makers to command mass audiences. This provides one way in which to organize our thinking about movies. But I don't think that all our theoretical questions about movies can be assimilated into this framework. For instance, my discussion of sight gags in this section isn't subsumed under the larger questions that I deal with under the label of "the power of movies."

Despite the fact that much of the discussion in Part II revolves around film, I mean it to apply to mass market TV as well. And the essay on soap operas, of course, deals directly with TV. I also suspect that many of the devices that I discuss in this section will also figure in CD-ROM and other computer-imaging technologies, where their operation will be accountable pretty much in the ways that I've suggested they already work in film and TV.

Part III concentrates on avant-garde film and the documentary. This is a traditional way of carving up the field and I've followed it. Nevertheless, I admit that this may not be the best way of proceeding. Avant-gardists and documentarists often complain about being segregated in this way. But I, at least, have no ax to grind here. This grouping is purely a matter of tactical convenience; it is not my point to marginalize or ghettoize these modes in any way.

This section comprises a mixed bag of concerns. On the one hand, it addresses certain perennial questions raised by these modes, namely, can nonfiction films be objective, and are avant-garde films really theoretical? My answer to the first question is *yes* and to the second question, it is *no*. I suspect that neither of these answers corresponds to received wisdom. Perhaps they will serve to reopen the debate.

The rest of Part III is involved in isolating and analyzing several mechanisms of figuration in motion pictures, including what I call ampliation, the verbal image and film metaphor. I have included them in the section on the avant-garde because figuration is often associated with the avant-garde and because many of my examples of these cinematic figures come from avant-garde films. But, of course, this grouping is a bit arbitrary, since the devices in question can also appear in movies and in documentaries as well. And, of course, many of the narrating strategies that I've discussed in the section on movies can also appear in avant-garde and documentary films. So, as I've already indicated, the division between Part II and Part III is a matter of convention, not theory.

During my career, I have gained a reputation as a dogged critic of contemporary film theorists. But now let me say one (brief) kind word about them. Even though I think their theories have been consistently misguided, many of the topics that they have put on the table for discussion are good ones. Many of my own theories about the movies, for example, were developed in response to questions that they raised for which I sought better answers. In no other section of this book than in Part IV am I more indebted to contemporary film theorists, since without their persistent concern with ideology and gender I might not have appreciated the urgency that led me to initiate my own theories about these issues. In Part IV, as always, I am very critical of contemporary film theory, but even I must acknowledge the contribution involved in placing these items on the agenda. I should also add that the essays in Part IV are somewhat programmatic, sketching research which I intend to amplify in future writing.

Part V is devoted to essays on the history of film theory. It comprises essays on Hugo Munsterberg, Hans Richter and Hollis Frampton. Perhaps because of my background in philosophy, I have always tended to read theorists from the past as part of a continuing dialogue. Thus, in the essays on Munsterberg and Richter I have tried to locate issues in their theories that are relevant for contemporary discussions. And, I have addressed their theories critically, as I might address a living theorist. The essay on the late Hollis Frampton is a different matter, since, as a practicing artist, his theorizing was not so much devoted to developing a theory of film in general as it was to theorizing his own film practice. Thus, my article on him is concerned with exposition rather than criticism; it is an attempt to reconstruct interpretively his theory from the inside, given what I take to have been his philosophical presuppositions.

Part VI includes several polemical exchanges with contemporary film theorists, or at least my half of them. Some of the articles are responses to criticisms of my previous objections to contemporary film theory. The article entitled "Cognitivism, Contemporary Film Theory and Method" tries to debunk some of the leading aspersions cast in my direction. It also sets out what I think is a decisive framework for conducting the debate between psychoanalytic film theory and cognitivism – a theoretical stance with which I am often associated, due to my tendency to defend cognitive explanations (explanations that do not advert to the Freudian unconscious) over psychoanalytic ones (especially with regard to film comprehension). However, Part IV

does not only restage old battles; I also try to provoke a new one by criticizing Kaja Silverman's theory of the acoustic mirror.

As a coda, in Part VII, I have included some of my earliest attempts at film theory. Since I am no longer satisfied with them, my first thought was to exclude them from this volume. But at the urgings of anonymous readers, I have incorporated them, since they are still quoted in the literature and since the publications where they originally appeared are hard to come by. I hope that the reader will be able to discern the progress I've made since these early writings. If not, I'm in trouble.

Preparing these essays for republication has been an exercise in autobiography for me. Most of that is of no importance for the reader. However, there is one aspect of my public biography that may merit comment. I began my academic career in film studies in the seventies, but in the eighties I moved into philosophy. And probably, my allegiance to philosophy, especially what is called analytic philosophy, is evident in these pages. However, one would be mistaken if one regarded this text as primarily philosophical. For in spite of the fact that some of the essays are philosophical and even though there are philosophical arguments throughout, the bulk of the text is film theory, not philosophy, where by film theorizing (or theorizing the moving image) I have in mind the activity of proposing substantive hypotheses of a general empirical nature about motion pictures (and images). I do not wish to draw a hard-and-fast line between philosophy and theory; philosophy has a role to play in theory as I conceive it. But at the same time, it should be clear that this volume is not, first and foremost, a series of exercises in conceptual analysis – however much conceptual analysis it contains – but is rather preoccupied most often with developing broad empirical conjectures (substantive theories) about moving pictures (and images).[2]

As well as being identified as a philosopher, I am also often identified as a cognitivist. It is a label that has several senses. As I understand its application to me, the label does not characterize a specific theory. It does not mark my commitment to a determinate body of ideas. It does not mean that I am what is called a cognitive scientist. It does not signal that I am a connectionist. What it indicates is my fixed opinion that many of our questions about film – especially concerning comprehension and reception – can be answered without resorting to psychoanalysis. This is, I believe, the major bone of contention between me and most current practitioners of film theory in the United States and Britain today.

My opposition to psychoanalytic film theory rests on my understanding of psychoanalysis. Psychoanalysis, it seems to me, is a practice that concerns the breakdown of rationality or of ordinary cognitive processing. Thus, psychoanalysis is only appropriate when there is a discernible breakdown in rationality (that is not attributable to somatic malfunction). The domain of psychoanalysis is the irrational. Therefore, if we are able to explain some behavior or some mental phenomena in terms of rational psychology (or somatic malfunction), then there is no pressure to search for psychoanalytic explanations; there is no conceptual space for psychoanalysis to inhabit. It is my diagnosis that a great many (I suspect most) of the questions that film theorists have about film comprehension and reception can be answered in terms of rational or cognitive (and perceptual) psychological hypotheses, or, at least, many of the questions raised by contemporary film theory can be so answered. Thus, in my view, psychoanalysis has been as inappropriate in recent film theory as it has been popular. Indeed, one can read an implicit argument running throughout this book. For every time I launch a theory based on a psychological conjecture in virtue of some rational or cognitive processes, I am in effect arguing for the redundancy of psychoanalysis in the domain in question.

Another point of tension between many contemporary film theorists and me has to do with style. One of the reasons that I left film study for philosophy was my frustration with what I experienced as the predominance of obscurantism in contemporary film theory. Theories were written in a style that was so impossible to understand that it made it difficult to evaluate the claims theorists were advancing. Thus, in my own writing, I have attempted (not always successfully) to be as clear as possible and to outline what I take to be the context of the discussion. I do not think that clarity proves my points. Rather, I think that by being clear, I can make it easier for others to find my errors. For my own conception of theorizing is that it involves a constant process of dialectical criticism and exchange in which the elimination of error is one important, if unspectacular, source of progress.

These essays span nearly two decades. Thus, there are some minor inconsistencies in them, since my views have changed (I hope they've matured) on some issues over time. In some cases, I speak of the medium or of resemblance in ways that diverge from my present views. I also sometimes refer to unconscious processes in the nontechnical, nonpsychoanalytic sense – something I would not do today. However, I have left these minor inconsistencies in the text. Where the reader finds them, she may take my considered view to be generally the one found in the later articles.

I think that, to a large extent, I have been regarded most frequently as a critic of theories, rather than as a constructive theorist. The reason for this is twofold. Some of my best-known articles have been critical; and many of my constructive theoretical pieces have been scattered in small-circulation journals or in journals outside the precincts of cinema studies. Thus, I welcome this opportunity to collect my theorizing in one place. For it provides an occasion to show that my inveterate nay-saying to contemporary film theory does not spring from mean-spiritedness, but from my conviction, based on the research in this volume, that there are better ways of doing theory. With that research assembled in one place, others may now judge for themselves whether my cause has been justified.

Notes

1. Because, as will become evident shortly, I eschew the use of the term "cinematic" in an essentialist or medium-specific manner, I should be specific about what I mean when I use locutions like "mechanisms of cinematic articulation" or "cinematic devices" or "film structures." For me, a cinematic device or mechanism or structure or strategy is simply a device or mechanism or structure or strategy that is used in film. Adjectival modifiers like "cinematic" or "film" carry no implication that the devices, structures, mechanisms, strategies, and so on are unique to film, essential to film, specific to film, peculiar to film, etc. A cinematic device is merely one that we recognize to be in use in film practice. Phrases like "cinematic devices" or "cinematic mechanisms" imply none of the theoretical baggage that go with theories of the peculiarly or uniquely cinematic nature of the film medium. My use of the term "cinematic" in such cases is simply historical. It picks out devices commonly associated with film while acknowledging that similar or parallel devices may also play a legitimate or central role in artforms other than film.

2. By asserting that this volume is primarily theoretical and not philosophical, I mean to be drawing a contrast between it and something like Gregory Currie's immensely interesting and important book *Image and Mind: Film, Philosophy and Cognitive Science* (Cambridge University Press, 1995).

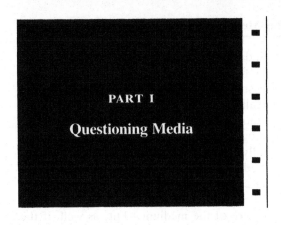

PART I

Questioning Media

When I began graduate studies in film in the early seventies, there was still an abiding obsession with "the cinematic." Certain directors, like Hitchcock, were cinematic; others, like Bergman, were not. Sometimes we called those other directors "literary." It was not a polite way of speaking.

To be cinematic was to exploit the unique features of the medium – to use film as film. It seemed self-evident at the time that the best films were the most cinematic, that they were the best because they were cinematic, and that if anything were to succeed as film, it would be necessary for it to employ the peculiar features of the so-called medium.

This prejudice in favor of the cinematic was not merely a critical bias. It also appeared to be reflected in the major theoretical texts that were available to us – notably Arnheim, the Russians, Bazin, and Kracauer. These theorists thought of film as a unique medium and they appeared to presume that the nature of the medium had stylistic implications. Moreover, this approach to cinema was also reinforced by theoretical approaches in the other arts; the influential aesthetics of Greenberg with respect to painting and sculpture stressed the essential specificity of the medium as well.

Undoubtedly, the doctrine of the specificity of the medium also served what might be called academic-ideological purposes. In those days, there was an initiative to form academic departments of cinema. And the notion of medium specificity was a powerful rhetorical lever for lifting film departments into existence. For if film was a unique medium with a unique practice – one different from literature, theater and fine art – then surely it required its own experts, housed in their own department. People in other disciplines, with approaches geared to other media, were obviously not equipped to understand film as film. Or, so we said. We needed our own discipline in order to study our own unique medium.

I lived inside this view long enough to start to see where the bodies were buried. Teaching it – attempting to make sense of it to others – made me acutely aware of where the doctrine lapsed into incoherence. I could hear myself uttering hypotheses aloud that I realized were only a step or two away from nonsense – assertions frozen midair that I knew would crack under the slightest logical pressure. And that is how the first section of this anthology came to be written. The articles here register my gradually growing skepticism about medium specificity talk. Indeed, the final article in this series worries about whether the notion of *the* medium is of any theoretical use to us whatsoever and suggests that it is not.

The first two articles – "Medium Specificity Arguments and Self-Consciously Invented Arts" and "The Specificity of Media in the Arts" – are overlapping attempts to undermine the view that film and the other arts each possess a *unique medium that has stylistic implications about what should and should not be made in it*. The scope of the third essay – "Concerning Uniqueness Claims for Photographic and Cinematographic Representation" – is more narrow than the previous two essays, insofar as it only focuses on photographic and cinematic *representation*. But it is obviously related to the others, since the putatively unique nature of cinematic representation – its photographic realism – is often cited as the relevant feature of film for our consideration by medium specificity theorists.

The last essay – "Defining the Moving

Image" – returns to the issue of medium specificity with new arguments. Also, it advances a preemptive strike against potentially new briefs for photographic realism. Specifically, it examines how recent reconsiderations of photography by people like Walton, Scruton and Maynard might be used to reinstall the case for photographic realism in cinema and then it goes on to block such a hypothetical attempt.

Of course, even if the doctrine of medium specificity and the sort of essentialism it espouses are false, it still may be the case that cinema has an essence. "Defining the Moving Image" explores that possibility and arrives at five necessary conditions for film, or, as I prefer to call the phenomenon, "the moving image." This falls short of essentialism, though I think that it makes a positive contribution to the ontology of film. So, despite the fact that most of the first part of this anthology is critical, it ends on a constructive note.

This first section has a pivotal role to play for the remainder of this book. Dialectically, it displaces one type of film theorizing in order to make space for another. Part I, in effect, is dedicated to dismantling medium specificity theorizing in order to prepare the stage for the type of piecemeal theorizing that follows in the rest of this volume.

As an approach to film theory, the presupposition of medium specificity has several advantages. Not only does it promote a unified approach to theory, criticism and filmmaking, it may also be used to suggest an evolutionary model for film history, inasmuch as the medium may be thought, in Hegelian fashion, to develop in such a way that it discovers its own unique potentials over time.

The medium specificity model has a tidy theoretical agenda: locate the unique style-implying features of the medium and then find its application across every dimension of film articulation – find the devices that best realize it, or the way in which it can be realized in the deployment of every cinematic device.[1] However, this highly unified program depends ultimately upon successfully locating the specific nature of the medium. And there's the rub. Not only have successive theorists failed to do this – often advancing conflicting candidates as to the nature of the medium – but, as well, if the arguments in this section are correct, it can't be done. And without this particular keystone, the project of medium specificity theory, no matter how pretty in principle, falls apart.

But even if we inhabit the ruins of medium specificity, theory still has enough space in which to thrive. For it remains possible to develop theories of the various devices, modes, genres, techniques, and mechanisms of film, even if they are not referred back to some conception of the overarching essence of cinema. These theories will be piecemeal in contrast to the systematic theories of film organized around conceptions of the specificity of the medium. Thus, Part I disposes of Film Theory in order to make room for the film theor*ies* presented in the rest of the volume.

Notes

1. Though I reject the notion of the "cinematic" as it is used in the opening paragraphs of this section, often throughout the book, I talk about cinematic devices. When I use that phrase, all I mean by it are devices used in film practice. It has no connotations of "uniquely cinematic devices" or "essentially cinematic devices." All I am talking about are historically cinematic devices – devices we recognize as being used in film (whether or not they are used elsewhere as well).

CHAPTER I

Medium Specificity Arguments and the Self-Consciously Invented Arts: Film, Video, and Photography

There are no muses. All the arts were invented by humans. However, in many cases – such as music and dance – that invention (or that process of invention) has been forgotten, lost, as it were, in history. Yet in other cases, arts have been self-consciously created. Sometimes this has been the result of hybridization – the combining of pre-existing artforms, as in opera. Or, as in the case of film, video and photography, artforms have been erected upon the technological discovery of new media. My purpose in this paper is to examine an aspect of the latter cases – the transformation of technological media into artforms. I am especially concerned with the way in which this process has recurrently led the defenders of emerging artforms to resort to medium specificity arguments – i.e., arguments that purport to establish that the new media have a range of aesthetic effects peculiar to them whose exploitation marks the proper avenue of artistic development within the medium in question.

In studying the emergence of film, video and photography as artforms – and in studying the polemics that attend these emergences – one is struck by certain arresting regularities. Each of these artforms appears to undergo an initial phase in which each attempts to legitimatize itself as art by aping the conventions, forms and effects of pre-existing arts. Film initially imitates theater; photography painting; and video imitates film.[1]

However, this strategy for legitimatizing the new medium as a prospective art – i.e., for getting the culture to take the new medium seriously by proclaiming it an ART – eventually evokes a countermovement, one predicated on a purist program. Proponents of this purist program argue that if the medium in question is to be truly regarded as an art, then it must have some range of autonomous effects, effects that are its own and that are not merely copied from pre-existing, established artforms. The purist then specifies the range of effects peculiar to a given medium, and goes on to urge that artists within that medium focus their energies upon experimentation within this range of effects. Needless to say, different theorists will identify different potentials of that medium. Thus, at stage two in our scenario, we are greeted by contesting recommendations about the correct line of stylistic development within that medium – recommendations, moreover, which are each putatively based upon having isolated the peculiar potentials or capacities of the medium in question.

The intent of this paper is to examine the role of medium specificity talk in the debates and criticism of self-consciously invented arts. My major aim is to discredit the philosophical foundations of such talk. I will also try to characterize why proponents of emerging arts are drawn to medium specificity talk, while offering, as well, an account of what I believe such talk really amounts to. However, before embarking upon a critical assessment of medium specificity talk, I think it will be instructive to canvas a wide variety of historical and contemporary examples in order to underscore the extreme extent to which medium specificity talk suffuses, at the very least, certain stages in the development of the self-consciously invented arts of film, video and photography.

Let us begin this review with the history of film. Early film theorists, reacting to charges that film merely mechanically reproduced theater, sought to identify effects said to be unique to film that could serve as a basis for cinematic expressiveness, while also differentiating film from theater. One leading figure in this enterprise was Rudolf Arnheim. He held that in various ways cinematic representation diverged from perfect recording, and, moreover, that by exploiting these divergences – that is, the unique limitations on perfect recording found in cinema – the artist would discover a necessary condition for expression. A close-up, for example, can make an object appear enormous in a way that would not occur in natural perception; a filmmaker, in turn, can exploit this cinema-peculiar failure of perfect reproduction to impart a feeling of power or giganticism in regard to the object photographed. Arnheim writes

A film art developed only gradually when the movie makers began consciously or unconsciously to cultivate the peculiar possibilities of cinematographic technique and to apply them toward the creation of artistic productions.[2]

Summarizing his approach to cinema in a recent article, Arnheim says

The strategy was, therefore, to describe the differences between the images we obtain when we look at the physical world and the images perceived on the motion picture screen. These differences could then be shown to be a source of artistic expression.[3]

So Arnheim believes that cinema has certain medium specific limitations – also, misleadingly I think, spoken of as possibilities – and that artistic expression will derive from cultivating these peculiarities. At the same time, Arnheim believes that the cinematic medium has a special subject matter, rooted in its peculiar nature, which he identifies as the depiction of animated action. (However, Arnheim never explains how this domain of subject matter logically follows from, or otherwise emerges from the types of cinema specific limitations – such as the lack of constancy of scale – which he spends most of his time analyzing.)

Like Arnheim, many Soviet montage theorists, such as Lev Kuleshov,[4] believe that the nature of the cinema medium can be specified and that that specification can direct artistic decision making. For them, montage is the essence of film and stylistic choices in any film concerning scripting, set decoration, lighting, etc., must be subordinated to facilitating rapid editing.

In opposition to the highly assertive stylistic recommendations that Arnheim and montage-essentialists made about the truly cinematic use of film, a group of succeeding theorists, often called realists, identified photographic representation as the essence of the film medium. Such theorists include, most notably, André Bazin and Siegfried Kracauer. Bazin held that a realist style, one that aspires to the impression of passive recording, follows from the essential photographic nature of film. For realists, the assertive, declamatory approach to stylization found in Arnheim and the montagists runs counter to cinema's essential nature as a recording device. Almost the reverse of Kuleshov, Kracauer argues that all the elements of film, such as plot construction, should be subservient to the photographic element, because that element, rather than montage, is the essential ingredient of cinema. Proper film style, for both realists and their predecessors, depends on its basis in the nature of the medium, though, of course, they disagree in their accounts of the nature of cinema.

Nor does the opposition between realists and montagists exhaust the range of essentialism in film. Especially during the seventies, undoubtedly influenced by the sort of gallery essentialism propounded by Clement Greenberg, filmmakers identified their task as that of reflexively revealing or foregrounding the essential conditions of their medium. This, of course, involves identifying film's essential characteristics and conditions. Thus, we encounter works such as Anthony McCall's *Line Describing a Cone*, a thirty-minute film which begins as a line of light which widens until it becomes a cone of light. The purpose of the film is to demonstrate an essential condition of the medium. McCall says *"Line Describing a Cone* deals with one of the irreducibly necessary conditions of film; projected light."[5]

As might be expected, given the fact that photography is a constituent element of cinema, essentialist arguments concerning photography often mirror those concerning film. In *Camera Lucida* Roland Barthes, for example, offers an account of the nature of photography that sounds surprisingly like Bazin's – i.e., photography as an emanation of past reality. And, he, Barthes, conjoins this with an aesthetic preference for photos that afford the viewer the pleasure of discovering unexpected details, a preference again reminiscent of Bazin's *parti pris* for depth-of-field cinematography.[6]

Other, nonconverging accounts of the nature of photography also abound. Paul Strand grounds his defense of the "straight" approach to photography on the notion of medium specificity. He writes

The full potential power of every medium is dependent on the purity of its use, and all attempts at mixture end in such dead things as color-etching, the photographic painting and, in photography, the gum print, oil print, etc., in which the introduction of hand work and manipulation is merely the expression of an impotent desire to paint.[7]

And, he adds,

The photographer's problem therefore is to see clearly the limitations and at the same time the potential qualities of his medium, for it is precisely here that honesty, no less than intensity of vision, is the prerequisite of a living expression. This means a real respect for the thing in front of him, expressed in terms of chiaroscuro . . . through a range of almost infinite tonal values which lie beyond the skill of human hand. The fullest realization of this is accomplished without tricks of process or manipulation through the use of straight photographic methods.[8]

Like Strand, Edward Weston was also opposed to photo-painting – photography that imitates the strategies and conventions of painting. Weston bases his attack on photo-painting in a firm belief in medium specificity. He says

Each medium of expression imposes its own limitations on the artist – limitations inherent in the tools, materials and processes he employs.[9]

Weston goes on to claim that "among all the arts photography is unique by reason of its instantaneous recording."[10] The conception of photography in this light leads Weston to uphold shooting, in opposition to optical or chemical manipulation, as the proper terrain of the photographer.

Continuing this inventory of "essential natures," essentialist grounds have also been proposed for photographic styles inimicable to straight shooting. Laszlo Maholy-Nagy believed that his photograms, directly produced by deploying objects on light sensitive paper, produced perceptions attainable only by means of photography. He holds

The photogram, or cameraless record of forms produced by light, which embodies the nature of photographic process, is the real key to photography.[11]

This recognition is supposed to guide our concern with the productive rather than the reproductive aspect of photography. Moholy-Nagy contends that with photography, light and shadow were for the first time fully revealed.

Through its black-white-gray reproductions of all colored appearances, photography has enabled us to recognize the most subtle differentiations of values in both the gray and chromatic scales: differentiations that represent a new and hitherto unattainable quality in optical expression. This is, of course, only one point among many, but it is the point where we have to begin to master photography's inward properties, and that at which we have to deal more with the artistic function of expression than with the reproductive function of portrayal.[12]

Though essentialist accounts of film and photography continued throughout the seventies, the popularity of medium specificity arguments in these fields has been often superceded by politicized, semiotic accounts of a generally antiessentialist bent. However, medium specificity characterizations remain strong in the area of video, where what is and has been at issue since the beginning of the attempt to create an art of video has been its differentiation from film. Frank Gilette writes

As you investigate videotape you enter into another reality. You investigate taped reality in a way which is peculiar to itself. No other medium quite gives you the advantages. What I'm trying to do is to develop a grammar, a syntax. A way of relating evolves from this probing, this experimentation with the media in terms of holistic phenomenon. In terms of the language of television, one assembles some kind of aesthetic that is intrinsic to television.

What I'm consciously involved in is devising a way that is structurally intrinsic to television. For example, what makes it *not* film? Part of it is that you look *into* the source of light, and with film you look *with* the source of light. In television, the source of light and the source of information are one. . . . What I'm involved with is designing frameworks where work with television can pertain to its own linguistic references, its own syntax, its own way of making sense, its own shared premise. Where it no longer parrots film. The content of my work is looking for a language with which to speak with videotape.

I believe in context not content. The context of what I do is to make sense of the state of information and evolve a way of navigating through it. That best relies on what I refer to as a set of circumstances that can be extrapolated from the series of changes. And not from my prior history or from my anticipated future but out of my immediate circumstances. Videotape is the medium par excellence for that.[13]

One area of video theorizing where medium specificity arguments occur with great frequency is in advocacy of image processing. Hollis Frampton writes that film

. . . builds upon the straight cut, and the direct collision of images, or "shots," extending a perceptual domain whose most noticeable trait we might call successiveness. (In this respect film resembles history.) But video does not seem to take kindly to the cut. Rather, those inconclusions of video art during which I have come closest to moments of real discovery and peripeteia, seem oftenest to exhibit a tropism toward a kind (or many kinds) of metamorphic simultaneity. (In this respect, video resembles Ovidian myth.)

So that it strikes me that video art, which must find its own Muse or else struggle under the tyranny of film, as film did for so long under the tyrannies of drama and prose fiction, might best build its strategies of articulation upon an elasticized notion of what I might call – for serious lack of a better term – the dissolve.[14]

Of course, from a very early date the potential of video for use in terms of what is called instantaneous transmission has also led many to claim for the medium a special advantage, or maybe even a destiny, in the service of certain forms of documentation, such as news reportage.

. . . the most distinctive function of television is its ability to show distant events at the moment when they are taking place. The Kefauver hearings, with a close-up of the hands of gangster Frank Costello; the Army–McCarthy hearings; the complete coverage of orbital shots; the presidential nominating conventions; the Great Debates of 1960; the live transmissions from Europe and Japan via satellite – this is television doing what no other medium can do.[15]

Positive reference to the exploitation of the special nature of the video medium, as an automatic form of commendation, also appears frequently in video criticism. Lizzie Borden writes

Some of the closed-circuit environments by Nauman have been among the most abstract works in video: given properties inherent in the medium, such as simultaneity of feedback, these pieces create their own conditions of presentation, independent of externally determining frameworks such as broadcasting or the monitor within an arbitrary display situation.[16]

And more recently, John Hanhardt has explicated the importance of Nam June Paik's *TV Buddha* and *TV Chair* in terms of video's distinctive "ability to show on a monitor in real time what the camera is recording."[17] Such criticism implicitly assumes that cultivating the inherent, unique properties of the medium is prima facie, aesthetically valuable.

What film, video and photography share, along with being technologically complex media for the production of visual imagery and representations, is an historical circumstance in which each attempts to have itself taken seriously within the culture by means of promoting itself as an artform. Given this situation, the strategy appears to be to mount the claim that the forms in question have a right to the mantle of art because there is something that, in virtue of their respective media, they can do that other arts cannot, or that these forms can do better than other arts. That is, since by dint of their media, these enterprises achieve something new and/or better than what is found in existing arts, they deserve recognition as new arts – ones that do not or should not copy existing forms and which are, therefore, autonomous. Medium specificity arguments are attractive for the purpose of transforming a new medium into a new artform, because they appear to provide a way of individuating arts and, thereby, isolating new ones. At the same time, this operation is based upon a close look at the medium in question, which, in these cases, at least provides an agreed upon starting point for disputants to discuss.

Of course, it is not my claim that medium specificity arguments are the only type of arguments used to legitimatize arts like film, video and photography. One also finds arguments in support of each of these media based upon various cognitive-value claims – e.g., that these arts bring about the possibility for new perceptions, that they change perception, or that they incar-nate the mind or consciousness, or that they exemplify some new form of consciousness. But now I will only consider medium specificity arguments.

The most popular source for medium specificity arguments is Gotthold Ephraim Lessing's *Laocoön*, a treatise that crystallized one major trend in eighteenth-century aesthetics. Lessing wrote

> I argue thus. If it be true that painting employs wholly different signs or means of imitation from poetry – the one using forms and colors in space, the other articulate sounds in time – and if signs must unquestionably stand in a convenient relation with the thing signified, then signs arranged side by side can represent only objects existing side by side, or objects whose parts so exist, while consecutive signs can express only objects which succeed each other, or whose parts succeed each other, in time.
>
> Objects which exist side by side, or whose parts so exist are called bodies. Consequently, bodies with their visible properties are the peculiar subjects of painting.
>
> Objects which succeed each other, or whose parts succeed each other in time, are actions. Consequently, actions are the peculiar subjects of poetry.[18]

Corresponding to the practice of art of his time, Lessing's theory is stated in terms of imitative representations. Due to the structure of the constituent forms of its medium, each art has a specifiable domain of things that it most suitably represents. Generalizing his position to abstract art, we can read Lessing's theory as claiming that each art, in virtue of its medium, has a uniquely appropriate range of effects such that only that medium can discharge.

If Lessing supplies the locus classicus of medium specificity arguments, it is also true that avant-garde filmmakers and video makers of the sixties and seventies were led to the advocacy of medium specificity because of the influential theory of Greenbergian modernism as regards the fine arts. Many film, video and photographic artists (not to mention critics) had backgrounds in the fine arts, or practiced their trade in the context of the gallery, the museum, the art school, or other artworld venues. This tempted them, as it did dancers and performance artists of the same period, to model their polemics on the dominant modernist line of the art world, which, in Greenberg's, Fried's and their imitators' formulations, were highly essentialist.

Interestingly, by taking their marching orders from gallery tastemakers, the proponents of arts such as film selected incongruous candidates for the essential characteristics of their medium. For they often chose candidates that really seemed to be merely extrapolations from the choices made by theorists of painting.

For example, people came to be interested in making films that acknowledged their surface, though a surface doesn't seem to be an attribute that one can literally apply to film images. For, there is no surface to speak of in regard to film images – the screen is not the surface of the film image, nor is the chemical configuration on the film strip the film's surface. Oddly enough, by emphasizing what they thought of as "the film's surface," for the sake of purism, such filmmakers were actually imitating another medium, viz., painting.

Even where filmmakers, video artists, dancers and performance artists do not apply the categories of Greenbergian essentialism so blatantly, they nevertheless tend in general to be influenced by the origin of the theory in the fine arts, insofar as they emphasize the *visual* dimension of their medium. Thus, a piece of performance art might engage in reflexively stressing the frontality and shallowness of theater space. Also, recalling painting, a video image might be said, rather peculiarly, to foreground its status as a real-object. But such enterprises at least hint at a striving after the effects of modernist painting at the same time that this is done, curiously, in the name of medium-purism. The derivation of the polemic in the gallery renders these quests

for purism strangely self-defeating, practically speaking.

But apart from the local ironies and incongruities that beset the Greenbergian derived medium specificity polemics of film, video and photography in the sixties and seventies, it must be stressed that any version of the medium specificity theory confronts enormous – I think insuperable – problems.

The medium specificity approach has two components – an internal component, which specifies the relation between a medium and an artform embodied in this medium in terms of a domain of legitimate avenues of representation, expression and exploration; and a comparative component, which specifies the relation between one artistic medium and other artistic media in terms of the legitimate domains of effects of all the parties canvassed by our comparisons.* The internal component identifies the range of effects that accord with the special limitations and possibilities of the medium in question, while the comparative component holds that there should be no imitation of effects between media. We can pursue the problems inherent in this position by first considering the perplexities caused by the internal component of the approach and then by turning to the difficulties of the comparative component.

The internal component examines the relation between the medium and the artform embodied in it. Each medium has a distinctive character, conceived of in terms of limitations and possibilities, which sets the boundary for stylistic exploration in the artform embodied in the medium. Our earlier inventory of medium specificity talk indicates how easily proponents of this line shift from speaking of limitations to speaking of possibilities and capacities. But these

---

*The internal component considers what a medium does best of all the things it does. The comparison component considers what a medium does best compared to other media.

are hardly the same sorts of things. Why should the limitations of a medium be grouped with the medium's potentials? How do these things fit together? Some theorists, like Arnheim, hold that limitations create possibilities – i.e., limitations in terms of representation make expression possible. But this is a controversial thesis because, contra Arnheim, expression in film seems possible without exploiting the limitations of the medium but through exploiting its representational powers – e.g., its powers of recording already expressive objects and scenes. There is, however, a broader point to be made here – namely, unbeknownst to most proponents of medium specificity, they are often simultaneously espousing two different theories – one that a medium has special limitations – limitations on what it can represent perfectly – which are supposed to direct stylization, and secondly, that a medium has special potentials – potentials for best representing certain subject matter – which mark what endeavors should be pursued in the medium. Arnheim primarily holds a limitation theory of medium specificity while Lessing holds a special power theory. These approaches may not be easily connectable since one is based on the idea that a medium imperfectly represents certain things while the other holds that there are certain things that the medium most adequately represents. But it is by no means clear that we can be sure that these two different approaches can always be coherently combined to lead to the same results. Arnheim says that cinema has a special capacity to represent animated action, but it is not apparent how that follows from the representational limitations of the medium. Indeed, isn't this very power the opposite of anything we could meaningfully construe as a limitation of cinema?

There are other problems with the notions of "limitations" and "possibilities" in these theories, apart from the ambiguities involved in attempting to combine them.

For example, if we read the idea of medium-limitations in a literal way, the medium specificity thesis appears trivial. For it the notion of medium limitations amounts to "Do not make a medium do what it cannot," then the slogan is otiose since it is quite frankly impossible to make a medium do what it can't. It is a waste of energy to warn artists not to do the impossible, since if the enterprise in question is literally impossible, it will never be executed. A famous example of Lessing's concerns the sculpture "Laoc- öon" which attempts to depict a movement-packed action in the face of the fact that it is impossible for figures in stone to move. But, of course, the statue neither attempts or achieves something impossible. It tries to project the impression of movement, as Lessing recognizes, by designing a frozen movement in a way that suggests continuity with the past and the future of the action in question. Nothing literally impossible is at stake. If we say that the statue is full of movement, we are employing a useful metaphor but we are not saying that the sculpture has done something literally impossible or violated either a law of logic or physics. The sculptor can't do anything that violates logic or physics. And there's the end to one strong reading of the medium specificity thesis.

Similarly, a strong reading of the "possibility" variation on the medium specificity approach shows it toothless. For if the slogan is to be "only aspire for effects that are possible in your medium," the same objection suffices; for we can be certain that no artist will ever execute anything that is literally unattainable, literally not possible, in his medium.

The answer, of course, to the preceding objection is to note that it rides on construing the medium specificity thesis in terms of logical possibility, whereas what might be meant by medium specificity theorists is that when speaking of the possibilities of the medium, they are speaking of the special powers of the medium, i.e., what the medium achieves with great ease or with little resistance. Thought of this way, the medium specificity thesis becomes "Aim at those goals that the medium most perspicuously facilitates." A similar rewriting of the notion of "limitation" might yield the slogan "Do not pursue effects that are difficult within the medium." However, these rewritings do not, I think, bolster the credibility of the medium specificity thesis. For even if we do not buy into the myth that the production of any work of art should entail a struggle, I do not see how, given art as we know it, we can accept principles that presume that the best line of production in art is the line of least resistance or the easiest approach.

Moreover, these reformulations of the medium specificity thesis will also be difficult to implement because we will be hard put to determine what is easy or difficult in a medium. Here, perhaps, we will have to abandon purely internalist considerations and speak of ease and difficulty via comparisons between media. But this will quickly lead us back to the sorts of issues we have just been considering. Certain action-packed events, like chariot races, are said to be easier to mount and to execute convincingly in film than they are in theater. But chariot races in theatricalizations of *Ben Hur* were staged on treadmills in the first decades of this century. If these chariot races were exciting, suspenseful and spectacular, what difference does it make that they would have been easier, in some sense, to execute in film? Similarly, it may be easier to convincingly dissolve a staked vampire into smoke in film than it is in theater, but an effect of this sort was quite breathtaking in Gorey's recent stage version of *Dracula*. Why should comparative difficulty make any difference if the final effect is excellent? Of course, it might be said that the overall effect of a work that fails to exploit the specific potentials of a medium cannot, of necessity, be successful. But this is to elevate the issue to a matter of logic, which it clearly is not. Whether embracing a difficult effect in a medium will result in

success or failure cannot be prejudged; we must simply wait and see what the outcome is. And failure in such cases need not be attributed to the medium; it may rather be said that artists in that medium have not yet discovered a convincing way to secure the effect in question.

Perhaps it will be urged that even if these medium specificity slogans are not without exception, they are our best rules of thumb for making recommendations about the projects artists might embark upon. It may be argued that if one does not pursue that which the medium facilitates, then things are likely to go badly for the artist. So the best line of attack is generally the easiest. In some sense, of course, this may be the safest way for artists to proceed. However, it is not customary, I think, for us to encourage artists to minimize risks. Also one wonders whether the rules of thumb adduced in such cases are really based on the nature of the medium or whether they really refer to the routine practice in the medium? Of course, an artist has a better chance at a limited form of success if he repeats what has already been done. But who would accept adherence to existing stylistic formulas as an imperative for all art?

A related modification of the medium specificity thesis would be to say that specification of the medium's powers helps us explain why certain works succeed and others fail. It is often said, for example, that stage plays or screenplays with much dialogue and restricted movement are not easily acquitted in cinema. Such attempts, often disdained as "canned theater," result in awkward films. But it is important to notice that often our paradigm cases of "canned theater" – viz., early talkies – were not simply bad movies; they were also bad theater. Their directors used their actors, sets, props and dramatic materials unimaginatively or inconsistently. As theater productions they would have been just as execrable onstage as they were onscreen. The problem was not that the film medium was being used to do something that the medium resisted but that the dramatic execution of these works were inept, banal and, at times, ridiculous. What are often problems that supposedly derive from the attempt to force a medium to what it cannot do, or cannot do easily, it seems to me, are problems, such as canned theater, which are better described in terms of unimaginative or lame execution. We do expect from works of art that they be wrought in such a way that their elements have multiple significances and functions which multiplicity is partially captured by Goodman's notion of relative repleteness. Examples of canned theater generally lack such added layers of meaning and design. Their problem is they are impoverished. But if a film, recall the courtship scene in *Henry V*, is theatrically rich to an appreciable extent, then we have no call to disparage it.

And we obviously have quite successful stage adaptations, and also dialogue-laden films, such as *Lifeboat* and *My Night at Maude's*. It may be difficult to make films under the constraints the latter two films accept. But that is no reason to avoid attempting such works. Moreover, that certain attempts of this sort have been successful suggests that the unsuccessful ones may not be indicative of failures of the medium but of failures of artistry. That is, the artists in question have failed to figure out an imaginative and compelling way of mounting their dramas.

The issue of forcing a medium to do what goes against its grain raises another major internalist problem for the medium specificity approach, namely, how does one identify what the grain of a medium actually is? Lessing tells us that the units that comprise poetry – words – are organized sequentially and that, therefore, the medium is suited to representing actions since they too evolve over time. Poems should not be viewed with a timeless gaze like a painting or a statue.

Lessing's account, of course, is quite wrong, for he is just mistaken that the

sequential organization of words can only represent actions rather than, say, states of affairs. Nor does his idea of the necessity of a "convenient" relation between the structure of a sign and its referent seem much more than question-begging, given the indisputable existence of things like the "Laocoon" statue. But of even greater importance is the question of how Lessing knew to choose the temporal dimension of poetry – written poetry – over its spatial-design possibilities. Presumably, Lessing would object to concrete poems like Ian Hamilton Finlay's "The Horizon of Holland," whose typography suggests windmills, or Jackson Maclow's "Jail Break," which looks like the facade of a prison.[19] These works can be viewed holistically as a single image, scanned like a painting with no preordained sequence of glances. But a theorist of Lessing's persuasion cannot conceivably maintain that these concrete poems are unnatural to the medium. For this type of poetry grows naturally out of the significance of typography for written poetry, which, in turn, grows out of conventions concerning the importance of line endings which, of course, is connected to one of the levers of temporal control that the writer exercises over the reader of poetry. But if this is the case, how does one ascertain that the temporal potential of poetry is more natural than the potential for spatial elaboration? The potential for spatial elaboration is as much a part of the poetic sign system of the practice of written poetry as is the potential for temporal elaboration.

Proponents of medium specificity arguments generally proceed as if identifying the sort of effects an artform should explore is self-evident, once one examines the physical structure of the medium in which the artform is embodied. Lessing isolated words as the building blocks of poems and from that he extracted that the temporal elaboration of actions was the proper domain of poetry. But, even aside from the issue of identifying words as simply physical constituents, one also wants to note that words, like

11

splashes of paint, appear next to each other. How, then, did Lessing know that spatial representation was not a primary area of experimentation in poetry?

The issue will not be settled by asserting that the proper direction of the medium will follow from the identification of its essence, where that essence is construed as the physical feature that defines entities as being instances of that medium. For though a flexible celluloid base is the physical characteristic that defines entities as film, nothing follows from that concerning what it is proper to represent in film, or concerning what effects are cinematic. What this example is meant to show is that even if media have essences, which is itself a controversial issue, it is far from clear that an ostensible essence of a medium has any directive force regarding how the medium is used, let alone how it should be used. Obviously the uses, including contradictory uses, of a flexible celluloid base are too innumerable to provide a focused recommendation, or even a family of recommendations, about the proper evolution of the medium.

Medium specificity theorists often write as if the various media they investigate had only one component, or, at least, only one basic component worth considering for aesthetic purposes. But in terms of the first assumption, it is important to stress that every medium has more than one component. In our previous discussion of Weston, he appears to presume that optical and chemical processing are not really a part of photography. This is an eminently self-serving view, given the style of photography he wishes to advocate, but can the developing and printing of photos really be excluded from the basic components of the medium in a non-question begging fashion? The notion that media have basic or lead elements, to which other elements must be subservient, also runs into justificatory problems. Film is composed, at least, of photographic images and a flexible band that is projected in time. Both of these features can be sensibly

proposed as fundamental constituents of photographic cinema – i.e., elements without which there would be no photographic cinema. But, then, on what basis does a realist such as Kracauer know that editing should subserve the purpose of a certain kind of photography, or does a montagist such as Kuleshov hold that photography should subserve the exigencies of organizing the celluloid strip sequentially in a certain way?

Of course, even if there were a single or basic component for each medium, we would still confront the problem of specifying the dimension or property of that element that is relevant for artistic elaboration. Kracauer connects fortuitousness with photography, but why should this be more significant for a photographer than the types of planned precision effects the medium makes available to the photomontagist? And furthermore, even if we could decide that there were a basic dimension or property or effect of the medium, we would still be at a loss for a decision procedure that would enable us to choose the stylistic enterprise best suited to cash in on it. Suppose that immediacy is the special property of video. This would nevertheless give us no indication of whether the medium should exploit this potential in terms of the immediate feedback possibilities of image processing, the immediate feedback possibilities vis-à-vis introspective explorations of psychological processes, the possibility for real time monuments, the possibility for the on-the-spot transmission of news, and so on.

Of course, the deepest problem revealed by these examples is not simply that the nature of the medium may be indeterminate in regard to alternative stylistic approaches, but that the medium may support conflicting and even contradictory avenues of development. In film, the montage style is construed as the opposite of the deep-focus style of realism. And in practice, it seems difficult to imagine both being pursued simultaneously and wholeheartedly in the same sequence of the same film. Similarly, the aesthetics of image processing appear inimicable to the purpose of location news coverage. The medium specificity theorist, it would seem, has no non-arbitrary way to choose between conflicting aesthetic programs that may be equally grounded in the complex of possibilities afforded by the medium. Nor is this problem a merely academic one. For very often contesting artistic programs attempt to vindicate themselves by means of invoking the nature of the medium. But this is of little moment, because the media we are considering can each support contradictory programs. A medium does not ordain a single style or even a single family of styles, but generally affords the opportunities for a plethora of incompatible styles. Thus, invoking the medium in defense of a particular line of stylistic development is not an especially advisable starting point.

The picture that believers in medium specificity generally labor under is that the medium has some significant, often thought to be essential, feature or features that dictate the proper line of development in that medium. The facility for special effects entails a commitment to image processing in video; the facility for juxtaposition signals the centrality of editing for film; the causal relation between image and referent suggests an objective style for photography. Yet, as we have seen, we can just as easily adduce several competing and even incompatible programs for each of these arts, and each of these will be connected to some possibility of the medium, i.e., each will, at the very least, be logically and physically possible within the medium. What this indicates is that the nature of the medium does not have any determinate directive force concerning the way in which that medium is to be developed. In fact, in any sense of the "nature of the medium" that relates to artistic styles embodied in the medium, there is no nature of the medium where that is conceived of as predating and determining the uses we find for the medium.

We have noted that each medium is complex – complex in its constituents, its effects, the properties of its constituents, and in the ways styles are related to these properties and potential effects. The medium specificity theorist promotes the myth that these complex alternatives can be narrowed down to a coherent artistic program simply by looking at the medium. If we look at poetry, it has been proposed, we will see that sound rather than space is its essence, and that musicality rather than spatial design is its proper terrain. However, antecedent to some use we have for the medium, it is not clear that such decisions have any rational foundation. Of course, if we have a use for a medium the problem becomes malleable. That is, if poetry is meant to be spoken aloud rather than read silently, then it makes sense for the musical dimension to be prized over the spatial possibilities. But here it is the use we have for the medium that determines which aspects of the medium are relevant, and not the medium that determines the use. If we want imagistic art then we will focus upon the special effects capacity of video over other possibilities. But it is not the capacity for special effects that commits us to imagistic video. If we desire to encourage an active exploratory mode of spectatorship toward film, then the exploitation of hard-focus, long shots is emphasized. But if the effect we seek is heightened control over the sequence of the audience's perceptual responses, certain editing possibilities are recommended. It is the use we find for the medium that determines what aspect of the medium deserves our attention. The medium is open to our purposes; the medium does not use us for its own agenda.

An artist may determine a particular, original use for the medium. But generally an artist embraces pre-existing uses and purposes as those are found in extant and emerging styles, genres and artististic movements. Most of the time when we are told that someone has transgressed his or her medium, what is actually meant, if anything, is that the typical effects of a certain genre or style have been contravened. For example, it may be claimed that direct address by a character to a camera is inherently uncinematic. But it is perfectly appropriate in a film of autobiographical dimensions – such as *Journeys from Berlin* – for the author to appear and to speak to us in a long take. If one criticizes a shot like this as uncinematic, then one is probably assuming that all films should be committed to exposition in terms of dramatic action à la Hollywood International – i.e., in terms of revealing thoughts and feelings through action rather than soliloquies. But that is a stylistic preference, not a preference based upon what it is possible for a medium to do.

The genre, style or artistic movement a work inhabits determines whether one's choices are appropriate or not. What hitherto have been identified as mediumistic questions are in fact stylistic questions. In answer to this, I may be asked where styles, genres, movements and their subtending purposes come from. Well, not from the medium. The medium is initially tongue-tied as regards these issues. Rather the purposes we find for the medium derive from the preoccupations of the culture at large as well as the particular momentums – artistic revolutions and long term developments – that inhere in the artworld at a given point in time.

Placing emphasis on the use or purpose of the medium entails certain consequences for the issue of evaluation. For if we evaluate the objects produced in a medium in virtue of use, then our assessments will tend to be of two sorts; evaluations of whether the object implements the purposes it is aimed toward, and appraisals of whether such purposes are worth pursuing. The former sort of evaluation is more narrowly formalistic, while the latter involves general humanistic considerations that touch upon the aesthetic, moral and intellectual concerns of the life of a culture.

That a given artwork exploits an inherent capacity of video, for example, is besides the point not only because in some sense every video work does, but also because, until it is said why doing that is important or worthwhile in a given context, we have no cause for interest.

Thus far I have concentrated on what I earlier called the internal component of the medium specificity thesis. This internal component is the notion that there is some special range of effects, derived from the distinctive features of the medium, which should be pursued by an artform embodied in that medium. But the thesis also has a comparison component. Each artform embodied in a different medium should pursue a different range of effects than artforms embodied in other media. Generally, it is added that each artform should pursue those effects which it acquits best of all artistic media. It may be felt that once we add the comparison component, many of the questions I raised earlier about the medium specificity thesis can be solved. For if we wish to know what feature of the medium is important, or which of conflicting programs in a medium should be pursued, we may be told to apply one of the two following directives: (1) focus on those features that differentiate the medium in question from other media, or (2) focus on the program that results in the range of effects where the medium in question excels when compared to other media.

The first of these directives identifies the distinctive feature of the medium and the distinctive program of the medium as those that differentiate it from other media. Positively, the directive encourages pursuit of whatever differentiates media while negatively it directs media not to duplicate each other's effects.

Taken at face value, the negative formulation of this standard is as vacuous as the directive to pursue only what it is possible to accomplish in a given medium. Medium specificity theorists, such as Bernard Bosanquet, often argue that each medium is physically different than others and will perforce impart different qualities.[20] A polemicist like Weston often begins with this assumption. But of course if this notion is taken literally, then there is no reason to worry that one medium will duplicate another. For each physical medium will automatically impart qualities that are different from those of other media. A silent, black and white, edited film like *The Cabinet of Dr. Caligari* cannot be taken as a duplicate of a stage rendition of the same drama, for it has properties, such as certain types of cinematic illumination, depth and continuity, that are discernibly different from a comparable stage production. There is no reason to implore artists in different media to differentiate their effects; they will do so without trying.

The positive formulation of the directive – "exploit that which differentiates media" – though perhaps not vacuous is certainly puzzling. Why suppose that what differentiates media – their defining features – leads in any way to interesting aesthetic results. Nor is it at all clear that the program that can only be realized in a specified medium will be an interesting or worthwhile one. For example, some video artists, such as the Vasulkas, appear to believe that an image is significant just because it is video-pure. But just because a given image or effect can only be made by means of video does not give us any reason to expect that that fact alone guarantees that the image will be aesthetically interesting. Presumably what the medium specificity theorist is offering us is a guideline for determining fruitful avenues of aesthetic research, and as well, a logical basis for critical evaluations of a certain sort. But it is difficult to see how the injunction to pursue differentiation per se successfully fulfills either of these roles. Moreover, if it is said that the correct formulation here is that the medium should pursue that which differentiates the media and which is also interesting, then we would want to know why we should

ask for anything more than interest from artworks?

Of course, if the comparison component of the thesis is framed in terms of what a medium is said to excel in – when compared to other media – then some of the preceding questions about the value of differentiation disappear since by speaking of "excelling," we already know that the specific differentiae in question have some aesthetic value. However, if the preceding questions appear to recede a different set of problems remain. For medium specificity proponents tend to presume that what a medium does best among media is what it can be said to do best in some univocal sense. But this is not evident. Indeed, following the demand for differentiation we may arrive at something that is less than the best in certain respects.

Let us draw a distinction between two ways in which a medium does something "best." The first is the differentiation sense of "best": what a medium does best is what it does better than any other medium. But by "what it does best" we may also be referring to that which a medium does best of all the things it does. Call this the mediumistic sense of "best." Clearly these two senses need not coincide. What photography may excel in, in the differentiation sense, is the detailed representation of very small things. But suppose what it excels in in the mediumistic sense is portraiture. Yet painting of all the arts excels in this regard. So the differentiation requirement directs us to expect from photography not what it does best but only what it does uniquely well – offer detailed representations of very small things. Likewise if narration were the best mediumistic use to which video could be put, even though this does not differentiate the medium from film, AND there is some special effect that video can achieve more compellingly than film, we will have to sacrifice the best (in one sense) that video might offer and to settle for its lesser virtues as those would be mediumistically construed. The medium specificity theory does not assure us that each artform will aspire to be as interesting as it can be, even though this sounds like our most basic expectation regarding the arts. Rather the medium specificity theory maximizes purity instead of excellence.

Of course, it may be felt that where there is purity, excellence correlates and vice-versa. But this is false. As a matter of fact, however theatrical, W. C. Fields' monologues remain excellent enshrined in celluloid.

Broadly speaking what appears to be most problematic about the medium specificity approach is that, due to its comparison component, it enjoins us to forgo potential excellence for the sake of purity. Had *Waiting for Godot* been originally proposed as a videotape, many medium specificity polemicists would have vetoed the project, while for some medium specificity proponents, a film such as *Animal Crackers* should not have been made. Moreover, the medium specificity theorist would have us foreclose such historically indisputable avenues of artistic creativity as the inspiration of one artform by another. Cinematic city symphonies, based on musical analogs, and works like *L'Age d'Or*, derived from strategies of Surrealist poetry, would be inadmissible. But what warrants all these sacrifices? Clearly medium purity is not a morally significant ideal such that it overrides any competing aesthetic interests. So why should we sacrifice all manner of aesthetic excellence in order to secure the purity of the medium?

In fact, very little reason is offered for the injunction to differentiate art forms. Rather, it seems to be proposed as self-evident. Undoubtedly it is based upon the metaphor of the division of labor. In order to maximize the efficient use of scarce resources, to avoid waste in terms of unnecessary duplication, and to meet a set quota of needs, society and business parcel out tasks, ideally to those best suited for them. Similarly, medium specificity theorists seem to rely

implicitly on a value placed on the type of efficiency afforded by the division of labor. Analogized to society the arts are urged to avoid waste by avoiding duplication.

Certainly this picture of the division of labor does not capture the way the arts really are. The arts are marked by many trans-art endeavors. Many arts are devoted to narrative, and rhythm, as well, is an effect variously shared by different media, from Glass's *Einstein on the Beach* to Mondrian's *One Way Boogie-Woogie*. Furthermore, the history of art has been beneficially served by innumerable trans-art movements, such as German Expressionism, in which artists attempt to translate one theme or set of concerns into a number of different media. Thus, since the arts do not already approximate a neat division of labor, the medium specificity thesis must be construed as a recommendation that artists embrace a division of labor.

But it is not clear that the model of the division of labor is really appropriate to the arts. For example, there is no real problem of potentially wasteful duplication in the arts. If we are confronted by a massive number of excellent narratives – produced by several media – we would regard ourselves as lucky rather than as suffering from a wasteful glut. Whereas a society might produce too many cars to be used, it is not obvious what would constitute too many interesting stories. We certainly have never reached such a point, though many media have been working at full steam for quite a long time producing narratives. That wasteful duplication is not a problem for the arts is a decisive disanalogy with those practices where a division of labor makes sense. A division of labor, therefore, need not be imposed on the arts.

Also the notion of a division of labor puts a premium on the efficient use of scarce resources. And, though the resources humanity has for producing art may be limited, it is not the case that efficiency is something we care about when it comes to artworks. For it is the results and not the process of production that counts with artworks. All manner of inefficiency, waste, self-indulgence and so on will be accepted in the production of satisfying art. Perhaps this is because with the arts we have no antecedently defined set of aesthetic needs or precise quota of specific aesthetic interests, however true it may be that we may have some general aesthetic interests that may be satisfied in diverse ways. But where there is no exactly defined output, the notion of efficiency loses its applicability to a large degree. Yet the medium specificity theorist has little more than some vague appeal to efficiency to recommend his or her program.

Indeed if we need a model for the arts that is drawn from notions of the social organization of work, then perhaps it is not the division of labor we should look to, but rather to the utopian pictures of Fourier and Marx in which the worker of tomorrow, a generalist to the core, pursues diverse activities, hunting in the morning and philosophizing in the afternoon. This picture corresponds better to the various sorts of freedom the arts are thought to enshrine both in their consumption and their production. Applying this metaphor to media, unfettered by the claims of efficiency, one would envision each medium exploring all available effects, including those achieved in other media.

Though the division of labor image is an unsupportable one in regard to the arts, it is clearly the idea behind the medium specificity attempt to legitimatize emerging arts like film, video and photography. Employed as an offensive strategy, the position asserts that these media have a right to exist because they can do something – perform some task – that no other art can do. But, of course this is a suspect maneuver. Just because a medium can do what no other does hardly recommends it to us, unless that which it does has some worth. But if that which it does has worth, then that alone, rather than the medium's uniqueness, is what attracts us to works in that

artform. If new media proffer work that is interesting, aesthetically interesting, then the new media will be established as art. Film came to be established as an art because masterpieces, such as the highly theatrical work of Chaplin, were produced in that medium. It is not the possibility of purity or the efficient production of a unique effect that wins a medium a place among the arts, but the creation of interesting, though often "impure," works.

The medium specificity theorist may also rely on the division of labor notion as a defensive gambit. That is, opponents of emerging media may claim that a new medium is extraneous, since an existing artform already does what the new medium aspires to. Of course, when a new medium emerges, it will most likely imitate existing artforms, insofar as that is the natural place for artists in the new medium to turn in order to get ideas about how to use the new medium. And, as a matter of fact, many works produced at this early stage will be bad imitations or slavish imitations of their sources – e.g., the early *Films d'Art*. To remedy this situation, the medium specificity theorist urges that the new medium pursue those unique effects that it executes best. Thus, we avoid such violations of the ideal division of labor as bad duplications of theater in film. However, this way of thinking confuses issues. For what is problematic about things such as *Films d'Art* is not that they are imitations – for imitations can be healthy, exciting and progressive – but that they are bad and slavish imitations. Here the problem is not a matter of medium for surely one can have bad, slavish and inept imitations within the same medium. The defect of slavish and inept imitation belongs to the artist, not the medium. It is incidental whether an inept imitation occurs trans-media or within one medium. Of course, where the imitation – construed perforce as an imitation in certain respects – results in a successful piece or a masterpiece, the question of extraneousness just disappears.

There is no point to caring whether Julia Margaret Cameron's photos of Tennyson and Longfellow duplicate strategies of portraiture in painting. It is enough that they were made, and that they move us.

In favor of the division of labor metaphor, the medium specificity theorist may ask what reason there would be for the existence of different arts, unless they were meant to have different purposes? But the question itself is inadmissible. It presupposes a view of the history of the arts as the rational unfolding of a grand plan. But, in fact, we have the arts we have as the result of discrete chains of events. Film was invented because Edison thought it would be profitable to have visual accompaniments for his phonograph records, and not because he discerned a lacuna in the system of the arts. Perhaps dance was born when a burly Neanderthal accidentally stepped into his camp fire and, while hopping about on one foot, his clansmen clapped rhythmically in appreciation. That we have the arts we have and that they evolved as they did are contingent matters, often related to separate chains of events, and not the fruition of some grand dream Apollo hatched in an Olympian arcade.[21]

Moreover, in terms of the way that medium specificity polemicists generally proceed, it is clear that they are not really concerned to neatly demarcate each artform from all the other arts. Usually such polemicists are only exercised by differentiating one artform from another art, one which, for contextual reasons, is perceived as a rival. Most film theorists are vexed by the problem of sharply cleaving film and theater, but they are scarcely moved to differentiate film from the novel and the short story, or film from photography. And if a film theorist or artist worries about novelistic or literary cinema that is generally because he or she is championing an alternative style of cinema. Ironically, often a cinema based on musicalist analogies is urged over literary cinema in the name of

purism. But what is important here is that while making medium specificity arguments, polemicists are usually, although inconsistently, disturbed by overlaps between certain arts, while overlaps with other arts are either ignored or treated as benign. Obviously, the real question in such cases is not one of the theoretical differentiation of the arts across the board, but a question of dividing up a turf, generally between two arts or two arts movements that perceive themselves as competing for the same audience. Film worries about theater and vice-versa; photography worries about painting; painting worries about sculpture; video worries about film.

The discussion of the competition between the arts may appear to supply at least a compelling excuse or vindication of the use of mediumistic arguments and recommendations by proponents of arts such as film, video and photography. Beleaguered by competitors accusing the new media of insignificant and extraneous imitation, these new media seek some differentiating effect in order to silence the polemics raised against them. In this they accept the presupposition of their detractors – viz., that there must be division between the arts – which the medium specificity proponent goes on to explicate. Thus, it might be argued that for purposes of first legitimatizing a medium as an art, it is rhetorically persuasive to accept the major premise of detractors of the medium, and to demonstrate that the medium can perform as a unique art. Once a medium is accepted as an art, once the struggle for legitimacy is won, it might be said, artists in that medium can go on to do whatever they like, trafficking in polymorphous mixtures with other arts. For once a medium is acknowledged as an art, the uniqueness issue dissipates. If film and photography won their campaigns to be regarded as art, then no one thinks twice about the theatricality of Rohmer's *Perceval*, or the painterly and cinematic dimensions of Duane Michel's work. Perhaps, on the horizon, video artists, once their medium is unequivocably accepted, will cease worrying about the uniqueness of their form. Thus, given this story, medium specificity polemics might appear to have a valuable sort of work to do, i.e., have an acceptable function to perform, in the historical and social context of the emergence of an artform, especially from a reproductive technology. In other words, medium specificity arguments and their related recommendations may seem to have a legitimate use at least in certain situations.

But this defense of the medium specificity approach has several flaws. First, I see no reason to accept the division of labor model for art, even as a debater's point. Rather, the defender of the new medium is better advised to deny the pressure for a division of labor, and point to the accomplishments – the works of aesthetic excellence – that the medium has produced as evidence that the medium is an established art. Of course, if a medium has no compelling accomplishments yet, it is idle to claim it is an established art.

Another problem about the preceding defense of medium specificity recommendations is that it really misconstrues what is generally at stake in such situations. Most often, perhaps in all cases, medium specificity recommendations turn out to be not defenses of a given medium per se, but briefs in favor of certain styles, genres and artistic movements. Weston is advocating a style of photography, straight photography, over another style, photo-painting; he is not really defending photography per se. As well, the debate between montagists, realists and modernists in film is not a matter of a defense of the medium, but of defenses of contesting styles and their subtending aesthetic, intellectual and moral commitments. But if one wishes to defend a style, a genre or an artistic movement, the way to do that is to show the value or worth – aesthetic, intellectual and moral – that derives from embracing the specific commitments involved in the practice of that style.

At this point, a final vindication of medium specificity arguments may seem to present itself almost naturally. Medium specificity arguments, it might be said, do not legitimatize emerging media as art, but they do function to perform the valuable service of legitimatizing new styles, genres and movements. There are at least two things wrong here. First, medium specificity arguments can be marshalled just as easily to defend established styles as they can be to defend new and innovative art. Herbert Read, for example, uses medium specificity intuitions to oppose the linear sculpture of Muller, Stankiewic, Kneals, Uhlman and Baldessari, among others, by invoking sculpture's supposedly essential concern with mass,[22] while there is the infamous case of Arnheim's rejection of sound in film in the name of the medium's commitment to animated action. Clearly, medium specificity arguments are not always on the side of either the angels or the future. Nor does it seem defensible to claim that medium specificity arguments are acceptable when used to support stylistic innovation but invalid when used for the sake of tradition. The medium specificity approach should be neutral between the claims of the past and the future.

Of course, my second objection to the notion that medium specificity arguments have an acceptable role to play in the defense of innovative styles has been the major theme of this paper. If a style, genre or movement has some aesthetic, intellectual and/or moral value of what added significance is the fact that it exploits some unique feature of the medium? And if a style, movement, or genre has no compelling aesthetic, moral or intellectual value, why should we care about it, even if it is true to the inherent possibilities of its medium, whatever they are? If a style, like image-processing in video, is to be defended, then that defense must be based on showing the aesthetic, intellectual and moral values available in this style. Medium specificity arguments have no defensible role to play in aesthetic debate in the realm of self-consciously invented arts, nor in the realm of those arts whose origins are submerged in the haze of history.

Appendix

Though medium specificity arguments would appear to be inadvisable in any form, two philosophers have recently attempted to make limited claims on their behalf. Their aim has been to find whatever truth there may be in such arguments. Thus, they have tried to find at least some restricted cases where such arguments are legitimately persuasive. The purpose of this appendix is to question even such minimal endorsements of medium specificity arguments.

Edward Sankowski has attempted a modified defense of at least some cases of the medium specificity argument on the grounds that, purportedly, the thesis provides a strategy for (1) assuring plurality and diversity in art as well as a strategy for (2) guaranteeing that the original achievements of a given artform will be sustained and developed.[23] Sankowski is claiming that on some occasions the medium specificity thesis can be advocated on the pretext that it will promote the overall aesthetically desirable end of encouraging the creation of novel kinds of art. Sankowski is also claiming that some medium specificity arguments can be justified on the grounds that abiding by the directives of the medium specificity thesis guides present-day artistic activity in such a way that the original achievements in the artform in question will be conserved and expanded upon in an optimum fashion.

First let us consider Sankowski's plurality argument. He begins by postulating that it is aesthetically important that we have diversity among our artworks. Sankowski points out that one way of insuring this is by encouraging artists in one field to avoid duplicating the types of patterns that artists in other fields are creating. This, Sankowski holds, can be implemented by advocating that artists take advantage of only those properties of one's artform that are unique to it. As a result, at least one form of aesthetic duplication will be avoided. So where we are concerned to enhance the diversity amongst the artworks we have, the medium specificity approach can be seen as an artistically fruitful means to that end.

Several things about this argument require comment. First, it assumes that one can isolate the unique features of a medium. I, on the other hand, submit that the supposedly unique features of a medium are those features that are relevant to certain styles, genres, and the purposes presupposed by them. Thus, if we want plurality we are better advised to advocate the creation of new genres and styles than to look to the medium as our guide. After all, Sankowski's account really appears to be based on coming up with the best policy recommendation we can make in certain circumstances of artistic impoverishment. And calling for new styles seems more germane than medium specificity briefs.

Secondly, the acceptability of Sankowski's defense of the medium specificity thesis also presumes a premium placed on having a diversity of novel kinds of artworks. This premium on diversity may be connected to both a concern for originality in artistic creativity and a desire for a range of variegated aesthetic experiences for artgoers. Of course, the plurality of aesthetic value is a stated preference in the artworlds of North Atlantic industrial cultures. But one can envision other cultures wherein a certain homogenizing similarity between various artforms is sought. Indeed, one can even recall in our own culture moments of both such consolidation and of the desire for such consolidation. And in contexts of these sorts, medium specificity arguments that are grounded in the desire to maximize diversity are undercut.

But let us assume with Sankowski both the viability of the project of isolating the unique characteristics of the medium, and situations in which artistic diversity is valued. We will immediately note that the uniqueness approach is just as likely to obstruct the creation of novel kinds of positively valuable art as it is to facilitate it. For example, one can easily imagine the seven or eight arts busily pursuing that which each agrees are its unique potentials so that the work in each artform is arrestingly similar to other works in the same artform. There is no reason to believe that medium specificity or uniqueness arguments will be conducive to a variety within artforms. And therefore, the medium specificity approach may contribute to an extremely regular and lamentably predictable artistic landscape.

The medium specificity approach, if it guarantees any diversity, guarantees only one sort, viz., the differentiation between artforms. However, there are other important modes of artistic diversity, ones, indeed, that commitments to medium specificity may in fact impede. For example, often the basis for the creation of novel art is the result of breaks with historical traditions, e.g., the shift from Classicism to Romanticism. Moreover, with the introduction of a new, innovating artistic movement – such as German Expressionism, Surrealism, or Minimalism – it is often the case that there is one lead art, which other arts emulate. For instance, with Minimal Art, the example and theory of fine art inspired dancers and filmmakers to contrive equivalents of the type of work gallery artists pursued.[24] The result was novelty and experimentation but this is in clear violation of the often explicit stricture of medium specificity proponents who claim that the arts should not imitate each other. Medium specificity theorists appear to believe that loyalty to the medium is a way of increasing the likelihood that novel art will be produced. But it may be that imitation and interanimation between the arts are as reliable if not more reliable than medium specificity for propagating circumstances in which novelty flourishes.

Contra medium specificity proponents, it seems to me that the arts often do imitate each other with productive effects. An example of this is the case of stylistic movements where the concerns and strategies of one art infect others. The aims and purposes of the style, as it emerges concretely in one art, are used by artists in other arts, which adapt their forms to converge on the effects of the lead art. Often the analogies between arts of the same stylistic movement can be quite striking, as each art applies the imperative of the movement, as derived from a lead art, to its medium. Also the spread of a stylistic movement in this way can be quite positive and valuable. Insofar as the medium specificity thesis closes off this obvious source of creativity, the thesis seems open to objection. Of course, this sort of imitation is not the only kind that might persist between arts. One art might imitate another art for expressive effect. A film might imitate theatrical style in order to appropriate the connotations of the notions of theater in our culture, e.g., present "theatrical" acting in order to symbolize that the characters of the fiction are "playing roles." Of course, this is not to say that all types of imitation between media are acceptable. Some imitation across arts will be boring, rote, and unimaginative. But then the problem is that the work is boring, rote, and unimaginative, not that there are overlaps between media. Indeed, there is nothing wrong, in principle, with imitation across the arts unless one mistakenly assumes that imitation, per se, is unimaginative.

Sankowski's defense of a limited number of cases of the medium specificity argument seems to be that in some instances we will be able to enhance the diversity of art by telling artists to take advantage of the properties unique to their medium. As I have argued, it is by no means apparent that loyalty to the unique properties of one's medium is likely to generate the most abundant or fruitful diversity. Nor do I think that loyalty to the medium, rather than stylistic innovation, is the straightest path to the creation of a plurality of novel artworks. In fact, at best, in Sankowski's account, medium specificity is an indirect means which in some cases leads to artistic pluralism. But then, it is a tactic, not the principle its proponents often presume. It will be dispensable in circumstances where it does not have the desired effect. Sankowski will undoubtedly be satisfied by this conclusion since he only claims that "some" medium specificity arguments are defensible. However, I wonder, even in cases where we desire to bring about diversity, whether a policy based on medium specificity is practicable. For we still will be confronted by the problem of isolating unique characteristics of the medium. Again, calling for stylistic innovation seems to be the more direct means of bringing diversity about. In fact, if I am correct about the claim that one does not really ever isolate independently determinable, "unique" features of the medium but only elements of prevailing styles, then Sankowski's purported reworking of the medium specificity argument is less an argument than a "gambit" based on a myth that directs artists to return to the styles of their several arts in the guise of pursuing the quidity of each art. This course of action, moreover, is favored (questionably) in opposition to and as superior to obvious prospects for diversity attainable through the pursuit of a single cross-art style (or movement), or a delimited set of such stylistic explorations as such is shared across various arts.

Another goal that Sankowski feels medium specificity arguments could be said to bring about is the sustaining of the achievements within a certain tradition. Sankowski writes "the uniqueness arguer often could be construed as claiming that if creative activity proceeds as his uniqueness argument enjoins, the original achievements of the art form will be sustained and/or developed. . . ."[25] This claim appears to be false. Very often medium specificity arguments are made in the context of polemics wherein the advocacy of medium specificity is meant to break with the forms of the past. Medium specificity arguments are the battering rams of aesthetic revolution. Sankowski himself cites Jerzy Grotowski's *Towards a Poor Theatre*, while in film an essentialist brand of realism denied much of the achievement of silent cinema. In these cases and others, medium specificity claims break with tradition rather than developing from it. Also, the role that Sankowski attributes to medium specificity arguments vis-à-vis traditions appears at variance with the role he attributes to such arguments in regard to artistic diversity. In one case, medium specificity is to stimulate a profusion of different kinds of art, whereas in the second case the allegiance to medium specificity is to lead to the production of more of the same kind of art. One wonders how the same sort of argument can be justified by its performance of such conflicting functions. Here, Sankowski may answer that there is no conflict, because what he intends by the adoption of medium specificity is that there should be diversity between the arts but also uniformity within each art. However, this is very close to just assuming the medium specificity argument which Sankowski is supposed to be defending; for example, he never explains why uniformity and diversity should be distributed in just this way.

Indeed, one also wants to ask why Sankowski thinks he is justifying uniqueness arguments rather than simply indicating what people sometimes are trying to bring about by making such arguments. By saying that one uses a uniqueness argument to bring about a legitimately desirable state of affairs one hasn't shown that an argument is a good one, but only that the person who makes it has commendable practical reasons for presenting such arguments.

In his "Uniqueness of the Medium," Donald Crawford argues that though medium specificity claims do not play a logical role in supporting evaluative judgments about works of art, the notion of medium specificity is relevant to judgments we make about artists. Speaking of the idea that the works of one medium should not imitate those of another, Crawford holds "this criticism is, I think, a disguised criticism of the artist rather than the work itself. When stainless steel flatware is criticized (for imitating silver), I suggest that we are really criticizing the artists for being unimaginative, or for prostituting his creative talents to a fairly simple functional task when he need not have: he's responding to a commercial market rather than *creating* a demand for an artistic product. . . ."[26] Crawford may be correct in his assessment of the motive behind the medium specificity language in such cases; however, it is not obvious that the real issue in these cases has anything to do with claims about the uniqueness of the media. Rather, it is equally persuasive to maintain that the problem is with the motives behind and the intelligence of the imitation. It is not a problem of what is being imitated by what, as the medium specificity proponent avers. It is a question about the qualities – both moral and intellectual – to be found in the particular act of imitation at issue. We may complain that, in a given case, the cross-media imitation has no point or is shallow duplication. But these are the same sorts of challenges we will bring against imitations within a specified medium.

Notes

1. At the rhetorical level, rather than simply at the level of practice, this process of legitimatization-through-imitation takes place as polemicists analogize their favored medium to existing arts. In film, Vachel Lindsay's *The Art of the Moving Picture* (New York: Macmillan, 1922) is an early, salient, American example of this.

   Also, the play of differentiation/imitation involved in the emergence of the self-consciously invented arts of film, video and photography somewhat recalls the way in which painting strove to differentiate itself from the crafts while simultaneously valorizing itself through analogies with poetry. See Paul Oskar Kristeller's "The Modern System of the Arts," in *Art and Philosophy*, ed. W. D. Kennick (N.Y.: St. Martin's Press, 1979), p. 17.

2. Rudolf Arnheim, *Film as Art* (Berkeley: U. of Calif. Press., 1967), p. 35.

3. Rudolf Arnheim, "On the Nature of Photography," *Critical Inquiry*, 1 (Sept., 1974), p. 155.

4. Lev Kuleshov, *Kuleshov on Film*, trans. and ed. by R. Levaco (Berkeley: U. of Calif. Press, 1974).

5. Anthony McCall, "Two Statements," in *The Avant-Garde Film*, ed. by P. Adams Sitney (N.Y.: New York University Press, 1978), p. 250. For those who think that essentialism is long behind us in film, consider the eponymous essay in Christian Metz's *Imaginary Signifier* (Bloomington: U. of Indiana Press, 1982). I discuss Metz's methodological essentialism in my review of the *Imaginary Signifier* which is forthcoming in the *Journal of Aesthetics and Art Criticism*. That Metz's methodological essentialism is indisputably in vogue is evinced by the way it is uncritically parrotted in books like John Ellis's *Visible Fictions* (London: Routledge and Kegan Paul, 1982).

6. Roland Barthes, *Camera Lucida* (N.Y.: Hill and Wang, 1983). Similar recent essentialist views of photography can be found in Susan Sontag, *On Photography* (New York: Delta Books, 1973), and Stanley Cavell, *The World Viewed* (N.Y.: Viking, 1971). I criticize the Barthes-Bazin-Sontag-Cavell position in my "Concerning Photographic and Cinematic Representation," which is in the journal *Dialectics and Humanism*. This essay is also included in this volume.

7. Paul Strand, "Photography and the New God," in *Classic Essays on Photography*, ed. by Alan Trachtenberg (New Haven: Leete's Island Books, 1980), p. 142.

8. Ibid.

9. Edward Weston, "Seeing Photographically, in *Classic Essays on Photography*, p. 170.

10. Weston, 171. Ansel Adams would also be an example of the straight-shooting school. See his "I am a Photographer," in *The Camera Viewed*, ed. by P. R. Petruck (N.Y.: Dutton, 1979), Vol. II, pp. 25–40.

11. Laszlo Moholy-Nagy, "A New Instrument of

Vision," in *The Camera Viewed*, Vol. I, p. 166.

12. Moholy-Nagy, 167.

13. Frank Gilette, *Video Process and Meta-Process* (Syracuse, N.Y.: Everson Museum of Art, 1973), pp. 21–22.

14. Hollis Frampton, *Circles of Confusion* (Rochester, N.Y.: Visual Studies Workshop, 1983), pp. 166–67. For a similar affirmation of the medium-based potential of special-effects video, see the interview with Richard Lorber, "From Cimabue to Cunningham," in *Millennium Film Journal*, 10/11 (Fall/Winter 1981–82), p. 7. And Bill Viola reasserts the importance of medium specificity in the interview with him in *Sightlines,* Spring, 1983, p. 24.

15. Edward Stasheff and Rudy Bretz, *The Television Program: Its Writing, Direction and Production* (N.Y.: A. A. Wyn, 1961), p. 3.

16. Lizzie Borden, "Directions in Video Art," from *Video Art*, ed. by Suzanne Delehanty (Philadelphia: Institute of Contemporary Art, 1975), p. 88.

17. John Hanhardt, "Paik's Video Sculpture," in *Nam June Paik*, ed. by John Hanhardt (Whitney Museum of American Art, 1982), p. 98.

18. Gotthold Ephraim Lessing, *Laocoön* (N.Y.: Noonday Press, 1969), pp. 91–92.

19. These examples can be found in *Anthology of Concrete Poetry*, ed. by Emmet Williams (N.Y.: Something Else Press, 1967), n.p.

20. Bernard Bosanquet, *Three Lectures on Aesthetics* (London: Macmillan and Co. Ltd., 1915).

21. A more expanded version of this particular argument can be found in my "The Specificity of Media in the Arts," in *The Journal of Aesthetic Education*, Vol. 19, n. 4 (Winter, 1985). This essay is also included in this volume.

22. Herbert Read, *A Concise History of Modern Sculpture* (N.Y.: Oxford University Press, 1964), pp. 247–257.

23. Edward Sankowski, "Uniqueness Arguments and Artist's Actions," in the *Journal of Aesthetics and Art Criticism* (Fall, 1979), pp. 61–74. Sankowski's "plurality" argument can be found on pp. 66–67; his argument from tradition is on p. 71.

24. For an example of a dancer influenced by Minimal Art see Yvonne Rainer's "A Quasi Survey of Some 'Minimalist' Tendencies in the Quantitatively Minimal Dance Activity Midst the Plethora, or an Analysis of Trio A," *in Minimal Art*, ed. Gregory Battcock (N.Y.: Dutton, 1968), pp. 263–273. The influence of Minimalism is also richly documented in Sally Banes' *Terpsichore in Sneakers* (Boston: Houghton Mifflin Co., 1980). For examples of filmmakers who are influenced by gallery aesthetics see P. Adams Sitney, *Visionary Film* (New York: Oxford U. Press, 1979), especially pp. 369–397.

25. Sankowski, 71.

26. Donald Crawford, "The Uniqueness of the Medium," *The Personalist*, 51 (Autumn, 1970), p. 467, parenthetical information added. Additionally, I should also like to object to a remark that Crawford makes on page 461. He says, ". . . The film has a facility for organizing temporal relations and spatially disparate representations unequalled by any other medium." I do not understand the basis of this assertion. Surely literature can leap through time and space as easily as film. Indeed, my own prejudice is to suspect that literature is even more adaptable than the cinematic conventions we presently have in regard to complex spatial and temporal juxtapositions. Just in regard to time, for example, it should be remembered that literature has a much richer battery of explicit tenses to play with.

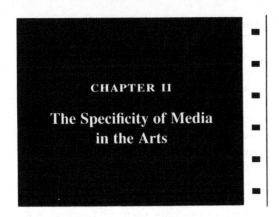

I

The idea – which I shall call the medium-specificity thesis – that each art form, in virtue of its medium, has its own exclusive domain of development was born in the eighteenth century, almost at the same time that the distinctions between the aesthetic and the nonaesthetic and between the fine arts and the practical arts crystallized. Yet despite its age, the medium-specificity thesis continues to exercise a tenacious grip on the imaginations of artists and theorists alike. On the contemporary art scene, this is perhaps most evident in the arena of video aesthetics, where one group, the image processors, advocate their stylistic explorations on the grounds that they are concerned with the basic attributes of video. Summarizing their position, Shelley Miller writes: "Electronic image processing uses as art-making material those properties inherent in the medium of video. Artists work at a fundamental level with various parameters of the electronic signal, for example, frequency amplitude or phase, which actually define the resulting image and sound."[1]

Undoubtedly many video avant-gardists are predisposed toward the medium-specificity thesis because, given backgrounds in the fine arts, their thinking has been and is swayed by the still influential tenets of Modernism à la Clement Greenberg. This approach to painting and sculpture is strongly essentialist. Greenberg proclaims:

A modernist work of art must try, in principle, to avoid dependence upon any order of experience not given in the most essentially construed nature of its medium. This means, among other things, renouncing illusion and explicitness. The arts are to achieve concreteness, "purity," by acting solely in terms of their separate and irreducible selves.

Modernist painting meets our desire for the literal and positive by renouncing the illusion of the third dimension.[2]

For Greenberg, optical, two-dimensional effects are the medium-specific domain of painting, while tactile, three-dimensional effects are the domain of sculpture. And video artists, influenced by this version of Modernism, believe that the proper direction of their art form will be involved in the isolation and definition of the quidity of the video medium. Moreover, with Greenberg, these medium-specificity proponents are advocating that the differences between media should supply us with a standard of what art should and should not be made. And, if medium-specificity is transgressed, the medium-specificity critic is thought to have a reason to evaluate a given work of art negatively.

Contemporary photographic criticism also shows some recurrent tendencies toward upholding the medium-specificity thesis. For example, in his extremely popular book, *Camera Lucida*, Roland Barthes argues that photographic representation is essentially different from representation based on analogy or copying, i.e., the kind of representation found in painting. Barthes writes: "The realists, of whom I am one and of whom I was already one when I asserted that the Photograph was an image without code – even if obviously, certain codes do infect our reading of it – the realists do not take the photograph for a copy of reality, but for an emanation of *past reality*: a *magic*, not an art."[3] Furthermore, realist aesthetic preferences appear connected to Barthes's realist account of photographic representation -- specifically, his taste for photos that afford the opportunity for the spectator actively to discover uncoded details.[4]

The persistence of the medium-specificity thesis has significance for educational policy as well. For when video makers and photographers strive to form their own academic departments or divisions, a prospect already before us, they are likely to do so by asserting their autonomy from other arts on the basis of medium-specificity arguments.

II

The medium-specificity thesis holds that each art form has its own domain of expression and exploration. This domain is determined by the nature of the medium through which the objects of a given art form are composed. Often the idea of "the nature of the medium" is thought of in terms of the physical structure of the medium. The medium-specificity thesis can be construed as saying that each art form should pursue those effects that, in virtue of its medium it alone – i.e., of all the arts – can achieve. Or the thesis might be interpreted as claiming that each art form should pursue ends that, in virtue of its medium, it achieves most effectively or best of all those effects at its disposal. Most often the medium-specificity theorist unconsciously relies upon (and conflates) both these ideas. Each art form should pursue *only* those effects which, in virtue of its medium, it excels in achieving. The thesis holds that each art form should pursue ends distinct from other art forms. Art forms should not overlap in their effects, nor should they imitate each other. Also, each art form is assumed to have some range of effects that it discharges best or uniquely as a result of the structure of its physical medium. Each art form should be limited to exploiting this range of effects, which the nature of the medium dictates.

The idea that each art form has its own domain and that it should not overlap with the effects of other art forms hails from the eighteenth century, when theorists such as

Jean Baptiste Dubos, James Harris, Moses Mendelsohn, and most famously, Gotthold Ephraim Lessing revolted against the kind of art theory proposed in Charles Batteux's tract entitled *The Fine Arts Reduced to the Same Principle*.[5] As Batteux's title should suggest, pre-Enlightenment art theorizing tended to treat all arts as the same – e.g., as striving for the same effect, such as the imitation of the beautiful in nature. Enlightenment proponents such as Lessing, possessed by the epoch's zeal for distinctions, sought to differentiate the arts in terms of their medium-specific ingredients. Using the concept of a *sign* in advance of semiology, Lessing felt that the proper subject matter of each medium could be extrapolated from the physical properties of its constituent signs: poetry, whose words are encountered *sequentially*, is a temporal art, specializing in the representation of events and processes, while painting, whose signs, daubs of paint, are encountered as only spatially contiguous, should represent moments.[6]

The impression that proponents of the medium-specificity thesis impart is that one need only examine the physical structure of the medium, and the sort of effects the art form based in that medium should traffic in more or less jumps out at one. Paint is the major ingredient in painting. Therefore, painting should primarily exemplify flatness (or, at least, be constrained to exemplify only effects that are consistent with flatness). However, it is far from clear that one can move so neatly from the physical medium to the *telos* of the art form. For example, if anything can lay claim to being the physical trait that essentially defines film, it is its flexible celluloid base. But what does this suggest to us about the kinds of things that could or should be represented or expressed in the medium? Indeed, why suppose that the essential characteristics of a medium necessarily have any directive consequences for the art made in that medium? Of course, this point also pertains when we are speaking of other than essential aspects of the physical medium. If some sort of writing instrument, e.g., a typewriter (or, to be more up-to-date, a word processor), and some material surface, say paper, are the customary, basic materials of the novelist, what can we extrapolate from this about the proper range of effects of the novel?[7]

Perhaps we will be told that language rather than print is the novelist's basic material. But then what different effects should poetry and the novel pursue, insofar as they have the same basic material? Maybe a move will be made to suggest that sound is the basic material of poetry, whereas events and actions are the basic material of the novel. Of course, it is very difficult to understand why we are to construe actions and events as *physical* constituents of a medium on a par with candidates like the paint of paintings. And, undoubtedly, the medium-specificity theorist, at this point, will tell us that we need not be committed to a simple notion of the medium restricted solely to its physical characteristics. But once we abandon a supposedly physicalist account of the medium, how are we to determine what the basic elements or constituents of the medium are? Whether or not it is true that actions and events are the basic elements of the novel, of course, is not my concern. My interests in the preceding dialectic lie in what it reveals about medium-specificity arguments, viz., that it is not an easy task to identify the basic materials of a medium, let alone to move from a simple enumeration of a medium's physical elements to the effects the art form embodied in the medium should be committed to explore. Indeed, it is often difficult to know at what level of analysis we should focus our attention vis-à-vis medium-specificity accounts. For though they generally suggest that their starting point is some physical element or constituent, medium-specificity discourse also easily drifts into consideration of nonphysicalistic elements or constituents: space and time, for example, are often said to be the basic ingredients of film. But why

are these more pertinent to the medium-specificity theorist than the flexible-celluloid base of cinema?

Of course, if we already have a specific use for a medium, say poetry, then we may be able to say that features of the medium, even what physical features, are relevant for serving that purpose. However, here it pays to note that a feature, like sound in language, might be better characterized as a feature relevant for the purposes of poetry rather than as the basic, determinant feature of the medium. Basic-feature talk seems to imply or connote that prior to any uses of the medium, a medium could have a feature that would be more important and more indicative than any other of its features concerning what ranges of expression the art form embodied in the medium should explore. But, in fact, we have no idea of what features of the medium are important unless we have a use for the medium.

Furthermore, once we realize that it is our purposes that mold the medium's development and not the medium that determines our artistic purposes, we realize that the problem of overlaps between media is vitiated. We may have a purpose, such as the dramatic portrayal of human action, that will cross media, selecting the features of each medium that best facilitate our purpose. These features in each medium, in turn, either may resemble or may sharply contrast with those of other media. The provisional purposes we designate for a medium may in fact be *best* pursued by imitating another medium. Thus, Jean-Marie Straub, in his film *The Bridegroom, the Actress, and the Pimp*, mimes theater outright in order to make – quite effectively, I might add – his reflexive point that all film is "staged." Moreover, it is likely that when we introduce a new medium like video or photography, we will have to begin by attempting to adapt it to already existing purposes and strategies, e.g., portraiture, whose implementation perforce will recall the effects of other media. With such incipient arts, that is, practitioners will have to begin somewhere. The evolution of the medium will depend on the purposes we find for it. The medium has no secret purpose of its own.

Another way to approach this point is to remember that all media have more than one constituent component. To simplify, let us say that paint, paint brushes, and canvases are the basic materials of painting. How does the medium-specificity theorist know to identify paint as the pertinent element in this group? And, having identified paint as the lead element, how does the Modernist know to identify the potential for flatness, as opposed to impastos of ever-widening density, as the relevant possibility of paint that is to be exploited? Clearly paint itself cannot dictate how it is to be used – paint can be adapted for covering houses, covering canvases, portraying funerals, or proffering color fields. Paint does not determine how it will be used, but the purposes for which paint is used – art and/or Modernism – determine the relevant features of the medium for the task at hand. Flatness, for example, could be made to express Modernist ideals of purity and rigor. In short, the purposes of a given art – indeed, of a given style, movement, or genre – will determine what aspects of the physical medium are important. The physical medium does not select a unique purpose, or even a delimited range of purposes, for an art form.

The fact that a medium is generally composite in terms of its basic constituents leads to other complications for the medium-specificity thesis. For different features of the medium may suggest radically different directions of artistic development. Film has photography as a basic element, which has led many to designate it as a realist art. But the appearance of movement generated by the sequential structure of the film strip is equally basic to cinema, and it has led some to champion cinema as a magical art. In such cases, which aspect of the medium should be emphasized? Can the medium-specificity theorist offer a nonarbitrary basis for selecting the program suggested by one basic feature of the medium over another? Perhaps the medium-specificity theorist will opt for the program suggested by that element of the medium that is a *sine qua non* of the medium. But in our film example, both photography and the sequential structure of the film strip are *sine qua nons*.

Of course, the medium-specificity theorist may argue that no problem arises for him because basic elements of the medium suggest different lines of development. For, it may be said, the artist can pluralistically pursue more than one line of development. However, there are often cases where the candidates for the basic features of the medium suggest programs of development that conflict with each other. Both cinematography and editing are counted as among the basic elements of cinema, ones purportedly enjoining radically opposed styles: realism versus montage. Here it is impossible that the artist can fully explore the range of effects his medium excels in, because it is impossible simultaneously to exploit the cinematic potentials of rapid editing and deep-focus, realist cinematography. Similarly, video's capacity for immediate transmission makes it a useful device for creating certain news documents, while its potential for instant feedback enables it to be employed for abstract image processing. But one cannot make an abstract, image-processed news document.

A medium may excel in more than one effect, and these effects may be incompatible, thus making it impossible for the artist to abide by the medium-specificity thesis by doing what the medium does best. For it is not possible to do all that the medium does best. Nor does the medium-specificity thesis have a nonarbitrary way to decide which of conflicting "medium-based" styles is to be preferred. Obviously, one will gravitate toward the technique that serves one's purposes best. What aspects of the medium are to be emphasized or exploited will be determined by the aims of the artists and the purposes of the art form. If poetry is to be read silently on the page, then it makes sense to emphasize certain aspects of the medium, such as where each line ends; if poetry is primarily to be declaimed aloud by bards, however, line endings will not be a very determinant feature of the medium, even if our poets compose their songs ahead of time on paper. A medium is used to serve the purposes of an art form, a style, or a genre. Those purposes make different aspects of the medium relevant, rather than vice-versa.

In response to my claims about the priority of use, it may be asserted that there are certain uses to which a medium cannot be put. And this, is might be said, is the basic truth of the medium-specificity claim. However, if the force of *cannot* here is that of either logical or physical impossibility, then the medium-specificity thesis is nothing but a truism, one irrelevant to art criticism or art making. For if it is literally impossible for a given medium to be put to a given use, then it never will be. Thus, since there is never any likelihood that media will overstep themselves in terms of what is logically or physically possible for them to do, there is no reason to warn them to be wary in this regard.

Clearly the existing output of any medium will only consist of objects designed to serve uses that it is logically and physically possible for the medium to perform. Use determines what aspects of the medium are relevant for aesthetics, rather than some essential trait of the medium determining the proper use of the medium. But if the use of the medium is key, then effects will be evaluated in terms of how well they serve presiding purposes. Some uses of painting, landscape, for example, enjoin the exploitation of *pictorial* depth – obviously a logical and physical possibility of the medium. Such instances of pictorial depth, then, will be evaluated in light of the degree to which they serve the purposes to which they are connected. Our landscape paintings with their depth cannot be rejected on the grounds that paintings *cannot* disregard the essential flatness of the medium. Quite clearly some paintings do and, therefore, can ignore the Modernist's constraints concerning pictorial flatness. In such cases, excellence in the service of a definable purpose – e.g., accurately portraying recognizable landscapes – will be our leading criterion for accepting each modification of the medium, at least where there is agreement about how to use the medium. Moreover, where there is not agreement, reference to traits of the medium will have little sway concerning alternative styles, since traits of the medium are only significant vis-à-vis uses. Rather, we will have to find other reasons for advocating one use over others.

It may be felt that whatever persuasiveness the foregoing account has, it can be resisted on the grounds that there are straightforward examples where artistic failure can be incontestably ascribed to ignoring the medium-specificity thesis. Imagine a silent film drama in which we see a gun pointed at X, followed by an intertitle reading "Bang!," followed by an image of a prostrate, dead X. One explanation of what has gone wrong here is that the filmmaker has failed to execute the scene in terms of what the medium does best – viz., showing things. However, we must ask whether the putative error here would be an error in any kind of film or only in certain types or genres of film with very special purposes. Put this way, I think we see that the sequence just described might be a brilliant invention in a comedy or in a film striving after Brecht's vaunted alienation effect. On the other hand, the sequence is an error within the Hollywood style of the action genre for which, among other things, considerations of pacing as well as of spectacular effects would favor showing the gunshot. Style, genre, and art form, and the purposes rooted therein, determine what elements of the medium will and will not be relevant.

That is, contra the medium-specificity thesis, there are no techniques that are unavailable to an artist because of a failure to exploit certain characteristics of a given medium (or because of overlaps with other media). Rather there are styles, genres, art forms, and their presiding purposes, which determine the viability of a technique within a context of use. Where certain artistic failures occur – such as in cases of canned theater – we are not confronting transgressions of the medium but errors within prevailing styles that cannot be recuperated by references to other existing styles or other defensible purposes.

Earlier I assumed that the "cannot" in the medium-specificity thesis – i.e., "Make no medium do what it cannot do" – signalled either logical or physical impossibility. However, there is another sense of "cannot" that the medium-specificity theorist is banking on. According to the medium-specificity approach, we are told that if one wants to identify the aspects of the medium that a given art is to exploit, then one must look to those aspects that differentiate the medium in question from all other media. Thus, it is the purported flatness of paint that distinguishes it from sculpture. So painting-as-surface is the painter's proper arena. Here we see that the medium-specificity thesis is to be read normatively – "Do not make an art form do what it cannot do" means "Do not make it do what it ought not do because some other art does it." Thus, the medium-specificity formula is an injunction.

As an injunction, the medium-specificity thesis has two components. One component is the idea that there is something that each medium does best – alternatively, best of everything else a given medium does or best in comparison with other media. On both counts, Lessing thought that painting represented moments best and poetry actions. Rudolf Arnheim thinks that films represent animated action best.[8] Also, the medium-specificity thesis holds that each of the arts should do that which differentiates it from the other arts. We can call these two components of the medium-specificity thesis the excellence requirement and the differentiation requirement, respectively. There are many problems with the medium-specificity thesis. Some of these are a direct result of the combination of the differentiation and excellence requirements.

An underlying assumption of the medium-specificity thesis appears to be that what a medium does best will coincide with what differentiates media (and art forms). But why should this be so? For example, many media narrate. Film, drama, prose, and epic poetry all tell stories. For argument's sake, let us say it is what each of these arts does best – i.e., what each does better than anything else it does. Yet, narrative will not differentiate these art forms. What does the medium-specificity thesis tell us to do in such a situation?

If film and the novel both excel in narration, (1) should neither art form narrate since narration fails to differentiate them? or (2) should film not narrate since narration will fail to differentiate it from the novel and the novel claimed the domain of narration first? or (3) should the novel give up narration and let the newcomer have its chance?[9]

The first alternative is simply absurd. It would sacrifice a magnificent cultural invention – narration – for whatever bizarre satisfaction we can derive from adherence to the differentiation requirement. That is, to what end would we be forgoing artistic excellence in cases like this? Clearly attainable excellence will always be more important to us than differentiation for its own sake.

The second alternative is also unattractive. In this case, the medium-specificity theorist would appear to confuse history with ontology. Film is to foreswear narrating just because literature already has that turf staked out. But surely this is only an accident of history. What if movies had arisen before writing? Then would novels have to find some occupation other than narrative? And what might that have been?

Clearly, accidents of history should not preclude an artistic medium from exploring an area in which it excels. Nor should accidents of history be palmed off as ontological imperatives, another proclivity of the medium-specificity thesis. That is, according to one very natural construal of the medium-specificity thesis, the special subject matter of each art form follows from the nature of the medium it is embodied in. However, in fact, we have seen that the medium-specificity thesis is even more complicated than this because a medium is supposed to specialize in what it excels in as a result of its nature, but only where that area of special achievement differentiates the medium in question from other media. So, the question of differentiation is not simply a question about the nature of what a medium in isolation excels in, but a question about the comparison of arts. And it is quite possible that a new art may be invented which excels in an area where an older art already excels.[10] To award the older art the domain just because it is already established seems arbitrary, as does the third alternative above – awarding the domain to the younger art just because it is younger. If two arts both excel in an area it seems natural to permit them both to explore it. What reason do we have to be against this option? Following this policy, we will enrich ourselves by multiplying the number of excellent things we have. This is surely the case with narrative. The world is richer for having novels *and* fiction films *and* epic poems *and* drams *and* operas *and* comic books *and* narrative paintings, etc., though the differentiation component of the medium-specificity thesis would seem to urge us to forsake some if not all of these treasures should we choose to regard the medium-specificity thesis as a guideline for deciding what art can and cannot be made.

The specificity thesis has both an excellence component and a differentiation component. Perhaps one interpretation of the theory is that each art form should pursue those projects which fall in the area of intersection between what the art form excels in and what differentiates the art form from other art forms. But this does not seem to be an acceptable principle because, among other things, it entails that an art form might not be employed to do what it does best just because some other art form also does it well or, for that matter, can merely do it passingly. Again, the specificity thesis seems to urge us willingly to sacrifice excellence in art on principle. But I think that excellence is always the overriding consideration for deciding whether or not a particular practice or development is acceptable.

Indeed, I believe that what could be called the priority of excellence is the central telling point against the specificity thesis. To dramatize this, let us imagine that for some reason the only way that G. B. Shaw could get backing for *Pygmalion* was to make it as a talking picture – perhaps in the possible world we are imagining, Shaw was only reputed as a successful screenwriter. Let us also suppose that in some sense it is true that theater is a better showcase for aesthetically crafted language than talking pictures. Would we decide that *Pygmalion* should not be made, even though film will afford an adequate mode of presentation for it? I think our answer is "no," because our intuitions are that the medium-specificity thesis should not be allowed to stand between us and excellence.

Nor need the excellence be a matter of the highest excellence achievable in a given medium. One interpretation of the medium-specificity thesis urges that a medium pursue only that which it does best of all the things it does. But if a medium does something well and the occasion arises, why should an art form be inhibited especially just because there is something that the art form does better? Certain magical transformations – weaklings into werewolves – can be most vividly executed in cinema. But it can also be done quite nicely on stage. Should this minor excellence be forgone in a stage adaptation of *Dr. Jekyll and Mr. Hyde* either because language, not transformation, is what theater handles best or because film can make the metamorphosis more graphic?

The medium-specificity thesis guides us to sacrifice excellence in art. We should eschew Groucho Marx's movie monologues because they more appropriately belong to theater, just as the *Laocoön* should have been poetry. But is there reason to give up all this real and potential excellence? There is the medium-specificity argument conceived of as a rule that tells us what art should or should not be made. But on what grounds? It is not a moral imperative. So what is its point? What do we gain from abiding by the medium-specificity dictum that compensates or accounts for the sacrifices of excellence the medium-specificity theorist calls for? Here it is important to recall that the medium-specificity thesis has often been mobilized to discount acknowledged artistic accomplishments.[11]

The medium-specificity theorist may maintain that his position is basically committed to the proposition that each medium should only pursue those effects that it acquits better than any other medium. This not only raises the question of why a medium should only pursue that which it is thought to do better than any other (in opposition to what it is merely thought to do as well as other media, or what it does well but not as well as other media are thought to do); it also raises the question of whether it makes sense to compare arts in terms of whether they are more or less successful in performing the same generic functions. Can we say whether film, drama, or the novel narrates best, or is it more appropriate to say they narrate differently? Moreover, the relevant issue when commending a given artwork is not whether it is an instance of the medium that is best for the effect the artwork exemplifies, but whether the artwork in question achieves its own ends.

Surprisingly, there is little by way of defense for the medium-specificity thesis, especially when it is thought of as a way of determining what art should and should not be made. The thesis usually succeeds by appearing to be intuitively self-evident. Undoubtedly, the medium-specificity theorist leads listeners to accept the thesis through an implicit analogy with tools. Tools, for example, a Philips-head screwdriver, are designed with functions in mind, and efficiency dictates that we use the tool for what it is designed for. If you wish to turn a screw with an *x*-shaped groove on top, use a Philips-head screwdriver. If you wish to explore the potentials of aesthetically crafted, dramatic language, employ theater. If your topic is animated action, use film. Likewise, just as you should not, all things being equal, use a Philips-head screwdriver as a church key (though it can open a beer can), you should not, all things being equal, use cinema to perform theater's task and vice-versa.

But I think that to carry over the tool analogy to an art form is strained. Art forms are not tools, designed and invented to serve a single, specific purpose, nor are they even tools with a delimited range of functions. Most art forms were not self-consciously invented and, therefore, they are not designed.[12] Painting was not invented to celebrate flatness. Moreover, even with self-consciously invented arts like photography, film, and video, it was soon realized that these media could perform many more tasks than they were expressly and intentionally designed for. Indeed, our interest in an art form is in large measure an interest in how artists learn or discover new ways of using their medium. But the idea of the artist discovering new ways of using the medium would make no sense if the medium were designed for a single, fixed purpose, as the strongest variants of the medium-specificity thesis seem to suggest.

An art form is embodied in a medium which, even in the cases of the self-consciously invented arts, is one whose many potentials remain to be discovered. But discovery would not be a relevant expectation to have of artists, nor would an interest in it be relevant to an art form if the task of the art form were as fixed as that of a Philips-head screwdriver. A correlative fact against the idea of the fixedness of function of art forms is the fact that art forms continue to exist over time, obviously because they are periodically reinvented and new uses are found for them. But if art forms were as determinately set in their function as are things like Philips-head screwdrivers, one would expect them, like most tools, to pass away as their function becomes archaic. That art forms are constantly readapted, reinvented, and redirected bodes ill for the central metaphor suggested by the medium-specificity thesis: that of the art form as specialized tool.

Furthermore, the notion of "efficiency" as it figures in the allure of the medium-specificity thesis is suspect. For it is not clear that if film undertakes the task of painting – showing a still setting – it will be inefficient in the sense of incurring more labor. Nor is it obvious that expenditures of time, material, or labor are really relevant in the appraisal of artworks. Excellence of effect is what we care about. Moreover, if "efficiency" is thought of as "operating competently," then it is difficult to see how the medium-specificity theorist can employ it in a non-question-begging fashion since things such as the *Laocoön* do support some measure of aesthetic experience even if they supposedly transgress their medium.

One way to attempt to defend the medium-specificity thesis is by asking, "Why else would there be different art media if they were not supposed to pursue different ends?" The medium-specificity thesis is, in this light, an inference to the best explanation. Given the fact that we have a number of arts, we ask "why?" The answer that seems most reasonable is: "Because each art has, or should have, a different function." Again, there is some underlying idea of efficiency.

An important presupposition of this argument is that it is legitimate to ask why we have different arts. It also supposes that it is legitimate to expect as an answer to this question something like a rational principle.

To paraphrase Wittgenstein, where there is no question, there is no answer. We can, I think, use this principle to rid ourselves of the preceding argument. For its question, when stated nonelliptically, is not "Why are there diverse arts?" but "What is the rationale that explains or justifies our possession of exactly the diverse arts we have?" Now there may be an answer, or, better, *a series of* answers to the former question – answers of an historical and/or an anthropological variety. For example, we have film because Edison wanted an invention to supplement the phonograph. Perhaps we have painting because one day a Cro-Magnon splashed some adhesive victuals on a cave wall and the result looked strikingly like a bison. And so on. But we have no answer to the second question – "What is the rationale for having exactly the several arts we have?" Rather, each art arose due to a chain of events that led to its discovery or invention and to its subsequent popularization. The result is the *collection* of arts we have, which we only honorifically refer to as a system. The arts are not systematic, designed with sharply variegated functions, as the medium-specificity thesis holds. Rather, they are an amalgamation of historically evolved media whose effects often overlap. There is no rationale for the system, for in truth, it is only a collection. Thus, we have no need for the explanation afforded by the medium-specificity thesis.

As I mentioned earlier, one area where it will be tempting to resort to medium-specificity arguments is in the justification of the formation of new arts-educational departments, such as film, video, photography, holography, and so on. Proponents of such departments will argue that their medium is distinct from the other arts in such a way that it will not receive its due if condemned to existence in departments dominated by specialists in literature, theater, and fine art. Furthermore, it may be added that the medium-specificity thesis is of great heuristic value insofar as it entreats students to think deeply about the specific elements of their trade.

I do not wish to demean the fact that the medium-specificity myth has and can have useful results. But I wonder whether the students who benefit from this myth are really doing something as simple as considering the materials of their arts rather than the "state-of-the-art" techniques, conventions, and styles that dominate their practices. And, furthermore, the medium-specificity thesis can result in undesirable consequences. Students can become mired in the prevailing traditions of their medium, closed to the possibility of innovating inspiration from the other arts. Indeed, my own prejudice is to suspect that once students have mastered the basic techniques of their medium, their best strategy is to explore not only the history of their art, but other arts and culture at large for new and stimulating ideas.

Concerning the usefulness of medium-specificity arguments for the justification of new academic departments, it can be said that this is a rhetorical matter, not a logical one. That administrators may be persuaded by such arguments, or that the proponents of new arts-educational disciplines feel they need such arguments, does not show that the medium-specificity thesis is valid. On the other hand, such departmental realignments can be defended without reference to medium specificity. We may argue that the practice in question has become or is becoming so important to the life of our culture that it warrants intensive and specialized study, even if the enterprise does overlap

with the practices of preexisting forms such as theater, literature, or fine art.

III

In concluding, I would like to emphasize that the strongest and most pervasive instances of the medium-specificity argument maintain that the various media (that art forms are embodied in) have unique features – ostensibly identifiable in advance of, or independently of, the uses to which the medium is put – and, furthermore, these unique features determine the proper domain of effects of the art form in question. However, it seems to me that what are considered by artists, critics, and theorists as aesthetic flaws, traceable to violations of the medium, are in fact violations of certain styles, the purposes of those styles, and their characteristic modes of handling the medium. That medium-specificity arguments are often connected with advancing the cause of one artistic movement or use of the medium should indicate that what is urged under the banner of medium specificity is linked to implicit conceptions of preferred artistic styles.

Even when analysts are not concerned with saying how a medium should be used but are only attempting to describe the unique, artistically pertinent features of a medium, I suspect that they are really speaking of styles within the medium. If we are told, for example, that temporal manipulation is the artistically relevant, unique feature of film, our informant clearly is thinking of film in relation to certain styles of filmmaking. For real-time exposition is also a feature of the medium, one pertinent to alternate styles of filmmaking, which, of course, have different purposes.[13]

Similarly, if we are told that the potential for wordless action and spectacle, rather than ornate language, is the key element of an authentic, nonliterary theater, then it is evident, I think, that we are being asked to advocate one style of theater while being confused about the reasons for doing so. We are led to believe that our decision is based upon some facts about the nature of the theatrical medium rather than assessing the purposes of the style of the nonliterary theater we are asked to endorse.

The task of the theorist of an art is not to determine the unique features of the medium but to explain how and why the medium has been adapted to prevailing and emerging styles and, at times, to either defend or condemn the prevailing or emerging purposes artists pursue. Such debate should not proceed by arguments about what the medium dictates, but rather by finding reasons – artistic, moral, and intellectual – that count for or against those styles, genres, artworks, and their subtending purposes which confront us in the thick of the life of the culture.

Notes

1. Shelley Miller, "Electronic Video Image Processing: Notes toward a Definition," *Exposure* 21, no. 1 (1983): 22.
2. Clement Greenberg, "The New Sculpture," from his *Art and Culture* (Boston: Beacon, 1961), p. 139.
3. Roland Barthes, *Camera Lucida*, trans. Richard Howard (New York: Hill and Wang, 1981), p. 88. I criticize this position on photography in my "Concerning Uniqueness claims for Photographic and Cinematic Representation," in the journal *Dialectics and Humanism*, no. 2 (1987). This essay is also included in this volume.
4. See Barthes's discussion of the photographic *punctum* in *Camera Lucida*, esp. pp. 51–60.
5. The historical remarks here follow the account offered by Monroe C. Beardsley in his *Aesthetics: From Classical Greece to the Present* (New York: Macmillan, 1966), pp. 160–63.
6. Gotthold Ephraim Lessing, *Laocoön*, trans. E. Frothingham (New York: Noonday Press, 1969), pp. 91–92.
7. In the paragraph above, I am accepting the frequent presupposition of specificity theorists that media can be individuated on the basis of their physical structures. But this does seem problematic. Why claim that daguerreotypes should be grouped in the same medium as celluloid-based photography? The physical structure and certain of the physical potentials of these processes are so different. Why not claim there are at least two media here? Obviously, the question of individuating media is not simply a matter of physicalistic considerations. Media are cultural and historical constructions. The topic of the way in which media are individuated is too large to include in this paper. For the purposes of my argument, I am hypothetically assuming the adequacy of our present distinctions between media. But for further discussion, see my "Defining the Moving Image," in this volume.
8. Rudolf Arnheim, *Film*, trans. L. M. Sieveking and F. D. Morrow (London: Faber and Faber, 1933).
9. It is interesting to note that most often when medium-specificity claims are advanced in support of the program of a particular art, generally, the theorist does not contrast the art he champions with every other art – which one would expect given the theory – but only with selected arts. Thus, painting is contrasted with sculpture, or video with film, or photography with painting, or film with theater, etc. Film, for example, is not usually contrasted with the narrative novel in order to find film's proper domain of effects, nor is video contrasted with music. The theory is only applied to certain neighbors of the art in question, normally ones with which the art in question is competing for attention and for audiences. The differentiation requirement, in such contexts, does not seem to be a matter of ontology but a rhetorical lever in aesthetic power struggles. This is discussed at greater length in my "Medium Specificity Arguments and Self-Consciously Invented Arts: Film, Video and Photography," in *Millennium Film Journal* nos. 14/15 (Fall/Winter, 1984–85). This essay is also included in this volume.

   Parenthetically, it is worth pointing out that most frequently medium-specificity arguments are used in the context of comparing only two arts. This may be the cause of the fact that it is difficult to find elaborately articulated statements of the general thesis.

Rather, the general thesis is most commonly assumed as a premise for the purposes of a more local argument.

10. Here we are not speaking of the arts excelling relative to each other but excelling in terms of one thing that they do compared to other things that they do.

11. For example, see Erwin Panofsky's attack of *The Cabinet of Dr. Caligari* in his "Style and Medium in the Motion Pictures," in *Film Theory and Criticism*, ed. Gerald Mast and Marshall Cohen (New York: Oxford University Press, 1970), p. 263.

12. Here an analogy with human beings may be helpful. Human beings are not designed with a fixed function and, as a result, we do not attempt narrowly to constrain, the ways in which they can fruitfully develop. We accept a range of alternative, even competing, life-styles. Likewise with the artforms embodied in artistic media.

13. Another reason that I advocate the priority of stylistic considerations over mediumistic ones is that our stylistic aims, needs, and purposes lead to changes in the very physical structure of media. It is because we are committed to certain stylistic aims that we mold dancers' bodies in a certain way; it is because we already are committed to certain styles of realism that various technical innovations, like cinemascope, are introduced into the film medium. The physical structure of a medium does not remain static. It is modified as a result of the needs and imperatives of our existing and emerging styles, genres, and art movements. Those often literally shape the medium, rather than the medium dictating style.

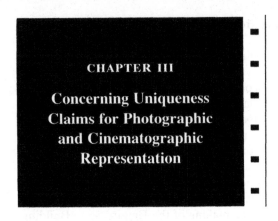

CHAPTER III

Concerning Uniqueness
Claims for Photographic
and Cinematographic
Representation

The Issue

One long-standing and still persistent view of photographic and (photographically based) cinematographic representation (i.e., the frame and the shot) is that they are essentially distinct from other forms of pictorial representation, notably painting. Whereas painting is thought to rely upon a resemblance relation between the referent and its representation, the photographic arts, including cinema, are believed to sustain an identity relation between their referents and their representations. André Bazin writes

Before the arrival of photography and later of cinema, the plastic arts (esp. portraiture) were the only intermediaries between actual physical presence and absence. Their justification was their resemblance which stirs the imagination and helps the memory. But photography is something else again. In no sense is it the image of an object or person, it is its tracing. Its automatic genesis distinguishes it radically from the other techniques of reproduction. The photograph proceeds by means of the lens to the taking of a luminous impression in light – to a mold. As such it carries with it more than a mere resemblance, namely a kind of identity – the card we call by that name being conceivable only in an age of photography.[1]

and

The photographic image is the object itself. . . . It shares by virtue of the process of its becoming, the being of the model of which it is a reproduction; it *is* the model.[2]

Stanley Cavell, in turn, sympathizes with Bazin's notion of some sort of identity relation between the photographic image and its referent when he urges "A photograph does not present us with 'likenesses' of things; it presents us, we want to say, with things themselves."[3]

Once the relation between the image – the photograph or the cinematic shot – is thought of as some sort of identity relation, the ruling idea of representation becomes *re*-presentation, i.e., the image is thought to *present again* some object or event from the past. Bazin writes

The objective nature of photography confers on it a quality of credibility absent from all other picture making. In spite of any objections our critical spirit may offer we are forced to accept as real the existence of the object reproduced, actually re-presented, set before us in space and time.[4]

Bazin's re-presentational theory is echoed by Roland Barthes when, writing of himself as a realist, he says ". . . the realists do not take the photograph for a 'copy' of reality, but for an emanation of past reality. . . ."[5] For proponents of the re-presentational theory, the photograph has a special bond with reality. Susan Sontag claims ". . . a photograph is never less than the registering of an emanation (light waves reflected by objects) – a material vestige of its subject in a way that no painting can be."[6]

From these quotations, it is possible to derive the key elements of the re-presentational theory of the photographic and cinematic image. First, it is essentialist, claiming that the nature of photographs and cinematic shots is unique, distinct, that is, from drawings, paintings, etc. Second, some sort of identity relation is held to persist between the photograph or film image and its referent *because*, third, the film image or photograph is directly produced or is caused to be by its referent. And, lastly, the photographic image has singular, existential import because it is produced from something that existed which caused it to be. That is, in photographic and cinematic representation, something is always thought to be re-presented – either the object itself, a pattern of light rays, an emanation, a trace, or an imprint.

The purpose of this paper is to examine the re-presentational theory, and several subsidiary hypotheses and arguments that are associated with it, and, finally, to offer an alternate approach to photographic and cinematographic representation.

Problems with the Re-Presentational Theory

The re-presentational theory of photographic and film representation purports that there is an identity relation between the image and its model. Sometimes this notion is unpacked by the metaphor of a mold. What are we to regard as the "mold" in this context? One option, a likely one it seems to me, is to think that the raw film stock functions as the mold. That is, the mold "fits" both the final image and its model. These are related in the manner of two subway tokens. This metaphor, in turn, could be further explicated by taking the identity claim of the re-presentational theory to hold that the photograph or film image is identical to its singular referent in terms of the pertinent patterns of light, emanating from the referent, which gave rise to the image. Thus, a strong version of the re-presentational theory maintains that: For any photographic or film image x and its referent y, x represents y if and only if (1) x is identical to y (in terms of pertinent patterns of light), and (2) y is a causal factor in the production of x. The term *pertinent* is included in the formula in order to attempt to accommodate the transposition of color scenes into black-and-white photography.

This theory of re-presentation has certain advantages over the simple forms of resemblance theories attacked by Nelson Goodman.[7] It cannot be reduced to absurdity by pointing to the symmetrical nature of identity. For by making reference to the causal process of photography, the symmetrical relation of identity, in this formulation, is blocked from entailing that "If a model y is identical with its image x then the model y represents the image x" because it is not the case that the image is a causal factor in the production of the model. That is, a photo of the Empire State Building was not a factor in the making of the Empire State Building.

If the re-presentational theory diverges from a simple resemblance approach, it also diverges from our ordinary concept of representation, including photographic representation. Indeed, the re-presentational theory is merely homonymous with our everyday sense of representation. For example, the re-presentation sense of representation is broader than our ordinary notion. It maintains that a cinematic shot and its referent are identical because the image is a causal effect of the light reflected by the model. It is in this sense that photographic representation is said to be re-presentational. Yet, by this standard, we must endorse many kinds of images that we do not ordinarily count as representational. A close-up of a square inch of a bare, undifferentiated wall is a re-presentation putatively, but it is hardly what we usually call a representation. Obviously, recognizability is key to our ordinary concept of representation. Re-presentation, however, proposes itself as a physicalist analysis without psychological dimensions. Therefore, all manner of shots – like the close-up of the wall – satisfy the requirements of re-presentation without being what we generally think of as representational images. Thus, the operative concept of re-presentation here is broader than our ordinary concept of representation in that shots we would typically count as non-objective and contrary to the style called representationalism, the re-presentational theory must count as representational in its very sense of the word.

It may be felt that the re-presentational

theorist's stipulation that photographic and cinematic representation is defined by identity of light patterns between image and model will enable him to pick out only recognizable images via his theory. This, however, is not true. Angle and distance from the subject of the shot may preserve identity of light patterns to a station point but they in no way guarantee recognizability. This is especially true of very close shots, very long shots and unfamiliar camera angles.

Not only is the re-presentational theory broader than our ordinary concept of representation, it is also more narrow. This can be seen by recalling the emphasis the theory places on the existential import of the photographic and cinematic image. Every such image supposedly re-presents a singular referent that actually existed. Now consider process shots, especially where these shots are made via an optical printer. Certainly, we ordinarily think of these shots as representational. When Gary Cooper gallops along on his horse to the accompaniment of a back-projection, that is representational. Moreover, the image would remain representational if the image was achieved by means of an optical printer rather than back-projection. All those optically constructed images in *Star Wars* are representational in terms of our ordinary concept of representation as is Alexander Shitomirski's photomontage "Dieser Gefreite führt Deutschland in die Katastrophe." Yet if we construe representation as re-presentation a problem arises – viz., what is the existential import of the printed shots or the photomontage? What is the *one* place in the world that is being re-presented? Even if there is an answer here it is certainly a radically different sort of answer than the one we normally supply to the question of what is represented by such "trick photography," process shots and photomontages. My own guess is that certain types of process shots will not count as representations under the re-presentational analysis because of the requirement of

existential import that is presupposed by the re-presentation thesis. Thus, the re-presentation thesis is narrower than our ordinary concept of representation because there are cases of trick photography which we ordinarily regard as representations but which are not re-presentations of actually existing events and objects.

The issue of singular existential import also raises questions about whether the preceding definition of photographic and cinematic representation is able to logically support the overall re-presentational thesis. That is, are the conditions in that thesis enough to pick out a singular, actually existing referent for each photographic or cinematic image? I think they are not.

The re-presentation theory, outlined earlier, proposes something like identity of light patterns as a condition for singular re-presentation. Yet such identity is not a sufficient condition for singular representation because it is not enough to show that an image and a model deliver identical light patterns to a station point in order to establish that the image re-presents a given model. The reason for this is that many models will have the same identical patterns of light.[8] This is borne out by several of the Ames experiments in perception.[9] That is, it has been shown experimentally that we can, for example, build all sorts of different, distorted rooms, among other things, which deliver to a prearranged, monocular station point the same patterns of light as a normal room. In this respect, in terms of identity of light patterns alone, one cinematic image could be identical with many models. Which one would it re-present?

The proponent of the re-presentation thesis would undoubtedly answer that our cinematic image re-presents the model that was involved in its causation. But this proposal is easily confounded. Let us gather three shots of three different Ames-type rooms, each of which delivers an identical batch of light patterns to a camera. We have three different shots, each representing a different, actually existing place. Now let us superimpose these three shots in printing so that all the contours within the shots match. The shots, though of different places, are all identical. And by superimposition, each place becomes a causal factor in our fourth image which, in turn, is identical with the other three shots. In such a case, it is impossible for us to say that image x (our fourth shot) re-presents a model y (one of the models for the first three shots) even though x and a given y are identical in terms of patterns of light and though y is a causal element in x's production. Here we see that identity and causal efficacy are not jointly sufficient to guarantee singular re-presentation.

Admittedly the preceding counter-example presents a highly specialized case. However, there are even deeper problems that beset the re-presentational thesis, ones that defeat at least the preceding formulation conclusively. Let us photograph a man with a 16mm motion picture camera. Let us take three shots in which we keep the man the same size in the finished frame of each shot while also varying the focal length of the lens in each shot. We may take one shot with a 9mm lens, one with a 17mm lens and one with a 100mm lens – i.e., one shot with a normal lens, one with a wide-angle lens and one with a telephoto lens.[10] The result will be three shots each of which, all things being equal, one would expect to be re-presentations of the self-same subject. However, as a matter of empirical fact, the patterns of light will differ – differ grossly enough that the disparities can be detected even by the untrained eye. They all putatively re-present the same subject, yet each delivers a different pattern of light, not because of physical changes in the subject but because of changes in the focal length of the lens. The re-presentational theory commits us to viewing each of these shots as identical, "to a mold," with its subject. However, identity is a transitive relation – if x is identical to y, and y is identical to z,

then x is identical to z. Hence, each of these shots if they are identical to the referent, must also be identical to each other. But as a matter of fact the shots will not be identical in terms of the light patterns they deliver. Thus, the re-presentational thesis, formulated in virtue of identical light patterns, when combined with some mundane facts of photography, leads to a contradiction. Consequently, this version of the thesis must be abandoned.

It may be thought that the thesis can be saved by arguing that what is re-presented is not a pattern of light but rather a certain view from the past, a view, for example, that would have been available of the object from a certain position, under certain conditions, such as through a certain type of lens. This alternative, however, is unattractive. For it asks us to countenance in our ontology the existence of such things as views-of-objects in addition to accepting the individually existing objects themselves. But one doubts that there are such things as views-of-objects over and above the objects that we view. Moreover, if there are such things then there are an infinite number of them for there will be a view of every object there is from every point in the universe as well as a view from every conceivable lens as they are stationed at every point in the universe. Ontological parsimony, in short, urges us not to proliferate *actually existing views* to be re-presented in photos and films.

Another option might be to say that what is re-presented is a trace from the past.[11] However, the problems here are similar to those encountered in the formulation based upon identical patterns of light. For a tracing, in any full-blooded sense, suggests matching contours between the original and the medium that traces it. But the requirement of matching contours again prompts us to consider the disparate "tracings" that different lenses will afford of the object. Thus, though each tracing supposedly identically matches the original, contradictorily, the tracings will not identically match each other. Nor is it helpful to claim special authority for the rendering of the "normal" lens, for what has been considered the "normal" lens has changed over history.

At this point, it may seem that the best manoeuver for the re-presentational theorist is to drop the suggestion of an outright identity relation between the original and the image and to say that the process of projection re-presents the exact imprint or impression of light that was reflected by objects and people in the past. This is probably true enough, but it makes out-of-focus shots, wildly underexposed shots, shots with mounds of vaseline on the lens, flash-pans, in fact, every kind of shot, no matter how distorted or unrecognizable, representational. That is, to define cinematic and photographic representation in terms of re-presentations of luminous impressions from the past makes every photograph and cinematic shot representational whether or not they are of the sort normally categorized as representational. This is to sap the concept of photographic representation of any significant contrast and to make its application exorbitantly uninformative. This also renders the concept logically useless for someone like Bazin who hopes to ground his advocacy of a specific cinematic style of realism on the notion of re-presentation insofar as cinematic representation conceived of as the re-presentation of an imprint is any shot in any style. The re-presentation thesis of photographic representation must be rejected, therefore, because, under the likeliest interpretations, it either leads to contradictions or it is vacuous.

Subsidiary Arguments Concerning Uniqueness Claims for Photographic Representation

The Automatism Argument

For proponents of the idea that photographic and cinematic representation are essentially distinct from other forms of pictorial representation, it is extremely important that the photographic process is a mechanical process. Bazin, Sontag and Cavell believe that since photographic images are made automatically via a physical process, they are objective, objective in a way that is impossible, for example, in painting. This objectivity, moreover, is taken by someone like Bazin to indicate that the filmmaker is committed to realism as the proper aesthetic direction for the film medium.

Bazin writes

Originality in photography as distinct from originality in painting lies in the essentially objective character of photography. (Bazin here makes a point of the fact that the lens, the basis of photography, is in French called the "objectif," a nuance that is lost in English. Tr.) For the first time, between the originating object and its reproduction there intervenes only the instrumentality of a nonliving agent. For the first time an image of the world is formed automatically, without the creative intervention of man. The personality of the photographer enters into the proceedings only in his selection of the object to be photographed and by way of the purpose he has in mind. Although the final result may reflect something of his personality, this does not play the same role as is played by that of the painter. All the arts are based on the presence of man, only photography derives an advantage from his absence. Photography affects us like a phenomenon in nature, like a flower or a snowflake whose vegetable or earthly origins are an inseparable part of their beauty.[12]

From these considerations, Bazin surmises that ". . . the cinema is objectivity in time."[13] And it is this connection with objectivity that determines the proper use of the medium for him. Bazin says

The aesthetic qualities of photography are to be sought in its power to lay bare the realities. It is not for me to separate off, in the complex fabric of the objective world, here a reflection on a damp sidewalk, there a gesture of a child. Only the impassive lens, stripping its object of all those ways of seeing it, those piled-up preconceptions, that spiritual dust and grime with which my eyes have covered it, is able to present it in all its virginal purity to my attention. . . ."[14]

This argument appears to be that since cinematography and photography are mechanical/automatic processes, they are objective – both in the sense that their images are objects, the products of natural processes, and in the sense that they are not subjective, i.e., not personal visions. For Bazin, this objectivity, furthermore, makes a certain kind of realism possible – namely it makes showing things without preconceptions possible. And, given that this is a unique power of cinema, it follows for Bazin that cinema should be used to implement a realist project.

The first thing to note about this argument is that it does not give logical support to a style of realism. At most the conclusion favors a form of realism conceived of as the showing of things without preconceptions. This corresponds to the way that Bazin characterizes some aspects of Italian Neorealism but it does not entail endorsement of such favored Bazinian techniques as long-takes and medium shots. Nor does this notion of non-preconceived presentation correspond to some enshrined variety of realism-as-such. Zola, for example, thought that the realist was committed to the scientific viewpoint of things rather than being committed to an eschewal of any viewpoint.[15] Thus, even if cinematic images were such that they show the world without preconceptions, no existing style of realism can be grounded in this fact and this fact alone.

However, an even deeper error besets the argument from the start. Its basic premise is that some sort of objectivity is built into the photographic medium because it is an automatic or mechanical process. The automatic nature of photographic reproduction is thought to be objective in the sense that the photographic image is a natural product – like a snowflake – and in the sense that once the photographic process is set in motion, subjectivity is excluded, so to speak, from the machine. These dimensions of objectivity are said to be special to the photographic media. But are they special to photography and film in any way that marks a real difference between the photographic arts and other representational arts?

When I write a novelistic description of a room and my fingers touch the keyboard of my IBM, the process of printing the words is automatic. Is the mechanical process between me and the final text any less automatic with the IBM typewriter than with the camera? Indeed, there is a way in which it is appropriate to describe a typewritten (or even a handwritten) page as a natural product, if what one means by that is that the page is a result of a causal process. Likewise the fine arts have physical, natural, causal dimensions. When a sculptor hammers his chisel or a painter daubs oil on his canvas, certain physical processes come into play. In both cases the media in question have physical dimensions whose mechanical manipulation involves natural causal processes. Every representation in every media is, in some sense, a product of a causal process. Cinema and photography are not alone in this respect. Every medium in some degree has a physical-process dimension and, therefore, has some aspect of "the automatic" about it. Thus, at best, the sort of objectivity that Bazin attributes to cinema can only differ in degree rather than kind from a similar type of objectivity to be found in all representational media.

But one wonders whether Bazin can sustain even a mild claim for cinema's relatively greater objectivity. One problem with Bazin's position is his peculiar notion of "objectivity." When someone claims that cinema is objective what we really want to know is whether or not cinema's mechanical processes either guarantee objectivity or exclude subjectivity where those terms are used in their normal epistemic senses. We are not concerned with the sense of "objectivity" through which the photographic image can be construed as a natural product/object. And when we focus on the epistemic sense of objectivity, it is apparent that it is not true that cinema's mechanical processes either guarantee objectivity or exclude subjectivity. They cannot guarantee objective results because the processes, in and of themselves, can't guarantee any sort of success, objective or otherwise. An attempted photo of a room may be overexposed beyond all recognition – and that as an automatic result of the process of photography. That is, photography as a set of physical reactions doesn't guarantee objective results insofar as it doesn't guarantee any recognizable results. To get recognizable results requires a photographer adjusting the camera mechanism, the lighting, etc. However, once this is admitted then it is clear that the photographer can set the "automatic" process in action in such a way that the results are highly subjective and personal. Imagine a photographer with a phobia for vegetables – following Weston's monumentalizing examples, he could easily transform a green pepper and some carrots into a giant threatening insect, armored and horned. This is not to say that there cannot be objective photographs – e.g., those of Cartier-Bresson. The point is rather that the question of the objectivity or subjectivity of a photograph or a film cannot be settled by reference to the automatic mechanical processes of the medium. Thus, realism does not follow from the supposed "automatic objectivity" of the medium because there is no such automatic objectivity. Moreover, it should be pointed out that even if Bazin had succeeded in establishing that the cinematic image is, in some distinctive sense, objective in terms of being the product of a natural process, this would have no implications for realism. It would show that cinematic images can be called *real* in certain specifiable respects, not that they are or should be *realistic*.

The Re-presentation of Objects

Bazin believes that a photo, and, by extension, a cinematographic image have existential import. A photographic image is always an image of something – specifically it is an image of the objects, places, events and persons that gave rise to it. A photographic image re-presents its model. The image is rooted in reality. Thus, Bazin, and certain of his followers, such as Stanley Cavell, hold that with regard to photographic images – in contrast to paintings and drawings – it always makes sense to ask what lies beyond the photographic image: what is *behind* the objects in the image and what is *adjacent* to the image.[16] Undoubtedly, the belief that the photographic image is a slice out of the continuum of reality is one reason that many Bazinians champion the idea of lateral depth of field in opposition to the painterly and theatrical conceptions of the frame as an enclosed box. But it is important to recall that this stylistic choice is purportedly defensible by reference to an ontological fact about photographic images – that they represent places, events, persons, in short, objects.

Bazin himself does not really supply an argument for this point. However, the leading contemporary Bazinian, Stanley Cavell, does. Cavell initiates his argument by asking what it is that films reproduce? He sees two major alternatives: either films reproduce the very objects that give rise to the image or the film reproduces the sight or appearance of the object represented by the image. Cavell writes

We said that a record reproduces a sound, but we cannot say that a photograph reproduces a sight (or a look, or an appearance). A sight is an object (usually a large object like the Grand Canyon) . . . objects don't make sights or have sights . . . they are too close to their sights to give them up for reproducing.[17]

And apart from these ordinary language considerations, Cavell also argues that "sights" are rather queer metaphysical entities that might be better banished from one's ontology in the name of simplicity – indeed, imagine how very many "sights" each object, viewed from an infinity of angles, will have. But if it is not the "sight" or the "appearance" of the object that a photographic image re-presents, then it must be the object itself that is re-presented. That is, Cavell assumes that a photographic image must either re-present the sight of the object or the object itself. And, since there is no such thing as a sight of an object (independent of the object), then it must be that photographic images re-present objects.

The obvious problem with this argument is the assumption of the premise that photographic images either re-present objects themselves or sights of objects. The problem here is not that Cavell has failed to give us enough alternatives. Rather the problem is that the premise begs the question about the nature of cinematic representation by assuming that the photographic image must re-present something from the past, and by assuming that the task of analysis is simply a matter of determining what that something is – is it an object or a sight? But I think that we can ask why we must believe that anything is in fact re-presented via photographic representation. The idea of re-presentation is doubtless a powerful metaphor for the phenomenon of representation. But we must ask whether it is literally true that anything – whether an object or a sight – is re-presented or reproduced by photography or cinematography. In fact, in an earlier section of this essay the very intelligibility of the concept of "re-presentation" was called into question.

A representation, I want to say, *presents* a stand-in or a proxy of a model; it does not re-present either the model or the sight of the model. Cavell may be right when he says that the sight or appearance of the object is "too close" to the object to be pried off for re-presentation. But he is wrong to surmise

from this that the only alternative that is left is to say that then it must be the case that it is the object that is reproduced. For instead we may say that what photography does is to *produce* a recognizable proxy for its model. Therefore, the image does not literally re-present anything whatsoever.

It should also be noted that re-presentationalists are fond of connecting the supposed existential import of photographic images to an essential distinction between paintings and films. It is urged that with paintings it does not make sense to ask what is adjacent to an image – such is the significance of the framing convention in fine art – whereas it always makes sense to ask what is offscreen with film.

However, I see no reason to believe that it never makes sense to ask what is adjacent to the view portrayed by a painting – i.e., what we would see if the painting did not end where it does but continued on. To support this, imagine a painting of the battle of Waterloo. I see Napoleon's grenadiers repulsed by Wellington's thin red line. I am taken by the historical accuracy of the work. I turn to the painter and ask him "where are the Prussians?" It seems perfectly reasonable to me for him to point to a place on the wall two feet from the left of the painting and say "they'd be about here given the scale and orientation of the painting." Indeed, since this painting is one that is committed to historical accuracy, this answer makes more sense than possible alternatives such as "in the world of this painting, there are no Prussians at the battle of Waterloo." I am not denying that a painter could portray a fictional battle of Waterloo where there were no Prussians. But this would be the special case, one, indeed, that the painter would have to flag in some way if he wanted viewers to delete the Prussians from his Waterloo.

On the other hand, it is not true that it always makes sense to ask what is adjacent to a photographic or cinematographic image. Again the problem of fiction looms in a way that makes this issue almost unintelligible. For re-presentationalists believe that cinema literally re-presents the models that give rise to the image. Thus, if it always makes sense to ask what is adjacent to cinematic images, we may arrive at some very perplexing answers. What's next to the land of Oz? The MGM commissary. And apart from these obvious problems, it seems to me that there are films, just as there are paintings, whose internal structures are designed to imply that a viewer should not ask what is adjacent to what is on-camera because the film presents its imagery as that of a fantastic realm or of a realm completely constructed by conventions rather than in terms of the mimesis of the normal space of physics. *Blood of a Poet, Andalusian Dog* and *Heaven and Earth Magic* are examples of the former. Rohmer's *Perceval* is an example of the latter. Rohmer's images do not signal that they are to be regarded as realistic. They are completely conventionalized, making direct allusions to theatrical staging and the scale changes of medieval painting. We are best advised not to assume that there are spaces adjacent to those on camera. We are indeed best advised to regard the frame line as a proscenium insofar as this accords with the overt theatricality of the rest of the film. Moreover, this theatricality is rigorously enforced to give the film its aura of artificiality, decorum, containedness and delicacy. To say of *Perceval* that it always makes sense to ask what is immediately offscreen, it seems to me, is a profound mistake. It makes no more sense than to ask what is next to Swan Lake – that is, just beyond the leg curtains – in the ballet of the same name. It is the purpose of the work or genre in question that determines whether it makes sense to ask what is adjacent to the action represented on-screen, on canvas or on stage. The issue is not an ontological one.

An Alternative Approach to Photographic and Cinematic Representation

Perhaps the most peculiar feature of the concept of re-presentation, which is held by people like Bazin and Cavell, is the characterization it implies of what is represented by fictional films and photographs. The re-presentational theory maintains that films have existential import – the film re-presents some *x* from the past. Film images, in supposed contrast to all painting, represent things in a unique way – i.e., they re-present things – which compels us to accept their referents as real. A re-presentationalist would seem to have to defend this claim by saying something like "*Citizen Kane* re-presents Orson Welles." But this is a curious thing to say since what is most relevant to viewing the fiction *Citizen Kane* is that it represents Kane. It certainly does not re-present Kane nor does it "fictionally represent" Welles. If it does re-present Welles, that seems beside the point if we are interested in appreciating the film as a fictional representation – in which case it is about Kane and not Welles.

A photo of Tip O'Neill might be said to re-present Tip O'Neill – photos, in our culture, are generally used to document. Re-presentationalists extrapolate from this *conventional* use of the photo – documentation – to an account of all photographic and cinematic representation. But, of course, the presupposition that even photography – let alone feature films – can only be used to document or to literally re-present is quite mistaken. Richard Avedon's recent advertisements for Christian Dior are miniature fictions replete with three characters: Wizard, Mouth and Oliver. The character of Wizard is modeled by the avant-garde dramaturg André Gregory. Yet when I look at one of these ads, I may be forced to accept the fact that the character, The Wizard, had to have some model who existed at some time and some place, but this admission does not entail that one characterizes the ad as a representation of André Gregory. That André Gregory plays the role of The Wizard is irrelevant to the fictional representation at work in the photo. The re-presentational conception of photography, on the other hand, seems to say that what is important about any photographic image – whether in a fictional context or otherwise – is what it re-presents. Yet what is literally re-presented in a photographic fiction may be completely irrelevant to what the fiction represents. That is, when confronted with fiction, the re-presentationalist theory implies strange results by ontologically misplacing, so to speak, the focus or our attention – e.g., having it that it is the re-presentation of André Gregory rather than that it is the fictional representation of The Wizard that concerns the Avedon series.[18]

This anomaly in regard to photography escalates when we turn to the issue of feature films. At least with photography, documentation rather than fictionalization is usually thought of as the primary role or purpose of still photography in our society. It is easy to see how, in our culture, one could confuse the pervasiveness of the snapshot with the essence of photography. But it is harder to see how the theorist can overlook the possibility of fiction when it comes to the feature film because fiction is surely the most visible purpose for which film is used in our culture. What is most bizarre about the re-presentationalist theory is that it is strangely ill-suited to account for what is represented in fictional films. Films seem to become records of actors and actual places; their fictional referents dissolve, in a manner of speaking. *M* is about Peter Lorre rather than about a psychopathic child killer; *The Creature From the Black Lagoon* is not about a rivulet off the Amazon but about Wakulla Springs, Florida. Films you thought were representations of castles, graveyards and forests are really about studio sets. The re-presentationalist theory,

in short, departs radically from what we would normally describe as the reference of fictional movies.

The problem that the re-presentationalist theory confronts with the issue of fiction is a function of its implicit assumption that there is only one form of cinematic representation. But like other media, artistic and otherwise, there is more than one mode of representation in cinema. In fact, we can mobilize some of Monroe Beardsley's terminology in order to illustrate that there are at least three types of representation in cinema which we must distinguish before we can appreciate the representational range of the medium.[19]

The first level of cinematic representation is *physical portrayal*. That is, every shot in a live-action photographic film physically portrays its model, a definite object, person or event that can be designated by a *singular* term. It is in the physical portrayal sense that it can be said that *Psycho* represents Anthony Perkins rather than Norman Bates – it was Anthony Perkins who served as the source of the image. Every live action shot will physically portray its model. This is obviously the point re-presentationalists have in mind when they speak of films representing the past. Because of the way such images are produced, every shot in a live action film physically portrays whatever people, places and things caused the image. Such shots are called "recordings" in the most basic sense of the term if the only representational function that they perform is physical portrayal. A physical portrayal is a representation of the particular person, object or event that caused the image. Traditional realist film theory is preoccupied with physical portrayal to the extent that this mode of representation is taken to be either the only use of shots or the most essential, most important or most fundamental use of shots. As a result, the use of shots in fictional representations becomes utterly mystified and confused since the realist must give an account of what is represented in a fiction in terms of physical portrayal.

But physical portrayal is not the only mode of representation in film and photography. A film, for example, not only physically portrays its source – a particular person, place, thing, event or action – but it also *depicts* a class or collection of objects, designated by a *general* term. A shot from *Psycho* physically portrays Anthony Perkins while also depicting a man; likewise a shot of the Golden Gate Bridge in *Attack of the Killer Tomatoes* physically portrays *the Golden Gate* but also depicts *a bridge*. Every shot of a live action film physically portrays its model – some specific individual – while also depicting a member of a class, describable by a general term – man, bridge, fire, cow, battle, etc. A film may be important in terms of what it physically portrays – e.g., a record of President Reagan's oath of office. Or a shot may be important in terms of what it depicts. Imagine, for example, a montage introduction to an evening news program. Let us say that this montage includes an image of a fire – one that occurred on the northwest corner of 23rd Street and Lexington Avenue in New York City on 12/11/72. But what is important in this prologue to the news program – important in terms of what is being communicated – would not be the portrayal of a particular fire (i.e., the fire of 12/11/72), but rather that the image stands for, represents, depicts *a fire*, which is the *kind* of thing – more specifically news – with which the program is concerned. A film image can depict a class as well as physically portray an individual. And in some contexts of communication it may be the case that only what the image depicts is relevant for communication. That is, the shot's relation to its model can be communicatively irrelevant.

What is theoretically important about depiction – as a mode of cinematic representation – is that it splits the shot, as a communication element, from its source, and it is this split that makes our third mode of cinematic representation, *nominal portrayal*, possible. A shot that physically portrays Anthony Perkins in *Psycho* depicts a madman while also, given its place in the context of the story, it nominally portrays Norman Bates. A shot is a nominal portrayal of a person, object or event when it represents a *particular* person, place or thing different from the person, place or thing that gave rise to the image. Nominal portrayal in film is a function of such factors as voice-over commentary, titles, an on-going story or editing. These devices establish that the objects, persons and events shown in the image "stand for" particular objects, persons and events other than the ones that caused the image. For example, in the fictional world of the story of *Psycho*, the images stand for Norman Bates rather than for Anthony Perkins, the actor whose presence in front of Hitchcock's camera brought those images of Bates into existence. Nominal portrayal is the most important mode of representation in terms of the way our culture uses film – i.e., uses feature films – since nominal portrayal is the basis of all fiction films.

By advocating that cinematic and photographic representation be seen as participating in nominal portrayal and depiction as well as in physical portrayal, I am, of course, giving up the prospect of defining a unique form of representation that is peculiar or specific to only the photographic media. For nominal portrayal and depiction, as well as various techniques of physical portrayal, are available in other than photographic media. Nor should we be surprised that the photographic media share the range of modes of representation available to other media. For the technologies of photography and cinema arrived after other media had already refined a series of modes of representation. Subsequently, the practitioners of the new media looked to already existing media to find purposes and projects to which the new photographic technologies could be applied. Fictionalization, for example, especially in regard to film, provided one such preexisting purpose. Thus, film became a technology for producing the nominal portrayals of Rhett Butler and Scarlet O'Hara, of King Kong and Dracula. The modes of representation that are relevant to consider in the analysis and appreciation of cinema and photography are determined by the uses to which these technologies are put. There is not an essence of photographic media or of photographic representation that directs the evolution of these media or our proper appreciative responses to these media. The media rather are adapted to the cultural purposes and projects we find for them. The relevant types of representation we observe in photography and cinema are not a function of the ontology of the photographic image but of the purposes we have found respectively for still and moving photography.

Notes

1. André Bazin, *What is Cinema?*, trans. H. Gray, Vol. I (Berkeley: University of California Press, 1967), pp. 96–97.
2. Bazin, 14.
3. Stanley Cavell, *The World Viewed* (Boston: Harvard University Press, 1979), p. 17.
4. Bazin, 14.
5. Roland Barthes, *Camera Lucida*, trans. Richard Howard (New York: Hill and Wang, 1981), p. 88.
6. Susan Sontag, *On Photography* (New York: Delta, 1978), p. 154.
7. Nelson Goodman, *Languages of Art* (Indianapolis: Bobbs-Merrill, 1968), p. 4.
8. Goodman, pp. 11–12.
9. W. H. Ittleson, *The Ames Demonstrations in Perception* (Princeton: Princeton University Press, 1952).
10. For a concrete example of this see Plate 44 in *Guide to Filmmaking* by Edward Pincus (New York: Signet, 1969). This plate also demonstrates that identity of light patterns is not really a necessary condition for photographic representation.
11. Both Bazin and Sontag explicitly evoke the notion of a trace.
12. Bazin, 13.
13. Bazin, 14.
14. Bazin, 15.
15. Emile Zola, "The Experimental Novel," in *Modern Literary Realism,* ed. George Becker (Princeton: Princeton University Press, 1969), pp. 162–196.
16. Cavell, 23.
17. Cavell, 19–20.
18. In *The World Viewed,* Cavell appears to connect the re-presentationalist consequence that we view actors, such as Bogart, in feature films to the phenomenon of the star system. Thus, one surmises, Cavell does not find it odd to say that in viewing feature fiction films we are, among other things, viewing – at the level of our appreciative response – Katherine Hepburn, Cary Grant, Buster Keaton, et al. Indeed, Cavell seems to want to correlate what he takes to be the camera's natural affinity for individuals to the flourishing of the star system as an expressive dimension of cinema. It is as if the star system is thought to flow from the photographic nature of the medium. However, the star system does not correlate exclusively with film. Theater, opera and dance, indeed all the performing arts, have star systems. Star systems, it seems to me, are a function of institutional arrangements rather than of the ontology of any medium. Moreover, whenever a medium is representational and it has a star system, it appears reasonable to allow that a spectator is responding both to a character *and* to the star portraying the character – e.g., both to Faust and to Richard Tucker. The kind of dual attention implied by star systems does not seem peculiar to photographic arts.
19. Monroe Beardsley, *Aesthetics* (New York: Harcourt, Brace and World, 1958), especially Chapter VI, section 16. See also Göran Hemeren, *Representation and Meaning in the Visual Arts* (Lund: Scandanavian University Books, 1969) especially Chapter II.

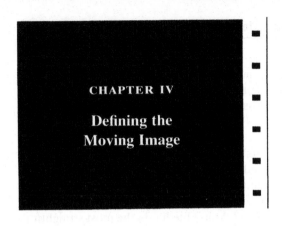

CHAPTER IV

Defining the Moving Image

I. Background: The Problem of Medium-Essentialism

"What is cinema?" has been one of the presiding questions that has agitated many film theorists throughout much of the twentieth century. The aim of this essay is to try to provide one sort of answer to this question. Namely, I shall attempt to defend a definition of the class of things – moving images – to which film belongs and in which, I believe, film is most appropriately categorized. My reasons for preferring the idiom of "moving images" over "cinema" or "film" will emerge as my argument proceeds. Moreover, I should also warn the reader that though I intend to define the moving image, my definition is not what is called a "real" or an "analytical" or an "essential" definition – i.e., a definition in terms of necessary conditions that are jointly sufficient. Instead, my definition comprises five necessary conditions for the moving image. I do not claim joint sufficiency for them. For I suspect that would involve more precision than the subject will bear. And, like Aristotle, I think that it is advisable to respect the limits of precision available in a given domain of inquiry.

If you have read the preceding articles in this book, it may appear peculiar to you that I should now embark upon the enterprise of attempting to answer the question "What is cinema?" or, at least, a question very much like it. For the question "What is cinema?" is generally taken as a request

for an essentialist answer, and my position has been stridently anti-essentialist. Am I now contradicting my earlier position? Not really. The sort of essentialism that film theorists have traditionally sought is misguided, as I hope I have shown. But that does not preclude the possibility that film has some necessary, general features whose explicit acknowledgment is useful in locating (though perhaps not pinpointing) the place of film among the arts. Thus, I intend to approach the question "What is cinema?" while at the same time avoiding an essentialist answer to that question.

Of course, saying only this is somewhat obscure, since essentialism comes in many shapes and sizes. So in order to clarify my own approach, I should be overt about the varieties of essentialism that I wish to eschew. First and foremost, in answering the question "What is cinema?" I want to avoid the pitfalls of what might be called medium-essentialism, which is the variety of essentialism to which I believe film theorists have been most prone. My answer to the question "What is cinema?" also falls short of what might be called real-definition essentialism, on the one hand, and Grecian essentialism, on the other hand. But more on that later. For now it is most instructive to indicate how my approach grows out of a response to medium-essentialism, since it is medium-essentialism that has been of primary concern for film theorists.

What is medium-essentialism? Roughly it is the doctrine that each artform has its own distinctive medium, a medium that distinguishes it from other other forms. This is a general doctrine, espoused by many theorists across the arts. Perhaps it was especially attractive to film theorists because it began to suggest a way in which to block accusations that film was merely a subspecies of theater.

Furthermore, essentialists of this ilk regard the medium as an essence in the sense that it, the medium/essence, has teleological ramifications. That is, the medium *qua* essence dictates what it is suitable to do with the medium. A weak, negative version of this is the "limitation" view that maintains that in virtue of its identifying medium, certain artforms should not aspire to certain effects. Thus, Lessing reproached the attempt to simulate hyperactivity in stolid, unmoving stone.

Alternatively, a stronger version of medium-essentialism holds that the medium dictates what will function best – in terms of style and/or content – for artists working in that medium, and that artists ought to pursue those and only those projects that are most efficiently accommodated by or even mandated by the nature of the medium. For example, it might, on this basis, be urged that painters specialize in representing still moments rather than events.[1]

Medium-essentialism is an exciting idea. For it promises not only a means for differentiating artforms, but also for explaining why some artworks fail and others succeed. Some fail, it might be said, because they do not heed the limitations of the medium, often by attempting to do something that some other medium is more essentially suited to discharge; while other artworks in a medium succeed because they do what the medium is essentially suited to do – they realize the telos inherent in the medium. Medium-essentialism may also be enticing because it addresses artists where they live. This is not dry philosophy cataloguing what is after the fashion of some ontological bureaucrat. Medium-essentialists give the artist helpful advice about what the artist should and should not do.[2] Medium-essentialism is not a bland, pedantic exercise in definition. It has explanatory and pragmatic value. Unfortunately, it is false.

Medium-essentialism depends on a number of presuppositions, many of which are extremely controversial. Some of these include the following: that each artform has a distinctive medium; that the material cause, so to speak, of an artform – its medium – is also its essence (in the sense of its telos); that

the essence of an artform – its medium – indicates, limits or dictates the style and/or content of the artform; and, finally, that film possesses such an essence.

The view that every artform has a distinctive medium appears false on several counts. First, it is not clear that every artform has a medium at all. Does literature have a medium? Words, you might say. But are words the right sort of thing to constitute a medium? Aren't media, in the most straightforward sense, physical, and are words physical in any interesting way? But put that set of questions aside for heuristic purposes. Even if words can be taken to constitute the medium of literature, would they amount to a distinctive artistic medium? For words are shared with all types of speech and writing, on the one hand, and with other artforms like theater, opera, song, and even some painting and sculpture, on the other hand. Likewise, if one says that the medium of literature comprises human events, actions and feelings, that, for similar reasons, would be hardly distinctive.

So, as a general theory of the arts, medium-essentialism is false in its first premise. Not all artforms have distinctive media. Literature does not – nor do its various parishes, including the novel, poetry, and the short story. But perhaps the position can be qualified in a useful way as merely stating that some artforms have distinctive media and those that do, in fact, possess the teleological structure that medium-essentialism describes. Then, the question for us becomes whether film is such an artform? And that, of course, depends on what one takes the medium of film to be. If it is identified as light and shadows, then film has no distinctive medium, since light and shadow are also arguably the medium of painting, sculpture, photography, magic lantern shows, and so on. Similarly, and for the same reason, light and shadow could dictate nothing by way of film-specific style and content.

Of course, yet another reason that the

premise that each medium has its own distinctive medium is mistaken is that – in the most literal senses of what a medium might be – many artforms (most? all?) possess more than one media, some of which are hardly distinctive. That is, the view that each and every artform must have a single medium that is uniquely and distinctively its own must be erroneous, since artforms generally involve a number of media, including frequently overlapping ones.

For example, if we think of the medium as the material stuff out of which artworks are made, then painting comprises several media: oil paints, water color, tempera, acrylic, and others. Also, in this rather straightforward sense of media, sculpture comprises a wide range of media, including at least bronze, gold, silver, wood, marble, granite, clay, celluloid, acrylic (again), and so on.

On the other hand, if we think of a medium as an implement used to produce an artwork, painting can be made by brushes, palette knives, fingers, and even human bodies (remember Yves Klein); while sculptures can be made by means of chisels, blowtorches, casts, and, among other things, fingers. Perhaps every musical instrument is a discrete musical medium in this sense, but, then, so is the human voice, and, once again, so are fingers.

Thus, it cannot be the case that every artform has its own distinctive medium since many (most? all?) artforms possess more than one medium, many of which themselves have divergent and nonconverging potentials. Nor, as these examples should suggest, are these media always distinctive of one and only one artform. Plastic acrylic figures in painting and sculpture; celluloid in film and sculpture; bodies in painting, sculpture and dance; and fingers, in one way or another, everywhere. Furthermore, if we think of the medium of an artform in terms of its characteristic formal elements, then the cause is altogether lost. For features like line, color, volume, shape, and motion are fundamental across various artforms and unique to none.

Obviously, what is meant by the phrase "artistic medium" is highly ambiguous, referring sometimes to the physical materials out of which artworks are constructed, sometimes to the implements that are used to do the constructing and sometimes to the formal elements of design that are available to artists in a given practice. This ambiguity alone might discourage us from relying on the notion of the medium as a theoretically useful concept. Indeed, I think that we might fruitfully abandon it completely, at least in terms of the ways in which it is standardly deployed by aestheticians. Be that as it may, it should be clear that most artforms cannot be identified on the basis of a single medium, since most artforms correlate with more than one medium.

Film is certainly like this. If we think of the medium on the basis of the materials from which the images are made, our first impulse might be to say that the medium is obviously a film strip bearing certain photographic emulsions. But flicker films, like Kubelka's *Arnulf Rainer*, can be made by alternating clear and opaque leader, sans photographic emulsion. And one can paint on a clear film strip and then project it. Moreover, in principle, video may be developed to the point where in terms of high definition, it may be indiscernible from film, or, at least, to the point where most of us would have little trouble calling a commercial narrative made from fully high-definition video a film. And, of course, if films can be made from magnetized tape, film would share a medium with music.

If we think of the film medium in terms of the implements typically employed to make cinema, cameras undoubtedly come to mind. But as our previous example of flicker films and painted films indicate, cinema can be made without cameras, a point reinforced by the existence of scratch films. And one could imagine films constructed completely within the province of CD-ROM; while, at the same time, formal features of film – such as line, shape, space, motion, and temporal and narrative structures – are things that film shares with many other arts. Consequently, it should be clear that, strictly speaking, there is no single medium of film from which the film theorist can extrapolate stylistic directives; at best there are film media, some perhaps which await invention even now.

It may seem counterintuitive to urge that we think of media where heretofore we have referred to the medium. But it shouldn't. There can be little question that photography is comprised of many media such as the daguerreotype and the tintype, on the one hand, and the polaroid, on the other. How fine grained we should be in individuating media may be problematic. Are panchromatic and orthochromatic film stocks different media? Are nitrate and ascetate both film? Is the fish-eye lens a different medium than the so-called normal lens? One can imagine respectable arguments on both sides of these questions. But such disputes notwithstanding, the observation that artforms involve multiple media, which, in turn, may be frequently mixed, is incontrovertible. Talk of *the* (one and only) medium with respect to an artform, then, is generally a misleading simplification or abstraction. Indeed, it seems to me that there is no way to stipulate selectively (from the various media that comprise a given artform) an hypostatized medium for the artform at the physical level of media that would not be guided by a notion of the proper function of the artform, a notion, moreover, that is informed by one's stylistic interests.

Of course, by denying that artforms possess a medium in the way that idea is standardly used, I do not intend to say that artworks lack a material basis or that they are not fashioned by physical implements. My point is simply that artworks in a given artform may employ different media, sometimes simultaneously, and that they may be constructed through various implementati-

ons. To hypostatsize this diversity under the rubric of something called *The Medium* obscures the richness and complexity of the relations of the artform to its material base(s). Undoubtedly some might resist my skepticism about the medium here on the grounds that my construal of medium talk is far too narrow. However, at this point in the dialectic, the burden of proof rests with them to come up with a concept of the medium that is immune to my objections.

So far I have been challenging two presuppositions of medium-essentialism, viz., that each artform has a unique, singular medium and that this is so of film. But the other presumptions of medium-essentialism are also worthy of scrutiny, often for reasons connected with the issues we have already broached.

The medium-essentialist thinks that the so-called medium of an artform is also the essence of the artform in the sense that it carries within it the distinctive telos of the form, somewhat in the manner of a gene. This is a surprising doctrine because many of the candidates for the medium that one encounters are not only shared by different artforms, but because in many cases – like oil paint or celluloid – the candidates seem to underdetermine the uses to which they might be put.

But the doctrine can also be challenged when one recalls that artforms do not generally possess a single medium but are better thought of in terms of media. For if artforms possess several media, there is no reason to suppose that they will all converge on a single effect or even a single range of effects. The media that comprise a single artform may sustain different, nonconverging potentials and possibilities. There is no antecedent reason to think that all the media that comprise an artform gravitate toward the same range of effects. Indeed, the more media that comprise an artform, the more likely statistically it will be that their assortment of effects may diverge. Thus, the fact that the media of an artform are multiple tends to undermine the supposition that a single medium (out of all the media) of the artform in question could define the telos of the artform as a whole. This is not to deny that even a single medium might have a nonconverging range of effects such that it might fail to specify a single coherent end for the artform. Rather when that possibility is added to the problem that artforms are composed of multiple media, the probability that the putative medium might correspond to an essence or telos of an artform becomes immensely dubious.

In commenting on the multiplicity of the media that may comprise an artform, I noted that some of the relevant media may not have been invented yet. Media are added to artforms as times goes by. Bellini could not have known that plastic would become a medium of sculpture. Moreover, it almost goes without saying, when media are added to an artform they may bring with them unexpected, unprecedented possibilities, ones that may not correspond to the already existing effects familiar to artists. Drum machines and samplers have recently been added to the arsenal of musical media in order to imitate existing sounds, but it was soon discovered that they could also be used creatively to produce heretofore unimagined sounds. For example, with a sampler one can combine the attack of a snare drum and the sustain of a guitar by means of a careful splice. That an artform is not static – at least because it can acquire new media with unpredictable, nonconverging possibilities – indicates that one cannot hope to fix the telos of an artform on the basis of one of its constituent media.

It may be that artforms do not possess coherent essences in the way in which the tradition has supposed. But even if they did, no single medium constitutes the essence or telos of an artform. Perhaps theoreticians in the past have missed this because they have tended to select out one medium of a given artform and treat it (or, as they say, "privi-lege" it) as *the* medium. This maneuver at least superficially makes the derivation of a coherent telos for the artform appear more plausible. But this ignores the fact that artforms are constantly expanding their productive forces. New media are, in principle, always available to artforms, thereby opening new possibilities to the practice. One can no more shackle these developments by means of theories that privilege a single medium in a given artform than one can shackle the means of production by means of ideology.

One does not identify the essence or telos of an artform such as film, on the basis of something called the medium, nor does this alleged medium indicate or mandate the legitimate domain of exploration in terms of style or content with respect to an artistic practice. One way to see the inadequacy of the medium-essentialist's view in this regard is to compare the implications of the medium-essentialist's view for stylistic development with reality.

The strongest version of mediumistic essentialism appears to regard artforms as natural kinds outfitted with gene-like programs that mandate stylistic developments. The artform has an unalterable nature – inscribed in the medium – and this unalterable nature dictates style. But this is clearly a false idea. An artform is not analogous to a natural kind. Artforms are made by human beings in order to serve human purposes. Artforms are not unalterable; they are frequently adapted, altered and reinvented, often to serve preordained stylistic purposes. And this, moreover, is exactly the opposite course of events from that predicted by the medium-essentialist.

Consider musical instruments. They have a fair claim to be considered artistic media in the sense that they are physical implements used to construct artworks. They are media in the same sense that chalk and crayon are media. Furthermore, new musical instruments are constantly being invented and readapted. And, in many cases, these developments are driven by stylistic interests. The piano, for example, was introduced at a time when composers were becoming increasingly interested in sustained crescendos. Here, stylistic interests figure in the alteration of the very shape of the medium. Likewise, individual musicians adapt musical media to suit their stylistic aims as did the jazz performer Jack Teagarden when he took the slide off his trombone and cupped the horn with a whiskey glass. In such cases, the medium does not fix the parameters of style, but stylistic ambitions dictate the production or reinvention of media.

Nor is this phenomenon unique to music. In film, the move to various wide-screen processes was undertaken, to a certain extent, in order to facilitate certain "realistic" stylistic effects that practitioners had observed imperfectly realized in earlier formats.[3] Likewise, in the late 1910s and early 1920s, as Kristen Thompson has shown, filmmakers introduced the use of portrait lenses and gauze over the lens to create noticeably soft images for certain stylistic effects.[4] And there is also the case of the reintroduction of the use of arc lamps for black-and-white cinematography that Welles and Toland pioneered for stylistic effects involving depth of field in *Citizen Kane*, which others picked up in the 1940s. In such cases, the "medium" is modified or reinvented in order to serve stylistic purposes. The so-called medium is physically altered to coincide with the dictates of style, rather than style docilely following the dictates of some fixed medium.

What cases like this suggest, of course, is that, contra the medium-essentialist, stylistic developments need not follow the "directives" of the so-called medium (even if one could identify said "directives") because in many cases, it is stylistic considerations that influence the invention, adaptation and reinvention of artistic media. This is not to deny that sometimes artists arrive at their distinctive stylistic choices by contemplating features of the medium (or "the media," as I

prefer to say). I only wish to dispute the crucial premise of the medium-essentialist, who maintains that style is determined by the structure (notably the physical structure) of the medium. That must be false because sometimes it is style that determines the very structure of media.

I hypothesize that medium-essentialism derives a great deal of its appeal from its association with the apparently commonsensical view that artists should not attempt to make a medium do what it cannot do. Once the medium-essentialist secures agreement with this negative prognostication, he then goes on to suggest that one can also specify certain determinate things that an artist ought to do with the medium. But two points are worth noting here.

First, there is no way logically to get from the truistic, negative prognostication to some robust, positive prescription of any determinateness about what artists should do with the medium. Second, the negative prognostication itself is idle. It is an empty admonition for the simple reason that if something truly cannot be done with a certain medium, then no one will do it. No one can do the impossible. The case is closed. But also, again, from the vacuous warning that no one should do what it is impossible to do with the medium, nothing follows about what live possibilities of the medium an artist ought to pursue. Medium-essentialists who leave the impression that their positive recommendations are implied by the negative injunction to refrain from making a medium do what it cannot are simply trading in non sequiturs.

I have spent so much time disputing the presuppositions of medium-essentialism because of my conviction that this approach has unfortunately dominated previous attempts to answer the question "What is cinema?" Thus, in what follows, I will define film, or what I call the moving image without reference to a specific physical medium, and, furthermore, my definition will not have stylistic ramifications for what film artists should and should not do. The problems of medium-essentialism become, in other words, constraints on my theory, demarcating certain areas of speculation where I shall not tread. By way of preview, what I intend to produce are five necessary conditions for what I call the moving image. Moreover, as I will try to explain, this does not amount to the assertion of a new kind of essentialism – of either the real-definition or Grecian variety – for reasons that I shall defend in my concluding remarks.

II. Revisiting Photographic Realism

In this section, I shall attempt to introduce one necessary condition for what I call the moving image. I shall try to argue on behalf of this condition dialectically by showing how a case for it can emerge in the process of demonstrating the shortcomings of one traditional view of the essence of cinema, namely photographic realism (a view discussed in the preceding essay in this volume).

As is well know, André Bazin answered the question "What is cinema?" by stressing the photographic basis of film. For him, photography was what differentiates the film image from other sorts of pictorial art, such as painting. He maintained that whereas handmade pictorial practices like painting portrayed objects, persons, and events by means of resemblance, machine-made pictures, like photographs and films, literally presented or re-presented objects, persons and events from the past to viewers. If the relation of paintings to their objects is resemblance, then the relation of photos and, by extension, film images to their referents is identity. The photo of Woodrow Wilson is Woodrow Wilson presented again in his visual aspect to contemporary witnesses. Film and photography provide us with telescopes, so to speak, into the past. Bazin says: "The photographic image is the object itself. . . . It shares by virtue of the process of its becoming, the being of the model of which it is a reproduction; it is the model."[5]

Among other things, what Bazin intends to achieve by emphasizing the photographic basis of film is to mark the essential difference between film and other picture-making processes like painting. Those traditional picture-making processes are representational, and what is distinctive about representation, in Bazin's opinion, is that it is rooted in resemblance. But film, like photography, is presentational, not representational, according to Bazinians. It presents objects, persons and events again, and, in consequence, there is some kind of identity relation between photographic and cinematographic images of x and x itself. Moreover, this distinction between presentational images, on the one hand, and representational images, on the other, is connected for Bazin to the fact that photographic and cinematographic images are machine-made whereas more traditional images are handmade.

Is there really such a vast difference between a machine-made picture and a handmade picture? In order to bolster the intuition that there is a deep difference lurking here, the Bazinian can invite us to consider the following comparison.[6] Quite frequently, objects that the photographer never noticed in the profilmic event appear in photos and cinematic images. This can be quite embarrassing when, for example, a Boeing 707 turns up in the background of a shot from *El Cid* or a telephone pole appears in *First Knight*. But even when it isn't embarrassing, photographers often admit finding things in photos of which they were unaware when they snapped the shutter and exposed the film. The reason for this is simple. Photography is a mechanical process. The apparatus will record everything in its field of vision automatically, whether or not the photographer is alert to it.

But, on the other hand, the Bazinian might suggest that such an occurrence is impossible in painting. One simply can't imagine a painter returning to her canvas and being shocked at finding a building there. Painting is an intentional action such that every object portrayed in the painting is there because the painter intended it to be there. There will be no surprises of the sort that photographers typically encounter when the painter looks at her painting – unless she has amnesia or unless someone else has tampered with it – because every person, object or event in the painting is there as a result of her intentions.

Because a painting is man-made, or woman-made, in a way that is dependent upon the maker's intention to portray this or that, it is, so the story goes, impossible that a painter could be shocked by the discovery of a Boeing 707 in her portrait of the Cid. But that very sort of shock is not only possible, but fairly routine when it comes to photography. Many scenes from movies must be reshot when things from the profilmic situation – which no one noticed at the time of shooting – wander into the frame. A director may demand to know "How did *that* get into my shot?" when she reviews the dailies. But the painter never has to ask. She knows already since she put it there – whatever it is.

Thus, the Bazinian surmises that the difference between machine-made and handmade pictures is not a trifling matter of alternative techniques. It is situated on an ontological fissure that goes deep into the very structure of the world at the level dividing what is possible from what is impossible. And since what is possible in film (because it is machine-made) is impossible in painting (because it is handmade), the Bazinian photographic realist believes that he has discerned a fundamental differentiating feature that separates traditional pictorial representations from photographic presentations.

Undoubtedly, the photographic realist can marshall some very powerful intuitions on his side. But until recently, as we argued in the previous article in this volume, this position has also been encumbered by a number of liabilities. One of these is that Bazin himself was never very helpful in explaining how we are to understand the supposed identity relation between a photo or shot of x and x itself. Patently, a shot of Denzel Washington is not the same thing as the man himself. So, in what sense *is* the image its model? Unless a reasonable answer can be supplied to this question, photographic realism seems dead in the water.[7]

Secondarily, photographic realism, as advanced by Bazin, represents a variation on the medium-essentialist refrain, and, therefore, involves many of the shortcomings rehearsed a moment ago in this essay. Consequently, added to its potentially incoherent account of the relation between the cinematic image and its referent, Bazinian photographic realism is also open to the charge that it attempts to mandate aesthetic choices on the basis of spurious ontological claims.

Yet these problems may not be so daunting. On the one hand, the photographic realist may detach his position from the medium-essentialist biases of Bazin. He may agree that his position has no stylistic implications about what must or must not be done by way of cinematic style at the same time that he maintains that cinema is essentially photographic. That is, photographic realists can argue that the photographic basis of film is the essential feature of the cinema without committing themselves to the idea that this logically implies a determinate style or range of styles for filmmakers.

Moreover, turning to photographic realism's other problem, a number of philosophers – including Roger Scruton, Kendall Walton and Patrick Maynard – have begun to work out the sort of identity claims which were only obscurely hinted at by Bazin in a way that makes them intelligible, if not compelling.[8] Thus, if they are able to provide a coherent account of the way in which photography is a presentational, rather than a representational art, then it may once again be plausible to ask whether or not photography is an essential feature of cinema, one that sets it off from traditional forms of pictorial representation, like painting.

A new defense of photographic realism could begin by analogizing film to telescopes, microscopes, periscopes and to those parking-lot mirrors that enable you to look around corners. When we look through devices like these, we say that we see the objects to which these devices give us access. We see stars through telescopes; bacteria through microscopes; aircraft carriers and atomic blasts through periscopes; and oncoming traffic through parking-lot mirrors. Such devices are aids to vision. As such, we may regard them as prosthetic devices.[9] Moreover, these prosthetic devices enable us to see things themselves, rather than representations of things.

When I look through my theater glasses at the ingenue, I see the ingenue, rather than a representation of the ingenue. Devices like these glasses, and the ones mentioned above, enhance my visual powers. They enable me to see, for example, what is faraway or what is small. Indeed, they enable us to see the things themselves, not merely representations of these things. These devices are not, in principle, different from the eye glasses we use to correct our vision. They enable us to overcome visual shortcomings and to make direct visual contact with objects otherwise unavailable to us.

But if we are willing to speak this way about microscopes and telescopes, the photographic realist asks, why not regard photography in the same light? Photography and cinematography are prosthetic devices for vision. They put us in direct visual contact with persons, places and events from the past in a way that is analogous to the manner in which telescopes put us in direct visual contact with distant solar systems. A photograph enables a wife to see her dead husband on their wedding day once again. A shot from an old newsreel enables one to see Babe Ruth at bat.

The argument here takes the form of a slippery slope. If a periscope enables us to see directly over a wall into an adjacent room, why not say that a video set-up does the same thing. One's first response is to say "But we don't see the contents of the adjacent room directly when we look at a video monitor." But what does it mean "to see directly?"

One thing that it means is that our perception is counterfactually dependent on the visible properties of the objects of our perception – i.e., had the visible properties of those objects been different, then our perceptions would have been different. There is a causal chain of physical events between the objects of our perception and our perceptions such that if the starting point in that network had been different, our perception would have varied accordingly. For example, I see the redness of the apple because the apple was red, but had the apple been green, what I would have seen would have been green. And had the object been a banana, rather than an apple, what I would have seen, all things being equal, would have been a banana.

Similarly, when I look through the periscope, what I see is also counterfactually dependent on the objects that give rise to my perception. This is why I am willing to say that what I see through a periscope or through a pair of opera glasses is seen directly. These devices boost the powers of direct perception. They are on a continuum with unaided sight inasmuch as what they give us access to possesses the property of counterfactual dependence. What we see through them would have been different if the visible properties they are aimed at were different. The causal chain of physical events involved in looking through a pair of opera glasses may have an added step when contrasted to unaided vision. But the step is not different in kind. It is still a causal process that preserves the feature of counterfactual dependence. It is on a par with prosthetically unaided vision and so we are willing to say that opera glasses, like unaided vision, put us in direct (counterfactually dependent, causal) contact with objects.

But, then again, is the situation so different with photography and cinematography? Photographic and cinematographic "visions" and unaided, "normal" vision are as strikingly analogous as opera glass "visions" and "normal" vision insofar as all three exhibit the relation of counterfactual dependence with respect to the objects of which they are "visions." We expect a photograph of x to present the visible properties of x in such a way that if x's visible properties had been altered, the photograph would have been altered in corresponding respects. For example, we expect a photograph or a cinematic image of a white church to be white, though if, counterfactually, the church had been black, then we would have expected the photographic depiction to show it as black, at least in cases of straight shooting.

This, of course, once again correlates with prosthetically unaided visual experiences of x where it is presumed that my visual experience of x depends on the visible features of x in such a way that had the visible features of x been different, my visual experience would differ – had the tan lion been red, I would have seen a red lion. Both prosthetically unaided vision and photography are counterfactually dependent on the visible properties in the same way because of the particular physico-causal pathways between these sorts of vision and that of which they are "visions." We say that we are in direct visual contact in the case of vision unaided by opera glasses and vision aided by opera glasses because of the kind of physico-causal processes involved. Since the same kind of physico-causal processes are involved in photographic and cinematic vision, we have no reason, in principle, to say that they do not directly show us those

things to which they give us visual access – such as JFK's assassination.

One might say "Not so fast; what about the temporal difference between the events in newsreels and the events themselves?" But the photographic realist can respond that this is not really so different theoretically than the case where the images of stars delivered to us by telescopes – through which we see directly – come from the past.

Given this argument, the photographic realist maintains that photographic and cinematic images are transparent – we see through them to the objects, persons, and events that gave rise to them.[10] It is this species of transparency, one conjectures, that Bazin had in mind when he talked about the relation between the photographic image and its referent in terms of identity. By means of transparency, we see through the photograph to that of which it is a photograph. The photograph is a transparent presentation of something from the past which we see directly in the sense of counterfactual dependence – i.e., had the relevant objects been different, the photography would have been different in corresponding ways as a result of the kinds of physical processes involved in photography.

Furthermore, traditional picture-making practices, like painting, are not transparent in this way. Paintings need not be counterfactually dependent upon the visible properties of what they portray. They are dependent on the beliefs the painter holds about those objects. The chain of events from objects to paintings of objects are not physico-causal chains like those found in what I have called unaided, "normal" vision. The relation is mediated by the beliefs and intentions of painters. A green apple in a painting would have been blue had the painter intended the apple to be otherwise; something other than "natural" physico-causal chains of events are involved. This is why drawings are not accepted as evidence in court in the way that videotapes are. A drawing of Rodney King being beaten would not have possessed the evidential power of the videotape for this reason.

We do not see directly through paintings. Paintings are representations. They are mediated by intentions. They are not transparent presentations. A painting offers us a representation of an object, whereas a photograph, and, by extension, a cinematic image, provides us the object that gave rise to the image in the same way that a microscope boosts our perceptual powers in a way that is continuous with "normal" vision so that we directly see tiny things. What photography and cinematography enable us to see transparently are the very things from the past that started the mechanical processes that caused the images in question.

In order to "see through" a picture, it is a necessary condition that the photographic process put us in contact with its object by purely mechanical means. But though this is a necessary condition for something to count as a transparent photographic presentation, it is not sufficient. Why not? Well, imagine a computer that was capable of scanning a visual array and then printing out a description of it. It need not be a complicated visual array; it might be comprised of very simple geometric shapes. Surely, there would be no problem in constructing a computer that could recognize such shapes and correlate them to simple descriptions. Yet in such circumstances, it would appear that we are in the sort of mechanical contact with the array that warrants attributions of transparent seeing. But something is wrong here, since descriptions are not transparent pictures for the simple reason that they are not pictures at all. So what then must be added to mechanical contact to differentiate between computer-generated descriptions of the sort imagined here and the kind of image that we might be able to see through?

One way to get at this difference is to note some of the ways in which we might be confused by a picture versus the ways in which we might be confused by a description. Reading, for example, we might confuse *mud* for *mut* because the lettering is so similar; such a mistake might come quite easily if we are confused or hasty. However, when out in the world, viewing objects in nature, so to speak, it appears nearly impossible to mistake an unsculpted mud puddle for a mongrel canine, if the light is good, our eyes reliable, our distance from the objects in question reasonable and our command of visual categories in place.

On the other hand, when it comes to seeing in nature, it may be easier to mistake the back of a garage for the back of a house, whereas even when fatigued it is difficult to mistake the word "garage" for the word "house." What accounts for these differences? One very plausible hypothesis is that confusions between objects in the case of natural seeing is rooted in real similarities between the objects in question, whereas the confusions between the words is based on similarities in lettering which is, in one sense, perfectly arbitrary. Thus, the photographic realist may say that seeing through a photographic process obtains only where confusion over the object in the photographic or cinematic image is a function of real similarity relations. Descriptions, even if mechanically generated, do not provoke visual confusion on the basis of the real similarities between the objects that they refer to, but only through confusion over lettering, which lettering is arbitrary. Transparent presentations, in contrast, traffic in real or natural similarities, whereas descriptions do not.

Consequently, in order to block counter-examples like mechanically generated descriptions, the account of transparent seeing or seeing through pictures must be supplemented by the stipulation that the presentations in question preserve real similarity relations betwixt the photo and that of which it is a photo.

So, summarizing: x is a transparent presentation if only if (1) x puts us in mechanical contact with its object, and (2) x

preserves real similarity relations between things. These conditions are individually necessary and jointly sufficient conditions for transparent pictures or transparent presentations. Moreover, the first condition provides the crucial differentia between *representations,* like painted pictures, and transparent presentations like photographs.

We have traveled this rather long and winding path in order to indicate that, unlike Bazin, the contemporary photographic realist can give an intelligible account of what it is to see through a photograph to its referent. The photographic realist, thus, can advance the claim that transparent seeing is the essential feature of photography or, at least, a necessary feature. And arguing that the photographic basis of cinema is an essential feature of film, the photographic realist could, if he wished, then go on to argue that transparent seeing is the essential feature of film or, at least, a necessary feature, thereby reinstalling something like Bazin's insight, albeit in a theoretically more sophisticated framework.

But even if the claims of photographic realism can be rendered intelligible in the way indicated, it does not seem that transparent seeing can be accepted as an essential or necessary condition of cinema or even photography. For photography is not the only medium of film. Cinema (and photography) can be computer generated, as the stampeding dinosaurs of *Jurassic Park* amply demonstrate. These images are certainly cinema, but there is nothing for the viewer to see directly by means of them. The first computer-generated sequence appeared in major motion pictures, like *Star Trek II* in the eighties and computer simulations have been deployed increasingly since then, as in Roger Corman's *The Fantastic Four.* Since the eighties, some shots in films have been wholly composited: several matte paintings, animation and so on have been "jigsawed together," without any photography of three-dimensional objects having been involved. The array we see, in such cases, corresponds to no independently existing spatial field, in part or whole.

Perhaps, the photographic realist will protest that every constructed image must have some photographic elements through which we see directly. But surely we are on the brink of completely digitally synthesized films. Matt Elson's animation short *Virtually Yours,* starring the completely constructed Lotta Desire, substantiates this possibility.[11] Moreover, the exorbitant costs of film actors nowadays provides an awesome financial incentive for film to turn toward the development of fully computerized characters.[12]

The future of film may become, in large measure, the future of digitally synthesized images, where the notion of seeing directly has little or no purchase, since such images need not possess a model in nature that we can see directly. There is no reason in principle why this cannot come about.[13] The epoch of photographic film, then, may represent nothing but a brief interlude in the artform. But even if these prophecies fall on fallow ground, seeing directly is neither an essential or a necessary feature of film even now, since we already have *some* fully computer-generated images. Nor need the only source of our counterexamples be contemporary. Hollywood has used matte shots – another technique that problematizes the notion of direct seeing – for decades, and though these shots are often only partially constructed, there is no reason in principle why a fully constructed matte shot or "composite" should not count as an instance of film as we know it.[14] In this case, as in the case of computer-generated images, film approaches the status of painting.

But what of earlier intuition pumps that suggested that film shots and paintings must be essentially different, since filmmakers could be surprised at finding Boeing 707s in their images, but painters could not? In truth, the intuition was premature. There is no principled difference between film shots and paintings here. Picasso tells the story of finding the outline of a squirrel in a painting by Braque.[15] Braque was unaware of the presence of the squirrel, since it inhabited the "negative" space in the image, rather like the vase that inheres in some pictures of facing profiles. Switch images like these – and the duck/rabbit and the old woman/young woman – are well known, and we have no problem imagining a painter who, while knowingly drawing one of the aspects of such an image, also unknowingly draws the other aspect. Something like this apparently happened to Braque. As Picasso tells the story, it is comical. But it is also theoretically important. For in documenting the possibility, Picasso shows how a painter could be as surprised as a cinematographer at finding some creature or object, that he had not intended to be there, lurking in his picture.

For the photographic realist, the cinematic image is a presentation, not a representation in the standard sense of that term as it pertains to things like paintings. The cinematic image presents us with things that we see directly; it is a transparent presentation. It is a transparent presentation because it puts us in mechanical contact with what we see and it preserves real similarity relations between things. But one wonders whether this is really sufficient for calling something a presentation rather than a representation (in the standard sense of that term).

Imagine a railyard. Suppose we build a point-by-point model of the railyard. Suppose also that we link every square inch of the railyard to a super computer so that every change in the surface of the railyard registers a change in the model. Next imagine that we interpose the model between us and the railyard so that we do not see any part of the railyard directly and so that the model occupies our field of vision at the angle and scale the railyard would, were the model not standing in the way between us and the railyard. In such a case, we would be in direct mechanical contact with the railyard, and every change we perceived in the model would notate a change in the railyard. Moreover, where we might tend to confuse objects (like spades and hoes) in the railyard, we will also tend to confuse objects in the model, because the model preserves real similarity relations between things.

Will we be disposed to call the model a presentation of the railyard, rather than a representation (in the standard sense) of it? Will we say that we see the railyard directly through the model? The answer to both questions, I predict, will be no. Thus, the conditions that the photographic realist proposes to identify a class of transparent presentations that are ontologically discrete from the class of representations are not adequate to the task, which, in turn, implies that the story the photographic realist has told so far about transparent presentation is insufficient to bear out claims about the uniqueness of photographic and cinematic images.

The photographic realist maintains that cinematic images are transparent presentations, not representations (in the standard sense of that term). We see through them. This conclusion is advanced by analogies between photographs and film, on the one hand, and microscopes and telescopes, on the other. If we are willing to say that we see through the latter, why should we be hesitant about saying the same thing with respect to the former? The photographic realist has us on a slippery slope. Do we have any principled reason for regarding telescopes as visual prosthetic devices while withholding the same status from photographic and cinematic images? I think that we do.

If I look through a pair of binoculars at a brace of horses racing to the finish line, the visual array I obtain, though magnified, is still connected to my own body in the sense that I would be able to find my way to the finish line, were that my wish. That is, when I use binoculars, I can still orient myself spatially to the finish line. My bodily orientation to the things that I perceive is preserved. The same story can be told about typical microscopes and telescopes. When I look through them, I can still point my body approximately in the direction of the bacteria and the meteors that they reveal to me.

But the same cannot be said of photographic and cinematic images. Suppose that I am watching *Casablanca* and what I see on the screen is Rick's bar. I cannot, on the basis of the image, orient my body to the bar – to the spatial coordinates of that structure as it existed some time in the early forties in California (nor could I orient my body by means of the image to the putative fictional locale [in North Africa] of the film). Looking at the cinematic image of the bar, I will not know how to point my body toward Rick's bar (the set) or away from it. That is, I would not know, looking at the image on the screen, how to point my body in the direction that I would have to take in order to walk, or drive or fly to Rick's bar (i.e., some set on a sound stage in L.A.). The image itself would not tell me how to get to the set, presuming that it still exists, nor how to get to the place in the world where, if it no longer exists, it once did. For the space, so to speak, between the set of Rick's bar and my body is discontinuous; it is disconnected, phenomenologically speaking, from the space that I live in.[16]

Following Francis Sparshott, we might call this feature of viewing cinema "alienated vision."[17] Ordinarily, our sense of where we are depends on our sense of balance and our kinesthetic feelings. What we see is integrated with these cues in such a way as to yield a sense of where we are situated. But if we call what we see on the silver screen a "view," then it is a disembodied view. I see a visual array, like Rick's bar, but I have no sense of where the portrayed space really is in relation to my body. On the other hand, with prosthetic devices like binoculars, telescopes and microscopes – at least in the standard cases – I can orient my body in the space I live in to the objects these devices empower me to see. Indeed, I submit that we do not speak literally of seeing objects unless I can

perspicuously relate myself spatially to them – i.e., unless I know (roughly) where they are in the space I inhabit.

Yet if this requirement is correct, then I do not literally see the objects that cause photographic and cinematic images. What I see are representations in the standard sense or displays – displays whose virtual spaces are detached from the space of my experience. But insofar as cinematic images are to be understood as representations in the standard sense of the term or what I call "detached displays," they are better categorized with paintings and traditional pictures, rather than with telescopes and mirrors.

Photographic realism, then, is mistaken. Photographic and cinematic images are not instances of transparent presentations that afford direct seeing. Photographic and cinematic images cannot be presumed to be on a par with binoculars as devices through which the sight of remote things is enhanced. For authentic visual, prosthetic devices preserve a sense of the body's orientation to the objects that they render accessible; whereas photographic and cinematic images present the viewer with a space that is disembodied or detached from her perspective. Nor can we speak of direct seeing here either, for the same reasons.

Undoubtedly the photographic realist will respond by saying that the feature of "normal" vision and of prosthetic vision that I have stressed as essential is an adventitious feature that should not be used to block the analogies the photographic realist underscores. However, I cannot agree. Surely it is the fact that normal vision connects us spatially with its objects that accounts for its evolutionary value. That vision informs us how to move toward what we want and away from what threatens us explains, in part, why vision, as we know it, is an adaptively selected attribute. Apart from the pressure of common sense, then, another reason to think that the feature of vision that I have emphasized in order to draw a brake along the photographic realist's slippery slope is not an avoidable one is that the feature in question plays a significant role in the evolutionary theory of vision. Nor can the photographic realist object that the analogy does not hold because mirror-vision is direct and yet there are some arrangements of mirrors where light is relayed along such a complicated pathway that we could not locate the source in nature of the image reflected before us. For though we may be said to see directly through some mirrors, I see no reason to believe that we see directly before any imaginable arrangement of mirrors. The mirror arrangements that make spatial orientation implausible, indeed, are just the ones we do not see through.

I have spent a great deal of time disputing the photographic realist's candidate for an essential or necessary feature of film.[18] But though the argument has been primarily negative so far, the outcome has had at least one positive result. For in the course of challenging the photographic realist's account, we have discovered a necessary condition of the cinematic image: all photographic and cinematic images are detached displays. It is this feature of such images that block the claim that photographic images are not representations in the standard sense of the term, but rather are transparent presentations that enable us to see through them to the objects they display. But this feature, insofar as it blocks the photographic realist's account across the board, also reveals a telling attribute of all film images – that they all involve alienated visions, disembodied viewpoints, or, as I prefer to call them, *detached displays*. That is, all cinematic images are such that it is vastly improbable and maybe effectively impossible that spectators, save in freak situations, be able to orient themselves to the real, profilmic spaces physically portrayed on the screen.

What of a situation where a video monitor shows us what is going on in a room on the other side of a wall? Isn't this a counterexample to our thesis concerning detached displays? No: because it is not the image itself that provides the orientational information, but our knowledge of the placement of the camera in addition to the information available in the image. We might be easily deceived in such cases, were the image of an identical room being broadcast to our monitor from a remote location.

One necessary feature of a motion picture image, then, is that it is a detached display. Something is a motion picture image only if it is a detached display. Such an image presents us with a visual array whose source is such that on the basis of the image alone we are unable to orient ourselves toward it in the space that is continuous with our own bodies. We are necessarily "alienated" from the space of detached displays whether those displays are photographs or cinematic images.

However, though this feature of film – that it projects detached displays – is a plausible necessary condition for motion picture images, it does not yet provide us with the conceptual wherewithal to distinguish film from other sorts of visual representation, such as painting. To that end, we must introduce consideration of another necessary condition of film.

III. The Moving Image

Even if it is a necessary condition of a film image that it be a detached display, this feature does not enable us to draw a distinction between motion pictures and paintings. For a painting of a landscape is typically a detached display or a disembodied viewpoint in the same sense that a moving picture is. For we cannot orient our bodies spatially to the vista in nature that the painting portrays on the basis of the painting. That is, sitting in my study in Madison, Wisconsin and looking at a painting of a street scene in Mexico City, I do not know, on the basis of the painting, how to walk to that street. Like a cinematic image, the painting is a detached display. So what then differentiates paintings from film images?

A useful clue is already available in ordinary language, where we call the phenomena in question *motion* pictures or *moving* pictures.[19] But we should be careful in the way that we exploit that clue. Roman Ingarden, for example, maintained that in films things are always happening whereas paintings, drawing, slides and the like are always static.[20] But this is not perfectly accurate. For there are a number of films in which there is no movement, such as Oshima's *Band of Ninjas* (a film of a comic strip), Michael Snow's *One Second in Montreal* (a film of photos) and his *So Is This* (a film of sentences), Hollis Frampton's *Poetic Justice* (a film of a shooting script on a tabletop with a plant), Godard and Gorin's *Letter to Jane* (another film of photos), and Takahiko Iimura's *1 in 10* (a film of addition and subtraction tables).

A perhaps better-known example than any of these is Chris Marker's *La Jetée,* a film of almost no movement whose time-travel narrative is told primarily through the projection of still photographs. Of course, there is one movement in Marker's film, but it should be easy to imagine a film just like *La Jetée* but with no movement whatsoever.

Some may respond to cases like these by saying that surely the prospect of such movies without movement is oxymoronic or perhaps even self-contradictory. Such experiments, it might be charged, are little more than slide shows mounted on celluloid, maybe for the purpose of efficient projection.

But there is a deep difference between a film image of a character, say from our imagined version of *La Jetée,* and a slide taken of that character from *La Jetée.* For as long as you know that what you are watching is a film, even a film of what appears to be a photograph, it is always justifiable to entertain the possibility that the image *might* move. On the other hand, if you know that you are looking at a slide, then it is categorically impossible that the image

might move. Thus, if you know what you are looking at is a slide and you understand what a slide is, then it is unreasonable – indeed, it is conceptually absurd – to suppose that the image can move.

Movement in a slide would require a miracle; movement in a film image is an artistic choice which is always technically available. Before *Band of Ninjas* concludes – that is, until the last image flickers through the projection gate – the viewer may presume, if she knows that she is watching a film, that there may yet be movement in the image. For such movement is a permanent possibility in cinema. But if she knows that what she is looking at is a slide, it would be irrational for her to entertain the possibility that it might move. It would be irrational, of course, because if it is a slide, it is impossible for the image to move, and if she knows what a slide is, then she must know this.

Furthermore, the difference between slides and films applies across the board to the distinction between every species of still picture – including paintings, drawings, still photos and the like – and every sort of moving picture – including videos, mutoscopes, and movies. When it comes to still pictures, one commits a category error, if one expects movement. It is, by definition, self-contradictory for still pictures to move. That is why they are called *still* pictures. Thus, to watch what one understands to be a painting with the expectation that it will move is absurd. But it is eminently reasonable – and never irrational – to expect to see movement in films because of the kind of thing – a moving picture – that a film is. Even with a static film, like *Poetic Justice,* it is strictly reasonable to wonder whether there will be movement until the last reel has run its course.

With a film like *Poetic Justice,* it is an intelligible question to ask why the film-maker, Hollis Frampton, made a static film, since he had movement as a genuine option. But it makes no sense to ask why Raphael foreswore literal movement in his *School of*

Athens. Unlike Frampton, he had no other alternative. Asking why Raphael's philosophers don't move is like asking why ants don't sing *The Barber of Seville*.

Of course, once one has seen a static film from beginning to end, then it is no longer justifiable to anticipate movement in repeated viewings, unless you suspect that the film has been doctored since your initial viewing. On first viewing, it is reasonable, or, at least, not irrational to wonder whether there will be movement on the screen up until the film concludes; on second and subsequent viewings, such anticipation is out of place. However, on first viewings, one can never be sure that a film is entirely still until it is over. And this is what makes it reasonable to stay open to the possibility of movement throughout first viewings of static films. But to anticipate movement from what one understands to be a slide or a painting is conceptually confused.

Why categorize static films as films rather than as slides or as some other sort of still picture? Because, as I've already noted, stasis is a stylistic choice in static films. It is an option that contributes to the stylistic effect of a film. It is something whose significance the audience contemplates when trying to make sense of a film. It is informative to say that a film is static; it alerts a potential viewer to a pertinent lever of stylistic articulation in the work. Contrariwise, there is no point in saying of a painting that it is a literally still painting. It is thoroughly uninformative. It could not have been otherwise. To call a painting or a slide a still painting or a still slide is redundant.

Indeed, one can imagine a slide of a procession and a cinematic freeze frame of the exact same moment in a parade. The two images may, in effect, be perceptually indiscernible. And yet they are metaphysically different. Moreover, the epistemic states that each warrants in the spectator when the spectator knows which of the categories – slide or film – confronts him are different. With motion pictures, the anticipation of possible future movement is reasonable, or, at least, conceptually permissible; but with still pictures, such as slides, it is never conceptually permissible. The reason for this is also quite clear. Film belongs to the class of things where movement is a technical possibility, while paintings, slides and the like belong to a class of things that are, by definition, still.

Ordinary language alerts us to a necessary feature of films by referring to them as "*moving* pictures." But the wisdom implicit in ordinary language needs to be unpacked. It is not the case that every film image or every film leaves us with the impression of movement. There can be static films. However, static films belong to the class of things where the possibility of movement is always technically available in such a way that *stasis* is a stylistic variable in films in a way that it cannot be with respect to still pictures. Perhaps the label, "moving pictures," is preferable to "film" since it advertises this deep feature of the artform.

Of course, the category of *moving pictures* is somewhat broader than that which has traditionally been discussed by film theorists, since it would include such things as video and computer imaging. But this expansion of the class of objects under consideration to moving pictures in general, in my opinion, is theoretically advisable, since I predict that in the future the history of what we now call cinema and the history of video, TV, CD-ROM and whatever comes next will be thought of as of a piece.

Nevertheless, there is at least one limitation in calling the relevant artform *moving pictures*. For the term "picture" implies the sort of intentional visual artifact in which one recognizes the depiction of objects, persons and events by looking. But many films and videos are abstract, or nonrepresentational, or nonobjective. Consider some of the work of artists like Eggeling and Brakhage. These may be comprised of nonrecognizable shapes and purely visual structures. Thus, rather than speaking of moving pictures, I prefer to speak of moving *images,* as the title of this article indicates. For the term *image* covers both pictures and abstractions. Whether the image is pictorial or abstract is less pertinent for this investigation than that it is moving imagery in the sense that it is imagery that belongs to the class of things where movement is technically possible.

So far then, we have not only recommended a change in the domain of investigation for film theory – from cinema to moving images – but we have also identified two necessary conditions for what is to count as a moving image. In answer to the question, "What is a moving image?" we argue that *x* is a moving image (1) only if it is a detached display and (2) only if it belongs to the class of things from which the impression of movement is technically possible. The second of these conditions enables us to distinguish film, or, as I call it, the moving image from painting, but this will not discriminate it from theater, since theatrical representations also warrant the expectation of movement. So what, then, differentiates moving images from theatrical representations?

IV. Performance Tokens

A theatrical performance is a detached display. Watching a theatrical performance of *A Streetcar Named Desire,* we cannot orient our bodies – on the basis of the images onstage – in the direction of New Orleans. The space of the play is not my space. It is not true of the play that Hamlet dies three feet away from me, even if I am sitting in the first row. Nor can I point my body toward Elsinor on the basis of the theatrical image before me.

Furthermore, though there may be literally static theater works – performances bereft of movement, such as Douglas Dunn's *101*[21] – in such cases, as in the case of moving pictures, it is reasonable for the audience to suppose that movement might be forthcoming up until the conclusion of the performance. For movement is a permanent possibility in theater, even in works that do not exercise it as a stylistic option. Thus, theater meets the two conditions that we have so far laid down for the moving image. Are there some other ways in which to signal the boundary between these two artforms?

Roman Ingarden locates the border between theater and film by arguing that in theater the word dominates while spectacle (as Aristotle would have agreed) is ancillary; whereas in film, action dominates and words subserve our comprehension of the action. But this ignores films like *History Lessons* and *Fortini-Cani* by Jean-Marie Straub and Daniele Huillet, and Yvonne Rainer's *Journeys from Berlin,* as well as Godard's videotapes, not to mention pedestrian TV shows such as *Perry Mason.*

Some photographic realists have attempted to draw the line between film and theater by focussing of the performer.[22] Due to the intimacy between the photographic lens and its subjects, some, like Stanley Cavell, think of film acting primarily in terms of star personalities, whereas stage performers are actors who take on roles. For Erwin Panofsky, stage actors interpret their roles, whereas film actors, again because of the intimacy of the lens vis-á-vis the actor, incarnate theirs. When it comes to movies, we go to see an Eastwood film, whereas with theater we go to see a Paul Scofield interpretation of Lear.

But this contrast does not seem to really fit the facts. Surely people go to the theater to see Baryshnikov dance and Callas sing no matter what the role, just as they did to see Sarah Bernhardt or Fanny Elssler. We may say that "Sam Spade *is* Bogart," but only in the sense that people once said that Gilette was Sherlock Holmes or O'Neill was the Man in the Iron Mask.

The difference, then, does not appear to reside in the performers in film versus those in theater. But it may reside in the token performances of the two artforms. Both theater and film have performances. On a given evening, we might choose to go to a live performance of Ping Chong's *Kindness* or a performance (a screening) of Robert Altman's *Ready to Wear*. Both might begin at eight. In both cases, we will be seated in an auditorium, and perhaps both performances start with a rising curtain. But despite the similarities, there are also profound differences between a theatrical performance and a film performance.

Undoubtedly, this hypothesis will seem strange to some philosophers. For they are likely to divide the arts into those that involve unique singular objects (e.g., paintings and sculptures) versus those arts that involve multiple copies of the same artwork – there are probably over a million copies of *Vanity Fair*.[23] And having segregated some artforms as multiple, philosophers frequently go on to characterize the multiple arts – like novels, plays and movies – in terms of the type/token relation. But on the basis of this distinction, theatrical performances and film performances do not look very different; in both cases, the performance in question is a token of a type. Tonight's film performance is a token of the type *Ready to Wear* by Robert Altman, whereas tonight's dramatic performance is a token of *Kindness,* a play of Ping Chong. Consequently, it might be concluded that there really is no deep difference between theatrical performances and film performances.

But, though the simple type/token distinction may be useful as far as it goes, it does not go far enough. For even if theatrical performances and film performances may both be said to be tokens, the tokens in the theatrical case are generated by interpretations, whereas the tokens in the film case are generated by templates. And this, in turn, yields a crucial aesthetic difference between the two. The theatrical performances are artworks in their own right that, thereby,

can be objects of artistic evaluation, but the film performance itself is neither an artwork nor is it a legitimate candidate for artistic evaluation.

The film performance – a film showing or screening – is generated from a template. Standardly, this is a film print, but it might also be a videotape, a laser disk, or a computer program. These templates are tokens; each one of them can be destroyed and each one can be assigned a temporal location. But the film – say *Toni* by Renoir – is not destroyed when any of the prints are destroyed. One might think that the master or negative is privileged. But the negative of Murnau's *Nosferatu* was destroyed as the result of a court order, and yet *Nosferatu* (the film, not the vampire) survives. Indeed, all the prints can be destroyed and the film will survive if a laser disk does, or if a collection of photos of all the frames does,[24] or if a computer program of it does whether on disk, or tape or even on paper or in human memory.[25]

To get to a token film performance – tonight's showing of *Pulp Fiction* – we require a template which is itself a token of the film type. Whereas the paint on Magritte's *Le Château des Pyrénées* is a constituent part of a unique painting, the print on the page of my copy of the novel *The Mill on the Floss* conveys George Eliot's artwork to me. Similarly, the film performance – the projection or screening event – is a token of a type, which token conveys *Pulp Fiction,* the type, to the spectator.

The account, however, is both different and more complicated when it comes to plays. For plays have as tokens both objects and performances. That is, when considered as a literary work, a token of *The Libation Bearers* is a graphic text of the same order of my copy of *The Warden*. But considered from the viewpoint of theater, a token of *The Libation Bearers* is a performance which occurs at a specific place and time. Unlike the film performance, the theatrical performance is not generated by a template. It is generated by an interpretation. For when considered from the perspective of theatrical performance, the play by Aeschylus is akin to a recipe that must be filled in by other artists, including the director, the actors, the set and lighting designers, costumers, and the like.

This interpretation is a conception of the play and it is this conception of the play that governs the performances from night to night. The interpretation may be performed in different theaters; it may be revived after a hiatus. For the interpretation is a type, which, in turn, generates performances which are tokens. Thus, the relation of the play to its performances is mediated by an interpretation, suggesting that the interpretation is a type within a type. What gets us from the play to a performance is not a template, which is a token, but an interpretation, which is a type.

One difference between the performance of a play and the performance of a film is that the former is generated by an interpretation while the latter is generated by a template. Furthermore, this difference is connected to another, namely, that performances of plays are artworks in their own right and can be aesthetically evaluated as such, whereas performances of films and videos are not artworks. Nor does it make sense to evaluate them as such. A film may be projected out of focus or the video tracking may be badly adjusted, but these are not artistic failures. They are mechanical or electrical failures. That is, a film projectionist may be mechanically incompetent, but he is not artistically incompetent.

In theater, the play, the interpretation, and the performance are each discrete arenas of artistic achievement. It is to be hoped, of course, that they will be integrated. And in the best of all cases, they are. Nevertheless, we recognize that these are separable stratas of artistry. We often speak of a good play interpreted badly and performed blandly; or of a mediocre play, interpreted

ingeniously and performed brilliantly; and every other combination thereof. This manner of speaking, of course, presupposes that we regard the play, the interpretation, and the performance as separate levels of artistic achievement – even where the play is written by someone who directs it and acts in it as well. The play by the playwright is one artwork, which is then interpreted like a recipe or set of instructions by a director and others in the process of producing another artwork or series of artworks.

But our practices with regard to motion pictures are different. If in theater, the play-type is a recipe that the director interprets, and the recipe and the interpretation can be regarded as different though related artworks, in film both the recipe and the interpretations are constituents of the same artwork. When the writer produces a play, we appreciate it independently of what its theatrical interpreters make of it. But in the world of moving pictures, as we know it, scenarios are not read like plays and novels, but are ingredients of moving pictures (or, more accurately, moving images). That is, to speak metaphorically, with movies, the recipe and its interpretation come in one indissoluble package.

Sometimes people say things like "many actresses can play Rosalind and the performance will still be a performance of the play type *As You Like It,* but it would not be an instance of the movie type *White Heat* without James Cagney." The reason for this is that Cagney's performance of Cody – his interpretation – in concert with the director Raoul Walsh is a nondetachable constituent of the film. The interpretation is, so to speak, etched in celluloid. The interpretation in the case of film is not separable from the film type in the way that interpretation is separable from the play type.

Whereas film performances are generated from templates which are tokens, play performances are generated from interpretation types. Thus, whereas film performances are counterfactually dependent on certain electrical, chemical, mechanical and otherwise routine processes and procedures, play performances are counterfactually dependent upon the beliefs, intentions and judgments of people – actors, lighting experts, make-up artists and so on. Though in modern Western theater, there is typically an overarching directorial interpretation of the playwright's recipe, the realization of the token performance on a given night depends of the continuous interpretation of that play, given the special exigencies of the unique performance situation. It is because of the contribution that interpretation makes in the production of the performance that the performance warrants artistic appreciation; whereas the performance of a film – a film showing – warrants no artistic appreciation, since it is simply a function of the physical mechanisms engaging the template properly. Or, in other words, it is a matter of running the relevant devices correctly.

A successful motion picture performance – the projection of a film or the running of a video cassette – does not command aesthetic appreciation, nor is it an artwork. We do not applaud projectionists as we do violinists. We are likely to complain and to perhaps demand our money back if the film emulsifies in the projector beam, but that is a technical failure, not an aesthetic one. If it were an aesthetic failure, we would expect people to cheer when the film doesn't burn. But they don't. For the happy film performance only depends on operating the apparatus as it was designed to be operated, and since that involves no more than often quite minimal mechanical savvy, running the template through the machine is not regarded as an aesthetic accomplishment. On the other hand, a successful theatrical performance involves a token interpretation of an interpretation type, and inasmuch as that depends on artistic understanding and judgment, it is a suitable object of aesthetic appreciation.

Moreover, if this is right, then we may conjecture that a major difference between motion picture (or moving image) performances and theatrical performances is that the latter are artworks and the former are not, and, therefore, that performances of motion pictures are not objects of artistic evaluation, whereas theatrical performances are. Or, another way to state the conclusion is to say that, in one sense, motion pictures are not a performing art – i.e., they are not something whose performance itself is an art.

This sounds bizarre and is apt to call forth counterexamples. Here are three. First, before motors were installed in projectors, film projectionists hand-cranked the performance, and audiences were said to come to prefer some projectionists over others. In these cases, it might be argued, the projectionists were performers whose performances elicited artistic appreciation. Second, the avant-garde filmmaker Harry Smith sometimes accompanied some his film screenings by personally alternating colored gels in front of the projector lens. Was he in this case any less a performing artist than a violinist? And lastly, Malcolm LeGrice presented a piece in the early seventies which he called *Monster Film*. In it, he walked – stripped to the waist – into the projector beam, his shadow becoming progressively larger (like a monster), while a loud crashing sound dominated the space. If *Monster Film* is a film, then surely its performance is an artwork.

However, these counterexamples are not compelling. Since the early projectionists who are usually cited are also said to have cranked the films they thought were tedious in such a way that the action was comically sped up, I doubt that their performances were actually performances of the film types advertised, rather than travesties or parodies thereof – that is to say comic routines in their own right. On the other hand, both Smith and LeGrice seem to me to have produced multimedia artworks in which film or the film apparatus play an important role, but which cannot be thought of as simply motion pictures.

What may be disturbing about my denial that moving pictures (and/or images) are instances of the performing arts is that motion picture types are generally made by people whom we standardly think of as performing artists – actors, directors, choreographers, and so on. But it is essential to note that the interpretations and the performances that these artists contribute to the motion picture type are integrated and edited into the final product as constituent parts of the moving image type.

When we go to see *Moby Dick,* we do not go to see Gregory Peck perform, but to see a performance of *Moby Dick*. And while Gregory Peck's performance required artistry, the performance of *Moby Dick* – the showing of it – does not. It requires nothing above and beyond the proper manipulation of the template and the apparatus. A performance of a play, contrariwise, involves the kind of talents exhibited by Gregory Peck prior to the appearance of the first template of *Moby Dick*. That is why the performance of a play is an artistic event and the performance of a motion picture is not.

Thus, there are important differences between the performance of a motion picture and the performance of a play. Two of them are that the play performance is generated by an interpretation that is a type, whereas the performance of the motion picture is generated by a template that is a token; *and* the performance of a play is an artwork in its own right and is an appropriate object of aesthetic evaluation, whereas the performance of the motion picture is neither. Moreover, the first of these contrasts helps us explain the second. For it is insofar as the performance of the motion picture is generated by engaging the template mechanically that it is not an appropriate object of artistic evaluation in the way that a performance generated by an interpretation or a set of interpretations is. These two features of film performance are enough to differentiate performances of moving images from performances of plays, and,

furthermore, the two differentia under consideration apply to all films, videos and the like, whether they are artworks or not.

V. Two-Dimensionality

So far we have identified four necessary conditions for the moving image. Summarizing our findings, we can say that x is a moving image (1) only if x is a detached display, (2) only if x belongs to the class of things from which the impression of movement is technically possible, (3) only if performance tokens of x are generated by a template that is a token, and (4) only if performance tokens of x are not artworks in their own right. Moreover, these conditions provide us with the conceptual resources to discriminate the moving image from neighboring artforms like painting and theater.

However, these conditions also seem vulnerable to at least one sort of counterexample. Consider what might be called moving sculptures of the sort exemplified by music boxes. Once wound up, the box plays a tune while mechanical figurines shaped like ballerinas cavort in a semblance of pirouettes. This is a detached display; the virtual space of the ballerinas is not our space. The image moves. It is manufactured from a template, and the mechanical dancing is not an artwork. But clearly this is not the sort of thing that we customarily think of as a moving picture or even a moving image.

In order to forestall cases like this we need to add a fifth condition to the preceding four, namely, that x is a moving image only if it is two-dimensional. Perhaps, it might seem unnecessary to supplement the preceding formula this way, since some may contend that two-dimensionality is already entailed by the fact that we are talking about moving pictures and moving images which are, by their very nature, two-dimensional. This may be right when it comes to pictures, but it surely cannot hurt to make it explicit that the images we have in mind, when speaking of moving images, are two-dimensional.

Here, of course, the weary reader may complain "Why wasn't two-dimensionality introduced earlier, since it would have given us the boundary between film and theater at a stroke?" "Why do we need all that extra paraphernalia about tokens generated by templates?" The answer I think is simple: theater can be two-dimensional. Consider the shadow-puppet plays of Bali (the Wayang Kulit), and of China. In order to count them as theater rather than motion pictures, we will require recourse to the notion that film, in particular, and the moving image, more broadly, are tokens generated by templates that are themselves tokens.

Concluding Remarks

I have proposed five necessary conditions for the phenomena that I am calling moving images. Of course, once one has accumulated so many necessary conditions, it is natural to wonder whether or not they might not be jointly sufficient conditions for what we typically call motion pictures. But they are not, for treated as a set of jointly sufficient conditions for what it is to be a motion picture, they are overly inclusive. Consider for example, the upper-right-hand page corners of Arlene Croce's *The Fred Astaire and Ginger Rogers Book*.[26] There you will find photographs of Astaire and Rogers dancing. If you flick the pages quickly enough, you can animate the dancers after the fashion of a flip book. Although the third condition of my theory – that token motion picture performances are generated by templates – excludes handmade, one-of-a-kind flip books from the category of moving images, the Astaire/Rogers example clearly meets the condition in question, as would any mass-produced flip book, whether it employed photographs or some other kind of mechanically produced illustrations. Similarly, Muybridge-type photographs of horses

animated by the nineteenth-century device known as the zoetrope fit the formula. But these do not seem to be the kind of phenomena that one has in mind when speaking of moving pictures in ordinary language, or of moving images in my slightly regimented language.

You might attempt to preempt this species of counterexample by requiring that moving pictures (and/or images) be projected. But that would have the infelicitous consequence of cashiering early Edison kinetoscopes from the domain of motion pictures. Obviously, it will be hard to draw any firm boundaries between motion pictures (and images) and the protocinematic devices that led to the invention of cinema, without coming up with difficult cases; indeed, we should expect to find problematic border cases in exactly this vicinity. But in any event, it does not seem obvious to me that we can turn the preceding five necessary conditions into jointly sufficient conditions for what is commonly thought to be a motion picture, without doing some severe violence to our everyday intuitions.

Thus, the characterization of moving pictures (or moving images) proposed in this essay is not essentialist in the philosophical sense that presupposes that an essential definition of cinema would be comprised of a list of necessary conditions that are jointly sufficient. That is, my account is not an example of real-definition essentialism. Nor is it what I earlier called Grecian essentialism.

By a Grecian essence, I mean a necessary condition for x whose citation a theorist believes is useful for understanding x. When Plato speaks of drama as essentially mimetic, he does not suppose that this is a unique feature of drama, but only that it is a necessary feature of drama (as he knew it) to which it is useful to draw our attention, if we wish to understand how drama works. However, though I have pointed out what I think are five necessary features of moving pictures, I do not think that they are particularly central to our understanding of how moving images function. For example, we don't – at least as far as I can see at present – derive any deep insights into the effects of movies or into film style by contemplating these five conditions.

And lastly, my position is not that of what I earlier called medium-essentialism. For, among other things, my analysis is not connected to any specific medium. Moving images, as I call them, can be instantiated in a variety of media. The moving image is not a medium-specific notion for the simple reason that the artform that concerns us, though born in film, has already undergone and will continue to undergo transformation as new media are invented and integrated into its history.

Furthermore, my position is not that of a medium-essentialist since the five conditions that I have enumerated have no implications for the stylistic directions that film and/or video and/or computer imaging should take. The preceding five conditions are compatible with any motion picture style, including styles that may conflict with each other. Thus, if I have indeed managed to set out five necessary conditions for moving pictures (and images), then I have also shown that contrary to previous traditions of film theory, it is possible to philosophize about the nature of moving images without explicitly or implicitly legislating what film, video, and computer artists should or should not do.[27]

Notes

1. The idea that each art has its own province and, thus, possesses unique features goes back at least to the Renaissance and the tradition of the paragone. It was also a prominent feature of turn-of-the century modernism. Thus, it may seem reasonable that theorists who were interested in justifying film as a fine art would naturally draw on premises already endorsed by the tradition of high-art.

2. This, at least, is how artists may regard mediumistic essentialist when they are enamored of it. Once disenchanted, they are apt to scorn it as a narrow-minded, unimaginative, intrusive, and altogether inappropriate exercise in proscription.

3. Such an interpretation is suggested by Charles Barr in his "Cinemascope: Before and After," in *Film Theory and Criticism: Introductory Readings,* second edition, edited by Gerald Mast and Marshall Cohen (New York: Oxford University Press, 1979). Of course, I don't mean to suggest that stylistic considerations were either the only reasons or even the most important reasons behind the adoption of realism. But they were, for the reasons Barr suggests, one motivating factor. At the same time, it should be noted that Barr's "realist/essentialist" reading of his preferred use of cinemascope can be readily challenged by considering the use that Sergio Leone makes of those cinemascope close-ups of Clint Eastwood's and Lee Van Cleef's eyes in the dazzling edited arrays in his spaghetti westerns.

4. See, David Bordwell, Janet Staiger and Kristen Thompson, *The Classical Hollywood Cinema: Film Style and Mode of Production to 1960* (New York: Columbia University Press, 1985), pp. 287–93.

5. André Bazin, *What is Cinema?*, vol. I, translated by Hugh Gray (Berkeley: University of California Press, 1967), p. 14. See also pp. 96–97. In conversation, David Bordwell has argued that the quotation above is a bad translation. However, even if this is true, the position represented by the translation is still worth debating, since it has given rise to what might be called a Bazinian position. And that position needs refuting, even if it is not Bazin's.

6. The shift to the idiom of the "Bazinian" here is meant to indicate that the following argument was not developed by Bazin himself, though I believe that if Bazin had thought of this "intuition pump," he would have been happy to use it.

7. For challenges to the coherence of Bazin's claims about the identity of the photograph to its model, see my essay "Concerning Uniqueness Claims for Photographic and Cinematographic Representation," in this volume.

8. Roger Scruton, "Photography and Representation," in *The Aesthetic Understanding* (London: Methuen, 1983); Kendall L. Walton, "Transparent Pictures: On the Nature of Photographic Realism," *Critical Inquiry* 11, no. 2 (December 1984); Patrick Maynard, "Drawing and Shooting: Causality in Depiction," *Journal of Aesthetics and Art Criticism* 44 (1985). In "Looking Again through Photographs," Kendall Walton defends his position against Edwin Martin's objections in "On Seeing Walton's Great-Grandfather"; both articles appear in *Critical Inquiry* 12, no. 4 (Summer 1986).

9. See David Lewis, "Veridical Hallucination and Prosthetic Vision," in *Philosophical Papers*, vol. 2 (Oxford: Oxford University Press, 1986) and E. M. Zemach "Seeing, 'Seeing' and Feeling," *Review of Metaphysics* 23 (September 1969).

10. This view should not be confused with the view of transparency employed by Althusserian-Lacanian film theorists. For them, viewers mistakenly take cinematic images to be transparent, but they really are not. Photographic realists, on the other hand, are committed to the view that photographic and cinematic images – or, at least, most of them – are actually transparent in pertinent respects.

11. See "Computer Technology and Special Effects in Contemporary Cinema" by Robin Baker in *Future Visions: New Technologies of the Screen,* edited by Philip Hayward and Tana Wollen (London: BFI Publishing, 1993).

12. See "Virtual Studio: Computers Come to Tinseltown," *The Economist* 333, no. 7895 (December 24, 1994–January 6, 1995), p. 88.

13. At this point, the photographic realist may argue that, nevertheless, there are some transparent pictures and that is really the bottom line in his theory. But if this is the view, then transparency cannot count as a necessary condition of cinematic images.

14. On mattes, see Fred M. Sersen, "Making Matte Shots," in *The ASC Treasury of Visual Effects,* edited by George E. Turner (Hollywood: American Society of Cinematographers, 1983); and Christopher Finch, *Special Effects: Creating Movie Magic* (New York: Abbeville, 1984).

15. Reported in *Life with Picasso* by Françoise Gilot and Carlton Lake (New York: Anchor Books, 1989), p. 76.

16. This disanalogy has also been noted by Nigel Warburton is his "Seeing Through 'Seeing Through' Photographs," *Ratio,* New Series 1 (1988), and by Gregory Currie in his "Photography, Painting and Perception," *Journal of Aesthetics and Art Criticism* 49, no. 1 (Winter 1991).

17. F. E. Sparshott, "Vision and Dream in the Cinema," *Philosophic Exchange* (Summer 1975), p. 115.

18. The reason for using the singular here – e.g., *an* essential feature of film is that the photographic realist will have to introduce at least one further feature in order to differentiate film from photography. Perhaps he might avail himself of the feature I defend in the next section, called "The Moving Image."

19. Here, and throughout this section I have been profoundly influenced by Arthur Danto's brilliant article "Moving Pictures," *Quarterly Review of Film Studies* 4, no. 1 (Winter 1979).

20. Roman Ingarden, "On the Borderline between Literature and Painting," in *Ontology of the Work of Art: The Musical Work, The Picture, The Architectural Work, The Film,* translated by Raymond Meyer and J. T. Goldwait (Athens: Ohio University Press, 1989), pp. 324–25.

21. For descriptions of this piece see Sally Banes, *Terpsichore in Sneakers* (Boston: Houghton Mifflin Company, 1980), p. 189, and Noël Carroll, "Douglas Dunn, 308 Broadway," *Artforum* 13 (September 1974), p. 86.

22. See, for example, Stanley Cavell, *The World Viewed: Reflections on the Ontology of Film,* the enlarged edition (Cambridge, Mass.: Harvard University Press), pp. 27–28; and Erwin Panofsky, "Style and Medium in the Motion Pictures," in *Film Theory and Criticism,* edited by Gerald Mast and Marshall Cohen (New York: Oxford University Press, 1985).

23. See Richard Wollheim, *Art and Its Objects* (Cambridge University Press, 1980), sections 35–38.

24. This would be true of a silent film. If we are talking about a sound film, the soundtrack would have to be retrievable as well.

25. If you can print the code out, then it is theoretically possible for it to be memorized,

if not by one person, then by a group – like the population of China. It is at least imaginable, therefore, that we might run something like the *Fahrenheit 451* scenario for film, with groups of guerrilla film buffs learning the programs of forbidden films in defiance of totalitarian censors.

26. Arlene Croce, *The Fred Astaire and Ginger Rogers Book* (New York: Vintage, 1972).

27. This paper represents a substantial rewriting and expansion of my "Towards an Ontology of the Moving Image," in *Film and Philosophy,* edited by Cynthia Freeland and Tom Wartenberg (New York: Routledge, 1995). I would also like to thank David Bordwell, Arthur Danto, Stephen Davies, Jerrold Levinson, and Alan Sidelle for their comments on an earlier version of this paper.

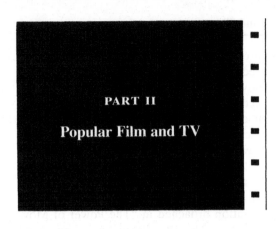

Historically, the notion that film was a unique artistic medium provided theorists with a program that was both straightforward and unified. Identify the unique features or function of the medium and then discuss its ramifications for every dimension of cinematic articulation. What kind of stories are best suited to the medium? What kind go against its grain? Is montage or deep-focus, long-take cinematography more genuinely cinematic? And so on. Such a program is immensely unified, since everything is referred back to the unique feature or function of the medium – usually as either an instance or a transgression thereof. If only that unique feature could be identified, everything else, it seems, would more or less fall into place.

But as we have seen in the previous section, establishing the credentials of a candidate as the unique feature of the medium – such that it entails stylistic directives – is an ill-advised project, burdened with conceptual and empirical difficulties. As a consequence, it is my contention that we must devise new ways of theorizing motion pictures. The alternative that I propose is piecemeal theorizing.

One of the strengths of the medium specificity approach to film theory was that it focused attention on film structures. Whatever its shortcomings, the approach illuminated the operation of all sorts of cinematic techniques. The problems with this approach were that it tended to characterize these techniques and structures in terms of cinematic

uniqueness, that it generally subsumed these structures into totalizing, though unsubstantiated, theories of film, and that it was often prescriptive. But, despite these problems, we should not overlook the fact that the enterprise of classifying and explaining the operations of specific devices, structures, mechanisms, and techniques is a worthwhile one. It is an objective that I think we should continue to pursue, albeit in a piecemeal way.

The approach that I advocate is piecemeal inasmuch as it recommends initially considering such devices – like point-of-view editing – one at a time, developing explanations of their operation without trying to fit those explanations into a totalized theory of film.[1] Of course, this does not mean that theorizing must remain atomic. Once we have various piecemeal analyses of film structures in front of us, we may then proceed to see whether they can be assembled into larger theoretical constellations -- i.e., whether there are generalizations that can coordinate our piecemeal analyses into larger frameworks. Yet even here I suggest that we should resist the expectation that all our small-scale theories will fit into one unified, overarching theory of film.

Much of what follows in this anthology are attempts at piecemeal theories of film. For convenience sake, this section and the subsequent one follow the frequent tendency in film studies to divide the field into different modes: the mainstream, commercial fiction, the avant-garde film, and the documentary. Under these headings, I attempt to offer various piecemeal theories of different film structures – such as suspense and metaphor – and to address certain longstanding questions – such as whether avant-garde films are theoretical and whether documentaries are objective. The articles in these two sections could probably be distributed differently under different headings. If readers do not like this way of divvying up the field, they should ignore the headings and just read the articles.

This section of the book focuses on

commercial narrative fictions or movies, under which label I also count TV fictions. The section looks at various devices or structures of film, including the cinematic image, variable framing, erotetic narration, point-of-view editing, suspense, modifying music, sight gags, and the sort of episodic narration associated with soap operas. A large number of these analyses and/or taxonomies may be read and evaluated in their own right. One may regard my theories of point-of-view editing apart from my hypotheses about the power of movies. But at the same time, several of these piecemeal accounts are also amalgamated into a larger hypothesis about what makes movies such an effective means of mass communication.[2] I refer to this hypothesis as the power of movies. But though I do advance a somewhat comprehensive theory under this rubric, it is not a total theory of film, nor even a total theory of the movies. For not only can theoretical questions not pertaining to the power of movies be posed about movies, but it is not even the case that all the piecemeal theories about movie structures advanced herein fit into my hypothesis about the power of movies. The essay about sight gags, for instance, does not.

In the first essay, "The Power of Movies," I advance accounts of the cinematic image, variable framing and movie narration, along with a conjecture about how variable framing and movie narration are standardly integrated. The essay also attempts to indicate how these structures serve the abiding aim of the movies – to command mass audiences. "Toward a Theory of Point-of-View Editing: Communication, Emotion and the Movies" and "Notes on Movie Music" pursue the piecemeal theorizing of film structures into further domains and, as well, speculate about the ways in which these devices advance the effectiveness of movies as a means of mass communication.[3] There is no presumption that the structures analyzed in this section exhaust the compass of movie

research, nor even that they are the only mechanisms that contribute to the power of movies. It is my hope that the essays in this section will encourage further piecemeal theorizing about movie devices and further discussion of the elements that comprise the power of movies.

"Toward a Theory of Film Suspense" and "As The Dial Turns: Notes On Soap Operas" develop from the notion of erotetic narration broached in "The Power of Movies." "As The Dial Turns" contrasts serial narrative construction with the typical construction of movie narratives in an effort to locate one of the enduring attractions of soap operas. "Toward a Theory of Film Suspense" begins with a consideration of erotetic narration as a foundation for proposing a theory of one of the most recurring emotional effects of movies, the elicitation of suspense.[4]

Though the other essays in this section are interrelated in various ways, "Notes on the Sight Gag" is freestanding. It does not link up with the other theories propounded in this section. Moreover, it is less an exercise in explanation than one in taxonomy. And it is more descriptive than it is systematic. I suspect that future researchers will do a better job organizing this field of phenomena than I have; I hope my halting attempt will both help and inspire them to do so. In this respect, the essay is perhaps best regarded as prototheoretical.[5]

Notes

1. Though my own theorizing tends to emphasize the analysis of cinematic structures of articulation, I do not believe that the ambit of film theorizing – including piecemeal theorizing – is limited to this domain of inquiry. Film theorists may also ask questions about film distribution, about film content, about film technology, and so on. I want to be fairly liberal about what counts as film theory. Roughly, if something is an explanation or taxonomy of sufficient generality about some

phenomenon of film practice, I am willing to countenance it as film theory – as a theory about something about film. Moreover, my liberalism here concerning film theory is probably also connected to my disposition toward piecemeal theorizing, since it seems fairly unlikely that every theoretical question we can ask about film – from accounts of the nature of camera movement to theories of the impact of film on American politics – will segue into one totalized theory.

2. This discussion itself is nested in a larger theoretical preoccupation. See Noël Carroll, "The Nature of Mass Art" and "Mass Art, High Art and the Avant-garde: A Response to David Novitz," *Philosophic Exchange: A Journal of the State University at Brockport,* no. 23 (1992).

3. When I use phrases like "film structures" in the sentence above, or terms like "cinematic devices" in what follows, I merely mean structures and devices that are used in film and are so recognized. Since in the preceding section, I have rejected the use of the appellation of "the cinematic" in the medium specific sense, my use of adjectives like "film" and "cinematic" should not be taken as having medium specificity implications. They are simply meant to inform the reader that the structures in question are ones that occur in film. Let there be no insinuation that they are specific, unique, or essential to film.

"The cinematic," in that sense, is alien to my positive theoretical conjectures.

4. For an expansion of my account of suspense, see Noël Carroll, "The Paradox of Suspense," in *Suspense: Conceptualizations, Theoretical Analyses and Empirical Explorations,* edited by P. Vorderer, H. J. Wuff and M. Friedrichen (Hillsdale: Lawrence Erlbaum Associates, forthcoming).

5. Tom Gunning has criticized one of the conjectures in this essay on the grounds that the sight gag is as old as cinema. But I don't believe that my essay denies this. It only claims that slapstick is more the mark of early cinema and that the sight gag (especially the intricately developed sight gag) is the aesthetically dominant structure in the twenties. This is a hypothesis about the differential degree of what was most important when. It is not an absolute claim about where you find sight gags versus where you find slapstick. Obviously, my conjecture does rely on certain aesthetic judgments about what I claim is aesthetically most important in different periods. But I don't think that my judgments are particularly idiosyncratic in this regard. For Gunning's criticisms, see his extremely interesting essay "The Origins of American Film Comedy" in *Classical Hollywood Comedy,* edited by Kristine Brunovska Karwick and Henry Jenkins (New York: Routledge, 1995), p. 361.

CHAPTER V

The Power of Movies

For much of its history, film theory has been obsessed with various notions of realism. In what has come to be called classical film theory, i.e., film theory until 1965, the writings of André Bazin evince the extreme form of this obsession. Bazin held that the film image was an objective re-presentation of the past, a veritable slice of reality.[1] In addition to this view of the ontology of film, Bazin also advanced the psychological corollary that spectators somehow regard the images on screen as identical with their referents. Contemporary film theorists reject Bazin's metaphysics concerning the nature of the film image; influenced by semiotics, such theorists deny there is any literal sense to be made of the idea that film is some kind of natural mirror onto reality. Yet contemporary film theorists do hold onto a portion of the realist approach, notably its psychological presuppositions. That is, contemporary theorists, while rejecting the notion that film is a slice of reality, nevertheless agree that in its standard uses, film imparts a *realistic effect* to its viewers. This effect, a psychological effect, is described by various formulas, including the notions that film gives the impression of reality narrating itself; film causes an illusion of reality; or film appears natural.[2]

Surely, contemporary theorists are correct in forsaking the extravagances of Bazin's ontology of film, the great influence of his theory notwithstanding. However, contemporary film theory's psychologizing of the realist approach, in terms of realist effects, is not very persuasive. For it requires attributing rather bizarre and frankly dubious mental states to spectators. Spectators are said to be under the illusion that the film image is its referent; or we are thought to believe that the film image is reality narrating itself; or that the film image is somehow natural. Some of these imputed psychological effects – for example, "reality narrating itself" – sound downright incoherent. But all of these variations on the realistic effect are suspect because they attribute to spectators states of belief that would preclude our characteristic forms of response to, and appreciation of, cinema. For, were we spectators ever to mistake the representations before us for the referents those images portray, we could not sit by comfortably, inactively, and appreciatively while buffaloes stampede toward us, while lovers reveal their deepest longings to each other, and while children are tortured.[3]

The realist approach to film theory, either as an ontological thesis or in its more contemporary, psychologized variations, is a dead end. However, the questions that motivated the realist answers may well be worth asking. That is, what is it that the various realist approaches in film theory are designed to explain, and is it worth explaining? At least two candidates seem key here. Realism, especially as a psychological effect, is supposed to play a role in explaining the way in which film disseminates ideology, according to contemporary film theorists. Second, the attribution of realism is meant to explain the power of movies, to explain why the moving picture, including narrative TV, is *the* dominant art form of the twentieth century.

Certainly, "How does cinema promote ideology?" and "What makes movies powerful?" are good questions. The purpose of this paper is to attempt to answer the second question, without resorting to the invocation of realism.[4] We shall try to explain what makes motion pictures our dominant mass art, one that is so widespread, internationally pervasive, and accessible across boundaries of class and culture. We shall furthermore attempt to explain what makes the response to movies *so intense for so many,* especially when compared to art forms such as opera and theater.

The hypothesis of realism was meant to deal with such questions by suggesting that since films appear to be slices of reality, they are widely accessible insofar as everyone is familiar with reality. But the reference to reality here won't give us much help with the intensity of our response to movies, because in large measure we conceive of the special intensity of movies exactly in contrast to our more diffuse responses to quotidian reality. Another way to put this, of course, is to point out that since our response to reality is so often lackluster, claiming that a film appears to be a slice of reality promises no explanation of our extraordinarily intense response to films. So another explanation, one not reliant upon realism, must be found to account for the power of movies.

To begin an account of the power of movies, some characterization of the phenomenon in question is relevant. First, the word "movies," as used here, does not refer to film or cinema at large – that is, to a body of cultural productions that includes, not only commercial, narrative films, but also industrial documentaries, medical training films, ballistics tests, experimental films, modernist art films, propaganda films, and so on. Rather, "movies" refers to popular mass-media films, the products of what might be called Hollywood International – films made in what has been dubbed the "classical style," whether they be American, Italian, or Chinese, and whether they be made for the screen or for TV. Movies, in this sense, are a genre, not the whole, of cinema. It is about this genre's power that my paper is concerned. Why speak of the power of a genre of cinema rather than of the power of the medium? Well, the answer to that is simply that the medium of cinema is not, in and of itself,

powerful; it is not the medium of cinema that has gripped such widespread audiences so intensely. Instead, it is the adaptation of the medium to the purposes of Hollywood International. When people speak of the power of the medium, they are, I believe, talking about the power of this particular genre or style. For it is the movies, and not modernist masterpieces or medical instruction films, that have captivated the twentieth-century popular imagination. It is the power of movies about which researchers are really curious.

To speak of movies rather than film or cinema deliberately eschews essentialism. Posing the problem in an essentialist idiom – i.e., what makes the *medium* of cinema powerful – would pervert the question. For neither the medium nor every style of film found in it is accessible to or intensely engaging of mass, popular audiences. Thus, plumbing the essence of the medium, if there is such a thing, would not provide the information we seek. Instead of comparing the medium of film to other media such as theater or literature, then, this paper will focus on the *genre of movies* in order to determine just what features of the stylistic choices of Hollywood International enable it to evoke a level of widespread, intensive engagement that is, ex hypothesi, unrivaled by other media, Indeed, this way of stating the project is not quite accurate; for it is not the case that the genre of movies is really to be contrasted with other media, but rather that movies will be contrasted with other *genres* within other media. We want to know what features of movies like *Red River, Psycho,* and *Blue Thunder* make them more appealing and more intensely engaging for mass audiences than, for example, plays like *King Lear* and *Hurlyburly,* ballets like *Giselle,* and novels like *Middlemarch.* My anti-essentialism amounts to a refusal to answer questions about the power of movies in terms of the specificity of the medium of cinema. It may seem that proclaiming this variety of anti-essentialism at this late date is so much redundant arm-waving. But I'm not sure. The influence of Christian Metz's recent essay, "The Imaginary Signifier," which proceeds methodologically in an essentialist manner, trying to isolate and analyze a cinema-specific feature of the medium which he identifies as a special sort of play of presence and absence, testifies to the persistent appeal of the essentialist approach.[5]

The power of movies comprises two factors: widespread engagement and intense engagement. This paper will attempt to explain the former in terms of those features of movies that make them highly accessible to broad audiences. It will also try to explain the intensity of movies by examining those features that enable movies to depict situations with a very high degree of clarity. In a nutshell, its thesis is that the power of movies resides in their easily graspable clarity for mass audiences.

We can begin to understand the general popularity of the movie genre by considering those features that make it generally accessible to mass, untutored audiences. A good place to start this investigation is with the image projected by the single-shot – a close-up of the hero's face, or a long-view of Castle Dracula. These images are, for the most part, representational, but, more important, they are *pictorial* representations. They refer to their referents by way of *picturing*, by displaying or manifesting a delimited range of resemblances to their referents. By recognizing these similarities, the spectator comes to know what the picture depicts, whether a man, a horse, a house, and so on.

Given that the typical movie image is a pictorial representation, what has this to do with accessibility? Well, a picture is a very special sort of symbol. Psychological evidence strongly supports the contention that we learn to recognize what a picture stands for as soon as we have become able to recognize the objects, or kinds of objects, that serve as the models for that picture. Picture recognition is not a skill acquired

over and above object recognition. Whatever features or cues we come to employ in object recognition, we also mobilize to recognize what pictures depict. A child raised without pictorial representations will, after being shown a couple of pictures, be able to identify the referent of any picture of an object with which he or she is familiar.[6] The rapid development of this picture-recognition capacity contrasts strongly with the acquisition of a symbol system such as language. Upon mastering a couple of words, the child is nowhere near mastering the entire language. Similarly, when an adult is exposed to one or two representational *pictures* in an alien pictorial idiom, say a Westerner confronting a Japanese image in the floating-point-of-view style, he will be able to identify the referent of any picture in that format after studying one or two representations of that sort for a few moments. But no Westerner, upon learning one or two linguistic symbols of the Japanese language, could go on to identify the reference of all, or even merely a few more, Japanese words. Moreover, historically the Japanese were eminently able to catch on to and replicate the Western system of perspectival picturing by examining a selection of book illustrations; but they could never have acquired any European language by learning the meanings of just a few words or phrases.[7]

Pictorial representations thus differ radically from linguistic representations. The speed with which the former is mastered suggests that it does not require special learning, above the realization, perhaps, that flat surfaces are being used to stand for three-dimensional objects. Rather, the capacity to recognize what a picture depicts emerges in tandem with the capacity to recognize the kind of object that serves as the model of the picture. The reciprocal relation between picture recognition and object recognition, of course, explains how it is possible for us, having acquired detailed visual information from pictures, to recognize objects and places we have never encountered in real life. And, of course, the fact that pictorial recognition does not require any special learning process would also explain how movies, whose basic constituent symbols are pictures, are immediately accessible to *untutored* audiences in every corner of the world. These audiences do not need any special training to deal with the basic images in movies, for the capacity to recognize what these images are about has evolved part and parcel with the viewer's capacity to recognize objects and events.

The technology of film could be adapted in such a way that the basic images of a film genre or film style were not pictorial representations. One could imagine a motion picture industry of changing abstract forms, after the fashion of Hans Richter's *Rhythmus 21,* or one of spectacles of color, such as Stan Brakhage's *Text of Light.* But that was not the road taken by the movies. Movies became a worldwide phenomenon – and a lucrative industry – precisely because in their exploitation of pictorial recognition – as opposed to symbol systems that require mastery of processes such as reading, decoding, or deciphering in order to be understood – they rely on a biological capability that is nurtured in humans as they learn to identify the objects and events in their environment.

The basic images in movies are not simply pictorial representations; they are, standardly, *moving* pictorial representations. But just as an audience need not go through a process of learning to "read" pictures, neither is its perception of movie "movement" learned. Rather, it is a function of the way stroboscopic or beta phenomena affect the brain's organization of congruous input presented in specifiable sequences to different points on the retina. Of course, following a movie involves much more than the capacity to recognize what its moving images represent. But we should not overlook the crucial role that the relative ease of comprehending the basic symbols of movies plays in making movies readily accessible.

The remarks thus far are apt to displease the majority of cinema researchers. For the contention that pictures (and, by extension, moving pictures) work by looking like their referents in those pertinent respects to which our perceptual system is keyed, goes against the contemporary received wisdom that pictures, like any other symbol, are matters of codes and conventions. Undoubtedly, some reader will recall an anthropology class in which he was told that certain non-Western peoples were unable to understand pictures shown to them by missionaries and other field workers. However, this evidence has never been entirely decisive. Complaints about the fidelity of the photographs involved have been raised, along with the more serious objection that what the subjects failed to understand, and then only initially, was the practice of using flat surfaces to portray three-dimensional objects.[8] Once they got the hang of that, they had no trouble in recognizing what hitherto unseen pictures referred to – assuming they were familiar with the kinds of objects displayed in the pictures.[9] Also, on the non-conventionalist side of the scale, we must weigh the psychological evidence of the child's acquisition of pictorial recognition, the easy cross-cultural dissemination of pictorial practices, and the zoological evidence that certain animals have the capacity for pictorial recognition,[10] against exotic anecdotes that are meant to demonstrate that the practices of picturing are cultural conventions that must be learned in the fashion of a language. We can consider our own cases. We all recall our own language acquisition, and we know how to go about helping youngsters to learn to speak and to read. But who remembers undergoing a similar process in regard to pictures, and what techniques would we employ to teach a youngster pictorial literacy? Yes, we may show a child a few pictures and say the name of the object portrayed. But very shortly the child just sees what the picture is of; the child doesn't "read" the picture or decode it or go through some process of inference. And from a meager set of samples, the child can proceed to identify the subjects of a plethora of pictures, because there is a continuum between apprehending pictorial representations and perceiving the world that does not depend upon learning anything like the conventional, arbitrary correlations of a vocabulary, or the combinatory principles of a grammar.

There is undoubtedly a temptation to think that picture recognition involves some process of decoding or inference because of the contemporary influence of the computational metaphor of the mind. We think that computers supply us with powerful insight into how the mind works. And if we were to build a computer to simulate pictorial recognition, it would require a complex information-processing system. But it does not follow that if computers employ complex information-processing systems in pictorial recognition, then humans must likewise possess such systems. It may rather be that our neurophysiology is so constructed that when stimulated by certain pictorial arrays, we see what the picture is of. John Searle notes that balance is controlled by the fluids in our inner ear. Were a robot to be built, balance would probably be governed by some complex computational program. But, for us, balance is a matter governed by our fleshy hardware.[11] A similar case might be made that biology – rather than information processing – may have a great deal to tell us about the workings of object recognition and picture recognition. And to the extent that pictorial representation is a matter of the way in which humans are made, a practice rooted in pictorial representation – such as the movies – will be widely and easily accessible to all humans made that way.

Many contemporary semiotically inclined film theorists resist approaching pictorial representation in the movies in the preceding fashion. Their resistance rests on a confusion, or rather a conflation, on their part of the ideas of code, convention, and culture; terms that in film studies are treated as equivalent. If something is coded or conventional, then it is regarded as a cultural production. This seems fair enough. But it is more problematic to presume, as film researchers do, the reverse; that if something is a cultural product, then it is an example of coded or conventional phenomena. Thus, if pictorial representations, including moving, pictorial representations, are cultural productions, which they certainly are, then they must be conventional. The difficulty here lies in the assumption that everything that is cultural is necessarily conventional.

Consider plows. They are cultural productions. They were produced by certain agricultural civilizations that had culturally specific needs not shared, for example, by hunter-gatherers. Is the design of a plow a matter of convention? Recall, here, that for semiotic film theorists, arbitrariness is a key defining feature of a convention. That is, a group creates a convention – like driving on the right side of the road – when there are a number of alternative ways of dealing with the situation *and* when the choice between these alternatives is arbitrary, a matter of fiat. But the adoption of the design of the plow could not have been reached by fiat. The plow had a purpose – digging furrows – and its effectiveness had to be accommodated to the structure of nature. It would have to be heavy enough and sharp enough to cut into the earth, and it had to be adapted to the capacities of its human users – it had to be steerable and pullable by creatures like us with two arms and limited strength. A device such as a plow had to be discovered; it could not be brought into existence by consensus. We could not have elected pogo-sticks to do the work of plows. The plow was a cultural *invention*, not a cultural *convention*. It was adopted because it worked, because it met a cultural need by accommodating features of nature and biology.

The point of introducing the concept of a

cultural invention here is, of course, to block the facile identification of the cultural and the conventional. Applied to the sort of pictorial representations found in movies, this concept suggests that pictorial representations may be cultural inventions, inventions that, given the way people are built, cause spectators who are untrained in any system of conventions to recognize what pictures stand for. The structure of such images is not determinable by a mere decision. Given the constraints of the human perceptual apparatus, we cannot decree that anything *looks like* anything else, though we may decree that anything can *stand for* anything else. It seems cogent to suppose that this limitation is in large measure attributable to human biology. And insofar as movies are constituted of a mode of representation connected to biological features of the human organism, they will be generally more accessible than genres in other media, such as the novel, that presuppose the mastery of learned conventions such as specific natural languages. Also, if the recognition of movie images is more analogous to a reflex than it is to a process like reading, then following a movie may turn out to be less taxing, less a matter of active effort, than reading. Perhaps this can be confirmed by recalling how much easier it is to follow a movie when one is fatigued than it is to read a novel.

The claim has so far been made that a crucial element in the power of movies is the fact that movies usually rely, in terms of their basic imagery, on pictorial representations that allow masses of untutored spectators easy access to the fundamental symbols in the system, due to the way humans are constructed. But is this not just a reversion to the kind of realist explanation we began by dismissing? Not at all. The Bazinian claims that the spectator somehow takes the film image to be identical with its referent, while contemporary film theorists hold that the typical film image imparts the illusion of reality, transparency, or naturalness. This

paper, though, has not invoked any of these realist, psychological effects, nor anything like them. It has instead claimed that the untutored spectator recognizes what the film image represents without reference to a code; it has *not* claimed that the spectator takes the pictorial representation to be, in any sense, its referent. Man's perceptual capacities evolve in such a way that his capacity for pictorial recognition comes, almost naturally, with his capacity for object recognition, and part of that capacity is the ability to differentiate pictures from their referents. Thus, we are not talking about a realist, psychological effect – the taking of a representation for its referent – but only about the capacity of movies to exploit generic, recognitional abilities. Another way to see the difference between this approach and that of the realists is to note how often their accounts of the power of movies emphasize the importance of the fact that movies are photographic, whereas in the account offered here the important technology for explaining the accessibility of movies is the non-cinema-specific technology of pictorial representation.

If up to this point anything can be said to have been demonstrated, then, admittedly, it must also be conceded that we are a good distance away from a full account of the power of movies. We have explained why movies are more accessible than genres like novels. But what features of movies account for their presumably superior accessibility and intensity in comparison with media and genres like drama, ballet, and opera, in which recognition of what the representations refer to is, like movies, typically not mediated by learned processes of decoding, reading, or inference? What standard features of movies differentiate them from the standard features of the presentation of plays, for example, in a way that make typical movies more accessible than typical theatrical performances? Our hypothesis is that due to certain devices developed early in the evolution of movies, the typical movie is, all things being equal, easier to follow than the typical play, i.e., theatrical performances as have so far been commonly encountered. This caveat is added because there is no reason to believe that theatrical devices that would be functionally equivalent to the movie devices about to be discussed could not be invented, thus changing the relative accessibility of typical movies and typical plays. Our anti-essentialist bias, however, demands that we not compare the eternal essence of the film medium with its putative theatrical counterpart, but rather the state of the art of movies with the state of the art of theatrical production.

Movies are said to be more accessible than plays. What does this mean? We have asserted that movies are easier to follow than plays. What is it that is distinctive about the way in which spectators follow movies? With the typical movie, given certain of its characteristic devices, notably variable framing, the movie viewer is generally in a position where he or she is attending to exactly what is significant in the action-array or spectacle on screen. Another way of getting at this point is to say that the filmmaker in the movie genre has far more potential control over the spectator's attention than does the theatrical director. The consequence of this is that the movie spectator is always looking where he or she should be looking, always attending to the right details and thereby comprehending, nearly effortlessly, the ongoing action precisely in the way it is meant to be understood. Due to various devices, such as variable framing, movies are easier to follow and, therefore, more accessible than theatrical productions because movies are more perspicuous cognitively. The element of cognitive clarity afforded by movies may well account, too, for the widespread intensity of engagement that movies elicit.

Of course, movies and standard theatrical productions share many of the same devices for directing the audience's attention. Both in the medium-long shot and on the proscenium stage, the audience's attention can be guided by: the central positioning of an important character; movement in stasis; stasis in movement; characters' eyelines; light colors on dark fields; dark colors on light fields; sound, notably dialogue; spotlighting and variable illumination of the array; placement of important objects or characters along arresting diagonals; economy of set details; makeup and costume; commentary; gestures; and so on. But movies appear to have further devices and perhaps more effective devices for directing attention than does theater as it is presently practiced. The variability of focus in film, for example, is a more reliable means of making sure that the audience is looking where the spectator "ought" to be looking than is theatrical lighting. Even more important is the use in movies of variable framing. Through cutting and camera movement, the filmmaker can rest assured that the spectator is perceiving exactly what she should be perceiving at the precise moment she should be perceiving it. When the camera comes in for a close-up, for example, there is no possibility that the spectator can be distracted by some detail stage-left. Everything extraneous to the story at that point is deleted. Nor does the spectator have to find the significant detail; it is delivered to her. The viewer also gets as close or as far-off a view of the significant objects of the story – be they heroines, butcher knives, mobs, fortresses, or planets – as is useful for her to have a concrete sense of what is going on. Whereas in a theater the eye constantly tracks the action – often at a felt distance, often amidst a vaulting space – in movies much of that work is done by shifting camera positions, which at the same time also assures that the average viewer has not gotten lost in the space but is looking precisely at that which she is supposed to see. Movies are therefore easier to follow than typical stage productions, because the shifting camera positions make it practically impossible for the movie viewer *not* to be attending where she is meant to attend.

Variable framing in film is achieved by moving the camera closer or farther away from the objects being filmed. Cutting and camera movement are the two major processes for shifting framing: in the former, the actual process of the camera's change of position is not included in the shot; we jump from medium-range views, to close views, to far-off views with the traversal of the space between excised; in camera movement, as the name suggests, the passage of the camera from a long view to a close view is recorded within the shot. Reframing can also be achieved optically through devices such as zooming-in and changing lenses. These mechanical means for changing the framing of an on-screen object or event give rise to three formal devices for directing the movie audience's attention: indexing, bracketing, and scaling. Indexing occurs when a camera is moved toward an object. The motion toward the object functions ostensively, like the gesture of pointing. It indicates that the viewer ought to be looking in the direction the camera is moving, if the camera's movement is being recorded, or in the direction toward which the camera is aimed or pointing, if we have been presented with the shot via a cut.

When a camera is moved towards an array, it screens out everything beyond the frame. To move a camera toward an object either by cutting or camera movement generally has the force of indicating that what is important at this moment is what is on screen, what is in the perimeter of the frame. That which is not inside the frame has been *bracketed,* excluded. It should not, and in fact it literally cannot, at the moment it is bracketed, be attended to. At the same time, bracketing has an inclusionary dimension, indicating that what is inside the frame or bracket is important. A standard camera position will mobilize both the exclusionary and inclusionary dimensions of the bracket to control attention, though the relative degree may vary as to whether a given bracketing is more important for what it excludes, rather than what it includes, and vice-versa.

There is also a standard deviation from this use of bracketing. Often the important element of a scene is placed outside the frame so that it is not visible on-screen, e.g., the child-killer in the early part of Fritz Lang's *M.* Such scenes derive a great deal of their expressive power just because they subvert the standard function of bracketing.

As the camera is moved forward, it not only indexes and places brackets around the objects in front of it; it also changes their scale. Whether by cutting or camera movement, as the camera nears the gun on the table, the gun simultaneously appears larger and occupies more screen space. When the camera is pulled away from the table, the gun occupies less screen space. This capacity to change the scale of objects through camera positioning – a process called "scaling" – can be exploited for expressive or magical effects. Scaling is also a lever for directing attention. Enlarging the screen size of an object generally has the force of stating that this object, or gestalt of objects, is the important item to attend to at this moment in the movie.

Scaling, bracketing, and indexing are three different ways of directing the movie spectator's attention through camera positioning. In general, a standard camera positioning, whether executed by cutting or camera movement, will employ all three of these means. But one can easily think of scenes in which the bracket is reoriented, but the scaling stays effectively the same, for example, a lateral pan as a character walks toward the edge of the frame. Likewise, a camera movement might be important for what it indexes rather than for whatever changes occur in the bracketing or the scaling: there are moving shots in the early Italian film *Cabiria,* for example, where the camera nudges a few feet forward in a spectacle scene in order to point the viewer's eye in a certain direction, though neither the bracket nor the scale of the objects in the scene are changed appreciably. Both the swamp scene and the trolley-car scene in *Sunrise* are artistically important for the way in which they call attention to the bracket, rather than for their scaling or indexing. However, bracketing, scaling, and indexing can be employed in tandem, and when they are, they afford very powerful means by which the movie-maker controls the audience's attention. We suddenly see a close-up of a gun, indexed, scaled, and bracketed as the important object in the scene, and then the bracket is changed – we see a medium shot in which the gun is being pointed at the heroine by the villain, telling us that now the important thing about the gun is its role within this newly framed context or gestalt. The constant reframing of the action that is endemic to movies enables the spectator to follow the action perfectly, and, so to say, automatically.

Adaptations of stage technology, of course, could probably establish theatrical means that would be functionally equivalent to the scaling, bracketing, and indexing functions of movies. Magnifying mirrors might be used to enlarge stage details at appropriate moments; the leg curtains could be motorized to constantly reframe the action; and indexing might be approximated by use of revolving stages that rotate the important characters and actions toward the audience. If these devices were not too distracting in and of themselves, they might provide the theater director with attentional levers that are functionally equivalent to scaling, bracketing, and indexing. However, these devices are not customary in theater as we presently know it, and our project here is to contrast movies as they are with theater as it currently is.

Of course, *films* can be made without variable framing; but *movies* rely on variable framing to automatize the spectator's attention. Also, variable framing is not unique to movies; other film genres employ

it. Yet it is key to why movies are accessible; as we have noted, it contributes to the intensity of engagement movies promote. Through variable framing, the director assures that the spectator is attending where and when she should. The action and its details unfold in such a way that every element that is relevant is displayed at a distance that makes it eminently recognizable and, in a sequence that is intelligible. Ideally, variable framing allows us to see just what we need to see at changing distances and at cadences that render the action perspicuous. The action is analytically broken down into its most salient elements, distilled, that is, in a way that makes it extremely legible. This kind of clarity, which is bequeathed to the audience automatically by variable framing, contrasts strongly with the depiction of action in theatrical representations. There, the depiction is not analytic but a matter of physical enactment, generally occurring in something approximating real time, and presented at a fixed distance to each viewer. Of course, theatrical action is abstracted, simplified, for the sake of legibility, often employing emblematic gestures. It is clearer, that is, than the actions we encounter in everyday life. But theatrical action is not as clear and analytically distinct as movie action as portrayed by variable framing. Movie action, given the way it can be organized through camera positioning, is also far more intelligible than the unstaged events we witness in everyday life. This is an important feature that helps account for the way in which movies grip us.

Our experience of actions and events in movies differs radically from our normal experiences; movie actions and events are so organized, so automatically intelligible, and so clear. The arresting thing about movies, *contra* realist theories, is not that they create the illusion of reality, but that they reorganize and construct, through variable framing, actions and events with an economy, legibility, and coherence that are not only automatically available, but which surpass, in terms of their immediately perceptible basic structure, naturally encountered actions and events. Movie actions evince visible order and identity to a degree not found in everyday experience. This quality of uncluttered clarity gratifies the mind's quest for order, thereby intensifying our engagement with the screen.

So far, our speculations about the sources of the power of movies have been restricted to what would have classically been considered the medium's "cinematic features": pictorial representation and variable framing. This, of course, does not reflect a belief that these elements are uniquely cinematic, but only that they are features that help account for movies' power, the capacity to engender what appears to be an unprecedentedly widespread and intense level of engagement. There is another core defining feature of what we are calling movies that needs to be treated: this is that they are fictional narratives. The question naturally arises to what degree this fact about movies can help explain their power.

The fact that movies tend to be narrative, concerned primarily with depictions of human actions, immediately suggests one of the reasons they are accessible. For narrative is, in all probability, our most pervasive and familiar means of explaining human action. If you ask me why George is watering the tulips, I may answer that George intends to have, or wants, a beautiful garden, and that he believes that he can't have a beautiful garden unless he waters the tulips. So I say he undertakes to water the tulips. You might ask me how he formed the desire to have a beautiful garden. I may refer to either his belief that this is a means to being a good citizen or his guilt about never caring for his father's garden, or both if his action is overdetermined. If you ask, where did he get the notion that the garden would not be beautiful unless he watered it, I say he read it in a book called *Beautiful Gardens* on May 17, 1953. Now if we tried to sum up this somewhat banal explanation of George's

action, a narrative would probably be the likeliest, though not the only, means of organizing our information: George, racked with guilt feelings about his father's tulips and convinced that a beautiful garden is a means to the coveted ideal of good citizenship, decided to have a beautiful garden; and when he read, on May 17, 1953, that such gardens could not be had without watering the tulips, he went out and watered the tulips (on May 18). We might add that he continued to do so happily ever after. Insofar as this sort of narrative is one of the most common forms of human explanation, and insofar as much movie narration belongs to this category, movies will be familiar and accessible. Moreover, the explanatory quality of such narration will also contribute to the clarity of movies.

Of course, the logical relations that subtend this sort of narrative, at crucial points, remind one, and are parasitic upon, those of practical inference. If I am George, for example, I reason thusly: I want a beautiful garden; I do not believe I can secure a beautiful garden unless I water the tulips; therefore, I proceed to water the tulips. What makes narratives of the sort that I told above explanatory is that they, at nodal moments, reflect processes of practical reasoning. Practical reasoning is part of everyone's life. And the actions of others are intelligible to me when I can see them as consequences of the sort of practical reasoning I employ. Insofar as movie narratives depict the human actions of characters in forms that are reflective of the logic of practical inference, the movies will be widely accessible, since practical inference is a generic form of human decision making.

Undoubtedly, this discussion of narrative may be too broad and too abstract to be of much use to the film analyst. In all probability nothing of great interest would be gained in film studies by showing that a series of scenes reflected a series of practical inferences on the part of characters. Rather, the film scholar will be interested in an analysis of the characteristic forms of plotting found in movies; she will want these described more specifically than they were in the preceding discussion. And she will want to know what it is about these forms, if anything, that contributes to the power of movies.

In a recent paper on film suspense,[12] I attempted to identify what I think is the most basic form of movie plotting, and I would like to take advantage of those speculations now. My position owes a great deal to the Soviet filmmaker and theoretician V. I. Pudovkin.[13] Pudovkin, like his teacher, L. Kuleshov, studied American movies, contrasting them with Russian films in order to discern what made the American films of the twenties more effective on popular audiences than were comparable Russian films. Pudovkin and Kuleshov undertook this investigation, of course, in order to calculate the best means for creating a new Soviet cinema for the masses. The theories of filmmaking they produced were meant to instruct other filmmakers in technique and praxis. As is well known, Pudovkin and Kuleshov tended to become very prescriptive in these matters, a tendency for which they have been duly chastised ever since. But whatever their dogmatism, we should not overlook the fact that beneath their debatable prescriptions about the way films should be made, they often had valuable insights into the way in which popular films, especially Hollywood movies, were actually constructed. What Pudovkin has to say about movie narration is a case in point.

A story film will portray a sequence of scenes or events, some appearing earlier, some later. A practical problem that confronts the filmmaker is the way in which these scenes are to be connected, i.e., what sort of relation the earlier scenes should bear to the later ones. Pudovkin recommends – as a primary, though not exclusive, solution – that earlier scenes be related to later scenes as questions are to answers. If a giant shark appears offshore, unbeknownst to the local authorities, and begins to ravage lonely swimmers, this scene or series of scenes (or this event or series of events) raises the question of whether the shark will ever be detected. This question is likely to be answered in some later scene when someone figures out why all those swimmers are missing. At that point, when it is learnt that the shark is very, very powerful and nasty to boot, the question arises about whether it can be destroyed or driven away. The ensuing events in the film serve to answer that question. Or, if some atomic bombs are skyjacked in the opening scenes, this generates questions about who stole them and for what purposes. Once the generally nefarious purposes of the hijacking are established, the question arises concerning whether these treacherous intents can be thwarted. Or, for a slightly more complicated scenario, shortly after a jumbo jet takes off, we learn that the entire crew has just died from food poisoning while also learning that the couple in first class is estranged. These scenes raise the questions of whether the plane will crash and whether the couple in first class will be reconciled by their common ordeal. Maybe we also ask whether the alcoholic priest in coach will find God again. It is the function of the later scenes in the film to answer these questions.

Of course, the narrative organization of Hollywood films is far more complex than these examples suggest, and I have tried to develop this subject with more precision elsewhere.[14] For present purposes, let us say that, as is suggested by the writings of Pudovkin, the core narrative structures of Hollywood-type films – the movies discussed in this paper – involve generating questions that ensuing scenes answer. Not all narrative films employ this approach. Often, modernist films generate questions – e.g., did I meet her at Marienbad before? – without supplying any answers. Or, I might chronicle my day at the beach: first I had a hot dog, then I put on suntan lotion, then I swam, then I went home. Surely we can conceive of a home movie like this, where none of the early scenes raised any questions, and where none of the later ones supplied any answers. Thus, to narrate by generating questions internal to the film that subsequent scenes answer is a distinctive form of narration. Admittedly, this is not a form unique to films or movies, for it is also exploited in mystery novels, adventure stories, Harlequin romances, Marvel comics, and so on. Nevertheless, it is the most characteristic narrative approach in movies.

How can this be proven? The best suggestion one can make here is to embrace the question/answer model of movie narration – what I call the *erotetic* model of narrative – and then turn on your TV, watch old movies and new ones, TV adventure series and romances, domestic films and foreign popular films. Ask yourself why the later scenes in the films make sense in the context of the earlier scenes. My prediction is that you will be surprised by the extent to which later scenes are answering questions raised earlier, or are at least providing information that will contribute to such answers. In adopting the hypothesis that the narrative structure of a randomly selected movie is fundamentally a system of internally generated questions that the movie goes on to answer, you will find that you have hold of a relationship that enables you to explain what makes certain scenes especially key: they either raise questions or answer them, or perform related functions including sustaining questions already raised, or incompletely answering a previous question, or answering one question but then introducing a new one.

Apart from the confirmation of the hypothesis afforded by this confrontation with empirical data, further support for the question/answer model might be gained by using it, not to analyze, but to develop movie scenarios. For when certain complexities and qualifications are added to the model of the erotetic narrative, it is a very

serviceable guide for producing stories that strike one as typically "movieish," especially in their economy. Partial confirmation of the question/answer model is its capacity to direct the simulation of movie scenarios.

If the model of the erotetic narrative captures the characteristic narrative form of movies, then perhaps we can note certain features of this mode of narration which will shed light on the power of movies. A movie scene or a series of depicted events make certain questions salient. An orphan wanders the street, importuning adults needfully. Will the orphan find a surrogate parent? This could be answered in the next scene, or it could take the entire film to answer. However, by characterizing the function of this scene as that of saliently posing a question, we have put ourselves in a position to account for one of the most notable features of audience responses to linear narrative movies, that is, expectation. Given the erotetic model, we can say what it is that audiences expect: they expect answers to the questions that earlier events have made salient – will the shark be stopped; will the jumbo jet crash? If it is a general feature of our cognitive make-up that, all things being equal, we not only want but expect answers to questions that have assertively been put before us, this helps explain our widespread, intense engagement with movies. Even if the question is as insignificant to us as whether the suburban adolescent in *Risky Business* will be found out by his parents, our curiosity keeps us riveted to the screen until it is satisfied.

Though space does not allow for a full elaboration of the matter, important distinctions can be made among the different types of questions that animate the erotetic movie narrative. One such distinction can be drawn between micro-questions and macro-questions. A scene or an event may raise a question that is immediately answered in the succeeding scene or by the succeeding event, or by a scene or event temporally proximate to the questioning scene. For example, some burglars trigger an alarm. This raises the question of whether the authorities will hear it. Next, there is a scene of two policemen reading magazines in their squad car; they look up and switch on their siren, raising the question of whether they will arrive at the scene of the crime on time, and so on. Such localized networks of questions and answers are "micro" in nature. They connect two individual scenes or a limited series of scenes and sequences. But movies are also generally animated by macro-questions, ones for which we await answers throughout most of the film, and which may be thought of as organizing the bulk of significant action in the movie – indeed, the micro-questions are generally hierarchically subordinate to the macro-questions. For an example of a macro-question, consider *Wargames;* at a certain point most of the action is devoted to answering the question of whether nuclear destruction can be averted. Of course, movies often have more than one macro-question. *Into the Night* asks both whether the romantic leads can escape the Middle Eastern villains *and* whether this couple will become lovers. Both macro-questions are answered by means of roughly the same sequences of action, and the micro-questions and answers that structure those sequences tend, finally, to dovetail with the answers to these presiding macro-questions. What is called "closure" in movies can be explained as that moment when all the saliently posed and sustained questions that the movie has raised have been answered.

A successful erotetic narrative tells you, literally, everything you want to know about the action being depicted, i.e., it answers every question, or virtually every question, that it has chosen to pose saliently. (I say "virtually" in order to accommodate endings such as that in the original *Invasion of the Body Snatchers,* where the audience is left with one last pregnant question.) But even countenancing these cases, an erotetic movie narrative has an extraordinary degree of neatness and intellectually appealing com-

pactness. It answers all the questions that it assertively presents to the audience, and the largest portion of its actions is organized by a small number of macro-questions, with little remainder. The flow of action approaches an ideal of uncluttered clarity. This clarity contrasts vividly with the quality of the fragments of actions and events we typically observe in everyday life. Unlike those in real life, the actions observed in movies have a level of intelligibility, due to the role they play in the erotetic narrative's system of questions and answers. Because of the question/answer structure, the audience is left with the impression that it has learned everything important to know concerning the action depicted. How is this achieved? By assertively introducing a selected set of pressing questions and then answering them – by controlling expectation by the manner in which questions are posed. This imbues the film with an aura of clarity while also affording an intense satisfaction concerning our cognitive expectations and our propensity for intelligibility.

The clarity imparted by the erotetic narrative in movies is, of course, reinforced by other clarity-producing methods, such as directing audience attention through the single shot or variable framing. These devices are the filmmaker's means of visual narration. They enable him to raise questions *visually:* the question "Will Jones be shot?" can be "asked" by focusing on a close-up of a gun. At the same time, the visual depiction of an action can either sustain or answer a question. "Will Eli Wallach die by hanging?" can be sustained by showing him teetering on a chair with a noose around his neck, or answered by showing us Clint Eastwood severing the rope in an act of super-human marksmanship. Of course, many of the pressing questions that drive movies forward are not primarily set forth visually but are stated explicitly in the dialogue, or are already implied in the scripting of the action. Nevertheless, the devices of visual narration, if not the original source of the questions, help make those questions salient.

The visual devices of movies were earlier described in terms of the type of clarity they afforded the audience, of how they enable the audience to see all that it is relevant for them to see at the appropriate distance and in the appropriate sequence. At the same time, another sort of clarity has been attributed to the erotetic narrative as a primary ground of the power of movies. How do these two "clarities" relate to each other? Well, generally in movies, devices such as scaling, bracketing, and indexing will be employed so that the first item or the first gestalt of items that the audience is led to attend to in a given shot is the item or gestalt that is most relevant to the progress of the narrative – to the posing, sustaining, or answering of those questions the movie elects to answer. The importance of variable framing for movies is the potential it affords for assuring that the audience attends to everything that is *relevant,* and that it does so automatically, so to speak. "Relevance" is here determined by the narrative, or, more specifically the questions and answers that drive the narrative, which in turn are saliently posed and answered in important ways by means of variable framing.

In order for this account to be adequate, certain qualifications need to be acknowledged. While generally processes such as variable framing are coordinated with the narrative for the purpose of emphasizing the first item, or gestalt of items, seen by the audience, there are standard deviations to this principle. These deviations are often employed in thrillers for shock effect: the important subject, say, the killer, is hidden in the shot in such a way that the audience only comes to see him belatedly (but unavoidably). In terms of our account, these deviations are not destructive counterexamples, because they still illustrate how the flow of narration is kept under strict control and the audience in rapt attention.

Standard movies also often contain much material that is digressive from the point of view of the erotetic narrative, for example, a melodic interlude from the heroine by the campfire in a Western. While this paper cannot fully develop a theory of such digressions, I suggest that the most important digressions typically found in movies are a function of the sub-genres the movies in question belong to (one could go on to explain those digressions by analyzing the sub-genres they most frequently appear in and, perhaps, proceed to analyze the power of those sub-genres).

We began by addressing the issue of the power of movies, which was understood as a question concerning the ways in which movies have engaged the widespread, intense response of untutored audiences throughout the century. We have dealt with the issue of the widespread response to movies by pointing to those features of movies that make them particularly accessible. We have also dealt with our intense engagement with movies in terms of the impression of coherence they impart, i.e., their easily grasped, indeed, their almost unavoidable, clarity. The accessibility of movies is at least attributable to their use of pictorial representation, variable framing, and narrative, the latter being the most pervasive form of explaining human actions. Their clarity is at least a function of variable framing in coordination with the erotetic narrative, especially where erotetic narration and variable framing are coordinated by the principle that the first item or gestalt of items the audience apprehends be that which, out of alternative framings, is most important to the narration. In short, this thesis holds that the power of movies – their capacity to evoke unrivaled widespread and intense response – is, first and foremost, at least a result of their deployment of pictorial representation, variable framing, and the erotetic narrative.

It will undoubtedly be noted that in this attempt to account for the power of movies, we have restricted our purview to features in movies which address the *cognitive* faculties of the audience. This is absolutely central to the argument. For only by focusing on cognitive capacities, especially ones as deeply embedded as pictorial recognition, practical reason, and the drive to get answers to our questions, will we be in the best position to find the features of movies that account for their phenomenally *widespread* effectiveness; since cognitive capacities, at the level discussed, seem the most plausible candidate for what mass-movie audiences have *in common*. That is, the question of the power of movies involves explaining how peoples of different cultures, societies, nations, races, creed, educational backgrounds, age groups, and sexes can find movies easily accessible and gripping. Thus, the power of movies must be connected to some fairly generic features of human organisms to account for their power *across* class, cultural, and educational boundaries. The structures of perception and cognition are primary examples of fairly generic features of humans. Consequently, it seems that if we can suggest the ways in which movies are designed to engage and excite cognitive and perceptual structures, we will have our best initial approximation of their *generic* power.

Some qualifications, of course, are in order. First, we are not claiming that people do not respond intensely to forms other than movies; indeed, some people respond more intensely to other art forms than they do to movies. There are opera buffs and balletomanes, after all. But this is compatible with the claim we are examining, that there is something special about the widespread and intense, though not necessarily universal, response that movies have been observed to command.

Next, we are not denying that there may be levers beyond those we have discussed that also figure in the account of the power of movies. Marketing structures, including advertising, are important elements, as well

as factors such as the transportability and reproducibility of movies. Research in these areas should not be abandoned. However, considerations along these lines do not obviate the present sort of speculation, since there must still be something about the product, so marketed, that sustains interest.

Pictorial representations, variable framing, erotetic narration, and the interrelation of these elements in the ways proposed will, at the very least, be constituents of any account of the power of movies. This paper does not pretend to have offered a *complete* account of why movies are powerful – its modesty is signaled by the hedge "at the very least." Perhaps movies employ other clarifying features, such as music, that require analysis. Furthermore, apart from the question of why movies are powerful, we may wish to pursue different, but related, questions about why certain movies or groups of movies are powerful for certain groups of people; how do movies, or at least certain varieties of movies, engage particular classes, nations, genders, and so on. Theoretical interest in these questions would undoubtedly lead to a focus on elements of structure and content that have not been addressed here, since we have been concerned with the *generic* power of movies, not the power of movies for specific times, locales, sexes, and interest groups. However, nothing we have said suggests an objection in principle to these more specific questions, which questions, of course, will, in all probability, lead to speculation about aspects of audiences over and above their cognitive faculties. Social conditioning and affective psychology, *appropriately historicized,* must be introduced to explain the power of given movies for target groups. Sociology, anthropology, and certain forms of psychoanalysis may be useful in such investigations. We can therefore continue to examine the power of movies by asking about the power of certain movies for historically specific audiences. However, if we wish to explain the power of movies for the world community, then pictorial representation, variable framing, and the erotetic narrative will be key elements in our account because of the ways in which they address common cognitive and perceptual capacities.

Notes

1. See André Bazin, *What is Cinema?* (Berkeley: University of California Press, 1971), especially vol. 1.
2. For an example of an author who employs these approaches, see John Ellis, *Visible Fictions: Cinema, TV, Video* (London: Routledge and Kegan Paul, 1982).
3. For detailed criticism of the Bazinian approach see my "Concerning Uniqueness Claims for Photographic and Cinematic Representation," which is included in this volume. For extensive criticism of contemporary attributions of realistic psychological effects to viewers, see my "Address to the Heathen," *October*, no. 23, 1982, and my "A Reply to Heath," *October*, no. 27, 1983; the latter article is included in this volume.
4. The question of film's ideological operation is also a good one, one I shall take up in another essay currently in preparation.
5. This essay is in Christian Metz's *The Imaginary Signifier* (Bloomington: University of Indiana Press, 1982). I criticize Metz's approach in a review of this book in the *Journal of Aesthetics and Art Criticism,* Winter 1984.
6. J. E. Hochberg and V. Brooks, "Pictorial Recognition as an Unlearned Ability," *American Journal of Psychology,* no. 75, 1962, pp. 624–628.
7. Ichitaro Hondo, "History of Japanese Painting," in *Painting 14–19th Centuries: Pageant of Japanese Art* (Tokyo: Tokyo National Museum, 1957), vol. II, pp. 54–55.
8. J. B. Deregowski, E. S. Muldrow, and W. F. Muldrow, "Pictorial Recognition in a Remote Ethiopian Population," *Perception,* no. 1, 1972, pp. 417–425.
9. John M. Kennedy, *A Psychology of Picture Perception* (San Francisco: Jossey-Bass; 1974), p. 79.
10. K. J. Hayes and C. Hayes, "Picture Perception in Home-Raised Chimpanzee," *Journal of Comparative and Physiological Psychology,* no. 46, 1953, pp. 470–474.
11. John Searle, *Minds, Brains and Science* (Cambridge: Harvard University Press, 1984), pp. 51–52.
12. Noël Carroll, "Toward a Theory of Film Suspense," in *Persistence of Vision: The Journal of the Film Faculty of the City University of New York,* no. 81, 1984. This article is in this volume.
13. V. I. Pudovkin, *Film Technique and Film Acting* (New York: Grove Press, 1960).
14. Carroll, "Toward a Theory of Film Suspense," op. cit.

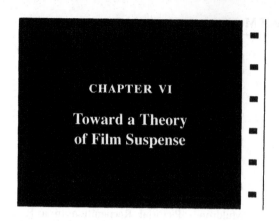

CHAPTER VI

Toward a Theory of Film Suspense

I. The Problem

For over eighty years, film audiences have thrilled to chases, races, escapes, and rescues. And a cursory glance at any nightly TV listing shows that younger generations are already being nurtured with a taste for suspense. But although suspense is one of the most popular modes of film, there is very little scholarly literature devoted to explaining what exactly it is. In a book like Gordon Gow's *Suspense in the Cinema,* one is often at a loss to understand what principle unites the heterogeneous group of films and scenes discussed – is the murder-by-default passage in *The Little Foxes* (1941) really an instance of suspense?[1] Moreover, looking for guidance from scholars in related fields can also be frustrating. In Eric Rabkin's *Narrative Suspense,*[2] anything that draws the reader through a story is treated as a suspense element. This is too broad. For example, it includes the continuation of a repeating motif of images under the label of suspense. In discussing artworks, critics seem prone to regard any structure that involves anticipation as suspense. But this is to mistake the species for the genus. Outside art, anticipation and suspense are discriminable. As Husserl points out, every experience involves anticipation to some degree.[3] But experiences of suspense are much less frequent. Likewise, when it comes to narrative art, it is advisable to keep the concept of suspense more narrowly defined than that of mere anticipation.

Undoubtedly some film scholars believe that we have little need to construct an original concept of film suspense because, they might argue, we already have a rigorous concept ready-to-hand in Roland Barthes's "Structural Analysis of Narratives."[4] There Barthes states:

Suspense is clearly only a privileged – or "exacerbated" form of distortion: on the one hand, by keeping a sequence open (through emphatic procedures of delay and renewal), it reinforces the contact with the reader (the listener), has a manifestly phatic function; while on the other, it offers the threat of an uncompleted sequence, of an open paradigm (if, as we believe, every sequence has two poles), that is to say, of a logical disturbance, it being this disturbance which is consumed with anxiety and pleasure (all the more so because it is always made right in the end). "Suspense," therefore, is a game with structure, designed to endanger and glorify it, constituting a veritable "thrilling" of intelligibility: by representing order (and no longer series) in its fragility, "suspense" accomplishes the very idea of language . . .[5]

This immensely turgid passage has many problems with it, some of which I will take up later. For the moment, however, let it suffice to note that in his concern to situate "suspense" on a continuum with (at least his own very dubious idea of) narrative in general and with language ("the very idea of language"!), Barthes has failed to distinguish suspense from his own (albeit vague and bloated) concept of narrative except to say that the former is a somewhat intense or privileged extension of the latter. This seems neither true – some narrative forms neither engender suspense nor do they resemble the structure of suspense – nor informative – what accounts for the occurrence of privileged moments of suspense over and above the mere experience of ordinary narrative linkages? At times, Barthes's supposed concept of suspense blends into ideas of tension, structural tension, and closure. Such a concept of suspense is too abstract to be useful. Thus, film scholars cannot hope to borrow a concept of suspense from Barthes because it is far from clear that he has one to lend them.

The only fully elaborated theory of film suspense that I know of is never mentioned in film scholarship. It was developed by Altan Löker and it is psychoanalytic in its orientation.[6] Space does not permit a detailed exposition and refutation of the theory, nor am I sure that the theory merits close critical scrutiny. Roughly, Löker sees suspense as a heightened state of ambivalence in which the audience is confronted by a dramatic conflict, staged in the film, which energizes an intrapsychic conflict within each spectator. That is, the drama triggers a conflict between the various Freudian-type forces within the self. For example, when danger threatens a character on screen, the danger may be desired by the spectator's demonic id but unwanted by the spectator's superego, which, in turn, induces fear in the ego. This complex psychological state of warring desires and fears is suspense.

It is not apparent to me that Löker's lengthy accounts of the interacting processes of his various intrapsychic forces are always internally coherent, or that each step in said processes is established by satisfactory argument. His postulation of all manner of psychological operations is generally *ad hoc,* and most often not compellingly motivated – if at all – by any evidence. For instance, Löker has it that part of the spectator's conflict in watching *The Stalking Moon* (1969) – a sort of *Cape Fear* (1962) of the Wild West – is that the audience feels guilt because (1) it wanted the character played by Gregory Peck to help the character played by Eva Marie Saint, and (2) the action endorsed by this desire has resulted in a series of terrible murders. No evidence for the audience's putative guilt-feelings is adduced, nor, given the manifest content of the plot, does there seem to be any reason for anyone outside the world of the film to feel any blame. Löker in general asserts non-obvious psychological responses

by spectators without grounding them in any documentation. Thus I question the proliferation of unconscious mechanisms to account for what I take to be invented data. Löker's theory posits a wealth of such subterranean processes. And to the extent that these are thoroughly unsupported speculations, unconstrained by evidence, his theory founders.

But a deep problem would remain with Löker's theory even if he were able to adequately show that all his various intrapsychic forces are clashing in the way he says. Namely, we should want to know why this intrapsychic tension and/or fear should be thought to add up to the specific affect called "suspense." Why, in other words, should this intrapsychic anxiety be cashed in as "suspense," and why should it redirect its target (or object) from, say, the ego to the plight of some character? Without making explicit the nature of the connection between intrapsychic anxiety and the ostensibly different emotion of suspense, Löker has left a logical lacuna in his reductivist theory that is serious enough to disqualify it as an explanation of suspense. That is, without saying why intrapsychic anxiety is phenomenologically and personally felt as suspense, Löker has explained nothing.

The purpose of this paper is to develop an adequate theory of film suspense.

II. Notes on Film Narrative

Before introducing the topic of suspense proper, it is necessary to consider certain notions about film narrative that can be used to describe film suspense. The approach to film narrative that I believe is especially instructive in this regard was suggested by Pudovkin,[7] but has not been developed further by later film scholars. Perhaps the reason for this is that Pudovkin's tone is prescriptive; he is telling prospective filmmakers how they ought to construct films; and such *overt* polemicism is often shunned by scholars. However, it is important to remember that Pudovkin, like Kuleshov,[8] was involved in distilling and conceptualizing central elements of what they observed in American cinema, (e.g., Kuleshov's points about the importance for rapid editing of succinct, uncluttered set design). That is, Pudovkin and Kuleshov clarified and articulated certain latent, stylistic principles that seemed to determine and were exhibited in American film practice. As recommendations about how cinema should be, Kuleshov's and Pudovkin's theories are open to question. Nevertheless, when examined for their crystallizations of the tendencies inherent in existing film practices, their remarks, reconceived as observations are often quite insightful. Specifically, I believe that Pudovkin's analysis of the approach to editing together or connecting scenes supplies us with a starting point for outlining the structure of one of the basic, if not the most basic, linear narrative forms in the history of cinema.[9]

Pudovkin suggests that the relation of earlier scenes and events in a film narrative to later scenes and events can be generally understood on the model of the relation of a question to an answer. One can grasp this by recalling primitive, two-shot narratives. In the first shot, a child might be kidnapped. This raises the question: "Will the child be saved or not?" The next and last shot answers the question; the police apprehend a racially stereotyped Eastern or Southern European, and the child is rescued. The basic narrative connective – the rhetorical bond between the two scenes – is the question/answer.

Since most film narratives involve a series of actions, it may seem natural to think that causation is the major connective between scenes in a narrative film. However, it is implausible to suggest that scenes follow each other in most film narratives via a chain of causal *entailments*. I would guess that most succeeding narrative scenes are causally underdetermined by what precedes them. Rather, the connection is weaker than a causal one. Earlier narrative scenes raise questions, issues, or possibilities that are answered or actualized by later scenes. A character robs a bank; this raises two well-structured possibilities: he will be caught/he will not be caught. In the next scene, the police, hitherto unseen, grab him as he exits the back door of the bank. The later scene is not causally implied by the earlier scene. Instead, the earlier scene raised a structured set of possibilities, one of which the later scene realized.[10]

Using the idea of a question to capture the idea of raising narrative possibilities seems appropriate since the most convenient way in ordinary language to state such possibilities is "Will x happen or not?" The concept of the question, as well, enables us to explain one of the most apparent audience responses toward linear film narratives: expectation. That is, the audience expects answers to the questions the film raises about its fictional world.

Some readers may balk at the preceding account on the grounds that it does not seem plausible to characterize the spectators of narrative films as engaged in a constant process of question-formation. Such spectators are not introspectively aware of framing questions nor are they moving their lips – silently speaking said questions – as scenes flicker by. So in what respect is it accurate to say that such spectators are possessed of the kind of questions discussed above?

Clearly I must say that such spectators frame narrative questions tacitly, and they subconsciously expect answers to them. The notion of an subconscious expectation – one we are unaware of until it is perhaps shortcircuited – should cause no difficulty. When we are told the plumbers will turn off the water for an hour, we still surprise ourselves by expectantly walking over to the sink. But maybe it is thought that some special problem arises when our subconscious expectation takes the form of a question (which awaits an answer) rather than being based on a reason or a belief.

True, reasons and beliefs are best represented by assertions rather than by questions. But then, of course, if anything really hinges on this grammatical point, we might think to recast our narrative questions as assertions – e.g., as predictions taking a disjunctive form such as "either x will happen or y will happen or x will not happen . . . ." But, in fact, to hold that a thought cannot be subconscious, depending on the grammatical format of its representation, is a highly unlikely hypothesis.

Needless to say, objectors to my characterization of spectators as question-formers may have in mind another issue – viz., that spectators are not involved in *explicit acts* of questioning when watching films. But here the error is to confuse having a question – which may be an implicit or tacit matter – with performing a self-conscious operation. Not all mental processes can be equated with consciously performed processes; nor are all mental states – such as having a question – to be equated with performing a mental action such as that of internal question-posing.

When following a narrative film, I want to say, a spectator internalizes the whole structure of interests depicted in the drama, and this structure includes alternative outcomes to various lines of action which the spectator must keep track of in some sense before one alternative is actualized in order for the film to be received as intelligible. I postulate that the spectator does this by tacitly projecting the range of outcomes as subconscious expectations which we can represent as questions. Thus, one argument in favor of the tacit question model is that it explains how spectators are able to regard films as intelligible. Another reason is supplied by the results of subverting the postulated expectations. If we stop a film midway, the tacit questions soon surface: "Well, did he marry the princess, or did she fly around the world?" greet us when the projector hum dies down.

At first glance, it may appear that the question/answer model is ill-conceived to handle flashback scenes; however, the purpose of most flashbacks is to answer (or to offer information in the direction of an answer to) questions about why characters are behaving as they do, or why they are as they are in antecedent scenes. Though further qualifications are necessary, my central hypothesis is that the major connective or logical relation in one of the most basic forms of linear film narrative is erotetic. You can turn on your TV any night of the week and find several films and weekly programs whose basic plot structure can be almost completely explained on the interrogatory model.

The ways in which a question is made salient by a scene or group of scenes is too diverse to examine in detail in this paper.[11] Much of the work is done in the writing, not only the dialogue and/or intertitles, but also in the choice of subject and the dramatic focus of given scenes – i.e., the dramatic organization of the scene will make clear that the major issue is, for example, "will x propose to y?" or "will z draw his gun?" This is not to say that nonverbal factors like gesture, framing, character, and camera position are not major components in leading an audience to regard a certain set of characters and their intentions as primary nodes of interest. Obviously, a whole ensemble of stylistic choices, often redundant ones, prompt the audience to identify this or that issue as central in a scene. Suppose a telephone is off the hook in the distant, blurry background of a shot while a character is begging for a loan from a rotund banker, center-frame foreground, in a well-lit, large medium close-shot. We know the question the scene raises is whether the petitioner will receive the loan (or, more broadly, will he get the money he needs?) and not whether the phone will be hung up. And we expect ensuing scenes or events to answer that question.

Though the question/answer structure is fundamental to certain linear film narratives, such narratives are not comprised baldly of simple questions and answers. Not every scene or event in the narrative can be described as a simple question or answer. Most linear narratives have scenes with more complicated functions than providing a simple question or answer. The following is an inductive characterization of the scenes in an idealized, erotetic, linear narrative: an event or scene in an erotetic narrative is:

1. an establishing scene – an event or a series of events or a state of affairs that introduces characters, locales, etc., or that establishes important attributes of a character, locale, etc. and that, perhaps, but not necessarily, raises a question. An establishing scene often initiates a film but one can come at any point in the film when the story involves the addition of new characters, locales, etc.
2. a questioning scene. (Any scene may, of course, introduce more than one question.)
3. an answering scene. (More than one question may be answered in such a scene.)[12]
4. a sustaining scene. A scene may continue and intensify an earlier question. The question "will x escape," is intensified by a subsequent scene in which we learn that, unbeknownst to x, he is surrounded. A scene that begins to answer a narrative question but then frustrates the answer – e.g., a detective follows up the wrong clue – is also a sustaining scene.
5. an incomplete answering scene. A partial answer may be given to a preceding question, e.g., "who killed Jones?" is partly but not completely answered when we learn that the killer is left-handed.[13]
6. an answering/questioning scene. A preceding question may be answered by a succeeding scene which *also* immediately introduces a new question. A man and a woman meet in such a way that in scene #1 the question arises whether or nor they will become a couple. Scene #2

opens on a confetti-strewn bed, answering the question of scene #1. But as the man stumbles into the kitchen for breakfast, he is surprised to meet a child, his new spouse's heretofore unmentioned son. Suddenly, the question arises as to whether or not this new variable will endanger the new relationship. Several ensuing scenes or an entire film could be built around answering this question.

By using the question/answer model as the core concept of this categorization of linear narrative scenes and events, I am not suggesting that it is a competitor with taxonomies based on temporal relations – e.g., parallel scenes, flashbacks, flashforwards, etc. The interrogative – will x be executed? – can be articulated by two alternating questioning scenes of parallel narration, e.g., *Intolerance* (1916). The idea of parallel narration describes a temporal relation in the fictional world of the film while the question/answer format describes the rhetorical-logical relation of scenes in the film's structure.

These six functions (plus the fulfilling scene discussed in note 12) give us a picture of the basic skeleton of a great many narrative films. Whether a scene or an event is part of the core plot of a linear narrative film depends on whether it is one of these types of scenes, i.e., on whether it is part of the circuit of questions and answers that powers the film. A scene that is not an establishing scene is a digression if it lies outside the network of questions and answers. A digression, of course, need not necessarily be something bad; digressions may enrich the film as a whole, as well as detract from it. But a scene in a linear narrative will be a digression, for good or ill, if it does not perform one of the core functions on our list.[14]

I hasten to add that I am not saying that all film narratives are or should be erotetic linear narratives. There are episodic narrative structures, such as one finds in *The Tree of Wooden Clogs* (1978) or *Amarcord*

(1973), in which scenes are generally linked, for realistic effect, by principles of rough temporal contiguity and often geographical propinquity, rather than in terms of questions and answers. This type of narration often has as its aim the desire to impart a holistic sense of a given milieu by itemizing or layering details concerning life in a certain culture or sub-culture at a given time. As in literary ventures, such as *Pictures from an Institution,* the importance of linear progression is deferred in favor of provoking an elaborate sense of the texture and tempo of the "world" depicted in the fiction. The film does not rush us forward along an arc of expectations but is said to invite us to "live in," to appreciate the rhythms of life of, to savor (and thereby understand) the milieu that it represents.

Films can forego a linear structure for all sorts of reasons. The scenes in *Satyricon* (1969) do not follow a question/answer logic, but that, of course, is exactly what engenders the alien, mysterious quality that Fellini sought when he created what he called this "science fiction" film of the past. Likewise, Welles's *The Trial* (1962) abruptly shifts scenes to instill a sense of arbitrariness. Fantasy films – whether supernatural or psychological – at times have scenes that cannot be mapped on the question/answer model; the apparitions of Death in *All That Jazz* (1979) could not plausibly answer any questions any spectator could have as the film proceeds; they are there to signal the egocentric view Bob Fosse has of himself as a special someone in touch with an eruptive, exclusive, transcendent reality. Modernist exercises like *Last Year at Marienbad* (1961) and *India Song* (1974) defy (literally) the erotetic model – they are all questions with no answers. Consequently, because of these and many other types of examples, the question/answer model does not apply to all narrative films, nor is it an evaluative grid with which we can measure the worth of every narrative film. But it is, at least, a description of the core structure

of a great many – the vast majority of? – linear narratives.

Yet the question/answer model may also represent something deeper. It may be a model of what we can call the basic film narrative. It may be what most of us have in mind when we hear the phrase "narrative film." Two considerations count in favor of this hypothesis. On the one hand, we do perceive a difference between a mere chronicle film – my home movie of my summer vacation in which each event follows the next simply because it was what happened next – and a film like *The Lonedale Operator* (1911). Clearly the difference between these different representations of human actions is one of structure.[15] The question/ answer model affords us one general structural differentia that we can use to distinguish the chronicle from something that we might consider a minimal narrative film. However, such considerations only lead us to regard the erotetic model as a candidate for the title "basic narrative."

The question/answer model gives us a means of differentiating one very simple narrative film type from a chronicle. But why should this type be considered more basic than the episodic film narrative or the other narrative variations alluded to earlier? One reason is that to a large degree we understand these alternative modes of film narration by comparing these modes to a more basic linear structure of the sort described by the erotetic model. The disjunctiveness of *Satyricon* and the attendant qualities we associate with it involve an implicit contrast with or deviance from more standard forms of conjunction – which, in turn, may be related to a propensity to form certain cognitive expectations (viz., that questions will be answered). The lack, omission, or foregoing of a structure that evokes expectation is a pertinent stylistic element or choice in a film because it is a contrast to a more basic, "normal" type in which certain connectives are expected. Even with the case of the episodic structure, as it developed as a major vehicle of film realism, we note that it was able to do so in lieu of its divergence from the linear forms of classical narrative cinema. That is, part of the reason why an episodic structure is held to have a special affinity with realism – i.e., why it is said to project the quality of realism – is because it is said to be looser ("more inclusive," and, therefore, "truer to reality") than the historically dominant, alternative mode of cinematic narration, viz., the linear narrative film which is based on the erotetic model.[16]

My point here is not to draw absolutely clean demarcations between erotetic narrative films and other sorts. Most films will mix elements of different narrative types. For example, a realistic film, like *The Tree of Wooden Clogs*, though predominantly episodic, employs the question/answer structure at crucial points; indeed, one of the most pressing issues in the film hinges on the question of whether the father will be caught and punished for cutting down "the tree of wooden clogs." Furthermore, it should be noted that even if I am wrong in asserting that the erotetic model describes the basic film narrative, the consequences of that mistake for this paper need not be disastrous, since the suspense film certainly falls under this model of the linear model, whatever "basic" or "non-basic" status we assign that model notwithstanding.

Before leaving the topic of the question/answer model of film narration, a distinction between the two types of narrative questions should be drawn. I have been emphasizing the question/answer model as a means of linking scenes. But questions are also a means for organizing whole narratives. Thus, it is worth drawing a distinction between macro-questions and micro-questions in film narratives. In Buster Keaton's *The General* (1926), there are three macro-questions – will Johnny Gray win his true love, will he recover his train, "The General," and will he eventually succeed in enlisting in the Confederate Army. In *The General,* these three questions are interrelated, of course. Gradually they dovetail with each other. When they are all answered, the film is effectively over.[17] We don't worry about whether or not the happy couple will have three children because that is not a question raised in the film. We say that a film is complete[18] and that we feel a sense of closure when all the macro-questions in the film have been answered.[19]

The General has three macro-questions but it also has a large number of micro-questions which connect scene to scene and fictional event to fictional event. For example, in one scene the Union hijackers scatter debris on the railroad track in order to frustrate Johnny's pursuit. This is undoubtedly related to the macro-question of whether Johnny will recover his engine – one might call it an instantiation of the macro-question – but at this point the answer to the macro-question is momentarily dependent on the answer to a micro-question – will Johnny be able to handle these obstacles and avoid derailment? – a question that following scenes or events answer. Suspense in film is generated by means of micro-questions and macro-questions.

III. Characterizing Film Suspense

We can begin to analyze suspense in film by means of the tools set out in our sketch of the basic film narrative. Suspense, in film, is generated as a concomitant of a question that has been raised by earlier scenes and events. The heroine is tied to the railroad tracks; the locomotive is steaming at her; will she be crushed or saved? Suspense arises when a well-structured question – with neatly opposed alternatives – emerges from the narrative and calls forth an answering scene. Suspense is a state that accompanies such a scene up to the point when one of the competing, alternative outcomes is finalized. But saying that suspense arises as a question in a basic plot is not enough to isolate suspense because, as I argued earlier, the question/answer nexus is a characteristic linkage in many narratives whereas most narrative linkages do not involve suspense. They may involve anticipation, but suspense is a subcategory of anticipation, not the whole of it. Anticipation may be a necessary condition for suspense, and a question/answer relationship is a necessary condition for narrative suspense. However, more must be added to the concepts of anticipation and questioning before we can arrive at a manageable notion of suspense.

Suspense in life, as opposed to film, is not just anticipation, but anticipation where something desired is at stake – a job, admission to a school, securement of a loan, passing an exam, escaping a nasty situation. Moreover, whatever is at stake has some psychological urgency partly because the outcome is somehow uncertain. Turning from life to film, we can see that in the largest number of the relevant film cases, the elements of everyday suspense – desirability and uncertainty – are still in operation; however, in the largest number of film cases, the range of each of these central elements has been narrowed so that the subjects of film suspense are the morally right (as the pertinent subclass of desirability) and improbability (as the pertinent subclass of uncertainty). In film, suspense generally obtains when the question that arises from earlier scenes has two possible, opposed answers which have specific ratings in terms of morality and probability. The actual outcome – the alternative answer which is eventually posited – is irrelevant to the question of whether a scene of a film involves suspense; whether the heroine on the tracks is saved or crushed is irrelevant to the issue of whether the moments leading up to that outcome are suspenseful. Suspense, rather, is a function of the structure of the narrative question as it is raised by factors earlier in the film. Specifically, suspense in the film generally results when the possible outcomes of the situation set down

by the film are such that the outcome which is morally correct in terms of the values inherent in the film is the less likely outcome (or, at least, only as likely as the evil outcome). That is, suspense in films, in general, is generated by combining elements of morality and probability in such a way that the questions that issue in the plot have logically opposed answers – x will happen/x will not happen – and, furthermore, that opposition is also characterized by an opposition of morality and probability ratings. The possible combinations of morality/probability ratings are as follows:

I. moral/likely outcome
II. evil/likely outcome
III. moral/unlikely outcome
IV. evil/unlikely outcome

My thesis is that, in general, film suspense occurs when the alternative outcomes – the alternative denouements of an answering scene – have the characteristics of II and III above. When our heroine is tied to the tracks, the moral outcome – her rescue – is unlikely, while the evil outcome – her destruction – is probable. I claim that, as an empirical matter, most suspense in film accords with this pattern. To summarize these hypotheses, I am holding that, in the main, suspense in film is (a) an affective concomitant of an answering scene or event which (b) has two logically opposed outcomes such that (c) one is morally correct but unlikely and the other is evil and likely.

It is to be hoped that this formulation will ring true for at least some simple examples. In *Way Down East* (1920), it is most likely that the heroine will go over the waterfalls; that is, as the scene unfolds, the boy's rescue attempt – hopping from one block of ice to the next – seems futile. Of course, after the scene is over, the probability of the rescue is one. But prior to that the prospect of saving the heroine is extremely low. Moreover, there is evil in the scene, a natural evil in theological jargon, since innocent human life and suffering are threatened by implacable natural forces. The moral effort – the rescue – is unlikely while an evil outcome – a natural evil in this case – appears inevitable.

In many cases, a moral human effort is opposed not by a natural evil but by an immoral human effort, e.g., *The Lonely Villa* (1909). Or, in *The Hills Have Eyes* (1977), two teenagers plant a liquid-propane gas bomb in their trailer in order to destroy a giant, subhuman maniac who is out to murder them. The giant hesitates at the door to which the bomb is rigged; suspense arises because when the maniac suspiciously sniffs the air, the likelihood of success for the teenagers' morally correct effort – obliterating this scourge – has been undermined. The finale of *French Connection II* (1975) provokes suspense by pitting Popeye Doyle's impossible crosstown run, righteousness verging on a coronary, against the elegant drug dealer's smooth escape on a conveniently situated bus and then a boat.

Though many examples of film suspense do hinge on whether or not a violent act will occur, the crux of suspense need not be violence. In *Red Dust* (1932), the philandering plantation manager, played by Clark Gable, wants to be noble and to trick the wife, played by Mary Astor, into once again honoring her husband. A shooting is involved in the scene, but the focus of the drama is not essentially whether the wife will fire but whether the husband, tramping through the jungle on his way to the plantation, will learn that his wife has been disloyal. The plantation manager's moral effort seems destined to ignominious defeat while the evil, the husband's learning of his wife's infidelity, appears unavoidable.[20]

Again, the actual, final outcome of a suspense scene is not relevant to whether it is a suspense scene. Most often the improbable moral alternative is victorious. But one still has suspense even if evil triumphs, e.g., *Von Ryan's Express* (1965), *Gallipoli* (1981), and the remake of *Invasion of the Body Snatchers* (1978). It will be noted that certain motifs like races, chases, rescues and escapes are staples of film suspense. One may wonder if these narrative contexts of themselves generate suspense without any special issue of morality arising. Races, in particular, may appear able to enjoin suspense while remaining essentially amoral. But races in films like *National Velvet* (1944) generally have some moral point. For example, in the recent *Chariots of Fire* (1981) Harry's stake in the Olympic races is connected to his desperate fight for an identity and to some kind of vindication of Judaism. No countervailing moral purposes are established for his opponents. Indeed, in the film the Americans are painted as vaguely guilty of something that is never made explicit. Given these circumstances, Harry's defeat would be an evil, though it is, up to the end of the race, as likely as his morally charged efforts to win.

If the above examples motivate a belief in the proposition that the alternative outcomes in suspense are primarily structured in terms of the moral/unlikely versus the evil/likely pattern, then, perhaps, some further cases will illustrate a subsidiary notion: that suspense does not generally correlate to situations where the outcomes are structured in terms of morally probable outcomes versus evil but improbable outcomes. When in *Dirty Harry* (1971), the eponymous super-cop stalks Scorpio in the baseball stadium, there is no suspense; Scorpio is limping and is no match for his righteous pursuer. The success of Scorpio's evil effort – his flight – is improbable; the odds are on the side of the avenger. When in *Tarzan and the Leopard Woman* (1946), the jungle king rescues the school teachers from the rafts of the leopard people, the scene is more risible than suspenseful precisely because Tarzan – a.k.a. Johnny Weissmuller – so outclasses the villains when it comes to aquatics. The last example suggests one of the dangers in designing suspense scenes in films with super-heroes. The powers of a

Superman, for example, are so great that much care must be taken to assure that an evil effort stands a chance against him. He must be matched against super-villains, or villains armed with kryptonite, or his feats must demand a level of physical effort that is taxing even for him – being in two places almost simultaneously or circumnavigating the globe in a matter of seconds. Posing a mob of gangsters, who tote nothing more than .38s, against Superman is more comical than suspenseful, a fact that the *Superman* series with George Reeves often intentionally exploited. The pattern of the moral, likely outcome versus the evil, unlikely outcome is not generally an efficacious one for suspense.

If these considerations capture the phenomenon of suspense as it generally exists in film, it still remains to be pointed out that there are various ways in which this notion of suspense can be applied to films. If a scene is suspenseful, then it is composed of a questioning event and an answering event, such that the possible narrative answers are logically opposed and have the previously defined morality/likelihood ratings. For example, in *The Gold Rush* (1925), the Tramp's cabin teeters on a precipice; he is unaware of this at first; the position of the cabin and the Tramp's initial unawareness of it raise the question: will he fall to his death or not? These same factors make it likely that an evil, the Tramp's death, will transpire, even though the final outcome of the scene is that the Tramp does not die. If a sequence of scenes is suspenseful, the earlier scenes raise a question or set of questions whose alternative answers have the structure outlined above. I have already offered several examples of this sort.

An entire film may be called suspenseful – or, more normally, a "suspense film" – for three different reasons. First, its macro-question (or questions) may have a suspense structure. Hitchcock's *The 39 Steps* (1935) is an example of this. As soon as Hannay's visitor, Anabella, is murdered, the

issues arise of whether he will be wrongly arrested or will escape, and of whether the secret agents will or will not successfully export their ill-gotten information. These questions and their ultimate answers are sustained throughout the film. At points, the question of whether Hannay will be wrongly arrested or not functions not only as a macro-question but as an often iterated micro-question linking sequences of scenes, e.g., Hannay's series of escapes after jumping through the sheriff's window. Nevertheless, the film as a whole can be seen as organized in large part by suspenseful macro-questions – plus the romantic micro-question of whether Pamela will believe Hannay and, then, come to love him – that are repeated again and again until the Mr. Memory scene at the Palladium where both Hannay's and Britain's dismal plights turn in a lightning reversal.

Cases where macro-questions in a film are suspenseful are perhaps the core instances of the suspense film. However, a film may also be called a suspense film if it is made up of a large number of suspenseful scenes or sequences of scenes even if these are not, in turn, strongly unified by a set of dominant macro-questions; serials, e.g., episodes of *Fantomas* (1913–14), and films composed of serial-like material, e.g., *Spies* (1928), are often of this sort – a string of separate suspenseful adventures, escapes and entrapments that are only very broadly connected under a vague rubric like "will good triumph or will evil?"

The last and loosest reason why some films may be categorized as suspense films is that their final or climactic scenes or sequences involve suspense as I have defined it. *The Birth of a Nation* (1915) might be considered a suspense film in this light. This is a weak sense of "suspense film" since a film like *Cops* (1922) is a suspense film in this respect. For this reason, it is probably best to discourage this use of "suspense film" and to speak rather of films of this sort as "suspenseful films." However, this use of "suspense film" is not completely fanciful because final and climactic scenes have extremely forceful effects in coloring our total sense of a film, and films with suspenseful scenes at the end, therefore, have more claim to the title "suspense film" than those films that merely have sporadic suspense scenes in early or middle portions of the narrative. Whether one wants to call films with terminating suspense scenes suspense films is a matter of stipulation. In terms of the theory in this paper, what is important is that if one decides to call such films suspense films, then it is because the terminating scenes are suspenseful according to our formula.

Now that the general theory of film suspense has been stated, time must be spent on clarifying certain of the central concepts in the theory. First on the agenda are "evil" and "moral." Both these terms are being used more broadly than one typically finds in ethical theory. Under "evil," I am including natural evils – any threats to human life and limb that result from natural causes and which need not be set in motion by evil agents. Films like *The Wages of Fear* (1955) and its remake *Sorcerer* (1977), are both predicated on human efforts in the face of probable natural disaster as trucks loaded with nitro-glycerin are precariously driven over bumpy, dangerous roads. The macro-question – will the trucks reach their destination (in one piece) or not? – is repeated in scene after scene. For example, in order to clear a turn, in *The Wages of Fear,* Mario has to back onto a rickety bridge overhanging a gorge. The bridge is rotten; its wooden planks are likely to break beneath him; he backs up too far because he won't believe his cowardly friend Jo's instructions to stop, as Mario eases off the bridge, his truck catches the suspension cable of the bridge and tightens it until it snaps; at exactly the moment the bridge collapses, Mario has just reached hard ground. The probability of natural evil – Mario's death – looms while at the same

time, Mario's effort is given as morally right in the film in the sense that, as a European stranded in South America with no chance of work and humiliated by the local tradesmen, driving this truck is Mario's only, albeit slim, opportunity to escape. Mario's effort as well is a result of exploitation by the oil company which has consciously lured financially desperate men by the promise of big money to do a job that the company realizes is most likely to end in death.

The Wages of Fear can be used to illuminate our operating concept of morality. The four drivers are not moral men in terms of normal Western standards of morality. Mario and Jo, at least, are hooligans. Yet, within the film's moral system, they are initially more moral than the other morally relevant forces in the town – the company and the manager of the store. Also, the situation of the Europeans in the town appears morally wrong; they cannot earn money to go home; the suicide of the Italian youth underscores the hopelessness of the foreign community in the town. And Mario and Jo, though petty thieves, do at first have certain virtues – bravado and the pragmatism versus the sloth and tyranny of established powers – that in the absence of countervailing virtues give them a purchase on representing what moral virtue there is in the film. By the time the other drivers become subjects of suspense, they too are emphasized in light of their virtue, their bravery (plus Bimba's anti-Nazism), so that the suspense of the driving scenes pits natural evil against human virtue.

Admittedly the film becomes very complex. Jo shows himself to be a coward. Interestingly, when this happens, he becomes more a subject of sympathy than of suspense. Moreover, even as Mario becomes increasingly crueler to Jo, he, Mario, still commands some positive moral force as a human steadfastly facing natural evil. Perhaps some viewers even believe that Mario is meting out Jo's just deserts. Of course, the last scene is underwritten by the belief that it is a tragic wrong that after all of Mario's tribulations he should die so carelessly.

In analyzing suspense films, it is important to keep in mind that the locus of morality is not always the ideological position or the ethical status of the projects of the characters in question. Caper films, for example, portray characters who are often involved in larceny. Their effort cannot be described as moral in respect of extant ethical codes or sets of categorical imperatives. However, the foci of suspense are nevertheless moral in the sense that they are marked by certain virtues that, in the absence of emphasis on countervailing virtues, claim our moral allegiance. These virtues – strength, fortitude, ingenuity, bravery, etc. – are often more Grecian than Christian, but they are virtues nonetheless.

Often in Hollywood films, a character is designated as good in terms of his courteous, respectful, and thoughtful treatment of supporting characters, especially ones who are poor, old, weak, lame, oppressed, children, etc. – that is, characters who are in some sense the protagonist's inferiors, but whom the protagonist treats with consideration. In *The 39 Steps* Hannay's kindness and attention to the oppressed Mrs. Jordan is an increment of Hannay's goodness as a character.

Democratic courtesy to one's inferiors as well as protectiveness of the weak, and an overall "niceness" are key virtues in many films – not only American ones – used to cue the audience to the characters and characters' efforts that, within the film's moral system are postulated as "good." We also note that villains are often segregated not only in terms of vices like brutishness, sadistic dandyism, arrogance, cowardliness, weakness, etc., but also by their discourteous and bullying attitude toward inferiors. Character, in other words, is the most integral factor in establishing the spectator's moral perspective on the action. Indeed, this is why one may watch a film like *The*

Wild Geese (1978), a saga of mercenaries in Africa, and be caught up in the suspense even if one is stridently opposed on moral grounds to the activities of soldiers of fortune in the Third World.[21]

If the protagonists are presented as possessing some virtues – especially if their opponents are not presented as having any virtues, or as having only negative personal and interpersonal attributes – suspense can operate because the efforts of the protagonists will be regarded as right in the moral system of the film, i.e., they have been marked as right. Most often the protagonist's purposes will be moral according to prevailing ethical norms. However, in a large number of standard cases where this does not hold, the protagonist's possession of saliently presented virtues will project the moral valuations of the films. Virtues are the basic means of establishing the moral sympathies of a film. Thus, even an antagonist, if provided with some virtues, can at times serve as an object of suspense.

It may be felt that a debit of my theory is that what is included under the labels of "moral" and "evil" in the formula for suspense turns out to be too broad. "Evil" is unpacked as human and natural evil. "Moral" encompasses ethical purposes and efforts, virtue, and simply opposition to natural evils. This is a far more extensive concept of "moral" than we find in ethical theorizing. Nevertheless, it does, I think, capture the wide range of things that people are wont to call "good" and "bad" in a nonpractical, nonprudential sense in everyday language. And it is not surprising that this expanded notion of goodness and badness, reflected in ordinary language, should be the relevant one for a popular medium like the movies.[22]

Let us now shift from the discussion of the scope of "the moral" in our formula for suspense to some specification of the pertinent concept of "likelihood." First, I am speaking of the likelihood the spectator assays for the alternative outcomes[23] of scenes relative to each other *before* one outcome is actualized in the narrative. Moreover, I am talking about the probability of the outcomes as they are presented by the film, not as they would be in similar situations in everyday life. And I am categorically excluding from the spectator's estimate of the relative probabilities, the audience's knowledge of such desiderata of filmgoing lore as that the heroine is generally rescued just in the nick of time. This talk of probability, I think, concretizes the essential truth of Alfred Hitchcock's emphasis on the importance of audience having knowledge for suspense (as opposed to shock) to succeed.[24] What I think the audience needs knowledge about is the relative likelihoods of the alternative outcomes of scenes.

The idea of probability that I have in mind in this formula is a non-technical one. For a spectator to believe that *x* is probable or improbable is not for the spectator to assign *x* some ranking or value in terms of the probability calculus. Rather it is for the spectator to believe that if *x* is probable then *x* is likely to occur, or can be reasonably expected to occur given all the available, permissible evidence on the screen. Nor does this imply that the audience is in its seat actively calculating probabilities of either the technical or non-technical sort. I see two cars – three feet apart and each traveling over sixty miles per hour – and I immediately form the belief that a crash is likely, indeed highly likely. Similarly, when the buzz saw is only nine inches from the heroine's neck and the hero is still in an anteroom battling six fulgurating ninjas, I, sans conscious calculation, presume that the heroine's moments, in all probability, are numbered.

Since the audience's appreciation of the relative probabilities is at the heart of suspense, it is necessary that the countervailing probabilities be not just stated, but constantly re-emphasized. The audience must be reminded and consistently have called to its attention these relative probabili-

ties if its grasp on the suspense is to remain firm. Thus, one can narrate a suspense scene by switching between shots that primarily add information about the relative probabilities. Even scenes which include shots of the agony of the victim of suspenseful machinations – in order to underscore the moral conflict in the scene – require the shots concerning probability information as their nucleus. Suppose character *x* is in one of those rooms whose walls close like a vise; character *y* is rushing to the rescue. The scene would typically be set out with shots of the walls inching inwards – thereby enhancing with each shot the probability of *x* being flattened – alternating with shots of *y*'s advance blocked by various stratagems – traffic, motor-trouble, guards, gates, etc., all of which make it less probable that *y* will arrive in time. Shots of *x*'s anxiety and *y*'s exertion may be included, but they need not be. The suspense sequence itself is most often primarily concerned with adding and re-emphasizing probability factors. In the average case, by the time the suspense sequence begins the morality ratings are already in place.[25]

One can easily go wrong by overadding improbability factors in a suspense sequence, thereby reducing the audience to giddiness. In John Cromwell's *Made For Each Other* (1939), the narrative alternates between scenes of a hospital in New York City, where a child is dying for want of a special medicine, and scenes of a flyer bringing the medicine from Buffalo. Time is running out on the kid. First, the flyer is caught in a blizzard, which is bad enough; then his plane crashes; then he crawls several miles to a farmhouse but he collapses before he can tell the locals what to do with his packet. By the time the farmer reads the address and calls the hospital in New York, the viewer is sobbing with tears of laughter. The contrivances of the improbabilities and their reversals in the delivery of the medicine are so overstated that they appear unintentionally parodic.

By focusing on the probability ratings in a suspense scene, I do not mean to say that other factors are beside the point. Often, suspense is accentuated by music. That is, as the narrative structure moves toward its completion, in the form of an answer, a corresponding musical system may be simultaneously moving toward closure so that the musical resolution reinforces the dramatic one.[26] Some of the favorite motifs in film suspense, like time-bombs, may seem analogous to suspense music in one regard; they afford a formalized countdown system that enhances the tension of the narrative. I, however, consider things like time-bombs as part of the probability structure of a suspense sequence; each tick makes it more likely that an evil will occur. Unlike most musical accompaniments in suspense films (I say "most" in deference to examples like *The Man Who Knew Too Much*, [1956]), time-bombs are causal constituents of, not merely temporal correlates of, the events depicted in the suspense scenes.

My emphasis on probability in suspense scenes is meant to stand in contradistinction to the idea that the core of suspense is a matter of temporal distension (Truffaut), or a simple delaying (Barthes) or forestalling of the final outcome of a suspense scene. I realize, of course, that in the process of adding and re-emphasizing probability information the narrative will most often cinematically distend some part of the represented action (in comparison to how long the event might actually take), and, in some sense it could be said that the addition of probabilities delays the outcome of a scene. But I think that these distensions and delays, when they occur, are contingent or accidental accompaniments of the more fundamental procedure for generating suspense – the adding and re-emphasizing of probability ratings. The "delays" that are centrally important in suspense are those that figure, quite literally, in the probability structure – e.g., the raised drawbridge that stalls the rescuer, something that one might want to

say "delays" the final outcome of the narrative, but which more significantly makes the rescue less likely. Also I am uncomfortable with the idea that film suspense distends or prolongs or delays events because this implies a comparison with some event – the delayed one – that is outside the film. But with fiction films there is no such independent event. The events only exist in the film. There is nothing for them to be "delayed" in relation *to*.

But perhaps the issue of whether probability ratings or temporal distensions are more important for suspense cannot be adjudicated conceptually. Some empirical research would be desirable. But, sans research, I would offer as pre-scientific evidence for my conjecture a consideration of the last scene in *Potemkin* (1925). We know that it is meant to be suspenseful, but neither I nor the numerous film classes I have watched it with have found it so. Nevertheless, it does rather elaborately "delay" the answer to the question of whether the fleet will open fire. I suggest the reason for the lack of suspense in the scene is that its probability structure does not include any information about the fleet during the entire detailed narration of the mutineers' preparation for battle. That the fleet will in all likelihood demolish the battle ship is never emphasized in the editing. There is only a brief glimpse of the fleet at the end of the shot chain. It is simply given that the fleet is likely to blow the "Potemkin" and crew out of the water. That prospect along with the awesome firepower at the fleet's command is never visually embodied or re-emphasized or woven into the heart of the sequence. There is a "delaying" of the climax in the narrative, but there is no effort to give the audience a sense of the likelihood of the Potemkin's destruction by repeated underlinings of the overpowering might of the countervailing moral force in the sequence. Likewise, the scene in *Meet Me in Saint Louis* (1944) in which the father decides not to move to New York does not seem suspenseful. His decision is "delayed," but the conclusion, a moral one in terms of the film, is foregone because no countervailing position – e.g., a colleague visiting and extolling the financial opportunities of New York – is incorporated in such a way that the morally right alternative seems improbable. In short, "delaying," if that is even the correct concept for the prolongation of audience anticipation, is not, on its own, sufficient for suspense.

The formula that I have sketched for suspense in film has immediate implications for film research. It can be used with a given film to isolate that film's suspense structure. I claim that suspense generally occurs in the context of an erotetic, dyadic structure – a question is posed that has alternate answers which in turn have contrasting moral/probability ratings. The logical opposition of the alternate answers and of the morality/probability ratings is what, at the level of form, gives rise to the "tension" of suspense. In approaching a completed suspense film, our task is: (1) to identify the presiding question and to enumerate the previous scenes and events that call for or sustain the question; (2) to isolate the scenes and events that establish the morality ratings of alternative answers; and (3) to itemize the scene, events, and shots that inform the spectator of the relative probability ratings. For example, in *Juggernaut* (1974), a splendid but underrated film by Richard Lester, the question – will the good ship "Britannic" sink or not – is voiced when the extortionist, Juggernaut, first calls the steamship line and informs it that he will destroy the ocean-bound vessel unless the owners pay his ransom fee. The greatest amount of energy in the film is spent trying to avert this disaster, but each sustaining scene, insofar as Juggernaut retains the upper hand, heightens the likelihood that the seven time bombs will go off. That is, most of the film is given over to developing the likelihood that the ship is doomed. From the start, Juggernaut's incomparable expertise is foregrounded – he apparently detonates a bomb long-

distance to display his prowess. The government's refusal to be coerced by Juggernaut also bodes badly for the fate of the ship. Shipboard scenes are counterposed to scenes in London with the police searching for Juggernaut. His electronic savvy stymies tracing his phone calls. The police admit that they do not have enough time to check the alibis of every bomb expert in London. At sea, the situation is even worse. The ship is beset by a storm; the demolitions crew barely survives its air-lift to the "Britannic." Once on board, they must attempt to dismantle all seven bombs at once without knowing whether all the bombs are wired the same way. The bombs are puzzles and they are booby-trapped. Two of them go off, one killing the assistant demolitions expert. Even the esperance of the cocky explosives chief, Fallon, flags. And time is running out; Juggernaut has terminated negotiations with the police because they attempted to arrest his bag man.

The moral elements in the suspense structure are elaborated in a number of ways. On several occasions it is reiterated that the lives of 1,200 people are at stake. Separate scenes are devoted to establishing the virtues of representative passengers and crew members: the garrulous politician who surprisingly turns out to be noble as well as touchingly eloquent in his dedication to his marriage; the cabin boy who considers the ship to be his country and who sacrifices himself to save a child; the entertainment director who struggles to keep everyone in good spirits. Characters who appear comic are, at second glance, virtuous. The vignettes given over to them function to promote the positive moral character of all the people on the ship for whom they stand. Some shipboard children – who coincidentally are the offspring of the chief investigator in London – figure often in the shooting, underscoring the innocence of Juggernaut's victims. An extended ball sequence is included to illustrate the indefatigable human spirit and courage of the passengers in the face of adversity. The evil of their situation is not only conveyed by Juggernaut's portrayal – on the telephone he sounds like your basic mad-scientist – but by the representation of the callous, underhanded government official who is willing to let the ship sink in order to show the world that Her Majesty's government will not be intimidated by terrorists.

In short, one could diagram the suspense structure of a film like *Juggernaut*. First, one would compose a sequential chart of the scenes and/or events in the film, designating those scenes and/or events in the question/answer network that terminate in the suspense scene/event – the bomb's ultimate defusing. One could then go through the film again connecting all those elements of character and action that contribute to the moral and probability ratings that are in tension in the creation of the alternate answers to the suspense questions. This would afford a picture of the structure of suspense within a given film such as *Juggernaut*. The formula I have presented, in other words, can guide research into a particular film and be used to pith its structure.

Having said this, I must hurriedly add that I do not think that, by introducing this formula for suspense, I have said the final word about studying film suspense. Though this formulation provides an initial inroad into analyzing suspense, many interesting discoveries may emerge when this mode of analysis is applied to individual films or particular groups of films. Individual films may find inventive or even subversive ways of manipulating this structure. And it may also turn out in studying genres or groups of films that there are significant sub-structures of suspense – e.g., ways of dovetailing probability factors and moral factors like *Juggernaut's* connection of the family on the ship and the police inspector – that are frequent enough to study in their own right. The formulation I have offered does not preclude all sorts of fascinating variations and complications. Rather, when this frame-work is adopted, such variations and complications are more readily seen in bold relief.

I have offered a characterization of suspense as it generally operates in film. My hypothesis will be, I hope, assessable in the light of film research. I claim the formula is comprehensive – that it is applicable to a very large number of films that we are pre-theoretically disposed to call suspenseful. The formulation should at the same time be replete, i.e., the inter-related factors I have isolated as central to the system of suspense should provide enough categories to segregate out the core suspense elements in a film, and suspense films should exhibit elements that correspond to each of the factors that I have enumerated. Lastly, the theory must be perspicuous enough that film researchers can employ its categories with relative agreement about the extension of the basic terms of the theory. Failure along any of these dimensions of evaluation are grave liabilities for this theory.

IV. Appendix A: Two Problem Cases

When I tried out this theory on colleagues and friends, two questions or problems continually recurred: what is the relation of suspense, on the one hand, to comedy and, on the other hand, to mystery? Given the frequency of these questions, some brief remarks seem appropriate here.

First, let us consider comedy. Suspense is often a major element in gags. A banana peel is cast on the ground; the audience sees it, but the character continues to walk towards the banana peel on his way to a pratfall. The problem is this: many theorists say that in comedy, the audience suspends its ordinary modes of moral thinking thereby taking pleasure in all sorts of sadistic spectacles – human beings falling, being beaten, stepped on, hurled, etc. Thus, the moral sense is in abeyance when comedy is at large. Therefore, the type of theory outlined above cannot explain comic suspense because morality ratings are not applicable to gags. In order to meet the full force of this objection, I will leave to one side the question of the truth of the suspension-of-morality theory of comedy. However, even if that view is correct, we may still ask whether our moral sense is idling in regard to every aspect of a gag or only in regard to some aspects. Many gags seem to demand an amoral response to their resolution – we laugh at rather than weep with a hero who falls on his head. Our *prima facie* moral reaction is neutralized in the outcome of the gag. But this does not mean that other dimensions of our moral sense are not engaged in our response to other aspects of the gag. Specifically, our categories for distinguishing characters, situations, and events as good or evil do not seem out of gear in regard to gags. In fact, a sense of the conflicts between goods and evils, or rights and wrongs, seems requisite for identifying the elements in a comic situation even though with comedy we may reward what would otherwise be an all-too-evil outcome with applause. That is, a man crushed by a Murphy bed is an evil and our recognizing it as such is a presupposition of a gag even if the gag also presupposes that our ultimate reaction to the situation will be levity rather than anxiety. The suspension-of-morality theory of comedy supposes that our basic moral reactions – in terms of attitude – are disengaged and not that our categorizations of characters and events as good or evil are inoperative. Insofar as my theory only requires the latter for morality ratings to take hold, the suspension theory of comedy does not present a problem for it.

The issue of mystery presents different conundrums. Mystery and suspense seem to be closely related phenomena. Often, mystery films are treated automatically as suspense films. But does the preceding theory of suspense really capture the quiddity of mystery? In a very broad sense, of course, it does. A mystery will have a macro-question – will the criminal be caught or not? Presumably the apprehension of the criminal will be a moral good which, due to the ambiguity of the evidence, seems unlikely. But this application of the suspense formula does not aptly characterize what is special about mystery, or, at least, what is called classical detective mystery.[27] The missing feature is that of the puzzle, which is the central element of the classical detective mystery. My solution to this problem is to claim that the classical detective film, while loosely in the realm of suspense, is better conceived of as a category unto itself which in its most important respects is distinct from suspense. In distinguishing suspense from mystery, I am making a distinction analogous to that made in the analysis of crime literature by Todorov when he divides thriller stories from detective stories.[28]

Given my formula, we can zero-in on the difference between suspense and mystery by considering the structure of the suspense question versus that of the classical mystery question. The suspense question has two competing answers. But the typical mystery question – who did it? – has as many answers as the film has suspects. The bulk of the mystery film is devoted to introducing an inventory of ambiguous leads and to a review of all the suspects who might have committed the crime. But the culprit, whose revelation we anticipate, is not unmasked until a scene near or at the end of the film. To a limited extent the character of our anticipation is suspense at this point – we wonder whether the criminal will be found or not. But at the same time, our anticipation is less focused on an outcome and more focused on a *solution,* a solution to the whodunit puzzle. Moreover, this puzzle can have many more than two alternative answers – it has as many potential answers as it has suspects. Thus, at the end of *The Thin Man* (1934), everyone at the dinner table might be the culprit; the detective weighs the evidence in regard to each of them in a *tour de force* of speculation. Our anticipation is not structured in terms of two possible outcomes but is distributed over a handful of possible solutions. In *Murder on the Orient Express* (1974), if I remember correctly, we have ten alternative solutions before the investigator's summing up, the quintessential moment in the classical detective genre. Thus, though overlapping in some respects, the suspense film and the classical mystery film might better be considered as distinct forms whose difference can be stated by reference to the different structures of their animating questions. In suspense, the animating question calls forth two contrasting outcomes, whereas in a mystery, the key question asks for a solution which is not limited to two contrasting answers but has as many different potential answers as there are suspects.

V. Appendix B: The Case of Hitchcock

The general theory of film suspense stated in this paper claims that suspense occurs when a moral outcome is improbable and, conversely, that suspense does *not* occur when an immoral outcome is improbable. Though the latter claim does seem generally accurate, it may not hold universally. For there are some ambiguous but troublesome counterexamples to it, clustered especially in the work of Alfred Hitchcock. Hitchcock presents (and, indeed, in the interviews claims to have intended to present) suspense in scenes where the audience worries because the success of some immoral action – "immoral" even in terms of the film's point of view – is imperiled. That is, Hitchcock has made, and, if he is to be believed, he has intentionally striven to create suspense scenes where immoral outcomes are improbable – scenes where there is suspense even though the moral outcome appears likely.

Examples of this – though complicated ones – can be found in *Strangers on a Train* (1951). Bruno drops Guy's cigarette lighter into a sewer. As he struggles to retrieve it, there seems to be suspense, though such suspense would appear to revolve around

the sudden improbability of the success of an immoral effort – Bruno's attempt to frame Guy. Personally, I am not sure that the preceding is an apt characterization of the sequence. For though there is suspense in the scene, it is not clear to me that it is generated simply by Bruno's misfortune. Guy's tennis match is intercut with Bruno's reaching for the lighter. So the suspense in the scene may still be traceable to the obstacles that prevent Guy from saving himself. Admittedly Bruno's momentary loss of the lighter causes a shift in the relative probabilities of the alternative outcomes. Guy's prospects are better than they were – he now has more of a fighting chance versus Bruno. However, it is not the case that Guy's endeavors are made clearly probable by Bruno's accident. Nevertheless, the intensity of the scene is certainly connected to the shift in the weights of the competing probabilities. But it is not evident that suspense is generated because Bruno's efforts are now improbable. His success, it seems to me, is only less probable than it had been.

However, even if the lighter-in-the-sewer-scene fails, there are more examples where that came from. At one point in the film, we are led to believe that Guy will indeed kill Bruno's father. In general, the suspense in this scene is explicable by our general formula. An immoral outcome – Guy's submission to Bruno's mad scheme – appears probable. Yet, there are moments in the scene where a contrary type of suspense has been claimed to arise by some viewers. As Guy walks up the staircase, a huge, initially menacing dog awaits him. Some spectators assert that they feel suspense at this point.[29] If this is the case, it must be said to occur in a context in which an ostensibly immoral effort – Guy's apparent complicity in an attempt at murder – is improbable. We can, of course, debate whether this is in fact what is at stake in this scene. Perhaps what is endangered is something moral – the time or the opportunity Guy might be thought to need to rethink and to renege upon what upright viewers take to be his untoward decision to throw his lot with Bruno. But whatever our conclusion about this complicated scene, it does, nevertheless, raise the theoretical possibility that suspense may occur where an immoral act is portrayed as improbable.

What does this do to the general theory of film suspense defended so far? First, it shows that the theory is only, at best, general – pertaining to the large majority of cases – but that the theory is not universal. Another related way of making this point is to claim that the formula for suspense offered in this paper is sufficient for identifying cases of suspense but that it does not supply necessary conditions for isolating cases of suspense. One way to augment the theory – given the Hitchcock cases – so that it will be universal (supplying necessary conditions for all cases of film suspense) is to alter the morality component of the formula and replace it by the notion of desirability. Suspense then will be the affective concomitant to scenes in which – given the film – *desired* outcomes (rather than moral ones) are improbable and *undesired* outcomes likely. If Guy's danger on the stairway results in suspense, that must be because we desire – against the immediate, perceptible odds – that Guy remain unscathed. The universal theory of film suspense will – to deal with cases like this – be stated in terms of desirability rather than morality, thereby supplying necessary as well as sufficient conditions for film suspense. In order to analyze suspense in film we must identify the features of given films which mark certain outcomes as desirable and others as undesirable. And, of course, in dealing with film suspense in terms of the concept of desirability, we are treating it in a way that is very close to our idea of suspense in life (apart from art).

Having sketched a universal theory of film suspense, one may ask, "Why bother detailing the general theory of film suspense?" In many respects, I think that the general theory of film suspense is a more important discovery than the universal theory, for it pinpoints the centrality of morality in the vast majority of suspense films. Furthermore, it presents morality as a determinant, *functional* feature of most suspense films, rather than as a general but *accidental* feature of most suspense films. In this, the general theory reveals a crucial factor about how most suspense films actually operate. On the other hand, the universal theory, insofar as its central term is broader, may in fact obscure the importance of morality ratings in normal suspense films.

In fact, in some ways, the general theory of film suspense presented in this paper is more helpful than the universal theory even in the analysis of the Hitchcock cases. For the general theory gives us a picture of the normal case of film suspense – what we may consider to be the base-line against which we plot deviations and subversions. With the general theory of film suspense in hand, we are able to see what is specifically distinctive about the often commented upon Hitchcock cases, namely that they are *repudiations* of the ordinary way of contriving film suspense, the norms for which are captured by the general theory. That is, in general, film suspense is constructed by contrasting morality ratings with improbability ratings and immorality ratings with probability ratings. If what is claimed for Hitchcock is true, then at times Hitchcock turns this structure topsy-turvy, making the moral probable and the immoral unlikely in contexts that are still suspenseful. This subversion of the normal mode of film suspense gives such scenes an arresting, memorable, and even disturbing quality. As subversions of the normal mode of film suspense, these scenes accord with what we know of Hitchcock's formalist bent – i.e., his willingness to contravene received wisdom about cinematic form (e.g., don't attempt to make films in contained spaces like lifeboats). Moreover, the particular subversions of normal suspense in these scenes are connected to Hitchcock's moralism. Hitchcock is said to be a filmmaker who shows his audiences that the line between being moral and immoral is slim and easily crossed. This point is underscored in films where what is conventionally the functional position of a moral effort is replaced by an immoral effort.

The full force of Hitchcock's repudiation of the normal method of creating film suspense is only brought into sharp focus when we consider the kinds of scenes in question through the optic of the general theory of film suspense. Thus, even in the case of Hitchcock, it may turn out that the general theory of film suspense has more to offer interpretive criticism than the universal theory.

Notes

1. Gordon Gow, *Suspense in the Cinema* (New York: Barnes, 1968), p. 43.
2. Eric Rabkin, *Narrative Suspense* (Ann Arbor: University of Michigan Press, 1973).
3. Edmund Husserl, *The Phenomenology of Internal Time-Consciousness* (Bloomington: Indiana University Press, 1964). On page 76, Husserl writes "Every primordially constitutive process is animated by protentions which voidly constitute and intercept what is coming, as such, in order to bring it to fulfillment."
4. For an example of such a film critic, see Stephen Neale, *Genre* (British Film Institute, 1980). On page 28, Neale unquestioningly endorses Barthes's characterization of suspense and goes on to apply it almost axiomatically to genres like the thriller film.
5. Roland Barthes, "Structural Analysis of Narrative," in *Image-Music-Text* (New York: Hill and Wang, 1977), p. 119.
6. Altan Löker, *Film and Suspense* (Istanbul, Turkey: Istanbul, Matbassi, 1976).
7. V. I. Pudovkin, *Film Technique and Film Acting* (New York: Grove Press, 1960).
8. L. Kuleshov, *Kuleshov on Film* (Berkeley: University of California Press, 1974).
9. It should be noted that it was not Pudovkin's purpose to proffer a picture of only one basic plot structure. Rather he intended to enumerate an exhaustive account of the principles that justify the insertion of a scene in a narrative film. He believes a scene can be added to a film if it is (1) an answer to a previous question; (2) a parallelism; (3) symbolism; (4) an instance of simultaneity; or (5) a leit-motif. Only 1 and 4, I presume, are relevant to the discussion of the basic linear narrative. Tangentially, it is interesting to speculate that perhaps Pudovkin (mistakenly) believed that film is a language because his formulation of these principles for legitimately adding scenes to a film bear a passing resemblance to (recursively stated) grammatical rules. This is not to say that Pudovkin discovered a grammar of narrative or of film, but that he stated his recommendations in a way that suggests something like a recursive definition for well-formed sequences – rules for licitly adding scenes to scenes.
10. John Holloway calls this "proponing" in his *Narrative and Structure: Exploratory Essays* (Cambridge University Press, 1979).
11. In Part V of my "Film History and Film Theory: An Outline for an Institutional Theory of Film," in *Film Reader* no. 5 (Northwestern University), I discuss what I call the economic-psychological method of medium shot composition which I posit as a baseline strategy of most narrative film composition. Combining the economic-psychological model of composition with the notion of basic film narrative offered in this paper (along with an outline of how salience is achieved through editing and camera movement), I think would give us all the fundamentals of a unified theory of the simplest form of ordinary film narration. The portrait, of course, would be an idealization – perhaps no existing film would satisfy every tenet of the theory – but it would reveal the underlying tendencies of the average narrative film. "Film History and Film Theory" is included in this volume.
12. In some cases, the questions that are answered by a scene or an event may not feel very acute. For example, the causal circumstances in an earlier scene may appear so implacably set out (a typhoon is heading toward an island, for instance), that we don't

have much of a question to ask. Or, a character may state emphatically what he intends to do in the next scene – "I'm going to the saloon to shoot Billy Ringo." The eventuations of such causes and intentions in later scenes seem better described not merely as answering scenes but as fulfilling scenes – i.e., scenes that fulfill what is predicted, not simply asked, by earlier scenes. Consequently, one should perhaps enter a special subcategory – that of the fulfilling scene – to the above list. Yet one should also recognize that it is a subcategory of the answering scene since in film fiction it is always possible for causal and intentional trajectories to make unexpected, hairpin turns. There is always a question – will the typhoon hit? – (though sometimes a slightly felt one) that underwrites a fulfilling scene.

13. In many cases, an incomplete answering scene may not be recognized as such at first glance. We may only retrospectively realize that such a scene gave us a partial answer to a preceding question. Many of the "clues" in classical detective films function in this way. We might want to call such scenes ambiguous, incomplete answering scenes; they are ambiguous because their initial significance is different from their retrospective significance.

14. Pudovkin's parallelisms, leit-motifs, and symbols are digressions from this point of view. Also, a saloon chanteuse singing a barroom ballad in a western of a certain period would count as a digression. It would be interesting to investigate the types of digressions that appear mandatory in given genres in stipulated historical periods. One might be able to develop a list of recurring types of digressions in popular film. Needless to say, digressions in a linear narrative should not be viewed mechanistically as automatic deconstructions of classical cinema; they are very often part and parcel of the form a filmmaker is working in.

Because of digressions, because of the various types of questioning scenes, because of the insertion of establishing scenes after the film is on its way, and because of the possibility of complex temporal relations between scenes (e.g., parallel narration), we should not anticipate that answering scenes will always follow scenes that initiate a question. Were we to diagram many films in order to outline their question/answer plan, we would often discover that we would have to leap-frog, so to speak, several scenes in order to connect question scenes with their answers. The question scene still cognitively generates the need for an answering scene but the answer may not appear immediately after the question in the film. A question scene may be followed by a digression, followed by an establishing scene, followed by another questioning scene before we get an answering scene that correlates with our first question, for example. The more leap-frogging the film involves, the more complex (and less basic) we tend to think the narrative structure is. By the same token, if a question is raised that is presented as important – what will happen to character x? – and it is not answered, even via a complex process of leap-frogging, then we tend to find the film incomplete. And if we cannot justify that incompleteness in terms of some meaningful point or quality that the film is projecting, then we tend to see such incompleteness in a negative light.

15. Arthur Danto employs the distinction between the chronicle and the narrative in his *Analytical Philosophy of History* (Cambridge University Press, 1967). The account of the basic fiction film narrative in this paper, however, differs from Danto's account of historical narration.

16. For example, in *Theory of Film* (New York: Oxford University Press, 1960), Kracauer often attempts to illustrate the nature of the episodic form by contrast to what he calls "the intrigue" and to studio-fabricated plots. I am less concerned with whether Kracauer's argument is sound than with the fact that the episodic structure/realism association is pervasive.

One might argue that the episodic form has the best credentials for being considered the basic film narrative because of its close resemblance to the chronicle. And undoubtedly the episodic form is supposed to appear to be a chronicle. But, it is in fact a highly mediated imitation of a chronicle rather than a chronicle pure and simple since the events it strings together are selected not because they happened one after another but in order to make a point – e.g., "love is fleeting" in *La Ronde* (1950) – or, to evoke a quality – e.g., a sense of a social totality in *The Tree of Wooden Clogs*. The kinds of spectator responses required to properly engage such episodic structures and to divine their purpose is far more demanding and complex than that required by an erotetic linear narrative.

17. After the last macro-question is answered, and Johnny becomes a Confederate lieutenant, there is one more scene in the film, the saluting gag. From the viewpoint of the core structure of the linear, erotetic film plot, such scenes are optional, though, of course, they may greatly enrich the film as a whole. For an analysis of the thematic significance of the saluting scene and its relationship to the rest of the film, see my unpublished doctoral dissertation, "An In-Depth Analysis of Buster Keaton's *The General*" (New York University, 1976).

18. The notion of "completeness" is discussed by Monroe C. Beardsley in *Aesthetics* (New York: Harcourt, Brace & World, 1958), and in Nicholas Wolterstorff, *Art in Action* (Grand Rapids, Michigan: William Erdmans Publishing Company, 1980).

19. In *The General,* the battle sequences toward the end – through which Johnny wins his uniform – may appear tacked on. One reason for this is that the macro-question of whether Johnny will be allowed to enlist has not been as sustained as it might have been throughout the film. The battle seems extraneous to the most animated questions the film has raised and the film might have successfully terminated when Johnny makes it safely to town. In retrospect, we recall that his girlfriend has made enlistment a condition for their relationship, but as the film unravels the issue gets lost and thus gives the battle scenes, wherein the uniform is won, an aura of superfluousness.

Isolating the macro-questions in a film – something most easily achieved after one has knowledge of the complete film – provides a powerful perspective from which to analyse the entire narrative structure of a film. We observe what questions are answered last in a film and then back-up and enumerate all the scenes that set forth and sustain the question

that elicits the final answer. For example, looking at the last scenes of *Bride of Frankenstein* (1935), we see that they answer three narrative questions: will Baron Frankenstein be persuaded to perform the experiment? (he will); will the monster finally have a friend? (he won't); will the Baron and his wife escape? (they do). Of these questions, the last one is a micro-question generated by the specific circumstances of the experiment scene. The other two questions, however, are alternatively the basic issues of the majority of scenes in the film. The monster keeps searching for a friend in scene after abortive scene – thereby reasserting the question – while Dr. Pretorius tempts Frankenstein in alternating scenes. Finally, the questions converge when the object of the experiment becomes the creation of a female, potential friend for the monster.

What I am calling macro-questions would be referred to by many film scholars as "enigmas." This terminology derives from Roland Barthes's *S/Z* (New York: Hill and Wang, 1974). At best, this characterization is misleading. Most narrative questions are not obscure or unfathomable mysteries. Identifying them as such seems to be a rhetorical gambit that enables the psychoanalytic structuralist critic to conflate narrative questions with things that one might more appropriately think of as enigmas, e.g., the nature of the subject. Perhaps by calling such narrative elements macro-questions, we can make a contribution to short-circuiting some of the most flagrant arguments by equivocation that are rampant in film scholarship today.

20. For examples of melodramatic suspense, see my "The Moral Ecology of Melodrama," in *The New York Literary Forum, The Melodrama Issue* (The City University of New York, 1980).

21. I am not claiming that everyone who is politically opposed to mercenary intervention in the Third World will be seduced by the suspense in such a film. Some will feel only outrage. Rather, I am trying to explain why some people, who would oppose certain activities – theft, freebooting, etc. – as criminal and immoral in the world outside the film, can be induced to regard the same activities in a film with a pro-attitude.

22. In the above remarks, it might be noted that I have studiously avoided any reference to the concept of identification. This omission is intentional. I do not believe that we need as elaborate a piece of psychological machinery as identification to account for audience responses to suspense scenes. The idea of moral allegiance will do our work for us. Just as we can have moral allegiance to a foreign nation – e.g., people who espouse either Arab or Israeli causes – without somehow psychologically merging with that nation, so we can agree with and root for a character in a film on the basis of shared moral commitments with that character. We do this on the basis of holding similar moral values to the characters in question. Perhaps, this is why virtues are so important in determining the moral system of the film. For in a given twentieth-century cultural system, we are more likely to agree on what the positive virtues are than we are likely to agree on political and moral precepts.

In film, I contend that what is generally called identification is best explained in terms of an audience's allegiance to a given character on the ground that that character exemplifies personal virtues that the audience has a pro-attitude toward. The spectator retains his/her identity during a film, i.e., does not somehow dissolve into the protagonist, but rather is prompted to applaud the protagonist because that character champions things that the spectator sees as moral goods, usually of the nature of virtues. This seems to me a better description of so-called identification than formalist accounts that trace audience sympathy to devices such as point-of-view shots in which the spectator's vision supposedly "fuses" with a character's. This can't be right since we often "see through" villainous point-of-view shots without taking up that character's cause, e.g., the steadycam shots in *Halloween I* and *II* (1978, 1981).

Obviously, space does not allow for thorough refutation of the concept of cinematic identification at this time. My general reservations about the concept are that: (1) often it is employed in a vague way; (2) when its workings are theorized, for example by someone like Stephen Heath, the steps involved in the putative operation of identifica-

tion seem very *ad hoc;* (3) normal viewers do not believe that they are about to be crushed by a train, pushed off a building, knifed, and so on when a protagonist is threatened – if they did, they would run screaming from the theater; (4) the concept of identification is logically incorrect to describe the phenomenon at issue since very often spectators do not have or share the identical or same emotions of the characters in question – the characters are in pain or enraged and we feel suspense or, in related kinds of cases, pity (that is, the logical asymmetry of the spectator/character relation in terms of the feelings imputable to both make it impossible to characterize the relation as one of identification); (5) the concept of moral allegiance is a simpler, less mysterious, and perfectly adequate way of dealing with the phenomenon. Using allegiance in this context in no way denies that our responses to film can be very intense; we often have very extreme pro-attitudes when it comes to values. For those who claim that allegiance itself must be explained by identification, there are two retorts: first, even if that is ultimately true, moral allegiance or value agreement might still be the proper description of the specific mechanism of reaction at the level of film viewing, and, second, the burden of proof – that all moral allegiance can be reduced to some form of identification – rests with the identificationists.

23. That is, one outcome is relatively more probable than the other, or one seems no more likely than the other.

24. Hitchcock discusses the distinction between suspense and shock in *Hitchcock/Truffaut* (New York: Simon and Schuster, 1967).

25. Sometimes suspense sequences also include credibility factors, i.e., elements that make the final, improbable denouement a little more plausible than it would be otherwise. For example, loquacious villains often megalomanically rant on for just enough precious minutes for aid to reach our beleaguered hero.

26. It might be said of this paper that it is a theory of narrative suspense in film rather than a theory of film suspense. A theory of film suspense would be a *unified* theory of all the elements – music, camera placement, edit-

ing, color, acting, etc. – that go into and are coordinated in producing suspense film. I can only say that if such a unified theory is possible, then I believe that the narrative will be the lead element in it. That is, all the other elements in creating film suspense will have to be subordinated to the functional requirements of the narrative structure of suspense.

Upon hearing the preceding claim, some critics have said that mine is really a literary theory of suspense. This is to misdescribe the case. I have dwelt on the structure of narrative suspense. It is true that that structure – insofar as it is a structure of narration – can be instantiated in film or in writing. But that does not mean that I am imposing a literary structure on film. In fact, I believe that there are certain differences in the technical means of literary suspense and film suspense that make the bald extrapolation of the former to the latter problematic. In literary suspense, for example, I have found that suspense is often narrated by going into the mind of the characters to give us a direct, elaborate and extended account of what the characters feel and of what they think their prospects are. Characters' thoughts, directly presented, supply us, for instance, with assessments of the likelihood or improbability of various outcomes. But that kind of portrayal of suspenseful scenes is awkward and ponderous in film, and would work against conveying suspense cinematically.

I should add that I believe that the formula for suspense offered in this paper can be used by filmmakers in a relatively straightforward way to churn out suspense scenes. I take it as partial confirmation of my formula that it can be used routinely to simulate simple cases of suspense.

27. The notion of the classical detective mystery is developed in John Cawelti's *Adventure, Mystery and Romance* (Chicago: University of Chicago Press, 1976).

28. In "The Typology of Detective Fiction, "*The Poetics of Prose* (Ithaca, New York: Cornell University Press, 1977).

29. My own personal response to this scene is not to feel suspense but simply utter confusion. Jolted by Guy's apparent moral *volte-face,* I feel at sea through most of the scene, concerned only that Guy change his mind. Others, however, have informed me that they find the moment with the dog highly suspenseful. Hitchcock himself cites the scene in *Frenzy* (1972) where the psychopath wrestles the corpse for a piece of jewelry to be an instance wherein the audience feels suspense over a scene in which the odds are against evil succeeding. Again, my personal reaction to the scene is at variance with the claim. I find the sequence a hilarious, surreptitiously obscene, and sustained exercise in black humor. In this case, my laughter interferes with any feeling of suspense on my part. But it is likely that others have responded differently.

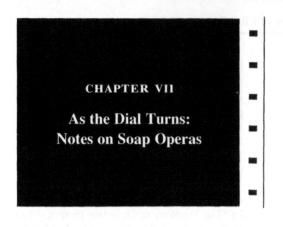

Tina Roberts, alienated from the affections of her husband Cord, is being tried for the murder of her ruthless mother-in-law, Maria. There is plenty of circumstantial evidence, but as yet no motive. The prosecutor believes that Maria was blackmailing Tina, but Tina denies it. He has planted a Latin American woman in the front row of the courtroom – a maneuver that unnerves Tina. The prosecutor demands to know whether Tina recognizes the woman. Hectored, she finally breaks down and divulges a secret that would make any blackmailer's mouth water.

The Hispanic woman was there when, as a result of going over a waterfall in South America, Tina had a miscarriage. At the same time, another woman, Gabrielle, had a child by a man, Max Holden, who Gabrielle believed – wrongly – was Tina's husband.

Tina had persuaded Gabrielle to turn the child, Al, over to her care – which Gabrielle did because she believed that in that way the child would be raised by its true father. Tina, however, put Cord's name on the birth certificate – in order to deflect his attentions away from his dissatisfaction with their marriage (and his girlfriend), and toward "their" new-born son.

Will this revelation turn the jury against Tina? Who will take custody of Al? Will Max, who didn't know that Gabrielle was pregnant, forgive his one-time lover for depriving him of his parental prerogatives – and will his new-found sense of indignation make a better man of him? Stay tuned for future installments of *One Life to Live,* one

of the quintessential American TV soap operas.

And, of course, millions *do* stay tuned – not only to *One Life to Live* but also to the horde of other soaps that crowd the daytime TV schedule, each one weaving, at a dizzying rate, its own web of personal crises compounded of marital infidelity, sudden sickness, accidents, bankruptcy, business scams, family estrangement, abortions, job problems, love affairs, illegitimate children, envy, intrigue, betrayal, and all manner of interpersonal entanglement.

Though for most of us mention of soap operas makes us think of TV, the form originated in radio, and to a surprising degree many of the features of the genre have persisted since the thirties. In all, the soap opera has been with us for at least fifty-five years, which is quite an impressive life span, given the fickleness of popular culture. We hardly recall break-dancing, let alone most of the fads of the early thirties. What accounts for the tenacious grip of the soap opera on the popular imagination? I believe that the answer has to do with the structure of the genre and the ways it addresses the moral life of viewers – ways, in fact, that are in place in the earliest soaps.

The soap opera, by which I generally mean daily, weekday, daytime serials of continuing stories concerned primarily with interpersonal problems and relations, is, as noted, a product of radio. In 1929, with *Amos 'n' Andy,* NBC Radio inaugurated nationally a broadcast serial story form that aired six days a week for fifteen minutes per installment. Its success provided a model to be imitated. The earliest soap operas followed its pattern. For example, *Painted Dreams,* the saga of an Irishwoman and her household, was created in 1930 for WGN by Irna Phillips (whose apprentice, Agnes Nixon, later originated such TV serials as *One Life to Live),* while *Just Plain Bill* began as an evening program in 1932 but became a daytime offering in 1933. By that time, there were nine daytime shows of this sort. A few years later, in the 1937–38 broadcast season, thirty-eight such programs were available – of which one, *The Guiding Light,* would continue as a TV soap starting in 1952. In their recent Sage Publication monograph *The Soap Opera,* Muriel Cantor and Suzanne Pingree observe that "The consensus is that in 1940 about 20 million women (approximately half the women at home during the day) listened to two or more serials daily."

Radio soaps were unabashed exercises in moral didacticism. In a 1938 script from *Today's Children* (also produced by Irna Phillips), Dot testifies that ". . . no matter what problems we might have to face in the future, somehow I feel for the first time since Terry and I have been married that we'd know how to meet them because we've experienced a similar problem and solved it," while Kay identifies the source of all this wisdom in the program's central character, saying "Mother Moran, somehow I think your friends should know that your wise teachings over the past five and a half years have given each of your Today's Children a foundation that nothing can destroy. You've shown us a road on which we know that our footing is sure."

Of course, the advice these programs brokered was not merely moral but, more important, it was commercial, taking the form of advertisements that could even be segued into the episodes. The soaps were expressly directed at female audiences, and they afforded guaranteed access to the primary purchasers of household goods; the very title of the form, set by about 1939, attests to this: the sobriquet "soap" alludes to some of the major sponsors – and, in certain cases, the actual producers of these programs – such as Procter and Gamble.

Radio soap operas continued until 1960, but by the early fifties the shift to television as the major venue for the form had begun. And despite initial, predictable worries that the soap opera as a verbal form would not translate visually onto the TV screen, its growth has been tenacious and steady. "Today the audience for network television soap operas is estimated to be fifty million persons, including two-thirds of all American women living in homes with televisions; the cumulative audience for soap operas over the past fifty years is inestimable. This enormous audience today provides more than $900 million in revenues for the three commercial television networks – one sixth of all the profits," notes media historian Robert Allen in his authoritative *Speaking of Soap Operas.*

The impact of the soaps can be seen on any newsstand, marked by the presence of such "fanzines" as *The Best of Soap Opera, Soap Opera's Stars, Soap Opera People, Soap Opera's Greatest Stories and Stars,* and so on. These specialize in interviews with and biographies of the actors who star in the soaps – thereby providing, in a manner of speaking, further stories about the stories that make up the soaps. Especially useful for anyone who wishes to follow the soaps is *Soap Opera Digest,* which carries, among other things, synopses of the major programs, so if you miss an installment you can always catch up on the plot.

Like it or not, soap operas saturate our culture. One reason is simply the amount of air time they get. Whereas a prime time TV program presents in the neighborhood of twenty-two episodes a year, a daytime soap may deliver as many as two hundred and sixty. *Soap Opera Digest* lists twelve major daytime soaps, which air five days a week. The number of soap operas on the air in any given year, of course, fluctuates. But the stories keep coming day after day. More stories have been told than are in memory or on record. By any standard, the output of the soap opera must represent a substantial proportion of our culture's narrative activity.

Of course, the soap opera has undergone

many changes during its long history. Radio soaps, for example, included much more authorial intervention, in the form of comments and insinuations on the part of the announcer, than do TV soaps. And in more recent years, TV soaps have begun to incorporate action-adventure subplots such as Jesse's undercover police work in *All My Children* and Elena's spy network in *General Hospital,* along with the more traditional interpersonal focus. Such changes certainly reflect the need for the soaps to readjust to shifting circumstances in order to sustain their appeal. But, at the same time, there persists a basic design of the genre, one that has enabled it to command such intense allegiance on the part of such a large audience for so long.

Why do soap opera viewers go on staying tuned? Undoubtedly the typical themes of the soaps – interpersonal relations, romance, health – touch common interests. But this feature alone, I think, cannot account for the addictiveness the form engenders. The very structure of these narratives is also a major contributing factor in the hold that soap operas have over their substantial audiences. That is, it is not just the stories, but the way the stories are told – their form – that keeps the fans coming back for more.

In determining what is distinctive soap opera storytelling, an initial, intriguing clue comes from Lorraine Broderick, one of the chief writers in charge of plotting for ABC's *All My Children.* In an interview with this author, Ms. Broderick remarked that a frequent criticism that soap writers level at a prospective story-line is that the plot is "too movie-ish." From Broderick's point of view, there are essential differences between soap plotting and movie plotting, and some of them work to the advantage of the soap opera. For example, the format of the soap facilitates detailed development of a plot over a long period; Mark's recovery from his drug addiction (which has recently raised

the prospect of AIDS) on *All My Children* – what Broderick refers to as a "public service" subplot – evolved over six months. On the other hand, Broderick notes, the scale and structure of soap narration does not encourage the neat tying-up of loose ends typical of a well-made Hollywood movie.

Broderick's contrast between movies and soaps is suggestive and can be further expanded in ways that not only point to what is characteristic about soap opera narration but also hint at its power of attraction. For movie narratives and their standard effects are something about which, at this time, we know a great deal, and we can use that knowledge to illuminate the less-studied soap opera form.

The most obvious contrast between soap operas and contemporary movies is that soap operas are serials and movies are not. (Of course, there was a time when the serial form was a major staple of movies as well.) The serial form, in whatever medium, relies on the same principle: the narrative generates certain questions that the audience expects will be answered either in the present installment or a subsequent one. Will the hero, in one of those old movie serials, escape from that cellar flooding with water, or will Casey, in *As the World Turns,* fall in love again with Taylor Baldwin and reject Lyla? The answer will come in some future episode.

Although movie serials are almost unheard-of today, the plots of feature films are still based on the question-and-answer principle. Earlier scenes and sequences in a movie pose questions that will be answered by ensuing scenes. If a film opens with a murder, we expect it to be solved before the movie ends. Moreover, the kinds of questions that a movie poses have a certain hierarchical order. Some of them tie together local actions and scenes; if the wagon train is surrounded by Indians, we wonder whether the pioneers will be saved, and this question begins to be answered when we cut to a sequence of the cavalry mounting up and riding to the rescue. Call these micro-questions, which elicit micro-answers.

However, movie narratives are also sustained by larger, macro-questions, questions that animate the film as a whole. Whether Jeff Bridges is a murderer is the fundamental question of *Jagged Edge*. All the actions and events in the plot, tied together by micro-questions, are ultimately subordinated to delivering an answer to this question. Of course, feature films may have more than one animating question. Watching *Bringing Up Baby,* we may wonder whether Grant and Hepburn will become lovers, whether the intercostal clavicle will be found, and whether Grant will "open up." In movies the action will typically be funneled in such a way that these interlocking questions are all resolved by the end of the film.

Feature movies, in other words, have closure. They proceed by generating one or more macro-questions and then answering them. When a movie has answered all the basic questions it has posed, it is over. Moreover, the ending has a sense of finality or fitness about it, for everything you wanted to know about the fictional world it presented has been answered. At the end of Chaplin's *The Gold Rush* you don't wonder whether he will invest in Standard Oil of New Jersey, for that question was never posed. What happens between the Tramp and Georgia is what the story has induced you to be concerned with, and once you learn about that, the story is finished.

Soap opera narration presents a different kind of temporal structure, one without the finality, climax, and closure that movies have. In soap operas, plots and subplots need not be hierarchically structured but may unfold simultaneously without presiding macro-questions to bond them together. Although individual subplots may pretend to a kind of quasiclimax – like Viki Buchanan's return from heaven in *One Life to Live* – they can always, in principle, be interrupted. Clearly, the kind of climatic closure appropriate to the movie form would be dysfunctional in a serial where tomorrow really always is another day. Whereas the movie narrative is ideally *closed,* the soap opera narrative must be *open.* Soap operas do not adhere to Aristotle's requirement that drama have a beginning, a middle, and an end; as Dennis Porter notes, the soaps belong "to a separate genus that is entirely composed of an indefinitely expandable middle."

The expandable middle characterizes soap operas but not necessarily all TV series. Prime time serials, such as *Miami Vice,* tend more toward the movie model in temporal organization; each episode is devoted primarily to the solution of a dominant crime, and this promised solution functions as the macro-question of the installment. Where a series braids together a set of continuing, disparate stories and perplexities from show to show, as *Hill Street Blues* does, the narration begins to feel open, like a soap opera. Of course, there are also evening soaps, like *Dynasty,* with a structure very like that of daytime soaps, even though a show that appears once a week cannot involve its audience the way one that airs five times a week can.

Movies and soaps differ not only in their temporal structure – closed versus open – but in the time of their telling. Most movies last about two hours and they are (with luck) projected without interruption. The movie narrative is compact, indivisible, and integral. The story as a whole is told in one sitting. Clearly the internal temporal structure of the movie narrative, its closure, and the external time structure of its narration, its compactness, are related in the production of perhaps the most characteristic effect of mass movies, their narrative economy.

Soaps, on the other hand, are obviously full of gaps in their manner of presentation. Aired daily, each installment comes at least twenty-three hours after its predecessor. So the open narrative structure in soaps is matched by a porosity in their mode of presentation, and taken together, these two features give soap operas a very different impact from the effect that movies have on their audiences.

Some feminists have even seen the soap opera as a proto-radical form, arguing that closure is associated with an omniscient male mode of reception while the "openness" of the soap provides a feminine mode of viewing for a predominantly female audience – a mode of viewing marked by anticipation and by a diffusion of interest and tolerance that might be described as motherly. One should hesitate over facile thematizations of narrative structures into dubious "essentializing" categories like male and female. Nevertheless, the openness and porosity of the soap opera narrative does allow for qualitatively different kinds of responses than do the temporal structure of movies.

The gaps in soap operas from day today open a kind of space for speculation that is effectively impossible with movies. Given its mode of presentation, the action in the movie is integral and complete. We don't really have much time to speculate whether a character will or should do this or that, because as the movie converges on its climax, what she does and whether, on balance, it was correct have already been settled. Of course there are moments of uncertainty in virtually every film, but the degree to which these may be speculatively explored is severely limited by the pacing of the plot structure, which demands resolutions in one sitting – thereby making it effectively impossible for us to debate with other viewers about what will and should be done.

Soap operas, on the other hand, allow and even encourage such speculation and discussion. The time between episodes gives viewers the opportunity to test with others their assessments of what they have seen. Yes, this character – say, Erica on *All My*

Children – is a stinker, and that one an angel, and Melissa *(General Hospital)* is headed for trouble if she accepts Zak's offer of drugs as a way of dealing with her fears and frustrations about her mother – although her mother is acting in an understandable way considering her daughter's behavior. Soap operas, in short, invite gossip. They encourage us to talk about the rights and wrongs of the argument Robert and Anna *(General Hospital)* are having over her career, and about what would be best for baby Al and what would be just for his assorted parents on *One Life to Live*. Indeed, soap operas supply an interpersonally available community on which we can practice our moral and prudential skills of evaluation – and then they give us the time to do so.

It is somewhat odd to think about gossiping about the characters (as opposed to the stars) and events in movies. What they have done and what they ought to have done appears already fixed, due to the closure and compactness of the form. Furthermore, the movie is over by the time we might start gossiping. One could argue that the characters *should* have behaved otherwise, but the fact that the book is closed makes such a dispute a matter of swiftly diminishing returns. Very shortly, that is, one has marshalled all the relevant facts from the fictional world that there are to be had, and the discussion reaches if not agreement then stalemate. But the openness of the soap opera – including the potentially continual addition of new facts – as well as its porosity makes sustained conversation seem natural.

We don't gossip about strangers, for the most part. Gossip, in general, requires most of us to have some knowledge of the people we are gossiping about. One function of soaps is that they supply viewers with familiar figures about whom to gossip – figures to whom they may apply standards of character and action, and about whose circumstances they can predict likely outcomes as well as evaluate them.

Gossip performs an important function in the moral realm. In *Moralities of Everyday Life,* John Sabini and Maury Silver contend that "gossip brings ethics home by introducing abstract morality to the mundane. Moral norms are abstract. To decide whether some particular, concrete, unanalyzed action is forbidden, tolerated, encouraged, or required, principles must be applied to the case." Gossip provides a setting in which individuals, in concert with others, are able to understand their moral principles and practical (i.e., prudential) guidelines by connecting them to concrete situations and characters. Through gossip, that is, one comes to realize the extent of abstract moral rules on one hand, abstract views of the vices and virtues, on the other, through a conversation over cases. Gossiping enables us to articulate abstract moral and practical views in detail, thereby, in a sense, helping us to discover our moral perceptions at the same time that we commit ourselves to them. Soaps, because they prompt gossip, also promote this social process, and that is a large part of their attraction.

That appeal is quite wide these days. Men and women are equally drawn to gossip. If at one time the topics for gossip placed on the agenda by soaps were traditionally thought of a "women's talk," indulged in primarily by housewives, recent studies show increases in college-age and male audiences that suggest the potential for soap opera's appeal across age, class, and gender.

Although soaps can be a very active social lubricant, the intense interest they evoke is not confined to people who have the opportunity to talk about them. Soap operas are also watched, avidly in many cases, by people who have little occasion to expatiate on them – for instance, the elderly who live alone. However, even in such cases, soap operas invite the exercise of moral and practical powers of synthesis and insight in ways that afford the viewer a sense of participation in a moral community. In *The*

Public's Use of Television, R. E. Frank and M. G. Greenberg maintain that viewers isolated from other adults derive a feeling of social integration from soaps, while Suzanne Pingree's findings indicate that viewers of daytime soaps are more active participants in relation to the ongoing story than any other type of TV viewer. The line of speculation we have pursued so far suggests a way of unifying these observations; daytime soaps engender a sense of communal integration because the activity they most invite is the exercise of social skills related to practical and moral judgement.

This doesn't mean that soap operas are necessarily forces for moral enlightenment, particularly in their plot material. On social issues, soaps tend toward a safe liberal view, but they also gravitate toward conventional moral attitudes that often deserve to be challenged. In recent soaps I have detected a pervasive "me-generation/go-for-it" ethos coexisting uneasily with a more traditional commitment to the primacy of family loyalty. Thus, I would not want to defend the moral contribution of the soaps on the basis of their explicit or implied ethical stances but rather for the way in which they open a space for the exercise of moral perception.

Feminists such as Ellen Seiter have suggested that women can interpret soaps against the grain, against the way in which such stories ask to be read. I have no idea how many people interpret such stories subversively, but I agree that the genre readily affords this possibility through its formal structure because it invites the play of active moral judgement – it invites gossip – and this must be one of its attractions. Whether the moral reactions it elicits always coincide with the forces of light is another question.

Of course, it is not simply a matter of form; content certainly plays a decisive role as well. The typical themes of the soaps – family, romance, sex, and sickness – are of especial moral concern to their still predominantly female audiences, and so the spaces opened by the temporal structures are also filled with living issues. As well, the soaps are written with an eye to topical problems – drug addiction, child abuse, teenage sex, wife-beating, abortion – that make them even more seviceable as grist for ethical exercise.

Given the contemporary critical disposition to explain the artifacts of mass culture in terms of realism – artifacts ranging from advertisements to detective novels – it may seem surprising that I have not attributed the allure of soap opera to realism. Some might claim that there is a realism operating in the soaps, rooted not only in their topicality, but also in their concentration on everyday life. But if "realism" in such formulas is supposed to signal that the viewer regards popular representations as very like reality, then I don't see how realism could explain the intensity of our response to these objects, since most people's encounters with reality are marked by indifference. And in any case, soap operas are not particularly realistic; their world is populated by too many doctors and nurses, while the rhythm of catastrophe is too pronounced.

Though clearly artificial, soap operas are no less engaging for that. Specifically, for many, they provide a stimulant for exercising moral skills. In a world of anonymity and fragmentation, they supply their viewers with an electronic front porch on Main Street, a world to judge.

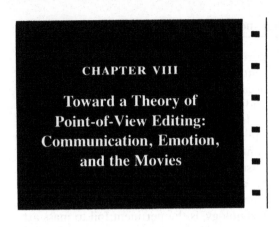

CHAPTER VIII

Toward a Theory of
Point-of-View Editing:
Communication, Emotion,
and the Movies

I. Introduction

Movies, under which rubric I include narrative TV, represent the paradigmatic popular art form of the twentieth century; each decade is memorialized in our collective archive by the images and styles of its distinctive movies – such as the gangster films of the thirties. The purpose of this article is to analyze one of the key devices of the movies, point-of-view editing, in order to suggest, in the course of that analysis, something about what makes movies so popular, specifically in terms of the structures, such as point-of-view editing, toward which the movies gravitate.

Moreover, the reader who is unfamiliar with the theoretical fashions of the cinema studies establishment should be forewarned that the methodological approach represented in this paper is at odds with the received wisdom of the English-speaking academy of the present. Whereas the dominant tendency in film studies, and in what is coming to be called "cultural studies," relies upon psychoanalysis (often Lacanian psychoanalysis) as its preferred explanatory framework, my own work along with that of others, such as David Bordwell, explores the relevance of alternative areas of psychology for answering questions about the structures of communication and reception of cinema in particular and mass art in general.

Furthermore, since the types of psychological and philosophical research this work favors attempts to avoid resorting to the postulation of irrational processes, whenever such hypotheses are redundant or ill-advised, the approach found in this paper has been called "cognitivist." I have argued for the superiority of the cognitivist approach elsewhere at great length.[1] So rather than repeat those arguments here, perhaps the success of the ensuing article in explaining the ways in which point-of-view editing serves the purposes of popular art can stand as testimony on behalf of the cognitivist approach.

But before taking up point-of-view editing proper, some clarification of terminology is in order. I have said that movies represent a paradigmatic popular art. However, this may not be the most insightful way of putting the matter. For, on the one hand, this formulation traditionally suggests a contrast with serious art, which contrast provides hardly a sufficient contrary since something, including certain movies, can be serious *and* popular. And, on the other hand, this way of characterizing the umbrella category groups movies together with rural medicine shows, thereby missing what is probably the most significant feature of movies, viz., that movies are *mass* art.

Rather than referring to movies as popular art, I believe that it is more instructive to refer to it as mass art. In many of its typical forms, mass art is thought to evolve out of popular arts or popular entertainments, such as vaudeville. But not all popular art has been transformed into mass art.

As an initial approximation, mass art is popular art or popular entertainment wedded with a technology – such as radio, film, or sound recording – that enables it to be distributed on a mass scale. Moreover, given its potential for mass distribution, mass art tends to be not as class-specific as earlier popular entertainments were. Mass art seeks as large an audience as is available, and, therefore, ideally strives to address general audiences. One might say that the function of mass art is to command mass audiences. And this function, in turn, not only influences the content of mass movie entertainment, but also influences the choice of its structures, such as point-of-view editing, as well.

Of course, not everything produced in a mass medium is a mass art in the sense that I use that notion. There have been and continue to be avant-garde films, videos, radio broadcasts, and so forth. That is, the technologies of mass media may be used to produce high art. But, nevertheless, we need to draw a distinction in terms of art produced by a mass medium (which would include the works of Nam June Paik *and* Elvis Presley) and art designed for mass consumption (which is also delivered by means of a mass medium). The latter is the narrow sense in which I wish to employ the idea of mass art.

Such art includes the work of Elvis Presley but not the work of Nam June Paik. For even if Nam June Paik wishes he had a mass consumer audience, he would have to admit, polemics aside, that he has not yet designed his video works in a way that would secure such an audience in the world as we know it. Some producers of mass art proper may also fail to elicit the mass response they wish because they have misapplied the formulas or strategies designed to entice mass followings. These artists differ from Nam June Paik, however, since he not only chooses to eschew such formulas, but he actually experiments with strategies that subvert them.

Mass art, then, as I would construe it is, at least, art produced by a mass medium and designed to elicit mass consumption or with the reasonable expectation of eliciting mass consumption. In order to elicit mass consumption, the products of a mass medium aim to be consumable by a maximum number of people employing minimum effort. Stated more formulaically, x is an instance of mass art if and only if it is (1) art that (2) is delivered by a mass technology that (3) is designed in such a way that its structural choices (modes of representation, types of narration, and perhaps to some extent content) gravitate toward that which is easily accessible by large numbers of untutored audiences.[2]

In terms of the major aesthetic debates of the twentieth century concerning high art in contrast to so-called low art/popular art/kitsch, I think that the real contrast is between mass art and the avant-garde.[3] That is, avant-garde art, even if it deploys a mass technology, is the pertinent foil to mass art. For, put summarily, avant-garde art is designed to be "difficult" and typically requires special background training in order to be understood, whereas mass art is said to be "easy" and (optimally) requires little or no background training.

Movies are paradigmatically mass art in this sense. By characterizing movies as mass art, rather than merely as popular art, we are alerted to one of their primary functions. This, moreover, puts us in a position to explain why certain of its central devices serve the purposes of the movies so well. For as we shall see, point-of-view editing, for reasons to be discussed below, is especially suited to address mass, untutored audiences expeditiously. Thus, starting from a functionalist perspective, which regards the elicitation of mass consumption as a central aim of movies, we shall illuminate the role of point-of-view editing in virtue of the ways in which it facilitates this overarching goal.[4]

The focus of this paper is point-of-view editing as it serves as a functional element in mass arts, including movies and narrative TV.[5] Our aim is to explain, at least in some respects, its serviceability in securing the purpose of the movies, that is, in effectively addressing mass audiences.

When referring to point-of-view editing, I have in mind minimally a structure which involves two shots – what Edward Branigan calls a "point/glance" shot and a "point/object" shot.[6] The point/glance shot is of a person looking, generally offscreen; the point/object shot is putatively of whatever the person sees.[7] The elements of this structure can be iterated in various, expanded ways, and the point/glance shot may precede the point/object shot and vice-versa, in what Branigan respectively calls prospective and retrospective structures.[8]

My first purpose in discussing this structure is to attempt to explain how it is suited for communication (notably, for mass communication), in general, and for the communication of emotion, in particular. Secondarily, I will try to explain how this structure fits into the overall goal of popular movie narration. I distinguish my aims from those of Edward Branigan in his influential writings insofar as his energies, it seems to me, are spent on the description of point-of-view editing, whereas mine are aimed at explanations. This is not said in order to criticize Branigan but only to signal that I have a different, and perhaps complementary, interest.

What follows is divided into three parts, each of which develops a different hypothesis about point-of-view editing. The first hypothesis rests on characterizing point-of-view editing as a cinematic elaboration of ordinary perceptual practices. The second hypothesis tries to show the way in which the structure of point-of-view editing is deployed to represent the emotional states of characters. And the third hypothesis, exploiting the observations of the earlier two, speculates on why point-of-view editing serves the purposes of mass movie narration so well.

II. Point-of-View Editing and Ordinary Perception

One adaptive behavior of many animals (especially mammals) upon encountering another animal is to direct attention to the target of that other animal's attention.[9] In doing so, the mammal attempts to derive information about the newly encountered animal in terms of what interests it evinces and, in consequence, in terms of its practical intents. This behavior obviously has high survival value. And it is present in humans as well as other higher primates. We humans, of course, automatically mobilize this behavior not only with respect to other species but with respect to each other.

Norbert Wiener comments

Suppose I find myself in the woods with an intelligent savage who cannot speak my language and whose language I cannot speak. Even without any code of sign language common to the two of us, I can learn a great deal from him. All I need to do is to be alert to those moments when he shows signs of emotion or interest. I then cast my eyes around, perhaps paying special attention to the direction of his glance, and fix in my memory what I see or hear. It will not be long before I discover the things which seem important to him, not because he has communicated them to me by language, but because I myself have observed them.[10]

Moreover, this tendency to explore another's glance for information about her interests appears to take hold in infancy. George Butterworth and Lesley Grover, for example, have observed the relation of children to their mothers in rooms full of objects. Invariably, children follow the trajectory of their mother's glance to its target object.[11] This behavior begins to manifest itself in infants of two or three months of age. Butterworth and Grover's research concerns the conditions of verbal communication and one of their points is that looking where an interlocutor is looking is crucial. But their findings have relevance to communication and information gathering outside the context of verbal communication, since this virtually preprogramed response of following the glance of others is likely to be a means, perhaps bred in the bone, that humans possess for discovering the intent of others.

Undoubtedly, in certain cultures, people may be trained not to look at other people. But where such prohibitions are not in force, humans gravitate toward looking at what other humans are looking at as natural means of information gathering. A common practical joke when I was in grammar school was for a group of us to look up into the empty sky in order to "trick" some hapless passerby into doing likewise.

Let us suppose, then, that it is generally a natural human perceptual behavior, in the relevant circumstances, for a person x to follow the gaze of person y to its target. It would appear that this is a typical way in which we secure information about other persons and the environment. In this respect, this tendency is clearly an adaptive asset that, in all probability, is innate.

Moreover, it is a perceptual practice that can be readily represented in cinema. Recall the shot in *Rear Window* (directed by Alfred Hitchcock, 1954, USA) where the character played by Jimmy Stewart observes the character played by Raymond Burr gazing downward intently from his window; the camera follows Burr's line of vision to its target, a small dog, and this sets both Stewart and us to conjecturing about the way in which this small dog's activities figure in Burr's practical concerns.

In this example, the camera movement literally traces the trajectory from Burr's gaze to the dog, thereby representing what I have claimed to be a type of natural perceptual behavior. What happens in point-of-view editing – at least of the minimal, prospective variety – is that the camera movement between the gaze and the target is deleted.

In *Rear Window,* for example, a skeptical Grace Kelly suddenly looks surprised and asks Stewart to repeat his suspicions about Burr. This is followed by a shot of Burr tying up a piece of luggage, a shot we regard as showing us what earlier surprised Kelly. Or, in *Stagecoach* (John Ford, 1939, USA), just after the character played by John Carradine drapes his coat over the body of a dead women, we see him look up with concerned curiosity. There is a cut to signaling on the nearby hills, which we surmise to be the object of Carradine's concern.[12]

In these cases, despite the deletion of the camera movement, we are still able to recognize the structure as a representation of a typical perceptual behavior; indeed, we find it hard to resist regarding a cut from a gaze to an object as such, perhaps because when we naturally engage this sort of perceptual behavior it is the endpoints of the activity, and not the space between, that command our attention.

Our difficulty in seeing this representation otherwise, of course, is often exploited by avant-garde filmmakers. In Peter Kubelka's *Mosaik im Vertrauen* (Peter Kubelka, 1954 – 55, Austria), for example, at different times, the chauffeur and the bum appear, improbably, to be looking at the crash at Le Mans. That is, in the avant-garde film, the point-of-view format can be insistently used to link together "magically" spaces that cannot be thought to coexist.

As a first approximation, thinking along the lines of Hugo Munsterberg, we might think of point-of-view editing as an automatization, via editing, of our own natural perceptual reaction to track a glance to its target.[13] This structure is readily picked up and applied, virtually by reflex, because it has our own ingrained perceptual behavior as its prototype. It so closely simulates our perceptual behavior that we somehow take it as objectifying our own (would-be) perceptual responses.

But though this way of thinking is both suggestive and certainly not completely wrong, it needs some refinement. For the point-of-view structure is a *representation*. We do not take it to be the automatization of an act of seeing with one's own eyes, but rather recognize it to be a representation of perception.[14] At the same time, it is, like many "mimetic" pictures, a representation whose recognition is hard to avoid, since it is keyed in intimate ways to our perceptual makeup.

Structurally, it delivers the glance and the target, the nodal points of our perceptual prototype, while functionally it serves the congruent purpose of supplying information about the agent whose gaze concerns us. The correspondences between this cinematic device and ordinary perceptual behavior undoubtedly make it immensely accessible and almost irresistible, but without leading the viewer to mistake a communicative showing for her own perceptual activity.

In discussions of point-of-view editing, stress is often put on the importance of eyeline matches for this device. Undoubtedly, there are important historical conventions that emphasize eye-line matching and overall geographical plausibility to point-of-view editing. But these conventions can be violated without notice by the spectator and without any loss of recognition on the part of the audience of the communicative function of the structure.[15] In the voyage in *Dracula* (Tod Browning, 1931, USA), for example, there is a cut from the vampire as he comes on deck, looking hungrily, one presumes, to a mismatched shot of the crew fighting a storm. But despite the sloppiness of the editing, the audience has no problem drawing the correct conclusions, since we recognize that what is being represented is a natural perceptual path from a glance to its target – a pathway that has internal to it the expectation that a glance will be followed by its target. The audience's appreciation that point-of-view editing is a representation and thereby possibly a fictional representation is what makes such conventionally aberrant exercises such as *The White Gorilla* (Harry Fraser, 1945, USA) possible.[16]

Our first hypothesis, in summary, is that point-of-view editing is a representation rooted in our recognition of an innate perceptual behavior that moves from a gaze to its target. This perceptual behavior occurs naturally in situations where we are gathering information about our environment. The human gaze in such situations, as encountered naturally, may or may not be intentionally motivated to communicate information to us. With point-of-view editing, however, the gaze and the gaze-to-target structure is

prima facie communicative, a possibility that is based on the fact that it is always, *ex hypothesi*, informative. That is, an information delivering practice is turned into an intentionally communicative practice in point-of-view editing. Stated baldly, point-of-view editing can function communicatively because it is a representational elaboration of a natural information-gathering behavior. That is, point-of-view editing, of the prospective variety at least,[17] works because it relies on depicting biologically innate information-gathering procedures. This is why the device is so quickly assimilated and applied by masses of untutored spectators. Or so I hypothesize. Moreover, this hypothesis fits neatly with empiricial findings about the ease of comprehension of edited arrays by first-time viewers such as members of the Pokot tribe of Kenya.[18]

III. Point-of-View Editing and the Communication of Emotion

My first hypothesis concerned a claim about the way in which point-of-view editing functions in general as a medium of communication. Now I would like to develop a more particularized hypothesis about how this structure communicates information about the emotional states of the characters, specifically the characters portrayed in the point/glance shots. In the previous section, the target was emphasized as a source of information. In this section, both the face in the point/glance shot and the target will be discussed in terms of the ways they interact to yield information about the agent in the film who is doing the viewing. What I want to develop is an account of the different contributions that the point/glance shot and the point/object shot make to conveying information to the audience about the emotional state of the character in question.

In the lore of film theory, a story, called the Kuleshov experiment, has been passed down about how an actor with no change in his facial composure was taken to be expressing different emotions simply by virtue of juxtaposing his glance to diverse scenes.[19] When the actor's face was correlated to a bowl of soup, for example, he was thought to express hunger, while the selfsame face, composed in the same way, but juxtaposed to birds and clouds was thought to express a yearning for freedom.

Yet if this story is true in its details, which I doubt, it does not correspond to the typical deployment of point-of-view editing. For standard point-of-view editing uses the character's face to give us information about her emotional state with respect to what she sees. That is, the character's face is not, as standard versions of the Kuleshov experiment claim, emotionally amorphous, merely awaiting emotive shaping from ensuing shots.

In the point/glance shot of a character seeing a monster in a horror fiction, the character's face will generally register the disgust she feels toward the creature she is looking at: her nose may wrinkle, her upper lip is raised, her teeth are clenched, and her head and torso start backward in a withdrawal response. That is, before we see the monster in the point/object shot, we have already been given information about the character's emotional assessment of it. The question before us is how this can happen.

For nearly two decades, psychological investigation into the expression of facial emotion has amassed a compelling amount of data to the effect that for certain *basic* ranges of emotional expression, there is a surprising degree of cross-cultural uniformity.[20] That is, when members of different cultural groups, including preliterates unfamiliar with mass-media representations, are shown pictures of facial expressions of emotion, they tend to agree in their categorizations of the emotion in the pictures at rates far above what one would predict on the basis of chance.[21] Especially relevant to any discussion of point-of-view editing is the fact that this convergence increases when

the photos in the experiments have been posed. This is not to say that every imaginable emotion can be transculturally recognized, but only that there is a great deal of convergence across certain basic ranges of affect, including interest/excitement, enjoyment/joy, surprise/startle, distress/anguish, disgust/contempt, anger/rage, shame/humiliation, and fear/terror. This research lends credence to the conjecture, defended long ago by Darwin, that the recognition, and the expression, of emotion, at least along certain very basic dimensions, has an innate, biologically rooted origin.[22]

Turning from psychology to film theory, it seems reasonable to suppose that where part of the function of the point/glance shot is to convey information about emotion, it is generally able to do so, at least in some measure, by engaging the spectator's innate capacities to recognize the gross category into which the character's expression falls. That is, the point/glance shot is a device designed to activate our capacities of recognition in such a way that we identify the global emotional state of the relevant character. That this capacity is keyed to very basic emotional ranges is not a liability to postulating its activation with respect to movies, since in movies the emotions portrayed are quite basic.[23]

Here, of course, it is not my intention to deny that audiences may also determine the emotional state of a character in virtue of the narrative context but only that in addition to the narrative context the look of the character's face is of major significance in determining the character's emotional state in the vast number of cases. Moreover, in mass movies, the narrative context and the look of the character's face will generally provide redundant, reinforcing information about the character's emotional state. And, indeed, in some cases where the narrative context has not yet been elaborated to any significant degree, it will be the audience's ability to discern broad emotional states that will carry a primary burden in the audience's broad identification of the relevant emotional state of the character.

If the citation of this capacity of recognition provides part of an explanation of how point-of-view editing can convey information about emotion, it is nevertheless not the whole story. For, as noted, this capacity detects emotional states in terms of global or gross categories, whereas the emotions we find in movies are more often fine grained. The fear etched on Jimmy Stewart's face is not fear *simpliciter,* but vertigo, in the film of the same name. And the look of anger on the sailor's face when he glares at the plate he is about to smash in *Potemkin* (Sergei Eisenstein, 1925, USSR) is more specifically moral indignation. So the question becomes how does the point-of-view structure get us from global emotional attributions to more fine-grained ones?

Here it is important to recall that emotions are characteristically marked by intentionality. That is, they are directed, or, to speak more technically, they have objects. One is not simply angry; one is angry at someone or something. Often, though hardly always, the object of an emotion is coincident with its cause.[24] And with respect to point-of-view editing I would hazard the guess that the particular object of the character's emotion is generally a cause of the emotion. Moreover, in order to identify the emotional state a person is in with any precision, one needs to specify the object of the emotion in question. Emotions, to revert again to technical jargon, are identified primarily by their objects. To determine whether an emotional state accompanied by an accelerating heartbeat is to be identified as an instance of fear or amusement depends in large measure on the object of the emotion, for example, an assault rifle aimed at one's head, on the one hand, versus a clown taking a pratfall on the other.

This feature of emotions – that they have objects that serve to individuate them – has an important bearing on the representation of emotional states. Encountering a picture of a person in an emotional state, such as those found in Charles Le Brun's *Conférence sur l'expression général et particulière des passions,*[25] the viewer may have a global sense of the kind of emotion portrayed, but, as Richard Wollheim notes, there is "likely to be in the spectator's mind uncertainty, vagueness, or ambiguity, about the corresponding emotion."[26] The *particular* emotion portrayed, in other words, is somewhat underdetermined. What disambiguates or specifies the particular emotion for us is the apprehension of the object, which in pictorial representation is most often coincident with the cause, of the emotion. For example, the look of fear or shock or surprise on Seleucus's face in Ingres's painting *Antiochus and Stratonice* can be specified as a shock of revelation when we connect his glance to its cause or object, the waning Stratonice.[27]

So, the human face can give us very broad, generally reliable information about the emotional states of others. But this information can be ambiguous in certain respects: sometimes it may be difficult to differentiate closely related emotions like fear and surprise, and, in any case, when one only sees the face, it will be hard to specify the emotion in a fine-grained way – that is, to say what variety of fear or surprise or joy is at issue. In order to arrive at a more fine-grained and unambiguous characterization of the emotion, we depend on knowing the object or cause of the emotion in question.

Returning to point-of-view editing, my hypothesis is that the function of the point/object shot is to supply the viewer with the cause or object of the character's emotion in order to specify that emotion in a fine-grained way. In point-of-view editing that is devoted to conveying the emotional state of a character, we move from the glance to the target in order to ascertain the particular emotion of the character. In *Vertigo* (Alfred Hitchcock, 1958, USA) there is a scene in which the Jimmy Stewart character tries to overcome his affliction gradually. He climbs a short kitchen step ladder. Suddenly his face, shown in a point/glance shot, is gripped by fear or terror or anguish. The point/object shot shows us what he is looking at – the street several stories below. With this knowledge of the object or cause of his emotional state, we can specify it. It is not fear or anguish globally it is vertigo most particularly. This, of course, is not to deny that the narrative context of the event plays an extremely important role in our interpretation here. Nevertheless, the point/object shot still plays the crucial role in fixing and confirming that interpretation.

The relation of the point/glance shot to the point/object shot, where point-of-view editing is used to portray emotional states, has a reciprocal structure. The point/glance sets out a global range of emotions that broadly characterize the neighborhood of affective states the character could be in. The point/object shot, then, delivers the object or cause of the emotion, thereby enabling us to *focus on* the particular emotion within the broad categories of the affective range made available by the point/glance shot. That is, the point/object shot focuses or selects the particular emotion being portrayed. Using jargon we may say that the point/glance shot functions as a *range finder,* and the point/object shot functions as a *focuser,* specifying the relevant affect as a particular emotion within the range set forth by the point/glance shot.

In addition to this particular reciprocal relation between the point/glance shot and the point/object shot, there are other functional relationships within the point-of-view structure. For in setting the range of the emotion in question, the point/glance shot also, again in a broad way, primes (undoubtedly, most often, along with other elements of the narrative context) the spectator's reception and interpretation of the point/object shot. The manner in which this works relies on certain structural features of emotions.

Given emotions are elicited by objects that share certain general features. The emotion of disgust, for example, is elicited by objects that the emoter regards to be noxious or impure. If we have no reason to believe that an emoter takes an object to be impure or noxious, we will not attribute disgust to her. This is not to say that we must assess the object to be noxious, but that we must think that the emoter does. Emotions, that is, have formal criteria of applicability – what are sometimes, perhaps confusingly, called formal (as opposed to particular) objects.[28]

Thus, when a point/glance shot sets forth a character possessed, broadly speaking, by fear, that recognition on the viewer's part comes with the expectation that whatever is eliciting the fear, of whatever sort of fear it is, will meet certain evaluative criteria: for example, that in the subject's view the object in question is believed to be harmful. When the point/object shot arrives, the viewer will survey it in terms of those features of the situation that appropriately correspond to the kinds of emotion the point/glance shot makes available. The point/glance shot, in other words, provides a rough guide to what is salient, emotionally speaking, in the point/object shot.[29] For example, if the point/glance shot in a horror sequence initiates our recognition that the character is disgusted by what she sees, then when the point/object shot arrives, we will attend to the open sores on the zombie's body and not to his designer jeans.

One way to see the importance of the point/glance shot in guiding the reception of the point/object shot is to think about the difficulties we have in trying to follow a film like Dreyer's *Vampyr* (Carl Theodor Dreyer, 1931–32, France/Germany). One of the problems that we encounter with this film, I submit, is the blankness of David Grey's face. In point/glance shot after point/glance shot we have no inkling of what his reactive affect is to what he sees, and this leaves us at a loss about how to interpret the point/object shots of what he sees. Of course, in stressing the importance of the point/glance shot in setting up a broad expectational horizon with respect to the point/object shot, I am not denying that those expectations can be subverted. This can be done for intentional comic effect, as in *The Return of the Killer Tomatoes* (John De Bello, 1988, USA) when the visage of an elderly woman in a paroxysm of horror is emotionally mismatched with a shot of a smallish, lone tomato on a plate.

At the same time that the point/glance shot makes certain features of the point/ object shot apposite, the point/object shot clarifies and deepens the recognition of the emotion in the point/glance shot. In Gance's *Napoleon* (Abel Gance, 1927, France), when Camille Desmoulins enters the chamber of the triumvirate with a copy of *La Marseillaise,* we see a shot in which his face is tinged with consternation and fear; when we see the point/object shots of what he is looking at – the triumvirate in animated conversation – we are able to specify Desmoulins's look as the deferential fear of being intrusive.

The point of this section has been to explain how information about the emotional states of characters can be conveyed by point-of-view editing. By exploiting certain facts about emotion recognition and about the structure of the emotions, we can hypothesize that character affect is represented in point-of-view editing through reciprocal, functional relationships between the point/glance shot and the point/object shot such that the point/glance shot *sets the range* of the relevant emotion and *guides the reception* of the point/object shot while the point/object shot *focuses* or *specifies* the particular emotion represented. The point/ glance shot is able to set the range of the relevant emotion in virtue of our innate capacity to recognize certain basic, broad emotional categories from facial displays, and the point/glance shot shapes our reception of the point/object shot in virtue of the

fact that along with the recognition of an emotion comes a conception of the kinds of features appropriate to the elicitation of the emotion. The point/object shot specifies the emotion in question as a particularized emotion by supplying the viewer with the object or cause of the emotion as the target of the glance as discussed in the previous section.

IV. Point-of-View Editing and the Movies

If the two hypotheses we have developed with respect to point-of-view editing are persuasive, then maybe they can be further exploited to advance a third hypothesis about why point-of-view editing is such a serviceable device in movies. By movies, here, I mean popular commercial mass-market narratives in the style loosely designated Hollywood International, or more academically labeled the Classical Cinema.[30] Indeed, for my purposes, as noted earlier, the term *movies* applies to the products of narrative TV as well as to the products made for theatrical distribution.

Since movies are, by definition, aimed at mass markets, movie makers are apt to favor design elements that will render their narratives accessible to large audiences. That is, ideally, movies will exploit structures that make them susceptible to fast pick-up by untutored audiences. Elsewhere, I maintained that the fact that movie narration proceeds, to a great extent, by pictorial representation is a particular advantage in this respect.[31] For picture recognition is an innate capacity that evolves in tandem with object recognition. That the basic symbols in movies are pictures, then, provides mass, untutored audiences with virtually immediate access to the events portrayed in movies. Part of the mass appeal of movies, that is, results from the fact that audiences can apprehend the basic symbols in this mode of communication without learning a language – like code or specialized forms of inference or decipherment. At a certain level of visual narrative action, mass audience spectators can follow movies because of their innate capacity to recognize pictures. This is far from the whole story of how audiences understand movies. Nevertheless, our biologically rooted capacity to recognize pictures supplies an important element in any explanation of how mass audiences understand movies.

Similarly, we have hypothesized several ways in which point-of-view editing is connected to very basic features of perception. On the one hand, the glance to target trajectory, of which the point-of-view structure is a compelling representation, recapitulates a very fundamental perceptual practice; it is easy to pick up and to follow by mass, untutored audiences exactly because it tracks information in the way we naturally track information and, consequently, can be recognized as a representation thereof.

Likewise, mass audiences, lacking any special training in detecting facial expressions, can nevertheless *generally* derive information about the emotional states of characters portrayed in point-of-view structures because certain very basic ranges of emotional expression are transculturally legible.[32] That blind children evince certain emotional states by means of facial expressions very similar to those emitted by sighted people worldwide strongly suggests that said expressions are innate, and, in consequence, that would explain their cross-cultural intelligibility.[33]

That these aspects of point-of-view editing can operate by exploiting and elaborating biologically rooted capacities imbues the structure with a high degree of legibility for mass audiences untrained in specialized codes or processes of reading or inference. This is not to deny that the point-of-view structure is a symbolic artifact of communication; rather, it is a symbol system that functions in large measure by engaging generic human capacities of recognition.

Moreover, since these sorts of capacities are the sort of thing that mass audiences are most likely to have in common, they provide particularly expeditious means to the ends of mass movie communication.

Put succinctly, then, our last hypothesis is that point-of-view editing serves the purposes of movie narration so well because to the degree to which it is keyed to biologically rooted and transculturally distributed features of perception, it guarantees fast pickup and a high degree of accessibility to mass untutored audiences, crucial desiderata for the persistence of any device in the economy of the movies.

This hypothesis should not be regarded as an example of biological determinism. It is not our claim that movies were destined to adopt the communicative structure of point-of-view editing. Movies without recourse to point-of-view editing can and have been made. We do not assert that the emergence of point-of-view editing was mandated by human nature. There is, for example, no reason to reject the possibility that point-of-view editing might never have been discovered.

Rather our claim is that, given certain of our biological propensities, point-of-view editing, once discovered, was an extremely viable and compelling means of visual communication in general and of emotional communication in particular. For supposing that the aim of mass movie entertainment is to engage (numerically) mass, untutored audiences, point-of-view editing is a ready source of communication because of the way in which it taps into or exploits biologically rooted, perceptual behaviors.

Of course, the filmmakers who introduced point-of-view editing did not do so on the basis of the theoretical conception articulated in this paper. They embraced point-of-view editing because it worked – because it facilitated the rapid pickup and visual understanding of their product by audiences worldwide who lacked any training in the so-called language of the medium. That point-of-view editing is keyed to our biological makeup undoubtedly enhanced the reception of the point-of-view structure. This is not to say that every successful communicative structure deployed by the mass arts will be biologically rooted, but only that biologically rooted structures, like point-of-view editing, will be attractive devices, for by-now obvious reasons, in promoting visual comprehension on a mass scale.

We began by noting that movies are a paradigmatic mass art form. In order to function in this way, movie structures, such as point-of-view editing, must facilitate the possibility of mass consumption. This requires that the structures be accessible to an international audience that has not been explicitly trained in the reception of a language-like code. One way for movies to achieve this end – as exemplified by point-of-view editing – is to engage generic perceptual tendencies. For a design element predicated on generic tendencies is, *ceteris paribus*, a likely candidate for mass consumption. Future research into the effectiveness of mass art may benefit from this analysis of point-of-view editing by attempting to isolate further features of mass arts, including the movies, that succeed by exploiting our biological inheritances. Undoubtedly, this will not provide us with the whole story of the reception of either movies in particular or mass art in general. However, it may enable us to appreciate certain crucial features of mass art that have been hitherto ignored due to the obsession with codes, construed as arbitrary, that has hypnotized cultural studies for the last two decades.[34]

Notes

1. See Noël Carroll, *Mystifying Movies: Fads and Fallacies in Contemporary Film Theory* (New York: Columbia University Press, 1988); and Noël Carroll, "Cognitivism, Con-temporary Film Theory and Method," reprinted in this volume.

2. This conception of mass art is defended at greater length in: Noël Carroll, "The Nature of Mass Art," *Philosophic Exchange* (1992); and Noël Carroll, "Mass Art, High Art and the Avant-Garde: A Response to David Novitz," *Philosophic Exchange* (1992).

3. Noël Carroll, "Philosophical Resistance to Mass Art," in *Affirmation and Negation in Contemporary American Culture,* edited by Gerhard Hoffman and Alfred Hornung (Heidelberg: Universitätsverlag C. Winter, 1994).

4. I have developed similar functionalist analyses of the roles played by pictorial representation, variable framing, narrative, and music in the movie system in other writings, including Noël Carroll, *Mystifying Movies;* "The Power of Movies"; and "Notes on Movie Music." The two essays just cited are reprinted in this volume.

5. The point-of-view format can also function in other media such as comic book illustration and photojournalism.

6. Edward Branigan, *Point of View in the Cinema* (New York: Mouton, 1984), p. 103.

7. Branigan, here, intends to follow Mitry. (See Branigan, p. 103; and Jean Mitry, *Esthetique et psychologie du cinema* (Paris: Editions Universitaires, 1965 vol. II, p. 212). With minor variations, I follow Branigan's and Mitry's stipulations for the narrow phenomenon I designate.

8. Branigan, p. 111.

9. This general claim about mammals has been advanced by Robert Gordon in his book, *The Structure of Emotions* (Cambridge University Press, 1987), p. 148. There is also evidence that the piping plover tracks the gaze of intruders. See, for example, Carolyn A. Ristau, "Aspects of the Cognitive Ethology of an Injury-Feigning Bird, The Piping Plover" in *Cognitive Ethology: The Minds of Other Animals,* edited by Carolyn A. Ristau (Hillsdale: Lawrence Erlbaum Associates, 1991), pp. 102–04. Perhaps indirect evidence that animals naturally track the glance of other animals for information is the way in which some animals inhibit their attention in order to mislead other animals about their intentions. Jane Godall tells the story of the

chimpanzee Figan who hid so that his glance would not give away his interest in a certain banana to Goliath, another chimpanzee. See: Jane Godall, *In the Shadow of Man* (London: Collins, 1971); Alison Jolly, "Conscious Chimpanzees? A Review of Recent Literature," in *Cognitive Ethology*, p. 240; and A. Whiten and R. W. Bryne, "The Manipulation of Attention in Primate Tactical Deception," in *Machiavellian Intelligence,* ed. by R. W. Byrne and A. Whiten (Oxford: Oxford University Press, 1988). At the level of annecdote, I have also been told by Arthur Danto of a case of a young monkey who, in order to flee from his elders, looked off into the distance; when the elder monkeys followed his glance to its target, the younger monkey used the opportunity to run away in the opposite direction.

10. Norbert Wiener, *Cybernetics* (Cambridge, Mass: MIT Press, 1978), p. 157.

11. George Butterworth and Lesley Grover, "Origins of Referential Communication in Infancy," in *Thought without Language,* edited by Lawrence Wiskrantz (Oxford University Press, 1988).

12. An interesting but slightly more complicated case occurs in Carné's *Les visiteurs du soir* (Marcel Carné, 1942, France). In the banquet scene, during the dance, the character Ann looks offscreen and her jealous suitor follows her glance. Once the jealous suitor is locked into the trajectory of her gaze, there is a cut to Gilles returning her attention, which, in turn, heralds the birth of a love triangle. Figuratively speaking, one might say that the jealous suitor enacts the role that this paper attributes to the ordinary viewer with respect to point-of-view editing in general.

13. Hugo Munsterberg, *The Film: A Psychological Study* (New York: Dover, 1969).

14. In stressing that with point-of-view editing the spectator is recognizing a representation of perception I mean to be averting the claim that some process of identification is involved in assimilating point-of-view editing. This sets me off from contemporary film theorists like Daniel Dayan and his version of suture theory. For statements of the suture approach, see Daniel Dayan "The Tutor Code of Classical Cinema," in *Movies and Methods,* edited by Bill Nichols (Berkeley and Los Angeles: University of California Press, 1976), and Jean-Pierre Oudart, "Cinema and Suture," *Screen* 18 (Winter 1977–78). For criticism of the identification/suture approach to point-of-view editing see: David Bordwell, *Narration and the Fiction Film* (Madison: University of Wisconsin Press, 1985); William Rothman, "Against the System of Suture," in *Movies and Methods;* Barry Salt, "The Last of Suture," *Film Quarterly* (1978); Noël Carroll, *Mystifying Movies,* pp. 183–98.

15. Here I believe that I differ from theorists like Nick Browne in the importance (or the lack thereof) that I place on spatial position for understanding the point-of-view figure. See Nick Browne, "The Spectator in Text," in *Narrative, Apparatus, Ideology*, edited by Philip Rosen (New York: Columbia University Press, 1986).

16. This is, in effect, a film composed of two films: a silent jungle adventure serial attached to a nineteen-forties, sound framing story. The nineteen-forties footage is segued with the earlier footage through the point-of-view shots of the narrator in the framing story; what he supposedly sees is the stuff of the silent jungle serial.

Edward Branigan has suggested to me that a similar point might be made with respect to the better-known film *Dead Men Don't Wear Plaid* (Carl Reiner, 1982, USA). Like *The White Gorilla,* this film interweaves footage from earlier movies – generally detective films – with contemporary footage of Steve Martin playing a private eye. And, in some cases, the segue between the earlier footage and the more recent footage is secured by means of the sort of point-of-view structure described in this paper. For example, the shots between Martin and Edward Arnold (from a sequence of *Johnny Eager* [Mervyn Leroy, 1941, USA]) are linked via point-of-view editing.

17. On this account, retrospective point-of-view editing is understood as a variation on prospective point-of-view editing. Prospective point-of-view editing seems to me to be more basic. One reason that I have for suspecting this is that very often it seems to me that a point-of-view figure that is introduced with a point/object shot very often follows the point/glance shot with another point/object shot.

This functions to establish that the framework is basically that of point-of-view by literally incorporating the prospective structure in the retrospective structure.

18. This point has been defended by Renee Hobbs, Richard Frost, Arthur Davis, and John Stauffer. See Renee Hobbs et al. "How First Time Viewers Comprehend Editing Conventions," *Journal of Communication* 38 no. 4 (1988). Paul Messsaris and the National Institute of Education have also produced interesting discussions of ways in which viewers come to comprehend edited arrays. See Paul Messaris, "To What Extent Does One Have to Learn to Interpret Movies," in *Film/Culture*, edited by S. Thomas (Metuchen: Scarecrow Press, 1982); and *National Conference on Visual Information Processing* (Washington, D.C.: Report to the National Institute of Education, 1974).

19. Lev Kuleshov, *Kuleshov on Film*, edited by Ronald Levaco (Berkeley and Los Angeles: University of California Press, 1974), pp. 53–54.

20. Though there are debates in the literature and though I do not subscribe to every claim found in the literature, there does seem to be agreement that there is noteworthy cross-cultural convergence in the identification of basic emotions. See: Carroll Izard, *The Face of Emotion* (New York: Appleton Crofts, 1971); Paul Ekman, Wallace Friesen and Phoebe Ellsworth, *Emotion in the Human Face* (Cambridge University Press, 1972); Paul Ekman and Wallace Friesen, *Unmasking the Face* (Englewood Cliffs: Prentice-Hall, 1975); Paul Ekman, "Cross-Cultural Studies in Facial Expression," in *Darwin and Facial Expression*, edited by Paul Ekman (New York: Academic Press, 1973); Paul Ekman, "Expressions and the Nature of Emotion," in *Approaches to the Emotions*, edited by Klaus Scherer and Paul Edkman (Hillsdale: Lawrence Erlbaum Publishers, 1984); Paul Ekman, Robert Levenson, and Wallace Friesen, "Autonomic Nervous Activity Distinguishes among Emotions," *Science* 221 (September 1983); and R. B. Zajonc, "Emotions and Facial Efference: A Theory Reclaimed," *Science* 228 (April, 1985).

21. Ekman, "Expression and the Nature of Emotion."

22. See Charles Darwin, *The Expression of Emotion in Man and Animal* (Chicago: University of Chicago Press, 1965); and Paul Ekman, "Cross-Cultural Studies of Facial Expression."

23. As are the situations – concerning life and death suspense, and romance – that movies so often depict. Perhaps the content of movies is also influenced by the concern for mass appeal. Crude life-and-death struggles are possibly basic enough to be recognized and followed by wide-ranging audiences, irrespective of their different cultural backgrounds.

24. This assertion runs afoul of a well-known doctrine of Hume's to the effect that the objects of emotion cannot be their causes. Grounds for suspecting Hume's claim have been advanced by Helen Nissenbaum in *Emotion and Focus* (Stanford: Center for the Study of Language and Information, 1985), pp. 15–21.

25. As is well known, Le Brun was interested in developing a system of emblems for the emotions; this endeavor, with certain qualifications, would not seem, in principle, completely outlandish, given the findings of some of the psychologists cited above. See Charles LeBrun, *Conférence sur l'expression général et particulières des passions* (Verona, 1751). Stephanie Ross has also published a very interesting in-depth discussion of Le Brun's project. (Stephanie Ross, "Painting the Passions," *The Journal of the History of Ideas* 45 (January/March, 1984).

26. Richard Wollheim, *Painting as Art* (Princeton: Princeton University Press, 1987), p. 88.

27. Wollheim, p. 257.

28. William Lyons has provided an extremely clear discussion of the formal object of emotion. See William Lyons *Emotion* (Cambridge University Press, 1980), pp. 99–104.

29. Ronald DeSousa has provided a useful discussion of the way in which the emotion "gestalts" a situation. See: Ronald DeSousa, "The Rationality of the Emotions," in *Explaining the Emotions*, edited by Amelie Okensberg Rorty (Berkeley and Los Angeles: University of California Press, 1980), pp. 142–43.

30. See David Bordwell, Janet Staiger, and Kristin Thompson, *The Classical Hollywood Cin-*

ema (New York: Columbia University Press, 1985).

31. Noël Carroll, *Mystifying Movies,* pp. 138–46.

32. Of course, I have never maintained that all emotions are transculturally recognizable. There are many that are not. In order to apprehend these, contextual features, rooted in the narrative, rather than mere facial dis-play, as well as information about the culture, will be required by the nonnative viewer (e.g., the European watching a Japanese film).

33. Izard, p. 61.

34. I would like to thank Richard Shusterman, Edward Branigan, and David Bordwell for their comments in response to an earlier version of this paper.

CHAPTER IX

Notes on Movie Music

Movie music often fails to receive proper attention in film analyses and film theories. Perhaps one reason for this is that the highly technical language of musical analysis intimidates the film expert. The non-musically trained analyst of film realizes s/he is unable to explore a movie's music in the professionally preferred idiom, and, debarred from the *lingua franca* of music criticism, decides to say nothing at all. The purpose of this short paper is to supply a musically-nontechnical way of speaking about one use of movie music, which we call modifying music. We shall attempt to describe the structure of this sort of music, to explain how it works and how it fits into the system of popular expression called the movies.[1]

There are, of course, many different functions that music can perform in relation to movies. Aaron Copland suggested five broad functions: creating atmosphere; underlining the psychological states of characters; providing neutral background filler; building a sense of continuity; sustaining tension and then rounding it off with a sense of closure.[2] These do not seem to be necessarily exclusive categories, nor do they exhaust the range of functions that music can perform in movies. This is not said in order to criticize Copland, for, in fact, we intend to follow his example. We shall analyze *a* function of movie music, freely admitting that there are others, and, moreover, we shall not deny that this function may also be yoked together with the performance of other functions, such as those Copland enumerates.

The type of music we have in mind is quite central in popular movies; it is a basic use of music, if not the most basic. To approach it, let us consider some examples. In *Gunga Din* (dir. by George Stevens; music by Alfred Newman), there is an early scene where the British, led by Cary Grant, Douglas Fairbanks Jr. and Victor McLaglen, enter a seemingly deserted village in search of foul doings. Indeed, the village has been raided by the nefarious Thugs, and those dastardly followers of Kali are lying in wait for the British. We have been somewhat alerted to this insofar as the scene is initiated by the use of an oboe in imitation of the sort of double-reed instrument associated with snake charmers, thereby signaling the presence of the Thugs in the deserted village. There is an ambush. During the ensuing battle, there is a recurring theme that is associated with the efforts of Grant, McLaglen and Fairbanks. Earlier, we had heard the same theme accompanying their drunken brawl over a treasure map. In the ambush scene, an interlude of strings will be followed by horns at a scherzo-like tempo. Often this theme comes in when our soldiers of fortune gain the upper hand, but not always. The horns are bouncy, light and playful. The battle scene, full of death and danger, could be the object of high anxiety. But the use of the horns in this theme color the scene in such a way that we come to view it as a lark, as a game, as comic rather than potentially tragic. This, of course, corresponds to one of the views of war and manhood that the film promotes – i.e., war as an outlet for boyish, beamish energy. Of course, from our point of view, what is important about the scene is the way in which the scherzo-like refrain directs the audience to view the mayhem as jaunty – almost comic – good fun.

In *Rebel without a Cause* (dir. by Nicholas Ray; music by Leonard Rosenman), we find a wholly different feeling associated with the onscreen violence. Underlying the confrontation and the fight, called the "blade game," which occurs after the visit to the planetarium, is atonal music, marked by odd time signatures and dissonant blaring brass. The use of the timpani and horns, along with the timing, give the music a Stravinsky-like flavor. As well, the music is sometimes recorded low, and, then, abruptly, the recording level is raised. The dissonance imparts a brooding feeling to the scene, a sense of latent, almost muscular violence that flashes out when the brass blares or the recording level shoots up. The uneasy, unstable quality of the music serves to characterize the psychological turmoil – the play of repression and explosive release – with which the scene is concerned.

For an example not involved with violence, consider the opening of *The Yearling* (dir. by Clarence Brown; music by Herbert Stothart). The camera displays views of the Everglades, as Gregory Peck, playing a Civil War veteran, recalls how he came to make his home there. The score is dominated by strings which have strong connotations of richness and lushness reflecting, of course, the way in which the narrator feels about this place. What Peck's voice and the visuals may fail to make you realize about the landscape, the music enables you to grasp. Also, the strings have a slightly haunting flavor and a sense of pastness which coincides with the appearance this film suggests of being swathed in memory. When we are introduced to the juvenile lead, Jody (played by Claude Jarman Jr.), the music sounds somewhat pentatonic, like an elongated country melody, conveying a feeling that is both lazy and dreamy. This not only corresponds to what we immediately see of Jody – he is playing listlessly with a toy windmill – but to what we learn of Jody throughout the film, viz., that he is a dreamer. In terms of the subject matter of the film, a major source of tension between Peck and his wife, played by Jane Wyman,

develops because Peck believes that youth *should* be a time when the imagination is given its head, before the hardships and responsibilities of practical life force one to turn to sterner things. Wyman resists this, and the battle between youth and imagination on the one hand, versus adulthood and practicality, on the other, is staged over Flag, the yearling from whom the film derives its title. Throughout *The Yearling,* the use of the strings repeatedly stresses the theme of the imagination by underscoring and characterizing the various spoken reveries and gambolings of characters in terms of an undeniable, albeit very nineteen-fortyish, feeling of dreaminess.

These examples are not alike in every respect. The theme from *Gunga Din* functions narratively as a leitmotif, whereas the example from *Rebel without a Cause* does not. However, the three examples share a very basic function, one which in fact enables the theme from *Gunga Din* to do its more specialized work so well. Namely, in each of these examples the music characterizes the scene, i.e., imbues the scene with certain expressive properties. This may be a matter of enhancing qualities that are already suggested in the imagery, but it need not be; the music may attribute an otherwise unavailable quality to the visuals. Nor does the expressive quality in question have to be grounded in the psychology of a character; in the *Gunga Din* example the *jauntiness* of the music appears to attach first and foremost to the action rather than to internal states of characters. And, lastly, the expressive qualities projected in these examples are in the music. We do not suddenly become dreamy when we hear the strings of *The Yearling.* Rather the dreaminess of the music characterizes Jody as dreamy to us. If we are pro-dreaminess, the way Gregory Peck and the film are, then we are apt to feel sympathetic (rather than dreamy) in regard to Jody. That is, by speaking of the projection of expressive qualities, we are not claiming that the music arouses in the spectator the self-same expressive qualities that it projects.

We can call this use of movie music *modifying music*. The music modifies the movie. The music possesses certain expressive qualities which are introduced to modify or to characterize onscreen persons and objects, actions and events, scenes and sequences. To use a crude analogy, one which must be eventually abandoned, the visual track is to a noun as the music is to an adjective, or alternatively, the visuals are to verbs as the music is to adverbs. Just as adjectives and adverbs characterize, modify and enrich the nouns and verbs to which they are attached, modifying music serves to add *further* characterization to the scenes it embellishes. This is a very pervasive use of movie music. Let us now turn to a discussion of its origin and its internal dynamics.

Movie music involves co-ordinating two different symbol systems: music and movies, the latter including not only visuals but recorded sounds, both natural and dialogic. In the case of modifying music, these two symbol systems are placed in a complementary relationship; each system supplies something that the other system standardly lacks, or, at least, does not possess with the same degree of effectiveness that the other system possesses.

Music, for example, is a highly expressive symbol system. This is not to say that all music is expressive or that it should be expressive, but only that much music is expressive. For example, that the Prelude to *Tristan and Isolde* is expressive of yearning or that the "Great Gate of Kiev" from *Pictures at an Exhibition* is expressive of majesty are part of the incontestable data of aesthetic theorizing. To say that the music is expressive is to say that it projects qualities describable in anthropomorphic, emotive terms. The symbol system of music is also sometimes thought to have more direct access to the emotive realm than any other symbol system. Nietzsche called music "the immediate language of the will."[3]

At the same time it is often noted that nonvocal music – orchestral music – though quite effective in expressing a broad palette of emotions, is not the ideal means for particularizing the feelings it projects. That is, a piece of nonvocal orchestral music may strike us as sorrowful or even more broadly as "down" but we generally cannot specify much further the kind of dolors or dumps the music projects. Is it melancholic, neurasthenic, suicidal, adolescent, etc.? That is, nonvocal music standardly lacks what music theorist Peter Kivy calls emotive explicitness.[4]

This lack of emotive explicitness has figured in numerous debates in the history of music. Some, like Johann Adam Hiller, took it as a limitation to be overcome, urging that if music is to become intelligible, i.e., emotively explicit, it must be combined with speech.[5] A similar view was espoused by James Beattie, who held that "the expression of music without poetry is vague and ambiguous."[6] Peter Kivy has brilliantly demonstrated that the development of the expressive arsenal of orchestral music, as we know it, was the result of solving the *perceived* problem of music's emotive inexplicitness through text setting.[7] In a different mood, Eduard Hanslick argued against the expression of emotion as a goal of music because he believed that music cannot express definite emotions,[8] while Nietzsche, staking out an altogether different position, sees the emotive inexplicitness of music as the path to some coveted form of universality: ". . . whoever gives himself up entirely to the impression of a symphony, seems to see all possible events of life and the world take place in himself."[9]

The vicissitudes of the preceding positions are less important to us than their recurring assumption, which we shall state weakly as follows: typically, nonvocal music is expressive of emotive qualities but ones that are inexplicit, ambiguous and broad. A theoretical explanation of why this should be is also readily available. Emotions are directed, directed at persons, objects, states of affairs and events. Indeed, it is in virtue of the objects to which emotions are directed that we individuate emotions.[10] I am afraid *of being run over by a train;* you are in love *with Bob;* we are angered *by apartheid.* For an emotion to be fully explicit and particularized, it must be aimed at some object. The object may be real, like South Africa, or fantasized, e.g., you may be terrified of The Green Slime. To become explicit, that is, the emotion must be referred to something. To say whether the joy in the music is hysterical or utopian, we would have to know toward what the joy was directed. And, of course, it is this sort of reference that is most commonly absent from music, that is, nonvocal music. Insofar as representation is not a primary function of standard orchestral music, most music of this sort will lack the logical machinery to secure emotive particularity. This is not to say that orchestral music cannot be representational: e.g., *Wellington's Victory,* Honegger's *Pacific 231* and the use of percussion to *refer* to King Kong's offscreen footsteps in the film of the same name.[11] And where the music is representational, a measure of emotive explicitness may be achievable. However, as we have said, as a matter of fact, most nonvocal music lacks the logical machinery which emotive explicitness requires.

So far we have claimed that orchestral music of the sort often employed in movies is a symbol system that makes a powerful yet broad and inexplicit emotive address. And this inexplicitness, in turn, is a result of the fact that generally such music is non-referring. Movies, on the other hand, are symbol systems with numerous overlapping referential dimensions, including the cinematographic image, dialogue, narrative and synched sound. Wedding the musical system to the movie system, then, supplies the kind of reference required to particularize the broad expressivity of the musical system. The *dreaminess* of the strings in *The Yearling* is specified as Jody's dreaminess, as the

dreaminess of a young boy prior to the hard lessons of life.

The relation between the music and the movie in the case of modifying music is reciprocal. The movie – the visuals, the narrative, the dialogue and the synched sound – serve as *indicators.* At one level, these elements establish what the scene is about. They indicate the reference of the scene. The music then modifies or characterizes what the scene is about in terms of some expressive quality. In a manner of speaking, the music tells us something, of an emotive significance, about what the scene is about; the music supplies us with, so to say, a description (or presentation) of the emotive properties the film attaches to the referents of the scene.

In our *Gunga Din* example, the movie establishes the subject, the battle, and the music imbues it with a feeling, that of jauntiness. The musical element, which we call a *modifier,* fills-in the subject matter in terms of the feeling the filmmaker finds appropriate to the scene. However, at the same time, the movie elements, what we have called indicators, stand in an important relation of influence to the musical component. The music on its own is bouncy, light and comic. When conjoined with the movie elements those feelings become further particularized as manly, daredevil bravado. The musical system, so to speak, carves out a broad range or spectrum of feeling, in this case, one that is positive, lively and energetic. The movie elements, the indicators, then narrow down or *focus* more precisely the qualities in that range or spectrum that are relevant to the action. The music no longer signals mere energy but more precisely bravado. This focusing operation of movie-as-indicator, in turn, enables the music-as-modifier to fill-in the action as a highly particularized feeling.

It might be initially helpful to think of the relation of the movie-as-indicator and the music-as-modifier on the model of the subject-predicate relation: the music says

". . . is jaunty" and the movie specifies the blank with "the battle." However, though suggestive, this analogy cannot be taken too seriously because the movie elements perform functions other than referring and focussing, and because the linguistic notion of predication seems to be strictly inapplicable to the image track in cinema (i.e., pictures lack discriminable subject-predicate elements and show objects with their properties, all-at-once, so to speak). Thus, though modifying music resembles linguistic predication loosely, it should not be taken as a literal example of it.

Another possible avenue of misunderstanding modifying music would be an oversimplification that regards music as exclusively expressive and the movie components as exclusively representational. As was earlier remarked, music can be used representationally. Similarly, movie elements have myriad means of expression – not only through acting, but through lighting, camera movement, camera angulation, cutting, etc. Indeed, the generally referential soundtrack can be "musically" arranged in order to aspire to musical expressivity, e.g., the natural sounds at the opening of *Street Scenes* and the dialogue in *Force of Evil*. Thus, it is not the case that the movie is pure representation to be supplemented by means of musical expression. However, in reaching out for music, the movie is seeking to incorporate an added, particularly powerful, augmented means of expression along with the visual, narrative, and dramatic means already at its disposal. The addition of music gives the filmmaker an especially direct and immediate means for assuring that the audience is matching the correct expressive quality with the action at hand. This is not to say that music is the film's only expressive lever; rather it is a notably direct and reliable one. It enhances the filmmaker's expressive control over the action.

If adding music to the movie enhances one's expressive control over the action, it is also the case that the movie imagery intensi-fies the impact of the music by particularizing its affective resonance. The unnerving, shrieking strings in *Psycho* are cruel, painful and murderous when matched with Norman Bates's descending knife. Here, the reference afforded by the movie elements serves to individuate the emotive content of the music in the way that the narrative and pantomime do in ballet, and as the words do in a popular song or opera.

Modifying music is one of the major uses of music in popular movies. It may be used to embellish individual scenes and sequences, or it may be integrated into leitmotif systems, etc. Structurally, modifying music involves the use of movie elements – photography, narrative, dialogue, and synched sound – as *indicators* that fix the reference of a shot, scene or sequence. The associated musical elements are *modifiers* which attribute expressive qualities to the referent, thereby characterizing it emotively as, for example, dreamy or jaunty. Functionally, the addition of musical modifiers to the scene augments the expressivity of the scene, though this does not preclude the possibility that the scene already possesses many nonmusical expressive devices. Nevertheless, music is a particularly privileged means of direct, expressive augmentation. The musical modifiers function to *fill-in* the scene expressively, to set the expressive tone the filmmaker takes to be appropriate to the scene. The music "saturates" the scene expressively. At the same time that the musical modifiers influence the reception of the movie, the movie indicators also reciprocally influence the reception of the music. For music typically, sans referential machinery, projects a very broad and inexplicit range of emotive qualities. Thus, in *The African Queen,* when the boat is stuck in the canal, the slow, spaced out drum beats project a generic, plodding feeling while the movie elements specify that feeling as Bogart's effort, an effort charged with all his hopes and commitments. Thus, as the music fills-in the movie, the movie *focuses* the emotive content of the music, particularizing and intensifying its effect which, of course, also abets the filling-in work that the musical modifier does.

We have attempted to explain the way in which modifying music operates. Modifying music is not employed, of course, only in movies – it occurs in other sorts of films, such as art films, as well as in other artforms, such as ballet. As well, it is not the only use of music found in movies. Yet, though the relation between modifying music and the movies is not unique in any sense, there is a way in which modifying music serves the aims of the movie symbol system quite expeditiously. That is, there is something especially fitting about the relationship between the modifying music and the movies. Thus, we will conclude by sketching the way that modifying music segues into the economy of the movies.

Movies are a means of popular expression. They are aimed at mass audiences. They aspire for means of communication that can be grasped almost immediately by untutored audiences. Another way of putting this is to say that movie makers seek devices that virtually guarantee that the audience will follow the action in the way that the filmmaker deems appropriate.[12] The movie close-up, for example, assures the filmmaker that the spectator is looking exactly where she should be looking at the appropriate moment. And, the close-up guarantees this automatically. Similarly, modifying music, given the almost direct expressive impact of music, assures that the untutored spectators of the mass movie audience will have access to the desired expressive quality and, in turn, will see the given scene or sequence under its aegis. Secondly, an important element accounting for the power of movies is the clarity that movies bestow upon the events that they depict. In contrast to our encounters in everyday life, movie events have an unaccustomed intelligibility and lucidity; movies, that is, are so much more legible than life.

Modifying music contributes to the clarity of movies in several different respects. The filling-in function of the music modifier keeps the expressive quality of the scene constantly foregrounded, thereby supplying a continuous channel of information about the emotional significance of the action. Unlike our quotidian experience of events, the music constantly alerts us to the feeling that goes with what we see. Whereas in life, the affect that goes with an observation is so often unknown, in movies, we not only have some affect but also the appropriate affect tied to virtually everything we see, through modifying music. The movie-world is emotionally perspicuous through and through.

Reciprocally, the focusing function of the movie indicators render the emotive content of the music more and more explicit, again enhancing clarity in yet another way. The concerted interplay of the music and the movie yields images replete with highly clarified, virtually directly accessible, expressive qualities. Thus, though modifying music is not a unique feature of movies, its capacity for promoting immediately accessible, explicit and continually emotive characterizations of the ongoing, onscreen action makes it *so suitable* to the presiding commitments of mass movie communication that *it would be a mystery* had movies failed to exploit it.[13]

Notes

1. For a discussion of what is meant by "movies" in this paper, see Noël Carroll, "The Power of Movies," in *Daedalus,* no. 114 (Autumn, 1985). This article is in this volume.

2. Aaron Copland, "Tip to Moviegoers: Take off those Ear-Muffs," in *The New York Times,* Nov. 6, 1949, section six, p. 28. This article is discussed at length in Roy M. Prendergast's *Film Music: A Neglected Art* (New York: Norton, 1977), Chap. 6.

3. Friedrich Nietzsche, *The Birth of Tragedy and the Case of Wagner,* translated by Walter Kaufman (New York: Random House, 1967), p. 103.

4. Peter Kivy, *The Corded Shell* (New Jersey: Princeton University Press, 1980), p. 98.

5. Johann Adam Hiller, "Abhandlung von der Nachahmung der Natur in der Musik," in *Historisch-Kritische Beyträge,* ed. by Friedrich Wilhelm Marpurg (Berlin, 1754), Vol. I, p. 524.

6. James Beattie, *The Philosophical and Critical Works* (Hildesheim and New York: Georg Olms, 1975), p. 463.

7. Kivy, *The Corded Shell.*

8. Eduard Hanslick, *The Beautiful in Music,* translated by Gustav Cohen (New York: The Liberal Arts Press, 1957).

9. Nietzsche, *Birth of Tragedy,* p. 102.

10. A source for this view of the emotions is Anthony Kenny, *Action, Emotion and Will* (London: Routledge and Kegan Paul, 1963).

11. For a thorough account of musical representation see Peter Kivy, *Sound and Semblance* (New Jersey: Princeton University Press, 1984).

12. For an amplification of the view of the movie system asserted above see Carroll, "The Power of Movies," which is included in this volume.

13. Though we stress a functional relation between sound and image in movies, our position should not be confused with the one propounded in *Composing for the Films* by Theodor Adorno and Hans Eisler. Our position is *closer* to that articulated by Schopenhauer when he writes in the Third Book of *The World as Will and Idea* that "Suitable music played to any scene, action, event or surrounding seems to disclose to us its most secret meaning, and appears as the most accurate and distinct commentary upon it."

CHAPTER X

**Notes on the
Sight Gag**

Although claims about "firsts" always seem disputable when it comes to the history of film, a case can be made that the first film was a comedy – depending on whether one dates *Fred Ott's Sneeze* as having been made in 1889 or 1892. In any case, comedy appeared early in film history. Thomas Edison provided peep shows of clowns and a kinetoscope series entitled *Monkeyshines,* which, at least, suggests comic doings. In terms of films made for the screen, the first Lumière show in 1895 contained one comedy, *L'Arroseur Arrosé,* in which a hapless gardener gets a face full of water when a prankster toys with his hose.

Comedy of a sort, of course, also figures largely in the films of Georges Méliès – although not comedy of the variety one usually associates with gags or jokes. It is more a matter of joy borne of marvelous transformations and physically impossible events: bodies blown apart and then reassembled – with unwanted fat emulsified. This is comedy that derives from exploiting the magical properties of cinema, a comedy of metaphysical release that celebrates the possibility of substituting the laws of physics with the laws of the imagination. Méliès's experiments gave rise to the early genre of the trick film, which promotes levity by animating the inanimate and by visualizing a fantastic physics. Here, the undeniably high spirits evoked seem less concerned with what we typically call humor and more involved with indulging a newfound freedom, the power of molding the physical world in accordance with the fancy – in short, a kind of cosmic wish fulfillment.

Early comedy also gravitated toward roughhouse and slapstick. Here the major theme was mayhem. Buffoons, marked by only slightly disguised clown outfits, would be set into exaggerated fisticuffs, discharging pistol shots into each other's behinds, jabbing each other with pitchforks, and clunking each other on the head with bricks. Because these clowns were signaled to be not quite human, they could be pummeled, dragged, hurled, hosed, burned, and stomped with impunity. Their fantastic biologies allowed the free reign of sadism in terms of either comic debacles or sprawling accidents, after the fashion of the Keystone Kops. In these cases, comedy was generally less a function of structure than of the transgression of social inhibitions about the proper way in which to treat the human body.

Whereas the trick film transgressed the laws of physics, films by people such as Mack Sennett tended to transgress the laws of society, especially in terms of the norms of respect appropriate to the handling of persons. In both cases, the comedy in question proceeded simply by displaying transgressive material. Gradually, however, a more structural type of comedy became a major source of humor in silent film. This was the sight gag.[1] And it is about the sight gag that this article is concerned.

The sight gag is a form of visual humor in which amusement is generated by the play of alternative interpretations projected by the image or image series. Sight gags existed in theater prior to their cinematic refinement, and sight gags, although they are regarded as a hallmark of the silent comedy, can occur in films that are neither silent nor comic. To orient our discussion, consider a famous example of a sight gag in Alfred Hitchcock's *The 39 Steps* (1934). The character played by Robert Donat has been manacled to a woman who positively hates him. They come to an inn, where the landlady takes them to be intensely affectionate newlyweds. Their closeness is in fact mandated by the handcuffs, and when Donat pulls his prisoner toward him, this is in order to get more control over her. The landlady misinterprets these gestures as further signs of the "lovers'" infatuation, although we hear them exchanging hostilities. The scene is shot and blocked in such a way that we not only know how things actually stand between these "lovers," but we also simultaneously see how someone in the landlady's position could systematically misinterpret the situation. Our amusement is generated by the fact that the scene is staged to show not only what is actually going on but how that set of events could also visually support an alternative, and in this case conflicting, interpretation. And it is this play of alternative, often conflicting interpretations, rooted first and foremost in the visual organization of the scene, that primarily causes the amusement that attends sight gags.

The type of humor of which the sight gag is a subcategory is often analyzed in terms of incongruity. On this view, amusement is provoked by the juxtaposition of incongruous elements. Comic duos, for example, are often composed by pairing a very fat man (or woman) with a thin man (or woman), or a tall, thin actor with a short, fat one, and so on. In the preceding example from Hitchcock, what is juxtaposed are two incompatible interpretations: that of a loving couple versus that of a hateful couple.

Stated schematically, the incongruity theory of humor says that comic amusement is an emotional state. Like all, or at least most, emotional states, comic amusement is identified by its object. The object of comic amusement is humor, where among the central criteria for what can be humorous – its *formal object*, to revert to philosophical jargon – is incongruity. The perception of incongruity in an event or situation amuses us, which in turn causes the risible sensations – laughter, for example – that we feel in response to humor. With sight gags, the loci of the relevant incongruities are the alternative, generally opposed interpretations put in play visually by the image.

Sight gags differ from verbal jokes. Verbal jokes generally culminate in a punchline that at first glance is incongruous by virtue of its appearing to be nonsense. Once the punchline is delivered, however, the audience has to give it an unexpected, although latently predictable or retrospectively comprehensible, interpretation that makes sense out of the incongruity. Succeeding in this, the audience is amused and the result is standardly laughter. For example: what do you get when you cross a chicken with a hawk? Answer: a quail. At first, this answer is nonsensical until you realize that "quail" is a pun on "Quayle" and that "chicken" and "hawk" are being used metaphorically, not literally. In order to appreciate this joke, one must reinterpret the riddle in light of the punchline in a way that effectively amounts to retelling the joke material to oneself. One is initially stymied by the incongruity of the punchline, which leads to a *re*interpretation of the joke material that makes it incomprehensible.

Sight gags also involve a play of interpretations. But with sight gags, the play of interpretation is often visually available to the audience simultaneously throughout the gag; the audience *need not* await something akin to the punchline in a verbal joke to put the interpretative play in motion.

To get a better handle on the nature of the sight gag, let us examine some major recurring types of this sort of cinematic humor. The following list does not pretend to be exhaustive; nor would I claim that some of these categories might not be so interwoven in specific cases that classifying a given gag neatly under one or another of my labels might not become daunting. In other words, I am aware of some conceptual slippage in this incomplete taxonomy, but I offer it nevertheless in the hope that future researchers will use its shortcomings to develop more precise formulations. So, without further ceremony, some leading types of sight gag include the following.

(1) The mutual interference or interpenetration of two (or more) series of events (or scenarios). This is far and away the most frequent form of the sight gag. It does not originate in cinema; in 1900 Henri Bergson identified it in his book *Laughter* with respect to theater. Nevertheless, this form is a staple of cinema, especially of the Golden Age of Silent Comedy. The previous example from *The 39 Steps* exemplifies this type of sight gag. One way to characterize it is to say that it is staged in such a way that an event, under one description, can be seen as two or more distinct, and perhaps in some sense mutually exclusive, series of events that interpenetrate each other. Thus, the event of the couple's seeking lodging at the inn in *The 39 Steps* can also be seen as two events – one from the perspective of the landlady and the other from the perspective of the couple – which events interpenetrate each other (i.e., have overlapping elements) in such a way that two interpretations of what is going on are comprehensible. This is not to say that even within the fiction both interpretations are equally sound, but only that we can *see* how both could be plausible, often plausible relative to different points of view.

Many of the most famous sight gags in silent comedy fall into this category. For another concrete example, let us look at the second gag depicting Harold's arrival at Tate College in Harold Lloyd's *The Freshman* (1925). Harold, yearning to be popular, has just mistaken a group of students at the train station to be welcoming him to Tate. Then a tight shot follows of a man at the train window lighting his pipe. He strikes a match along the edge of the window, and he drops the match out of the frame. Next there is an extreme close shot of the match landing on a white woolen

background. The ensuing medium shot identifies the white woolen background as Harold's sweater. Lloyd cuts back to the shot of the match; the sweater is starting to burn. Back to the medium shot – the man with the pipe looks down and sees that his carelessly dropped match is burning Harold's sweater. The man with the pipe bends out of the train window and slaps Harold on the back in order to snuff out the flame. The blow is a hard one, and it momentarily knocks Harold off balance. By the time Harold turns around to see who hit him, the man with the pipe has recomposed himself and sits reading his paper. Standing behind Harold is a man previously identified as the Dean of Tate. His back is turned toward Harold; he is talking to a distinguished-looking group. To Harold's mind, we suppose, the Dean is the only possible person who could have slapped him on the back, a slap by the way, that Harold seems to interpret as a robust greeting. Harold hits the Dean on the back, nearly knocking him over. Lloyd cuts to a close shot of the Dean's face; he is astounded and enraged. Lloyd cuts to a close shot of Harold attempting to introduce himself. The ensuing close shot of the angered Dean, identifying himself, bodes badly for Harold's future at Tate.

Within this single event – call it Harold slapping the Dean on the back – there are three interlocking events or scenarios, each correlating with the perspective of one of the scene's leading agents. There is the event of the smoker stanching the fire, the event of Harold reciprocating a welcoming slap on the back, and the event of the Dean being insulted. Each of these events or scenarios causally interpenetrates the others in significant ways; none of the characters appears to be aware of the views of the event alternative to his own. Indeed, none of the characters has the overall interpretation of the event that the audience has, for the simple reason that none of the characters is positioned in the fiction to see everything we see. Moreover, some of these event descriptions, as relativized to characters' points of view, directly conflict. Harold thinks that he is making a friend just as he is making an enemy. And it is this incongruous conflict of interpretations rooted visually in the play of points of view that gives the scene its humorous edge.

Because this particular type of sight gag is so pervasive, discussion and analysis of a further example of it may be fruitful. Johnnie's entry into Northern territory in Buster Keaton's *The General* (1926) comes to mind here. The scene begins with the title, "The Southern army facing Chattanooga is ordered to retreat." There is a shot of Southern cavalry troops waving a retreat signal. Then a shot of the Union spies shows them crouching in the cab of The General (the hijacked locomotive). Finally we see Johnnie. In an overhead shot over the timber car, he can be seen cutting wood. Keaton then cuts to a shot of the retreating Southerners. Initially it is a long shot. Then all of a sudden the front of The Texas (the locomotive with which Johnnie is pursuing The General) pulls into the foreground from screen right. The Texas drives past the camera, revealing that Johnnie is still chopping wood with his back to the battle. This is quite an ingenious shot not only in its use of foreground and background to set out the significant facts of the situation but also in its channeling of the relevant facts to the audience sequentially, thereby effectively replicating the detailed, phased selectivity available in editing in the context of the realism of the single shot.

The battle ensues behind Johnnie's back. The Southerners retreat entirely, and the Union troops triumphantly spill onto the field behind Johnnie. Now he is in enemy territory. Yet he continues to chop. At one point, he breaks his ax handle. But even at this rupture in his work pattern, he remains unaware that he is completely surrounded by hostile Union troops. In all, it takes twelve shots before Johnnie realizes his predicament. He is so absolutely engrossed in his work that he never once glances outside his narrow work area.

Here again there is a striking incongruity between two interpretations of the shot, both of which are made visually comprehensible to the audience. On the one hand, Johnnie's fortunes have changed dramatically; he is in the grip of the enemy. On the other hand, from his perspective, which we can understand by noting the fixity of his attention, his position remains relatively benign. The disparity of viewpoints, made evident in the staging of the action, gives rise to a play of conflicting interpretations of the situation, and this gives rise to amusement.

Key to this Keaton gag, as to many other Keaton gags, is the character's inattention or unawareness of the surrounding environment – an inattention that is palpably portrayed in the shooting.[2] Often sight gags rest on this sort of monumentally unaware character. We laugh at the clown headed for a pratfall as he approaches a discarded banana peel because we see the banana peel and he doesn't *and* because we see that he doesn't see the banana peel. This gives birth to two divergent interpretations of the scene: one in terms of what we see is the case and another in terms of what we see the protagonist sees and takes to be the case. This incongruity, available visually to the spectator, is the source of humor in the situation. Our amusement is not purely sadistic pleasure at someone taking a fall. Rather, the pleasure comes of a visually motivated conflict of interpretations over the nature of the scene. Two different interpretations of an event collide, or, to put the matter differently, the actual situation or event interferes with the protagonist's imagined picture of the event, with the net effect that the protagonist's expectations have been reversed.

Yet another way to put this is that the event progresses under two scenarios – here, notably, that of the comic butt, on the one hand, and of "reality," so to speak, on the other. For our purposes, we will require of candidates for this sort of sight gag that there be at least two scenarios (visible in the image or image series), that these scenarios be at odds with each other, and that the disparity between them portends a mishap (i.e., one of the scenarios *interferes* with the other).

Generally, sight gags of the mutual interference of two series of events (or scenarios) variety often occur where the character's view of the situation diverges from the reality of the situation. Thus, the relevant conflict of interpretations emerges from the disjunction of the character's point of view – which is a function of the situation being laid out in such a way that the spectator can see why the character fails to see it properly – and the way the situation is. Again, this structure differs from the standard case of verbal jokes. For with verbal jokes, our second interpretation deals with the incongruous punchline, whereas with this sort of sight gag we have two or more alternative and often conflicting interpretations before us throughout most of the gag.

(2) The mimed metaphor. Silent film, of course, employed a great deal of pantomime. Sometimes pantomime was engaged to produce a very special sort of sight gag, one in which the audience came to see an object metaphorically equated with something that it was not. Mime functioned figuratively to produce visual similes between disparate sets of objects. In *The Gold Rush* (1925), Charlie Chaplin treats a boot as a meal. The shoe laces become spaghetti; the nails, bones; the sole, a filet. In the same film, candle wicks become eggs. In *The Rink* (1916), Chaplin holds a chicken aloft in a way that suggests a bird in flight; when the stuffings fall out of the rear and hit a customer in the eye, it is hard to resist seeing them as bird droppings from on high. And in *The Pawnshop* (1916), Chaplin does a virtuoso number with an alarm clock. His surrounding gesticulations make the clock seeable as a heart and then as a sardine can.

And when its inner cogs rush about on the counter like so many insects, Chaplin turns his oil can into an insecticide. Earlier in the same film, Chaplin transforms doughnuts into barbells and teacups into dish towels. In such cases, humor arises through seeing objects in their literal aspect at the very same time that the miming gesticulation enables us to see them otherwise: to see cogs as bugs or nails as turkey bones. The operation here is essentially metaphorical; disparate objects are identified for the purpose of foregrounding similes, in this case visual similes. This abets the play of incongruous interpretations. For the self-same object can be seen either literally or figuratively.

The preceding examples all hail from Chaplin. And this is no accident. For Chaplin is particularly invested in the theme of imagination, and it is an essential feature of his character that he can see things differently from others, that is to say, imaginatively. But the device is evident throughout silent comedy. In *Cops* (1922), Keaton beautifully metamorphoses an accordion extension (of the sort associated with telephones) into an arm while also portraying a ladder as a seesaw and then as a catapult. This type of sight gag is probably more popular in silent film than in sound film – in contrast to the mutual interference gag, which is crucial to both – but it has exemplars in sound film as well. One recalls the house with eyes in Jacques Tati's *Mon oncle* (1958) and the tire as funeral wreath in his *Mr. Hulot's Vacation* (1953);[3] there is also the metaphor of glass as nothing in *Playtime* (1967), when the doorman with only a handle to speak of, acquits his duty as if he had a door at his disposal. And, indeed, the very glass he has not got, shattered as it is, is recycled as ice cubes.

With the mimed metaphor, the audience is invited through the prompting gesticulations of the mime to consider objects under alternative interpretations. This is not akin to the famous duck-rabbit examples discussed by psychologists, however, for we can see the nail as a bone at the same time we see the nail as a nail. The humor in the situation rides on the possibility of its simultaneous play of interpretations, which interpretations are nevertheless delightedly opposed, allowing and even encouraging alternative – literal versus metaphorical – views.

In speaking of mimed metaphors, a distinction is meant to be marked here between what is mimed and mimes that provoke metaphors, that is, mimes that are implicit similes. When Keaton's Steamboat Bill, Jr., attempts to tell Steamboat Bill, Sr., that he has given him a saw, he mimes sawing off his thumb. This is not a mimed metaphor. For no object is being analogized to a disparate object. This is miming pure and simple. With mimed metaphors, it is important that the audience has before it, imaginatively speaking, radically disparate objects that are being equated for the purpose of analogizing them in a context where the point – the very wit in question – is that the audience appreciates the success of the analogy in the face of its unlikelihood. Ordinarily, this will require that we be able to identify the literal object and the metaphor independently and that we speak of two objects. Chaplin's "sailboat" turns constitute a real problem here. For when he pivots, throwing out his leg as if to shift a sail, it is not easy to describe that movement literally – that is, independently of saying it is a "sailboat" turn. Perhaps a different category – body metaphors? – will have to be introduced to accommodate examples such as this.

Mimed metaphors may also function by evoking linguistic idioms or verbal metaphors. In *College* (1927), Keaton plays a high school valedictorian who speaks on the evils of sport. As his diatribe revs up, he lurches exaggeratedly from left to right while standing in place. We note that the assembled local dignitaries in the background shift position with him. Keaton is, so to speak, "swaying the audience," and

we view this scene both literally and under the aegis of the unexpected and amusing metaphor.[4]

Mimed metaphors differ from mutual interference gags in that the alternative points of view need not be relativized to any characters, that they need not result in mishaps, and that they are directed more at objects than at events, although as the last example from Keaton indicates, they may operate on situations.

(3) The switch image. A famous shot in Chaplin's *The Immigrant* (1917) shows the Tramp leaning over the railing of a boat and lurching to and fro. We think he is seasick and vomiting; but he turns around, and we see that he has been struggling to land a big fish. Or, again from Chaplin – more than once – we see his shoulders heaving. We infer sobbing and sorrow. But the figure seen frontally is mixing a drink. In Lloyd's *Safety Last* (1923), we initially think that we are to be witnesses to an execution, but we soon realize that we have been fooled into regarding a farewell scene as death row, just as in Keaton's *Cops* we initially think that the suitor is in prison when he is only on the other side of a gate. Or Tati shows us an airline terminal that we initially think is a hospital waiting room. Likewise, in Keaton's *The Boat* (1921), we first take him to be caught in a storm at sea, whereas a subsequent image shows him to be the victim of his children pulling on the ropes in his garage.

In these cases, the image is given to the audience under one interpretation, which is subverted with the addition of subsequent information. The initial image is subsequently shown to be radically underdetermined. At first, it seems to mean one thing unequivocally in terms of its visual information, but then it means something entirely, and unexpectedly, other. Switch images are lessons in visual ambiguity.

Unlike most mimed metaphors, switch images pertain to events rather than objects, and their dual aspects are generally perceived sequentially rather than simultaneously. Unlike mutual interference gags, switch images need not be relativized to any character, and they may involve no mishap. Switch images may be thought of as the interpretation of visually distinct events without interference. That is, the two alternative interpretations of the scene – the literal and the metaphorical – are not embedded in the narrative in such a way that disaster befalls anyone. Or, to put it differently, the alternate interpretations are not narrativized in a way that they causally impinge upon each other.

Switch images tend to be found at the *beginnings* of films and sequences. An obvious reason for this may be that at such points the filmmaker does not have a large number of narrative commitments and implications that need to be camouflaged in the imagery.[5] But, there is no reason in principle that a switch image cannot occur in the middle of a shot, perhaps by way of playfully deceptive scale variation.

In some ways, the switch image resembles a verbal joke. For once the initial image is subverted, part of our pleasure involves noting the way in which our first identification of the image was misguided. That is, switch images abet a limited play of reinterpretation. Nevertheless, switch images are distinct from verbal jokes in that the first image, unlike the punchline of a joke, need not be absurd or incongruous.

(4) The switch movement. In Chaplin's *The Pawnshop,* the Tramp spends a great deal of time fighting with his office mate. On one occasion, the boss walks in, and, midair, the Tramp's punch changes its trajectory and heads for the floor, where he falls to his knees and begins scrubbing. One movement – the punch – is transformed into another – washing the floor – in one seamless line of movement. Or, again, the Tramp has his adversary straitjacketed between the rungs of a ladder. He feigns high-class, dancerly boxing poses, torturing his helpless opponent with tweaks on the nose. A cop appears behind the Tramp, and, aware of the cop's presence, the Tramp's pugilistic dodges become swaying, waltzlike steps – as if the whole time he had been dancing rather than street-fighting. The Tramp, continuing this deception, glides back into the pawnshop, and seeing the disapproving visage of his boss, he transforms his prancing pivot into a businesslike strut.

In all these cases, the Tramp is out to deceive an authority figure by seamlessly metamorphosing a questionable movement activity into an innocent one – as if to say, for example: "You thought I was fighting, but I was only dancing," or "You thought I was dancing, but I am really off to work." Such switch movements often occur in narrative contexts of deception, although they need not.

Switch movements are to actions as puns are to sentences. They derail one line of thought and send it in another direction. The gesture or series of gestures upon which a switch movement pivots are like a pun in that they can take different meanings in different movement contexts. Switching from one meaning potential of a movement to another provokes an alternative interpretation of initial action. Just as our earlier pun – quail/Quayle – plays on the aural similarity of two different words in order to prompt interpretive amusement, the Tramp exploits the visual similarity of boxerly dancing with ballroom dancing to compel a reinterpretation of his activity.

That this reinterpretation is purportedly "forced" onto observers, like the policeman, shows, as indicated previously, that different types of sight gags can be segued in larger comic constellations. For insofar as we attribute the reinterpretation of the action not only to ourselves but also to the cop, this byplay can also be seen as a mutual interference gag.

Switch movements are like verbal jokes in that they involve a sequential play of reinterpretation. But they are unlike verbal jokes insofar as they are not prompted by anything like an incongruous punchline. Indeed, we start out initially unaware that we are interpreting an action, and we only become retrospectively aware of our initial interpretation when it is undercut. That is, unlike a verbal joke, our reinterpretation of the gag does not begin with the perception of nonsense. Nevertheless, our amusement at the gag still rests on the incongruous play of interpretation. For we are delighted by the way in which one line of movement may be made to yield two, often conflicting, glosses, for example, the Tramp wasting his boss's time fighting versus dutifully washing the floor. Switch movements often reverse the interpretive meaning of an action; but they need not. They may merely transform one action into another as when a silent comedian, beaned on the head, turns his doddering into a modern dance à la Isadora Duncan.

(5) The object analog. This category is very much like the mimed metaphor. Some readers may in fact see little point in drawing a distinction here. A famous example of the object analog is the moment in *The Pawnshop* when the Tramp drops his cane into the tuba as if it were an umbrella stand; or in the same film when he puts his derby in a bird cage as if it were a hatbox; or in *The Rink* when he removes his coat from an oven as if it were some kind of closet. In these cases, one object is equated with another. One object, that is, can be seen under two aspects: one literal and the other metaphorical.

Essentially, the comic dynamic here is the same as in mimed metaphors. I have not assimilated these examples to the mimed metaphor, however, because they do not seem to require mime to do their work. They do not need enabling gesticulations of the sort that must accompany the perception of a doughnut as a barbell. The objects analogized bear their similarities close enough to the surface, so to speak, that the metaphorical interpretation does not require much staging. Unlike verbal jokes but like mimed metaphors, the object analog affords a simultaneous play of interpretation – seeing the object literally and metaphorically at the same time. In the Chaplin example, the audience focuses on the visual similarities of tubas and umbrella stands while remaining peripherally aware of their differences.

The object analog gag should not be confused with another technique common to much action-oriented comedy (silent and otherwise). Call this technique the refunctionalization of objects. Very often at the height of an action sequence, when disaster seems inevitable, a comic will seize upon an object and use it triumphantly in a way that deviates from its ordinary employment. For example, when the back of the boat breaks away in *College,* Keaton realizes that he can use his behind for a rudder. Or, for a less action-packed example, in *The Navigator* (1924) Keaton redeploys crab traps to cradle boiling eggs in the galley's outsized cauldron. Here an object is used successfully for a purpose for which it was not designed; the object is, in a manner of speaking, refunctionalized.

Such refunctionalizations are undoubtedly amusing, but I am not sure that they should be considered *sight* gags. For the object is not being redeployed in order for the audience to see it as something else. With object analogs and mimed metaphors, the point of the humor appears to rest on visual metaphors; refunctionalization of objects does not. The humor in the latter case rests on the comic's unexpected – incongruous but sufficient – ingenuity rather than on any particular visual byplay. In *The Frozen North* (1922), when Keaton turns the guitars into snow shoes, or the snow shoe into a tennis racket, the point of the routines (which I count as mimed metaphors) is to remark on the physical resemblances of the items in question. Refunctionalizing objects would not necessarily have this dimension of paraverbal wit. That said, however, let me also admit that the refunctionalization of an object may also be yoked to the projection of an object analog or a mimed metaphor. At the end of *College,* Keaton uses a pole supporting a laundry line as a vaulting pole and a lamp as a javelin. These involve not only refunctionalization but mimed metaphors, for in the context of the film it is hard to miss the similarity, indeed the visual similarity, that is being drawn between these events and the earlier sporting episodes.

(6) The solution gag. The discussion of the refunctionalization of objects reminds me of another type of gag, albeit rare, that appears in comic films – the solution gag. I am of two minds as to whether it should be considered a *sight* gag, for like refunctionalization it concerns unexpected, indeed brilliant, reversals based on practical ingenuity rather than play with the presentation of visual ambiguities. But I may be too narrow-minded in this case. So I will discuss the structure of the gag and leave it to the reader to determine whether it belongs on this list.

The most famous example of what I am calling a solution gag occurs in Keaton's *The General.* Johnnie (aka Buster Keaton) sees a railroad tie strewn on the tracks in front of him. The Union spies have thrown it there, hoping to derail him. Johnnie slows his locomotive down and runs along the side of the engine. Carefully, he slides down the cowcatcher of his locomotive. He runs to the foreboding tie, and with much difficulty, pulls it off the track. Unfortunately, he has not worked fast enough. His engine has inched up behind him while he struggled with the tie. By the time he lifts it, his locomotive scoops him off his feet, and he falls on the top of the cowcatcher. The beam he removed from the track, moreover, is so heavy that it pins him to the front of his own engine. Suddenly, he sees there is another railroad tie on the track less than ten feet ahead of him. The locomotive seems destined to derail with him on the front of it. Yet Johnnie, but not the audience, in a flash

of brilliance sees an avenue of escape. He realizes that the tie on the track is straddling one of the rails. Thus, if he can hit the overhanging end of the tie on the track, he can catapult it out of the way of the oncoming train. He lifts the tie on his chest overhead and bangs it down on the beam on the track, thus casting two worries aside with a single blow.

This is an immensely amusing routine. And its effect rests on the lightning reversal of one interpretation of the situation by means of an unexpected, economical, and effective reconceptualization of the situation. It depends on Johnnie seeing that the beam on his chest is not a burden but a tool. Johnnie sees this, but the standard viewer does not until Johnnie demonstrates it. The reconceptualization of the situation surprises the audience, which also would appear to derive pleasure from the situation by reinterpreting the scene in light of the absolute fitness of Johnnie's action. If Johnnie's lifting the beam, rather than, say, trying to roll off the cowcatcher, strikes us as initially incongruous, once the beam is flung, the action strikes us as the most perfect and neatest solution available. In this respect, the solution gag is akin to a verbal joke insofar as it enables the viewer to pleasurably reconceive the situation, although the solution gag is not exactly like a verbal joke because in the process of appreciating the gag and the sequential reconceptualization of the scene, the audience does not exercise its own wit but rather admires the wit displayed by Keaton.

Whether this gag counts as a sight gag probably depends on the degree to which one thinks a sight gag depends on visual play. On this basis, one might reject it as a sight gag because the gag is more a matter of physics than of perception. Or if one takes the gag to derive from a kind of visual thinking – seeing the situation as a catapult – one might be prone to call it a sight gag. Moreover, if one wants to use the phrase "sight gag" to denominate all the recurring gag structures of the great silent comedians, then this sort of solution gag counts as a sight gag.

Nevertheless, however one decides this terminological point, it is important to note that the solution gag does differ interestingly from the standard cases of mutual interference gags. For with mutual interference gags, it is generally some comic character in the fiction whose interpretation of the event is limited, whereas with solution gags, it is the audience whose vision is limited. Moreover, with solution gags the play of alternative interpretations comes sequentially, whereas with mutual interference gags and switch images the audience can contemplate incongruous alternative interpretations simultaneously.

The preceding taxonomy of sight gags is admittedly rough. It does not claim to be exhaustive, nor are the categories as precise as I would like them to be. Furthermore, it is not systematic in the sense that these distinctions could be deduced from an underlying set of formulas. The lack of systematicity in part derives from my method, which has been primarily descriptive. Whether a system could be developed for the sight gag really depends upon getting a more comprehensive picture of the range of variations within this form. The purpose of advancing this confessedly informal cartography of the sight gag is to elicit the kind of criticism and refinement of terms that will foster a more comprehensive and rigorous classification of the phenomena, which may in turn allow systematization.

It is also important to note that this essay does not pretend to say why the sight gag is amusing. Rather, I have attempted to assimilate the sight gag to the incongruity conception of humor. Thus, explaining why the sight gag is funny relies on an account of why humans find incongruity amusing. Though by attempting to assimilate the sight

gag to the humor of incongruity we have not *explained* the sight gag, we have, however, I believe, enhanced our understanding of it by situating the sight gag in the appropriate conceptual framework.

I began by noting that the sight gag appears in artforms other than cinema, in films other than comedies, and in periods other than that of the silent cinema. At the same time, however, most of us probably have very strong associations between the sight gag and silent film. One reason that might be offered for this is that this is just where you happen to find sight gags. However, I distrust this answer. Sight gags are everywhere in the history of film (and television), and they recur frequently in our own day in films such as *Back to the Future* (1985), *Big* (1988), and the works of PeeWee Herman, not to mention their standard use in all sorts of television comedy shows. So in concluding, I would like to speculate on whether there might be a deep thematic connection between the sight gag and silent film that underlies our sense that these phenomena, so to speak, "go together."

In looking over the preceding taxonomy of the sight gag, I see that one motif running through all the examples is what might be called the "double (or multiple) aspect." Sight gags seem to presuppose the possibility of visually interpreting the image in two (or more) ways. I have argued that the incongruousness of these interpretations is the feature of these gags that gives rise to amusement. But at the same time, the theme of the multiple aspect is relevant to important debates about the artistic prospects for film in the silent era.

As is well known, early film suffered what might be called "the anxiety of photography."[6] That is, because film is a product of photography and photography cannot be art, then film is not art. The reason for supposing that photography could not be art was that it was believed that photography could only slavishly reproduce reality. The task of silent filmmakers and of theoreticians of the nascent artform was generally to refute these charges by showing that film need not slavishly reproduce reality; it could also creatively reconstitute it.

Within this context, I hypothesize that the sight gag, with its exploitation of the multiple aspects of the image, has an especial, symbolic pride of place. For the donneé of the sight gag is that the film image is open to various interpretations, can show more than one point of view, and can be creatively ambiguous (albeit in a highly structure way). In other words, the sight gag flies in the face of the prejudice that movies can only brutishly recapitulate from a single point of view what stands before the camera. In celebrating the ambiguity of appearances, sight gags in effect undermined the uninformed conviction that cinema was capable only of mechanically, unequivocally, and unimaginatively recycling something often infelicitously called "reality." The ethos of silent film culture – its commitment to cinema as a means of interpretation rather than of recording – was, in other words, the operating premise of the sight gag. This, I submit, is the reason silent film theorists generally have an affectionate, if sometimes unexplained, place in their hearts for the masters of the sight gag. At the same time, I think that the rest of us may intuit some of the urgency of this dialectic when we laugh at the great silent clowns. That is, we feel them trying to transcend what were often perceived as the period-specific limitations of their medium. We do not feel the same about sight gags in our own time, however, because we are as yet unaware of our limitations.

Notes

1. The historical claims here are meant to be quite tentative. Roughly, it seems to me that the earliest stages of film comedy were aimed at generating laughter through an exploitation of the fantastic capacities of cinema and/or through a kind of amoral, antisocial transgressiveness. But this is only to speak of major tendencies. Sight gags – for example, Feuillade's *Une Dame Vraiment Bien* (1908) – were certainly in evidence in early film.

   Similarly, when I speak of sight gags emerging as a key form of silent comedy, I do not mean to imply that trick films and roughhouse slapstick ceased to be made. I merely wish to note the prominence that the sight gag form gradually assumed as it was refined by people such as Chaplin, Lloyd, and Keaton. Of course, the sight gag form is not inhospitable to either the machinations of the trick film or roughhouse. The sight gag often incorporates these elements in the kinds of structures discussed in this chapter: Keaton's disappearance in *Sherlock, Jr.* (1924) is surely one of many survivals of the trick film in the period of the sight gag, and a great many sight gags are basically structured roughhouse. And, as well, films notable for their sight gags can also employ trick devices and sadistic slapstick independently of their sight gag structures.

   Given all these qualifications, one might begin to wonder about the point I am trying to make. It is this: the sight gag, although evident in very early comedy, gradually comes to be refined in such a way that it, rather than trick comedy or slapstick pure and simple (the more dominant earlier tendencies), is seen as the most important form of silent comedy. This is a process that gains steam in the later half of the 1910s so that by the 1920s the sight gag is the leading type of film comedy.

   Needless to say, the preceding historical hypothesis may require even further modification as we learn more about very early film comedy, such as the work of the Italians.

2. For further discussion of the role of inattention in Keaton's humor, see Noël Carroll, *An In-Depth Analysis of Buster Keaton's The General* (New York: Ph.D. thesis for New York University, 1976).

3. Mention of Tati's wreath gag gives me the opportunity to make a comment about comic conventions, especially with respect to sight gags, not discussed above. Clearly, this gag with the tire succeeds in large measure because we are dealing with a black-and-white

film. In a color film, a tire with wet leaves stuck to it would not be visually confused with a funeral wreath; this sight gag is persuasive only because the film is black and white.

But this leads to an interesting point – that the characters in the world of the fiction insofar as they are confused by the tire appear to be seeing their world in black and white. This suggests that there may be an implicit convention with respect to sight gags – that the perceptual capacities of the characters in silent films are presented as roughly the same as the perceptual capacities of the silent film audience, unless otherwise signaled. That is, just as the silent film spectator cannot hear, smell, or feel cues in the fiction, so the silent film character, unless otherwise marked, is similarly deficient in these regards.

This would explain the comprehensibility of the spectacular inattention that characters in, for example, mutual interference gags often evince. In *Fatty's Magic Pants,* a comedy of the middle 1910s, for instance, someone sews a rope down the seam of Arbuckle's slacks from behind. And he does not notice this! Nevertheless, it seems to be accepted by the audience. Why? I hypothesize that it is because it is being implicitly supposed by the filmmakers and the audience that Arbuckle

has available to him only the perceptual capacities that are available to the film viewer with respect to the fiction – here, specifically vision. In this gag, his touch receptors are bracketed just as in the Tati gag the characters' color receptors are bracketed. And unlike real-world humans, characters in silent film with astounding frequency seem to be unaware when other people and animals are standing behind them. We might call this convention perceptual leveling. Whether there actually, rather than hypothetically, is such an implicit convention, however, is a topic for further research.

4. For a discussion of this sort of interplay between word and image, see Noël Carroll, "Language and Cinema," in this volume.

5. In *Wild and Woolly* (1917), the film begins and ends with switch images, ones with reversed significations. In the opening we initially take Fairbanks to be on the range but then learn he is in the city; at the conclusion, we think he is in the city, but he is really out West. For analysis of this, see David Bordwell, *Narration in the Fiction Film* (Madison: University of Wisconsin Press, 1985), pp. 166–69, 202–03.

6. This is discussed at greater length in Noël Carroll, *Philosophical Problems of Classical Film Theory* (Princeton: Princeton University Press, 1988), chap. I.

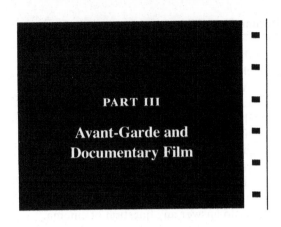

Students of the avant-garde cinema and the documentary film often complain that their subjects are marginalized – marginalized in terms of being treated apart from the massively distributed fiction film discussed in the previous section and marginalized by being thrown together as a kind of miscellaneous, catchall category, that is, as a kind of afterthought. I sympathize with their protests that they are underappreciated. I have grouped them together, though I mean no disrespect in this. I hope the range of reference to avant-garde and documentary films in this section will exonerate me of suspicions in this regard. I hope that they show that I have been an avid follower of developments in these traditions. In fact, in my days as a journalist, my primary "beat" was the independent cinema.

"Causation, the Ampliation of Movement and Avant-Garde Film," "Language and Cinema: Preliminary Notes for a Theory of Verbal Images," and "A Note on Film Metaphor" can be read as a continuation of the pursuit of piecemeal theories of specific film devices and structures that was initiated in the previous section. Of course, the structures discussed in this section are not unique to the avant-garde film. But since many of my examples come from avant-garde film and since figuration of the sorts discussed in these articles is generally associated with avant-garde film, I have placed these essays somewhat but not completely arbitrarily in this section.

In "Causation, the Ampliation of Movement and Avant-Garde Film" I have tried to explain the basis of apparent motion and apparent causation in various editing figures and to show some of the ways in which these phenomena can be and have been exploited expressively in certain avant-garde films. In some ways the essay is more interpretive than it is theoretical. Moreover, I now suspect that my concluding remarks in the essay about the limits of cinema studies are way too conservative.

In "Language and Cinema," I attempt to isolate a mechanism of figuration that I christen "the verbal image." Critics frequently assume the existence of such a device in their interpretations, but the device has gone untheorized for the most part. The purpose of this essay is to identify this device, to say what it is, and how it works. In retrospect, I think that my categorization of the device as a para-illocutionary act was probably not a good idea. It was suggested to me by the late Monroe Beardsley and I latched onto it too hastily and without considering how badly it fit the overall framework of speech-act theory. On the other hand, I think that my appropriation and freestyle modification of the speech-act approach in terms of constitutory conditions and facilitating conditions add a useful dimension of precision to the discussion, even if the phenomenon is not really profitably classified of as a kind of speech act. However, if I were to rewrite the article I would probably rework these conditions in the spirit of the analysis in "A Note on Film Metaphor."

"A Note on Film Metaphor" introduces a theory of at least one kind of film metaphor. It may not be the only candidate for the title of film metaphor, but I think that it is a fairly clear-cut candidate. As my footnotes in this article indicate, I think that there is further research to be undertaken in this area. Nevertheless, I think that the analysis of this rather straight-forward case of film metaphor can limn the outline of an approach to less obvious candidates.[1]

Though "Avant-Garde Film and Film Theory" is centrally concerned with the question of whether such films propound theories, this essay might also be regarded as a contribution to the piecemeal theorizing of mechanisms of signification inasmuch as the attempt to come to terms with the notion that avant-garde films are theoretical leads me to the identification and elucidation of various structures of reference that connect certain avant-garde films with theories.

Of course, piecemeal theorizing need not only concern the isolation and explanation of specific structures. It may also attempt to address certain localized problems and to answer certain presiding questions that arise out of film practice. This essay approaches the localized question of whether avant-garde films make theory – a question that was made urgent by the discourse about avant-garde film in the precincts I inhabited especially in the seventies – and the essay comes to the conclusion that, strictly speaking, they don't.[2] This conclusion is not meant to disparage avant-garde filmmaking aesthetically, however, since I think that avant-garde films are interesting, even if they are not really theoretical. Moreover, from the perspective of this anthology, this essay is perhaps instructive insofar as it illustrates that one can pursue a theoretical problem independently of constructing an entire theory of film.

"From Real to Reel: Entangled in Nonfiction Film" is not an inquiry into operation of cinematic devices. It confronts a question indigenous to or localized to the practice of documentary filmmaking. Common wisdom – shared by film theorists and high school students alike – assures us that it is impossible for nonfiction films to be objective.[3] I argue that these conclusions are precipitate.[4] A coda – "Reply to Carol Brownson and Jack C. Wolf – follows "Real to Reel" and it enables me to correct some

of the errors I made in the earlier essay and to clarify some of my earlier contentions.

As with the case of isolating devices, mechanisms, and structures, I think that dealing with localized questions or problems of film practice makes film theorizing manageable. Compared to the more traditional ways of constructing film theory, it relieves the theorist from the onus of having to have an answer about every question of cinema in order to answer any question of cinema.

Piecemeal theorizing makes film theorizing feasible, since the attempt to solve a single problem or to explicate the operation of a single device is less overwhelming, and more definable a task than devising a global approach to cinema as a whole. And apart from eminent practicability of piecemeal theorizing, it also makes good sense, since we have no reasons to believe – and many reasons not to believe – that every question about film (or the moving image) is connected.[5]

Notes

1. For further discussion of my approach, see Noël Carroll, "Visual Metaphor," in *Aspects of Metaphor*, edited by Jaako Hintikka (Dordrecht: Kluwer Academic Publishers, 1994). If there is one limitation that I now feel with respect both to this article and "A Note on Film Metaphor," it is the suggestion I may leave that the species of metaphor that I discuss is the whole story. It is not, and I know it isn't.

2. For a continuation of the discussion of the relation of the avant-garde to theoretical discourse, see Noël Carroll, "Avant-garde Art and the Problem of Theory," *The Journal of Aesthetic Education* (Fall 1995).

3. Concerning this essay, I should like to note that I am no longer satisfied with the possible-world talk in it. What I was trying to get at in those portions of the text will need to be reworked and cleared up in a future essay.

4. Since "From Real to Reel" was written, new arguments for the impossibility of objectivity in the nonfiction film have emerged. I

address these in Noël Carroll, "Postmodern Skepticism and the Nonfiction Film," in *Post-Theory: Reconstructing Film Studies,* edited by David Bordwell and Noël Carroll (Madison: University of Wisconsin Press, 1995).

5. That is, if we begin to compile a list of all the theoretical questions we might wish to ask about film, as the list grows longer (and more diverse in its topics), the likelihood that a single set of principles will be suitable for answering them diminishes.

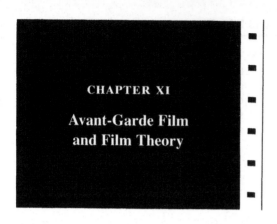

CHAPTER XI

Avant-Garde Film and Film Theory

In a recent discussion with Howard Guttenplan, director of Millennium, I suggested that an issue of the Workshop's film journal be devoted to the topic of film theory. He said he thought that would be redundant, arguing that every issue was already about theory since theory is so intimately bound up with the nature of avant-garde film. Admittedly the word "theoretical" abounds in discussions of the avant-garde. But in reading the literature and viewing the films in question, it often becomes hard to ascertain whether what is described as "theoretical" in one film is the same type of phenomenon that is described as "theoretical" in another film.

Part of the problem is that what is called "theoretical" in one work is often on a different level of theory than what is considered "theoretical" in another. One film may be correlated to a metaphysical theory, e.g., about the nature of the self, whereas another is correlated with an epistemological view, e.g., about the nature of intentionality. Or, one film may go with an aesthetic position, e.g., about the imperative of each art to emphasize its own essence, while another work is associated with a stance from film theory, e.g., about the true (read "flat") nature of cinematic space. Thus, the claim that a given film is "theoretical" is ambiguous until you specify the kind of theory you intend to correlate with it.

But the idea that an avant-garde film is "theoretical" is also ambiguous in the sense

that the ways such a film may relate to different orders of theory are also multiple. The task of this paper is to elucidate some of the relations that avant-garde films may have to theories. I suspect that the paper is not exhaustive in this regard. But I will attempt to be skeptical. I will argue that some of the most prevalent relations between avant-garde film and theory (especially film theory) are not adequately described by the adjective "theoretical" where this term is meant to imply that the films in question are vehicles for making theories.[1] I have no doubt that fully theoretical films could be made, perhaps after the fashion of *Ways of Seeing*. But I do not believe that this is what we encounter in the most prominent examples of what are called "theoretical" avant-garde films.

Before charting the kinds of relations that hold between the avant-garde and film theory, let me try to delineate my terms. To say a film is avant-garde is to say something about the form of a film. Specifically, it is to say that the form of a given film is different, but more importantly, that it is in advance of existing cinematic practice. It is in advance of prevailing technique not simply because it deviates from antecedent practice but because it in some way opposes or repudiates antecedent practice. It points to some possibility of the medium that is not only ignored in prevailing practice but arguably is repressed. To interpret a given film as avant-garde demands that one establish how it deviates from existing practice and how that deviation counts as an advance by being a repudiation that liberates a distinct possibility of the practice that has been hitherto repressed.

Kubelka's *Adebar, Schwechater* and *Arnulf Rainer* are avant-garde because they are predicated on (a) foregrounding rhythmic structures and (b) emphasizing the single frame, rather than the shot, as the basic unit of film articulation. Both these stylistic deviations, but especially the emphasis on the single frame, are clear repudiations of most existing forms of cinema. Likewise, Renoir's use of lateral reframing, depth-of-field and zig-zag panning amounted to avant-garde in repudiations in the Thirties.

Needless to say, the above formulation falls short of capturing all the films we would intuitively want to classify as avant-garde. Why? Because there are avant-garde genres. For example there are films by young structuralist filmmakers, like Vincent Grenier and Tom DiBiaso, that someone might argue are not really repudiations of prevailing practices but rather merely repetitions or amplifications of the existing, well-entrenched stylistic frameworks set forth by people like Frampton, Gehr and Snow. In short, these younger filmmakers are not repudiating a prevailing practice but embracing one.

Nevertheless, I think that we want to denominate developing practitioners of the structural film as avant-garde. Part of the reason for this is that we regard the genre as a whole as a repudiation of a larger, more dominant form of cinema. But I think that we also want to call Grenier and DiBiaso avant-garde because we believe that there is a strong, genetic lineage (in terms of influence) between them and the earlier, more innovative instances of the genre. How long a genre like structural film can continue and still be appropriately called avant-garde is a perplexing question to which I have no answer. However, for the purposes of this paper, I will assume what I take to be at least a semi-clear characterization of an avant-garde film as one that repudiates prevailing cinematic practice and/or is in the direct lineage of such a film.

I will not attempt to characterize film theory completely; I have tried that elsewhere with mixed results.[2] For the purposes of this paper, however, we need not have a complete definition of film theory in order to examine its relation to avant-garde film. Rather I will mention only a few features of film theory that seem pertinent to the discussion. First, film theories presuppose a level of generality. If they do not pretend to deal with all film, then they at least deal with large classes of film. A film theory is not a theory of a single film though a film theoretician may examine a single film for the sake of illuminating a generic possibility of the cinema. Film theories present evidence for their positions. And they are explanatory; they explicate the ways in which a given film, technique or genre moves or communicates to spectators.

Given these admittedly rough notions of the avant-garde film and film theory, we can begin to outline the kinds of relations that can exist between the two.

First, avant-garde films can provoke theory change. That is, a given avant-garde film can cause either the expansion or contraction of a theory. Of these two modes, the provocation of expansion is, I believe, more typical. A given avant-garde film can serve as counter-evidence or as a counter-example to existing theories by manifesting a possibility or aspect of the medium hitherto ignored by theorists. In this role, the avant-garde film operates as a piece of new data that forces theory to expand its analytic framework in order to assimilate it.

This capacity of avant-garde film is well-precedented in the art of the twentieth century. Duchamp's *The Fountain* caused a crisis in art theory; it revealed a crucial component feature of what it is to be a work of art that previous theories had overlooked – namely, the importance of the social context as a condition for an object's being a work of art. The force of *The Fountain* is that today any plausible theory of art must be sensitive to the social dimension of the practice of art. In Godard's *Pierrot le Fou* we see two alternative scenes of how the major characters could escape. This editing, between parallel modalities rather than between parallel temporalities, adds a possibility to film editing which every contemporary theory must analyze in order to propose an adequate theory of film.[3]

Related to provoking theory expansion,

though rarer I think, would be the use of avant-garde film to contract prevailing theory. That is, a work by an avant-garde filmmaker could operate as a *reductio-ad-absurdum,* premised on shearing off a theoretical excess. One has the feeling, for instance, that this is part of the aim of Tony Conrad's ironic "delicatessen" pieces like *Pickled Wind.* Conrad treats celluloid like food, on occasion cooking and processing it so that it cannot be projected. He does this, I submit, as a *reductio-ad-absurdum* of the waffling notion of "material" in film theory. These works might be understood as proposing that if film theoreticians really want to talk in terms of the "material" basis of film, they should really be talking about celluloid pure and simple since it is the least ambiguous candidate for the category. Thus, Conrad's pranks can be interpreted as an attempt to chasten theory by illustrating an inadequacy, excess or vagueness in theoretical discourse.

Though avant-garde films may be called "theoretical" insofar as they provoke theory change, I think that if one considers the work in question, one immediately realizes that this is not the primary way in which the term is used. Most often films are dubbed "theoretical" because in one way or another they make reference to an existing theory or theoretical proposition. Here the theory may be a theory of film, of art, or, as very prevalent nowadays, some metaphysical theory – for example, some idea of the subject as it is to be deciphered from what is metaphorically called the position of the spectator in the text.

Just as there is more than one way for an avant-garde film to cause theory change, there is more than one way for avant-garde films to make reference to theories. But before speculating on these ways of reference, I want to raise an important issue about this idea. To wit, is an avant-gardist making theory when he or she makes reference to a theory? A related question also should be broached: Is identifying the theory to which a film makes reference a theoretical or a critical response?

One way an avant-garde film makes reference to theories is by exemplification, i.e., by being a sample or example of the kind of film or work of art that a given theory either endorses, implies or stipulates. To hold that a given avant-garde film exemplifies a given theory is to hold that the theory can be seen as generating the film. That is, the theory is seen as providing a set of principles that determine the articulations in the film. In practice, we perform such an identification by arguing that we arrive at our best explanation of the film in question when we hypothesize that the film presupposes the relevant theory.

Like many structural films, *Zorn's Lemma* can be correlated with a Kantian aesthetic theory. Few previous films make the tension between unity and diversity so palpable and so rich. Its strong internal relations seem to exemplify the idea of a form of purposiveness that is itself purposeless. Contemplative spectatorship is virtually required by the film. As we watch, we constantly discover emergent structures of interrelations. We note that Part One has sound but no image while Part Two has images but no sound. Part Three reconciles this dichotomy – it has both sound and image – but it also carries the contrastive organization to other dimensions. It can be described as a "realistic" film in opposition to Part Two, which is a "montage" film, as well as a landscape versus a city film. The wealth of disparate diverse details plus the sorts of emergent structures that bind them (including the alphabetical replacement patterns in Part Two) engender a variety of cognitive and perceptual play that corresponds to the basis of a Kantian notion of the foundation of aesthetic experience. In terms of film theory, avant-garde works often presuppose discernible theoretical stances. For instance, Gehr's *Reverberation* appears premised on the idea that film is primarily a real object.[4] In both the Frampton and the

Gehr cases, when we say their films are theoretical, we mean they exemplify theories, i.e., postulating the theory in question as generative gives us our best explanation of the work.

One way a film makes reference to a theory is by exemplification. But is exemplification of a theory the same as the construction of a theory? My suspicion is that it is not because it is difficult to understand how the existence of a film, especially one designed with an eye to exemplifying a given theory, could ever stand as evidence for the theory in question. How would such a film argue for the veracity of its generative theory except in a viciously circular manner? How would such a film have any generality?

Identifying a certain theory as the basis for the organization of a given film is a piece of criticism, not a piece of film theory. I am not denying that filmmakers make theory – read Gidal, Le Grice, Wollen, and Sitney's two anthologies for myriad examples. But the question is whether when they make films that exemplify those theories, those films are also works of theory. I believe that they are not.[5] Clearly they are not evidence for any general theory – one flat film would hardly show that all films are really flat, for instance.

It might be proposed that such exemplifications are theoretical recommendations that all films should be made a certain way. Two problems arise here, however. First, making a flat film does not supply a reason for making other flat films, though such a reason is requisite if a recommendation is to be theoretical. Second, if we presuppose that avant-garde films theoretically recommend a specific direction of filmmaking, aren't we committed to admit that typical Hollywood films are theoretical recommendations in the same way since they will exemplify certain classical theories of film and narration? This is not to suggest that there are not interesting theoretical questions here. Theory hopefully will be able to explain how and when a film recommends a

new direction in cinema. But such questions have neither been raised nor answered by existing avant-garde films that have exemplified specific theories.

A second way that an avant-garde film makes reference to a theory is by literalizing it. For example, Bill Brand's *Works in the Field* evokes the notion that classical narrative editing is a code by juxtaposing sequences employing a random dot matrix superimposed over images with sequences of a French documentary about Indochina. The random dot matrix sequences allude (through their structure) to information theory with its very strong notion of a code. Cut against the cleanly edited documentary, the "coded" image section elicits the idea that the editing is a code – at least for those of us who know such a theory exists. We infer the association because the idea of a code is something that has linguistic applicability to both parts of the film and thereby serves as a perfect means for making Brand's juxtaposition of the two parts coherent. Brand's alternating structure evokes a theory, virtually literalizes it, as might a charade.

Why not say that Brand is doing theory in *Works in the Field?* First, we note that from Brand's film we have no idea of what the codes of classical editing are; that is, nothing has been explained. Furthermore, in order to divine the proposed theoretical import of the film you would already have to have an inkling of the theory being referred to. For instance, you would have to know that there is a theoretical posture that regards classical editing as precisely coded in a way that is analogous to the kinds of phenomena information theory studies. It seems to me that much avant-garde film that is called theoretical is of this variety; it literalizes an antecedently developed theory but only for those of us already somewhat familiar with the theory.

Another way to argue that Brand's film is miming rather than making theory is to point out that the film, in terms of the theory it literalizes, is not its own best explanation. That is, the film in part relies on prompting an associative identification between the notion of a code in information theory with the notion of what we call in the trade "codes of classical editing." This particular type of associative operation is not broached in the theory as the film literalizes it. Thus, somewhat paradoxically, the film as a putative theory doesn't explain itself – among other things an embarrassing way to lack generality.

It is not my intention to say that films should not literalize or exemplify theories of film, of art, of metaphysics, of psychoanalysis, etc. My only aim is to stress that making reference to theories is not the same as theorizing. Many avant-garde films do make reference to theories; if this is what commentators mean when they call such films "theoretical," it seems perfectly reasonable. The problem or rather the confusion only begins to arise when commentators begin to slip into presenting such films as vehicles for the construction of theories.

Generally, films that make reference to theories presuppose audiences that are already familiar with the theory in question. Structural/Materialist film purportedly redefines the role of spectatorship, making it active in a way that has political ramifications. How can a film have such significance? Part of the story, to use a favorite adverb of one of the movement's major polemicists, is that Structural/Materialist films vehemently eschew narrative. Furthermore, the denial of narrative is a means of denying certain associated features of narrative. For these British filmmakers, this includes passive spectatorship which is correlated with illusionism and ideology. That is, the strident repudiation of narrative in Structural/Materialist film expressively functions as a means to deny what narrative is most saliently correlated to in British film culture. The associative process which literalizes this supposedly new conception of the subject is based on a set of associative contrasts, viz., narrative is to nonnarrative, as illusion is to antiillusion, as passive spectatorship is to active spectatorship. No Structural/Materialist film either proves or explains the correlation between narrative and passive spectatorship nor does any illuminate the relationship of active spectatorship and politics. Yet, I agree that these films have the symbolic import that their polemicists attribute to them because of prevailing theoretical associations with narrative in British film circles. But this is only to say that these films have a kind of allegiance to a film theory, not that they produce film theory. Indeed, they are the emblems of a set of film-theoretical prejudices, but they have not made film theory.

I do not wish to dismiss films that make references to theories as uninteresting. They are theoretically significant but not in the way that they are often taken to be. They are not vehicles for making theories in the sense of offering arguments or evidence. Rather, they attempt to incorporate prevailing theories in unique, elliptical symbol systems that in some way mirror or express the theoretical preoccupations of the culture or sub-culture from which they emerge. In short, they are examples of something quite common across the arts – the urge to reflect the concerns of a given culture or sub-culture in the various symbol systems of each artform. That is, each culture or sub-culture, and, for that matter, often each generation has a tendency to attempt to differentiate itself by producing unique symbol systems that relate, in complicated ways, to prevailing issues and presuppositions.

Panofsky sees the structure of the Gothic Cathedral as an exemplification of monastic patterns of reasoning. Likewise, postmodern dancers, such as Yvonne Rainer, responded to the reductionist fervor of the Sixties by literalizing the notion that dance is essentially movement to the exclusion of expressive gesture and choreographic composition. They did this by adopting a dance vocabulary composed of everyday actions and macaronic phrasing.

In film, we can see the Soviet montagists as well as the Constructivists as opting for a style that emphasizes assemblage in order to literalize the idea of the artist as worker. Vertov talks of his filmmaking organization as a "factory of facts." The montagists in general favored metaphors for their style that described them as artisans and engineers. Their style expressed their interest, derived from Marxist theory, in identifying themselves as makers of a certain sort, namely, workers piecing together the artifacts of modern industry and science. Their style symbolized their theoretical allegiance to the proletariat. In the same way, I believe the well-known contemporary avant-garde films that make a reference to theories can be seen as part of a more generic social tendency in art towards resonating particular, pressing intellectual issues, fashions and concerns across every key of the culture.

Successive generations of avant-garde filmmakers have made films which correlate with very different kinds of theories ranging, for example, from Romantic poetics, Jungian psychology, modernist aesthetics, phenomenology, different brands of film theory, the philosophy of language and Psychoanalytic-Marxist-Semiology. These films have not made direct contributions to the theories they refer to; however, they have symbolically differentiated, and, in that sense, enriched and reinforced the cultural context from which they arose.

To my knowledge, avant-garde films that refer to theories have not been vehicles for making theory. Nevertheless, they are particularly interesting subjects for theoretical research in terms of the kinds of processes, and contextual and articulatory structures that make it possible for the often elliptical symbol systems of the avant-garde film to make reference to theories. Needless to say, in making reference to theories an avant-garde film frequently becomes theoretical in the sense of provoking theory change by

means, for instance, of introducing new techniques or exploiting new possibilities of the cinema in its attempt to exemplify a theory.

Though I think that the four categories outlined above describe the most important relations between theory and the avant-garde film, I will conclude by briefly mentioning two other candidates. Often one film may be described as "answering" another film or type of film. For instance, Robert Nelson's *Suite California Stops and Passes* begins by parodying Hollywood story films. It could be called a polemic for the diary film. One wonders whether this metaphor of "answering" implies that the film is "theoretical." Undoubtedly films do "answer" films. But again the question arises of how by simply manifesting a specific stylistic and/or theoretical allegiance a film would straightforwardly constitute evidence or argument for a general theory.

Lastly, some films, which do not make reference in any way to a given theory, may nevertheless be strongly compatible with a certain theory. For example, the Camera Obscura Collective champions the films of Yvonne Rainer on the grounds of a shared preoccupation with identity in Rainer's themes and those of the currently popular conglomeration of metaphysics, psychoanalysis, politics and film theory associated with Lacanian semiology. In this case, it is especially hard to see how Rainer's films, which I believe are extremely important, can be theoretical since there is nothing in them or in the context of their production to associate them with the specific theories that are being mobilized to valorize them.

I began pessimistically by admitting that I would probably not be able to enumerate every kind of relation between avant-garde film and theory. I confess that if I were more imaginative, I might have been able to discern some way in which we could say films make theory. For the present, however, my provisional conclusion is that in most cases, the avant-garde films that fascinate us are more involved in making reference to theories than in making theories.

Notes

1. In arguing that avant-garde films are not theoretical (in the sense of making theory), I do not mean to imply that they are uninteresting. I do not mention a single film in this paper that I do not believe is a good film.

   An example of a critical interpretation of an avant-garde film which claims that the film makes theory is P. Adams Sitney's gloss of Brakhage's *The Animals of Eden and After* in "Autobiography in Avant-garde Film," in *Avant-garde Film* (New York: NYU Press, 1978), pp. 220–24. Though Sitney has disagreed with this characterization of his "reading," I believe, after several re-readings, that the text can only be understood as claiming that in the film Brakhage develops a theory of metaphor as a process of *aftering* one shot by another.

   Other examples of the idea that avant-garde films make theory include the popular charge that some works are "idealist," which implicitly indicates that what is wrong with the films amounts to philosophical or theoretical errors, i.e., that the theory they make is misguided.

   The claim that avant-garde films make theory is also advanced by Edward S. Small in *Direct Theory* (Carbondale: Southern Illinois University Press, 1994).

2. In "Film History and Film Theory: An Outline for an Institutional Theory of Film." This article is included in this volume.

3. Editing in terms of parallel modalities is discussed in my "Toward a Theory of Film Editing," pp. 86–87, in *Millennium Film Journal* no. 3. This article is included in this volume.

4. This interpretation can be found in "Program Notes" by Ernie Gehr in Sitney's *Avant-garde Film*, pp. 247–48.

5. Some readers of this paper have argued that the reason I am unable to accept avant-garde films as theory is that I believe that theory must be linguistic rather than imagistic. I do not think, however, that this is the crux of the matter. Rather the problem may be that the demand that avant-garde films be formally innovative implies that they must be highly elliptical symbol systems which are capable only of allusion to rather than articulation of theories. For further argumentation in the vein, see Noël Carroll, "Avant-garde Art and the Problem of Theory," in *The Journal of Aesthetic Education* (Fall, 1995).

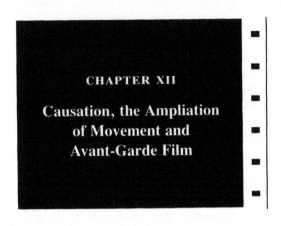

CHAPTER XII

Causation, the Ampliation of Movement and Avant-Garde Film

I. Introduction

In Martin Ritt's recently released film, *Back Roads,* there is a scene in which the male protagonist, Elwood Pratt, floors a moronic, gigantic heavyweight named Marvin Bleitz. The situation is comic. Before the boxing match begins, Elwood learns that Marvin, a high school dropout version of Miles Gloriosus, is always late to leave his corner, too busy is he basking in the audience's adulation. Elwood rushes on Marvin as, unawares, the giant turns from his public, and Elwood flattens the lummox in a single stroke.

The action is represented in three shots, all in slow motion. The first has Marvin partially in close-up in the foreground as a diminutive Elwood stalks him in the background, approaching the camera while Marvin has his back to him. The difference in cinematic scale rehearses your basic David and Goliath theme. Next, Elwood is in range of Marvin; he throws a punch that travels from screen right to screen left and lands on Marvin's jaw. Lastly, there is a shot of Marvin flying screen right and hitting the mat. Later in the film, in the last fight scene, a brawny, bearded trucker in a roadside bar bashes Elwood. The trucker's fist sails right to left but we don't see its impact because the stunt is done in such a way that the antagonist's shoulder shields it. In the next shot, Elwood hits the floor in the same direction as the trajectory of the punch. We have as strong an impression of the causal

interaction as we did in the case of Marvin's defeat even though we have not seen a representation of the fist meeting Elwood's chin.

Both of these shot interpolations are quite effective though neither is particularly distinguished. In both cases, the impression of causation in the representational array is heightened by matching the directions of the movements in the successive shots that stand for the cause and effect stages of the actions at hand. The use of match cutting is quite common and is a basic device for presenting cases of proximate causation in narrative films. The device is so efficacious, in fact, that the matched directionality of the cut in our second example is capable of accentuating our sense of causation even though we have not seen the trucker's hand touch (or even appear to touch) Elwood. Here, of course, the narrative context contributes to our intuition of causality. Nevertheless, we are all familiar with cases where matched directionality in and of itself can give rise to the impression of causation. Undoubtedly, this is the reason why matched directionality has become a fundamental ingredient in the representation of proximate causation in film.

The psychological factors involved in the suggestion of causation by matched direction cutting seem related to, though not identical to, those discussed in Albert Michotte's famous study, *The Perception of Causality.*[1] Michotte designed a series of experiments in order to disprove David Hume's dictum that

Suppose two objects be presented to us, of which the one is the cause and the other the effect; it is plain that from a simple consideration of one or both of these objects, we shall never perceive the tie by which they are united, or be able certainly to pronounce, that there is a connexion between them.[2]

Against Hume, Michotte believes that in certain cases and under certain conditions, we do perceive causation. Michotte describes these cases in terms of a process called ampliation which he defines thusly: "Ampliation is the creating or establishing of a movement onto the second object of the already existing movement of the first object."[3] Michotte arrived at the concept of ampliation primarily through the examination of two phenomena which he dubbed the Launching Effect and the Entraining Effect.

The Launching Effect occurs when a subject views a projected object, A, say a rectangle, moving at and then touching another projected object, B, which until contiguous with A is stationary but which when A arrives begins to move. At certain speeds, movement intervals, etc. – all exhaustively studied by Michotte through endless experiments – subjects report that object A *causes* object B to move. The subjects know that in reality there is no causation.[4] They know they are watching the independently projected movement of two independently projected figures. But they report that, phenomenally speaking, they see A push or launch B.

The Entraining Effect occurs when a projected object or group of objects, A, passes a stationary, independently projected object, B, which begins to move when A and B are aligned. Subjects recount that A "picks up" B. The force or impetus for B's movement appears to come from A.

In both the Launching Effect and the Entraining Effect, in Michotte's experiments, there is no question of actual causation between A and B. Both are projected figures whose movement is completely independent of each other – they start and stop as the experimenter manipulates the projection apparatus. Yet, the subjects report strong impressions of causation. B's movement in both cases *appears* dependent on A's.[5] Here the basis of phenomenal causation (as opposed to actual causation) is the apparent leap or transfer of properties (namely movement or propulsion) from one object to another.

Michotte attempts to explain both forms of ampliation in terms of a variation on the Gestalt idea of *Prananz*. He argues that the subjects see causation in order to maintain good continuity in their visual field. B's movement is amalgamated with A's as a matter of *conservation of process,*[6] i.e., A's movement is conserved by seeing it evolve or become B's. With both the Launching Effect and the Entraining Effect, the subject integrates the two movements into one process, seeing the movement of B as a prolongation of and extension of the movement of A – just as one amalgamates a series of dots into a straight line, reducing them to one figure for the sake of economy. Michotte adds that this is not a matter of interpretation but of perception.[7] The impression of causation results from the conservation of process which leads us to assimilate two independent movements into one event in which A's movement is transformed into B's while maintaining its initial identity; the movement, in other words, is transferred from A to B, or A's energy is imparted to B so that we see A's movement produce B's. Our constitutional tendency to conserve process gives rise to the imputation of production. And the concept of "production," of course, is nothing but a virtual cognate or purely, systemic *definiendum* of causation.[8]

It is not at all clear that Michotte proves everything he wants. Whether he defeats Hume is doubtful since in Hume's argument the notion of perception is being used epistemically in the sense of "truly perceive" whereas what Michotte establishes are merely cases of phenomenal perception. The explanatory power of the gestalt-type account given to ampliation, as well, is open to question as is the strictness of the concept of interpretation in Michotte's argument that we are perceiving causation rather than entering a causal interpretation in cases of ampliation. And Piaget has charged – rightly I believe – that the idea of ampliation itself is only descriptive and not explanatory.[9] But these are issues for philosophers and psychologists. Film scholars, on the other hand, can still benefit from Michotte's research because it supplies a framework for discussing the impressions of causation engendered by shot chains such as those introduced in my opening paragraph, since these seem related to the Launching Effect.

I say "related to" rather than "examples of" for several reasons. First, Michotte contends that the figures in his experiments are "real" as opposed to "representational" objects; thus, he writes ". . . the causality sometimes perceived on the cinema screen may represent the causality exercised by one 'real' object on another 'real' object; but from a psychological point of view it is still one phenomenal causality representing another." Second, in Michotte's experiments the subject is initially presented with two objects whereas in film we often see the objects of the represented interaction successively.[10] For example, we might see a row of men wielding a battering ram in one shot and in the next shot a hitherto unseen door buckles in the direction of the blows. Also, because of the synthetic nature of the space of editing and because of the diminution of spatial information due to the monocular viewpoint of the single shot, the necessity for spatial contiguity in cinematic ampliation is rather an ambiguous issue. That is, in opposition to most of Michotte's cases, temporal succession, or simultaneity, matched speeds and directionality seem enough to cue a cinematic launching effect. Cinematic ampliation, therefore, is better seen as a derivative and modification of ampliation per se.

Of Michotte's effects, Launching is clearly the most important in casual editing.[11] The use of matched movement editing in order to enhance the impression of causation is straightforwardly describable as a case of cinematic ampliation. By using the word "impression," I do not, of course, mean to imply that spectators are deceived – for ideological purposes or otherwise – into believing they are witnessing actual in-

stances of causation, but only that by using matching directions and often matching speeds film editors can accentuate their representation of causation by exploiting some of the cues or conditions of ampliation per se. Cinematic ampliation is the selective imitation of some of the necessary features of ordinary ampliation. Like ordinary ampliation, cinematic ampliation is a structure that involves an approaching or launching movement, which can be set out in either one shot or a group of shots, followed by withdrawal movement in the same direction and generally at a similar speed as the approaching movement. This structure has been used in conventional films since the twenties and though often exhilarating, it is also quite banal. However, there is a variation of cinematic ampliation – that has also been with us at least since the twenties – that is a bit more interesting. That is the suggestion of causation between represented objects or events that could not possibly – given the laws of physics or the information in the film – be interacting causally. Here, I am not referring to the representation of magical causation in a horror film because such a film will posit the event as lawful, maybe Higher Lawful. Rather I have in mind the use of ampliation in avant-garde film where what is represented via matched movement is a case of unrecuperated, impossible causation. A man – a teacher? – is shot in a famous scene in *Un Chien Andalou* and in the next shot he falls, clutching the naked back of a woman. The impression or suggestion of causal continuity is vivid despite the fact that we firmly believe that the represented event is totally implausible. This use of cinematic ampliation – not to enhance the sense of causation between conceivably connected events, but to create the sense of connection between palpably disjunct events – is a staple device, one might even say a trope, of avant-garde film. This is not to claim that it never occurs outside avant-garde film; it can figure, for instance, as a flashy scene connective in a stylish thirties' narrative. But in general, this use of cinematic ampliation is more a matter of ornamentation or decoration in most conventional narratives (where it appears) while avant-gardists who tend to employ it use it as a basic structural and expressive device.

We can find a prototype for the cinematic ampliation of impossible events in Michotte's experiment #28 in which a real ball appears to launch a projected circle; Michotte notes "We know perfectly well that a 'real' ball cannot drive away or 'launch' a reflected image or shadow"; so Michotte concludes that the experiment "shows that the 'status' of the objects in no way alters the impression of causality and that the objects belong to different 'worlds' . . . does not act as a segregative element in these experiments."[12]

An example of the use of the cinematic ampliation of an impossible event can be found in Stuart Sherman's *Flying*. The second shot is of a metal railing – an airport bannister – that runs horizontally across the screen; on the left, a hand mysteriously holds a suitcase handle, sans suitcase. The camera moves rapidly along the railing from left to right. Then, there is a cut to a shot of a plane taking off in the same direction. This shot is executed from the perspective of a passenger. As the camera rises at a gradually expanding acute angle, the hand is superimposed on the image. This is an elegantly elliptical symbol for travel, charged by the haunting partial absence of the traveler and his belongings, which, among other things, functions as a verbal image[13] for the "absence" departure entails. Cinematic ampliation is crucial to the creation of this symbol. To use Michotte's terminology, the separate movements of the two shots undergo a "fusion because they are kinematically similar."[14] The action of "rushing" to the plane becomes, or is united with, or is transformed into, the action of the plane's lift-off. More than that, the energy of the first shot appears, impossibly

enough, to be propelling the upward movement of the camera. Unlike Michotte's examples, here we do not have visible objects in seeming interaction, but rather movements – i.e., camera movements. Nevertheless, there is still a strong impression that the first camera movement has transferred its thrust to the second and that the first camera movement is driving the plane skyward.

The preceding case of the cinematic ampliation of an impossible event is a case of strong cinematic ampliation which we can define as a case of ampliation that results in an impression of a causal push, or shove, or energy transfer from one shot to another. There is also, in regard to the suggestion of impossible events, a weaker form of cinematic ampliation which occurs when, as the consequence of matching screen directions, the independent movements of two or more shots appear continuous, appear to compose a single line of movement across tangibly disparate locales and/or "through" patently different objects. This second type of cinematic ampliation is weak only in the sense that it doesn't instill a sense of causation. Nevertheless, it does trigger the appearance of a fusion or extension of an earlier movement to a later movement. Together, the strong and weak ampliations of impossible events provide very standard linkage devices in avant-garde editing. But though they are standard devices in one respect, they can be used to signal unique, expressive commitments when embedded in particular contexts. In order to explore the expressive potential of these devices, let us examine two films – *Man with a Movie Camera* by Dziga Vertov and *Rude Awakening* by Warren Sonbert – which employ both weak and strong instances of cinematic ampliation as essential expressive and organizational devices. (N.B.: Often in what follows I will use the simpler phrase "cinematic ampliation" for brevity rather than the more accurate phrase "the cinematic ampliation of an impossible event." However, the context should make it clear when the ampliation is of the impossible variety.)

II. *Man with a Movie Camera*

Man with a Movie Camera is a film in which many of the main themes are worked out in terms of movement. The overall course of the film is one from stasis through activity – first work activities, then leisure activities – and, finally, hyperactivity – by the end of the film, the Soviet Union, as a whole it seems, rushes breathlessly toward its future. After a prelude where we are introduced to the cameraman and the movie theater, the film-within-the-film begins by showing us Russia at rest. We see barren streets, empty fire-escapes, sleeping babies and all sorts of quiescent objects – an abacus, a typewriter, an elevator, cars, mannequins, gears, etc. There is an overhead shot of an auto arriving to pick up the man with the movie camera; as they start off to work, the city awakens. People dress, travel to their jobs and the still objects viewed earlier are set in motion. The work day accelerates only to halt and be replaced by an ever-accelerating play day. The montage and camera speed increase velocity, communicating an overwhelming sense of energy and well-being. Cars, horses, pedestrians, trains, trolleys, bicycles approach the camera and then turn and hurtle away. The steam engine, a symbol of modernity (and industrialization), keeps reappearing, grounding the racing imagery as an emblem of progress. The intense movement comes to stand for The Movement – the movement of history, the movement of socialism toward, what promised to be in 1928, a glorious future. *Man with a Movie Camera* attempts to picture an entire society – a society *moving* toward utopia.

Matched movement editing is key to developing the central movement metaphors in *Man with a Movie Camera*. An inventory of all the uses of motion in the film deserves an essay all to itself, though I think it is safe to say that there are three major strategies for movement editing that Vertov relies on. They are comparative movement cutting, weak and strong ampliation. Each of these techniques, in different ways, attempts to transform unique, localizable movements of the film into occasions for general statements; that is, they attempt to visually assimilate the movement of individuals into the movement of society as a whole, thereby illustrating one of the film's major ideas, viz., that all movements are co-ordinated or concrease into one Movement under socialism.

The comparative movement editing is the easiest to identify. The literal movements – of work and play – of all different walks of Soviet life are analogized in groups of successive shots in which the activities recorded either belong to the same category – e.g., washing – and/or they look alike. A significant proportion of these analogies is devoted to the visual similarities of the Soviet film workers' activities and those performed by other workers. Editing is compared to sewing; cranking a camera is rhymed with working a cash register and massaging a scalp; turning rewinds is likened to turning the drive shaft of a sewing machine; scraping emulsion is collated to shaving and manicuring, etc. And throughout the film there is a motif of juxtaposing moving square objects – matchbooks and train windows – to moving film strips that are, of course, sectioned into frames; thus, the filmmakers' production is also visually analogous to that of other workers.

Not only does the Soviet film worker go everywhere the average Soviet citizen goes; not only does he participate in every social activity (from fire-fighting to sunbathing); and not only is the film worker represented as involved in activities that are categorically similar to those of ordinary workers;[15] at the same time, the Soviet film worker is shown to be engaged in work that looks just like the work of the ordinary citizen. The view of the artist here is not Romantic and elitist but egalitarian. The artist is a worker, like anyone else; the artist worker and his comrades in other fields participate in the *same movement.*

Of course, the film not only sets forth movement similes between film artists and workers but also between a wide range of all sorts of work and play. Washing in preparation for work is categorically compared to washing street hydrants and ash cans, while, via fast motion photography, folding cigarette boxes, running a switchboard and typing are imbued with the same movement qualities. Motorcycle racing and merry-go-round riding are equated in virtue of cycloid movement. And as Russia exercises its way into a healthy future, the various strenuous games of the body politic are reviewed in rapid cutting that stresses their similarities. Again, the effect is to promote a vision of Soviet life as both concerted and democratic.

Through the use of weak ampliation, Vertov is able to forward the theme of unified movement along another front. Not only are the movements from shot to shot similar in *Man with a Movie Camera;* but at points, the screen directions and comparative velocities from one shot to the next are such that their movements seem to blend or fuse into each other. For example, in the sporting sequence, a man hurls a javelin from screen right to left in one shot. There is a cut to a soccer goalie defending his net. As the goalie maneuvers, it is difficult to resist the feeling that the javelin is about to skewer him. When the soccer ball enters the frame, spinning screen right to left, it seems to be the same line of movement as the javelin. It is as if the spear metamorphosed into a ball in transit. And it feels as if the spear thrower's energy powers the ball. This case borders on strong ampliation but falls somewhat short, perhaps because of the time interval that is left between the beginning of the second shot and the entry of the ball. But even as a case of weak ampliation, the cut is able to carry its rhetorical point. All these sports – here, specifically, hurling the javelin and soccer – are part of the same

process, the rejuvenation of Russia. Since the ultimate reference of *Man with a Movie Camera* is not to individuals but to the Soviet Union – the film is "a day in the life of the Soviet Union" – the vitality of the sporting scenes stands for the vitality of the young socialist nation. The use of the weak cinematic ampliation of impossible events not only serves to visually fuse disparate events in order to polemically connect them, but it also operates as a means of cuing the more generic reference of the images by "upsetting" the particularity of the individual events recorded. That is, since we realize that we cannot take the weak ampliations literally – because they suggest impossible events – we must take them figuratively and generically.

Weak cinematic ampliation also binds work processes in *Man with a Movie Camera.* An ax is sharpened, the blade cutting across the screen in such a way that its movement elides with that of workmen in a succeeding shot. Again, the impression of the blending of these movements into one impossible event is to prime the discursive point that all work in the Soviet Union is of a piece, the unity of movement heralding a unity of purpose. Weak cinematic ampliation, of course, is a perfect visual device for making this assertion, substituting phenomenal fusion for teleology. Throughout the film, movements seem to merge as the result of similar rhythms and screen directions. A revolving door swings counterclockwise and a long shot of a thoroughfare seems to have traffic continuing the same movement. The movement of a strip of film over the editing table seems to blend into the scarped movement of a train – movies are thus phenomenally incorporated into the rush of progress.

Cases of strong cinematic ampliation are statistically less frequent than weak ampliations in *Man with a Movie Camera.* One early example is quite humorous. A woman rolls uncomfortably in bed and this is matched twice with a shot of a train executed by a similarly "tossing" camera. The woman's rustling appears literally earthshaking. Later a case of beer swings in such a way that it elides with the wobbly camera movement of the next shot which reviews a scene of churches. Phenomenally, the beer seems to send the camera bobbing; polemically, the camera movement is "drunken." Vertov has found a stylish way through strong ampliation to realize Trotsky's call for cinema to tackle the twin intoxications of religion and alcohol.[16]

One of the most important instances of strong ampliation occurs in the section on the work day which begins with the comparisons between the beauty salon/barbership imagery, on the one hand, and those analogizing shots of workers applying mud to buildings, washing clothes, etc., on the other. This is one of the most important sequences of the film insofar as it is Vertov's richest and most condensed compendium of work. The montage picks up speed, cataloguing a wide selection of work in textile factories, cigarette plants, switchboard offices, etc. Cranking cameras, stropping razors, turning spindles, sharpening axes enter the stream of imagery setting up a rhythmic pulse of energy that gravitates to and fro but whose propulsion seems directed primarily to the right. Suddenly a group of factory or mine workers is included; they heave a heavy beam to the right in a movement that seems to impart force to a hand in the next shot that moves the rotary of a sewing machine. The workers' energy, in other words, seems to cross the boundaries of the frame.

Perhaps the most famous image of the film – that of the cameraman at the center of a mandala of whirling machinery – likewise is a case of strong ampliation. For as the cameraman turns – in the direction of the vortex – one can't help but see him as being rotated by the changing machines. They supply the "motor," as it were, that is moving him. Here, it is not simply a case of seeing the independent movements as unified, but of seeing the initial, dominant movements of

the machines as supplying the "shove" that motivates the cameraman's movement. He is presented as a cog in a machine, though his "stature" is in no way diminished by this.

These last two examples of the strong cinematic ampliation of an impossible causal interaction are key means by which Vertov establishes his view of the nature of the Soviet state. In the parlance of political science, Vertov's conception of the state is that it is an organic whole.[17] The different activities of Soviet life are presented as inextricably interdependent; the "parts" of the new Russian society mutually interact in chains of cause and effect. The energy of the workers seems to push the hand of the textile worker and the cameraman is "moved" by machinery. In a manner of speaking, we can say that Vertov is attempting to portray instances of remote causation – like the relation of the cameraman to industry – as cases of proximate causation. That is, causal, social processes – the sorts of things that usually are of such a scale that it is impossible to see them in a single glance – are cinematically transformed into what appears phenomenally as a piece of direct causation. Thus, the inter-relatedness of the parts of the social whole is dramatically depicted; the "organic interdependency" of distant parts and activities within the Soviet state is "made visible."

It may strike some readers as rather oxymoronic to say that Vertov's metaphor for the state is an organism because, on the face of it, it is obvious, just in terms of the imagery, that Vertov is equating the state with a kind of gigantic machine whose magnificently calibrated parts interlock "miraculously" via strong cinematic ampliation. And, of course, since we tend to construe "organism" and "machine" as polar opposites, it appears somewhat perverse to associate Vertov's vision of the state as an elegant, ideal, powerful, synchronised engine with an organic metaphor. Yet, it is important to remember that the core element of the organic/machine contrast hinges on the opposition of an immanent principle versus the formalist application of an external principle. Hence, as early as 1679, Dryden, in his "Grounds of criticism in tragedy," rebukes neoclassicists for their "mechanic rules." In political philosophy, the organic society is one in which the community is integrated by a common goal rather than one in which the citizenry is a bundle of egoistic individuals legalistically and bureaucratically governed from above. Through the employment of both the strong and weak ampliation of impossible events, Vertov's symbolism emphasizes the mutual, interdependent effort of the Soviet people as united and as involving a reciprocal, co-operative, inter-related system of causes and effects that connect all strata of Soviet society. If the new Russia was to be a machine for Vertov, we can also say, without contradiction, that it was to be an organic machine, i.e., the metaphor of the machine society is mobilized to point to the same features that were made salient by the older organic metaphor.[18]

Causation is a major topic of *Man with a Movie Camera,* one explored across many different dimensions of the film. There is, for example, a macro-structure in the editing which traces effects to their causes, moving from buses and trains to the factories, mines and hydroelectric plants that made and/or power them. This corresponds to what might be thought of as a search for origins in the film, i.e., an answering of questions like "where do trolley cars come from?" in an effort to render mass society less alienating for the viewer. The didactic revelation of the causes and origins of the film itself is a dominant motif of this overall preoccupation.

Annette Michelson has pointed out in her brilliant, pioneering article, "From Magician to Epistemologist," that Vertov uses the device of hysteron proteron as a central means for displaying causation in a distinctly illuminating manner.[19] Strong and weak ampliation provide equally important strategies for Vertov to use in his pursuit of causal

themes. Their full significance can be grasped by considering them in the context of another form of causal representation that recurs often in the film but which so far has not been mentioned, viz., the use of synecdoche to imply causation between presumably disparate, independent events.

Often we see a tight shot of a lever being pulled or a wheel being turned, followed by a shot of a machine starting. Though not a matter of ampliation, we nevertheless have a strong sense that the lever or wheel has "switched on" the machine. Or, we may see a machine rapidly whirring in manic arcs cut against the shot of the cameraman being raised in a cable car over a dam. It is hard to suppress the intuition that the machine is powering the ascent. In both these cases, we infer mechanical causation as the linkage between the represented events not because we know that the first shot is the source of propulsion for what is in the second shot, but because this format of representation is deeply associated with the conventional presentation of mechanical causation in film. Indeed, in many of the pertinent cases, one is pretty sure that the shots are not representing parts of the same mechanical process – the machines in question don't look like they are designed to perform the task at issue. But the tension between the implication of causation, on the one hand, and its probable unlikelihood, on the other, enables Vertov to make the point that all the machines in the Soviet Union are, in some generic sense, causally interrelated in the production of socialism; he does this by suggesting visually that machines with very discreet functions are "magically" bound up in the same supposedly localizable process.

In the examples of the preceding paragraph, Vertov is using the same structure that Eisenstein adopts in *The General Line* when at the bovine wedding, Tommy charges at his offscreen bride, followed by a cut to an explosion, followed by shots of water churning at a hydroelectric plant. At one level, the explosion stands for intercourse and the roiling waters for sperm. But, at the same time, the union of these events into one "fantastic" whole illustrates forcefully the interdependency – the causal interdependency – of Soviet agricultural productivity with the industrialization of Russia, a major tenet of state policy in the twenties.[20] More cattle facilitates the building of more power stations – symbolised by the land-clearing explosion and the water-power/ sperm. Eisenstein, in other words, is attempting to represent an instance of remote causation, a social process, as proximate causation in order to hammer home the needful, intimate connection between city and country.

Vertov and Eisenstein are, indisputably, the two Soviet filmmakers who are most obsessed with jumping out of the concrete here-and-now of photography into the realm of essayistic generalization. Vertov, like Eisenstein, returns often to the use of impossible synecdoches of causation between different units of the industrial complex in order to establish the theme of interdependency. In this light, the strong ampliations of *Man with a Movie Camera* are sterling devices for stressing the functional interdependency of physically disjunct processes because they promote phenomenally compelling images of proximate causation. Weak ampliation, which occurs in the film more frequently than strong ampliation, projects organicism in another sense, the unity of movement conveying a perceptible unity of purpose. In Aristotelian jargon – as found in both the *Physics* and the *Metaphysics* – strong ampliation of impossible events affords the impression of (virtual) efficient causation while weak ampliation affords the impression of (virtual) final causation.[21] Both devices, in turn, promulgate an overarching vision of the Soviet Union as an organic system of reciprocal causal processes, while also realizing the goal of early Soviet cinema, i.e., the illustration of the general via the manipulation of the photographic particular.

III. *Rude Awakening*

Warren Sonbert's *Rude Awakening* is a very accomplished example of a strategy often used in avant-garde editing – what might be called "polyvalent montage." Sonbert has relied heavily on this device since *Carriage Trade*. In this mode of editing, it is particularly important that each shot is polyvalent in the sense that it can be combined with surrounding shots along potentially many dimensions. That is, this style begins in the realization that a shot may either match or contrast with adjacently preceding or succeeding shots in virtue of color, subject, shape, shade, texture, the screen orientation of objects, the direction of camera or object movement, or even the stasis thereof.

In Sonbert's *Divided Loyalties,* a shot of a group of opera singers bowing is contrasted immediately to a shot of a bridge rising which is symmetrically followed by the singer bowing again; later a shot of a single singer bowing is matched to a shot of the arm of an oil well slowly lowering. In *Rude Awakening,* an image of *white* clouds is cut to a shot of a *white* goat being *milked*. In another shot, the camera plows past a naked model to take the measure of the gleaming glass façades across the street; they are analogized to an arboreal pond, the forest reflected on its surface.

In polyvalent montage, the linkages between shots can be along more than one dimension, and can simultaneously involve comparison *and* contrast. In *Rude Awakening,* an animal tamer has one lion leap from screen right to left over a host of fellow felines; this is cut against a shot of the top of a convertible rising in the opposite direction while the car itself starts to move ever so slightly to the left side of the frame. Later, two golfers – a man in the foreground in a red sweater and a woman in the background in a yellow sweater – both putt; the balls go left to right; there is a cut to a patch of red and yellow tulips over which the camera pans right to left.

Nor do the linkages in polyvalent montage simply hinge on comparison and contrast. A crowd of spectators looks upwards in *Rude Awakening;* this is juxtaposed to a plane in flight; the suggestion that the people in the first shot are watching it. And, of course, I have chosen to speak of *Rude Awakening* because cinematic ampliation is a major connective tissue throughout the film.

Essential to how polyvalent montage is practiced by contemporary avant-gardists is the tendency to incessantly shift the rationale of the cutting to new associative pathways, both over the course of the entire film and even from shot to shot. Polyvalent editing is a kind of overtonal montage in spades because either the tonal dominant is always changing, or because there are so many equipotent associative links between the shots that there is no tonal dominant. Polyvalent montage progresses as a dense broken line, often pivoting, leaving behind units of development of generally uneven proportions.

Polyvalent montage has existed since the twenties; its history stretches from *Ballet Mecanique* and the city symphonies to works of our contemporaries from Brakhage to Abigail Child. Certain images – like fairgrounds – are especially conducive for obvious reasons to polyvalent montage and they recur with surprising regularity.[22] Many of the formal variables crucial to polyvalent montage were isolated by Eisenstein in his "collision" period.[23] Of course, the Russians most often exploit the various relations of similarity and contrast within a formal arrangement in the spirit of the rhetorical principle of decorum, perpetrating what in literature Yvor Winters fallaciously decries as the "fallacy of imitative form."[24] So in the Odessa Steps sequence of *Potemkin* the contrasting upward/downward movement emphasized in the editing mirrors the conflict between the people and the police, while in *Alexander Nevsky* the rising soundtrack echoes the compositional line of the

shots.[25] Indeed, much of Eisenstein's invention as a critic as well as a filmmaker is a product of what we can easily identify as a compulsive concern with correlating content and style, i.e., with "imitative" or "expressive" form. And Vertov, if the preceding analysis is correct, is similarly preoccupied, particularly in his use of cinematic ampliation. The use of the polyvalent possibilities of editing for the sake of imitative form never completely disappears in the work of contemporary practitioners, especially Brakhage's. But at the same time, the importance of imitative form is less foregrounded in the polyvalent montage of the seventies. Instead, the play of polyvalent variables is probed and expatiated in a reputedly autotelic pursuit of a heightened or refined visual sensibility.

The opening four shots of *Rude Awakening* contain many of the themes of the rest of the film; they provide a kind of prologue. In the first shot, a man draws a long bow, aims and sends an arrow at a target on screen right. There is a dissolve to a bridge; the camera is mounted, presumably in a car, and it moves screen left to right toward the bridge. Next we see a parade, the most striking item of which is a float with a large statue in a yellow cloak on it; the float is moving right to left. Lastly, there is a shot of an airplane wing, shot from the cabin of a jet that is flying right to left. In terms of subject matter, the motifs of sport, carnival and travel are major topics throughout *Rude Awakening*. Moreover, in the inter-relations of the movements of these four shots, the preoccupation with movement also looms. Shots one and two are analogized in their rightward vector while shots three and four head toward the left. In turn, these two sets of shots are contrasted insofar as they pull in opposite directions. And finally, in each set of shots we find that the first shot involves object movement within a static frame followed by a moving camera shot in the same direction. This is of special significance for the kind of cinematic ampliation that supplies an important part of the formal backbone of *Rude Awakening*.

As the prologue prophesies, the contrast and comparison of movement provides much of the "logic" of *Rude Awakening*. Entire blocks of shots are edited in terms of alternating, successive screen directions – from right to left to left to right – thereby building a rhythmic counterpoint. As well, different types of movement are juxtaposed – a circular movement, e.g., children revolving on a playground wheel, with directional movement, e.g., a plane sailing cross-country. In some of these circular/directional contrasts, there is a persuasive suggestion that the repetitive, circular movement is supplying the energy for the directional movement both when the directional movement is vertical and when it is horizontal.

Movement comparisons in *Rude Awakening* can be very subtle. A whirling shot from inside a fairground saucer ride is matched with a fashion model turning, displaying her wares. The circular movement of the lithe model is then contrasted with the shot of a dumpy gasoline truck traveling away from the camera. Symmetrically, another shot of a model appears. She wheels around in front of the camera, her blue dungaree hot pants dominating the center of the image. As she struts away from the camera, there is a cut back to the gasoline truck. The shots are connected by similar movement and by the outlandishly incongruous visual equation of the model's bottom with the oil tank.

Another example of delicate movement comparison occurs in a sequence of three shots that begins with a shot from a car moving right to left. This is followed by a shot of an artist, Robert Indiana, slowly outlining an "O" with his paintbrush. The two movements are likened in terms of direction which makes their contrast in terms of velocity feel especially sharp. Next a subway train leaves a station, exiting at the left side of the frame. Its gradual acceleration, eventuating in a speeding blur, summarizes the contrast of the two preceding shots.

Shots with simultaneous movement in two opposite directions are also compared, e.g., a traffic scene is followed by an enormous game of team tag. And, shots describable in related movement terms, as well, are matched, e.g., a basketball player driving in for a lay-up inscribes a *curved* path on the court and this is replaced by the image of a ferris wheel turning *round* and *round*.

The importance of all the comparative movement editing in *Rude Awakening* for cinematic ampliation should be obvious. Since comparative movement editing relies quite often on matching shot directions, it sets out conditions in which the probability of the cinematic ampliation of impossible events is high. In fact, one might say, for this reason, that cinematic ampliation is a "natural" wherever movement analogy is a structural theme in the editing.

Weak cinematic ampliation recurs throughout *Rude Awakening*. After one basketball player sinks a foul shot, another whizzes the ball left to right so that it can be "taken out." This matches the movement of the ensuing, yellow tinted traveling shot of Calvary Cemetery in New York. The two independent movements blend into one. Likewise, a shot from a merry-go-round – a perennial favorite in polyvalent montage – fuses with a hand-held survey of a barbecue. At times, Sonbert cuts as many as six shots of matching movement together. The viewer gets the feeling of a virtual line of movement expanding through a series of disparate shots. Sonbert may then stop the movement with a static shot and follow it with weakly ampliated movement in the opposite direction.

Throughout *Rude Awakening,* there is a tendency to organize blocks of shots in virtue of movement/direction themes. In order to understand the significance of weak ampliation in this context, it is worthwhile to call attention to the musicalist sensibility that subtends all of *Rude Awakening*. That is, the film is predominantly structured around the play of correlation and contrast between sensuous variables like color, shape and direction. These seem to build into thematic units that are underscored by counterpoints. Perhaps because music is generally regarded as the paradigmatic non-representational temporal art in our culture, we tend unavoidably to depend on it to characterize the kind of unities intuited in *Rude Awakening*. Thus, Sonbert's work since *Carriage Trade* is sometimes called fuguelike. In *Rude Awakening,* the grouping of similar sensuous qualities is easily ana-logized to a melody. Moreover, the thrust of *Rude Awakening* demands something akin to musical appreciation, i.e., a discerning response to the phenomenal interplay of perceptual properties in terms of tempos, echoes, contrasts, elisions, etc. In respect to the rough, musical metaphor that *Rude Awakening* rejoins, the weak cinematic ampliation of impossible events serves to literalize the musical ideas of a movement or a melodic line. That is, through weak ampliation the (phenomenally) same move-ment is distributed over shots of disparate events in a way that is loosely but insistently like the distribution of a thematic movement over different parts of an orchestra. The suggestion of unified movement plus the ostensibly non-representational motivation for such movement, in other words, flesh out the musicalist conceit of the film by organizing many of the "movements" and "developments" in the editing in visual concatenations of shots that are appre-hended as part and parcel of the same movement.

Rude Awakening also contains numerous instances of strong cinematic ampliation. A boy pushes a shuffleboard puck left to right and this concords with a cut to an airplane take-off, shot from inside the jet and moving in the same direction as the puck would have, save for the splice. The result is the appearance of an impossible piece of causation – the child seems to have launched the plane into flight. A golfer in

a red sweater and plaid pants putts away from the camera and this is followed by a stuttered series of shots of camera move-ments traveling down a country road in such a way that the golfer seems to be the source of the camera's propulsion. Later, and conversely, a man pushes his shuffle-board stick in the direction of the camera and in the next shot the camera is rushing "toward" the audience. Or, for yet another example, the dancer, Douglas Dunn, alone in his studio, pushes himself, balanced on one leg, into a position where from head to toe he is exactly parallel to the floor. As he swings into this perfectly horizontal pose, the editing matches his movement with that of a camera throttling across a bridge in a way that suggests that Dunn's dip, an *arabesque penchée* à la *Giselle,* powered it. In all these cases, movement within a static frame is seen as launching camera move-ment in an ensuing shot. Moreover, the camera movement is launched by a "lei-sure" activity – a gesture of play or art – and the movement so caused is such that it would require far more initiating energy than is supplied by the activity emanating from the "leisure" movement.

At times, strong ampliation occurs be-tween two statically framed shots. For exam-ple, the shot of a handball being driven against a wall is juxtaposed to a shot where a line of chorines, from *The Million Dollar Mermaid* segment of *That's Entertainment,* dive sideways into a swimming pool as if the man's serve is displacing them like a row of bowling pins. Even though camera move-ment is not a key element in this image, as in our earlier examples, we observe a sporting activity that via strong ampliation appears to cause an impossible effect which, among other things, would require far more energy than a handball serve even if it were mechanically plausible.[26]

A repeated theme of most of the strong cinematic ampliations in *Rude Awakening* is that of a kind of magical burst of force, i.e., a human effort, appears to give rise to a far more awesome physical effect, like the boy launching the plane. The strong ampliations portray their human agents as superhuman. In some of our examples, the human effort is almost casual, so that its apparent momentous consequences propose an arresting fantasy of strength but more importantly of ease. Even where the initiating action is somewhat strenuous, its putative result is so greatly disproportionate that the implicit vision of the human body is still that of a source of incredible power. Where objects appear to be displaced by human initiating actions, those objects acquire a tangible quality of lightness. When camera movement follows the initiating action, its velocity often has a very fluid character as if the movement is flowing or streaming from the human action. All of these factors conspire to promote a very distinct sense of "effortless effort" and ease which corresponds to a major theme of the film, i.e., relaxation.

The theme of relaxation is developed in *Rude Awakening* in several ways. The iconography is culled predominantly from what, in our culture, is considered the realm of leisure, e.g., travel, art, play, sport, popular amusements, etc. And, the kind of attentiveness demanded of the spectator by the polyvalent montage is what we typically regard as "aesthetic," i.e., attentiveness to the formal play of elements and to the expressive qualities and impressions of the art object. This type of attentiveness, of course, is also associated with leisure, with the relaxed and leisurely contemplation of the sensuous properties and design of an object. I am not arguing here the philosophical point that there is something called aesthetic attention that is distinct from ordinary attention. Rather, I am saying that *Rude Awakening* presupposes attentiveness to such things as are historically regarded to be the targets of aesthetic attention. Nor am I denying that this variety of perceptual activity is often very exhausting. However, for all sorts of complicated historical reasons, it is often touted as a form of play or leisure, something pursued in a "disinterested," "free" and relaxed way. *Rude Awakening* is a testament to this notion of "the aesthetic." The strong ampliations fit within this expressive context not only because they project a sense of ease and "effortless effort" but because the magical causation they suggest champions a vision of the human body freed from the normal constraints of physics and its frictions.

The themes of ease, relaxedness, and "effortless effort" in *Rude Awakening* can be highlighted by briefly comparing it with Brakhage's *Western History*. Brakhage, of course, is the grand master of polyvalent montage and his films often include cinematic ampliations. In *Western History,* there are several sequences of airplane trips. Each of these comprises several shots ranging from bright, blue daylight to a scorching, red sunset. Most of these sequences are weakly ampliated[27] – the trips are represented as a single line of movement. The second plane trip, however, is strongly ampliated. The camera movement from shot to shot phenomenally fuses and in the last aerial shot the line of movement turns downward for a landing. The camera's descent picks up speed. This is cut against a violently shaking image of the New York skyline. The movement of the descent elides with the visual earthquake in such a way that it seems that there has been some sort of collision. I have heard viewers describe this by saying "it's the end of the world" or "it's like a rocket hit the city." These are colorful ways to capture the sense of causation, indeed of upheaval, that the strong ampliation engenders. In contrast to Sonbert's, Brakhage's strong ampliation is not instilling a feeling of ease but one of stress and conflict. This obviously correlates with Brakhage's other choices throughout *Western History.* Where Sonbert generally favors a clean, medium long shot, Brakhage often returns to a tight close shot, one that is only gradually focused. In Brakhage, the process of coming to visual clarity is agonic. The movement from visual obscurity to recognizability is markedly dramatic, a struggle, as if Brakhage were constantly tearing the scales from his eyes. If *Rude Awakening* leaves a feeling of effortless effort, *Western History* incarnates a sort of stressful or effortful effort. Where Sonbert's camera movements are for the most part even Brakhage's handheld shots frenetically rush hither and thither, the zoom lens played like an abstract expressionist slide trombone. Likewise the employment of strong ampliation in each film accords with the overall expressive design – Brakhage is using it to enhance the sense of stress already apparent across several dimensions in *Western History* and Sonbert is using it to develop a feeling of ease that reinforces the comparatively relaxed quality of the rest of *Rude Awakening*.

IV. Concluding Remarks

Cinematic ampliation is a standard editing device for the representation of causation in conventional narrative films. From one commercial film to another the use of this device generally stands for causation. In avant-garde films strong cinematic ampliation is often adopted to suggest impossible events, i.e., instances of causation that defy the laws of physics. The significance of these cinematic ampliations is highly dependent on their context. In Vertov, strong cinematic ampliation is a means to communicate themes that can be easily formulated into propositions, e.g., "the Soviet industrial worker powers the nation." In Sonbert and Brakhage, however, the meaning of the ampliations is less susceptible to paraphrases in the form of complete sentences. Rather, the strong ampliations suggest expressive qualities that are best described by single words or phrases, e.g., "ease," "stress," "effortless" and "effortful effort." Whether the ampliations of impossible events in avant-garde film are of the order of themes or of expressive qualities, their meaning is generally a matter of their

relation to the film (they are in) as a whole, whereas in conventional film strong cinematic ampliation usually has a fixed meaning, viz., "*x* causes *y*." Of course, in avant-garde film, the ultimate significance of a strong or weak ampliation will be related to the impressions of causation or fused movement that the ampliations engender. The sense of ease in Sonbert's *Rude Awakening* results as a particular quality of *causal* agency in the cutting. Thus, the range of themes and expressive qualities that the cinematic ampliation of impossible events can project is somewhat governed or determined by the basic impressions of fused movement and/or causation. Nevertheless, the important aspect, quality or point of a particular suggestion of causation – its final meaning so to speak – depends on the larger context of the film.

In concluding, it is useful to consider quickly the relation of this essay to psychology. It should be clear that though I have derived certain ideas from psychological research, this is not psychology paper. Such a paper would concern itself either with the measurement of the comparative intensities of cinematic ampliation as the cues that constitute it are experimentally modified, or it would be devoted to plumbing the genesis of cinematic ampliation. I have done neither of these things. I have adapted some of the vocabulary of psychology and, in a broad way, I have defined cinematic ampliation. Most of my energy has been spent in unraveling the meaning of specific cases of ampliation. My focus has been hermeneutics, not psychology. Certainly there is a place for a psychology of film. But most of us in cinema – with backgrounds in literary studies or art history – are in no position to make an original contribution to such a field because we lack training and experimental experience. And, in the related case of psychoanalysis, we lack clinical experience, the empirical basis of that branch of psychology. Psychology may help film scholars up to a point, but, in general, we are more concerned with charting systems of signification rather than unearthing causal generalizations. Obviously I do not mean that we should forsake psychology but only that the difference between cinema studies and psychology should be acknowledged. And, if we wish to embark on a psychology of film, we must ground our hypotheses in the empirical practices of that discipline. In other words, render unto psychology what is psychology's and unto cinema studies what is its own.

Notes

1. Albert Michotte, *The Perception of Causality* (New York: Basic Books, 1963).
2. David Hume, *Treatise of Human Nature,* vol. II (London: Everyman), p. 161.
3. Michotte, 143.
4. Michotte, 86.
5. Michotte calls this the hierarchy of priority, which means that the object that moves first is the one that is seen to supply the "motor" for the phenomenon.
6. Michotte, 227.
7. Michotte, 223.
8. Myles Brand, "Introduction: Defining Causes," in *The Nature of Causation,* ed. M. Brand (Urbana: University of Illinois Press, 1976).
9. J. Piaget, *Les mecanismes perceptifs* (Paris: Presses Universitaires France, 1961). Piaget explains perceived causation genetically in terms of the acquisition of operations. In *Understanding Causality* (New York: Norton, 1974), he writes

"As Michotte himself admits, we see nothing passing from an active A mobile to a passive B mobile. We do see an 'effect' dependent on speeds, durations and displacements. We shall add, then, that this impression of production results from an elementary composition according to which in the course of transformation, what B gained A lost. If operations are still not involved, there is at least a preoperational construction by perception on sensori-motor regulations and not a perception of an actual transmission. . . . These perceptive impressions would also be unexplainable if they did not come from a displacement in terms of visual indices, from tactilo-kinesthetic perceptions linked to the sensi-motor action itself. This leads us back to action.

Effectively, starting with the sensori-motor level, we witness the formation of a causality linked to the actions of moving, pushing, pulling, balancing, etc. and therefore we can see in it a whole development prior to that of operations. . . . On the other hand, from the first causal behavior of pushing, pulling, etc., these actions constitute products of composition starting with prehension and spatial relationships. It is enough to say that in every sensori-motor causality we find at work a system of *Schemes* of intelligence and their general coordinations, which is the first form of what will later constitute operations."

10. Michotte's experiments allow for a roughly analogous situation. In some cases, the launching object, A, was made to disappear before reaching B, but when B moved, subjects still reported ampliation. On page 138, Michotte writes ". . . the movement of an object is liable in some circumstances to survive phenomenally the removal of this object and there is an apparent continuation of the movement of an object which has ceased to exist. . . ."

11. The Entraining Effect seems more important in dance than in film. In dance, it supplies the basis for a much used choreographic pattern – the ensemble moves across the stage and picks up a stationary dancer or group, i.e., they suddenly fall into the movement of the ensemble. This use of "pick-up" is a fundamental strategy in Doris Humphrey's *New Dance.* This is interesting in relation to Vertov's *Man with a Movie Camera. New Dance,* like *Man with a Movie Camera,* attempts to project a vision of a utopian society. Both works use phenomenal causation to communicate a sense of the organicity of the ideal society. Vertov uses the Launching Effect and Humphrey employs the Entraining Effect.

In terms of dance theory, the use of the Entraining Effect is undoubtedly a motivation for Susanne Langer's erroneous but provocative argument that ". . . a realm of Powers, wherein purely imaginary beings from whom the vital force emanates shape a whole world of dynamic forms by their magnet-like, psycho-physical actions, lifts the concept of Dance out of all its theoretical entanglements with music, painting, comedy, carnival or serious drama and lets one ask *what belongs to dancing* and what does not."

From *Feeling and Form* (New York: Scribners, 1953), p. 184.

12. Michotte, pp. 84–86.

13. For a discussion of verbal images, see my "Language and Cinema: Preliminary Notes for a Theory of Verbal Images," *Millennium Film Journal, no. 7/8/9.* This essay is included in this volume.

14. Michotte, p. 218.

15. For a discussion of categorical editing see my "Toward a Theory of Film Editing," *Millennium Film Journal,* no. 3 (Winter/Spring 1979). This essay is reprinted in this volume.

16. Leon Trotsky, "Vodka, The Church and the Cinema," from *Problems of Everyday Life* (New York: Pathfinder Press, 1973), pp. 31–35.

17. See Karl Mannheim, "The History of the Concept of the State as an Organism: A Sociological Analysis," in *Essays On Sociology and Social Psychology,* by Karl Mannheim, edited by Paul Kecskemeti (London: Routledge & Kegan Paul, 1953), pp. 165–182, for a brief outline of this notion as well as for valuable bibliographic references to its development in the 19th century.

In terms of *Man with a Movie Camera,* it is interesting to note a correspondence between Vertov and Schelling. Schelling thought of both states and artworks on the model of organisms. In fact, he analogized the ideal organic unity of the state with that of an artwork, conceiving of the state as in artwork. Vertov introduces the same notion into *Man with a Movie Camera.* As the film charges into its finale, there is a shot of the film editor glancing downward in such a way that you take it that she is looking down or looking over all the material that subsequently flashes on the screen. The Soviet Union is presented as an artwork – a film! The device Vertov deploys here is an impossible point-of-view schema rather than a cinematic ampliation of an impossible causal event. A similar use of editing appears in Lang's *Spione.* The Secret Agent discards a cigarette and this is retrieved by a disguised, enemy spy. This shot is followed by a close-up of Haghi that implies that he is watching the earlier event. Ensuing shots reveal that this is impossible. But through this cut, and others like it, *Spione* establishes the maleovolent

omniscience of Haghi – the evil genius is presented as seeing (or seeming to see) everything. Lang insinuates an impossible point-of-view to make a symbolic comment. Likewise, Vertov suggests that the editor watches over Russia in order that he, Vertov, can work out the organicist condensation of the state as an ideal artwork, a masterpiece.

18. I am not advocating the adoption of the organic metaphor for the state but only claiming that Vertov espouses it.

My interpretation of *Man with a Movie Camera* makes Vertov much more sanguine about the Soviet Union than the interpretation offered by Stephen Crofts and Olivia Rose in "An Essay Towards *Man with a Movie Camera*" in *Screen,* Vol. 18, no. 1, Spring 1977. In this essay, especially in "IIB The Film's Theoretical Reconstruction of the Contemporary Social Formation," Crofts and Rose portray Vertov as a social critic. I believe that they are right to a certain extent and that to that extent they have added a new and valuable insight to the discussion of *Man with a Movie Camera.* Vertov does make a point of acknowledging certain social problems of the Soviet Union, including unemployment and alcoholism. But, at the same time, his overall vision seems to be optimistic; the Soviet Union is pictured as heroically and robustly hurrying into the future. Crofts' and Rose's attempts to find a more pervasive tendency toward social criticism in the film seem to me to rest on three mistakes: First, an inability to distinguish good-humored teasing from corrosive satire (e.g., their discussion of the "weightwatchers"); second, a penchant for distorting the meaning of a shot chain by describing only part of it, lifting certain images out of their full context so that they can be twisted to say what the writers want (e.g., the account of The Day's Work Section which they fail to note also goes on to equate various activities of the service sector of the economy with heavy industry); and third, a bizarre correlation between bad/bourgeois/capital intensive industry versus good/proletariat/labor intensive industry. Personally, I see no evidence for a systematic connection between capital intensive industry and the new bourgeois class in the film. Aren't workers going to use electricity too? Also, the very idea of a negative view toward capital intensive industry seems sentimentalist rather than Marxist. Attributing such an association to Vertov not only ignores his ebullient representation of such capital intensive items as hydroelectric plants but it makes Vertov sound more like William Morris than the materialist Crofts and Rose claim him to be. Their murky understanding of the capital intensive/labor intensive distinction reflects the fuzzy, confused and imprecise use of technical terms so common on the pages of *Screen*.

19. Annette Michelson, "From Magician to Epistemologist," in *The Essential Cinema,* ed. P. Adams Sitney (New York: New York University Press, 1975), pp. 94–111. As in so many other things, throughout this essay I am especially indebted to my teacher, Prof. Annette Michelson. She introduced me to Vertov, taught me how to think about him and showed me the importance of causation in his editing.

20. After the revolution, the Soviets hoped to rapidly industrialize their country. To get capital to finance the international procurement of heavy machinery, they intended to increase agricultural production so that they would have something to export. Eisenstein illustrates this plan in *The General Line;* not only is Tommy's "productivity" connected to clearing the land, perhaps for a hydroelectric plant; also there is a theme of multiplication – contrasting to the divisions of the opening – of cattle and tractors; they proliferate in tandem, as it were. Of course, the hero of *The General Line* – the tractor – was a key element in the attempt to expand agricultural production; it was used to entice peasant participation. In many ways, *The General Line* is like a wish fulfillment dream of Soviet planners – maybe it's no accident that Marthe "sleeps" her way to the state dairy. For information about Soviet agricultural policy in this period see Erich Strauss, *Soviet Agriculture in Perspective* (New York: Praeger, 1969).

21. This is not to say that the strong ampliation of impossible events cannot also suggest (virtual) final causation. In the *Physics,* 198a 24, Aristotle notes that often the formal, efficient and final causes correlate to each other.

22. Images of travel – particularly train and plane rides – and images of sport are also staples of polyvalent montage.

23. Sergei Eisenstein, "A Dialectic Approach to Film Form," in *Film Form,* edited and translated by Jay Leyda (New York: Harcourt, Brace & World, 1949), pp. 45–63.

24. Yvor Winters, "The Experimental School in American Poetry," in *Defence of Reason* (New York: The Swallow Press & William Morrow and Co., 1944), p. 41. Winters' reasons for finding imitative form a fallacy include the idea that it is redundant and that it can lead to absurdity – the adoption, for example, of a ridiculous style to ridicule a ridiculous subject. The second objection, of course, does not show that the practice is always in error, but that it can lead to error. The charge of redundancy is also misguided, not because it misdescribes imitative form but because it misses one of the enduring points of poetry – to saturate itself with meaning in such a way that the reader re-reads it with an ever increasing awareness of coherence.

A more radical objection to imitative form is offered by Dr. Johnson, in what we could think of as his Nelson Goodman mood. Alexander Pope claimed that in poetry "The sound must seem an echo to the sense" ("An essay on criticism"). Johnson held "sound can resemble not but sound" (*Rambler,* no. 94, 2/9/1751). But Johnson overlooks the *fact* that there are conventions for associating formal attributes and meanings. Portraits don't resemble people except under a set of conventions that tell us where to look for analogies and where not to look. One convention of poetry tells us to look for form/content correspondences where a line ends. Taking our cue from Johnson's remarks on Berkeley, we refute him thus

> A few leaded panes, old beams
> Fur, pleated muslin, a coral ring rung
> together
> In a movement supporting the face, which
> swims
> Toward and away like the hand
> Except that it is in repose. It is what it is
> *Sequestered.*
> John Ashbery
> *Self-Portrait in a Convex Mirror*
> (italics added)

I am spending so much space on the issue of imitative or expressive form because if indeed there is something wrong with the idea then much avant-garde filmmaking and even more criticism is based on an error. The various uses of disjunction, from Surrealism to Lacanian Marxism, all presuppose the expressive significance of form. It is true that often the "contents" that the form refers to in avant-garde film are issues or polemical themes that dominate the avant-garde filmworld rather than themes that can be read off the work itself. This is to say that expressive form in avant-garde film is often extended, in the sense that its thematic reference is to something outside the work it appears in. Nevertheless, expressive form is a basic presupposition of avant-garde film practice. Individual filmmakers may reject it; but is hard to conceive of the history of the avant-garde as a whole without it. So, if expressive form is in some way fallacious, then so is all the art that rests on it.

25. Sergei Eisenstein, "Form and Content: Practice," in *The Film Sense,* edited and translated by Jay Leyda (New York: Harcourt, Brace & World, 1942), pp. 173–216.

26. Sonbert seems particularly interested in "impossible images" in *Rude Awakening.* For example, he superimposes the sun and the moon as well as fire on water.

27. In "*Western History* and *The Riddle of Lumen,*" *Artforum,* 1/73, p. 68, Fred Camper seems to be arguing that the sky/city sections of *Western History* assert the purity of the individual image over any kinds of abstracting techniques or substitutions. If the section I have discussed is the same one he is referring to, and if his discussion of the completeness and independence of the "image" refers to shots, I think he is wrong. Especially in the second sky/city approach, I believe that it is hard not to see the sequence as an example of ampliation. I have also, unscientifically, asked innocent bystanders what they thought of the sequence, and they have concurred with me. I think that in regard to this sequence Camper may be confusing what he knows about the shot chain with what is phenomenally perceptible on the screen.

CHAPTER XIII

Language and Cinema: Preliminary Notes for a Theory of Verbal Images

I. Introduction

Cinema is not a language. Nevertheless, language plays an intimate role in several of the symbolic structures used in cinema. The purpose of this paper is to explore one such language/image relation. It has been given various titles in the literature, including metaphor, literalization, literalism, dramatization and concrete imagery.[1] Since it is not always clear that these names refer to exactly the same phenomenon, I will coin a new phrase for it – viz., the verbal image – in the hope that by defining it anew we will get a better sense of what it is. I do not claim to have discovered verbal images, so that what follows is hardly the first word on the matter. Nor is it likely to be the last. At most I hope to say some helpful things mid-debate.

What are verbal images? Indeed, do they even exist? One way to tackle these questions is to consider a near relative of the verbal image – the primed verbal image – whose existence is beyond doubt.

Larry Rivers' lithograph *An Outline of History* is a primed verbal image. It is an outline copy of John Trumbull's well known painting *Signing of the Declaration of Independence* that also alludes to the title of H.G. Wells' once popular book on world history. The word "outline" in the caption directs our attention immediately to the style of the picture which, in turn, gives the title a second meaning for us that the picture as a whole literalizes. This effect is often exploited in movies – in cartoons, for example, a character may complain of "falling apart" and then do so half a second later. Nor are primed verbal images found exclusively in non-photographic media. In *Scorpio Rising* the song "Wind Up Toy" alerts us toward seeing a biker turning a gear box as a child with a toy. Furthermore, primed verbal images can be used dramatically as well as comically. In *Electric Horseman,* the camera pops back for a scenic long shot while the wandering, bedraggled lovers sing "America The Beautiful." Needless to say, the vista behind them is not merely "spacious" but "purple." The words of the hymn become images and this at least is meant to be patriotically inspiring.[2]

In the case of primed verbal images, the accompanying words lead us to focus on specific features of the pictures. Metaphorically we could say that we see the pictures through the words. With verbal images proper, however, we find the words through the pictures. There is no accompanying text; rather, we supply it. For example, in *The Thin Man,* the police begin a nation-wide search. There is a cut to a map of the U.S., and a net shoots out of New York covering the country. The image forcefully suggests the word "dragnet" to the spectator.[3] In *Bigger Than Life,* the central character is suffering immense psychological pressure due to the wonder drugs that he gorges recklessly. As he stands in the bathroom, his wife slams his medicine chest shut with such power that the mirror smashes. The camera notes this in an emphatic close-up of his fractured simulacrum. This elicits the word "shattered" from the spectator which, of course, has figurative applicability to the character's emotional state as well as to the literal condition of the mirror. Likewise *Apocalypse Now* begins with a shot of the major character apparently "upside down" as a comment on the Vietnam war.

An example of a verbal image from an avant-garde film can be found in J. Hoberman's *Cargo of Lure.* The film is a record of a day's outing on a Circle Line boat that tours the coast of the South Bronx. Hoberman shoots the journey in one 400 ft. take, aiming the camera so that the shoreline occupies the top half of the frame while the lower half comprises the river with likenesses of the waterfront shimmering on the surface. The shot summons up the word "reflection" not only as a description of what we see but as a theoretically charged quotation of a particular view of the nature of cinema as a reflection of reality.[4]

Whereas primed verbal images give us words that shape our understanding of images, verbal images proper produce the recognition of the words behind the images. Or, to speak more directly, verbal images proper are images (or succession of images) that evoke words or strings of words (phrases, sentences, clichés or proverbs). By "evoke," I mean that the images suggest or allude to specific words, that they prompt or introduce the words for consideration. I do not mean that the images cause the words to reverberate in our heads. (How this prompting is possible will be discussed in the fourth part of this essay.)

II. The Extent of Verbal Images

Before examining cinematic verbal images in detail, it is important to emphasize that the phenomenon is not specific to film. It occurs in every medium that has visual elements. In fine art Brueghel is a rich source for this mode of expression. Approximately one hundred proverbs have been identified in his *The Netherlandish Proverbs*.

One can start on the proverbs anywhere; on the left the eye is caught by the white shirt of a man who runs his *head against the wall.* The literalness of the visual translation makes suicidal obstinacy real. The man will *die in harness* and he is accordingly buckled into armor. The associations gather momentum; his head in its stone-colored cap is halfway to wall-color and following the impetus we come to the personification of futile bellicosity *armed to the teeth.* Quite literally, for he bites on iron, *on a bullet* as we say

(not many of the proverbs need much translating). He is a parody of courage; he is *belling the cat,* fumbling with a bell that is incongruously large. It is almost the only point at which Brueghel distorts the literal reconstruction just as Magritte might distort it and in the same interest, the dream-like potential of the same kind of bell. They belong to the same culture and nothing dies in art.

As the associations proliferate the wall becomes one side of a stone-colored dwelling for a whole vocabulary of follies. The pugnacious cocks on the next ledge are eluding a miserable visionary who *counts his chickens before they are hatched.* Further on there is a cell for the duplicity that *speaks with two mouths;* the face is hideously cleft. Then the fantasy breaks loose in a fatuous dream. The inside of the house becomes bright and out staggers an idiot with his burden steaming like soup; he is *bringing basketfuls of light into day,* like coals to Newcastle. The shining doorway is magical, like Magritte's reversals of day and night and an Italianate tabernacle is built on to the house to shelter the perverse associations. Under the pink canopy one man lights *candles to the devil;* another *has the devil for a confessor,* and so on. As one follows the train of thought one realizes what is being represented so graphically. Men are saddled with these formulations precisely because they are the captives of propensities too vicious, mad or boring to be spelt out *en clair.* When we meet the peasant in the white shirt again on the right of the picture we discover the practical consequence. *He cannot reach from one loaf to another* – he does not know where his next meal is coming from.[5]

For a possible modern instance of a verbal image in fine art consider Gert Schiff's interpretation of Picasso's *Portrait of Dora Maar.* He writes,

Instead of merely distorting, he [Picasso] *displaced* ever more radically the most sensitive organs – eyes, ears, noses, breasts – achieving effects that can be as frightening as certain manifestations of insanity. That the analogy is not quite unwarranted can be proved by linguistic reference: the German word for "mad," *verruckt,* has the literal meaning "displaced."[6]

Of course, Schiff's exegesis here depends on the plausibility of presuming that Picasso had knowledge of the meaning of "*verruckt*" as "displaced." But even if Schiff's particular explanation is ill-founded, his willingness to entertain this kind of interpretation indicates the assumption of the continued existence of a convention of verbal image making in modern fine art.

Both theater and dance have important visual elements including movement, sets and costume that can be readily mobilized for the sake of verbal images. In Antony Tudor's *Jardin aux Lilas* the young lovers literally though demurely "incline" toward each other while on *pointe*[7] and in theater the blazing lighting – raised to full strength – evoked the theme of "blindness" during Peter Brook's *Lear*.[8] In both these cases, the words elicited by the visuals operate as annotations concerning the ongoing action.[9]

Turning from art in general to film, we note that verbal images can be propounded by every channel of articulation available to the medium including blocking, lighting, set design, camera placement, movement and angulation as well as editing, special effects and overall narrative organization.[10]

The first means for projecting verbal images involves the choice of actions and objects to be filmed. The kinds of actions and objects required for verbal images are ones which can be literally described by a word or string of words, which in turn also have an extended, often metaphoric, meaning. For example, in *The Last Laugh*, the doorman, wearing his stolen uniform, parades through his neighborhood unaware that his fellow tenants know he has lost his exalted position. The camera faces him frontally and in the background of this deep focus medium long shot we see people poking their heads out of their windows and jeering riotously. Quite literally they are "laughing behind his back," while at the same time this phrase is a cliché connoting slander and humiliation.

Objects can function similarly. Paul Willemen writes,

In Sam Fuller's *Pick Up On South Street*, there is a rather extraordinary and at first pointless camera movement in the scene when Candy (Jean Peters) and Skip (Richard Widmark) first kiss after he has knocked her down. The shot starts off in a close-up, then the camera backs away a little and travels a few yards to the left while still focussing on the kissing couple who haven't moved. In the course of the camera movement a new element has entered the image: two chains hooked together right in front of the camera, vertically dividing the frame. After holding this shot for a few seconds, the camera simply moves back to its starting point, the close-up of the couple (still kissing). Although up to that point in the film there is little in the film to suggest that Skip and Candy are falling in love, the hook which momentarily occupies the very center of the frame suggests they are "getting hooked." Simultaneously, we must bear in mind that Skip is "on the hook" (the police blackmailing him) as is Candy (she must retrieve the vital piece of microfilm).[11]

Verbal images may result not only as a function of what is in them but of how they are composed. Words of scale (large, small), of movement (especially in terms of anabasis and katabasis) and of position (up, down) are linked with virtually endless resources of metaphoric associations that are repeatedly mined through camera angulation and placement. In *The Last Laugh,* high and low angle shots render the doorman literally large and figuratively "magnificent" and, then, literally small with the connotation of "degradation"; in *The General Line,* the scale relationship between the rich kulak and Martha corresponds to the theme of domination; in *Sunrise,* the tininess of the housewife in the boat, cowering *under* the camera correlates to the sense of "small" as "helpless." Moreover, these devices are not just curiosities of the "expressionist" tendencies of the silent film period. In a realist, sound film, such as *The Heiress,* we find Wyler depicting Austen's savage evaluation of Catherine by means of a slightly low angle shot of the father berating his daughter who in a high angle shot looks small in a way that literalizes her humiliation. Scale metaphors can be mobilized through techniques other than camera angle. The czar's scale relative to that of the Russian people in the medium long shot at the end of *Ivan the Terrible,* Part I, makes him a "giant" – an appropriate metaphor for a great historical ruler – as effectively as the low angle shots valorize Charles Foster Kane in terms of the same rhetoric. Also, the enormous close-ups of the leading characters' heads carry forward the theme of the "giant" in both *Ivan* and *Citizen Kane.*

Screen position can, as well, be used to produce verbal images; Shiva's "higher" consciousness in *Inauguration of the Pleasure Dome* is signaled by placing him in the upper left quadrant of the frame. Of course, there are a multitude of compositional variations – other than those relying on scale and position – that yield verbal images. In the opening of *Red Desert,* in a shot over the hard focussed shoulder of the heroine, we see the blurred landscape, presumably as she sees it. The lack of "focus" undoubtedly refers to her psychological state.

Film editing has long been acknowledged as a major mechanism for generating verbal images. In Zinnemann's *The Search,* a voice-over narrator asks the refugee boy, Carol, "Why don't you speak?" This sets up for a flashback which begins with a shot of "flowing" water which, of course, functions as a metaphor for the "flow" or "stream" of memory. Later, when Carol has been befriended by an American soldier, he is confused and in his consternation he upsets a goldfish bowl. There is a cut to a close-up of the fish "floundering" out of water. The "floundering" is a comment on Carol's bewilderment. These examples are of a piece with some of the most famous (some say most notorious) cuts in film history: from *October,* Eisenstein's jump from Kerensky to the mechanical peacock ("Kerensky's as proud as a peacock"); and from

Fury, Lang's juxtaposition of gossips with a barnyard full of hens ("They are like hens"). These editing examples are all predicated on evoking similes – in fact, the above cases all picture more or less dead or clichéd metaphors. But editing also affords a means of proliferating fresh similes. The cut in Brakhage's celebratory birth film, *Window Water Baby Moving,* from Jane's vagina to a shot of a window from the inside of his home not only provokes the simile "her vagina is like a window" but also has original metaphoric impact, inviting us to grasp the selective affinities between the two terms of the cut which are both apertures and, significantly, passageways that lead out into the hard, cruel world.

Cine-similes involve adding a shot (or succession of shots) of an object, action or event that metaphorically comments on preceding shots. But this is not the only way that editing projects verbal images. The qualities of a given cut may elicit a description that has metaphoric applicability to the surrounding subject matter. In *October,* Eisenstein cuts from the lowering of a cannon from a factory rack to a soldier, hundreds of miles away. The movement qualities of the two shots suggest the artillery piece is physically "crushing" the soldier while the figurative import is that the arms industry crushes the life out of the common man.[12]

Though I began this section by observing that verbal images are found in every visual medium, it should be clear that film does possess certain unique means for projecting verbal images since film (and TV) employs some devices that are not shared with other media. In *Sunrise,* the camera "tracks" the steaming footprints of the nefarious lovers out of the swamp. It is not only literally a tracking shot but it suggests that the camera is "tracking" the plotters like a detective.[13] The variables of speed, direction and shape in camera movement can each be exploited to produce verbal images; Ophuls' circular movements in *Lola Montes,* for example, are "encirclements" in the sense of entrapments. Cinema-specific special effects also may yield verbal images. The obsessive opticals in DeLanda's vitriolic parody, *Itch, Scratch, Itch,* actually "wipe out" his reprehensible characters, but, as well, express his deisire to destroy them and what they stand for.

Since most of the preceding cases of cinematic verbal images are localizable – to particular objects, actions, angles, cuts, etc. – I will conclude this section on the range of verbal images with cases where the words and phrases motivate somewhat large scale choices in the organization of a film. The entire ending of *Safety Last* involves Harold – an aspiring young businessman – climbing up the side of the Bolton Building – a feat that will win him both $1000 and a wife. At the barest level of narrative description, we say that he is struggling to the top. But having said this we also have uttered a clichéd metaphor for success in business – one that we find immortalized, for instance, in books by Horatio Alger like *Struggling Upward or Luke Larkin's Luck.* A white-collar hero for the growing service sector of America in the 20s, Lloyd incarnates "rising" prospects in a narrative designed to make him "climb to success." His trajectory is also the most thrilling anabasis in silent comedy. In *Boy's Ranch,* one continuing subplot involves the character Butch literally "winning his spurs." In James Fargo's *The Enforcer,* there is also an overarching verbal image. The criminals sport a variety of army surplus weapons (including a bazooka!) leaving no doubt that throughout the film the forces of evil are quite literally "at war" with society. Similarly one feels that the beginning of *L'Age d'Or* is endorsed by a presiding verbal image, a playfully vicious subversion of "upon this rock I will build my church." (Matthew 16:18).

Snow's *Breakfast* represents a case of an animating verbal image that organizes an entire film but that does not derive from narrative elements. In this film the veteran of *Wavelength* behaves like Sherlock Jr. A camera with a telephoto lens approaches a tabletop piled with breakfast fixings, imitating the zoom in *Wavelength* through camera movement. The technical description of the optical effect such a lens has on the appearance of what it records is that it "flattens" or "contracts" space. Snow takes this jargon at its word and the objects in the frame – eggs, an orange juice container, etc. – are crushed and drop laterally out of the path of the camera as if the space were really shrinking.

III. Verbal Images and Inner Speech

Verbal images have been discussed in film literature at least since the 20s. Eisenstein's writings offer famous examples of the device. Apparently, in his classes he urged students to find verbal solutions of this sort for visual problems.[14] Eisenstein, however, does not offer us a theory of verbal images, i.e., an explanation of how they work or of why they exist in film. In all probability, he believed that verbal images have something to do with the putative psychological process called inner speech. Eisenstein refers to this concept in his 1935 essay "Film Form: New Problems,"[15] but he does not explicitly tie the notion of verbal images to that of inner speech. Nevertheless, a contemporary of Eisenstein's, Boris Eikenbaum does. Eikenbaum writes,

One more general question remains, concerning cases when the director must give commentary to the film in whole or in part, when "something from the author" must appear in a film over and above the plot itself. The easiest method is to give commentary in intertitles, but contemporary cinema is already making attempts to function by different means. I have in mind the appearance in cinema of metaphor, which sometimes even bears the characteristics of symbol. From the semantic point of view the introduction of metaphor into film is of particular interest because it confirms again the real significance of internal speech, not as an accidental psychological element of film perception, but as an integral structural element of film. Film metaphor is entirely dependent on verbal metaphor. The viewer can understand it only when he possesses a corresponding metaphoric expression in his own verbal baggage. Of course, it is possible that as cinema develops further it will create its own semantic patterns which can serve as the basis for the construction of independent film metaphors, but this will not change anything in principle.

A film metaphor is a kind of visual realization of a verbal metaphor. It is natural that only current verbal metaphors can serve as material for film metaphors: the viewer quickly grasps them precisely because they are already well known to him and because they are easily recognized as metaphors. For example, the word "fall" is used in language as a metaphor for the road to death; because of this usage, the metaphor in *Devil's Wheel* was possible. In this film the sailor Shorin chances into a tavern and joins a billiard game. His ball *falls* into the pocket. The absolutely episodic quality of this scene gives the viewer to understand that it is significant not for story-line development, but as commentary: the hero's fall begins.[16]

What I have called verbal images, Eikenbaum here christens "metaphors," arguing that the key for understanding this process lies in the operation of inner speech in the spectator. Eikenbaum's speculations have been embraced by current theorists.[17] Paul Willemen calls them "literalisms" in his article on the subject. He offers many examples of verbal images, as I did in the previous part of this paper. He connects literalisms with inner speech, urging

It would appear, therefore, that the phenomenal surface of the film text, with its multiplicity of overlapping, intersecting, redoubling, continuous codes . . . is enmeshed within the network of internal speech which presides over its production while internal speech is in its turn a product of what we are tempted to call thought work. . . . Filmic internal speech is quite probably a code specific to the cinema. . . .[18]

Both Eikenbaum and Willemen write as if by invoking the process of inner speech

they have explained verbal images. But I suspect that inner speech is nothing but a convenient theoretical carpet under which these theorists attempt to sweep their vaguely formulated though indisputable data. Or, to mix metaphors, I think that inner speech is an escape hatch in this context, a bogus answer to the question of the function of and reasons for verbal images.

In outlining my reservations about the inner speech approach, I will avoid a central issue, viz., is the concept of inner speech viable as a scientific construct? Though I am dubious about inner speech on this score, I intend to dodge the responsibility of defending my skepticism since I am a film theorist and not a psychologist. Rather, I will attack the inner speech approach by giving the devil its due (i.e., by agreeing to assume the existence of inner speech) and then by demonstrating that even if there is something called inner speech, it has not elucidated anything about verbal images in film.

There are four objections to the inner speech account of verbal images.

1. Inner speech, as analysed by Vygotsky,[19] is portrayed as a general intermediary process between thought and action. Non-figurative, instrumental and utilitarian thinking is mediated by inner speech. However, the thinking prompted by verbal images is a highly specific form of cognition that mobilizes metaphors. How does a generic process like inner speech explain anything about such a specialized psychological function? Clearly inner speech would have to be broken down into different modes – e.g., the inner speech of mechanical manipulation, of quantitative analysis, of metaphor etc. – before it would be a refined enough concept to explain how verbal images engage the spectator. Without differentiating types of inner speech, the claim that inner speech is related to our responses to verbal images is tantamount to saying that since inner speech operates generally in tandem

with thinking, it must be operative in relation to verbal images. But this is a perfectly uninformative position posturing as an explanation. Just as asserting that every event has a cause tells us nothing about how or why a given event occurred, pointing to inner speech, a supposedly generic component of cognition, in this context, does not illuminate the unique pattern of thinking involved with verbal images.

2. resembles our first objection. Eikenbaum believes that the film spectator is constantly involved in mental labor – he says we are incessantly connecting "frames" (though he probably means "shots") – and Eikenbaum relates this work to a continuous burble of inner speech.[20] This entails that inner speech characterizes our constant response to a film. But verbal images need not occur continuously throughout a film. In general, they transpire in isolated, discontinuous moments – they are extraordinary events that appear intermittently before the film reverts to non-metaphoric exposition. How can the process that is used to account for our ordinary response to the task of assimilating a film also explicate with any specificity our reaction to these extraordinary moments? Again, without a typology of inner speech, the concept sounds like a catchall phrase indiscriminately applied to everything. But if this is true, inner speech is too broad a framework to enlighten us about the unique workings of verbal images.

3. The closest example of something even loosely like verbal images that Vygotsky offers is a specimen of egocentric speech. He writes,

> A child of five and a half was drawing a streetcar when the point of his pencil broke. He tried, nevertheless, to finish the circle of a wheel, pressing down on the pencil very hard, but nothing showed on the paper except a deep colorless line. The child muttered to himself, "It's broken," put aside the pencil, took watercolors instead, and began drawing a *broken* streetcar after an accident, continuing to talk to himself from time to time about the change in his picture.

The child's accidentally provoked egocentric utterance so manifestly affected his activity that it is impossible to mistake it for a mere by product, an accompaniment not interfering with the melody. Our experiments showed highly complex changes in the interrelation of activity and inner speech.[21]

Vygotsky explains the function of both inner speech and egocentric speech as means of preparing for activity. But could this be the function of verbal images? Perhaps if a distinction were drawn between figurative and non-figurative processes of inner speech, the notion of inner speech as action-orienting could be used to explain how filmmakers come to make verbal images. But it would not account for why audiences respond to verbal images with inner speech just because movie audiences are not typically preparing to embark upon any other activity while watching a film. And yet, it is the spectator's response that Eikenbaum and Willemen intend to unravel by reference to inner speech.

4. None of Vygotsky's examples exactly match the phenomena we are calling verbal images. Verbal images seem to evoke a double play of meaning whereas Vygotsky's cases are of words that are freighted with what he calls "sense" as a result of being highly contextualized. These two phenomena are different though not always mutually exclusive. Moreover, the words evoked through verbal images need not behave according to syntactic laws of inner speech as sketched by Vygotsky. He writes,

> Predication is the natural form of inner speech; psychologically it consists of predicates only. It is as much a law of inner speech to omit subjects as it is a law of written speech to contain both subjects and predicates.[22]

However, the strings of words suggested by verbal images may indeed take the form of fully grammatical subject/predicate sentences, e.g., recall "Kerensky's as proud as a peacock" or "They're laughing behind his back." Or, for an example that doesn't involve a copulative verb consider the famous "the very stones roar" case from *Potemkin*. Consequently, either the "laws" of inner speech will have to be modified or another explanation of the response to verbal images must be sought.

None of the foregoing objections incontrovertibly establish that verbal images cannot be explained in terms of inner speech. Rather, they only show that unless the theory of inner speech is revised and refined, it is of no use for the discussion of verbal images. What we would need would be a distinction between different processes of inner speech which in turn could be used either to reductively explain or to match with responses to verbal images. If we cannot reduce our responses to verbal images to specific processes of inner speech or if we cannot analogize said responses to specific operations of inner speech, the invocation of the concept is hollow. Maybe some researcher will be able to overcome these shortcomings in the inner speech model. In all likelihood, that researcher should be a psychologist. Nevertheless, as a film theorist rather than a psychologist, I believe that we can explain the how and why of verbal images without holding our breaths, awaiting breakthroughs in the study of inner speech.

IV. An Alternate Approach: Verbal Images as Illocutionary Acts

A. Performative Utterances[23]

The late J. L. Austin introduced the idea of "performative utterances" into the study of philosophy of language. The acknowledgment of "performative utterances" could be seen as a corrective to the theory of meaning espoused by logical positivists who claimed that the only meaningful statements were those that were verifiable.[24] Austin pointed out that there was more to meaning than reporting truths. Meaningful utterances were also made to do things like promising,

challenging, inviting, ordering, asking, etc. Central to Austin's analysis of these utterances is the concept of an illocutionary act. An illocutionary act is what is performed in speaking or writing a meaningful utterance. The contingent effect produced in performing a locutionary act e.g., upsetting your boss by telling him "Be quiet" (an illocutionary act of ordering) is a perlocutionary act. The illocutionary act is what the utterance does in virtue of a background of rules, conventions and conditions. I perform the illocutionary act of promising when I perform the locutionary act of uttering "I promise to give Mary my print of *The Maniac*."[25] At the same time I may also perform the perlocutionary act of infuriating Myron who always asked for that print. The task of illocutionary act theory is to isolate the various illocutionary acts performed in language, to specify the rules, conventions and conditions that make them possible and to group these acts into types of illocutionary acts.

I believe that we can use the machinery of illocutionary act theory to describe the workings of verbal images. Some deviations from illocutionary act theory will, of course, be necessary, but the general outline for studying performative utterances will remain intact.

Images are not utterances in the normal sense of the word so each of the acts discussed in what follows should be understood as having "para" as a prefix. Throughout this analysis, I will assume that the acts of inserting verbal images into films are pictorial (para-) locutionary acts with the (para-) illocutionary force to evoke words or strings of words by means of images that remark upon a subject of the ongoing film. I am attracted to illocutionary act theory as a way of investigating verbal images for two reasons. First, filmmakers seem to use verbal images to make discrete, isolatable remarks or statements. The sense in which they can be said to make such "remarks" strikes me as only slightly metaphorical. Thus, it is appropriate to employ an analytic framework designed to study statements. Second, by adopting illocutionary act theory the direction our analysis must take is clearly demarcated. For any kind of illocutionary act to be generated, certain conditions must be met. "I now pronounce you man and wife" only performs the act of marrying if there is an institution of marriage, if the participants of the act are of the right sexes, appropriate ages, of the right legal standing, etc. To account for how a given illocutionary act does what it does, one must specify the conditions that make the act possible. I have claimed that verbal images perform the act of evoking words. My task is to enumerate the conditions a verbal image must meet in order to successfully bring off such feats.

I am not the first writer to attempt to apply illocutionary act theory to visual representations.[26] In general, I have been unpersuaded by earlier efforts. Søren Kjørup's "George Inness and the Battle at Hastings, or Doing Things with Pictures,"[27] for example, strikes me as an uninstructive exercise in redescription that uses the framework of illocutionary theory (plus Nelson Goodman's notion of exemplification) to transform virtually everything we are willing to say about pictures into statements pictures make. Kjørup does this by postulating a welter of conventions, many of which I find downright *ad hoc*. Unlike Kjørup, I do not intend to apply illocutionary act theory to all or even most of the questions of pictorial representation. I am only shooting for an account of verbal images; I do not pretend to know the degree to which illocutionary act theory can dispel other problems about visual representation.

B. Constitutory Conditions

The large number of examples from art in general and from film in particular have been cited in order to convince the reader that there is a rather widespread convention in our culture of getting words from pic-

tures. I have called these pictures verbal images and I am assuming that the practice of making them and of recognizing them is a well-entrenched, institutionalized process of symbolization in art. Artists, spectators and critics have not learned about verbal images through rule books; instead they have observed others making, recognizing and interpreting verbal images, and, proceeding from examples, they have gone on to make and/or to recognize verbal images on their own. Yet even though there is no rule book in existence governing verbal images, there do seem to be some basic rules or conditions that images must meet if they are to count as full blooded verbal images. No image is a verbal image as the result of an act of nature. An image is a verbal image in virtue of the institutionalized modes of making and interpreting images. Meeting the conditions for verbal imagery is what makes verbal images possible. In this sense, the conditions in question are constitutory, i.e., they create the possibility of verbal images.

An image is a verbal image if it meets all of the following conditions.

i) the image, or image part, or succession of images under consideration is literally describable by a certain word or string of words.

For example, *Strangers on a Train* opens with shots of the major characters' feet. Bruno's shoes are literally of a type called "Spectators." In retrospect, as his psychosis and his homoerotic infatuation with Guy, the tennis player, become clearer, we realize that this introductory image was a verbal image commenting on Bruno's character. But for this verbal image to come off it is requisite that the shoes -- what I would refer to as an image part -- must in fact be describable as "Spectators" and not, for instance, as sneakers. It is certainly true that images can be described in many different ways and by many different words. And it is equally true that getting the verbal image hinges on finding the right word or kind of word to describe the image.[28] Yet with all this latitude the verbal image is still condition bound. If the image can't be appropriately described by the word in question, it is not a verbal image.

ii) the word or string of words evoked as a description of the image must have some extended meanings beyond its literal meaning and at least one of those extended meanings applies as a comment on the subject of the image.

In *The Women* there are close shots of two small female dogs that get into a scrap. In a broader shot their owners, women, also begin to quarrel. This sexist verbal image is predicated first on the fact that the dogs are literally describable as "bitches" and second on the fact that "bitch" is also a slang metaphor for an unpleasant woman. Verbal images depend on the tendency of words or strings of words to accrue extended meanings above what they denote. These extended meanings include metaphoric uses, associations attached to the words through use in certain commonplaces and clichés as well as technical significances due to their employment in special communities of discourse. An example of such a "special significance" is the word "reflection" adduced earlier in the case of *Cargo of Lure*. It is a word associated with many debates in film theory and it marks one polemical approach of film. Hoberman signals allegiance to this Bazinian line of thought by arranging the shot so that "reflection" as a literal description of the image leads us to "reflection" in the technical sense as a marker of his position.

Verbal images are based in the shift between the literal, descriptive use of a word and an extended meaning of a word.[29] That extended meaning, in turn, functions as a scholium on the image, story or entire film that gives rise to it. In this regard it is important to stress that we do not usually grasp the meaning of an image or string of images in terms of the verbal commentary it evokes but in general (there are exceptions) we are able to find what component of

the extended meaning of a description-word applies in virtue of our already understanding both the film's subject and the film's attitude toward the subject. Verbal images are, in the main, parasitic means of cinematic communication.

iii) both the literal and extended meanings of the words or strings of words putatively evoked by the image must exist in the language (or languages) of the filmmaker (or filmmakers).

The motivation for stipulating this condition is straightforward. Since I am holding that films say things via verbal images, we must be certain that the assertion we attribute to a film is something that it could have said. In the previous example from painting, I worry about Schiff's analysis of Picasso just because it is questionable whether Picasso had "*verruckt*" in his verbal repertory. It is important to add that the basis for this condition is not a commitment to the position that an image can mean only what its maker intended it to mean. The point is that we can only attribute to a film what it is possible for it to signal. Support for this condition can be marshaled by imagining an analogous problem from language. Suppose there is a phrase in Martian that means "Be my guest" but when pronounced properly sounds exactly like "Yankee go home" in English. When the American exploratory team reaches Mars they will undoubtedly be confused – the Martians appear very accommodating and helpful but are always saying "Yankee go home." Sooner or later the confusion will be resolved. However, at no point, neither before nor after the clarification, will it make any sense to hold that the Martians, using their language, ever bade the earthlings homeward. It simply was not possible that the Martians could have been saying this given the rules and vocabulary of their language. Likewise, Martians landing in front of American embassies in the Third World will be wrong in presuming that the crowds they observe there are full of vociferously inviting persons. With images, we can only take them as saying *x* when *x* is something they could be saying.[30]

If I read Paul Willemen correctly, he would not agree with the necessity for condition iii). He appears to take it that the meaning of the image or string of images is determined by the spectator's response to the film-text. Though I do not believe that the meaning of the film is identical with the filmmakers' intentions neither do I believe that meaning or meanings reside in viewers' reactions. At the very least, that way lies contradiction – just imagine joining all the viewer responses into one long conjunction. Furthermore, it seems to me that Willemen's position on this issue is not ostensibly coherent. He points out that a filmmaker may proffer a literalism from a language different than the viewer's. Willemen then argues that this bodes badly for the idea that film is a universal language. But one wonders why Willemen makes this point when he seems to think that it is the viewer's production of the text rather than "the first production of the text" that is relevant to the issue of literalisms.[31] In other words, why not say film is a universal language if you believe that what is important from the textual point of view is that it universally elicits inner speech?

Though these three conditions cover most of the examples of verbal images we have introduced, there is one large class of instances that these conditions miss, viz., cine-similes of the sort found in *Fury* ("The gossips are like hens.") In such cases the string of words results, in part, because we have a strategy for understanding editing that tells us to insert the syncategorematic terms "like" or "as" in our description of juxtaposed shots with probable comparative import.[32] But nothing in the imagery evokes the word "like." Moreover, using Black's terminology,[33] in these cases the frame of the statement ("The gossips") does not undergo the type of metaphorical shift encapsulated in condition ii), only the focus ("hens") does. Here the symbolic formation is heterogenous, combining both the trope of comparative editing with verbal imagining. To handle this, we should add an auxiliary clause to condition ii) that states that "in cases of cine-similes and metaphors that are generated by conventions of cinematic articulation, only the word or string of words evoked in the description as the focus term must have some extended meaning that applies as a comment on the subject." With the addition of this codicil, we have stated the necessary conditions for a verbal image. In order to postulate the presence of a verbal image in a film we must be sure that our candidate meets these conditions. To project such an image, the filmmaker must do likewise, though meeting condition iii) probably just comes naturally, so to speak.

C. *Warranting/Facilitating Conditions*

Though the preceding conditions set forth what an image must be to be a verbal image, they in no way guarantee that an image bearing these traits will be recognized as such. The constitutory conditions say what makes a verbal image possible but not what makes its uptake probable. To discuss this matter I think we must introduce a further species of conditions. These can be thought of as warranting conditions. That is, as spectators we may be confronted by an image that meets all the conditions for verbal images. Nevertheless, we may feel nervous about attributing it to the film; the putative verbal image may seem too strained or outlandish. We will cast about for further justification before we feel comfortable in asserting the presence of the verbal image. In other words, we will search for reasons that make it more probable that the verbal image we think we've sighted is in the film, communicating to us in a significant way. These reasons warrant our claims and are warranting reasons. Furthermore, the types of reasons available to us do fall into a small number of definable categories that we use again and again in our hermeneutic enterprises. These categories and their use in interpretation have been institutionalized through practice. In this respect, they can be regarded as conditions which render interpretations more plausible – they are warranting conditions. In the case of verbal images, we refer to some of these warranting conditions in order to reassure ourselves and others that we do indeed have hold of the genuine article. But this is only to speak of the spectator's terminus in the circuit of communication. Working the other side of the street, we can see that warranting conditions are also relevant to the filmmaker since in order to facilitate the uptake of a verbal image by spectators, he/she will have to make an image in such a way that spectators will feel warranted in identifying it as a verbal image. The warranting conditions, in short, are also facilitating conditions, i.e., conditions the filmmaker meets to increase the probability of uptake by spectators. To the artist's question, "How does one enhance the likelihood that the audience will catch on to a given verbal image?" we answer "by taking the warranting conditions for recognizing said images as facilitating conditions for projecting them."

One reason for endorsing an image that meets our constitutory conditions as an operative verbal image is that the elements that give rise to the verbal image have formal prominence or salience in a given pictorial array in a way that calls for an explanation. If hypothesizing the verbal image in such a case gives us our best explanation of said prominence, then we are, *prima facie*, warranted in presuming its presence. For example, the close-shot of the mirror in *Bigger Than Life* gives the broken glass a dominating position in the imagery. We account for this by postulating the verbal image as our best explanation of Ray's formal choice. Close-ups are an obvious device for delivering verbal images because they give objects incontestable prominence. But there are innumerable other devices for establishing salience and most of them may be used for projecting verbal images. A disjunctive cut

away from the spatio-temporal co-ordinates of the ongoing story may suffice or a simple break in the causal flow of a narrative. Or the event or object that evokes the verbal image may be put along a compelling compositional vector like a diagonal. In *Journeys from Berlin/1971,* the background in the shots of the psychoanalytic session are presented in the film as fields for metaphoric invention; they are given salience by being isolated as discrete planes of action juxtaposed to the foreground. In one scene, an oriental carpet is unfurled behind the analysis – the broad movement in relative stasis catches our eye, giving it salience. Next people line up on the rug, though because of the way the shot is cropped we only see their legs. Their arrangement is very formal and they leave the frame one by one as if they were on a queue awaiting some off-screen interview. Literally, they are "on the carpet" and the appearance of a queue suggests they may be figuratively on one too. And, of course, being "on the carpet" metaphorically reflects upon the predicament of the analysand.

Verbal images are common parlance in film comedy. For example in *Lizzies of the Field,* the hero's rival has built an automobile whose passenger seat can shoot out, like an accordion, roughly twenty feet from the side of the car. He tools down the boulevard and when he spies a fetching woman, the seat flies out, scoops her off her feet, and zooms her back to our lurid inventor. The joke is that he has "picked her up." The verbal image functions punningly, jolting us into a laugh. The inventor's mechanism is given utmost salience so that the pun will be grasped in a flash of surprised recognition. Because the shift of meaning can have such strong comic effect it is a staple for directors specializing in sight gags. Since rapid apprehension is necessary to the laugh, the comic filmmaker will project verbal images with a degree of salience that in other genres may seem heavy-handed. I have heard audiences chortle at the "shattered" image in *Bigger Than Life.* Perhaps the unexpected shift from the literal to the figurative is so abrupt that it has the force of a joke. But despite the fact that some dramatic verbal images may suffer from too much prominence – from being delivered too quickly and too emphatically – verbal images do afford a useful symbol formation for dramatic films and dramatic contexts can be manipulated so that untoward hilarity is avoided. In *Potemkin* disjunctive editing is used to make the famous verbal image, "the very stones roar," salient, but the effect is not humorous perhaps because we have by that time already become so accustomed to Eisenstein's metaphoric approach throughout the rest of the film. Salience, in other words, may give rise to a comic effect but this seems contingent on surrounding factors. In any case, salience is a warranting condition for the attribution of a verbal image to a film. We can say that an image that meets the constitutory conditions is, *ceteris paribus,* a warranted verbal image if

a) the elements that give rise to the putative verbal image are salient and hypothesizing the verbal image gives us our best explanation of the otherwise unmotivated prominence of the elements.

To see the force of salience as a warranting condition, consider a hypothetical case where after a screening of *The Women* we leave the theater with a companion who is complaining that too much time and too much attention was lavished on those dogs in the beginning of the film. The film is about women, not dogs, our companion argues, and just because Cukor likes dogs, he/she continues, that is no reason to take up our time with them. We would answer by pointing out that the salience given to the dogs was the means for projecting the verbal image of "bitches" and that what our friend takes as excessive and digressive has a ready explanation. We feel, I think justifiably, that our companion has misunderstood the shot by not taking the salience as a cue for the verbal image.

A similar example shows how salience can be regarded as a facilitating condition. We talk to a filmmaker who remarks that he really hammered home that the central character in his film – a policeman – is a pig. We thought the character was treated sympathetically so we press the filmmaker to say exactly where he tried to convey the "pig" idea. We are told to remember a scene where the policeman arrests a mugger in the foreground while traffic rumbles past in the background. We remember. Now we are informed that one of those flatbed trucks was full of pigs and for a quarter of a second you could hear them oinking faintly. We're somewhat bemused. Did the filmmaker expect us to pick up so fleeting an allusion, especially since it does not correspond with anything else that has been indicated about the character? Next time, we urge the filmmaker, at least make the pigs more prominent if he wants uptake on that admittedly not-very-inspired verbal image.

Salience is not the only warranting condition for verbal images. In fact, in some films we find a tendency to thrust the elements that give rise to the verbal image into the background allowing the spectator to only gradually discover and decipher it. This is the kind of use of verbal images that we find constantly sponsored in Perkins' *Film as Film*. Writing of *Carmen Jones,* Perkins notes that the frontal view of a jeep containing Carmen and Joe gives way to a shot from the side.[34] The background of the latter is full of rapid movement and "fluid patterns" that refer to Carmen's mode of being-in-the-world. That Perkins applauds what might be called "hidden" or "camouflaged" verbal images is consistent with his general film aesthetic which is geared to the Hollywood variety of expressive realism. *Film as Film* is really a manual of the appropriate hermeneutic strategies for appreciating conventional (especially Hollywood) narratives. Nevertheless, apart from the role that such "camouflaged" verbal images play in Perkins' criteria for evaluating films, it is undeniably true that this sort of "subtle," "non-demonstrative," "unemphatic" verbal imagery exists and plays an important part in cinematic communication. But if we cannot use salience as a reason to argue for such an image's presence, what other grounds are available?

One group of prize contenders for this task are what we will call conditions of internal fitness. In condition ii) it was proposed that verbal images comment upon a subject. The conditions of internal fitness specify the kinds of subjects verbal images comment upon. A verbal image can comment on the ongoing narrative as in the examples from *Safety Last* and *The Enforcer*. A verbal image may comment on a character, as in *Carmen Jones* or *Journeys from Berlin*, or it may underscore a thematic point as in *Itch, Scratch, Itch*. In each of these cases, we believe that the fact that the purported verbal image fits with what we take it we know about the developing plots, characters and themes gives us evidence and encouragement to assert the presence of the verbal image. The verbal image, in other words, fits with the internal structure of meanings we already intuit in the film.

The problem with the earlier hypothetical example of the filmmaker's "pig" was not simply that it lacked salience but that it also lacked characterological fitness. The difficulty might have been overcome by augmenting both the salience and internal fitness of the verbal image or merely the salience or merely the characterological fitness. Where conditions of internal fitness ground the verbal image, the verbal images "live off" what we already know of the film rather than being productive of new messages. That the postulation of verbal images can be warranted vis-à-vis conditions of internal fitness gives us a way of grounding said hypotheses when the images are of the non-salient variety. We say an image is a verbal image when it meets the constitutory conditions and

b) its postulation fits as a coherent (i.e., consistent) remark upon the developing narrative

and/or

c) its postulation fits as a coherent remark upon a developing character

and/or

d) its postulation fits as a coherent remark in favor of a developing theme.

The warranting conditions for verbal images are not mutually exclusive. A verbal image must satisfy i), ii), iii) and may satisfy b), c), d) as well. In fact, condition a) may be satisfied along with b), c), d). In *Strangers on a Train*, the "Spectator" example meets conditions i), ii), iii) and a) and c). As a general rule, we can say that for a verbal image to be carried off successfully it must meet all of the constitutory conditions and *at least one* of the warranting/facilitating conditions. Of course, it can satisfy more than one or even all of the warranting/facilitating conditions. But it must meet at least one of them. That is, to successfully project a verbal image the filmmaker must assure that it meets the constitutory conditions plus at least one of the warranting/facilitating conditions; and for a spectator or critic to assert the presence of such an image he/she must show said image fulfills the constitutory conditions plus at least one warranting/facilitating condition.

Verbal images are not only warrantable in terms of salience and internal fitness but also by external or contextual conditions. That is, the likelihood that a given verbal image is present in a film may be grounded in the fact that the words or strings of words evoked are of particular moment in the discursive context in which the film is produced.

External fitness conditions are extremely important to generating images in avant-garde films. Like the avant gardes of other arts, avant-garde films tend to be elliptical and allusive. The ellipticality is implied by what it is to be avant garde. That is, by definition such films use structures that are innovative and unconventional. But the innovative structures must also defy past art and subvert the expectations about art that are derived from more traditional styles and forms. So the avant-garde film is rarely self-explanatory. The use of structures that go beyond the conventional leads to films that make us feel that something has been left out – meaning can't be teased off the surface of the work. But these films are embedded in rich polemical contexts. This is where allusiveness enters. In fact, it is the other side of ellipticality because we are able to unfold the initially enigmatic messages of these films by referring to the theories and debates that rock the world of the avant garde. For example, we associate the fragmented imagery of early Bunuel films with the surrealists' triumphant acknowledgement of the unconscious; the disjointed imagery is no longer utterly meaningless but is an emblem of the surrealists' very specific revolt against bourgeois culture. Since the citizenry of the avant-garde film culture is small, most moviegoers do not see past the elliptical structures to the meaning of the films. Historically the avant garde arose to outrage bourgeois sensibilities; the avant-garde film world remains hermetic, a community or fellowship of filmmakers and spectators who understand each other through knowledge of in-house debates about the nature of the medium and contending stylistic imperatives. One necessary, generic feature of the avant garde is that it requires a highly developed polemical background. It is this context that enables its elliptical symbol systems to acquire meaning. In terms of verbal images, we approach avant-garde films knowing the prevailing debates and theories of film and art that shape this community of discourse. The vocabulary of those debates and theories supplies us with a framework for scrutinizing the works. The situation is somewhat like that of primed verbal images except that no specific words need be supplied by the film though a range of vocabularies is by the context.

A related way of putting it is that with most varieties of avant-garde film we presume that one thing they are "about" is film art itself. That is, film and art are taken as one of the references for such films. These works pledge allegiances to different positions on the nature of film and art. Verbal images are a primary mechanism for signaling such commitments. By manipulating the visual medium the avant-garde filmmaker is able to latch onto polemically charged words and phrases from the tumultuous aesthetic arena that supplies the context for the films. For example, the filmmaker may submit images that are literally "flat" but that description then perks an association with the specialized meaning of "flat" in recent aesthetic discourse, viz., flat = real. In the Hoberman case earlier, the film evoked the description "reflection" which connects with an extended or specialized concept in the filmworld to the effect that "film is a reflection of reality." When considering avant-garde films we discover that often the descriptions of images in said films act as trigger words that, by means of evoking central words in prevailing debates, correlate to positions about the nature of film and art.

A recent exemplar is Sally Potter's *Thriller*. A British film, it can be situated in the polemical context of Marxist-Psycho-analytic-Semiology. The film mixes still-photos and moving images, emphasizing that it is a "construction" from single frames. It includes reproductions of a performance of *La Bohème*, thereby emphasizing its "artifice" and it is quite literally a "mystery." These words, in the context of the regnant theories in British film culture, are polemically loaded, locked in a skein of interrelated propositions, e.g., that film is constructed, that the ego is constructed, that the film constructs its subject (its spectator's position) while the subject reciprocally constructs the film, that films and subjects are artificial or made things and that pondering the nature of the self (and its construction) is The Mystery. The film itself does not yield these propositions directly but when informed of the context of the film we can see that Potter is telegraphing her commitments by producing images that hook onto the words used to set out crucial articles of faith of the milieu of the film's creation. This example should also indicate that the avant-garde film does not only allude, by way of verbal images, to theories of art and film. Theories from psychology, economics, philosophy, etc. are also in its reach as nodes of reference just because it is often characteristic for the avant garde as a community to combine speculations from many diverse sources in its discourse. Thus, in *Inauguration of the Pleasure Dome,* it is possible for Anger to communicate the idea that the ego is split by means of a Janus-faced image of the Scarlet Woman composed on a "split" screen. The film does not say that the ego is split but given its historical context, in which the proposition was nearly a commonplace, the provoking of the descriptive term "split" opens the way to the attribution of the associated, specialized application of the term as it figured in contemporary slogans. The polemical context beckons us to look for literalizations of words of some currency in the given community of discourse. Where attributing the extended meaning of a verbal image does not contradict anything else in the film we feel it is legitimate. Though the discussion of external fitness conditions so far has been exclusively of avant-garde film – where context is generally extremely important – conventional narrative films can also project verbal images based on prevailing catchwords in surrounding cultural spheres.[35] For both avant-garde films and more conventional ones we can say that an image in a given film is a verbal image when it meets the constitutory conditions and

e) its postulation fits the discursive context of the film's production and it does not contradict the overt meanings internal to the structure of the film.

In the subtitle to this essay, I call it "preliminary notes." The disclaimer is meant not only to acknowledge that the theory as stated needs tightening in a number of spots but also because I suspect that there are more warranting/facilitating conditions than I have proposed. Future research should aim at unearthing and clarifying these as of yet unidentified conditions. But even with the addition of further warranting conditions, I would conjecture that their role in relation to the constitutory conditions will remain approximately the same. That is, an image will be a verbal image when it meets *all* the constitutory conditions and at *least one* of the warranting/facilitating conditions.[36] This leaves open the possibility that an image may meet all the constitutory conditions and two or three or even all of the warranting conditions.

I claim that by outlining the conditions an image must meet to be a verbal image and to elicit uptake that I have offered an account of how verbal images are projected by filmmakers and recognized by spectators. I hazard that some readers will balk at my presumptiveness, complaining that I have not in any way explained how verbal images are made. That is, I have not supplied a recipe with directions showing how the filmmaker should choose this specific object or image if he/she wants to evoke this or that specific word. On this reckoning, very little has been said except to note the proclivity of images of scale, height, ascent, descent, movement, etc. to prompt metaphors. I have also offered a wide variety of other kinds of verbal images which the filmmaker might use as examples for inspiration. But it is true that we don't have anything approaching a set of rules – like a verbal/visual dictionary – for solving the problem of what image will get exactly the right word in a given context. This question will be grappled with at the level of practice – of fiddling about until the filmmaker feels he's got it. In general, it is probably easier to begin with the word or phrase and then arrange and rearrange one's cinematic material until the word "screams out." But obviously the story could go the other way. The word or phrase may "lurk" in the filmmaker's materials and suddenly "leap" at him. The precise process of choice that leads the filmmaker to use a given object or image to elicit a given word is a matter of discovery and creativity and as such is not rule-bound in the strictest sense. But though the process of finding the right word is not reducible to a single formula or set of formulae the matter of projecting and recognizing such verbal images is not the result of pure happenstance either. We can tell filmmakers what conditions the image must meet in order to be a verbal image – apart from what it is an image of. Also, we can tell the filmmaker how to assure uptake of his image by noting what institutionalized expectations spectators need to be satisfied in order to reassure themselves that they have hold of a verbal image. And this is an account of how the verbal image works as an institutionalized means of communication.

Before concluding the discussion of verbal images as illocutions, a word of warning is pertinent. The introduction of warranting conditions is a departure from traditional speech act theory. I feel that it is justified. Indeed, I believe that if we are to import speech act theory to certain problems of aesthetic communication, the idea of warranting conditions is particularly germane because it acknowledges the operation of interpretation and judgment in aesthetic communication whereas the more ritualized speech acts – such as "I promise" – can be explicated solely in terms of constitutory conditions. But a speech act theorist could respond that that is the very reason that I should not attempt to use speech act theory

to analyze verbal images – that I've missed the whole point of speech act theory.

By discussing warranting conditions – what makes uptake probable – I am liable to the charge that what I am calling the illocutionary force of the verbal image is really a matter of perlocutionary force. I cannot answer this accusation here in detail, nor do I want to engage the nettlesome issue of whether a sharp boundary can be drawn between illocutions and perlocutions. But I do think there is a difference between the uptake of a verbal image – which is guided by conventionalized interpretative strategies – and the anger that results when a student orders a teacher to leave the room. That is, verbal images seem more of the nature of conventionalized communications than of causal effects and to the extent that they resemble the former it appears appropriate to view them as illocutions.

I do not contend that I have sharply focussed the objections that a speech act theorist might bring against me nor do I think I have conclusively rebutted such objections. It is an open question whether illocutionary act theory is the correct conceptual apparatus to apply to the phenomenon of verbal images. I think the approach is defensible but also invite disgruntled readers to start here in criticizing me.[37]

D. Why Verbal Images?

Even if the preceding formulation is adequate as an account of how verbal images function communicatively (in light of certain institutionalized conditions), it does not explain why verbal images exist in art in general and film in particular. Several reasons immediately suggest themselves as likely explanations. To the extent that they do not contradict each other – or can be shown to be relevant to definably distinct cases – I am prone to accept them all as factors contributing to the persistence and pervasiveness of verbal images. Why presuppose that a symbolic structure perseveres as the result of a single cause?

The first purpose that verbal images may fulfill is to revivify dead metaphors and clichés. Hackneyed phrases – like "laughing behind someone's back," or, from *The Trial*, being "lost" in the legal system – become vivid again and their aptness shines forth when pictorialized. We experience the cliché afresh, as it were. This motivation for verbal images is somewhat opposed to their use in comic contexts where the cliché, proverb or dead metaphor is parodied, i.e., reduced to absurdity through the risible combination of gestures, postures and props it takes to visualize them.

Previously it was noted how often the identification of a verbal image depends on knowing that it is appropriate to a given film because we already understand that the film evinces the position or prejudice rehearsed by the verbal image. In this regard, verbal images generally seem somewhat redundant in terms of what is communicated, and the explanations we offer for them should accommodate this tendency.

One explanation that meets this requirement is the construal of verbal images as a form of aesthetic play. That is, the filmmaker adds the verbal image to the work as an elaboration, along another dimension, of something already in the film, and the spectator discovers this complication, this echo, in the course of his/her own interpretive or hermeneutic game. The presence of the verbal image thereby intensifies the reward of the spectator's cognitive and perceptual play. In other words, recognizing verbal images may be an end in itself, or better, a self-gratifying exercise like recognizing a recurring pattern in visual art or a recurring motif in music.

Though there are undeniable cases where verbal images act solely to instill aesthetic play, probably the most frequent motivation for them is to reinforce some concurrently evolving dramatic or thematic point. Like

the explanation in terms of aesthetic play, this notion of reinforcement accords with the observed redundancy of many verbal images but it posits an instrumental role to the images. We understand the perilous emotional condition of the leading character in *Bigger Than Life* before we get the verbal image of the "shattered self." The verbal image underlines the character's straits; perhaps it even increases the probability of spectators describing him as "breaking up" or being "shattered." The verbal image does not add new information but underscores, condenses, galvanizes and summarizes what is already known in one crystallized image.

The concept of reinforcement raises the question of whether or not all the verbal images projected by films are comprehended consciously. It appears more plausible to suppose that much of the reinforcement that goes on via verbal images is subliminal. After all, only critics and film students talk about literalizations; for the mass of filmgoers, verbal images seem to do their work "silently." Yet, if this is the case with reinforcement, what of the claim that verbal images are regulated by a set of institutionalized conditions? That is, how does the conventionalist thrust of our account square with the subliminal reception of many verbal images? Obviously, I have to hold that both the conventions ruling verbal images and, in some cases, the recognition of verbal images are tacit. Viewers are not able to expound the rules for recognizing verbal images nor can they pinpoint the origin in the imagery of the metaphors (derived from verbal images) that they use to describe what's going on in a film. Nevertheless, it is still reasonable to say that they are subscribing to tacit conventions just as few of us are able to localize the kinesic signals we receive in terms of discrete gestures even though those gestures are conventional.[38]

Lastly, it might be argued that if the conditions for recognizing verbal images are primarily tacit – which they must be if this paper justly claims originality for formalizing them – how did anyone – whether artist or spectator – ever manage to learn them? Sarcastically, one might cavil "by osmosis." But is that so wide of the mark? I would say that we learned to make and to respond to verbal images through examples and by practice, by talking and reading about art and images in ways that implicitly presuppose the projection and recognition of verbal images. We pick up on verbal images in the course of learning the institutionalized interpretive strategies of aesthetic discourse. The theory of verbal images herein is only a rational reconstruction of reasoning patterns we already, albeit tacitly, respect.[39]

V. What About Psychoanalysis?[40]

Some readers may have read the earlier sections of this essay surprised and maybe annoyed that no reference was made to psychoanalysis. For surely what I have called verbal images seem intimately related to a species of unconscious thought that Freud noticed more than once. Writing of Ferenczi, Freud observes in a *foot*note

One day, however, he (Ferenczi) was blaming himself for having committed a technical error in a patient's psychoanalysis. That day all his former absent-minded habits reappeared. He stumbled several times as he walked along the street (a representation of his *faux pas* [false step-blunder] in the treatment). . . .[41]

Freud also reports a similar parapraxis of his own.

There is a house where twice every day for six years, at regular hours, I used to wait to be let in outside a door on the second floor. During this long period it has happened to me on two occasions, with a short interval between them, that I have gone a floor too high – i.e., I "climbed too high." On the first occasion I was enjoying an ambitious day-dream in which I was "climbing higher and higher." On this occasion I even failed to hear that the door in question had opened as I put my foot on the first step of the third flight. On the other occasion, I again went

too far while I was deep in thought; when I realized it, I turned back and tried to catch hold of the phantasy in which I had been absorbed. I found that I was irritated by a (phantasied) criticism of my writings in which I was reproached with always "going too far." This I had now replaced by the not very respectful "climbing too high."[42]

And Freud is well aware of the importance of the play of meaning in his examples. He says

. . . falling, stumbling and slipping need not always be interpreted as purely accidental miscarriages of motor actions. The double meanings that language attaches to these expressions are enough to indicate the kind of phantasies involved, which can be represented by such losses of equilibrium. I can recall a number of fairly mild illnesses in women and girls which set in after a fall not accompanied by any injury, and which were taken to be traumatic hysterias resulting from the shock of the fall. Even at that time I had an impression that these events were differently connected and that the fall was already a product of the neurosis and expressed the same unconscious phantasies with a sexual content, which could be assumed to be the forces operating behind the symptoms. Is not the same thing meant by a proverb which runs: "When a girl falls, she falls on her back?"[43]

Unquestionably, there is some relation between these cases and verbal images. But can we explain verbal images by extrapolating from what Freud says about these examples? I think we cannot. First, Freud says precious little about how these word/action interpenetrations operate aside from noting that they ride on double meanings. At one time, Freud was interested in exploring the possibilities of a technique of "free imagery" but he dropped the practice and stayed with free association as his basic method.[44] Perhaps if Freud had continued with "free imagery," he might have had more to add about the specific structures of word/image interpenetrations of the sort we are discussing. But as it is, he's done little more theoretically than to note their existence; of course, therapeutically, he used his knowledge of their existence with unparalleled brilliance.

Current researchers are again interested in "free imagery" techniques.[45] But they seem less concerned with pithing the internal structure of the mental processes involved in "free imagery" than they are with other questions – for example, what causes more anxiety, free association or "free imagery?"[46] They have not elaborated on the workings of word/image associations beyond adopting what is already available in traditional texts. Thus, nothing would be purchased about the workings of verbal images by indenturing clinical psychology because that field appears not to have much to say about them.

Of course, clinical psychology does offer ideas about the role that word/action and word/image interpenetrations play in our lives. They function as vehicles of disguise that enable unconscious thoughts, fantasies and impulses to elude psychic censorship. But can we requisition this account of word/image interpenetrations in dreams and parapraxes for a theory of verbal images in art? No. Recall the example from *Pick-up on South Street*. It is absurd to think that Fuller and his crew rolled a heavy studio camera across a sound stage to that hook without full awareness of what they were doing. The notion that the kinds of verbal images we've discussed in this paper result from repressed, unconscious thoughts ducking a censor and welling up onto the screen just doesn't harmonize with the data. It strains credulity to envision Cukor in a funk when he arranged that verbal image in *The Women*. At the very least, it's difficult for a parapraxis to pass unnoticed before an army of producers, writers, actors and technicians.

The problem with commandeering the psychoanalytic explanation of word/image association for a theory of verbal imaging is that verbal imaging in art is to a large degree conventionalized an, thus, out in the open, so to speak. I would not gainsay that

verbal imaging in art probably has the kinds of word/image associations Freud considers as rough psychic prototypes – or as distant ancestors, to wax metaphoric. Like many conventionalized symbolic practices, verbal imaging may have originated in and evolved from a "natural" psychological process. But two things must be borne in mind. First, though it is pleasant to know where a symbolic practice hails from, that does not guarantee additional understanding of the process because once institutionalized the process is likely to change, especially in terms of the purpose it serves. Even if verbal images are sometimes "hidden," they are in works of art to be found as a means of enriching aesthetic experience; the word/image associations ferreted out by clinical psychologists are "hidden" more unyieldingly and designedly so. Second, though it makes sense to discuss verbal images in terms of warranting/facilitating conditions – just because they are public means of communication – it is ludicrous to suppose that our rollicking ids play by any rules, and certainly not by any rules that would make their ruminations more lucid. If born of dreams and parapraxes, verbal images in art have drifted away from the old sod and picked up new habits. And it is the new habits that it is the task of aestheticians to investigate.

Does this commit us to the position that psychology has no place in the study of verbal images in art? Not at all. By discriminating the types of interpretive thinking that go into making and recognizing verbal images, we have segmented the psychologist's data, offering him/her in gross outline some identifiable patterns of institutionalized reasoning whose subtending mental processes it is his/her job to differentiate.

VI. The Frontiers of Verbal Images

It has not been my intention to argue that the verbal image is the only or even the most central type of symbolic formation in film. It is one symbolic form among many. We have spent some time trying to say what it is. In conclusion, we will turn to what it is not, examining two of its neighbors, surveying boundary lines as a further means of clarifying our subject.

To the north of verbal images are iconographic images. These are visual images that have a one-to-one correspondence with an established meaning. During the Middle Ages, for instance, ostrich eggs symbolized man's forgetfulness of God.[47] Deciphering the meaning of an image of such an object in a work of art is a matter of what Panofsky calls "iconographical analysis in the narrower sense."[48] These images have a fixed association with an abstract idea or concept. The represented object, such as the ostrich egg, is correlated to the phrase "forgetful of God" as a word is paired with its dictionary definition. But verbal images are connected with a given word or string of words not because of an established or fixed or invariant bond between the represented object and the word but because the word or string of words evoked fits the context of the image. Iconographic images are to verbal images as context-independent, fixed associations between words and images are to context-sensitive hypotheses to the best verbal fit between word and image.

To the south of verbal images are expressive labels. We often communicate our reactions to all kinds of works of art, including films, by means of such anthropomorphic predicates as "melancholic," "fanciful," "spritely," "adventurous," etc. Since we use these metaphors in our description of works of art the temptation arises to think of them, where visual art is at issue, as some sort of overarching verbal image. However, it is important to realize that though we use expressive labels to synopsize aspects of our experience of artworks, it is not the point of an artwork to elicit expressive labels from us. It is the purpose of a verbal image to evoke a word or string of words. But it is the purpose of expressive qualities to engender

certain experiences rather than to invoke the nominal labels of those experiences.[49]

Verbal images sit between iconographic images and expressive qualities on the map of symbolic formations in the visual arts. Their relation to verbal language is more fluid than that of iconographic images but more dependent than that of expressive qualities. Though the verbal image can function in concert with other varieties of symbolic structures, it is a specific mode of symbolic communication in the visual arts – one whose surface has barely been scratched.

Notes

1. In my own writings I have made frequent reference to this type of symbolism. For example, see: "Mind, Metaphor and Medium," *Film Quarterly,* Vol. 31, no. 2 (Winter, 1977/78); "Welles and Kafka," *Film Reader* 3; "The Cabinet of Dr. Kracauer," *Millennium Film Journal* 2; "The Gold Rush," *Wide Angle,* Vol. 3 no. 2. In my "Toward A Theory of Film Editing." *Millennium Film Journal* 3, I attempted, somewhat unsuccessfully, to describe how this symbolic structure operates in editing. This last essay is reprinted in this volume.

2. I am aware that not all the examples in this paragraph operate in precisely the same way but a taxonomy of primed verbal images would require another paper.

3. Hopefully some of my examples should have already indicated that I do not believe that the production of a verbal image is necessarily a major aesthetic achievement. I am using the term – verbal image – to isolate a specific symbolic structure. It is a descriptive term not a commendatory one. There are good and bad, eloquent and forced verbal images. Nowhere in this essay am I implying that simply by having used a verbal image has an artist done anything of artistic merit.

4. See Jonathan Buchsbaum's review of Hoberman's work in *Millennium Film Journal* 6.

5. Lawrence Gowing, "Brueghel's World," in *Narrative Art,* ed. by Thomas Hess and John Ashbery (New York: Macmillan Co., 1970) pp. 16–19.

6. *Images of Horror and Fantasy* (New York: Abrams, 1978), p. 65.

7. The ballet is described in Margaret Lloyd, *The Borzoi Book of Modern Dance* (New York: Dance Horizons, 1949), p. 328. The dance is in the repertory of the American Ballet Theater.

8. Described in Margaret Croyden, *Lunatics, Lovers and Poets* (New York: Delta, 1974), p. 234.

9. Though literature is not a visual art, and, therefore, cannot project verbal images as such, literature, because it describes visual scenes, can use language in a way that resembles verbal images in the visual arts. That is, a novelist can describe a scene by words whose use evokes a literalization. In Sade's *Juliette,* Saint Fond has Juliette lick his anus; the scene turns into a literalization of the metaphor, sycophancy = coprophagy, when Saint Fond proclaims "Kneel and face it; consider the honour I do in permitting you to do my arse the homage an entire nation, no, the whole world aspires to give it!" I choose a ribald example, here, because the very structure of such obscenities often lends itself to literalization not only in literature but in everyday speech and, of course, verbal jokes.

    Digressing somewhat, it is worthwhile to point out that writers often design their texts to evoke specific words. These words need not be literalizations. Consider this stanza from Denise Levertov's "The Secret":

> I who don't know the
> secret wrote
> the line.

Ending the first line as she does prompts the question "what?" which, of course, corresponds to and headlines the very next word, accentuating its impact. Levertov achieves this by eschewing certain conventions for line-endings in free verse, including segmentation of a sentence syllabically, accentually or at units of syntax. By doing this she raises a special fermata at the end of the line.

    Music can also be used to evoke definite words; ascending and descending scales are often dragooned into literalizing – e.g., *The 1812 Overture.*

10. Though it does not always result in what we are calling verbal images, sound, in film – including verbal language, music and noise – can be used to evoke words and literalizations.

11. Paul Willemen, "Reflections on Eikenbaum's Concept of Internal Speech in the Cinema," in *Screen* (Winter 1974/75), pp. 64–65.

12. See my "Welles and Kafka" for an extended examples of this kind of verbal image in editing.

13. Alain Silver notes a similar use of camera movement by Lang as a result of the new technological possibilities of the 50s. He writes "Fritz Lang in discussing the camera movement in *The Blue Gardenia,* asserted that the film's fluid tracking shots, which *relentlessly pursue* (italics added) his guilt-ridden heroine, could not have been executed without the compact crab dolly." in *Film Noir,* ed. by Alain Silver and Elizabeth Ward (Woodstock, N.Y.: Overlook Press, 1979), pp. 2–3.

14. V. Nizhny, *Lessons with Eisenstein* (New York: DaCapo Press, 1979), pp. 103–104.

15. In *Film Form,* trans. and edited by Jay Leyda (New York: Harcourt, Brace and World, 1949), pp. 122–149.

16. Boris Eikenbaum, "Problems of Film Stylistics," trans. by Thomas Aman, in *Screen* (Autumn, 1974), p. 30.

17. See Ronald Levaco, "Eikenbaum, Inner Speech and Film Stylistics," and Willemen, "Reflections on Eikenbaum's Concept of Internal Speech in the Cinema," *Screen* (Winter 1974/75).

18. Willemen, 61.

19. L.S. Vygotsky, *Thought and Language,* trans. and edited by Eugenia Hanfman and Gertrude Vakar (Boston: MIT Press, 1962).

20. Eikenbaum, 14.

21. Vygotsky, 17. The "broken" wheel in this example is not really a case of what we have been calling a verbal image because, even if the picture elicited the literal description "broken" for either a spectator or its creator, the word would not spark any further connotative associations about the picture. To use Willemen's nomenclature, no "literalism" is involved.

22. Vygotsky, 145.

23. The bibliography for speech act theory is large and continually growing. The *locus classicus* is

J. L. Austin's *How to do things with words* (Boston: Harvard University Press, 1965). A truncated, starting list of other relevant sources includes: J. R. Searle, *Speech Acts* (Cambridge University Press, 1969); Searle, "A taxonomy of illocutionary acts," in *Language, Mind and Knowledge* (*Minnesota Studies in the Philosophy of Science* 7), edited by K. Gunderson (Minneapolis: University of Minnesota Press, 1975); Searle, "A Classification of Illocutionary Acts," in *Proceedings of the Texas Conference on Performatives, Presuppositions and Implicature,* edited by A.H. Rogers, B. Wall and J. P. Murphy (Arlington, Va.: Center for Applied Linguistics, 1977); P. Cole and J. L. Morgan (eds.), *Speech Acts* (*Syntax and Semantics* 3) (New York: Academic Press, 1975); Zeno Vendler, *Res Cogitans* (Ithaca: Cornell University Press, 1972); Jerrold Katz, *Propositional Structure and Illocutionary Force* (Boston: Harvard University Press, 1980).

In terms of aesthetics, literary theory has been a major center for the application of speech act theory. A handful of titles from this burgeoning enterprise includes: J. R. Searle, "The Logical Status of Fictional Discourse," in *New Literary History* VI (Winter, 1975); Barbara Herrnstein Smith, "Poetry as Fiction," in *New Literary History* II (Winter, 1971); Herrnstein Smith, "Actions, Fictions and the Ethics of Interpretation," *Centrum* 3 (Fall, 1975); Martin Steinman and Robert Brown, "Native Readers of Fiction: A Speech Act and Genre-Rule Approach to Defining Literature," *What is Literature?* ed. by Paul Hernadi (Bloomington: U. of Indiana Press, 1979); Martin Steinman, "Perlocutionary Acts and the Interpretation of Literature," *Centrum* 3 (Fall, 1975); Richard Ohman, "Literature as Act," in *Approaches to Poetics,* ed. by Seymour Chatman (New York: Columbia University Press, 1973); Monroe Beardsley, "The Concept of Literature," in *Literary Theory and Structure,* ed. by Frank Brady, John Palmer and Martin Price (New Haven: Yale University Press, 1973); Beardsley, "Aesthetic Intentions and Fictive Illocutions," in *What is Literature?;* Michael Hancher, "Understanding Poetic Speech Acts," *College English* 36 (Feb., 1975); Stanley Fish, "How to do things with Austin and Searle," *Modern Language Notes* (Oct., 1976); Terry Eagleton, "Ideology, Fiction, Narrative," *Social Text* (Summer, 1979).

24. See A.J. Ayer's *Language, Truth and Logic* (New York: Dover, 1935) for a statement of the logical positivist view of meaning.

25. For an account of promising as an illocutionary act see Searle, *Speech Acts,* pp. 57–62, or Searle, "What is a Speech Act," in *The Philosophy of Language,* ed. by J. R. Searle (London: Oxford University Press, 1971), pp. 46–53.

26. See David Novitz, "Picturing," *Journal of Aesthetics and Art Criticism* 34 (Winter, 1975); Søren Kjørup, "George Inness and the Battle of Hastings, or Doing Things with Pictures," *The Monist* 58 (April, 1974); Søren Kjørup, "Pictorial Speech Acts," *Erkenntis* 12 (January, 1978).

27. *The Monist* 58 (April, 1974).

28. I distinguish between "right word" and "right kind of word" here because with many verbal images it is not necessary that only one specific word be evoked but rather that a kind of word be evoked – namely, a kind of word that belongs to a class of words with roughly the same reference, and, more importantly, the same connotations. In the case from *Bigger Than Life* either "broken" or "shattered" will describe the mirror and comment metaphorically on the character.

29. To work out the "logic" of this shift, it is helpful to consider L. J. Cohen and A. Margalis, "The Role of Inductive Reasoning in the Interpretation of Metaphor," in *The Semantics of Natural Language,* edited by G. Harman and D. Davidson (Dordrecht: Reidel, 1972), pp. 722–740.

30. I do not wish to be understood as saying that if a filmmaker wishes to literalize a figure of speech he/she knows from a language he/she doesn't otherwise speak that this is impossible. On such an occasion, I would construe the figure of speech as part of the filmmaker's language.

31. Willemen, 66–67.

32. There are also superimpositions and dissolves where we conveniently insert the word "is" between the "represented objects" collated in the array. This can be the "is" of identity, e.g., the superimpositions of the different faces of the master criminals in both *Dr.*

Mabuse, The Gambler and *Fantomas,* or of Pat's face over the horse in *Pat and Mike.* Likewise, the "is" of metaphor is available, e.g., the heads of the spies over those of their animal personifications in *Strike.* Metaphoric superimpositions and dissolves appear in very early films – *Nymph of the Waves* – as well as modern film – the vulture/helicopters in *Capricorn I.* Since there are conventions for inferring "like," "as," and "is" in regard to cinematic contexts, cinema can create metaphors that are unprecedented in verbal language. Eikenbaum, on page 30 of his essay, seems to be saying that film metaphors must correspond to metaphoric expressions already in the spectator's verbal baggage. He says this principle remains true even if film develops its own semantic patterns. But given conventions for inserting "like," "as," and "is," I don't see how in any straightforward sense filmmakers are restrained from coining original metaphors and similes. Perhaps Eikenbaum has something more complicated in mind. He may believe that since literalization hinges on words having extended meanings in existing language, all film metaphors just repeat possibilities that already exist in verbal language. But this throws the baby out with the bathwater; surely it is too strong an argument. For it would compel us to say that there can be no original metaphors in verbal language since all verbal metaphors already exist in the semantic, componential structure of the focus word in the metaphor.

33. Max Black, "Metaphor," in *Philosophy Looks At The Arts,* edited by Joseph Margolis (Philadelphia: Temple University Press, 1978), pp. 451–457.

34. V. F. Perkins, *Film as Film* (Harmondsworth: Penguin, 1972), pp. 79–80.

35. Of course, as previous examples attest, the verbal images in avant-garde films need not always be affiliated with polemical debates. For example, "on the carpet" in *Journeys From Berlin* refers to a character and not to an artworld context.

36. This formulation may be a bit too neat. A dissenter might argue that all verbal images require *some* degree of salience since we must light upon the elements that give rise to the putative verbal image before we can decide whether it meets either an internal or external fitness condition. But perhaps what is at issue here is not salience but some notion of minimal perceptibility.

37. Monroe Beardsley has suggested to me that reference is an important ingredient in verbal imaging and that my warranting conditions are really constitutory conditions that make referring possible.

38. Subliminal reinforcement sounds like perlocution but I hold out for illocution because the event seems somewhat rule regulated.

39. The idea of reasoning patterns that we tacitly respect is not so strange. We could say of a student in an introductory logic class that he/she is about to learn *modus ponens,* a reasoning pattern he/she has practiced all his/her life and tacitly respected.

40. In this section I do not address the attempt to weld together Vygotsky's idea of inner speech and Lacanian psychoanalysis. I should say, however, that I find that, on the face of it, this project is curious because it seems contradictory. Vygotsky, as I read him, seems to believe that there is thought without language, whereas Lacan appears to believe that all thought is linguistic, e.g., Lacan's *Ecrits: A Selection,* trans. Alan Sheridan (New York: Norton & Co., 1977), p. 148.

41. Sigmund Freud, *The Psychopathology of Everyday Life* (New York: Norton & Co., 1960), pp. 156–157.

42. Freud, 164–165.

43. Freud, 174–175.

44. Joseph Reyher, "Free Imagery: An Uncovering Procedure," *Journal of Clinical Psychology* 19 (1963), p. 454.

45. E.g., Jerome L. Singer, *Imagery and Daydream Methods in Psychotherapy and Behavior Modification* (New York: Academic Press, 1974).

46. Joseph Reyher and William Smeltzer, "Uncovering Properties of Visual Imagery and Verbal Association: A Comparative Study," in *Journal of Abnormal Psychology* 73 (1968), pp. 218–222. By the way, "free imagery" wins.

47. Millard Meiss, "*Ovum Struthionis:* Symbol and Allusion in Piero della Francesca's Montefeltral Altarpiece," in *The Painter's Choice: Problems in Interpretation in Renaissance Art* (New York: Harper and Row, 1976) p. 107.

48. Erwin Panofsky, *Studies in Iconology: Humanistic Themes in the Art of the Renaissance* (New York: Harper and Row, 1939).

49. Some useful ideas for working out a "logic" of expressive labels can be found in *The Measurement of Meaning* by Charles Osgood, George Suci and Percy Tannenbaum (Urbana: University of Illinois Press, 1957), and *Cross-Cultural Universals of Affective Meaning* by Charles Osgood, William May and Murray Miron (Urbana: University of Illinois Press, 1975).

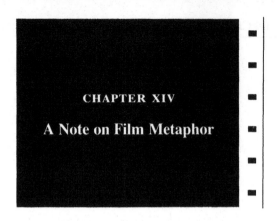

CHAPTER XIV

A Note on Film Metaphor

The purpose of this note is to propose a theory of what I take to be the most straightforward type of film metaphor. What has provoked me to compose such a theory is the fact that in his recent, excellent study – *Metaphor and Film* – Trevor Whittock advances a series of useful analyses of a whole battery of cinematic tropes, none of which, oddly enough, is the most obvious and clearcut example of filmic metaphor.[1] Moreover, an examination of the relevant literature convinces me that the structure that I think is the best candidate for the title of film metaphor has not been identified as such by theorists of the relation of metaphor and film.[2] Consequently, this paper will attempt to construct a case for a central type of film metaphor, one which heretofore has been untheorized.

It is probably useless to haggle over the term "metaphor." It has been used to describe a wide range of phenomena in film. Thus, I shall not claim that other theorists are wrong in their applications of the term nor that my usage is the only correct one. Instead, I will simply claim that what I am calling film metaphor is a central case – if not the most central case – of film metaphor, as well as the case which has the most compelling credentials for the title.

What is the type of metaphor that I have in mind? Let some famous examples initiate the conversation. In the third scene of Fritz Lang's silent film *Metropolis* we see a huge machine through the point of view of the son of the ruler of Metropolis. There are two enormous turbines at the foot of the machine and an awesome stairway, rising between rows of work stations, leads up to an open space dominated by some sort of pumping levers.

The machine explodes and the scene is swathed in smoke; as it clears, we not only seen maimed workers but – again through a point-of-view shot – we see the machine transformed into the monster Moloch. Via superimposition, the stairs become Moloch's tongue, while the space at the top of the stairs is Moloch's mouth and throat. In one shot, the turbines are replaced by Moloch's paws, though in subsequent shots we see the turbines as turbines, suggesting, perhaps, modernist versions of outsized votive candles.

The machine, or at least parts of it, has been transformed into parts of a monster, Moloch. Nevertheless, the machine is still recognizable as a machine. The monster elements and the machine elements are co-present – or homospatial – in the same figure. Moreover, the co-present monster elements and machine elements interanimate in such a way that we grasp the point of the image to be that the machine is Moloch, or, more broadly, that such modern factory machines are man-eating monsters. That is, we take the modern factory machine to be the target domain in the structure, and Moloch (or man-eating monster) to be the source domain in the structure, and then we selectively map aspects of what we know about the source domain onto the target domain – or, more colloquially, we see modern machinery as man-eaters.[3] Or, yet once more, we use what we know of man-eating monsters – that they devour people – to selectively focus our understanding of modern machinery.

Further, famous examples of this structure in film include Vertov's superimposition in *Man with a Movie Camera* of the eye over the camera lens – thereby propounding the metaphor that the eye is a camera (or that the eye should be a camera);[4] and Eisenstein's suggestion in *Strike,* through gradual dissolves, wipes and superimposition, that one of the spies is a monkey and that another is a fox. In *Man with a Movie Camera,* the point is that what we know (or, what Vertov thought we knew) of the camera (or cinema) – that it is the microscope and telescope of time – serves as the source domain through which we filter our understanding of what the human eye (or consciousness) either is now or (more likely) is to be – viz., that which is temporally transcendent; while in the case of *Strike,* Eisenstein proposes that one of the spies is a monkey and that another is a fox, thereby encouraging us to apply what we know of the source domains – monkeys, foxes, and their associated commonplaces – to focus and filter our understanding of the objects in the target domain – the two spies, respectively.[5]

Though the examples cited so far have all involved superimposition, the structure under discussion can be contrived by other means. Think of all these Popeye cartoons where after Popeye eats his spinach, the fact that he has regained his strength is signalled by images where his biceps become an anvil or his fist becomes a hammer. Clearly these are metaphors. His muscles are an anvil; his fist is a hammer. In both cases, the source domains suggest that we selectively reconceive Popeye's muscle and his fist to be incredibly hard; or, to put the matter more technically, we map an attribute of the source domain – the hardness of anvils or that of hammers – onto the target domain – Popeye's muscle or his fist.

Likewise, make-up can also be used to provoke this variety of metaphorical comprehension. For example, if you believe that the relevant scenes in David Cronenberg's *Videodrome* are hallucinations, then the scene in which the character played by James Woods has a video cassette inserted in his body propounds the metaphor that people are video cassette players. However ungainly this metaphor sounds in spoken language it is nevertheless appropriate in the

film *Videodrome,* where it is an element of an overarching theme that insinuates that modern societies are being programmed by TV. In effect, Cronenberg's visual metaphor says "people nowadays are no better that video recorders, their minds being video tapes produced elsewhere."

Furthermore, there are techniques beyond superimposition, drawing and make-up – including video-image processing, computer-generated imaging, set design, costuming, and so on – which facilitate the production of the sort of film metaphors exemplified above. For what the previous cases have in common is that they are all composite figures – machine/monster, eye/camera, fist/hammer, person/videoplayer – and one can construct composite figures by means of an indeterminate number of techniques.

But what is it about such composite figures that leads us to call them metaphors? To state my case succinctly, first, verbal metaphors are most frequently advanced by grammatical structures that propose identity relations – such as the "is" of identity or, apposition – and the film metaphors I have introduced likewise depend upon visual devices that portend identity – viz., what I have already called "homospatiality." Second, verbal metaphors generally turn out to be false when taken literally, whereas what I am calling film metaphors have an analogous property, viz., physical noncompossibility.[6] That is, it is not physically compossible with the universe as we know it that muscles be anvils, that people be cassette recorders or that spies be foxes.

To expand: just as verbal metaphors most often signal some sort of identity between the objects they relate or some intersection between the categories they mobilize – e.g., "man *is* a wolf unto man" – the relevant composite images in film deploy homospatiality to suggest identity; disparate elements (calling to mind disparate categories) are visually incorporated or amalgamated into one spatially bounded homogeneous entity. Elements are fused in a composite, but nevertheless self-identifiable, construct thereby visually indicating that these elements are elements of the self-same entity.[7] Verbal metaphor proposes identity by means of various grammatical devices. Film metaphor rides on the proposal of identity as well, though by means of homospatiality which, in turn, may be secured by an indeterminate number of devices, cinematic (e.g., superimposition) and otherwise (e.g., make-up).

The elements in such metaphors are features of the self-same entity in virtue of inhabiting the same space-time coordinates – in virtue of inhabiting the same body – i.e., being within the same continuous contour, or perimeter or boundary. The elements in the visual metaphor – machine parts and monster parts – are fused or superimposed or otherwise attached as parts of a recognizably integrated or unified entity.

Homospatiality is a necessary condition for the type of film metaphor about which I am talking. Homospatiality provides the means to link disparate categories in visual metaphors in ways that are functionally equivalent to the ways that disparate categories are linked grammatically in verbal metaphors. Where verbal metaphors appear to assert identity between distinct, nonconverging objects and/or categories, visual metaphors,[8] of which film metaphors are a subclass, suggest categorical identity by presenting nonconverging categories as instantiated in the same entity. Indeed, it is the way in which homospatiality plays the role as a visual equivalent to the appearance of asserted identity in verbal metaphors that supplies us with one of our reasons for speaking of certain kinds of film images – such as machine/Moloch – as film metaphors.

Through homospatiality a figure is presented that is a recognizably unified entity, but, nevertheless, in film metaphors certain of the elements that comprise the structure come from discernibly disparate categories –

in fact, categories that are not physically compossible in the same entity. A human arm could not support that big hammer that has become Popeye's fist. You can't replace a camera lens with a human eye and get a working anything.

Moreover, there is a consensus among researchers in the field that, generally, verbal metaphors are either false or not literally true. Film metaphors, of course, cannot be false or literally not true because they are not propositions. However, our film metaphors do possess a feature that roughly corresponds to falsity or apparent falsity. Namely, through homospatiality, our film metaphors identify disparate objects and/or link disparate categories that are not physically compossible, in terms of what we know about the universe, in the sorts of entities thereby concocted. While verbal metaphors are generally marked by falsity or apparent falsity, film metaphors represent homospatial entities comprised of features that are not generally physically compossible.

In addition to homospatiality, the physical noncompossibility of the elements in the putatively unified figure is also a necessary condition for film metaphors of the sort that I am isolating. And, of course, the analogy between the falsity or apparent falsity of verbal metaphors, and the physical noncompossibility of the elements of the kind of film metaphors I am talking about provide me with another important reason for me to call these filmic figures metaphors. Indeed, it is in virtue of these close structural affinities between images of the machine/Moloch variety and linguistic metaphors that leads me to claim that these images have the most compelling claim to the title of film metaphor.

With verbal metaphor the palpable falsity or apparent falsity of the putative assertion, among other things, encourages the listener to reassess it in order to make it relevant to the rest of a conversation. One strategy is to take the utterance as a way of getting the auditor to use it as an opportunity to rethink the target domain – to focus and filter it – in light of a source domain. Or, to put the matter more directly: confronted with an obviously false statement the auditor searches for some other significance that it might have – such as metaphorical or ironical significance – in accordance with Gricean-type principles of cooperation in conversation.[9]

Similarly, since the homospatially linked elements in film metaphors are physically noncompossible, the spectator of such a symbol explores alternative strategies to render the image intelligible, apart from relying on the laws of physical possibility. In the cases at hand, I conjecture that the spectator entertains the alternative that the physically noncompossible elements in the filmic array refer to the categories to which they belong and that those disparate, nonconvergent categories (or, to be more exact, members thereof) have been fused or connected in a way that defies physical possibility, not in order to represent a state of affairs in the world of the fiction, but to interanimate the categories the image brings to mind. That is, the viewer or, at least, the ideal viewer considers the possibility that the categories in question have been introduced in order for her to focus on aspects of one of the categories in terms of aspects of the other category. And when doing this is rewarding – that is, when an intelligible correspondence obtains – the viewer regards the filmic array metaphorically.

The physical noncompossibility of the homospatially fused but disparate elements in the visual array entices the ideal viewer to comprehend the image not as a portrayal of some physically possible state of affairs, but as an opportunity to regard one of the categories as providing a source domain for apprehending something about the other category, the target; or as an opportunity for regarding each of the categories as mutually informative (as alternatively the source and the target domain for each other). And, of course, it is the ease with

which the composite, homospatial, physically noncompossible film examples discussed previously can be assimilated into the model of metaphor as a mapping from source domain to target domain that provides me with yet another reason for calling these images film metaphors.

Given the way in which the play between physical possibility and physical noncompossibility figures in the communication of film images, I suspect that film metaphors must be what I call visual images – that is, intentionally made, human artifacts of the sort whose reference (or putative reference) is recognized simply by looking, rather than by some process of reading, decoding or the like. Watching *Moby Dick,* the spectator looks at the screen and recognizes that a whale is represented; the spectator looks at the top of the whale and recognizes that the whale has been jabbed with harpoons.

Visual images, needless to say, are symbols. But they are a special type of symbol insofar as their comprehension does not require codes nor could there be anything like a dictionary which would enable one to decipher or read such images. Rather, the audience looks at the screen and recognizes that which the images represent – at least whenever the spectator is capable of recognizing the referents of the image in what might be called standard perception (i.e., perception not mediated by coded symbols).

Because film metaphors are visual images, the audience is initially geared to taking the putative referent of the image to be some physically possible thing or state of affairs. Encountering something that is physically noncompossible instead, the spectator is encouraged to search or to explore some other way in which the symbol before her may be taken in order to make sense. And this leads her to test various metaphorical interpretations of the array.

So far, I have argued that a film metaphor is a visual image in which physically noncompossible elements co-habitate a homospatially unified figure which, in turn, encourages viewers to explore mappings between the relevant constituent elements and/or the categories or concepts to which the constituent elements allude. Nevertheless, more is required than these features, if we hope to identify a film image as a film metaphor.

A film metaphor is a visual image. This means that the figure as a whole is recognizable perceptually – recognizable by looking – and that the elements that the spectator uses in her metaphorical interpretations are recognizable perceptually as well. But, obviously, in order to grasp a film metaphor, the spectator must not only be able to recognize the relevant elements; her attention must also be drawn to them. The relevant elements must stand out; they must be visually salient; they must be prominent. Of course, we cannot theoretically predict all the ways in which filmmakers may secure salience. But we can argue theoretically that in order for a film metaphor to be identified by a spectator, all things being equal, the film metaphor and its pertinent elements must be salient.

These elements are parts of homospatially unified figures. But these spatially bounded wholes strike the spectator as anomalous, since certain of the saliently posed elements in the homospatial array defy our conception of physical possibility. A man cannot have an anvil embedded in a working arm; he could not move his hand, if he did. However, in determining whether the elements in the image are physically noncompossible, the spectator cannot rely simply on what the image in isolation shows and on what she knows about science and the world. She must also consider the context in which the image figures as well as the likely intentions of the filmmaker in presenting the image.

The reason that the spectator has to consider the filmic context and the filmmaker's likely intentions is that there are homospatial figures in film with apparently physically noncompossible elements that are saliently posed which are patently not film metaphors. For instance, in horror films there are many examples of creatures that are physically noncompossible – like the animal/vegetable in *Pumpkinhead* or the insect/human in *The Fly* – but, given the narrative context and the genre of the film, along with the evident intentions of the filmmaker, the spectator does not count these composite figures as metaphors. For given the narrative context of the film and the genre, such composite figures are compossible entities in what might be called the world of the fiction, or the world intended by the narrator.

We can imagine the machine/Moloch figure as a denizen in a fictional context in which it is, by dint of science fiction, a fleshy robot out to conquer the world. In that context, the viewer would take the image as intended to be physically compossible in the world of the fiction. Consequently, if the audience is to interpret a figure like machine/Moloch metaphorically, the audience must at least have grounds for believing that the filmmaker is presenting something that she intends to be taken as physically noncompossible and not as some physically possible entity in a fantastic, fictional world, ruled by physical laws at variance with our own. In order to explore a composite entity like machine/Moloch for metaphorical insight, the spectator must have reason to suspect that she is confronting a physically noncompossible entity, not one that is physically possible fictionally.

Needless to say, an apparently physically noncompossible entity may be introduced to serve intentions other than fiction making. A composite entity might be religiously motivated. Perhaps a devotional, Christian film presents us with the figure of Satan as part man and part goat. Here, though goat men are physically noncompossible, we will not interpret the image as a film metaphor if we suspect that some fundamentalist, Christian filmmaker is portraying the devil in the way that his religion maintains that one correctly conceives the look of the devil. That is, our hypothesis that the filmmaker does not intend to present us with a physically noncompossible entity, but one that his religion avows is physically compossible with higher truths than are available to our sciences, restrains our metaphorical exploration of the image.

A film metaphor rests on the shared recognition on the part of the filmmaker and the pertinent spectators that the disparate elements fused in the homospatially unified entity on the screen are physically noncompossible. In order to ascertain whether the homospatially fused image on the screen is to be taken as representing a physically noncompossible state, several, crucial conditions must be in place.

First, the filmmaker must believe that the film image represents a physically noncompossible object or state of affairs and, also, the filmmaker must expect that in presenting her image, she is producing the representation of something that is physically noncompossible, rather than something that is physically possible, religiously actual, fictionally possible, and so on. And furthermore, if the filmmaker intends her image to be taken metaphorically, she must believe, as well, that the standard, intended spectator also believes that the image represents a physically noncompossible state of affairs.

Moreover, it probably goes without saying that for a film metaphor to succeed – for it to secure uptake – the standard intended spectator will in fact believe that the state of affairs or object represented by the visual array is physically noncompossible and that it is intended to be taken as physically noncompossible, rather than as a representation of some supernatural actuality or as a state of affairs that obtains in the context of some fiction that abides by some laws alternative to those found in the universe as we know it. Thus, if a spectator takes the image of machine/Moloch to be a film metaphor, she

must believe that the filmmaker believes that machine/Moloch is a physically noncompossible entity and that the filmmaker is presenting machine/Moloch as physically noncompossible and not as some existing monster, some sci-fi monster, or as some god or demigod.

If the filmmaker intends a film metaphor, then the filmmaker believes that her juxtaposition of physically noncompossible elements in a homospatially unified array will serve as an invitation to the viewer to explore the ways in which the noncompossible elements and their corresponding categories illuminate each other when they are interpreted as source domains and target domains that are related by mappings onto each other. That is, the filmmaker must intend that the homospatially unified figure and its noncompossible elements have what Ina Lowenberg calls heuristic value.[10]

The filmmaker, in other words, intends the spectator to take the image as a proposal to consider the referents of the noncompossible elements and their related categories as interacting in an illuminating way. In creating the image, the filmmaker expects that the juxtaposition of elements will insinuate a relation or comparison or fact and will beckon or prompt the audience to notice or focus upon that relation or comparison or fact. The film metaphor has heuristic value in the sense that it facilitates the spectator's apprehension of the putative relation, or comparison or fact.

In creating a film metaphor, the filmmaker believes that her image has heuristic value. This does not mean that the image maker antecedently knows all of the discoveries that spectators may make in the process of exploring the image. Indeed, audiences may find more connections between the elements in the film image than the filmmaker imagined, just as in the case of linguistic metaphors, where there may be an indefinite number of resonances that no reader, including the author, ever fully appreciates.

The filmmaker invites the spectator to make these discoveries by saliently posing physically noncompossible elements. The juxtaposition of physically noncompossible elements prods the spectator to attempt to make the image – as a communicative act – intelligible. Though recognizable perceptually, the relevant film image cannot be taken to be a realistic representation. Thus, on the presupposition that the image has been proffered for the sake of making some point, the spectator will try to comprehend it by means of another sort of interpretation. In film metaphors, the saliently posed juxtaposition of the noncompossible elements, along with something like conversational principles of charity, give the spectator reason to explore the image in order to see whether it affords metaphorical insight.

Though the filmmaker guides the exploration of the image in many respects, the invitation that she extends to the spectator is a fairly open one. The audience expands the metaphor through its own interpretive play. The spectator tests to see whether the metaphor is only to be expanded in terms of the referents of the noncompossible elements in the figure or in terms of the categories or concepts to which the noncompossible elements belong. And, as is the case in verbal metaphor, the audience explores what Lakoff and Turner call the various "slots" of the source domain schema to see if they have any bearing on the target domain. Moreover, where the slots "click," the spectator is apt to derive heuristic value.

Summarizing our theory of film metaphor then, I contend that a filmmaker successfully presents a film metaphor if and only if (1) she makes a visual image in which (2) at least two physically noncompossible elements are (3) saliently posed in (4) a homospatially unified figure; (5) the filmmaker believes that what the figure represents is physically noncompossible and presents it as being physically noncompossible; (6) the filmmaker believes that the typical, intended spectator will believe that the figure is physically noncompossible; (7) the typical, intended spectator does believe that it is physically noncompossible; (8) the typical, intended spectator also believes that the filmmaker believes that the image is physically noncompossible; (9) the filmmaker believes that posing the noncompossible elements saliently in a homospatially unified figure has heuristic value in terms of potential mappings of the referents of the elements and/or their related categories onto each other; (10) the filmmaker intends the spectator to take the image as an invitation to consider the referents of the physically noncompossible elements and/or their related categories in terms of their heuristic value, and the filmmaker also intends the spectator to realize that she, the filmmaker, intends this; (11) the spectator believes that the filmmaker intends her to take the image as an invitation to consider the referents of the physically noncompossible elements and their related categories in terms of mappings onto each other.

Composite figures that meet all these conditions can be successfully identified as film metaphors. In my view this variety of filmic metaphor has the best claim to the title of film metaphor because, as I hoped I have shown, it bears extremely close structural affinities to linguistic metaphor. For example, it is closer structurally to linguistic metaphor than the juxtaposition of two shots of similar objects for the sake of comparison, since such cinematic juxtapositions carry no suggestion of an identity relation, whereas linguistic metaphors and what I call homospatially fused film metaphors do. Thus, I surmise that the sorts of filmic figures that I have been writing about represent a central case of film metaphor or what I would hazard to call *strict filmic metaphor* or *core filmic metaphor*.[11]

Upon hearing me christening what I'd like to call strict film metaphor, some may be perplexed, because they believe that they have reason to suspect that there can be no such thing as film metaphor, whether strict or otherwise. Thus, insofar as such prejudices are common, let me conclude by discussing the most likely objections to the proposition that there are film metaphors (of which strict film metaphors are the most central case).

There seem to be three main objections to the existence of film metaphors: (1) the concreteness objection, (2) the asymmetry objection and (3) the essentialist objection. Let me deal with each of these in turn.

(1) The concreteness objection.[12] This argument begins with the presupposition that the film image is always concrete in the sense that it is always the representation of a particular. However, it is then noted that metaphors require abstraction insofar as metaphors interanimate the relations between classes or categories. Thus, the argument continues, metaphors supposedly require that audiences free themselves from the apprehension of particulars and play imaginatively with categories. For example, in the metaphor "death is deep sleep," one is invited to map generic features of the source domain, deep sleep, onto deaths in general. Therefore, inasmuch as film images are concrete and particular, film images are incapable of serving as vehicles for metaphors, which, by their very nature, are abstract.

But clearly, the presumption that metaphors are abstract, in the sense in which it is presupposed in this argument, is absolutely false. Many linguistic metaphors refer to particulars. For example, one insider trader may say admiringly of another "When it comes to corporate takeovers, Jones is Attila the Hun." This is a perfectly unproblematic instance of metaphor, but note that both its target figure and its source figure are particulars. Nor is this feature only evident in invented examples. When Americans say that "George Washington is *the* father of *our country,*" they are referring to particulars as does Romeo when he identifies Juliet with the one and only Sun.

In addition, the second presupposition of

the concreteness argument is also false. Though every film image may be an image of a particular in the sense that (putting to one side the complexities of chemical and electronic processing) it is an image of a particular object, it is false that every film image refers to particulars. The image of a Ford motorcar in an advertisement does not refer to that particular Ford motorcar, but to Ford motorcars, or to some class of Ford motorcars in general. Thus the second presupposition of the concreteness argument is false, along with the first, and, moreover, given that the premises of the argument are so flawed, the concreteness objection has little to recommend it.

Of course, a friend of the concreteness argument might claim that I have misinterpreted it. The argument, it may be said, concerns psychology. The idea is that metaphor requires abstract thinking in terms of the interanimation of categories, but the particularity of film images blocks abstract thinking by keeping the spectator mired in the perception of particularity. This may not be a totally unreasonable piece of armchair psychology. But I see no compelling grounds for accepting it.

For I have already conjectured a rival hypothesis. I have argued that there is some mechanism in certain film images that prompts the audience to abandon their attempt to regard the image as a representation of a particular and to attempt to reinterpret it in terms of the interaction of categories. I claim that the physical non-compossibility of the disparate elements that have been fused homospatially invites and even prompts the spectator to find a way to assimilate the image as something other than the representation of a particular. I take it that this scenario is at least plausible. Therefore, unless some flaw can be found with my hypothesis, the burden of proof lies with the skeptic to show that film imagery thwarts abstract, metaphorical thinking.

(2) The asymmetry objection.[13] Linguistic metaphors are unidirectional. When I say of

a past king of England that "Richard is a lion," putatively I am saying something about Richard and nothing about any lions. I am not, for example, saying that some lion is Richard or even that some or every lion is like Richard. On the other hand, film images have no resources for fixing directionality. The genuine metaphors that we know from language are asymmetrical; they cannot be flipped. "Juliet is the Sun" cannot be reversed as "The Sun is Juliet."

Film images have no way of guaranteeing unidirectionaltiy. Putative film metaphors can be flipped – Vertov's "The eye is a camera" might just as easily be comprehended as "The camera is an eye." Therefore, since it is premised that genuine metaphors have undirectionality or asymmetry as an essential feature, and our putative film metaphors do not, then our candidate is surely not an authentic metaphor (nor are all the other film candidates, all of which also fail the unidirectionality test).

Of course, it is at least controversial whether all linguistic metaphors are unidirectional or not. If we take metaphors to be abbreviated similes, as Aristotle did, then there would appear to be the potential to flip all metaphors, for if "this book is garbage" is really an abbreviated way of saying "this book is like garbage" then the saying might also suggest "garbage is like this book." But, of course, in response the asymmetry theorist may maintain that this is a reason to deny that metaphors are abbreviated similes.

Nevertheless, might it not at least be plausible to read some metaphors as bidirectional? If I say "See the winter in his beard," I am asking you to see his old age in light of winter, and its associated commonplaces, but isn't it also the case that the statement may intelligibly guide you to recall that winter is the oldest, final stage of the year. We think of lives in terms of seasons in part because we think of years in terms of lives. Thus, I would find it unsurprising that one metaphor might draw

our musings in both directions. And finally, if "business is business" is a metaphor, then the asymmetry claim does not look completely universal.

The friend of unidirectionality not only assumes that all linguistic metaphors are asymmetrical, but also that none of our film metaphors are. But this doesn't seem right. Given the context of *Metropolis*, "the machine is Moloch" or "the machine is a living monster" seems correct, but "Moloch is a machine" or "the monster is a machine" seems an unlikely metaphorical communication. This is not because "Moloch is a machine" could not possibly be a metaphor; if someone says that their spouse is a machine, that is an acceptable, if unfortunate metaphor. But "Moloch is a machine" is not the operative metaphor in *Metropolis* because it doesn't make much sense given the overall film, while "the machine is Moloch," given the Luddite animus of the rest of the fiction, fits perfectly in context.

Moreover, this is analogous to the linguistic case. If we do not read "Richard, the Lion" as "the lion is Richard" or "the lion is like Richard" but as "Richard is a lion" or "Richard is like a lion" that is probably because in the relevant contexts this reading makes the most sense. If we are talking about King Richard, then it is more intelligible to think of the phrase in terms of Richard, the lionlike, rather than Lion, the Richardlike. But, in any case, if some of the examples that I contend are strict film metaphors are asymmetrical – such as "the machine is Moloch" – then there are some film metaphors, even strict film metaphors.

Furthermore, another strategy for dealing with the unidirectionality argument might be to say that even if most linguistic metaphors are asymmetrical, this might not be an essential feature of film metaphors. Perhaps Vertov's imagery leads us to think of cameras as eyes and of eyes as cameras. Maybe film metaphors always invite the spectator to explore them by, among other things, testing to see whether the putative target domains and source domains can be flipped. Or maybe film metaphors just invite this bi-directional exploration more frequently than linguistic metaphors. But this might only be a difference between film metaphors and linguistic metaphors, not grounds for disallowing the very possibility of film metaphor.

Conceding that film metaphors may involve more frequent bi-directional explorations than do linguistic metaphors does not, of course, concede that there are no unidirectional metaphors in film. For exploring an image like the machine/Moloch figure may result in one's conviction, given the contextual constraints of the fiction, that the metaphor is asymmetrical.

Whether a film metaphor is symmetrical or asymmetrical depends upon whether the viewer can produce a suitably constrained interpretation of the image that renders it intelligible when the source domain and the target domains are reversed. There is no reason to suppose that this procedure will not produce many asymmetrical film metaphors. Thus the asymmetry objection is wrong at least for some of the candidates for strict film metaphor that I advance. Moreover, since there seems to be little structural or functional[14] difference between my asymmetrical film metaphors and the symmetrical variations, I maintain that we have more reason to ignore the proponents of the asymmetry argument than to heed them. Let us call such images strict film metaphors whether they are asymmetrical or symmetrical, for this will economize our theoretical activity.

(3) The essentialist objection. I have talked about strict *film* metaphors. But in response, a critic might argue that there is nothing essentially cinematic about these metaphors at all. Metaphors just like these – rooted in homospatiality and physical noncompossibility – can be found in media other than film and, therefore, have no rightful claim to be called *film* metaphors.

Consider Man Ray's 1938 *Imaginary Por-*

trait of D.A.F. de Sade (oil on canvas). It is dominated by a composite image in the foreground: the head of de Sade and his shoulders. Moreover, as we inspect the image closely, we notice that the figure of de Sade is composed of stones – some of which are cracking. These stones, furthermore, are the same sort of stones that comprise the walls of the Bastille, a building which we see burning in the background of the image.

De Sade is clearly a composite figure; a human and a wall are fused in one homospatial unity which proposes a physically noncompossible being whose metaphorical significance is something like "De Sade is a prison, bursting apart." What has been repressed is smashing out of De Sade.

This example meets all the criteria stated above for identifying a successful film metaphor, but the example is not a film metaphor, since it is a painting, not a movie. This is true. What it shows is that my first condition above has to be rewritten as "she [the filmmaker] makes a visual image *in film*. . . ." And once this phrase – "in film" – is added, the theory will only identify visual metaphors that are film metaphors.

Undoubtedly, the essentialist critic will not be satisfied by this adjustment. For he expects that if there is anything worth calling a film metaphor then that will be something whose metaphorical structures themselves are uniquely cinematic. And this is not the case with the decisive structures for film metaphor – such as homospatiality and physical noncompossibility – that I have identified.

However, at this point in the dialectic, I must simply admit that I reject the essentialist's expectations. The metaphors that I have isolated are film metaphors because they are visual metaphors that occur in films. I see no reason to expect that film metaphors will possess some uniquely cinematic features that distinguish them from visual metaphors in other arts.

Melodramas in theater and melodramas in film employ the same melodramatic structures. An informative analysis of a film melodrama will point to the same melodramatic ingredients the theater analysis will point to in a play. There are no unique ciné-melodramatic characteristics – i.e., characteristics that appear not only in no other media, but also in no other film genre. Film analysis is no less effective for isolating melodramatic structures in films that are also found in theater.

Likewise, film metaphors belong to the larger family of visual metaphors which can encompass examples from every existing artistic medium that deals in visual images, including not only film, but painting, sculpture, photography, video, theater, dance, and so on. But this is not a problem. For in this case, as in every other I can think of, the film theorist benefits from thinking about what film has in common with other arts, just because we are able to bring to bear what we know of the other arts to the study of film.[15]

Notes

1. Trevor Whittock, *Metaphor and Film* (Cambridge University Press, 1990).
2. The literature that I have in mind includes: N. Roy Clifton, *The Figure in Film* (Newark: University of Delaware Press, 1983); Louis Gianetti, "Cinematic Metaphors," *Journal of Aesthetic Education* 6, no. 4 (October 1972); Calvin Pryluck, "The Film Metaphor Metaphor: The Use of Language-Based Models in Film Study," *Literature/Film Quarterly* no. 2 (Spring 1975); and Calvin Pryluck, *Sources of Meaning in Motion Pictures and Television* (New York: Arno Press, 1976).
3. For a discussion of the distinction between source domains and target domains, see George Lakoff and Mark Turner, *More Than Cool Reason* (Chicago: University of Chicago Press, 1989), p. 38.
4. This image is recognized by N. Roy Clifton, but he categorizes it as "inclusion:superimposition" (see p. 160). He does not count it as a metaphor, probably because it does not have to be "completed" by the spectator (see pp. 87–88). Nor does he recognize the image of the pistons superimposed over men stoking furnaces from John Grierson's *Drifters* as a metaphor; it also counts as inclusion: superimposition. See Clifton, *The Figure in Film.*
5. The notions of focusing and filtering above are adapted from Max Black's classic article "Metaphor," *Proceedings of the Aristotelian Society,* N.S. 55 (1954–55), pp. 273–94.
6. I have added the qualifier *generally* above since some commentators have argued that some metaphors are literally true. One example that has been proposed is "Business is business."
7. Note that the requirement here is that the physically noncompossible or disparate elements be literally co-present in the same object. This is to exclude certain cases that people may be tempted to call film metaphors, like the famous boot sequence in Chaplin's *The Gold Rush.* Due to Chaplin's miming, one may be inclined to entertain the thought that Chaplin's shoe laces are spaghetti. However, since the lace elements and the spaghetti elements of the image are not literally co-present in the object, the image is not strictly the sort of metaphor that I am talking about. For no spaghetti elements are ever actually fused with shoe lace elements.

Of course, there is a relation between Chaplin's miming and what I call visual metaphors. In both cases, two or more objects are "superimposed;" but in visual metaphor the fusion is literal, whereas in the Chaplin case, it is not. Rather than calling the Chaplin case one of visual metaphor, I prefer to call it a case of *mimed metaphor.* For an analysis of mimed metaphor, see: Noël Carroll, "Notes on the Sight Gag," in *comedy; cinema/theory,* edited by Andrew S. Horton (Berkeley: University of California Press, 1991). This article is also reprinted in this volume.
8. I present my theory of visual metaphors, of which the theory of film metaphor in this article is an application, in *Aspects of Metaphor,* edited by Jaakko Hintikka (Dordrecht: Kluwer Academic Publishers, 1994).
9. This notion is adapted from H. P. Grice, "Logic and Conversation," in *The Logic of Grammar,* edited by Donald Davidson and Gilbert Harman (Berkeley and Los Angeles:

University of California Press, 1975). See also, Edward Bendix, "The Data of Semantic Description," in *Semantics: An Interdisciplinary Reader,* edited by D. Steinberg and L. Jokobovits (Cambridge University Press, 1971).

10. See Ina Lowenberg, "Identifying Metaphors," in *Philosophical Perspectives on Metaphor,* edited by Mark Johnson (Minneapolis: University of Minnesota Press, 1981), pp. 175–6. Let me acknowledge that this section on the identifying conditions for film metaphor has been enormously influenced by Ina Lowenberg's account of the identification of linguistic metaphor.

11. In an earlier paper, I identified a phenomenon that I referred to as verbal imagery – film images predicated upon encouraging the viewer to think of the action in terms of linguistic phrases, often commonplace phrases. For example, in my Popeye example, the audience may think of the image in terms of commonplace phrases like "fists of steel." Obviously some film metaphors can be verbal images in the sense developed in my earlier paper, viz., those visual metaphors that rely on homospatiality and that, at the same time, illustrate commonplace metaphors. On the other hand, verbal images that illustrate commonplace metaphors, but not by means of homospatiality will not count as film metaphors. And, of course, many verbal images have nothing to do with metaphor because the linguistic idioms, phrases or sayings that they evoke do not involve metaphor. For an analysis of verbal images, see: Noël Carroll, "Language and Cinema: Preliminary Notes for a Theory of Verbal Images," *Millennium Film Journal,* nos. 7/8/9 (Fall/Winter, 1980–1981). This paper is also reprinted in this volume.

12. This position is often attributed to Siegfried Kracauer; see his *Theory of Film* (Oxford: Oxford University Press, 1960). The argument is discussed in the already cited texts by Pryluck, Giannetti and Whittock.

13. Pryluck, "The Film Metaphor Metaphor," pp. 117–18.

14. Here I have in mind the cognitive function of the figures to encourage insight into the concepts put forward for comparison by the metaphor. That is, Vertov's figure invites us to think about correspondences between eyes and cameras in the same way that it invites us to think about the way in which cameras are like eyes.

15. This paper has offered an anlysis of *strict* film metaphor. One reason I have used the label *strict* is because there are many examples of phenomena very much like the metaphors I have analyzed, but which also lack one of its central features. What I have in mind are images like the ones in Roger Corman's film *Gas,* where the football players are partially attired in Nazi regalia. The point of this imagery seems clear, if unflattering: "Footballers are Nazis." At the same time, however, this cannot count as a *strict* or *core* film metaphor because, though there is homospatiality, there is not physical noncompossibility. For though it is implausible that the footballers should have Nazi uniforms available to them, it is not physically impossible.

What I want to say is that such cases are not cases of strict film metaphor; they are not central cases. They do bear a strong family resemblance to central cases, however, and in virtue of that we may call them film metaphors, though not strict film metaphors. Physical noncompossibility, it seems to me, tracks the central or core cases of film metaphor, though in certain compelling cases, it may be that incongruously or implausibility juxtaposed elements which are nevertheless physically compossible elicit metaphorical thinking. This suggests that further research should be done into the type of incongruous, or implausible, or unlikely juxtapositions that, when saliently posed, can function like physical noncompossibility. Or, perhaps salience alone can elicit metaphorical thinking in some cases. But these are questions that may possibly require another theory and certainly another paper.

I. Introduction

Over the past twenty years, the nonfiction film has achieved a level of prestige and prominence unequaled in any other period of its history. Yet, for all the recent energy, thought and discussion devoted to this enterprise, the nonfiction film remains one of the most confused areas of film theory. Arguments of all kinds challenge the very idea of nonfiction film. The nonfiction filmmaker, it is observed, selects his or her materials, manipulates them, inevitably has a point of view and, *therefore*, cannot pretend to offer us anything but a personal or subjective vision of things. Objectivity is impossible if only because the medium itself – due to framing, focussing, editing – necessitates the inescapability of choice. Whether or not an event is staged, the act of filming involves structuring so that what results is an interpretation rather than the Real. The problem, according to this subjectivity argument, is not simply that the filmmaker can't jump out of his skin, one can't jump out of the film medium either.

A related set of arguments worries the distinction between fiction and nonfiction. On the one hand, it is charged that the nonfiction film shares narrative, dramatic and aesthetic devices, like parallel editing, climaxes and contrastive editing, with fiction films and that, consequently, it presents its subjects fictionally.[1] Or, in a variation on the strategy behind the subjectivity argument, it is proposed that filmmakers are trapped

within ideology, both in their forms and contents; that the posture of objectivity itself is a pose, indeed an ideologically motivated one; and that documentaries belong to the genus of social fiction. Some commentators go so far as to suppose that because any cultural event, photographed or not, is structured (according to roles and folkways), recording one merely captures the ideological "fictions" of a given time, place and people.[2] Perhaps the most extreme denial of the boundary between fiction and nonfiction film has been voiced by Christian Metz – he suggests that all films are fiction (purportedly) because they are representations, i.e., because, for example, the train you see on the screen is not literally in the screening room.[3]

To further complicate matters, there is a minority opinion that has it that all fiction films are actually documentaries;[4] *Casablanca* is *about* Humphrey Bogart in front of a camera as well as being an archaeological fragment of American mores and styles of the early forties. In fact, at least one theorist, a proponent of Jacques Derrida's notion of *différance*, advances the nonfiction-is-really-fiction approach while simultaneously insisting that fiction films are documentaries.[5]

The central concepts as employed in many of these arguments – including objectivity, subjectivity, fiction, document – are fraught with ambiguities and downright misconceptions. But before examining these problems critically, it is worthwhile to speculate about the way in which, historically, the discussion of nonfiction film reached its present state.

I think that the most important influence on the way that nonfiction film is currently conceptualized was the development of direct cinema (sometimes called *cinema verité*) in the sixties. The movement – associated with the work of Robert Drew, the Maysles Brothers, D. A. Pennebaker, Richard Leacock, Frederick Wisemen, Allan King, Chris Marker and others – proposed a new style of documentary filmmaking that repudiated prevailing approaches to the nonfiction film. These filmmakers eschewed, among other things, the use of scripts, voice-of-God narration, re-enactments of events, and staging and direction of any sort. They employed new, light-weight cameras and sound equipment in order to immerse themselves in events, to observe rather than to influence, to catch life on the wing. Many of the aims of direct cinema parallel the avowed objectives of the species of cinematic realism sponsored by André Bazin. Techniques and approaches were adopted that encouraged the spectator to think for himself, to take an active role toward the screen, to evolve his own interpretation of what was significant in the imagery rather than have the filmmaker interpret it for him. The new spontaneity of the filmmaker and spectator correlated expressively with some sort of new "freedom" in contradistinction to the "authoritarianism" of traditional documentaries. Often the new style was promoted as an epistemological breakthrough for cinema. Critics concerned with and, at times, participants in the direct cinema movement spoke as if the new techniques guaranteed the filmic representation of reality.

Of course, previous documentary filmmakers, such as John Grierson[6] and Dziga Vertov,[7] had never denied that they were involved in interpreting their subject matter. But for advocates of direct cinema, at their most polemical, that allegiance to interpretation, to telling the audience what to think, violated their conception of what it is to be a documentary. As a result, upholders of direct cinema evolved a style designed to minimize the types of control exerted in the older styles of nonfiction film.

But no sooner was the idea of *cinema verité* abroad than critics and viewers turned the polemics of direct cinema against direct cinema. A predictable *tu quoque* would note all the ways that direct cinema was inextricably involved with interpreting its materials. Direct cinema opened a can of worms and then got eaten by them. Almost concomitantly, a similar, and, in fact, related debate emerged in the somewhat narrow discussion of ethnographic film. Anthropologists who opted for filming in order to avoid the subjectivity of their field notes quickly found themselves confronted by arguments about selection, manipulation and eventually, by arguments about the inescapability of ideology. In regard to the anthropological debate especially, but also in regard to direct cinema, it was stressed that the very act of filming changed or was highly likely to influence the outcome of the events recorded. In order to grapple with both the arguments from subjectivity and related arguments about camera intrusiveness, some filmmakers, like Jean Rouch and Edgar Morin in *Chronique d'un Été*, included themselves in their work, acknowledging their participation, their manipulation and their intervention. In general, filmmakers and proponents of direct cinema now guard their claims. They have become the first to admit that they have a point of view, maintaining only that they are presenting their "subjective reality," i..e, their personal vision of reality as they see it. For example, Frederick Wiseman merely insists on the veracity of an honest, first-person statement for his work when he says "The objective-subjective argument is from my view, at least in film terms, a lot of nonsense. The films are my response to a certain experience."[8]

With the rise of direct cinema, two major wrinkles were added to the dialogue concerning the nonfiction film. First, direct cinema repudiated large parts of the tradition of nonfiction film because it was interpretive. Then, like a boomerang, the dialectic snapped back; direct cinema, it was alleged, was also interpretive and, *a fortiori,* subjective rather than objective (and, for some, fiction rather than nonfiction). The combined force of these maneuvers within the debate was to stigmatize all nonfiction film, both the traditional and direct cinema varieties, as subjective. Thus, we find Erik Barnouw concluding his history of documentary films with remarks such as these:

> To be sure, some documentarists claim to be objective – a term that seems to renounce an interpretive role. The claim may be strategic, but it is surely meaningless. The documentarist, like any communicator in any medium, makes endless choices. He selects topics, people, vistas, angles, lens, juxtapositions, sounds, words. Each selection is an expression of his point of view, whether he is aware of it or not, whether he acknowledges it or not.
>
> Even behind the first step, selection of a topic, there is a motive.
>
> . . . It is in selecting and arranging his findings that he expresses himself; these choices are, in effect, comments. And whether he adopts the stance of observer, or chronicler or whatever, he cannot escape his subjectivity. He presents his version of the world.[9]

More quotations could be added to Barnouw's, which represents one of the more or less standard ways of coming to terms with the polemics and rhetorical framework engendered by direct cinema.[10] But that Barnouw's position rebounds so naturally from the direct cinema debate is part of the problem with it, because, as I hope to show in the next section, the presuppositions of that discussion are irreparably flawed.

II. Nonfiction Films Ain't Necessarily So

A. Nonfiction Film and Objectivity

Though many of the preceding arguments appear to be designed to deal with issues specific to the nonfiction film, a moment's deliberation shows that they are far more generally devastating in their scope. The possibility of objectivity in the nonfiction film is denied because such films involve selection, emphasis, manipulation of materials, interpretation and points of view. In fact, these features lead commentators not only to withhold the possibility of objectivity from nonfiction film; they also prompt

commentators to reclassify such films as subjective. Yet, if these arguments have any force, they will not simply demolish the subjective/objective distinction in regard to nonfiction film; the lectures and texts of history and science will be their victims as well.

Historians, for example, are characteristically concerned with making interpretations, presenting points of view about the past, selecting certain events for consideration rather than others, and emphasizing some of the selected events and their interconnections. That's just what doing history is. Thus, if the nonfiction film is subjective, for the above reasons, then so is historical writing. Nor is science unscathed. It is hard to imagine an experiment without manipulation and selection, or a theory without emphasis and interpretation. In short, the arguments against objectivity in nonfiction film are too powerful, unless their proponents are prepared to embrace a rather thoroughgoing skepticism about the prospects of objectivity in general. The defense of such a far-ranging skeptical position would, of course, have to be joined on the battlefields of epistemology rather than in the trenches of film theory. Indeed, if such a skeptical position were defensible, the reclassification of the nonfiction film as subjective would simply be a footnote to a larger campaign. I mention this because I do not think that commentators who conclude that the nonfiction film is subjective intend their remarks as a mere gloss on the notion that everything is subjective. But that, I fear, is the untoward implication of their line of attack.

At the same time, another danger in collapsing the distinction between the subjective and objective is that we will still have to distinguish between different kinds of endeavors – in film, for example, between Frederick Wiseman's *Hospital* and Maya Deren's intentionally personal *At Land* – even if they are all said to be under the enveloping bubble of subjectivity. But how will these boundaries be drawn? Most probably by reinstating something very much like the subjective/objective distinction. Perhaps Wiseman's film would be called "*subjective*-objective" in contradistinction to Deren's "*subjective*-subjective." But two points need to be made here. First, the nonitalicized "subjective" and "objective" represent the basic concepts which are indispensable in this particular context of classification; if they are momentarily dismissed, they must inexorably return; and this provides a good reason not to dismiss them in the first place. Second, the italicized "subjective" is conceptually lazy; it does no work, and it serves little purpose. It is all-inclusive, so lamentably, it is not exclusive. For if there is no italicized "objective" to counterpose against it, the italicized "subjective" is trivial. It is a piece of excess theoretical baggage, easily disposable because it says nothing more than the obvious, namely, that all research and communication is man-made. But more on this later.

As an initial response to my opening objections, a subjectivist vis-à-vis the nonfiction film might try to argue that there is something special about film that makes it inevitably subjective in a way that history and science are not. Thus, when it is said that *Hospital* is "*subjective*-objective," the italicized "subjective" is being meaningfully contrasted to the objectivity of the texts and lectures of history and science. But what is that "something special?" One of the candidates is the notion that every shot in a nonfiction film perforce involves a personal viewpoint or point-of-view whether the filmmaker is aware of it or not; in other words, a life history of attitudes, feelings and beliefs determine where the camera is positioned and aimed, what lens is chosen and how it is set. Consequently, all film, including the nonfiction film, is necessarily personal, "*subjective*," in a way that historical and scientific writing is not. That is, each image is indelibly imprinted with the filmmaker's (or

filmmakers') personality whereas there are certain protocols and stylistic canons of exposition in history and science that enable practitioners of those disciplines to subdue if not totally efface their personalities.

Bela Balazs, for one, seems to hold a position on composition in the single shot (which he calls the set-up) that is like the above, proposing that a representational image can't be made without conveying a viewpoint that is the self-expression of the filmmaker. He writes, concerning fiction and nonfiction film alike, that

> Every work of art must present not only objective reality but the subjective personality of the artist, and this personality includes his way of looking at things, his ideology and the limitations of the period. All this is projected into the picture, even unintentionally. Every picture shows not only a piece of reality but a point of view as well. The set-up of the camera betrays the inner attitude of the man behind the camera.[11]

For Balazs, a personal point of view in every shot is unavoidable. But will this wash? I suspect not, for several reasons.

To begin, the idea of point-of-view in film is really a bundle of ideas, which are often literally unrelated. "Point-of-view" can refer to a specific kind of editing schema (a character looks off screen, there is a cut to what he sees, and then there is a cut back to the character); it can refer to the position of the camera (the camera's viewpoint, or point-of-view, or perspective); or it can refer to the narrator's and/or the authorial point of view or both – i.e., to the perspective of a character commenting on events in the film and/or to the implied perspective of the film toward said events – or it can refer to the creator's personal point-of-view. Undoubtedly there are shots in which all five concepts of point-of-view can be applied simultaneously; John Wayne's *Green Berets* would probably be a good place to search for examples. Nevertheless, these concepts are quite discrete. And this suggests that at the heart of the position – that a shot is, *eo ipso*, a point-of-view – lies the fallacy of equivocation. It is true that each representational shot, save those where the image is drawn on the film, has a point-of-view or a viewpoint or a perspective in the sense that the camera must be placed somewhere. This might be thought of as the literal meaning of the cinematic point-of-view, i.e., the camera's vantage point. A personal point-of-view is yet another matter; indeed, calling it a "point-of-view" is at root metaphorical, using the language of physical position to characterize the values and feelings of the film's creator toward the subject depicted. Proponents of the omnivorous point-of-view school conflate two separate ideas, fallaciously moving from the necessity of a camera viewpoint in each shot to the necessity of a personal viewpoint, suppressing the fact that the two phenomena, though bearing the same name, are distinct.

The debate, of course, does not end here. Rather, the charge of equivocation can be met with the claim that the two senses of point-of-view really are the same because the personal point of view determines the camera's view(ing) point in such a way that the resulting image is invariably and reliably symptomatic of the creator's underlying viewpoint. The viewing point inevitably betrays the personal viewpoint and, hence, is always revelatory. But this, it seems to me, is implausible. Cameras can be turned on accidentally, and their operators can leave them running without realizing it, thereby recording events upon which the creator has no opportunity to inscribe his personal viewpoint. Likewise, unexpected events can intrude into the viewfinder – e.g., Lee Harvey Oswald's assassination – before there is time for a personal viewpoint to crystalize, that is, unless we wish to ascribe lightning omniscience to the cameraperson's unconscious. Camera positions can also be determined by circumstances, like a police barricade, and a cameraperson pressed for time can shoot "wild," hoping to "get something" without having any ideas about or attitude toward what is happening.

One could attempt to assimilate these cases by means of a rather extreme psychological theory, arguing that when shooting wild the cameraperson is in something akin to a trance, unconsciously selecting and expressively framing exactly the details that accord with subterranean interests. However, this sounds *ad hoc,* imbuing the unconscious not only with a kind of omniscience but also of omnipotence. Freud is clearly correct in saying that *some* apparently random gestures reveal hidden motives, wishes and attitudes, but no one has shown that *all* gestures are meaningful signals of the psychopathology of everyday life. It seems to me an indisputable fact that a cameraperson can set up and move cameras with random attention – precisely like a remote-control video monitor in a bank – and that the result need not develop into a coherent personal viewpoint. In regard to adverse circumstances, like constraining police barricades, it might be argued that the cameraperson will always take up the position, out of all the available ones under the circumstances, that best suits his personal point-of-view. This – like the "trance" solution to "wild shooting" – is *ad hoc.* In both cases, what are we to make of complaints that the results of shooting were not what the cameraperson wanted or needed? One might say that they got what they *really* wanted (without knowing it), but one says this at the cost of making the original hypothesis suspiciously unfalsifiable. Needless to say, a filmmaker could successfully attempt to make either a fiction or nonfiction film in which every shot communicated a personal attitude. But it affronts credulity to purport that every shot in every film is necessarily of this variety.

Another problem with the set-up = personal vision approach is that often the "creator" of the film is neither the cameraperson nor the editor: so whose personal vision is being conveyed? And, more importantly, in both fiction and nonfiction film, directors and writers are typically assigned preordained points-of-view. Can't an atheist shoot and cut a reverential life of Christ, and can't a Blakean make an industrial film about computer technology without a glimmer of repugnance in any of the shots? Filmmakers, that is, can not only not have an attitude toward their assignment, but even if they have an attitude, it can be successfully repressed. There is a shot in *Kinesics* where the cameraman, according to the commentator, perhaps out of ingrained modesty, pulls away from the scene of a man making a pass at a woman. But this is neither evidence that all shots are under such guidance nor that the cameraman, contrary to his ordinary disposition, could not undertake a documentary film made up exclusively of squarely centered shots of public attempts at seduction. Perhaps it will be proposed that in the latter case a trace of disapproval or irony will always be visible, there to be unearthed by a complex exegesis. But such exercises in interpretation may actually be no more than face saving. The positioning of a shot is just not as indicative of a filmmaker's authentic point-of-view as some film theorists let on.

Lastly, even if the shot = a personal vision approach were true, it would pertain only to shots and not to films in their entirety. A theorist who moves from the putative fact that every shot in a given nonfiction film represents a personal point-of-view to the conclusion that every nonfiction film is a personal vision commits the fallacy of composition. For even if each shot were personally inscribed with a decision that fused the values and attitudes of a lifetime, such shots could be assembled and combined with each other and with commentary in ways that neutralize the attitudes inherent in the single shots. Most compilation films demonstrate that the supposedly intrinsic personal points-of-view in original individual shots don't add up to the point-of-view of the entire film that they inhabit. For

example, *The Fall of the Romanov Dynasty* has no difficulty turning whatever positive sentiments czarist cameramen might have expressed in their footage of the royal family into criticism of the monarchy, criticism that does not seem describable as subjective.

The argument that nonfiction film is subjective hinges not only on confusions about the concept(s) of point-of-view but also about the concepts of subjectivity and objectivity. The charge of subjectivity, as leveled at the nonfiction film, appears to mean one of two, often elided, things: first, that a film is personal, or stamped with a personal viewpoint; and second, that a film is not objective. When considering the first meaning of subjectivity, we must ask whether the way in which a film is said to be personal is problematic to the status of nonfiction film as objective as well as whether nonfiction films are personal in a way distinguishes them from nonfiction writing.

If by saying the nonfiction film is personal we mean that any assertions or implied statements made by such films are epistemologically on a par with statements like "I believe that x," then we would be tempted to reclassify the nonfiction film as subjective in the sense that its assertions and implied statements are only to be evaluated as honest or dishonest. But the mere fact that selection and interpretation are involved in a nonfiction film does not entail the first person status of its claims – no more than those features suggest that all historical writing is subjective. We have intersubjective criteria for evaluating the selections and interpretations in both cases.

Undoubtedly because film is a visual medium, commentators are enticed (incorrectly) into identifying the imagery (and even its flow) as a simulacrum or reproduction of what its filmmaker saw; and they jump from this to the proposition that "That's *how* the filmmaker saw it" (where seeing is non-veridical and involuntary), which, in turn, is regarded as something indisputable and subjective. They also seem to treat shots as a sort of celluloid sense data. This plays into the confusions over the point-of-view of the shot and personal vision. As a result the film-maker is left in a doxastic cocoon. But there is no reason to conceive of shots in film as celluloid sense data – either passively received or as unavoidable results of unconscious structuring – nor does the camera's point of view necessarily have to correspond to a personal vision. The confusion rests with comprehending photography as nonveridical vision and the camera as an eye – with the result that each shot is to be prefaced with "I see". Though a nonfiction filmmaker might adopt this metaphor – consider Brakhage's *The Act of Seeing with One's Own Eyes* – films are not typically made under this rubric nor are they presented in ways that necessitate the camera-eye (I) metaphor in order to be understood. *The Act of Seeing with One's Own Eyes* is an astonishing film in part because the camera strains for some sort of equivalence with the filmmaker's perception. Such a film may lead us to speak of lyric-nonfiction; but it does not force us to say that all nonfiction films are subjective.

In most cases, I believe, certain misconceptions about the photographic component in film supply the primary grounds for convincing some that nonfiction film is problematically personal in a way that verbal exposition in history and science is not. These notions arise (mistakenly) by equating the camera to nonveridical, involuntary perception. Without these presuppositions – camera point-of-view = personal vision, and shooting = seeing – we are left with elements like editing, narration and commentary as the possible sources of the putative special subjectivity of film. Yet, the selectivity and interpretation involved in these processes seem no different and no more subjective than the practices of nonfiction writers, since we can challenge the selections, exclusions and interpretations of nonfiction filmmakers by means of the same considerations that we use to evaluate the nonfiction writer.

For example, in *The La Guardia Story,* a David Wolper production for his TV series *Biography,* the Little Flower's first election as Mayor of New York is presented solely as a consequence of his attack on the corruption of Tammany Hall. On the basis of the information on the screen, the implied interpretation is that the people of New York, appalled by the perversion of the American system, carried their indignation to the polls and overthrew the bosses. But this interpretation excludes a key factor in La Guardia's election – one that doesn't accord nicely with the civics lesson idealism of Wolper's account: namely, La Guardia's victory was an important part of an ethnic conflict between Jews and Italians, on the one hand, and the Irish, on the other, for political, social and economic power in New York; in other words, many voted for La Guardia out of ethnic self-interest. We are not compelled to accept the rosier version of La Guardia's election as indisputably Wolper's personal vision and leave it at that. We can also ascertain the objective weakness of the interpretation on the basis of intersubjectively available facts and modes of reasoning of exactly the same sort that we would employ when reading a scholarly journal or a magazine article.

At times, some commentators seem to argue that nonfiction film is subjective not because said films are unavoidably personal but because they are not objective. The logic here is that anything that is not objective must fall into the only other operative category; the subjective becomes the catchall for everything that doesn't suit the criteria of the objective. But what is objectivity? In film debates, three notions seem to determine the course of the discussion: First, "objective" means "true"; second, "objective" means "representative of all – or at least all the major – viewpoints on the subject at hand"; and third, "objective" means "having no viewpoint – personal, political, theoretical, etc. – whatsoever."

These three different concepts of objectivity do not fit together neatly, though in the course of an informal discussion after a nonfiction film disputants may slip willy-nilly from one to another. The second concept of objectivity sounds more like a political principle of tolerance – "let every voice be heard" – than an epistemic criterion. And save for cases in which there is only one uncontested and incontestable viewpoint, or those in which unavoidable indeterminacy rules (or those in which we have ascended to the lofty position of Spinoza's god), the conjunction of all perspectives on a given topic amounts to cacophony, and contradiction rather than truth. Moreover, the second and third senses of "objective," as outlined above, are strictly incompatible with each other.

Nor does any one of these concepts of "objectivity" appear viable in and of itself. Canvassing every opinion on a subject may exemplify some ideal of fairness but historians can be perfectly objective in their discussions of Hitler's career without mentioning Heinrich Himmler's assessment of the Führer. The idea that objectivity coincides with presenting a topic from no perspective whatsoever runs afoul of objections from two different directions. First, assuming a liberal notion of a perspective, it is impossible to conceive of a subject totally unstructured by any conceptual framework; there is no utterly "given"; the unadorned facts are both "unadorned" and "facts" relative to a conceptual schema or point-of-view. In other words, it is self-defeating for us to demand that a nonfiction film be "untouched by human hands." Second, in some fields a string of supposedly unadorned facts unsystematized by a theory would be the paradigm of random, subjective observation. Thus, Lucien Goldman attacks *Chronique d'un Été* exactly because it is uninformed by a theoretically based principle of selectivity.[12] Finally, objectivity cannot be equivalent to truth. Such a requirement is far too strong. The history of science is littered with false theories which nonetheless were objective. I can

offer objective reasons – perhaps based on statistics – for the conjecture that there is intelligent life on other planets and, nevertheless, it could turn out that we are alone in the universe. In such an instance, my problem would be that I was wrong and not that I was overly subjective.

Though objectivity is not equivalent to truth, the two are related in an important way. In any given field of research or argument, there are patterns of reasoning, routines for assessing evidence, means of weighing the comparative significance of different types of evidence, and standards for observations, experimentation and for the use of primary and secondary sources that are shared by practitioners in that field. Abiding by these established practices is, at any given time, believed to be the best method for getting at the truth. With continued research, these practices undergo changes – for example, after Marx economic evidence became more important in the study of history than it had been previously. Yet, even while some practices are being revised, others are still shared. Thus, in virtue of their shared practices, researchers still have a common ground for debating and for appreciating the work of their peers. We call a piece of research objective in light of its adherence to the practices of reasoning and evidence gathering in a given field. It is objective because it can be intersubjectively evaluated against standards of argument and evidence shared by practitioners of a specific arena of discourse.

With this in mind, we can untangle some of the conceptual knots that tether the nonfiction film. The nonfiction film is not necessarily subjective; like nonfiction writing, it is objective when it abides by the norms of reasoning and standards of evidence of the areas about which it purports to impart information. This is not to say that a nonfiction film is one that always abides by said standards; that would be tantamount to proposing that the nonfiction film is necessarily objective. Rather, we should say that a nonfiction film is, at least, one that must be assessed against the norms of objectivity that are practiced in regard to the type of information the film presents to its spectators. Some may feel that this is not a very helpful definition; how will we pick out the nonfiction films from the fictions, on the one hand, and the purely lyrical films, on the other?

In defense of my partial definition, let me lead off by postulating that we can never tell merely by looking whether or not a film is a piece of nonfiction. This is because any kind of technique or verbal assertion that is characteristic of a nonfiction film can be imitated by a fiction filmmaker – *The Battle of Algiers* and *David Holzman's Diary* are famous examples of this. Both are fiction films but both imitate the look of documentaries for expressive purposes. In *Battle of Algiers* the documentary look helps to heighten the gravity of events and thereby stokes the viewers' outrage at French colonialism. In *David Holzman's Diary,* the documentary conceit underscores the contemporaneity and specificity of the subject – the movie-crazy sixties in New York at a time when the distinction between film and life passionately blurred for many. A spectator might be confused and believe, for a moment, that these films were nonfiction. But, like a sentence, a film cannot be classified at a glance as fiction or nonfiction. Rather, films are indexed[13] by their creators, producers, distributors, etc. as belonging to certain categories. When a film is indexed as nonfiction then we know that it is appropriate to assess it according to the standards of objectivity of the field of which it is an example. Different nonfiction films, of course, correlate to different sorts of nonfiction discourse – newspaper articles, newspaper editorials, human interest stories, science textbooks, instruction manuals, anthropological field notes, psychological case studies, historical narratives, etc.

"Nonfiction" is a term that is used in contradistinction to fiction but it would be a mistake to think it pertains only to one type of exposition. There are many different areas of nonfiction – each with its own methodological routines – and, therefore, there are a variety of types of nonfiction film, each beholden to the restraints employed in processing the kind of information the film presents. A nonfiction film can be mistaken; that is, it ain't necessarily so. Yet, such a film can still be objective insofar as its mistakes do not violate the standards of reasoning and evidence that constitute objectivity for the area of nonfiction which it exemplifies. To be a nonfiction film means to be open to criticism and evaluation according to the standards of objectivity for the type of information being purveyed. Interpretation, selectivity, etc, are, therefore, appropriate insofar as they heed intersubjective standards.

Where does this lead us? Does it imply – as suggested by Rouch and Fernando Solanes and Octavio Getino – that nonfiction films must not traffic in aesthetic effects? Not at all. Nelson Goodman's philosophical writings are full of playful alliterations and puns, and Edward Gibbon in the *The History of the Decline and Fall of the Roman Empire* employs semicolons to create very dramatic pauses within long sentences. Yet, despite these effects, neither Goodman nor Gibbon are writing fiction. Similarly, the elegant juxtapositions in *Song of Ceylon* and the monumental compositions of *The Plow that Broke the Plains* do not disqualify those works from the order of nonfiction. Art is not the antithesis of nonfiction; a nonfiction filmmaker may be as artistic as he or she chooses as long as the processes of aesthetic elaboration do not interfere with the genre's commitment to the appropriate standards of research, exposition and argument. For example, a nonfiction filmmaker cannot invent new events or eliminate ones that actually occurred for the sake of securing an aesthetic effect where this falsifies history. Imagine a documentary called *The Pearl Harbor Tragedy* in which the filmmaker changes history a bit by having a PT boat with a broken radio racing to Hawaii just behind the approaching Japanese air fleet in order to warn of the impending assault. Undoubtedly with enough crisp parallel editing, this invented episode could produce a great deal of suspense. But I think that no matter how much suspense is achieved in this way, we would not accept the aesthetic effect as a justification for changing history. A nonfiction filmmaker must be accountable to the facts and the prospect of heightened effects does not alter that accountability. This, of course, is a major difference between fiction and nonfiction. In fiction, the past can always be rearranged in order to enhance aesthetic effects; but, though aesthetic effects are legitimate in nonfiction, accuracy cannot be suspended in the name of art.

A nonfiction filmmaker is committed by the genre to conveying the literal facts, where "literal" is defined by the objective procedures of the field of discourse at hand. Another way of saying this is that the nonfiction filmmaker makes reference to segments of possible worlds,[14] albeit ones that, at times, closely resemble the actual world.

Despite Vertov's caveats against staging, there is no reason why nonfiction films cannot employ re-enactments – like the postal sorting in *Night Mail* – or even historical reconstructions of types of events from the past – e.g., a minuet in *Baroque Dance* – or even reconstructions of a specific event – e.g., the car robbery in *Third Avenue: Only the Strong Survive*. Likewise, re-enactments of the surrender at Appomattox, the Scopes Monkey Trial, the repeal of Prohibition, etc, can all be accommodated within the framework of the nonfiction film as long as such reconstructions are as accurate as possible given the state of available evidence. This raises questions about the boundary line

between nonfiction and some historical fiction, especially cases like *The Rise to Power of Louis XIV*. In this film, great pains were taken to insure the authenticity of detail as well as using actual memoirs and written documents of the period as a basis for dialogue. Yet, *The Rise to Power of Louis XIV* is still fiction because its creator, Roberto Rossellini, has invented a number of events in which historical personages mouth their writings at meetings and in imagined situations for which there is no historical evidence. In this way, Rossellini animates history, making the writings "come alive" supplying visual interest via intriguing background detail and character movement. History, in other words, is rearranged and altered for aesthetic effect.

The nonfiction filmmaker's commitment to objectivity does not disallow the use of devices like composite case studies. That is, one can make a nonfiction film of the experiences of the average army recruit, of the characteristic behavior of a schizoid, a representative case study of the plight of an unemployed (but composite) teenager, a day in the life of a medieval serf, and so on. The dramatization of corruption in *Native Land* is perhaps arguably an example of this sort of generalization. Such generalizing devices project theoretical entities meant to summarize the normal tendencies and types of events found in the kind of situation depicted. These devices are used in areas like journalism, history, sociology, and psychology, and they are legitimate in nonfiction film to the extent that they abide by the same constraints in their construction that analogous devices in nonfiction literature respect. Moreover, such devices are rooted in the attempt to portray the literal truth since they are generalizations subject to objective criteria in terms of intersubjectively accessible facts.

Throughout the preceding discussion I have relied on the idea that the nonfiction film can be objective, indeed that it is committed to objectivity, where objectivity is defined by the standards, routines and norms of evidence of particular disciplines and modes of exposition. To adopt this strategy, however, is to invite a predictable rebuke from Cine-Marxists who would claim that the disciplines I am invoking – both in terms of their content and their methodologies – are themselves so shot through, or, better yet, so contaminated with ideology that their purchase on objectivity is extremely tenuous.

The argument from ideology, like many arguments in film theory, is often underwritten by such inclusiveness in its central terms that it borders on vacuity. For many film scholars, ideology is virtually synonymous with culture; any nonfiction film is a cultural item – in semiotic jargon both in its signified and signifiers – and, therefore, it is unavoidably suffused with ideology.[15] Clearly, under these assumptions, everything is ideological and, consequently, the concept of ideology is open to the same variety of criticism we leveled earlier at the italicized concept of subjectivity. Furthermore, were one to employ a narrower notion of ideology, it is not clear that we would be easily convinced that every existing institution for the acquisition and dissemination of knowledge is irretrievably and necessarily ideological.

Another problem with the Ciné-Marxist approach is that it tends to proceed as though there were two social sciences, the Marxist variety and the capitalist, and it assumes that these two schools are completely disjunct, sharing no common ground. In the case of ideology, some Marxists speak as if only Marxists were aware of the distortive potential of ideology. Yet, non-Marxist social scientists have embraced Marxist ideas about ideology and, in turn, they scrutinize each other's findings for the possibility of errors due to ideological bias. That is, non-Marxist historians and social scientists are sensitive to the dangers of ideology and it is part of their methodological framework to be on guard against ideologically determined mistakes.

When I refer to the standards and routines of different disciplines, I do not conceive of these as static and unchanging. Rather, these standards and routines are often revised, sometimes in response to discoveries within the field, sometimes in response to changes in adjacent fields and sometimes as a result of innovations in general epistemology. Such revisions themselves are open to intersubjective debate and can be evaluated in light of factors like the added coherence they afford both within a given field and with other fields, in the increased explanatory power they provide, the degree to which they block certain likely avenues of error, etc. In reference to the ideology argument, I would hold that an important part of the Marxist perspective has been introjected into the practices of history and social science to the extent that social scientists are aware as a matter of routine of the threat of ideological distortion, and are, in principle, able to correct for ideological error. It is always fair game, in other words, for one social scientist to examine the work of another for ideological prejudices. This is not to say that all social science is free of ideology, but only that social scientists, as a matter of course, must answer charges that their work is misguided because of its ideological presumptions. Thus, the existence of ideology does not preclude the possibility of objectivity since cognizance of it is built into the practices of the fields where it is liable to emerge.

The issue of ideology, of course, raises that of propaganda. I have argued that the nonfiction film is such that its practitioners are responsible to the norms of reasoning and standards of evidence appropriate to their particular subject matter. What of propaganda films – like *Triumph of the Will* – that intentionally suppress all manner of facts – such as the purge of the S.A. – in order to endorse a given political position? Such films appear to be counterexamples to my characterization of nonfiction film, since they are expressly designed to violate standards of objectivity, using every rhetorical trick in the book to sway audiences to their viewpoint; and yet works like *Triumph of the Will* are classified as nonfiction.

To handle these cases we must distinguish between two senses of "propaganda." The first is derisory. We call something "propaganda" if it callously twists the facts for polemical ends. But "propaganda" can also be thought of as the name of a quasi-genre, cutting across the categories of fiction and nonfiction, devoted to persuasion, especially political persuasion. When "propaganda" is used in this second sense it need not be pejorative. A film may be successfully persuasive without bending the facts; I think that *Battle of Chile* and *The Selling of the Pentagon* are examples of this. Nevertheless, it is true that many films that are "propaganda" in the second sense are also "propaganda" in the first sense; unquestionably this is why the abusive meaning of the word took hold. But etymologies notwithstanding, it is important to note that propaganda films would only serve as counterexamples to my characterization of nonfiction film if nonfiction propaganda films in the second sense were necessarily propaganda in the first sense. That is, nonfiction propaganda films are problematic for my position only when the two senses of "propaganda" are conflated; by saying that nonfiction filmmakers are committed to objectivity, I have not implied that all of them respect that commitment; some lie, giving rise to the unsavory connotations of the word "propaganda"; but, in fact, it is only because it is possible to make nonfiction films of political advocacy that are objective – a subclass of "propaganda" in the second sense – that we bother to have the sordid name "propaganda" in the first sense. As a genre, nonfiction propaganda films are to be evaluated against objective standards just like any other nonfiction film. When they are caught out playing down and dirty with their materials, we castigate them as "propaganda" in the disdainful sense of the word.

For some, my attempt to connect nonfiction propaganda as a genre with objectivity may be unsettling. They might feel that propaganda as such is inimical to objectivity. There are at least two possible origins for this sentiment. The first harkens back to a concept of objectivity already discussed, viz., objectivity amounts to representing all points of view on a given subject. But, propaganda, by definition, champions one viewpoint, excluding contending positions. Therefore, propaganda cannot be objective. Secondly, one may feel that propaganda deals primarily with values rather than facts, and further hold that the realm of values – ethical, political, sexual, social – is subjective rather than objective. Again, the consequence is that nonfiction propaganda cannot be objective.

The first of these positions is questionable in respect to its concept of objectivity; it is really a principle of fairness rather than a principle with epistemic import. The second objection also seems mistaken in its presuppositions. Morality and, in the case of propaganda, politics are objective areas of discourse since they are governed by intersubjectively established protocols of reasoning. I do not say that we can easily resolve all our ethical (and meta-ethical) disputes, but we can pursue our disagreements objectively. Obviously, I cannot here satisfactorily develop an attack on the view that questions of value are inevitably subjective. But to the degree that that position is debatable, the argument that objective propaganda is impossible is unconvincing.

Besides propaganda, there are other genres of nonfiction that do not, on the face of it, appear well characterized by my formulations because the issue of objective standards for evaluating their claims does not seem relevant to the kinds of work they are. Two such genres are commemorations of events and people – like *The Eleventh Year, Man with a Movie Camera* and *Three Songs of Lenin* – and autobiographical films – like *Lost, Lost, Lost.* But are these films beyond the bounds of objective criticism in terms of the knowledge claims they make? In the case of commemorations, and, for that matter, sponsored travelogues, I think it is perfectly reasonable to say that they are flawed as nonfiction when they overlook unpleasant facts. One thing that is particularly attractive about *Man with a Movie Camera* is that it celebrates the progress and potential of pre-Stalin Russia while at the same time acknowledging persisting social problems like unemployment and alcoholism.

Nor are ciné-autobiographies epistemologically incorrigible. If we observe that Jonas Mekas is perfectly at home in the United States, that, according to reliable eye-witness testimony, he never evinced any sense of loss, and was a satisfied bourgeois, we would be in a position to raise objections against *Lost, Lost, Lost*. That is, there are objectively accessible facts that we could use to take the measure of the film. Of course, it might turn out in such a case that the purpose of the film was not to report Mekas' experience but to image the way a melancholic Lithuanian might respond to immigration and displacement. But then we are no longer dealing with a lyric nonfiction but with a pure lyric, which some commentators would argue is in the province of fiction proper.[16]

I have been falling back on the notion that there are standards of research, argument, evidence and interpretation incorporated in the routines and practices of the different fields of knowledge production. I have further argued that these constitute objectivity in a given area of discourse and that nonfiction films can be and are supposed to be objective in the same sense that nonfiction writing is. Such films, that is, are responsible to whatever objective standards are appropriate to the subject matter they are dealing with. This is not to say that nonfiction films are always true or even that they always meet the relevant standards of objectivity. But I do deny that nonfiction films are intrinsically subjective, as many film theorists claim. I deny this precisely because nonfiction films can meet the same

criteria that are met by nonfiction writing. I have not broached the problem that the standards of objectivity in any given area are not always easy to formalize nor have I offered a conclusive argument against the skeptical objection that my so-called standards of objectivity are really chimeras. But to attempt to grapple with these questions – important as they are – is beyond the scope of this paper, for these are issues about the possibility of objectivity in any form. My point is simply that there is no special problem of objectivity confronting nonfiction film because the concept of objectivity is the same for nonfiction film as it is for other nonfiction discourses. In fact, the standards of objectivity relevant to nonfiction film are bound to those of other modes of nonfiction exposition.

B. Nonfiction Film and Fiction

The arguments purporting to show that the nonfiction film is really or even necessarily fiction resemble previous maneuvers in the arguments about subjectivity. As such, they manifest many of the same weaknesses. A very liberal set of features, including manipulation, choice, structure, coding, the influence of ideology, is implicitly assumed or explicitly employed to define "fiction" in such a way that it is difficult to imagine anything that is not fiction. Jean-Louis Comolli, for example, virtually retreads earlier arguments, exchanging "subjectivity" for "fiction" in his assault on direct cinema. He writes:

In reality the very fact of filming is of course already a productive intervention which modifies and transforms the material recorded. From the moment the camera intervenes a form of manipulation begins. And every operation, even when contained by the most technical of motives – starting with the cameras rolling, cutting, changing the angle or lens, then choosing the rushes and editing them – like it or not, constitutes a manipulation of the film-document. The filmmaker may well wish to respect that document, but he cannot avoid manufacturing it. It does not pre-exist reportage, it is its product.

A certain hypocrisy therefore lies at the origins of the claim that there is antinomy between direct cinema and aesthetic manipulation. And to engage in direct cinema as if the inevitable interventions and manipulations (which produce meaning, effect and structure) did not count and were purely practical rather than aesthetic, is in fact to demand the minimum of it. It means sweeping aside all its potentialities and censoring its natural creative function and productivity in the name of some illusory honesty, non-intervention and humility.

A consequence of such a productive principle, and automatic consequence of all the manipulations which mould the film-document is a co-efficient of "nonreality": a kind of fictional aura attaches itself to all the filmed events and facts.[17]

The sort of argument attempts to have its cake and eat it too. It posits the celluloid reproduction of a *ding-en-sich* as the goal of nonfiction, notes the impossibility of the task and declares all film fictional rather than starting off with the obvious premise that in some sense all films are mediated and, then, attempting to ascertain which of these cases of mediation belong to fiction and which to nonfiction. In and of itself, following the above approach – that all films are fictional because they are produced – gives rise to the same vexations rehearsed in regard to the subjectivity argument. The only difference is that now we will be speaking of "*fictional* fictions" and "*fictional* nonfictions."

To see the line of counterattack in bold relief, recall Metz's assertion that all film is fictional because it represents something that is not actually occurring in the screening room. But if representation is a sufficient condition for fiction then Cyril Falls' book, *The Great War 1914–1918,* is fiction because there is no mustard gas in it. Metz's theory, taken at its word, implies that there are no books, or films, or speeches left that are not fiction, thereby making the concept of fiction theoretically useless.

This counterattack can be generalized to other versions of the fiction argument so that, *pari passu,* we can demonstrate that arguments based on manipulation, choice, coding, structure and the like lead us down the same garden path until at the end we discover the shrubbery growing wild and still needing to be separated into patches of fiction and nonfiction respectively. Perhaps the argument that all films are fictional due to ideological contamination is a bit more complicated since it generally not only assumes an expansive definition of fiction, i.e., fiction = ideology, but also an expansive definition of ideology, i.e., ideology = culture. Yet even with this addition, the moral of the story is the same; by theorizing with such undifferentiated concepts, nothing whatsoever is said. Even the argument that nonfiction films are fiction because they employ the same narrative devices as fiction suffers this liability. For narration is common to types of both fiction and nonfiction, and not a differentia between the two categories. To say nonfiction films are fictions because, for example, they use flashbacks, is to sweep much historical writing into the dustbin of fiction.

Many of the apparently paradoxical conclusions film theorists seem to derive result from the use of ill-defined and overblown concepts. The declaration that all nonfiction films are really fictions is a sterling example. To rectify the confusion requires a clarification of the central terms of the discussion. Nonfiction films are those that we evaluate on the basis of their knowledge claims in accordance with the objective standards appropriate to their subject matter. Producers, writers, directors, distributors, and exhibitors index their films as nonfiction, thereby prompting us to bring objective standards of evidence and argument into play. We don't characteristically go to films about which we must guess whether they are fiction or nonfiction. They are generally indexed one way or the other. And we respond according to the indices, suspending objective standards if the film is marked as fiction but mobilizing them if it is called nonfiction.

Moreover, these responses are grounded in an ontological distinction between the two forms of exposition. Nonfiction refers to the actual world. Thus, in principle, there could be evidence for each of the knowledge claims that such a film makes. Fiction, however, refers to segments of possible worlds. Insofar as many of the entities in fictions do not exist, there is no evidence that could serve to establish knowledge claims about them; hence, the issue of knowledge claims is generally dropped altogether.

Furthermore, the possible worlds referred to by fictions are incomplete: there are questions that might be asked about fictions – like the notorious "How many children has Lady Macbeth?" – that in principle have no answer, even within the fiction. It is impossible to deal with such questions because fictional worlds are not fully articulated. Fictions do very often contain correspondences with actual persons, places and events, but they also contain descriptions of ontologically incomplete possible persons or places or events, or of variations on actual persons or places or events, that transform all the entities in the fictional world into ontologically incomplete possibilities. We cannot know who, for example, was the landlord of Sherlock's Baker Street digs in the film *Pursuit to Algiers;* although we know the address of the apartments, we can say little of their history, save what Watson tells us. Because fictions are by nature ontologically incomplete it makes no sense to evaluate them according to objective standards of evidence; no fiction is designed to be entirely answerable to the canons of proof that are applied to discourses about the actual world. Thus, we disregard such standards of evidence *tout court* because fictions are not the kind of objects to which such canons are pertinent.

A word or two about indexing is in order. In the main, films are distributed so that the category they are intended to belong to is public knowledge before they are screened. A film is billed as a documentary, or an adaptation of a novel, or as (only) based on a true story, or as a romance, etc. Indexing a film as a fiction or nonfiction tells us what the film claims to refer to, i.e., the actual world or segments of possible worlds; and indexing tells us the kind of responses and expectations it is legitimate for us to bring to the film. In short, insofar as indexing fixes the attempted reference of a given film, indexing is constitutive of whether the given film is an instance of fiction or nonfiction, which amounts to whether it is to be construed as fiction or nonfiction.

Because issues of evaluation hinge on indexing, one would think it in the interest of producers, and distributors to be scrupulous in this matter. Since mistakes and errors are defects in documentaries, calling *Star Wars* nonfiction, a piece of intergalactic history, might have disappointing results in its critical reception. Yet, it does seem that there are cases in which we are tempted to say that films are indexed improperly. For instance, a nonfiction propagandist may stage an imagined enemy atrocity in order to drum up support for his country. Here we may feel that it is best to describe the initial indexing as incorrect and that it should be indexed as fiction. But I think that once it is indexed as nonfiction, it is more appropriate to say that the attributed atrocity is unfounded and that the film is being used to lie. The original indexing of a film is crucial; inaccurate nonfiction films cannot be rechristened as fictions in order to gain a second hearing, though a documentary director may take a long, hard look at the available footage and decide to cut it in a way different from what was planned and, then, initially index the result as fiction. From my perspective, the only time it is correct to speak of improper indexing would be when a comedy of mixed-up film cans results in something like *Logan's Run* being inadvertently screened on *Nova*. But in this case, we speak of that event as an instance of improper indexing because *Logan's Run* has antecedently and originally been indexed as fiction by its creators and promoters.

Films like *Citizen Kane* and *The Carpetbaggers* are indexed as fictions, but critics and viewers discover they bear strong analogies to the biographies of actual people. With such films it is easy to imagine a plaintiff suing for libel and winning. Here, one may be disposed to say that though the film was indexed as fiction, the verdict shows it is nonfiction. But I am not sure that we are driven to this conclusion. Rather, we might merely say that the film is libelous instead of claiming it is nonfiction where "libelous" means that the film, though fiction, affords a highly probable interpretation, based on analogies, that caused or tends to cause the plaintiff public injury or disgrace. What the trial proves is not that the film is nonfiction but that the film produced damages of a certain sort.

Ambiguously indexed films, certain docudramas like the TV series *You Are There*, also seem to raise problems for the attempt to differentiate fiction from nonfiction. In this series from the fifties, a fictional reporter would travel into the past to interview famous personages embroiled in momentous historical events, e.g., Washington at Valley Forge. Both the interview and the interviewer were completely invented, and their introduction renders the referents of the show ontologically incomplete. For example, it is in principle impossible to answer the question of whether the interviewer had previously met Washington, say in 1756. Consequently, I am inclined to say that though ambiguously indexed as a hybrid of fiction and nonfiction, *You Are There* is fiction. This may strike some as perplexing because the program seems obviously designed to offer information about the actual world and it also in some sense succeeds in its purpose. But in response, we must note that the very use of the interview indicates that the series was also designed to entertain

and that the desire to entertain was strong enough to encourage a high degree of poetic license on the part of its creators. Undoubtedly, this decision was motivated by educational as well as economic considerations, and it is true that education is often facilitated through entertainment. But the fact that *You Are There* is in part educational does not entail that it is nonfiction. People can learn things from fiction. That is, people can acquire new beliefs from fictions; what they cannot do is appeal to the authority of a fiction as a basis for justifying those beliefs.

In regard to the relation between fiction and nonfiction film I have stressed two basic points. First: the concepts of fiction employed by film theorists to show that nonfiction films are really fiction are unconvincing. Like the arguments for the necessary subjectivity of film, the arguments about fiction are advanced on the backs of overly broad concepts that deny the possibility of nonfiction in every medium and field of discourse. Second: I have tried to sketch briefly a narrower picture of the boundary between fiction and nonfiction in order to sustain the distinction between two kinds of film. Whatever inadequacies beset this latter attempt do not reflect on my first point; I may be wrong about the proper formulation of the concept of fiction and still be right that film theorists like Comolli need a much narrower concept than the ones they now employ.

III. Exposition and Evidence

The first section of this essay proposed that current confusions over nonfiction film arise from polemics about direct cinema. And though it is true that the debates about direct cinema brought these issues to a head, many of the presuppositions that energize the discussion are deep-rooted and long-standing.

One source of the invention of cinema was science, e.g., certain breakthroughs in the development of the motion picture camera resulted from work like Marey's in the recording of motion. Thus, the idea of film as a recording device has been with the medium since its inception. Early detractors dismissed cinema as a mere reproduction or automatic reproduction of reality. This dismissal was the *bête noir* of silent filmmakers and film theorists alike; in deed and word they strove to show that film could artistically rearrange the world rather than just slavishly and mechanically duplicate it. But with the influential writings of André Bazin the dialectic took a new turn.[18] The recording aspect of film was again seen as central, only this time around it was praised as a positive virtue rather than chided as a limitation of the medium. For Bazin, the crucial feature of film is mimetic photography which is defined as the automatic re-presentation of the world. Every film image is a trace of the past. It is this viewpoint on the nature of film that leads some of the theoreticians cited previously to claim that all film is nonfiction; *Gone with the Wind* yields evidence about Clark Gable insofar as it re-presents or is a trace of the man. For Bazin, it is the nature of film to re-present the world.

Bazin's position and its various reincarnations face stiff problems, which have been forcefully stated by Alexander Sesonske, in accounting for fiction film and animation.[19] But the position nevertheless has a special attractiveness for nonfiction film. The notion of the automatic reproduction of reality as part and parcel of the essence of film, for example, enjoined Caesare Zavattini to envision the ideal film as a storyless recording of ninety consecutive minutes of a day in the life of an ordinary man.[20]

Without question, the naïvete of the view that the essence or destiny of film is to automatically reproduce reality provoked the subjectivity and fiction arguments reviewed already. But the problem with these responses is that in attempting to show that cinema does not automatically reproduce reality they go too far, insinuating that cinema can never faithfully record, document or bear evidence about the world.

In order to deal with some of the problems that muddy thinking about nonfiction film it is profitable to consider the basic modes of representation in film. Adopting some of Monroe Beardsley's terminology,[21] we note that each shot in a representational photographic film physically portrays its source. In *Gone with the Wind*, the shots of Rhett Butler physically portray Clark Gable. Every shot in a representational photographic film physically portrays its source, a definite object, person or event that can be named by a singular term. This is the point that Bazin is making when he says that film re-presents the past; the shots in a representational photographic film, whatever our account of representation, physically portray the objects, persons and events that cause the image. If shots are only used to physically portray their sources, they are recordings in the most basic sense of the term. When we speak of films as evidence we primarily have physical portrayal in mind. The problem with various realist approaches to film theory is that they sometimes appear to propose that physical portrayal is the only use of shots, or that it is the essential or most important use.

But at the same time that a film physically portrays its source (some specific object or event) it also depicts a class or congeries of objects. A shot from *Gone with the Wind* physically portrays Clark Gable but it also depicts a man; likewise a shot of the White House physically portrays the White House but also depicts a house. Each representational shot in a film physically portrays its source and depicts a member of a class describable by a general term – a man, a fire, a house, etc. Thus, in a given film, a shot can be presented via its context in a way that what is discursively important about it is not what it physically portrays but what it depicts. In *Man with a Movie Camera* there is an image of a hammer thrower. What is discursively significant about it is that it is an image of a Soviet athlete, not that it is an image of a particular Ivan. Because film images depict classes as well as physically portraying individuals, they can be used to stand for kinds in communication contexts where their relation to their specific sources is irrelevant.

Depiction, so to speak, pries the individual shot from its specific referent and in doing so opens up another possibility of cinematic representation. The shot physically portraying Clark Gable depicts a man, and given the context of *Gone with the Wind,* it also represented Rhett Butler. This form of representation, which we may call nominal portrayal, occurs when a shot represents a particular person, object or event different than its photographic provenance, due to its context as a result of factors like commentary, titles, an ongoing story or editing. In light of film history, nominal portrayal is the most important use of shots. Obviously it is the *sine qua non* of fiction films. But it is also indispensable in nonfiction films, even those other than historical re-enactments. The use of stock footage, for instance, of strike breaking in *Union Maids* or naval bombardments in *Victory at Sea,* is based on shots that depict policemen and battleships so that they can be contextualized in order to nominally portray the specific events the film discusses. Furthermore, a shot of the Capitol Building taken in 1929 might accompany a soundtrack that states that such and such a bill was passed in 1934. Strictly speaking, this is a case of nominal portrayal since it represents the Capitol Building at a time other than that of the making of the shot. We do not take this use of such a shot (which is common in nonfiction production) to be a matter of lying – unless the commentary explicitly claims the shot was taken at the moment the bill was passed – because we understand that shots can not only be used as recording units but also as expositional units. And nominal portrayal is the representational practice that most facilitates cinematic exposition.

By distinguishing between physical portrayal, nominal portrayal and depiction, we can clarify some of the great debates of film theory. Realist theorists tend to overemphasize the importance of physical portrayal in film. Montagists, on the other hand, are proponents of nominal portrayal, especially of the way editing can function as an agency for this type of representation. The montagists did not invent nominal portrayal in film but they did aggressively conceptualize its relationship to editing. If the montagists erred, it is probably in their extreme deprecation of the photographic component in film. At times, in their enthusiasm, they seem to be not only denying the importance of physical portrayal in film but also claiming that a shot can be made to depict anything whatsoever (depending on its position in an edited sequence). But it is hard to imagine, given existing symbol systems, how any amount of editing could make a clean, medium long shot of Lenin depict an ice cream soda. In fact, what a shot depicts guides the montagist's selection of what shots will be chosen to nominally portray the persons, objects and events that comprise the subject of the film. Nevertheless, historically, the Soviets in de-emphasizing the importance of physical portrayal were more right about the direction of the cultural use of film than the realist theorists.

The distinction between different modes of cinematic representation also enables us to characterize a number of beliefs that sustain conundrums about nonfiction film. On the one hand, those who claim that every film is nonfiction do so on the basis that every shot physically portrays its source. But it does not follow that whole films made up of such shots are physical portrayals. *Casablanca* is composed of shots that individually portray Bogart, Bergman, Raines, Lorre, Dalio, Veidt, and Henreid, but it is not a recording of these people: to see *Casablanca* as a record of Bogart in front of a camera is as inappropriate as seeing a Catholic priest at the Offertory of the Mass as a toastmaster.

Arguments denying the possibility of objective nonfiction also often proceed from overemphasis on physical portrayal. These theoreticians presuppose that for a film to be an objective nonfiction means that the film will be a physical portrayal of its sources. Thus, they immediately suspect any use of nominal portrayal or depiction in a putative nonfiction film. Moreover, though it is easy to think of individual shots as re-presentations (in the sense of physical portrayal), the concept is not readily adaptable to whole films. This is one reason why editing presents problems to many nonfiction theorists, i.e., they begin to wonder how films can be said to genuinely re-present (physically portray) the past, given the ellipses of editing. Their problem, in part, is that they are using the individual shot, understood as a physical portrayal, as a model for what a nonfiction film should be, and then they find all the candidates wanting. It would be better to drop the intuition that the shot as physical portrayal is the paradigm of cinematic nonfiction.

The typical nonfiction film mixes physical portrayal, nominal portrayal and depiction. A film is not nonfiction in terms of the modes of cinematic representation it does or doesn't employ, but in terms of its commitment to the standards of argument, evidence and exposition that are appropriate to the type of information it presents. My key point in this regard is that what is important but sometimes forgotten about nonfiction films is that in general they are expository, and are to be evaluated in light of the assertions they are used to make. This is not to deny that films and footage can also be evidential in the sense that the shots within the film are all used to physically portray their sources and that their sequencing is presented as a reliable record of an event. But this type of nonfiction film is neither the whole of the genre nor a privileged or central instance thereof.

In many nonfiction films, it is impossible for the viewer to tell by looking whether the footage is a literal physical portrayal of the objects, persons and events it purports to represent, so we are best advised to greet such images as nominal portrayals. However, this is not to say that films do not often present footage as a physical portrayal of its source, i.e., as straightforward recording. Where footage is proffered as a recording it is open to questions about its authenticity. In this regard it is no different than any other document. Ultimately, some questions will not be answerable in terms of what is on the screen but will require recourse to production records and witnesses. But the fact that it can be difficult to tell on the basis of the film itself whether or not it is a legimate recording does not pose problems for the possibility of using footage as a record, since there are other means for authenticating its origins.

In some instances, footage will be used to provide a record of a specific event as well as evidence in support of an assertion about the situation it refers to. Here the footage is again open to questions about whether it is good evidence for the claims it is supposed to support. In *Chariot of the Gods* we are shown an image of a Mexican frieze that is meant to persuade us that Central Americans had knowledge of spaceships prior to the European invasion. The frieze depicts some whooshes sculpted onto the back of a chariot. But this is hardly enough to substantiate familiarity with interplanetary space vehicles, even if the footage is authentic.

Where sequences of footage are spliced together and are presented as reliable recordings of events, questions of authenticity arise again. The way the footage is edited can be open to dispute; the adequacy of an edited recording may be challenged in terms of witnesses and, as occurs in legal contexts, by a review of the out-takes.

In short, whether a nonfiction film is primarily expositional and uses its footage to nominally portray events or whether it presents its footage as physical portrayal, it is still responsible to established standards of objectivity, though in the latter case the film will be open to further criticism if it illicitly claims its footage is a physical portrayal of its alleged subject.

IV. Digression: Realism and Nonfiction

So far, I have stressed the shared rhetoric of the defense of deep-focus realism – the cinematic style of Renoir and the Neorealists, advocated by Bazin – and that of direct cinema. Indeed a recent anthology, *Realism and the Cinema,* at times shifts seamlessly from pieces on nonfiction to pieces on realism. The relation between the deep-focus style of realism and direct cinema, of course, is one of influence; practitioners of cinema-vérité adopted and adapted Renoir's (and Bazin's) conceptions of framing, of the importance of camera movement and of the value of spontaneity.[23] The interplay of the theory of deep-focus realism and documentary practice gives the impression that there is a link between one style of filmmaking and truthfulness, and that in virtue of that link one style of filmmaking is more appropriate to nonfiction film than any other.

The style of deep-focus realism is defended because it encourages spectators to participate more actively in the construction of meaning in a film than, for example, the style of montage filmmaking. Directorial control *appears* to be relaxed so that the spectator *appears* free to assimilate the succession of imagery in his own way. This freedom is called realistic because it is analogous to the kind of choice and freedom we experience when we scan everyday reality for information about how things stand. Purportedly, this style of realism enables us to make up our own minds rather than molding the world according to the filmmaker's preconceptions. And, of course, the notion of presenting the world without preconceptions is particularly alluring to the practitioner of direct cinema.

Yet, the idea that the style of deep-focus realism is truthful or has a special potential for re-presenting reality is problematic. No cinematic technique in and of itself guaran-

tees truth. For any film technique or set of techniques can appear in either a fiction or nonfiction film. Some techniques may be historically associated with documentaries; but they can always be incorporated for expressive effect in fictions, e.g., grainy, fast film stock. Deep-focus realism, in fact, is an ensemble of techniques that coalesced in fiction films, a strange place for a style that is truth-preserving to evolve.

The confusion between realism and truth is grounded in a misconception of what it means to consider a style of filmmaking realistic. In most writing, if an author calls a film or a style realistic, this is taken to signal a two-term relationship between the film and reality. Realism is thought of as a transhistorical category inclusively denominating any film or film style that corresponds to reality. Hence, if the deep-focus style is realistic, then it corresponds to reality, and insofar as the nonfiction filmmaker is committed to corresponding to reality, he is urged to employ this style.

But realism in film or in any medium is not a simple relationship between a representation and reality. First and foremost, realism designates a style and in this role it points to a difference between contrasting films, paintings, novels, etc. To call a film or a group of films realistic is to call attention to some feature that the items in question have that other films don't have. *Rules of the Game,* for example, employs a series of multi-plane compositions that induce the spectator to scan the frame for dramatic details and inflections. This differs from the type of composition found in Soviet montage or in the soft-focus of Hollywood films of the thirties. The term "realism" marks this contrast. But why is "realism" used to do the marking? Because spectator scanning, a possibility inhibited by Soviet montage or the soft-focus style, is taken to be *more like* our normal perceptual behavior than our reaction to the composition in alternate styles. But deep-focus realism does not correspond to reality. Rather it is more like some aspects of reality when compared to alternate approaches to filmmaking. A film or film style is realistic when it deviates from other specified films or styles in such a way that the deviation can be construed as like some aspect of reality that was hitherto repressed or merely absent in previous films or film styles. Realism is not a simple relation between films and the world but a relation of contrast between films that is interpreted in virtue of analogies to aspects of reality. Given this, it is easy to see that there is no single Film Realism – no trans-historical style of realism in film. Rather there are several types of realism. There is Soviet realism which because of its mass hero and details of proletarian life deviated from the individualism and glamour of Hollywood narratives in such a way that aspects of reality, class action and lower class living conditions, were foregrounded. Deep-focus realism emphasized yet another dimension of reality in film. Its arrival did not force us to stop calling the Soviet films realistic but only to recognize that another variety of realism had been introduced. Because "realism" is a term whose application ultimately involves historical comparisons, it should not be used unprefixed – we should speak of Soviet realism, Neorealism, Kitchen Sink and Super realism. None of these developments strictly correspond to or duplicate reality, but rather make pertinent (by analogy) aspects of reality absent from other styles. Furthermore, once we abandon the correspondence conception of realism, there is no reason to presume that one cinematic style is correct for all nonfiction film.

This is not to deny the importance of direct cinema's espousal of the Renoir/Bazin ethos of deep-focus and camera movement. The expressive effects of this choice were (and still are) far reaching. The spectator's role in relation to the screen was redefined, encouraging in us the active and spontaneous play of opinion, judgment and decision. In a film like *Warrendale,* it is left up to us to decide

whether the regime of that institution is barbaric and irresponsible, on the one hand, or curative and caring on the other. The relative freedom of the spectator and its precondition, the relative slackening of overt evaluation on the part of the filmmaker, may suggest one sense of objectivity – namely that of making a place where all opinions may flourish. But this is a political – in fact historically liberal – concept of objectivity, not an epistemic one. And indeed it is as an expressive emblem of egalitarianism, a major preoccupation of the sixties, that direct cinema's adoption of the Bazinian creed is most significant.

V. Concluding General Remarks

My overall strategy in this essay has been to argue that there is nothing special or essential to film as a medium that raises unique problems for the notion of nonfiction film. I have constantly compared nonfiction film with nonfiction writing in order to answer the charge that in some way the inevitability of the modes of selection, manipulation, etc., endemic to cinema produce special problems for film in regard to nonfiction. My approach, here, is part of a larger conception of cinema. I believe that film, perhaps because it is a recent medium, invented within living memory, has developed primarily by imitating and incorporating preexisting cultural practices and concerns. Cinema has been adapted to make narrative, to make drama and to make art as well as nonfiction. The medium, in short, discovers itself in the process of enlisting and assimilating previously established structures, forms, goals and values. Understanding film, therefore, most often depends on applying the concepts and criteria appropriate to the broader or older cultural projects that cinema mimes.

By urging this perspective I am going against the grain of much traditional film theory which centered on discovering and elucidating what is unique to film – what is peculiarly (and essentially) cinematic. The notion that subjectivity flows from the special processes of the film medium is, in fact, a variation, though a negative one, on this traditional theme; rather than outlining film's peculiar, positive potential, it means to acknowledge film's special limitations. My position on the nonfiction film, in contradistinction, is that no special epistemological problems result from the distinctive features of the medium. On the issue of the essential nature of film, I hold that film has no essence, only uses, most of which are derivative and subject to analysis and evaluation according to the categories that apply to their sources – art, drama, narrative, nonfiction, and so on.

In emphasizing the relatedness of film to larger cultural projects, I am not claiming that there are no differences between film and the other media in which those projects are pursued but only that in comprehending film as, for example, art, or nonfiction, the conceptual frameworks of those institutionalized endeavors are more fundamental than questions about the nature of film as film. Undoubtedly, the vivid portrayal of time and process in *Fishing at Stone Weir,* the immediate intelligibility of the construction of the igloo in *Nanook of the North,* and the revelation of the intimate interplay of the rhythm, economy and society of the !Kung Bushmen in *The Hunters* would be difficult, if not practically impossible, to duplicate in written accounts. Sometimes a picture is worth a thousand words, though, of course, sometimes a single word can do the work of a thousand pictures. The upshot of this is not that some topics categorically belong to cinema and some to language and that these can be antecedently plotted by establishing the unique potentials or limitations of the medium. There is no subject or project that is inherently adverse to cinema. Rather some films fail and others do not. Films can be artistic, objective, dramatic, etc. Or they can fail in these attempts. But this is a matter of individual cases and not of unique

features of the medium that dictate failure in advance.

To underscore film's indebtedness to broader cultural enterprises for its marching orders and to abandon the quest for the cinematic is not to deny that there is an important area of study called film theory. Questions still remain about how film is able to incorporate and implement the larger cultural frameworks that it is heir to. For example, how does narrative editing function as a system of communication? Furthermore, as film develops, pursuing the aims of projects like art, nonfiction and narrative, it evolves new means of expression whose operation it is the task of film theorists to illuminate. At certain junctures, like the rise of direct cinema, the onset of new stylistic options precipitates a dialogue or dialectic with traditional forms of filmmaking that the theorist must unravel and clarify. Film does not have a unique destiny, set by its essential possibilities and limitations. But it does have a unique history as it is used to articulate the enterprises of twentieth century culture. And the rhyme and reason within that process is the topic of film theory.

VI. Postscript: Miscellaneous Arguments

Since this article was completed several arguments against the nonfiction film have come to my attention which I had not encountered before, or which I had forgotten. I would like to review three of the arguments briefly because they are much in use at present.

I will approach two of the arguments by examining a passage from Stephen Heath's influential, recent book *Questions of Cinema.* The quotation pertains to making historical nonfiction films. Heath believes it is an idealist fallacy if such films pretend to depict the past accurately. Historical nonfiction films cannot achieve such a goal (1) because they are trapped in hermeneutic circles – i.e., such films always perforce are locked in a present standpoint, trapped in the needs and concerns of the now which distorts while determining the picture of the past that such films masquerade as portraying truthfully – and (2) because such historical films are in fact merely constructions of the past. Heath writes:

What needs particularly to be emphasized here is that history in cinema is nowhere other than in representation, the terms of representing proposed, precisely the historical present of any film; no film is not a document of itself and of its actual situation in respect of the cinematic institution and of the complex of social institutions of representation. Which is to say that the automatic conjunction of film and history as-theme, as past to be shown today, the strategy for a cinema developed to recover 'popular memory,' is an idealist abstraction, an ideal of film and an ideal of history. The present of a film is always historical, just as history is always present – a fact of representation not a fact of the past, an elaboration of the presence of the past, a construction in the present, for today. . . .[24]

As I have already noted, there are at least two arguments in this dense passage. One of these holds that the researcher's point-of-view, rooted as it is in the present, blocks an accurate view of the past. This is an argument from selection of a type with which we are already familiar. Historians and filmmakers who make historical films select and interpret. They screen out certain facts and connect others. In doing this screening out, this selection and this interpretation, they are governed by the interests of the present. Thus, the films they give us are not replicas of the past but are perspectively skewed representations of the past, indelibly imprinted by the issues of the present. Moreover, we are ensnared in such views because we have no access to the past save through the optic of the present. The historical filmmaker offers theses about the past from the concerns of the present *and also* selects his evidence for these theses on the basis of the concerns of the present. Countervailing evidence, not sensitive to present concerns,

will be overlooked. We cannot accurately retrieve the past. We are frozen in the present and our historical films really reflect contemporary preoccupations more than anything else.

The first point to be made against this mode of argumentation is that historical films are not supposed to be replicas of the past. Indeed, what it would take to be a replica of the past is unclear. Would it have to be a representation of the past and past events depicted exactly as they were seen, experienced and cognized by peoples in the past? If so, then history clearly has little to do with such replicas. For history need not be restricted to the purview of the past. Just because the Allies at Versailles in 1919 failed to foresee the consequences of the stern terms of the treaty does not mean that a nonfiction filmmaker should not make the appropriate causal connections in his cinematic account of the rise of the Third Reich. In fact we might even want to argue that historical films – as opposed to mere records – in general are expected to connect past events and actions to consequences that the historical agents who performed the actions were often unaware of. History – as opposed to chronicling – is about making connections between events and in many cases the later events being connected to earlier events are unbeknownst to the historical actors. This doesn't disqualify a film as accurate history even if the film is not a mysterious something called a replica.

If history is a matter of making connections between events and if often earlier events are connected to events in the present, we have still not shown that historical films are necessarily mired in the epistemologically suspect present. For even if past events are selected and combined with other events in line with present concerns, it is not the case that the claims made by histories and historical films are *substantiated* on the grounds that they satisfy present preoccupations. Whatever causal connections or threads of events that a historical film purports *must be supported by evidence*. Satisfying the needs of the present, that is, does not warrant a historical claim. Only evidence will support whatever claims a historical film makes. Nor is it true that the only evidence available to us is the evidence that we will select because of our present interests. For even if on our own we could only find such evidence as our present needs and concerns guide us to, there is nevertheless a vast accumulation of unavoidable evidence that has been bequeathed to us by past generations of historians whose "present" interests led them to amass the many details that our historical accounts – filmed or written – must gibe with. (Moreover, I must also object – hermeneutic circles notwithstanding – that it is possible for researchers to imaginatively transcend their ties to the present to conceive of the past from alternative viewpoints – both those of different times and of different cultures).

The second argument found in the Heath passage does not apply only to historical films but to nonfictions in general. Films are said to be constructions, specifically representations. Within contemporary film theory, this, in combination with the fact that such representations do not internally acknowledge their status as constructions entails that a film is a deception. A nonfiction film of this sort necessarily could not be objective because it is necessarily a lie. That is, nonfiction films that do not acknowledge that they are constructions *thereby* mask the fact that they are constructions. This is thought to be a deception that amounts to falsification.

Though this argument is very popular among contemporary film theorists, it is somewhat obscure. All films including nonfiction films are seen as falsifications unless they acknowledge that they are constructions by means of representations internal to the film (in the manner of the Godardian avant-garde). What does this mean? All films are constructions, it is said. "Constructions," one asks, "rather than what?" One

answer is: "rather than the very events – historical or otherwise – that the film represents." Of course, this is true. Indeed, it is so obvious that one wonders why the point has to be made – acknowledged – within the film itself. Often nonfiction films do, in fact, refer to the process of production which resulted in the film we are seeing – e.g., the arduous trip to such and such a mountain village is underscored. But even where this does not occur, wouldn't things like the title credits, advertisements, reviews, etc. tell normal viewers (as if they normally needed to be told) that the nonfiction films in question are constructions? Why, that is, is it necessary to represent or to acknowledge the process of the film's construction within the film itself? It simply is not the case – as some film theorists might hold – that viewers take films without such acknowledgments to be something other than constructions. And, as I have already pointed out, such films conventionally announce they are the construction of a team of filmmakers – who employed processes of production like editing – by means of the credits.

When many contemporary film theorists, like Heath, refer to a film as a construction or a production, they have in mind not that most films have been produced by a team of filmmakers – a fact the films supposedly mask and which must be reflexively revealed – but that films are constructed by spectators who make sense out of the films. Sometimes this process of making sense is called suture.[25] This suturing is unacknowledged or not represented within the film. Consequently, it is thought that this aspect of the film's construction is hidden from the spectator. Again, the charges of deception and falsification loom. The spectator thinks the film makes sense when in fact the spectator makes (or constructs) sense out of the film. An edited nonfiction film like *Turksib* is constructed by the spectator comprehending the meaning of and making connections between the shots in the film. However, the film does not acknowledge that the spectator is performing this operation. Therefore, the film lies, deceptively masking that it is a construction. The film's veracity is called into question because the film does not remind the spectator – through some process of representation internal to the film – that he is deciphering the meaning of the film.

This argument seems to rely on a false dichotomy, viz., either the film constructs its meaning, or the spectator does. It is also assumed that if the spectator's interpretive activity, his suturing, is not emphasized by the film, then the film deceptively insinuates that the film, not the spectator, is constructing its meaning. But clearly it is inappropriate to hold that there is a univocal sense to the phrase "construct meaning" such that we must decide a competition between mutually exclusive alternatives such as "either films or spectators construct meaning, but not both." A film is meaningful, intelligible, etc. in virtue of its structure. That is, the arrangement of its materials determines whether it has successfully "constructed meaning" in what we can think of as the *message* sense of that phrase. The spectator, in turn, in response to the film might be said to "construct meaning" where this signifies the operation of a cognitive process. We might call this the *message-uptake* sense of the phrase. Thus, it is compatible for the film to appear meaningful – to be the source of meaning – while it remains for a spectator to impute meaning to the film by mobilizing a cognitive process. That the film is meaningfully structured does neither preclude nor hide the fact that a spectator actively derives meaning from the film, i.e., "constructs meaning" (according to this mode of speaking). And surely every spectator knows that meaning in the sense of the spectator's recognition of meaning (i.e., message-uptake) requires a spectator's discerning and comprehending the structure of a film. That is, "the construction of meaning," where that refers to the *experience* –

via cognitive processing – of intelligibility, obviously has a spectator's portion. So why must this be acknowledged within the film? Moreover, the legitimate though different and compatible sense of "meaning construction" (the *message* sense), which refers to the structure or arrangement of a film's materials, does not imply that the spectator's cognitive processing of meaning is in any way effaced or hidden.

I was reminded of the final argument against nonfiction film while watching the recent movie *Lianna* by writer-director John Sayles. In this film, there is a portrayal of a college cinema class, circa, it seems to me, 1970. The lecturer repeats a point that was a popular slogan in regard to documentary film in the sixties and early seventies. He notes that quantum physicists discovered that by observing sub-atomic events they changed the course of the events they were studying by introducing unforeseen but necessary disturbances into the situation. Science shows, the lecturer in *Lianna* claims, that observation always alters the situation it strives to capture objectively. This generalization is then applied to film. Once a camera is introduced into a situation, the situation changes. People begin to behave for the camera, for example. Thus, the principle that rules the observation of the atom applies equally to the act of filming humans. No film can be objective – i.e., can render an event as it is typically, sans camera – because filming always changes events. This is, moreover, just one instance of a law that applies to every aspect and order of being in the physical universe. Observation must alter the behavior of whatever is observed.

This argument dubiously assumes that whatever holds as a matter of law at the sub-atomic level applies to every level and mode of experience. Therefore, since our presence can be felt drastically on the atomic level, it is hypothesized that it is also always felt drastically on the macroscopic level. In fact, however, the presence of an observer has little palpable physical effect at all on the macroscopic level. But this is not the most damning point to raise about the argument. For the argument proceeds by extrapolating from the *physical* effect of observation on an atom to a putative *behavioral* effect that a camera has on the people it films. But even if a camera did have some almost undetectable physical influence on every object in its vicinity, it need not have an influence on every person it films. The camera may be very far away or hidden, so that its subjects are unaware that it is observing them. Thus, it has no behavioral repercussions. Or perhaps the subject of the camera is habituated to the camera's presence and the subject acts naturally as a result. Maybe the subject is emotionally carried away and just doesn't modify his behavior because he doesn't care that the camera is nearby. These and hundreds of other reasons can be offered to show that in many cases the presence of an observing camera does not necessarily change the event from the way it would have been had the camera been absent. Nor can the discovery of the physical effects of observation on particles in quantum mechanics be used to support this claim. For even if the presence of the camera resulted in some physical changes in the situation, two adulterous lovers unaware of the private eye across the alleyway will not change their behavior despite the fact that a battery of cameras is pointed their way. I am not denying that the presence of a camera in a situation might change it. I am denying both that the presence of a camera must necessarily change a situation at the level of human behavior and that the claim that cameras must change human behavior can be gleaned from discoveries of the physical effects of observation upon atoms.

Notes

1. This argument was made from the floor at the conference, "Film, the False Sociology," at New York University, 1980.

2. Michael Ryan, "Militant Documentary: Mai-68 Par Lui," in *Ciné-tracts*, no. 7/8. On pages 18–19 Ryan writes

What *Mai 68* demonstrates is that even 'natural' life is highly technological, conventional and institutional. Its content and form is determined by the technology of language and symbolic representation. The so-called natural world of *Mai 68* is as much a construct as any fictional object.

For example, the various actions of the different groups involved in the events – workers, students, police, union hacks, etc. – all fall back upon what can be called a 'scenario,' that is, highly over-determined set of conscious and unconscious prescriptions, inscribed in language, modes of behaviour, forms of thought, role models, clothing, moral codes, etc., which give rise to and mark out the limits of what happened and what would have happened in May 1968. There was an unwritten rule that the students would not use arms. Likewise, the workers could not storm the National Assembly. Otherwise, the rule forbidding the police from mowing them all down would have been legitimately forgotten. The homes of the bourgeoise were not to be broken into. The battle was to be limited to the streets and the factories, the prescribed scenes of revolution. The city was not to be set on fire. . . .

Limits on action are determined by, among other things, role-giving concepts. The concept (in conjunction with the reality) "police" determines the behaviour of the men hired to carry out that epithet. . . .

The role of 'fictional' constructs in determining 'real' history is not clear in terms of institutions and of language. . . .

The events of *Mai 68* then, even if they can, *à la limite,* be called a real referent, are themselves constituted as a play of representations. They are real, but not 'natural' and uncontrived. History, but a history which is constructed. At the limit of nonfiction is another form of fiction, just as the goal or limit of fiction (in film) is a seemingly nonfictionalized event. . . .

My point, then, is that the presence of real history and objective fact which documentary supposedly renders is itself comprised of and constituted by representations. Fictional representation is shown to be historical. This would be the gesture of reducing fictional film to documentary. It is the Marxist ideology-critical moment of the analysis. The deconstructive equivalent of this moment is to show that the supposedly natural referent of non-fictional film can be itself described as a kind of fiction, a complex set of presentations – political, social, institutional, conceptual, physical, linguistic – whose reference one to the other in history is open-ended.

3. Christian Metz, "The Imaginary Signifier," *Screen,* Vol. 16, no. 2 (Summer 1975). On page 47, he writes "At the theater Sarah Bernhardt may tell me she is Phedre or if the play were from another period and rejected the figurative regime, she might say, as in a type of modern theater, that she is Sarah Bernhardt. But at any rate, I should see Sarah Bernhardt. At the cinema she could make two kinds of speeches too, but it would be her shadow that would be offering them to me (or she would be offering them in her own absence). Every film is a fiction film."

4. Richard Meran Barsam attributes this view to Andrew Sarris in *Nonfiction Film: A Critical History* (New York: E. P. Dutton and Co., 1973).

5. Michael Ryan, "Militant Documentary."

Derrida's concept of *différance* holds that two polar opposites when examined closely, deconstructed, reveal traces of each other such that the dichotomy collapses as the terms become each other (or manifest elements of each other). This is a function of the common origin of the terms. In *Of Grammatology,* Derrida writes "This common root, which is not a root but the concealment of the origin and which is not common because it does not amount to the same thing except with the unmonotonous insistence of difference, this unnameable movement of *difference-itself,* that I have strategically nicknamed *trace, reserve* or *différance,* could be called writing only within the historical closure, that is to say within the limits of science and philosophy." Jacques Derrida, *Of Grammatology,* trans. Gayati Chakravorty Spivak (Baltimore: Johns Hopkins University Press, 1974), p. 93. In *Positions,* Derrida defines *différance* as "a structure and a movement which cannot be conceived on the basis of the opposition presence/absence. *Différance* is the systematic play of differences, of the *spacing* (*espacement*) by which elements refer to one another."

Ryan wants to use this concept and the method of deconstruction to show that fiction films blur into nonfiction and vice-versa. See the last paragraph of note 2.

6. See *Grierson on Documentary,* edited by Forsyth Hardy (London: Faber and Faber, 1979).

7. Dziga Vertov, "Selected Writings," in *Avant-Garde Film,* edited by P. Adams Sitney (New York: New York University Press, 1978). On page 5, Vertov writes "My road is toward the creation of a fresh perception of the world. Thus, I decipher in a new way the world unknown to you."

8. Frederick Wiseman, an interview in *The New Documentary in Action,* by Alan Rosenthal (Berkeley: University of California Press, 1977), p. 70.

9. Erik Barnouw, *Documentary* (New York: Oxford University Press, 1974), pp. 287–288.

10. See for example Peter Graham, "Cinema Verité in France, *Film Quarterly,* 17 (Summer, 1964); Colin Young, "Cinema of Common Sense," *Film Quarterly* 17 (Summer, 1964); Young, "Observational Cinema" in *Principles of Visual Anthropology,* edited by Paul Hockings (The Hague: Mouton Publishers, 1975). In these articles the authors, though arguing that film is necessarily subjective, do not turn this into a rejection of the prospects of documentary filmmaking.

11. Bela Balazs, *Theory of Film* (New York: Dover Publications, 1970), pp. 89–90.

12. Lucien Goldman, "Cinema and Sociology," in *Anthropology – Reality – Cinema,* edited my Mick Eaton (London: British Film Institute, 1979), p. 64.

13. A somewhat similar, though not identical, concept of indexing is used in regard to artworks in "Piece: Contra Aesthetics" by Timothy Binkley in *Philosophy Looks at the Arts,* edited by Joseph Margolis (Philadelphia: Temple University Press, 1978).

14. The idea of segments of possible worlds derives from Nicholas Wolterstorff, "Worlds of Works of Art," *Journal of Aesthetics and Art Criticism* 35 (1976).

15. I recommend that film theorists use a narrower sense of ideology than they presently use. I would call an assertion – like "Those who are unemployed have only their own laziness to blame for their problems" – ideological when (1) it is false and (2) it is used to support some relation of social domination or oppression. Film theorists, of course, also want to describe entire symbol systems – like cinema or language – as ideological. Such systems are not true or false. But *if* an entire symbol system could be

characterized as ideological, I think it would be because it (1) excludes or represses the representation of certain social facts or relations and (2) is used to support social oppression in virtue of the exclusions it entails.

Some Marxists have also disapproved of the global concept of ideology used by film theorists. In their criticisms of the Althusserian tendencies of *Screen,* Kevin McDonnell and Kevin Robins write that ideology should become "a less total phenomenon than it is for Althusserians who identify it with the cultural or symbolic as a whole. We take ideology to be an *abstract* concept, referring only to the fetishised forms assumed by thought which uncritically confronts the necessary constraints of capitalist social reality. . . ." in "Marxist Cultural Theory" in *One Dimensional Marxism* (London: Allison and Busby Limited, 1980), p. 167. Though I disagree with much of McDonnell and Robins's position, I think their consternation with the reigning, inflated idea of ideology is correct.

Since the completion of this essay I have discovered another voice raised against the bloated concept of ideology used by film theorists – Terry Lovell, *Pictures of Reality* (London: British Film Institute, 1980). Like McDonnell and Robins, Lovell is a Marxist who is attacking the Althusserian mandarins of British film theory – apparently a sport of gaining popularity in England. Lovell's book is a mixed blessing. The account of trends in philosophy of science is not only turgid and questionably metaphoric but inept and riddled with error. For example, the definition of induction offered on page 11 is philosophically incorrect. On the other hand, Lovell has some salutary things to say about ideology. Lovell argues that ideology "may be defined as the production and dissemination of erroneous beliefs whose inadequacies are socially motivated." (page 51) Lovell also provides a useful service by showing that this conceptions of ideology dictates the form that ideological analysis should take, one which is reflected in Marx's method.

"To establish that a given body of ideas or theory serve class interests is always insufficient to justify the label ideology. It is always necessary *first* to apply epistemological criteria to evaluate the work. . . . The common practice of discrediting ideas by reference to their social origin is not what is meant by this critique. Questions of validity are always involved. We can learn a good deal here from Marx's own practice. His procedure is to first of all establish by theoretical analysis, argument and evidence, an account of whatever is in contention. He then goes on to show precisely in which respects a rival theory falls short of explanatory power. Only then does he attempt to relate those specific errors to class alignments and the class struggle. An example of this method is to be found in Vol. III of *Capital* where he considers the evidence given by bankers in the *Report of the Committee on Bank Acts of 1857.* He assesses this evidence in terms of its internal inconsistencies, and its theoretical and empirical inadequacies. He then goes on to argue that these views are to be expected from bankers within that structure of social relations because of the form which social relations take in general under capitalism, and because of the particular position of bankers within that structure of social relations and the interests which that position generates. His argument is, in effect, 'this is indeed how money and banking *would appear* to people so situated, and these are the categories they *would require* in their day-to-day conduct of their business activities. . . .' This procedure is exemplary, but is seldom followed by people wishing to explore the ideological underpinnings of their opponents' thoughts."

It is to be hoped that this invocation of the master will shame Ciné-Marxists into adopting a more rigorous approach to the analysis of ideology than the guilt-by-association (usually free association) tactics that are so prevalent nowadays.

In my own writings I have sometimes used a looser, Leninist concept of ideology in which "ideological" is interchangeable with "political." This is an acceptable, common usage. Under this variant, a Marxist might speak of "the communist ideology." Nevertheless, I think that the sense of ideology outlined in the preceding paragraphs is the most fundamental and correct. It is probably best to keep the critical edge to the concept. One should, therefore, announce that one is using the Leninist concept when one adopts it in an analysis.

16. Monroe C. Beardsley, *The Possibility of Criticism* (Detroit: Wayne State University Press, 1970).

17. In *Realism and the Cinema,* edited by Christopher Williams (London: Routledge and Kegan Paul, 1980), p. 226.

18. See especially vol. I of André Bazin's *What Is Cinema?* translated and edited by Hugh Gray (Berkeley: University of California Press, 1967).

19. "The World Viewed," *Georgia Review* (Winter 1974).

20. According to Eric Rhode in "Why Neo-Realism Failed," *Sight and Sound,* 30 (Winter 1960/61).

21. Monroe C. Beardsley, *Aesthetics* (New York: Harcourt, Brace and World, 1958), especially Chapter VI, section 16. Also see Göran Hermerén, *Representation and Meaning in the Visual Arts* (Lund: Scandinavian University Books, 1969) especially Chapter II.

22. *Op. cit.*

23. In *Cinema Vérité in America* (Boston: MIT Press, 1974), Stephen Mamber writes "Cinema verite adopts Renoir's idea of the camera and uses it as a recording tool, so that the events themselves, 'the knowledge of man,' become the standard we use to judge the film." (p. 18).

24. Stephen Heath, *Questions of Cinema* (Bloomington: Indiana University Press, 1981), pp. 237–238.

25. For analysis and criticisms of the concept of suture, see Noël Carroll, "Address to the Heathen," *October,* no. 23 (Winter 1982), sections IV and VI.

I

Let me begin by commenting on some points Carol Brownson makes that I think are correct and which have helped me to clarify for myself the nature of my own project. She says, "Rather than giving a partial definition of nonfiction, he has described a reasonable and respectable standard of evaluation applicable to films that lay claim to objectivity. . . ." I think Brownson is right that I should steer clear of attempting to define nonfiction for the very reason that it is not a homogeneous class of things but a bunch of things lumped together only because they are not fictions.

In my paper, I really had in mind using nonfiction as a label for all sorts of *films of purported fact* – historical films, anthropological films, films of current events, etc. I wanted to say, contrary to many contemporary theorists, that such films of purported fact can be objective as well as having certain other features in common – e.g., reference to the actual world. But I made these points by speaking as though nonfiction film was an essentially unified class, when it is not. I should have made my points by saying "historical films can be objective," "anthropological films can be objective," "sociological films can be objective," etc. rather than by speaking of nonfiction films *tout court*. My argument is really that films of putative fact can be objective and not that everything that is not fiction has some epistemic standard of evaluation – Ernie Gehr's *Serene*

Velocity is not fiction but it does not have an accompanying set of standards for epistemic evaluation. Throughout the essay, I generally use "nonfiction" to refer to various genres of films of putative fact (journalistic reports, historical films etc.). But at times I slip into talk of a homogeneous genre of nonfiction films which I suggest that I can partially define, when, indeed, all I actually should be claiming is that films of putative fact can be adjudged objective in terms of the prevailing standards of epistemic evaluation of the types of knowledge claims that the films that make said knowledge claims present. Also I am making the related generalization that this "genre" of nonfiction films makes reference to the world. Brownson's remarks on my confusions here are very useful.

On the other hand, I have great difficulty understanding Brownson's points about objectivity. She urges us to drop the objectivity/subjectivity dichotomy in discussing documentary film but never really explains why we should do this. She suggests that I have redefined the concept of objectivity in terms of adherence to intersubjectively assessable practices of reasoning and evidence gathering. But I am not sure that I have introduced a new meaning of "objectivity." Admittedly I do not mean by "objectivity" "self-evident certainty." But nor do many contemporary theorists. The contemporary concept of objectivity, dating back to Peirce and Husserl, it seems to me, centers on the notion of intersubjective validation. I haven't redefined "objectivity" but have employed one major prevailing conception of it.

Brownson also thinks that I am wrong in thinking that most commentators who conclude that film is necessarily subjective are restricting their arguments to film. She holds that indeed such commentators believe more broadly that all knowledge claims are subjective. There is no way to finally adjudicate this controversy save by counting cases. But in my favor I would point out that many of the theorists who hold that nonfiction films are subjective are Marxists. And Marxists, one supposes, can't hold that all knowledge claims are subjective insofar as their theory is proposed as being scientifically and objectively verifiable.

Much of Brownson's discussion of objectivity is preoccupied with sketching two arguments (that ultimately collapse into one) that she thinks might be leading commentators to claim that the nonfiction film is subjective. These, moreover, are arguments that I failed to foreclose. Both these arguments have as their crucial premise the notion that language is subjective. Thus, insofar as film is language-like, it too is always subjective.

Frankly, neither of the arguments persuade me, specifically because I do not know what to make of the idea that "language is subjective." Language is a shared tool of a cultural community. A language does not exist solely in an individual's mind. Indeed Wittgenstein has proven that a private language is impossible. What could it mean to say that language is subjective other than that it is in the province of a single consciousness? Indeed, I doubt the idea that language is subjective can be intelligibly interpreted. Thus, I do not believe that either of the arguments that Brownson invents are available for film theorists since both require the either unintelligible or impossible proposition that language is subjective.

The first argument states that since films do not mechanically mirror reality, they are intensional. If they are intensional, they are language-like. If they are language-like, they are subjective. I have already rejected the last proposition in this series as unintelligible. But I don't understand the earlier parts of the argument either. I am not sure that the fact that films don't automatically "mirror" reality shows they are "intensional." Indeed, I am not sure that I understand the meaning of the word "intensional" here. Is it that films must be understood as somehow analogous to referentially opaque contexts. But why? Don't some film images warrant inferences about things in front of the camera? What does the fact that the camera lens has to be adjusted – i.e., that the camera does not operate entirely automatically but requires some human manipulation – have to do with whether or not the reference of the shot is referentially transparent or opaque?

Brownson takes the supposed intensional dimension of film to support the claim that it is language-like. This seems to be very slim grounds for accepting a language/film analogy. And, of course, even if we do accept the language/film analogy, I doubt that sense can be made of the claim that language is subjective.

Brownson's second argument charges that I attribute too simplistic an error to those who believe that films have points-of-view. I argue that theorists are led to this belief either by equivocations on the concept of "point-of-view," or through a fallacy of composition – every shot has a literal p.o.v., therefore, the film as a whole has a viewpoint. Against my accusation of equivocation, she says that the different applications of the concept of point-of-view are related by metaphoric expansion. I agree. Indeed, some of the expansions are very nice metaphors. But what difference does this make? One can still not jump inferentially from a literal to a metaphoric sense of "point-of-view" and act as though one is still speaking univocally.

In answer to my argument that theorists commit a fallacy of composition when they move from the literal p.o.v. of the shot to the claim that the film as a whole has a personal vision, Carol Brownson suggests I have misconstrued what theorists really have in mind. They actually hold her first argument – films are not mechanical; thus, they are language-like; thus they are subjective because language is subjective. Again I think that the latter claim is unintelligible. I have rejected the claim that films are significantly language-like elsewhere as have other theorists.[1] And lastly, I think it is a mistake to treat "mechanical" and "language-like" as logical contraries that exclusively carve up the field of inquiry.

Brownson criticizes my approach because I do not allow for gentle criticism in cases such as *The Graduate* where the character is going in the wrong direction on the Golden Gate Bridge. I am tempted to respond that in the fictional world of *The Graduate* the relation between the fictional Berkeley and the fictional San Francisco is opposite that customarily experienced by California drivers.

Finally, Brownson seems worried that my way of treating the distinction between fiction and nonfiction suggests an endorsement of a cleavage between pleasure and knowledge. I don't see why she fears this. At several points in the essay I make clear that I do not believe that nonfiction writing and nonfiction film must eschew aesthetic ornamentation and elaboration.

II

One of Jack Wolf's biggest problems with my paper is his fear that I give film producers too much authority when I assign them full responsibility for indexing films as "nonfictional." At this point, Wolf complains "I do not agree with Carroll's position that the label of the producer is the one and only criterion acceptable for determining the category of [a] film. If the producer says the product is true to 'actual reality' and it is demonstrably false to that 'actual reality,' then it is fiction, an untruth, and the label should be rejected." Jack Wolf's dissatisfactions in this matter, I believe, underwrite the reservations he voices to my approach throughout his response. But I am not so sure that there is an outright disagreement between us rather than simply a misunderstanding.

Wolf uses the terms "fiction" and "nonfiction" differently than I advocate. For him "fiction" = "false" or "untrue," while "non-

fiction" = "true." Thus, he is worried that a producer empowered to index a film as nonfiction is being licensed to declare the film "true," as if merely saying something is so could make it so. Wolf says if we can show the film is false, then it is fiction – no matter how the producer indexes it.

But I do not correlate nonfiction with the truth, nor do I believe that it is advisable to equate fiction with falsity. It is not false that Scarlet O'Hara lived on a plantation called Tara. It is only – well – fictional. Nor does the fact that *Chariot of the Gods* is nonfiction make it true. It only makes *Chariot of the Gods* a candidate for evaluation in terms of literal truth or falsity – something the proposition "Scarlet O'Hara lived on Tara" is not.

We can call the use of the fiction/nonfiction dichotomy to commend or to disparage items as true or false the normative sense of the dichotomy. That is, it honors or ranks or grades the true and the false by means of the appellations "fiction" and "nonfiction." Throughout his comments Wolf has the normative use of these terms in mind. And given this he is upset because he thinks that I am giving filmmakers the right to establish that their films are true no matter what the rest of us clearly know the facts to be. Certainly Wolf is correct to reject such a prospect. But I don't think that my paper opens this particular Pandora's Box.

For I do not use the fiction/nonfiction distinction in the normative sense. I do not think that in indexing a film as nonfiction the filmmaker declares that it is true but only that it is to be evaluated against the standards of truthfulness. Indeed, when measured against those standards, a film that has been indexed as nonfiction may turn out to be false. At that point, moreover, I am not disposed to re-label the film as "fiction" as proponents of the normative usage might. I am contented to say simply that the film is false.

I would identify my use of the nonfiction/fiction distinction as classificatory not normative. To index something as fictional classifies it as belonging to a category of things to which truth and falsity do not pertain. In saying something is fictional I no more mean to chastise the film for being false than I mean to commend the truthfulness of other things by calling them "nonfiction." "Nonfiction" only signals membership in the class of things to which standards of truth or falsity can be applied; the badge, "nonfiction," does not prejudge the outcome of such appraisals.

If Jack Wolf were to review my approach with the recognition that I use the nonfiction/fiction distinction in the classificatory and not the normative sense, I think he might withdraw some of his objections. For, of course, I agree with him that it is utterly absurd to believe that a filmmaker can establish the truth of a documentary simply by asserting that it is true (or by saying it is "nonfictional," where this, inadvisably, is regarded as synonymous with "true").

Note

1. Noel Carroll, "Toward a Theory of Film Editing," *Millennium Film Journal,* no. 3 (1979). Also see Christian Metz, *Film Language* (New York: Oxford University Press, 1974). "Toward a Theory of Film Editing" is reprinted in this volume.

PART IV

Ideology

The birth and growth of the institution of film studies in the United States is coeval with the cultural revolution of the sixties and its vicissitudes. Many graduate students of my generation developed their passion for film and their passion for radical politics simultaneously. Understandably, they sought to fuse these two passions into one. This was undoubtedly abetted by their conviction that everything is political, and, in any case, the proposition that film has some ideological implications would appear hard to deny no matter what one's political stripe. As a result, ideological analysis, of which feminist analysis is a major subdivision, has dominated film theory for over two decades.

The view that still prevails in most graduate departments of film is that the ideological operation of film is best conceived in functionalist terms where the ideological function of film is to position or to construct or to suture subjects (and where the instantiation of the so-called male gaze is also a case of subject positioning). Psychoanalysis has been the preferred vocabulary for describing these processes. Under this dispensation, film structures – from the perspectival image, narration, and point-of-view editing to the very conditions of film projection – are psychoanalyzed to show how each triggers a series of psychological processes that culminate in the positioning of viewers as subjects for the purpose of oppressive social systems like capitalism and patriarchy.

As I have argued elsewhere at length,[1] contemporary film theory has, like medium-specificity theory, tended to be totalizing. Where earlier theorists spoke of the essence of cinema, contemporary film theorists think of film in terms of a central function or role, viz., the propagation of ideology through subject positioning. And where earlier theorists referred all their analyses back to the unique nature of the medium, contemporary theorists refer every analysis of a device or cinematic structure back to the ideological function of cinema. Indeed, contemporary film theorists tend to append the same scenarios about subject positioning to every filmic device, imbuing their theory with a great deal of unity, if not monotony.

Contemporary film theorists argue, in effect, that film – at the level of its structures of articulation – is inherently ideological, irrespective of narrative, imagistic or thematic content. If the Russians argued that film was essentially montage, contemporary film theorists maintain that film is essentially ideological, which, for them, means that film form intrinsically possesses an ideological content which is to be unpacked in the light of the laws of subject positioning. Film theory becomes a matter of showing the way in which each cinematic device or structure exemplifies the laws or universal pattern of subject positioning. And this yields a singular theory of film, since every cinematic device is subsumed under the same patent of subject construction.

I have never been a friend of subject position theory. One reason for this is that I have never been convinced that film form is *inherently* ideological. I remain wedded to the view that ideology is not a matter of form, but of content. I find it paradoxical to court the proposition that film form is intrinsically ideological, since I believe that it is evident that there are some films which are not ideologically pernicious, but whose formal structures and devices are congruent with films that are ideologically pernicious. But this would be impossible if films were ideological at the level of formal articulation.

Nor, though I am a child of the sixties, am

I persuaded by the slogan that everything is political. What I think the sixties may have taught us is that it is always prudent to consider whether politics is playing a role behind the scenes. But this is consistent with the finding that once we investigate for subterranean political machinations, we may discover none. One cannot simply define everything to be political. Some things are political as a matter of fact; some are not. You have to look and see. And I think that if you look and see, you will find that it is vastly implausible to believe that cinematic structures, like point-of-view editing, are inherently or intrinsically ideological. The use of point-of-view editing in a particular film may serve ideological purposes. But the structure itself is ideologically neutral.

I reject the notion that film forms are inherently or essentially ideological as I earlier rejected the notion that certain devices of film were essentially cinematic, and I reject the totalizing theoretical approaches which each of these parallel prejudices encourage. However, I would not wish to deny the obvious fact that films in particular and moving images in general are frequently involved in the dissemination of ideology and that explaining the ways in which films, indeed many films, can play this role is a legitimate theoretical ambition. However, I regard this type of theorizing as best pursued in a piecemeal fashion, attempting to isolate the structures that facilitate the dissemination of ideology in film and analyzing the way in which they work. The essays in this section are meant to initiate ways of analyzing *some* of the strategies that account for the ideological effects of film.[2]

In "The Image of Women in Film: A Defense of a Paradigm" I criticize one of the leading psychoanalytic accounts of the way in which sexism is advanced by the narrative cinema. But the essay is not merely negative. I also suggest how certain concepts from the contemporary theory of the emotions may be joined to the early-seventies idea of the image of women in film in order to provide a framework for talking about the ways in which films may promote sexism. One of my leading points in this essay is that, appearances notwithstanding, feminism need not be linked to psychoanalysis in order to interrogate cinema. Undoubtedly, psychoanalytic feminism may look like the only game in town. But there is no reason to suppose that a scholar cannot depart from reigning fashion and remain committed to feminism – at least in any politically meaningful sense of that term.

In "Film, Rhetoric, and Ideology," I summarize some of my objections to the dominant Althusserian-Lacanian model of political film theory. Rather than conceiving of film as inherently ideological, I consider the dissemination of ideology in film to be a matter of rhetoric, and I go on to isolate some of the rhetorical devices, such as the one I call the "narrative enthymeme," which I think explain how films dispense ideology. This essay, like the preceding one, is somewhat programmatic. But I hope that both essays at least suggest the plausibility of a piecemeal approach to the analysis of ideology and film.

Throughout my career as a film theorist, I have been denounced as a formalist. But if formalism is the doctrine that film has nothing to do with politics, then I cannot be thought to be an acolyte of that persuasion. For the articles in this section agree that film can be connected to politics and attempt to show that we can begin to theorize that connection. So I am not a formalist.

On the other hand, if one is putatively guilty of formalism if one does not believe that film is inherently political in its every aspect, then I suppose that since I think certain film devices are ideologically neutral, I could be called a formalist; though I would immediately want to add that this is an inflated and, I think, question-begging conception of formalism. For even if everything *might* be political, it remains to be shown that everything is political. That is as true of film as it is of interpersonal relations. And just as I believe that many aspects of our personal relations are not political, so I deny that every aspect of film is inevitably ideological.

In film studies, the charge of formalism is generally an exercise in political correctness. To call someone a formalist is to say they are politically incorrect. As I have already indicated, I do not think that I am a formalist because I acknowledge that film has political and ideological repercussions and that they can be studied theoretically. But I also do not believe that it is politically incorrect to analyze the operation of film metaphor without reference to its putatively inherent ideological implications. Metaphor in language can be used for ideological effect or not, and the same holds for film metaphor. To castigate or impugn a theorist for supposing this on what are alleged to be political grounds does nothing to help the oppressed, if that is one's aim. It only impedes the acquisition of knowledge about film.

Unfortunately, there is no area in academia that is more subject to the repressive reign of political correctness than film studies. In film studies, political correctness is wielded not only to suppress intellectual dissent, but to protect shaky thinking. To criticize Lacanian psychoanalysis or to question the statistical accuracy of certain general claims about the depiction of women in Hollywood film is to invite torrents of self-righteous political rage.

Theorists, it would appear, can say anything, no matter how preposterous, as long as they are perceived to be on the right side of the barricades. Thus, though I have attempted in this section to make theoretical contributions to the political analysis of film, I predict that I will be rebuked once again for being a formalist, since I am not perceived to belong to the right (academic) party. Perhaps the evidence will be that I complain about political correctness. But I confess that I find the prevailing political correctness in film studies intellectually self-serving, complacent, and smug. It not only inures the doctrines of the allegedly politically correct from criticism, it represses any original thinking on any terms that are not its own. It stamps out diversity in the name of difference. It is not a policy likely to promote the growth of understanding.

Notes

1. Noël Carroll, *Mystifying Movies* (Columbia University Press, 1988).
2. Though I hasten to add that these devices are not uniquely cinematic.

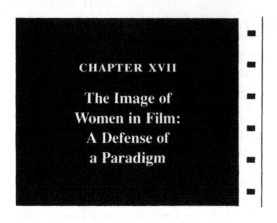

I. Introduction

Feminism is the most visible movement in film criticism today, and the most dominant trend in that movement is psychoanalytically informed. Psychoanalytic feminism came to this position in film studies at the very latest by the early to mid-eighties. Before the consolidation and ascendancy of this particular variety of feminism, earlier approaches to the study of women and film included the search for a suppressed canon of women filmmakers – a feminist version of the *auteur theory* – and the study of the image of women in films, primarily the image of women in films by men. Neither of these approaches mandated a reliance on psychoanalysis, though, of course, one could pursue these research programs while also embracing psychoanalysis.

My particular interest in this essay is to defend the study of the image of women in film, regarding that project as logically independent from the resort to psychoanalysis. In speaking of this approach to feminist film criticism, I have in mind writing on cinema from the early seventies like Molly Haskell's *From Reverence to Rape* which paralleled research in literary studies such as Kate Millett's *Sexual Politics*.

Work of this sort called to our attention the ways the imagery of women in our culture recurringly portrayed them through a limited, constraining, and ultimately oppressive repertory of characterizations. For example, in film, it was noted that very often the options for depicting were strongly structured by the dichotomy of the mother versus the whore. Insofar as the ways of representing women in popular media in some way influences or reinforces the way real women may be construed, the study of the recurrent imagery of women in film, especially where the relevant options were either impoverished and/or distorting, provided an inroad into one of the sources, or, at least, resources of sexism in the broader society.[1]

Clearly, the study of the image of women in film could proceed without commitment to psychoanalytic theory. However, that is not what happened. As a participant in the evolution of film theory and history, my own sense is that the project of studying the image of women in film was superseded by psychoanalysis due to a feeling that this project, as practiced by early feminists, suffered from being too naively empirical. It appeared to involve meandering from genre to genre, from period to period, and even from film to film, accumulating a mass of observations which however interesting, were also thought to be theoretically ragtag. Psychoanalysis, in contrast, provided a means to incorporate many of the scattered insights of the image of women in film approach (henceforth, generally called simply "the image approach"), while also sharpening the theoretical direction of feminist research. That is, psychoanalysis could provide not only a theoretical framework with which to organize many of the discoveries of the first wave of film feminism, but also a powerful program for further research.

This, of course, is not the whole story. Many film feminists were also interested in the origins and reinforcement of sexual difference in our culture, and in this respect, psychoanalysis, as a putative scientific discipline, had the advantage of having theories about this, albeit theories whose patriarchal biases would require modifications by feminists.

The purpose of this paper is to attempt to defend feminist film studies of the image of women in film approach, where that is understood as having no necessary commitment to psychoanalysis. In order to carry out this defense, I will try to sketch some of the shortcomings of the psychoanalytic model, but I will also attempt to indicate that the image approach can be supplied with a respectable theoretical basis drawn from the contemporary philosophy of the emotions. My strategy will be to consider psychoanalytic feminism and the image approach as potentially rival research programs; and I will try to show that the psychoanalytic approach has a number of liabilities which can be avoided by the image approach, while also attempting to show that the image of women in film model need not be thought of as irredeemably sunk in atheoretical naivete.[2]

The first section that follows will outline some of the shortcomings of psychoanalytic feminism in film studies, and the section that follows it will propose some theoretical credentials for the image of women in film model. I will not address the purported advantage of psychoanalysis to provide a theory of sexual differentiation. That would involve a discussion of the adequacy of psychoanalysis as a scientific theory of development, and I obviously do not have the space to enter that issue. Consequently, the objections I raise with respect to psychoanalytic-feminist film criticism will not depend on contesting the scientific pretensions of psychoanalysis, though I should add that I am very skeptical about them. Nevertheless, I shall try to restrict my objections to ones that can be adjudicated within the bounds of film theory.

Furthermore, I want to add that my opposition to the psychoanalytic model in feminist film criticism in no way implies either logically or as a matter of fact any opposition to feminism as such. The issue is between different models of feminist film criticism. I do not believe that an endorsement of feminism carries with it a theoretical commitment to psychoanalysis.

II. Mulvey, Psychoanalysis and Visual Pleasure

At present, as already indicated, it appears fair to say that the most active area in feminist film studies is psychoanalytic in orientation. Moreover, there are subtle differences and debates between the major, feminist-psychoanalytic film critics. As a result, it is impossible in a paper of this scale to chart all the positions that might be correctly identified as feminist-psychoanalytic film criticism, nor could one hope to develop objections to every variation in the field. Consequently, in this section of my paper, selectivity is unavoidable. Specifically, in developing my objections to psychoanalytic-feminism in contemporary film studies, I shall focus on Laura Mulvey's seminal essay "Visual Pleasure and Narrative Cinema."[3]

I have chosen this paper for several reasons. First, it can lay claim to being the inaugural polemic of feminist, psychoanalytic film criticism. Second, it is widely reprinted and widely taught. If someone knows just one essay of the psychoanalytic school, it is likely to be this one. And, even though many feminist film critics have registered objections to it and have tried to qualify and expand it, it remains perhaps the major introductory text to the field. One charge that might be made against my choice of this essay for scrutiny might be that it is somewhat dated in its specific claims. However, in response, I would maintain that many of the theoretical tendencies which I intend to criticize in Mulvey's essay continue to plague psychoanalytic film feminism, even in those cases where other psychoanalytically inclined feminists may explicitly wish to modify Mulvey's approach.[4]

The uncontroversial premise of Mulvey's essay is that the Hollywood cinema's success involves, undoubtedly among other things, the manipulation of the audience's visual pleasure. Moreover, Mulvey hypothesizes that the visual pleasure found in movies reflects patterns of visual fascination in the culture at large, a culture that is patriarchal. And she argues that it is important for feminists to identify those patterns of visual fascination, particularly in order to challenge them. Here it is useful to recall that Mulvey is a leading feminist filmmaker. So her meditations on the resources of visual pleasure in Hollywood film are explicitly motivated by an interest in developing a counter-cinema, one in which the patriarchal levers of visual fascination exercised by Hollywood will be subverted.

According to Mulvey, one place to look for a theoretical framework that will enable an interrogation of patterns of visual fascination is psychoanalysis. Psychoanalysis has a theory of visual pleasure or scopophilia; so it is at least a candidate for answering questions about cinematic visual pleasure. However, it must be noted that Mulvey's embrace of psychoanalysis seems to be unargued. Rather, she announces the need for theoretical vocabularies and generalizations, and then she endorses psychoanalysis simply because it has them. She does not ask whether there are rival theoretical frameworks to psychoanalysis which might also serve her purposes; she does not consider any problems concerning the scientific status of psychoanalysis; she does not weigh the shortcomings of psychoanalysis against the advantages of competing models. Her acceptance of psychoanalysis appears almost uncritically pragmatic: we need a theory of visual pleasure; psychoanalysis has one; so let's use it.

This unquestioning acceptance of the *scientific* authority of psychoanalysis is a continuing feature of epistemologically dubious merit in contemporary feminist film criticism.[5] Where psychoanalytic hypotheses are not marred by obvious sexism, psychoanalytic feminists tend to be willing to accept them without exploring their possible logical flaws, empirical shortcomings, or relative disadvantages with respect to other theoretical frameworks. In this, they follow Mulvey's lead. However, though I will not dwell on this issue now, I believe that this methodological oversight, in the opening moves of psychoanalytic-feminism, with respect to theory choice, compromises feminist-psychoanalytic film criticism fundamentally.[6]

From psychoanalysis, Mulvey inherits the observation that scopophilia is targeted at the human form. To this, then, she adds an empirical generalization, presumably one independent of psychoanalysis, that in film there is a division of labor in terms of the portrayal of the human form.[7] Men are characterized as active agents; women are objects of erotic contemplation – so many pin-ups or arrested images of beauty.

Women are passive; men are active. Men carry the narrative action forward; women are the stuff of ocular spectacle, there to serve as the locus of the male's desire to savor them visually. Indeed, Mulvey maintains, on screen, women in Hollywood films tend to slow down the narrative or arrest the action, since action must be frozen, for example, in order to pose female characters so as to afford the opportunity for their erotic contemplation. For example, a female icon, like Raquel Welch before some prehistoric terror, will be posed statue-like so that male viewers can appreciate her beauty. Backstage musical numbers are useful devices for accommodating this narrative exigency, since they allow the narrative to proceed – insofar as the narrative just involves putting on a show – while lavishing attention on the female form.

For Mulvey the female form in Hollywood film becomes a passive spectacle whose function is, first and foremost, to be seen. Here the relevant perceiving subject may be identified as the male viewer, and/or the male character, who, through devices like point-of-view editing, serves as the delegate, in the fiction, for the male audience member (who might be said to identify with the male character in point-of-view editing).[8] This idea may be stated in terms of saying that in Hollywood film, women are the object of the look or the gaze.

What appears to be meant by this is that scenes are blocked, paced, and staged, and the camera is set up relative to that blocking in order to maximize the display potential of the female form. Undoubtedly, as John Berger has argued, many of the schemata for staging the woman as a display object are inherited from the tradition of Western easel painting, where an elaborate scenography for presenting female beauty in frozen moments was developed.[9] Calling this scenography, which *does* function to facilitate male interests in erotic contemplation, "the look" or "the gaze," however, is somewhat misleading since it suggests that the agency is literally located in a perceiving subject, whereas it is literally articulated through blocking, pacing, and staging relative to the camera. What is true, nevertheless, is that this blocking, pacing and staging is governed by the aim of facilitating the male perceiving subject's erotic interests in the female form which could be said to be staged in a way that approximates maximally satisfying those interests. And it is in this sense – that the image of the woman in Hollywood film is constructed through scenography, blocking, pacing and so on in order to display her for male erotic contemplation – that feminist, psychoanalytic critics invoke when they say that the gaze in Hollywood film is masculine. Indeed, these practices of blocking and staging could be said to impose a male gaze on female spectators of Hollywood film, where that means that female spectators are presented with images of the female form that have been staged functionally in order to enhance male erotic appreciation of the female form. However, as already indicated, this is not simply a matter of camera positioning, and to the extent that talk of the look or the gaze

creates that impression, such terminology is unfortunate.

Women in Hollywood film are staged and blocked for the purpose of male erotic contemplation and pleasure. However, at this point, Mulvey hypothesizes that this pleasure for the male spectator is endangered. For the image of the woman, set out for erotic delectation, inevitably invokes castration anxieties in the male spectator. Contemplating the woman's body reminds the male spectator of her lack of a penis, which psychoanalysis tells us the male takes as a sign of castration, the vagina purportedly construed as a bloody wound. Unlike male characters in Hollywood cinema, whom Mulvey says make meaning, female characters are said to be bearers of meaning: specifically they signify sexual difference, which for the male spectator portends castration.

The male scopophiliac pleasure in the female form, secured by the staging techniques of Hollywood film and often channeled through male characters via point-of-view editing, is at risk in its very moment of success, since the presentation of the female form for contemplation heralds castration anxiety for the male viewer. The question, then, is how the Hollywood system is able to continue to deliver visual pleasure in the face of the threat of castration anxiety. Here, the general answer is derived from psychoanalysis, as was the animating problem of castration anxiety.

Two psychic strategies, indeed perversions, that may be adopted in order to come to terms with castration anxiety in general are fetishism and voyeurism. Similarly, Mulvey wants to argue that there are cinematic strategies that reflect these generic psychic strategies, and that their systematic mobilization in Hollywood films is what sustains the availability of visual pleasure – male scopophiliac pleasure – in the face of castration anxiety.

Fetishism outside of film involves the denial of the female's lack of a penis by, so to speak, fastening on some substitute object, like a woman's foot or shoe, that can stand for the missing penis. Mulvey thinks that in film the female form itself can be turned into a fetish object, a process of fetishization that can be amplified by turning the entire scenography and cinematic image into a fetish object; the elaborate visual compositions of Josef von Sternberg, in Mulvey's view, are an extreme example of a general strategy for containing castration anxiety by fetishization in the Hollywood cinema.

A second option for dealing with male castration anxiety in the context of male scopophilia, Mulvey contends, is voyeurism. Apparently, for Mulvey, this succeeds by re-enacting the original traumatic discovery of the supposed castration of the woman – though I must admit that I'm not completely clear on why re-enacting the original trauma would help in containing castration anxiety (is it like getting back on a horse after you've been thrown off of it?).

In any case, Mulvey writes:

The male unconscious has two avenues of escape from this castration anxiety: preoccupation with the re-enactment of the original trauma (investigating the woman, demystifying her mystery), counterbalanced by the devaluation, punishment, or saving the guilty object (an avenue typified by the concerns of the *film noir*); or else complete disavowal of castration by the substitution of a fetish object or turning the represented figure itself into a fetish so that it becomes reassuring rather than dangerous (hence over-valuation, the cult of the female star).[10]

If von Sternberg represents an extreme and clarifying instance of the general strategy of fetishization in Hollywood film, the radical instance of the voyeuristic strategy is located in the cinema of Alfred Hitchcock. Here, one finds cases like *Rear Window* which other commentators have often described in terms of voyeurism; moreover, Mulvey associates voyeurism with the urge for a sadistic assertion of control and the subjugation of the guilty. And here Hitch-

cock's *Vertigo* and *Marnie* come particularly to mind, films in which voyeuristic male characters set out to remake "guilty" women characters.

Needless to say, Mulvey's exemplification of the general strategies of fetishism and voyeurism by means of von Sternberg and Hitchcock is persuasive, at least rhetorically, for these are directors whom critics have long discussed in terms of fetishism and voyeurism, albeit using these concepts in a nontechnical sense. What Mulvey effectively did in her essay was to transform those critical terms into psychoanalytic ones, while also implying that cinematic fetishism and voyeurism, represented in the extreme cases of von Sternberg and Hitchcock, were the general strategies through which male visual pleasure in the cinema could be sustained, despite the impending threat of castration anxiety. And, as well, these cinematic strategies – if psychoanalysis is true – reflect patterns of visual fascination in patriarchal culture at large where visual pleasure in the female form depends on either turning her into an object or subjugating her by other means.

In summary, Mulvey situates the visual pleasure in Hollywood cinema in the satisfaction of the male's desire to contemplate the female form erotically. This contemplation itself is potentially unpleasureable, however, since contemplation of the female form raises the prospect of castration anxiety. Cinematic strategies corresponding to fetishism and voyeurism – and emblematized respectively by the practices of von Sternberg and Hitchcock – provide visual and narrative means to protect the structure of male visual pleasure, obsessively opting for cinematic conventions and schemata that are subordinated to the neurotic needs of the male ego. Feminist film practice of the sort Mulvey champions seeks to subvert the conventions that support the system of visual pleasure deployed in Hollywood filmmaking and to depose the hegemony of the male gaze.

I have no doubt that there are conventions of blocking and of posing actresses before the camera that are sexist and that alternative nonsexist styles of composition are worth pursuing. Moreover, as noted earlier, I will not challenge Mulvey's psychoanalytic presuppositions, though I believe that this can and ought to be done. For present purposes, the only comment that I will make about her invocation of psychoanalysis is that, as already noted, it does not seem methodologically sound. For even if psychoanalysis, or specific psychoanalytic hypotheses are genuine scientific conjectures, they need to be tested against countervailing hypotheses. Neither Mulvey nor any other contemporary psychoanalytic feminist has performed this rudimentary exercise of scientific and rational inquiry and, as a result, their theories are epistemically suspect.

Moreover, apart from her psychoanalytic commitments, Mulvey's theory of visual pleasure rests on some highly dubitable empirical suppositions. On Mulvey's account, male characters in cinema are active; females are passive, primarily functioning to be seen. She writes that a male movie star's glamorous characteristics are not those of an erotic object of the gaze.[11] It is hard to see how anyone could come to believe this. In our own time, we have Sylvester Stallone and Arnold Schwarzenegger whose star vehicles slow down and whose scenes are blocked and staged precisely to afford spectacles of bulging pectorals and other parts. Nor are these examples from contemporary film new developments in film history. Before Stallone, there were Steve Reeves and Charles Bronson, and before them, Johnny Weismuller. Indeed, the muscle-bound character of Maciste that Steve Reeves often played originated in the 1913 Italian spectacle *Cabiria*.

Nor is the baring of chests for erotic purposes solely the province of second-string male movie stars. Charlton Heston, Kirk Douglas, Burt Lancaster, Yul Brynner – the list could go on endlessly – all have a beefcake side to their star personae. Obviously, there are entire genres that celebrate male physiques, scantily robed, as sources of visual pleasure: biblical epics, ironically enough, as well as other forms of ancient and exotic epics; jungle films; sea-diving films; boxing films; Tarzan adventures; etc.

Nor are males simply ogled on screen for their bodily beauty. Some are renowned for their great facial good looks, for which the action is slowed down so that the audience may take a gander, often in "glamor" close-ups. One thinks of John Gilbert and Rudolph Valentino in the twenties; of the young Gary Cooper, John Wayne, Henry Fonda and Laurence Olivier in the thirties; of Gregory Peck in the forties; Montgomery Clift, Marlon Brando, and James Mason in the fifties; Peter O'Toole in the sixties; and so on.[12] Nor is it useful to suggest a constant correlation between male stars and effective activity. Leslie Howard in *Of Human Bondage* and *Gone with the Wind* seems to have succeeded most memorably as a matinee idol when he was staggeringly ineffectual.

If the dichotomy between male/active images versus female/passive images ill-suits the male half of the formula, it is also empirically misguided for the female half. Many of the great female stars were also great doers. Rosalind Russell in *His Girl Friday* and Katherine Hepburn in *Bringing Up Baby* hardly stop moving long enough to permit the kind of visual pleasure Mulvey asserts is the basis of the female image in Hollywood cinema. Moreover, it seems to me question-begging to say that audiences do not derive visual pleasure from these performances. Furthermore, if one complains here that my counterexamples are from comedies, and that certain kinds of comedies present special cases, let us argue about *The Perils of Pauline*.

After hypothesizing that visual pleasure in film is rooted in presenting the woman as passive spectacle through the agencies of conventional stylization, Mulvey claims that this project contains the seed of its own destruction, for it will raise castration anxieties in male spectators. Whether erotic contemplation of the female form elicits castration anxiety from male viewers is, I suppose, a psychoanalytic claim, and, as such, not immediately a subject for criticism in this essay. However, as we have seen, Mulvey goes on to say that the ways in which Hollywood film deals with this purported problem is through cinematic structures that allow the male spectator two particular avenues of escape: fetishism and voyeurism.

One wonders about the degree to which it is appropriate to describe even male viewers as either fetishists or voyeurs. Indeed, Allen Weiss has remarked that real-world fetishists and voyeurs would have little time for movies, preferring to lavish their attentions on actual boots and furs, on the one hand, and living apartment dwellers on the other.[13] Fetishism and voyeurism are literally perversions – involving regression and fixation at an earlier psychosexual stage – in the Freudian system, whereas deriving visual pleasure from movies would not, I take it, be considered a perversion, *ceteris paribus,* by practicing psychoanalysts. Mulvey can only be speaking of fetishism and voyeurism metaphorically.[14] But it is not clear, from the perspective of film theory, that these metaphors are particularly apt.

In general, the idea of voyeurism as a model for all film viewing does not suit the data. Voyeurs require unwary victims for their intrusive gaze. Films are made to be seen and film actors willingly put themselves on display, and the viewers know this. The fanzine industry could not exist otherwise. Mulvey claims that the conventions of Hollywood film give the spectators the illusion of looking in on a *private* world.[15] But what can be the operative force of *private* here? In what sense is the world of *The Longest Day* private rather than public? Surely the invasion of Normandy was public and it is represented as public in *The Longest Day.* Rather one suspects that the use of the concept of private in this context will turn

out, if it can be intelligibly specified at all, to be a question-begging dodge that makes it plausible to regard such events as the reenactment of the battle of Waterloo as a private event.

Also, Mulvey includes under the rubric of *voyeurism* the sadistic assertion of control and the punishment of the guilty. This will allow her to accommodate a lot more filmic material under the category of voyeurism than one might have originally thought that the concept could bear. But is Lee Marvin's punishment of Gloria Grahame in *The Big Heat* voyeurism? If one answers yes to this, mustn't one also admit that the notion of voyeurism has been expanded quite monumentally?

One is driven toward the same conclusions with respect to Mulvey's usage of the concept of fetishism. Extrapolating from the example of von Sternberg, any case of elaborate scenography is to be counted as a fetishization mobilized in order to deflect anxieties about castration. So the elaborate scenography of a solo song and dance number by a female star functions as a containing fetish for castration anxieties. But, then, what are we to make of the use of elaborate scenography in solo song and dance numbers by male stars? If they are fetishizations, what anxiety are they containing? Or, might not the elaborate scenography have some other function? And if it has some other function with respect to male stars, isn't that function something that should be considered as a candidate in a rival explanation of the function of elaborate scenography in the case of female stars?

In any case, is it plausible to suppose that elaborate composition generally has the function of containing castration anxiety? The multiple seduction jamboree in *Rules of the Game,* initiated by the playing of *Danse Macabre,* is one of the most elaborately composed sequences in film history. It is not about castration anxiety; it is positively priapic. Nor is it clear what textually motivated castration anxiety could underlie the immensely intricate scenography in the nightclub scene of Tati's *Play Time*. That is, there is elaborate scenography in scenes where it seems castration anxiety is not a plausible concern. Why should it function differently in other scenes? If the response is that castration anxiety is always an issue, the hypothesis appears uninformative.[16]

Grounding the contrast between fetishistic and voyeuristic strategies of visual pleasure in the contrast between von Sternberg and Hitchcock initially has a strong intuitive appeal because those filmmakers are, pre-theoretically, thought to be describable in these terms – indeed, they come pretty close to describing themselves and their interests that way. However, it is important to recall that when commentators speak this way, or even when Hitchcock himself speaks this way, the notions of voyeurism at issue are nontechnical.

Moreover, the important question is even if in some sense these two directors could be interpreted as representing a contrast between cinematic fetishism and voyeurism, does that opposition portend a systematic dichotomy that maps onto all Hollywood cinema?[17] Put bluntly, isn't there a great deal of visual pleasure in Hollywood cinema that doesn't fit into the categories of fetishism and voyeurism, even if those concepts are expanded, metaphorically and otherwise, in the way that Mulvey suggests? Among the things I have in mind here are not only the kind of counterexamples already advanced – male objects of erotic contemplation, female protagonists who are active and triumphant agents, spectacular scenes of the Normandy invasion that are difficult to connect to castration anxieties – but innumerable films that neither have elaborate scenography nor involve male characters as voyeurs, nor subject women characters to male subjugation in a demonstration of sadistic control. One film to start to think about here might be Arthur Penn's *The Miracle Worker* for which Patty Duke (Astin) received an Academy Award. (After

all, a film that receives an Academy Award can't be considered outside the Hollywood system.)[18]

Of course, the real problem that needs to be addressed is Mulvey's apparent compulsion to postulate a general theory of visual pleasure for Hollywood cinema. Why would anyone suppose that a unified theory is available, and why would one suppose that it would be founded upon sexual difference, since in the Hollywood cinema there is pleasure – even visual pleasure – that is remote from issues of sexual difference.

It is with respect to these concerns that I think that the limitations of psychoanalytic film criticism become most apparent. For it is that commitment that drives feminist film critics toward generalizations like Mulvey's that are destined for easy refutation. If one accepts a general theory like psychoanalysis, then one is unavoidably tempted to try to apply its categorical framework to the data of a field like film, come what may, irrespective of the fit of the categories to the data. Partial or glancing correlations of the categorical distinctions to the data will be taken as confirmatory, and all the anomalous data will be regarded as at best topics for further research or ignored altogether as theoretically insignificant. Psychoanalytic-feminists tend to force their "system" on cinema, and to regard often slim correspondences between films and the system as such that one can make vaulting generalizations about how the Hollywood cinema "really" functions. The overarching propensity to fruitless generalization is virtually inherent in the attempt to apply the purported success of general psychoanalytic hypotheses and distinctions, based on clinical practice, to the local case of film. This makes theoretical conjectures like Mulvey's immediately problematic by even a cursory consideration of film history. One pressing advantage, theoretically, of the image approach is that it provides a way to avoid the tendency of psychoanalytic film feminism to commit itself to unsupportable generalizations in its attempt to read all film history through the categories of psychoanalysis.[19]

III. The Image of Women in Film

The investigation of the image of women in film begins with the rather commonsensical notion that the recurring images of women in popular media may have some influence on how people think of women in real life. How one is to cash in the notion of "some influence" here, however, will be tricky. In fact, it amounts to finding a theoretical foundation for the image of women in film model. Moreover, there may be more than one way in which such influence is exerted. What I would like to do now is to sketch one answer that specifies one dimension of influence that recurring images of women in film may have on spectators, especially male spectators, in order to give the model some theoretical grounding. However, though I elucidate one strut upon which the model may rest, it is not my intention to deny that there may be others as well.

Recent work on the emotions in the philosophy of mind has proposed that we learn to identify our emotional states in terms of paradigm scenarios, which, in turn, also shape our emotions. Ronald de Sousa claims

my hypothesis is this: We are made familiar with the vocabulary of emotion by association with *paradigm scenarios*. These are drawn first from our daily life as small children and later reinforced by the stories, art and culture to which we are exposed. Later still, in literate cultures, they are supplemented and refined by literature. Paradigm scenarios involve two aspects: first a situation type providing the characteristic *objects* of the specific emotion type, and second, a set of characteristic or "normal" *responses* to the situation, where normality is first a biological matter and then very quickly becomes a cultural one.[20]

Many of the relevant paradigm scenarios are quite primitive, like fear, and some are genetically preprogrammed, though we continue to accumulate paradigm scenarios throughout life and the emotions that they define become more refined and more culturally dependent. Learning to use emotion terms is a matter of acquiring paradigm scenarios for certain situations; i.e., matching emotion terms to situations is guided by fitting paradigm scenarios to the situations that confront us. Paradigm scenarios, it might be said, perform the kind of cognitive role attributed to the formal object of the emotion in preceding theories of mind.[21] However, instead of being conceived of in terms of criteria, paradigm scenarios have a dramatic structure. Like formal objects of given emotions, paradigm scenarios define the type of emotional state one is in. They also direct our attention in the situation in such a way that certain elements in it become salient.

Paradigm scenarios enable us to "gestalt" situations, i.e., "to attend differentially to certain features of an actual situation, to inquire into the presence of further features of the scenario, and to make inferences that the scenario suggests."[22] Given a situation, an encultured individual attempts, generally intuitively, to fit a paradigm scenario from her repertoire to it. This does not mean that the individual can fully articulate the content of the scenario, but that, in a broad sense, she can recognize that it fits the situation before her. This recognition enables her to batten on certain features of the situation, to explore the situation for further correlations to the scenario, and to make the inferences and responses the scenario suggests. Among one's repertory of love-scenarios, for example, one might have, so to speak, a "West Side Story" scenario which enables one to organize one's thoughts and feelings about the man one has just met. Furthermore, more than one of our scenarios may fit a given situation. Whether one reacts to a situation of public recrimination with anger, humility or fortitude depends on the choice of the most appropriate paradigm scenario.[23]

I will not attempt to enumerate the kinds

of considerations that make the postulation of paradigm scenarios attractive except to note that it has certain advantages over competing hypotheses about the best way to characterize the cognitive and conative components in emotional states.[24] Rather, I shall presume that the notion of paradigm scenarios has something to tell us about a component of emotional states in order to suggest how recurring images of women in film may have some influence on spectators, which influence is of relevance to feminists.

Clearly, if we accept the notion of paradigm scenarios, we are committed to the notion that the paradigm scenario we apply to a situation shapes the emotional state we are in. Some paradigm scenarios – for example, those pertaining to the relation of an infant to a caretaker – may be such that recognition of them is genetically endowed. But most paradigm scenarios will be acquired, and even those that start out rather primitively, like rage, may be refined over time by the acquisition of further and more complex paradigm scenarios. There will be many sources from which we derive these paradigm scenarios: observation and memory; stories told us on our caretaker's knee; stories told us by friends and school teachers; gossip, as well, is a rich source of such scenarios; and, of course, so are newspaper articles, self-help books, TV shows, novels, plays, films and so on.

These scenarios may influence our emotional behavior. Male emotional responses to women, for example, will be shaped by the paradigm scenarios that they bring to those relations. Such paradigm scenarios may be derived from films, or, more likely, films may reflect, refine, and reinforce paradigm scenarios already abroad in the culture. One way to construe the study of the image of women in film is as an attempt to isolate widely disseminated paradigm scenarios that contribute to the shaping of emotional responses to women.[25]

The recent film *Fatal Attraction,* for example, provides a paradigm scenario for situations in which a married man is confronted by a woman who refuses to consider their affair as easily terminable as he does. Armed with the *Fatal Attraction* scenario, which isn't so different from the *Crimes and Misdemeanors* scenario, a man might "gestalt" a roughly matching, real life situation, focussing on it in such a way that its object, correlating to Alex (Glenn Close), is, as Dan (Michael Douglas) says, "unreasonable," and "crazy," and, as the film goes on to indicate, pathologically implacable. One might use the scenario to extrapolate other elements of the scenario to the real case; one might leap inductively from Alex's protests that her behavior is justified (you wouldn't accept my calls at the office so I called you at home), which are associated in the film with madness, to the suspicion that a real-life, ex-lover's claims to fair treatment are really insane. Like Dan, one guided by the *Fatal Attraction* scenario may assess his situation as one of paralysing terror, persecution and helplessness that only the death of the ex-lover can alleviate.

I am not suggesting that the *Fatal Attraction* scenario causes someone who matches it to a real life situation to kill his ex-lover, though embracing it may be likely to promote murderous fantasies, in terms of the response component. In any case, matching it to a real life situation will tend to demote the ex-lover to the status of an irrational creature and to regard her claims as a form of persecution. This construal of the woman as persecutrix, of course, was not invented by the makers of *Fatal Attraction.* It finds precedent in other films, like *Play Misty for Me,* and stories, including folklore told among men in the form of gossip.

Fatal Attraction provides a vivid exemplar for emotional attention that reinforces pre-existing paradigm scenarios. However, even if *Fatal Attraction* is not original, studying the image of the woman Alex that it portrays is relevant to feminists because it illuminates one pattern of emotional attention toward women that is available to men, which pattern of emotional attention, if made operational in specific cases, can be oppressive to women, by, for example, reducing claims to fair treatment to the status of persecutory, irrational demands.

That a paradigm scenario like *Fatal Attraction* is available in the culture does not imply that every man or even any man mobilizes it. But it does at least present a potential source or resource for sexist behavior. That such a potential even exists provides a reason for feminists to be interested in it. One aspect of the study of the image of women in film is to identify negative, recurring images of women that may have some influence on the emotional response of men to women. Theoretically, this influence can be understood in terms of the negative, recurring images of women in film as supplying paradigm scenarios that may shape the emotional responses of real men to real women.

Recurring, negative images of women in film may warp the emotions of those who deploy them as paradigm scenarios in several different ways. They may distort the way women are attended to emotionally by presenting wildly fallacious images such as the "spider woman" of *film noir*. Or, the problem may be that the range of images of women available is too impoverished: if the repertoire of images of women is limited in certain cases, for instance, to contraries like mother or whore, then real women who are not perceived via the mother scenario may find themselves abused under the whore scenario. The identification of the range of ways in which negative images of women in film can function cognitively to shape emotional response is a theoretical question that depends on further exploring the variety of logical/functional types of different images of women in film. That is a project that has hardly begun. Nevertheless, it seems a project worth pursuing.

I began by noting that the image approach might appear to some to be without proper theoretical credentials. I have tried

to allay that misgiving by suggesting that the program fits nicely with one direction in the theory of the emotions. From that perspective, the study of the image of women in film might be viewed as the search for paradigm scenarios that are available in our culture and which, by being available, may come to shape emotional responses to women. This aspect of the project should be of special interest to feminists with regard to negative imagery since it may illuminate some of the sources or resources that mobilize sexist emotions. Obviously, the theoretical potentials of the image of women in film model need to be developed. What I have tried to establish is the contention that there is at least a theoretical foundation here upon which to build.

This, of course, is not much of a defense of the image approach. So in my concluding remarks I shall attempt to sketch some of the advantages of this approach, especially in comparison to some of the disadvantages of the psychoanalytic model discussed earlier.

First, the image of women model seems better suited than the psychoanalytic model for accommodating the rich data that film history has bequeathed us. It allows that there will be lots of images of women and lots of images of men and that these may play a role as paradigm scenarios in lots of emotional reactions of all kinds. One need not attempt to limit the ambit of emotional responses to fetishism or voyeurism.

Of course, the image of women model may take particular interest in negative images of women in film, for obvious strategic purposes, but it can also handle the case of positive images as well. Whereas Rosalind Russell's character in *His Girl Friday* may be an inexplicable anomaly in the psychoanalytic system, she can be comprehended in the image approach. For this model allows that there can be positive images of women in film which may play a role in positive emotional responses to real women.[26] It is hard to see how there can be anything of genuine value in Hollywood film in Mulvey's construction. The image approach can identify the good, while acknowledging and isolating the evil.

The image of women in film model is less likely to lead to unsupportable generalizations. What it looks for are recurring images of women in film. It has no commitments about how women always appear in film.[27] Rather it targets images that recur with marked frequency. Moreover, it makes no claims about how all viewers or all male viewers respond to those images. It tracks images of women that reappear in film with some significant degree of probability and, where the images are negative, it can elucidate how they may play a constitutive role in the shaping of oppressive emotional responses to women. It is not committed to the kinds of specific causal laws that Mulvey must accept as underlying her account. It can nevertheless, acknowledge causal efficacy to some paradigm scenarios – indeed, it can acknowledge causal efficacy to paradigm scenarios of all sorts, thereby accommodating the richness of the data.

Indeed, it is interesting to observe that the image approach can accommodate certain of Mulvey's insights in a way that does not provoke the kind of objection Mulvey's position does. It can acknowledge that it is the case that there is a recurring image, of undoubtedly unnerving statistical frequency, of women in film posed as passive spectacles. Not all images of women in film are of this sort; but many are. Unlike Mulvey, the proponent of the image approach can point to this as a statistical regularity without claiming any over-reaching generalizations, and then go on to show how this sort of imagery reinforces a range of paradigm scenarios which mobilize a wide variety of oppressive emotional responses by men toward women, encountered on the beach, on the street, and in more ominous circumstances as well.

One objection that might be raised here, of course, is that I have presented the image approach as a rival to Mulvey's theory. But it might be countered that Mulvey's theory is about the pleasure taken from Hollywood cinema, and the image approach, as described so far, says nothing about pleasure. So though it may be a rival to Mulvey's model with respect to attempting to isolate the way in which Hollywood cinema functions in patriarchal society, it has not answered the question of how it is pleasurable.

One admittedly programmatic response to this objection is to note that insofar as the image approach is connected with engaging emotions, and insofar as indulging emotions in aesthetic contexts is generally thought to be pleasurable, then the proponent of the image approach can explain the pleasure to be derived from Hollywood films in virtue of whatever its defender takes to be the best theory or combination of theories that accounts for the pleasure we take from exercising our emotions in response to artworks, popular or otherwise. That is, where the rivalry between the image approach and Mulvey's approach is about pleasure, the supporter of the image approach has a range of options for developing theories.

On the other hand, I wonder whether the interest on the part of feminists in Mulvey's theory is really in its account of pleasure rather than in the way that it provides a means for analyzing the way film functions in patriarchal society. And if the latter is the real source of interest, two things need to be said: (1) the question of pleasure is only of interest insofar as it illuminates the function of film in abetting sexism, and (2) the image approach is a competing perspective in relation to that question, even if it makes the issue of pleasure less central to feminism than does Mulvey's approach.

Lastly, consonant with the preceding objection, it may be urged that Mulvey's theory is a theory of *visual* pleasure, and though we have spoken of images, even if we could advance a theory of pleasure, it would not be specifically a theory of *visual* pleasure, for *images* in the sense we have used it are not essentially or necessarily visual. Here, two points need to be made.

First, it is not clear that Mulvey herself is always talking about uniquely visual pleasure, nor that it is possible, with respect to Hollywood film images, to suppose that we can find some substratum of interests that are exclusively visual in nature.

Second, Mulvey's putative answer to the riddle of how viewers can take visual pleasure in the female form in cinema presupposes that there is a riddle here to be solved, which, in turn, depends upon the conviction that the image of a woman on screen, in some lawlike fashion, provokes castration anxiety in male viewers. There is no problem of visual pleasure without the supposition of regularly recurring male castration anxiety with respect to visual emphasis on female form. So if, like me, you are skeptical about this supposition, then Mulvey has not solved the problem of visual pleasure, for there was no problem to solve in the first place, and, therefore, no pressure on rival theories to address the issue.

Moreover, if, again like me, you are worried about accepting generalizations that are derived from psychoanalysis and treated like laws by film critics, then the image of women in film approach has the virtue of providing means for analyzing the function of film in the service of sexism without necessarily committing one to the still controversial tenets of psychoanalysis. This, of course, is hardly a recommendation that I expect committed psychoanalytic film critics to find moving. I offer it, without further argument, to concerned third parties.[28]

Notes

1. The distinction between *sources* and *resources* above is meant to acknowledge that it is generally the case that popular film more often than not reinforces rather than invents ideology, sexist and otherwise. Thus, film is primarily a *resource* rather than a *source* of

ideology. However, at the same time, I have no reason to assert dogmatically that a film could never invent ideology. If this happens, I suspect that it happens very, very rarely. But I have no investment in claiming that it could never happen.

2. I say a "potential rival" because, as already noted, one could marry the study of the image of women in film with a psychoanalytic perspective. Thus, the theoretical rivalry that I envision in this paper is between a study of the image of women in film that is neutral with respect to psychoanalysis and psychoanalytically informed film feminism.

3. This essay first appeared in *Screen* in 1975. It has been reprinted often, most recently, with respect to the writing of this essay, in Laura Mulvey's collection of her own writings entitled *Visual and Other Pleasures* (Indiana University Press, 1989). All page references to this article pertain to that volume.

4. It should also be noted that Mulvey herself has attempted to modify, or, perhaps more accurately, to supplement the theory that she put forward in "Visual Pleasure and Narrative Cinema." See, for example, her "Afterthoughts on 'Visual Pleasure and Narrative Cinema' inspired by King Vidor's *Duel in the Sun*" in *Visual and Other Pleasures,* pp. 29–37. The latter essay, while not denying the analysis of male pleasure in the former essay, offers a supplemental account of female pleasure with respect to narrative film. Space does not allow for criticism of that supplemental account. However, it is interesting that its structure is analogous to the structure of her psychoanalysis of male pleasure insofar as Mulvey attempts to "deduce" female pleasure at the movies from an earlier stage of psychosexual development whose masculine phase film narratives may, supposedly, reactivate.

5. I stress that what is accepted without sufficient critical distance in this matter is the *scientific* viability of psychoanalysis. Feminist film critics, including Mulvey, are aware of and seek to cancel the patriarchal biases of psychoanalysis. But unless the elements of the theory show sexist prejudices, they tend to accept its pronouncements on matters such as psychosexual development and visual pleasure without recourse to weighing psychoana-

lytic hypotheses against those of competing theories or to considering the often commented upon theoretical flaws and empirical difficulties of psychoanalysis.

6. I have discussed the tendency in contemporary film theory to embrace theoretical frameworks without considering rival reviews at some length in my *Mystifying Movies: Fads and Fallacies in Contemporary Film Theory* (Columbia University Press, 1988).

7. Indeed, John Berger makes such a distinction – between the male as active and the female as passive – with respect to the iconography of Western easel painting without invoking psychoanalysis. See his *Ways of Seeing* (London: Penguin, 1972), especially chapter 2.

8. Like many contemporary film theorists, Mulvey appears to believe that through point-of-view editing Hollywood film masks two other "looks" – those of the camera on the profilmic event and of the spectator on the finished film. Point-of-viewing editing, in this respect, functions to abet what contemporary film theorists call "transparency." I have challenged the overall advisability of hypotheses of this sort in my *Mystifying Movies;* see especially the discussion of suture.

9. Ibid.

10. Mulvey, "Visual Pleasure and Narrative Cinema," p. 21.

11. Ibid., p. 20.

12. Other commentators have also questioned Mulvey's generalizations in this regard. See Kristin Thompson, "Closure within a Dream? Point of View in *Laura*" in *Breaking the Glass Armor* (Princeton University Press, 1988), p. 185; and Miriam Hansen, "Pleasure, Ambivalence, Identification: Valentino and Female Spectatorship," *Cinema Journal* 25 (1986); 6–32.

13. Allen Weiss in the introduction to his unpublished doctoral dissertation on the films of Hollis Frampton (New York University, 1989).

14. Mulvey may reject this interpretation of her essay. She may think that she is using these psychoanalytic terms literally. In the "Summary" of her essays (p. 26), for example, she speaks of the neurotic needs of the male ego. But this seems tantamount to implying that

the male ego is, at least, in our culture, inevitably and essentially neurotic. And I am not convinced that this is the way that clinical psychoanalysts would use the idea of neurosis as a technical classification. Nor would the classification be of much scientific value if it applied so universally. Furthermore, Freud himself, in his study of DaVinci, talks of sublimation as an alternative formation to perversions like fetishism. Why has sublimation dropped out of Mulvey's list of options for visual pleasure?

15. Mulvey, "Visual Pleasure and Narrative Cinema," p. 17.

16. Christian Metz, perhaps the leading psychoanalytic film theorist, appears to hold such a view. For arguments against this hypothesis, see the second chapter of my *Mystifying Movies*.

17. Here one might object that Mulvey is not committed to regard the fetishism/voyeurism dichotomy as systematic; so I am attacking a straw position. But I think she is committed to the notion of a systematic dichotomy. For if the problem of castration anxiety with respect to the female form is general, and fetishism and voyeurism are the only responses, then where there is no castration anxiety, won't that have to be a function of strategies of voyeurism and fetishism? Perhaps Mulvey does not believe that there is always castration anxiety in response to the female form. But then we would have to know under what conditions castration anxiety will fail to take hold. Moreover, we will have to ask whether these conditions, once specified, won't undermine Mulvey's theory in other respects. Of course, another reason why one might deny that Mulvey's claims involve a systematic dichotomy between fetishistic and voyeuristic strategies is that she believes that there are other strategies for containing castration anxiety. But then the burden of proof is on her to produce these as yet unmentioned alternatives.

18. This film was, of course, based upon a highly acclaimed Broadway production. So, it is a counterexample that should also be considered by theater critics who wish to apply the generalizations of feminist film critics to the study of their own artform. Likewise, TV

critics, with the same ambition, should want to ponder the relevance of this example to the successful remake of the theater and film versions of *The Miracle Worker* for TV in 1979 by Paul Aaron where Patty Duke (Astin) plays the Anne Sullivan role.

Also, it should be obvious, contra Mulvey, that not all visual pleasure in film is rooted in sexual difference. Consider the visual pleasure derived from recognition, from detail, from shifts of scale, and, more specifically, from machinery, from casts of thousands, and so on (I owe these examples to Cynthia Baughman).

19. There is another line of argumentation in Mulvey's essay that I have not dealt with above. It involves a general theory of the way in which cinema engages spectators in identification and mobilizes what Lacanians call "the imaginary." The sort of general theory that Mulvey endorses concerning these issues is criticized at length in my *Mystifying Movies*.

20. Ronald de Sousa, *The Rationality of the Emotions* (MIT Press, 1987), p. 182. The idea of scenarios is also employed by Robert Solomon, "Emotion and Choice" in *Explaining Emotions,* ed. Amelie Rorty (University of California Press, 1980).

21. E.g., Anthony Kenny's *Action, Emotion and Will* (London: Routledge, 1963).

22. Ronald de Sousa, "The Rationality of Emotions" in *Explaining Emotions,* p. 143.

23. This example comes from Cheshire Calhoun's "Subjectivity & Emotions," *The Philosophical Forum* 20 (1989), p. 206.

24. See the de Sousa citations above for some of the relevant arguments.

25. Of course, there could also be a research program dedicated to studying the image of men in film for the same purposes.

26. Kristin Thompson, in conversation, has stressed that determining whether a paradigm scenario is positive or negative may crucially hinge on contextualizing it historically.

27. Whereas psychoanalytic-feminism, given its avowal of the *general* laws of psychoanalysis, is tempted to say how woman must always appear as a result of deducing film theory from a deeper set of "scientific" principles.

28. This paper was read at the 1990 Pacific Division Meetings of the American Philosophical Association where Laurie Shrage provided helpful comments. Other useful criticisms have been offered by Ellen Gainor, Kristin Thompson, David Bordwell, Sally Banes, Peggy Brand, Carolyn Korsmeyer, Sabrina Barton, and Cynthia Baughman.

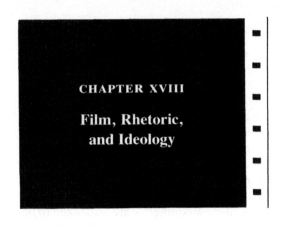

CHAPTER XVIII

Film, Rhetoric, and Ideology

Introduction

Until recently, the major recurring question of value that confronted film theorists was whether film could be an art, and, thus, a source of artistic value. In the earliest stages of film theory, this worry was made urgent by the existence of certain anti-mimetic prejudices with respect to photography. For photography was regarded to be a purely mechanical process of recording, and, hence, essentially inartistic. Consequently, film, whose central constituent is photographic, likewise found its artistic credentials under fire.

As a result, the self-appointed task of members of the first generation of film theorists, like Rudolf Arnheim,[1] was to demonstrate, often at length, the ways in which film could diverge expressively from what was thought of as the *mere* reproduction of reality. For in showing the ways in which cinematic devices creatively reconstructed pro-filmic events,[2] an inventory of artistic structures was enumerated.

Moreover, the task of establishing the artistic potentials of film proceeded under certain constraints. For it was thought that if film had genuinely artistic potentials, they would have to be of a uniquely cinematic variety. That is, film would not be shown to be an art were it simply mimicking theater. Rather, it had to be established that film had some range of essentially cinematic effects, possessed by no other art forms, which, at the same time, performed some demonstra-

bly artistic function (such as, for example, expression).

Thus, for much of its history, film theory operated within an essentialist framework. Theorists, of course, disagreed over what they took to constitute the essential features and powers of cinema: for Arnheim it involved the expressive reconstruction of reality, while for André Bazin it was a matter of the objective re-presentation of reality.[3] However, until the late sixties and early seventies, most of the conversation of what might be called classical film theory gravitated toward securing the artistic value of film by means of identifying its essentially cinematic capacities.[4]

But, as the sixties turned into the seventies, the essentialist project in film theory found itself embattled from two directions: a neo-Wittgensteinian suspicion of essences, on the one hand,[5] and semiotics, of an implicitly anti-essentialist sort, on the other. These pressures, along with a rising sense that film theory should leave off its primary preoccupation with aesthetics, and examine the role of cinema in society, spelled the demise of at least one sort of film theory. From the early seventies onward, film theory became less concerned with the aesthetic value of cinema and more obsessed with its social value. Moreover, the primary social role that film theorists came to attribute to film was negative. Film, particularly but not exclusively the mass entertainment cinema, was regarded as predominantly – and for many (ironically enough) *essentially*[6] – an agency of ideological manipulation, a means by which ostensibly oppressive systems, notably capitalism, sustain dominion. Thus, the leading hypothesis amongst contemporary film theorists is that film is an instrument of ideology, and their research program is a matter of identifying the relevant levers of ideological manipulation that cinema affords. As a result, the central preoccupation of film studies in the United States today concerns the ideological effect of cinema on its audiences.

Film studies in the United States became a widespread and established academic discipline in the seventies. Its preoccupation with ideology is a reflection of the conviction of the academic generation of the sixties and seventies that everything is political. Within contemporary film studies, it is typical to invoke a contrast between research into the ideological dimensions of film and a concern with aesthetics – of the sort one finds in earlier generations of film theorists – where, furthermore, a concern with aesthetics is often regarded as not merely old-fashioned, but potentially reactionary.

Moreover, not only are contemporary film scholars generally agreed that ideology is their central topic; they are also convinced that they have at their disposal a theoretical framework for analyzing the ideological effect of the cinema. For the sake of convenience, I will call this framework Althusserian.[7] My purpose in this paper is to suggest a rival approach to the analysis of ideology in cinema, to that of the dominant Althusserianism of contemporary film theorists. Unlike contemporary film theorists, I do not think that aesthetics is either beside the point or pernicious. But I do agree with them that film is (often) a vehicle for conveying ideology and that it is worthwhile to attempt to get some general (theoretical) understanding of the ways in which cinema performs this function. That is, I do not want to suggest that we abandon questions of aesthetic value with respect to film. But we may, at the same time, accommodate the concerns of contemporary theorists with the ideological operations of film. Indeed, I hope to introduce ways of thinking about the ideological operation of film – in terms of the notion of rhetoric – that are superior, theoretically, to what the reigning Althusserian model proposes.

The Althusserian Model

In order to set the stage for the rival approach that I wish to advocate, something needs to be said about the presuppositions of the Althusserian film theory. There are two fundamental tenets of this theory. The first is that ideology in film is not simply a matter of the content of films. Rather, ideology is, so to speak, built into the very instruments of cinema: the camera, especially in terms of perspective,[8] and the projection apparatus.[9] Moreover, narrative structure as well as the customary figures of film editing – such as point-of-view editing[10] – are also taken to be *inherently* ideological.[11] Thus, the first tenet of Althusserian theory maintains that what others might tend to call the formal conditions and formal structures of cinema are themselves ideological. In this sense, of course, using the word "formal" itself is a misnomer, since these structures are, *ex hypothesi,* primary disseminators of ideology. This tenet of Althusserian film theory can be summed up by saying that cinema is essentially or inherently ideological.

The second tenet of Althusserian film theory concerns the ideological *effect* of what I call, perhaps tendentiously, the formal elements of film. This effect is a matter of instilling in the film viewer the impression or illusion that he or she is a unified and autonomous subject. That is, film theorists believe that certain structures of cinematic representation, such as perspectival representation, impart or reinforce the viewer's faith in his/her identity as what contemporary film theorists label (dubiously, I think) a Cartesian subject or ego.

What does regarding oneself as what contemporary film theorists call a Cartesian ego have to do with ideology? Presumably, such a subject considers itself to be free. But contemporary film theorists think that this is false. Individuals are shaped by the cultures in which they are raised and their choices – including those which appear to them as free choices – are socially mandated. Given this, imparting the impression of freedom, it is thought, has a function for the status quo. It encourages the impression that the choices dictated by the culture at large are free choices, thereby encouraging the subject in the illusion that the roles, choices, and beliefs that are imposed upon her by the culture are really her own. The dominant social system functions smoothly, that is, by instilling the conviction in its subjects that their decisions are freely made, whereas, under the Althusserian dispensation, they are, in reality, completely constructed by the social system in the interests of the dominant order.

All cultural life turns out to be ideological in this framework. If something is cultural, it is ideological or, what amounts to the same thing, it is socially constructed. A primary function of ideology is to obscure the operation of social construction. Of central importance, in this regard, is inspiring the belief or, in the jargon of film studies, the *misrecognition* on the part of the subject that she is a unified, free agent rather than a consummate social construction. Cinema participates in this central function of ideology by deploying structures – such as the perspectival image, narrative closure, point-of-view editing, a certain type of projection arrangement – all of which are claimed to enhance the spectator's conviction that she is a unified, free subject.

Space does not allow the rehearsal of how this misrecognition is supposedly counterfeited in each case. But for illustrative purposes, let me say that it is widely believed that perspective putatively enjoins the viewer to embrace the illusion that she is at the center of an optical array – i.e., at the monocular station point of the perspectival image. This central position, moreover, is a *single* point in space, and it is supposed that the attending impression of singularity promotes the conviction of unity in the subject, thereby securing the principal ideological effect of the Althusserian theory.

There are a great many problems with the characterization of the operation of ideology endorsed by contemporary film theorists. I will briefly discuss a few of them in order to motivate the proposal of a rival conception

of the way in which we might think of the ideological operation of film.

The first tenet of the Althusserian theory – that film is *inherently* ideological – seems to me suspect. Undeniably, many films may function ideologically to celebrate the values and assumptions of the status quo. For example, many cavalry films of the forties and fifties valorized the conquest of the American West while dehumanizing the claims of the indigenous, native populations. However, it seems equally possible to make a film from an oppositional position that mobilizes the resources of conventional cinema and that at the same time contests the ideology of the status quo. However, if the film employs cameras and projection in standard ways; if it tells a story with a beginning, a middle and an end; and if it advances that story by means of continuity editing, it will, according to contemporary film theorists, be ideological. Thus, John Sayles's film *Matewan* could not avoid being ideological once certain decisions were made about designing it to be accessible for general audiences. It would appear that any film that is not an exercise in modernist reflexivity is unavoidably ideological (though, of course, many contemporary film theorists are also suspicious of the prospects of modernism for different reasons).

I believe that this is an extremely counterintuitive conclusion. Any approach to the analysis of ideology in film ought to resist the conclusion that film as such, or film of a certain form – say conventional narrative cinema – is inherently or essentially ideological.

The claim that film is ideological by virtue of its formal structures is putatively supported by the analyses that film theorists offer of the various structures in question. Without going through these analyses one at a time here, I shall merely say that I find them consistently ill-advised. For example, in my brief summary of the case against perspective, one immediately notes that the reasoning proceeds by means of a number of hasty inferences. Even if we suppose that a perspectival image imparts to the viewer a sense of being posited at a single monocular station point, we immediately wonder why thinking that one is occupying a single point in space would give one the impression that one was unified in the requisite sense – what does occupying a single point in space have to do with, for example, the impression of being an *autonomous* agent?[12] Indeed, the accounts that one finds by contemporary film theorists of the dynamics according to which interactions with formal film structures result in the film viewer misrecognizing herself as a Cartesian ego seem uniformly strained.

Of course, there is an even deeper problem here. The contemporary film theorist assumes that it is a necessary element of capitalist ideology that we all conceive of ourselves – via misrecognition – to be what they call Cartesian subjects, subjects who believe that they are unified in the sense of not being socially constructed and who, it is said, therefore, mistakenly take themselves to be autonomous agents. However, on the one hand, it is doubtful that a culture like capitalism requires that its citizens endorse any single conception of the subject of the generality of the film theorists' so-called Cartesian subject. Couldn't capitalism flourish if we were all behaviorists or if we thought of ourselves in terms of Hume's bundles? Couldn't a population of Zen Buddhists supply a coterie of happy workers? And, alternatively, couldn't the putative delusion that we are Cartesian egos underwrite a culture quite different than that of capitalism?

The contemporary film theorist wants to reduce metaphysics to politics. This is not only a problem because of the way in which these theorists attempt to "read" a metaphysics of the subject into the formal structures of cinema. But, in addition, the metaphysical commitments they supposedly discern are underdetermined with respect to the political purposes that they may serve.

Along with their assimilation of metaphysics to ideology, contemporary film theorists also, often expressly, conflate the notion of ideology with that of culture. To show that something is cultural, to show that it is a social construction, in their view, warrants the inference that it is ideological. Perhaps this presumption is underwritten by the notion that whenever society comes into the picture, the powers that be enter in such a way as to ensure that whatever conventions or conceptions we arrive at will be to the advantage of the status quo. This does not seem to be empirically plausible; surely there are practices and beliefs that arise outside the dominant culture – e.g., breakdancing and other subcultural expressions. Indeed, even within mainstream culture, it seems possible for ideas and practices to emerge that do not serve the status quo, such as the anti-war movement of the sixties. And, more importantly, the view of contemporary theorists presupposes that any culture, virtually by definition, is politically complicit, which, of course, makes the point of criticizing ideology from the perspective of a vision of emancipatory social relations pointless.[13]

However, there does seem to be a point in criticizing certain films as ideological. But in order to do this we need a trimmer conception of ideology than one that identifies the ideological with the cultural. Thus, the first step in constructing an approach that is rival to the Althusserian view is to specify what we mean by "ideology," and to assure that our conception of ideology does not conflate it with culture in general.

Ideology and Rhetoric

Originally "ideology" pertained to the study of ideas; Lockean epistemologists were ideologues in this sense.[14] However, the notion gradually narrowed so that it applied to political ideas or ideas that were politically significant, especially in terms of those ideas that were politically useful for supporting oppression.

Following this heritage, I want to restrict the domain of what is ideological to ideas, primarily: to beliefs understood as propositions held assertively – where the propositions may be vague, especially in terms of quantification (e.g., "People are funny") – and to categorical frameworks.[15] Taking beliefs first, I hypothesize that in order to be ideological, a belief or the way it is held must be in some sense epistemically defective. It is either false, or it is ambiguous, or it is connected to other beliefs in a way that is misleading or unwarranted.[16] "The unemployed are just lazy" is a straightforward example of such a belief.

Of course, it is not enough for a belief to be false or otherwise defective epistemically for it to be ideological: "2 + 2 = 1492" is false, but to my knowledge it has not, as yet, ever been employed ideologically. To be ideological an epistemically defective proposition has to be used in a certain way. Specifically, it has to be used as a tenet – as a slogan, a premise, a principle, etc. – in some system of social domination. To show that a proposition with its corresponding belief is ideological, one must show that it is epistemically defective and that its continued invocation plays a role in practices of social domination.

Stated roughly, x is an ideological belief if and only if (1) x is false (or otherwise epistemically defective) and (2) x is employed as a tenet in some system of social domination. Of course, as noted above, ideological ideas may not merely take the form of propositions, but may be of the order of categorical frameworks, i.e., ways of carving up phenomena.[17] For example, if a society like ours tends to portray African-Americans as either drug-crazy criminals or saints, then that grid distorts the way in which someone who employs this optic forms expectations and assessments about the behavior of African-Americans. This framework, moreover, may readily perform

a service in continuing social oppression since persons failing to evince sainthood are likely to be consigned to the criminal class and treated with suspicion. So a categorical framework is ideological if it is distorting, where that distortion performs some role in a system or practice of social domination.

In contrast to the Althusserian approach, then, showing that a film or a segment of a film is ideological is not a matter of indicating that it is a social construction, but of demonstrating that it promotes ideological ideas – either false beliefs or distorting categorical schemes that function to support some system of social domination. The Althusserian approach locates central levers of ideology in the formal structures of film. I have at least suggested some reasons why this is a problematic way to go. In contrast, I want to hypothesize that whether a film is ideological is a function of its internal organization or, more specifically, what I call its rhetorical organization, i.e., the particular organization of its narrative and pictorial elements in such a way that it promotes or encourages ideological beliefs or frameworks in viewers.

The idea that the locus of ideology in film resides in the way in which specific films articulate their stories and images is fairly commonsensical. It would not seem to be worth dignifying by the title of "an approach" were it not the case that, at present, most contemporary film theorists think that they have isolated a deeper level of ideological manipulation in film, viz., that of generic film structures, like perspective. This has the liability of being overly general in two ways: it makes all films – or at least all films that employ certain generic structures – ideological *and* it makes them all ideological in the same way, always encouraging spectators to misrecognize themselves as Cartesian subjects. Alternatively, the view that ideological beliefs are propagated by films through their specific rhetorical organization allows both that some films may not be ideological – if they promote no ideological beliefs – and that there can be quite a range of ideological beliefs, including ones that may not pertain to issues of personal identity.[18]

To say that ideological beliefs are propagated by films by means of their rhetorical organization is pretty uninformative, unless we have some idea of what the notion of "rhetorical organization" signifies. So, how do I understand rhetoric and how is that relevant to analyzing the ideological operation of film?

Rhetoric is a matter of influencing thought – a matter of persuasion, as a consequence of presenting material in a way that is structured to secure an audience's belief in certain conclusions, or, at least, their favorable disposition toward those conclusions. Those conclusions may be stated outright by the orator, or the listener may come to embrace them insofar as they are strongly implied by, insinuated by, or presupposed by the rhetoric in question. Moreover, many of the techniques of oratory can be adapted to narrative film-making so as to promote beliefs or openness to beliefs in audiences. From my perspective, where those beliefs are epistemically defective *and* where instilling them contributes to a system of social domination, they are ideological.

That rhetorical strategies may be implemented in narrative film should be fairly obvious. Aristotle, for example, points out that establishing one's good character is influential in securing a speaker's point of view.[19] Similarly, in narrative films, an ideological perspective may be advanced by a character, and the persuasiveness of the view may hinge, in part, on portraying the said fictional character as virtuous. In Hollywood films, these virtues – strength, fortitude, ingenuity, bravery – are more often Greek than Christian. However, quite frequently in Hollywood films, a character is designated virtuous in terms of his courteous, respectful, and thoughtful treatment of supporting characters, especially ones who are poor, weak, old, lame,

wrongfully oppressed, children, etc. – that is, characters who are in some sense the protagonist's "inferiors," but whom the protagonist treats with consideration (notably in contrast to the villain, who is apt to handle his social inferiors quite brutishly – kicking dogs, etc.). Democratic courtesy to one's "inferiors," as well as protectiveness toward the weak, and an overall aura of "niceness" (toward other "nice" characters) can function as a means of representing protagonists in such a way as to make the positions – which may be ideological – that they uphold attractive.

Likewise, Aristotle points out that a crucial form of rhetorical argument is the example, of which the fable or invented story is a major variation.[20] And clearly whole film narratives can serve as rhetorical examples. André Bazin took Orson Welles's *Citizen Kane* as an example supporting the contention that "there is no profit in gaining the whole world if one has lost one's own childhood."[21] Of course, this rhetorical function is not unique to film narrative; a narrative in any art form can operate this way. For instance, Arthur Miller's drama *Death of a Salesman* functions as an argumentative example, advancing the viewpoint that the American Dream and its corresponding cult of appearances are ultimately destructive. Nevertheless, where film narratives serve as argumentative examples for views that are epistemically defective and tenets in some practice of social domination, their rhetorical effect will be ideological.

Among Aristotle's insights into the rhetorical strategies of persuasion is the importance of the enthymeme – the syllogism that leaves something out and that requires the audience to fill in the missing premise.[22] Indeed, Aristotle thought that this form of rhetorical argument was the most effective one available. The advantage of this device for the rhetorician is that it engages the audience as participants in the process of argument in such a way that listeners, by what Arthur Danto calls "an almost inevitable movement of mind," supply what is needed for the argument to go through.[23] This enhances the credibility of the argument for the listener; in so far as she has the impression of reaching the missing segment on her own, she may regard it as her own idea. For example, rhetorical questions function as a means of bringing the listener to certain conclusions before the orator states them outright. And, when the orator does, subsequently, state them outright, the listener then greets them favourably as conclusions that she probably already formed on her own. That is, "when an arguer suppresses one or more parts of a rhetorical syllogism, the arguer invites an audience to complete it, thereby contributing to its own persuasion and exhibiting its rationality in the process."[24]

Narrative films are not arguments. But they often do presuppose ideas which the audience fills in in order for the narrative to be intelligible. Narrative films may be thought of as rhetorical, then, in so far as they are structured to lead the audience to fill in certain ideas about human conduct in the process of rendering the story intelligible to themselves. For example, in James Whale's film *The Bride of Frankenstein,* there is a scene in which the monster is alone, raging through the forest. At one point, he begins to hear offscreen music, issuing from an unseen fiddle. His demeanor changes from that of a rampaging monster to one marked by childlike yearning. In order for the scene to make sense to the viewer, one must realize and fill in what is being presupposed, namely a commonplace principle of behavior that goes something like "Music hath charms to soothe the savage breast."

That is, the narrative is structured in such a way as to elicit this presupposition – which is of the order of a cultural commonplace – from the audience in its own process of making sense of the action. We may call this operation the narrative enthymeme. Though it is not the only rhetorical structure available in film, it is a crucial one – one whose significance has not been extensively discussed. In the remainder of this essay, I want to explore this device further as a way of expanding our understanding of one very important way in which film, especially narrative film, disseminates ideology.

Narratives presuppose all sorts of vague generalizations as conditions of intelligibility. The audience must supply them as it supplies the missing premise in oratorical enthymemes. Moreover, where the unstated generalizations are made explicit, they have resonance because we have already been prompted in their direction by the structure of the story. Typical episodes of the eternally rerun TV series *Star Trek* exemplify this nicely. Very often, these programs will conclude with a vaguely liberal observation by Captain Kirk, which takes the form of a generalization that comprehends the action in terms of an organizing moral that is virtually on the audience's lips already – precisely because the story has been structured in such a way as to elicit it from the viewer.

For example, in the installment entitled "Let That Be Your Last Battlefield," race hatred is explored through the conflict between two aliens from the planet Charon. One, called Loki, is a revolutionist; the left side of his body, from head to foot, is black and the right side is white. His pursuer, Beal, represents the master race on Charon; he is black on the right and white on the left. Loki and Beal loathe each other and they are prone to denounce each other by means of racially loaded epithets. Of course, the difference between them seems insignificant to the viewer and we feel that Spock has merely verbalized our own conclusions when he remarks that they look as if they belong to the same race. The underlying theme of this episode – which the action illustrates – is that the kind of irrational, racial hatred that these two Charonites bear toward each other can only lead to their own destruction and the destruction of their respective races. This is borne out by the plot – indeed it is the presupposition that makes the plot intelligible – and when Capt. Kirk intones lines like "There's nobody alive on Charon because of hate" and "You both must end up dead if you don't stop hating," the audience hears its own surmises stated, thereby disposing it favorably toward Kirk's conclusions.[25]

Of course, this sort of structure is not only found in what might be thought of as the simplistic narratives of mass culture. When *Oedipus Rex* ends with the Chorus singing that we should count no mortal as fortunate until he/she is dead (and safely out of harm's way), we hear the articulation of the presupposition of the vivid example (the story of Oedipus) that we have just witnessed and which was predicated on bringing us to just this sobering viewpoint.

Also crucial to the rhetorician for securing conviction from audiences – as may already be evident from my examples – is the manipulation of commonplaces, clichés and what Aristotle called maxims. The rhetorician exploits what is common or familiar in order to gain the assent of the audience. That is, the rhetorician uses what the audience is already likely to believe or have cognitively available in order to encourage acceptance of the rhetorician's viewpoint. The use of commonplaces is also thought to encourage conviction because it leaves the audience with the impression that what it's heard is what it already believes and that the conclusions the rhetorician reaches are, again, its own conclusions. For the rhetorician has elicited these conclusions from the audience by way of generally accepted commonplaces and, indeed, the conclusion – which the rhetorician ideally tries to inspire in the mind of the audience even before it is uttered – is itself often couched in commonplaces. Of course, where the rhetorician has already inspired the commonplace in the mind of the audience before it is uttered, the effect of uttering it will be that the audience may

recognize the utterance as its own concurrent thinking on the matter.

The relevance of the role of commonplaces in oratory to what we can call narrative enthymemes is, of course, that the presuppositions that the narrative prompts the audience to fill in are generally of the nature of commonplaces or clichés or nostrums or platitudes of a general sort about the nature of human conduct and behavior. The narrative functions to dispose the audience toward mobilizing these commonplace generalizations in the process of rendering the narrative intelligible to itself, thereby reinforcing the audience's faith in them by virtue of the impression that the audience has reached these conclusions "on its own." And, of course, where these commonplaces themselves are ideological, the rhetorical operation of the film – here understood as importantly but not exclusively as prompting the filling in of commonplace presuppositions – is ideological.[26]

In order to clarify the application of these points about rhetoric to film, an illustration will be useful. Consider the original version of *Back to the Future*. The point of the film seems to be that anything can be altered by acts of individual will. This is the general principle or premise that the film dramatizes, and, in order for the film to make sense to audiences, they must embrace, or, at least, entertain it.[27] That is, if the film is to appear as a coherent whole to them, they will have seen it in the light of this generalization. In addition, this generalization is a commonplace of our individualist culture – a tenet of what is called positive thinking – and it is serviceable in a number of ways for upholding practices of social domination. For example, if someone finds himself in dire straits, such as homelessness, this is sometimes said to be ultimately his own fault – and not a product of social conditions – because he has failed to think himself positively out of his circumstances.

In *Back to the Future*, this commonplace is sowed early on in the film. Walking down the street with his girlfriend Jennifer, Marty says that Doc says "If you put your mind to it, you can accomplish anything."[28] At this point in the film it is cited tentatively; it is quoted by Marty, but it is not yet a matter of conviction for him. But it is repeated on two subsequent occasions. Marty offers it as a piece of advice to George, his father. And then at the end of the film, George – who had promised never to forget Marty's advice – repeats it when advance copies of his first novel arrive in the mail. By this time, the commonplace clearly expresses the viewpoint of the film. Moreover, the audience has been encouraged to see the events of the film under the aegis of this commonplace throughout, and it has been rewarded in adopting this generalization as a relevant presupposition about human behavior in so far as this generalization offers the most comprehensive explanation of the action in the film.

Obviously, the generalization applies to the exploits of the major character, Marty, who, among other things, is able to change the conditions of his own existence by putting his mind to it. This is achieved in large measure by changing his father, George, whose transformation, in turn, is achieved by virtue of his acceptance of the principle that willing enables you to accomplish anything, whether it be decking Biff or publishing a novel. Likewise, that Goldie Wilson becomes the first African-American mayor of Hill Valley is due, the film implies, to his go-getter attitude – to his commitment to making something of himself and to standing tall, while Doc, himself, is moved from the despondency over his history of failed experiments to enthusiasm by the challenge of putting his mind to sending Marty "back to the future."

Rhetorically speaking, *Back to the Future* plants the idea in the audience's mind that "if you put your mind to it, you can accomplish anything" – an idea, moreover, that is already a cultural commonplace. The viability of this idea, furthermore, is en-hanced at least in so far as that idea, as a presupposition of the plot, underwrites the narrative development of much of the action of the film. That is, this idea supplies a general principle that applies to a great deal of the action in the film, most notably to virtually all the successful activity in the film. The audience, in turn, comes to adopt it as its own hypothesis for the sake of comprehending the events of the film. And, finally, when the commonplace is uttered for the last time – when George receives his copies of his novel – the film iterates the commonplace to an audience which is likely to endorse it as its own thought insofar as it has already reached this view, if only as a generalization that best explains the events in the film.

Of course, this is not the only commonplace in the film. Another, made explicit by Goldie Wilson, is that you need to stand up to bullies and not let them walk all over you. This is connected to the notion that you can do anything to which you put your mind not only because it occurs in the context of Goldie's speech about making something of himself, but also because the road to George McFly's "accomplishing anything" is bound up with confronting a bully, namely, Biff. Bullies, that is, are defeatable by acts of will and this commonplace is, in turn, a particular instance of "If you put your mind to it you can accomplish anything," which includes defeating bullies.

A further particularization of the nostrum of positive thinking, which is crucial to the film, concerns the importance of taking risks or trying. This arises in several contexts, including Marty's paralyzing fear of rejection with respect to his music, and his father George's parallel fear about showing his science fiction stories to anyone; and, of course, the importance of trying is also related to George's asking Marty's mother, Lorraine, for a date and, later, to his exercising his will in confronting bullies such as Biff and, later still, the redhead at the dance. When characters complain of their fears of rejection, the audience is apt to think that the character will never know whether he can succeed unless he puts himself on the line. We almost subvocalize: "You'll never know unless you take a chance." The conversations in which these anxieties are expressed function in a way that is analogous to rhetorical questions – given the culture that we inhabit, they elicit a predictable answer to the character's plight. In addition, this answer underwrites the narrative action as a general principle – i.e., the characters do succeed when they try – and, furthermore, it is connected to the overarching commonplace that structures the film. For resolving to try, to take a risk, or to take a stand is part of what is required by "putting your mind to it."[29]

If this analysis of the rhetoric of *Back to the Future* appears convincing, then central to the film is the manipulation of commonplaces. Either these commonplaces are presented overtly to the audience or they are elicited by contriving situations to which the audience is apt to respond associatively with a well-worn truism (like "in order to succeed, you have to take risks"). Moreover, the audience uses these commonplaces to track the action; insofar as they have, in fact, structured the action, they account for it quite expeditiously. So by the time the leading commonplace is delivered as a conclusion, the spectator is apt to greet it as what she already thinks, for she has already come to it herself, albeit as the result of rhetorical promptings.

So one crucial element in the rhetorical operation of the film is that it instills its conclusion in its spectators in such a way that the spectator's conviction is reinforced by her sense that the conclusion is a matter of something that she is already disposed to embrace. The key to installing this conviction is that the view in question be rather of the order of a commonplace *and* that this commonplace – as a generalization about behavior or a principle of conduct – fit the events in the plot as the best way to make

sense of them. That is, the plot is rather like an example of the commonplace. The audience's acceptance of the commonplace is encouraged as it comes to recognize the story as an instance of the commonplace. This, in turn, has the net effect of reinforcing the commonplace – insofar as it appears successful in accounting for some behavior, even if fictional – while also concretizing the commonplace in the audience's mind in terms of a paradigm case which may guide application of the commonplace to actual situations.[30]

How generalizable are these observations about what I have called the rhetorical organization of *Back to the Future*? My hunch is that they can be extended to quite a lot of films, and that adopting the notions of rhetoric, presupposition and the use of commonplaces will provide a useful framework for isolating the ideological operation of a great deal of cinema. To support my hunch about commonplaces, two considerations come to mind. First, one notices that frequently the titles of conventional films are themselves commonplaces – *You Can't Take It with You, The Best Years of Our Lives, Cheaper by the Dozen, It's A Wonderful Life* – and, in these cases at least, the role clichés play in organizing the narrative seems to accord with our hypothesis about films like *Back to the Future*, where the commonplace is not featured in the title. Secondly, one would predict, on what might be called "design grounds," that the presuppositions that are favored in popular narratives would be something of the order of commonplaces and clichés since they would have to be familiar enough for mass audiences to have access to them.

That narratives involve presuppositions that the audience fills in, I conjecture, is something that most theorists accept. However, several qualifications about the relevance of filling in presuppositions with respect to the ideological operation of film need to be made. First, I am not claiming that narrative presuppositions are always ideological; they are only ideological where they meet the criteria stated earlier in this paper. Moreover, eliciting presuppositions from audiences is not the sole means of conveying ideology; films may have long speeches that state their ideological position quite bluntly. Rather, my claim is that the use of presuppositions, in terms of the way in which it involves the audience "finding the conclusion for itself," is a powerful rhetorical device for conveying ideology and a frequent one. Moreover, though sometimes the presupposition may be found stated somewhere in the dialogue or title of the film,[31] in other cases the commonplace remains tacit.[32]

Though the rhetorical organization of a film in terms of presuppositions and commonplaces may proffer ideological tenets to audiences, they do not, of course, guarantee their acceptance. For viewers who do not already accept the ideological presuppositions and commonplaces advanced by the film are unlikely to accept them. For such viewers, the film is apt to seem unintelligible or ridiculous, and, perhaps, worthy of indignation.[33] On the other hand, where viewers readily accept the rhetoric of the film, they probably already accept the ideological commonplaces, and the ideological operation of the film in such cases is probably best described as reinforcing existing ideology. My suspicion is that this is the most common operation of ideology in film.

One other case, however, is worth brief comment. There may be some viewers who, antecedently, neither accept nor reject the ideological commonplaces that the film elicits. What is the film's ideological effect on them? Here, I conjecture that the rhetorical operation of the film may at least tilt them toward the ideological premise in question by enhancing the viability of the commonplace in their cognitive stock of heuristics.[34] That is, human beings are optimizers.[35] When confronted with situations, we will often grasp for whatever heuristics – such as commonplace generalizations – are available to

us for the purpose of rendering the situation intelligible. That a film reinforces one of these heuristics with respect to some fictional behavior may then have some spill-over effect in the sense that when searching for a heuristic to apply to real circumstances, the heuristic in question is one whose availability is attractive because it has succeeded in the past in rendering some stretch of phenomena, albeit fictional, intelligible.

Moreover, recent research in cognitive and social psychology indicates that vivid information is more likely to be stored, remembered, and mobilized than is pallid information. Factors that contribute to vividness include the extent to which the information is, for example, emotionally interesting, concrete, and imagery-provoking.[36] Thus, heuristics wedded to films, in so far as they are characteristically conveyed vividly, will have a high degree of availability in the minds of viewers who are not ill-disposed toward the heuristic to begin with. And the availability of the said heuristics may incline viewers to access and apply them to actual cases.[37] And, of course, where the heuristic in question is ideological, a film's reinforcement of its availability amounts to an ideological effect.[38]

In conclusion, where contemporary film theorists attempt to locate the most important ideological effects of film in its formal structures, I propose that we think in terms of rhetorical structures, such as the ideological deployment of presupposition in the service of eliciting ideological tenets (which will often be of the nature of commonplaces). Commonplace and presupposition are not the only relevant rhetorical levers in film; further research in this area is required. However, thinking of the dissemination of film ideology in this way has the advantages of: (1) satisfying our intuition that not all films are necessarily ideological and (2) facilitating the recognition that ideology in film can be more than a matter of causing people to conceive of themselves as Cartesian egos.[39] Furthermore, the Althusserian approach suggests that the ideological effect of cinema is virtually unavoidable – that through its formal structures, cinema uniformly causes us to misrecognize ourselves as Cartesian egos. A final advantage, then, of a rhetorical approach is that, as indicated in the preceding paragraphs, it allows that the uptake of a film's ideology is variable, depending in large measure on the audience's predispositions.

Notes

1. Rudolf Arnheim, *Film as Art* (Berkeley: University of California Press, 1966).
2. A term of art, in film studies, for events staged or otherwise transpiring before the camera.
3. André Bazin, *What is Cinema?* (2 vols., Berkeley: University of California Press, 1971).
4. For a sketch of this conversation, see Noël Carroll, *Philosophical Problems of Classical Film Theory* (Princeton, NJ: Princeton University Press, 1988).
5. A primary representative of this sort of skepticism in film theory is Victor Perkins. See his *Film as Film* (Baltimore: Penguin Books, 1972). It should be noted that the case of Perkins here is somewhat complicated. For though he mounts anti-essentialist arguments against classical film theory, it is also possible to read his constructive proposals for the film theory of the future as a species of closet essentialism. See Carroll, *Philosophical Problems,* chapter 3.
6. I say "ironically" above because, though many contemporary film theorists are avowedly anti-essentialist, they believe that certain cinematic devices – like the perspectival image – are *essentially* ideological.
7. The label "Althusserian" has been chosen in order to signal the degree to which contemporary film theorists have been influenced by the framework for analyzing ideology that was introduced by the Marxist philosopher Louis Althusser in his "Ideology and ideological state apparatuses," in his *Lenin and Philosophy* (New York: Monthly Review Press, 1971). By employing this appellation I am not implying either that Louis Althusser endorses all the findings of contemporary film theorists or that contemporary film theorists have not essayed critical departures from the views of Althusser. However, I do believe that it is indisputable that the previously cited article supplies the fundamental framework within which contemporary film theory has developed and continues to develop. This much is admitted even by contemporary film theorists – for example, see Colin MacCabe, "Class of '68," in his *Tracking the Signifier* (Minneapolis: University of Minnesota Press, 1985), p. 13. Moreover, I doubt that any contemporary film theorist would deny that there is a historical link between Althusser's speculation on ideology and the emergence of contemporary film theory. For a further defense of this way of labeling contemporary film theory see Noël Carroll, *Mystifying Movies: Fads and Fallacies in Contemporary Film Theory* (New York: Columbia University Press, 1988). For a collection of many of the central documents of this variety of film theory see the anthology edited by Philip Rosen and entitled *Narrative, Apparatus, Ideology* (New York: Columbia University Press, 1986).
8. See, for example, Jean-Louis Comolli, "Techniques and ideology: Camera, perspective and depth of field," *Film Reader* 2 (January 1977).
9. See, for example, Jean-Louis Baudry, "Ideological effects of the basic cinematographic apparatus," in Theresa Hak Kyung Cha (ed.), *Apparatus* (New York: Tanam Press, 1980).
10. See, for example, Daniel Dayan, "The tutor-code of classical cinema," in Bill Nichols (ed.), *Movies and Methods* (Berkeley: University of California Press, 1976).
11. For a sympathetic overview of this position, see James Spellerberg, "Technology and ideology in cinema," reprinted in Gerald Mast and Marshall Cohen (eds.), *Film Theory and Criticism* (New York: Oxford University Press, 1985).
12. A similar argument can be found in David Bordwell, *Narration in the Fiction Film* (Madison: University of Wisconsin Press, 1985), pp. 25–26.
13. For a more thorough account of contemporary film theory, along with more detailed

criticisms thereof, see Carroll, *Mystifying Movies: Fads and Fallacies in Contemporary Film Theory.* As its title indicates, that book is a brief against Althusserian film theory. The present chapter is a continuation of that debate. Specifically, in order to challenge contemporary film theory, I believe that one must not only show its logical flaws and empirical shortcomings. One must also indicate that there are more fruitful lines of research than those developed by the Althusserians for answering the very questions that perplex them. That is, in order to defeat contemporary film theory decisively, one needs to engage it dialectically and to demonstrate that competing theories superior to the Althusserian model are available, i.e., theories that avoid the liabilities their theories incur while also explaining the data. One question that contemporary film theorists ask is how films disseminate ideology. This essay is an attempt to begin to develop an alternative answer to that question. Thus, this essay is an extension of the argument in *Mystifying Movies* to the terrain of the ideological effect of cinema.

14. For information on the history of the concept of ideology, see David McLellan, *Ideology* (Minneapolis: University of Minnesota Press, 1986); H. Barth, *Truth and Ideology* (Berkeley: University of California Press, 1977); Allen Wood, "Ideology, false consciousness and social illusion," in Brian P. McLaughlin and Amélie Oksenberg Rorty (eds.), *Perspectives on Self-Deception* (Berkeley: University of California Press, 1988).

15. I am also willing to entertain the extension of what counts as ideological to other cognitive phenomena, including what cognitive scientists have labeled scripts (Shank and Abelson), paradigm scenarios (de Sousa), schemas (Kelley), and personae (Nisbet and Ross), and perhaps even to prepropositional patterns of salience (Rorty). However, if such structures are to play a role in ideology, we must be able to specify the conditions under which each, in turn, is epistemically defective. See R. Shank and R. P. Abelson, *Scripts, Plans, Goals and Understanding: An Inquiry into Human Knowledge Structures* (Hillsdale, NJ: Lawrence Erlbaum, 1977); Ronald de Soussa, *The Rationality of Emotion* (Cambridge, MA: MIT Press, 1987); H. H. Kelley, "Causal schematas and the attribution process," in E. E. Jones (ed.), *Attribution: Perceiving the Causes of Behavior* (Morristown, NJ: General Learning Press, 1972); Amélie Rorty, "Explaining emotions," *The Journal of Philosophy* 75 (1978); Richard Nisbett and Lee Ross, *Human Inference: Strategies and Shortcomings of Social Judgment* (Englewood Cliffs, NJ: Prentice-Hall Inc., 1980), p. 35. I have attempted to apply the notion of a paradigm scenario to films in Noël Carroll, "The image of women in film: a defense of a paradigm," *The Journal of Aesthetics and Art Criticism* 4 (1990).

16. This last disjunct is introduced in order to allow for the role that true propositions may play in ideology. That is, a true proposition may be embedded in an otherwise ideological discourse in such a way that its import is, overall, misleading owing to its discursive contextualization.

17. Other candidates for the cognitive component of *ideological ideas* are mentioned in note 15 above.

18. Of course, the Althusserian does not deny this. Rather, for the contemporary film theorist the conviction of Cartesian egohood is the primary ideological effect of the cinema and, perhaps, a condition for the effectiveness of further ideological machinations. On our contrasting account, films may be ideological with no implications about the nature of the subject, and therefore, need not require the misrecognition of Cartesian subjecthood as a condition for other ideological effects.

19. Aristotle, *Rhetoric,* Book I, sections 8 and 9.

20. Aristotle, *Rhetoric,* Book II, section 20.

21. André Bazin, *Orson Welles,* (New York: Harper & Row, 1978), p. 66.

22. Aristotle, *Rhetoric,* Book II, sections 22–25.

23. Arthur Danto, *The Transfiguration of the Commonplace* (Cambridge, MA: Harvard University Press, 1981), p. 170.

24. Walter R. Fisher, *Human Communication As Narration* (Columbia, SC: University of South Carolina Press, 1987), p. 28.

25. In his *Rhetoric,* Aristotle regards the example and the enthymeme as distinct forms of argument; where they are both deployed in the same discourse, he advises that the enthymeme precede the example so that the

force of the former not be diluted. However, with what we are calling narrative enthymemes, it is generally the case that example and ellipsis work in tandem.

26. Needless to say, films may be rhetorical without being ideological. Films may propose genuinely moral (in the sense of upright) arguments by means of rhetoric. And, of course, the use of rhetoric in and of itself is not a sign of disvalue. The rhetorical operation of a film will only count as ideological if it meets the criteria laid down earlier. At the same time, we are also claiming that ideology in film is primarily disseminated through rhetorical operations of which the narrative enthymeme is one of the most important.

27. Or know that others in the given culture believe it.

28. There is a similar commonplace in *Back to the Future III* to the effect that your future is what you make it. This cliché is woven through the narrative in a way that is analogous to the example discussed above and, in addition, it is literalized by the special features of time-travel, as is the maxim that we are considering.

29. Interestingly, the characterization of the ideological operation of *Back to the Future* that I am advancing may appear to correlate with the kind of ideological effect that I claimed Althusserians find pervasive in film. That is, I have maintained that *Back to the Future* celebrates an exorbitant belief in personal agency and freedom. The question then arises as to how really distinct my analysis is from an Althusserian view of the same film. Here, I think that three differences are noteworthy. First, the beliefs that I find proposed in *Back to the Future* are more in the nature of folk platitudes which, contra the Althusserians, need not be thought necessarily to hook up to an entire ontology of the subject, nor can they be worked into a theory of the subject that you could label Cartesian, Husserlian, or even Idealist. Second, if these beliefs can be derived from *Back to the Future*, this is not – again, contra Althusserianism – a function of the fact that the film is projected by an apparatus, that it employs pictorial verisimilitude, perspective, narrative or continuity editing (including point-of-view editing). It is, rather, a matter of rhetoric – indeed, of the rhetorical/narrative organization of this specific film. And finally, though *Back to the Future* appears to traffic in ideology in terms of its notion of personal freedom, the method used to isolate this commitment does not privilege themes of agency as the *sine qua non* of ideology, and it allows that in other films there may be other sorts of ideological commitments, ones that may have nothing to do with personal efficacy, but that are conveyed by narrative enthymemes. On the other hand, I take it that the Althusserians are committed to the view that any film, of the classically constructed variety, is not only always ideological but, at the very least, involved in propagating an ideology of exorbitant personal agency.

30. Though further research on the matter is necessary, it would also appear that one way in which a film may function ideologically that differs somewhat from my examples so far is by concretizing a cultural commonplace – which in isolation may not be ideologically charged – by means of a misleading or tendentious example that, in turn, may come to influence the way in which the audience applies that commonplace in actual situations. For example, John Ford's *She Wore A Yellow Ribbon* is underwritten by the presupposition that the army is always the same. This refers, first and foremost, to its routinized activity and to the induction of successive generations of soldiers (primarily officers) into its routines and folk-ways. But there is also the suggestion that the army is always the same in the sense that the high moral purpose exemplified by the cavalry in the film is an enduring, eternally benevolent feature of the military. Thus, the example in question puts an ideological "spin" on the otherwise innocent and perhaps accurate maxim about military life. Further study of this "spin factor" with respect to tendentious and misleading narrative examples will, I believe, reveal a major source of the ideological operations of films.

31. For example, when Marty quotes Doc as saying "If you put your mind to it you can accomplish anything."

32. For example, in the original *Invasion of the Body Snatchers,* part of the horror of collectivist invaders is that they lack individuality. As vegetables, the pod people are alike – as

alike as two peas in a pod. That is, a commonplace about vegetables is exploited for horrific as well as ideological effect, though it is never explicitly stated in the film.

33. One advantage of what I am calling the rhetorical approach to film ideology versus the Althusserian approach is that whereas the Althusserian approach seems to present the ideological effect of a film as inevitable, the rhetorical approach allows that spectators may reject and resist the ideology proffered by a film. That is, on the Althusserian model, if a film has a certain generic structure, like perspective, this will inexorably cause the spectator to misrecognize himself as a Cartesian ego. However, in my account of the rhetoric of *Back to the Future,* there is no problem in acknowledging that a viewer may recognize the ideology of positive thinking that the film presupposes and reject it. That viewers are quite often aware of and ill disposed toward the ideological address of a film seems to me to be an indisputable fact. That the viewer is always duped, as the Althusserian model suggests, is just wrong. One strength then, comparatively speaking, of the rhetorical approach to film ideology is that it can explain how films dispose audiences toward various ideological stances, while also admitting that viewers do not always succumb to them.

34. For discussions of heuristics in human reasoning, see Amos Tversky and Daniel Kahneman, "Judgment under uncertainty: heuristics and biases," *Science* 185 (1974), 1124–1131; Amos Tversky and Daniel Kahneman,

"Availability: a heuristic for judging frequency and probability," *Cognitive Psychology* 5 (1973); Daniel Kahneman, Paul Slovic, and Amos Tversky (ed.), *Judgments Under Uncertainty: Heuristics and Biases* (Cambridge University Press, 1982); and Nisbett and Ross, *Human Inference.*

35. Shelley E. Tylor, "The availability bias in social perception and interaction," in Kahneman, Slovic, and Tversky (eds.), *Judgments Under Uncertainty,* pp. 190–191.

36. See Nisbett and Ross, *Human Inference,* chapter 3.

37. My use of terminology above differs somewhat from that of cognitive psychologists. They call vividness itself an example of the availability heuristic, i.e., a heuristic that privileges a biased inference or interpretation because it is available. Nevertheless, despite our slightly different uses of terminology I believe that our points of view amount to roughly the same thing.

38. Another case, which is at least worth noting, is that of the viewer who is unaware that the heuristic or commonplace conveyed by the film is ideological. Such a viewer might even be opposed to the ideological message of the film, if the ideological applications of the message were to be made apparent. The range of potential and logical effects on such viewers is too varied to discuss here, but will be developed in a future paper.

39. Since the ideological presuppositions and commonplaces that a film mobilizes may involve issues that don't involve questions of personal identity.

I have always found it both interesting and useful to reread the historical texts of film theory. For it seems to me that the history of film theory is not a closed book for film theorists in the way that the history of physics is a dead letter for physicists. That is, practicing physicists do not – as part of their training or as part of their customary practice – pore over the writings of Copernicus; one would not typically consult Kepler to help solve a current problem. But film theory is different. Its historical writings may maintain a relevance to present theorizing that is not paralleled by the historical texts of mature sciences like physics.

I am not sure why this is so. Perhaps part of the reason is that substantial portions of film theory still belong in the province of philosophy, and philosophical theories are not as susceptible to supercession as scientific theories. Philosophical theories are not decisively refuted in the way that scientific theories are.

Or perhaps it has to do with the immaturity of film theory as a field of inquiry. For though film theory has (arguably) been around for eighty-some years, it has only recently been organized as a coherent field of academic study. That is, much of film theory has been the work of inspired loners or of disconnected groups with little historical consciousness of belonging to a continuous conversation or tradition. Thus, one finds little dialectical engagement between the participants in the history of film theory. They do not work through each other's arguments and positions systematically. As a result, historical hypotheses have, more often than not, been bypassed, rather than defeated. Little has been definitively discarded. So what may be of use and what is plainly wrong has not been sorted out properly.

In the earlier section of this anthology on the movies, for example, I remarked more than once on my debts to Pudovkin. In this section, I claim that Hans Richter may have something of value to teach the contemporary avant-garde. But it is not the case that the history of film theory may only instruct us by providing insights that we may exploit today. The errors of the past film theory may also be instructive about theoretical options that continue to tempt us in the present.

In "Film/Mind Analogies: The Case of Hugo Munsterberg," I examine one of the most articulate early attempts at film theory, not only in order to clarify the issues that confronted silent film theorists and the strategies they adopted to address them, but also in order to raise problems with the enduring proclivity of film theorists to organize their thinking by means of analogies between film and the mind. In this, I see Munsterberg as a predecessor to contemporary film theorists, like Metz and Baudry. For though these latter-day theorists analogize film to the irrational aspects of the mind where Munsterberg analogizes film to the cognitive functions, all three share a confidence in the theoretical value of film/mind analogies. Thus rereading Munsterberg provides us with an opportunity for scrutinizing one of the most frequently recurring paradigms of film theory virtually at its inception.[1]

Whereas Munsterberg comes in for relentless criticism in what follows, in "Hans Richter's Struggle for Film," I find much to be admired in the clear-headed way in which Richter goes about setting up his theory for a politically committed, avant-garde film practice. Richter's theory is also interesting for the way in which it parallels Walter

Benjamin's thinking in "The Work of Art in the Age of Mechanical Reproduction." Like Benjamin, Richter appears to me to be involved in the attempt to map a materialist conception of history onto film history. Thus, my rereading of Richter enables me to work through some of the problems that are raised by attempting to apply historical materialism to art in general and to film in particular.

"A Brief Comment on Frampton's Notion of Metahistory" was originally a talk for a panel at the Museum of Modern Art which was organized by Annette Michelson in the spring of 1985 in order to honor the memory of the late Hollis Frampton. The essay is exegetical. It speculates about the role that Frampton's theory of the metahistory of film might have played for his filmmaking. I suspect that there may also be an undeveloped theoretical idea – or metatheoretical idea – of my own lingering in the background of this essay. It is that it may be useful to draw a categorical distinction between different kinds of film theories: those made by scientists or philosophers like Metz and Munsterberg, on the one hand, and those made by artists, like Frampton, Epstein, Brakhage, and perhaps Deren, on the other hand.

The first group of theories propose to tell us about film in general – or about certain kinds of film or certain film devices in general. But filmmakers often seem to make theories that are designed to rationalize or to make sense out of their own film practice and to discover an agenda. Thus, these theories do not really seem to have general import outside the filmmaker's practice.

Moreover, it strikes me that it may be appropriate to think and to talk about these different kinds of theories in different ways. Perhaps we should not have the same expectations and make the same demands of Brahkage's theories that we make of Arnheim's. Of course, the distinction that I have in mind is not an absolutely limpid one to apply, since authors like Richter and Eisenstein seem to be playing in the same ballpark as Benjamin and Kracauer. Yet, the matter is ambiguous, since the case could also be made that they are also just trying to make sense of their own practice. Nevertheless, there does seem to me to be some kind of a distinction somewhere around here. It is, as they say, a topic for future research.

Note

1. Munsterberg can also serve as the most completely analyzed example in this book of the sort of medium-specificity theorist whose position was challenged throughout Part I.

Though there is a strong tendency in the writing of our culture to assimilate cinema to notions of reality and realism, there is another tradition, at least equally persistent, that attempts to conceptualize cinema as an analog to the human mind – i.e., to characterize cinematic processes as if they were modeled upon mental processes.

Neither of these traditions seems to me an adequate perspective from which to develop satisfying film theories. However, neither tendency can be ignored, because both are so entrenched in our thinking about film, that, if not explicitly confronted, they will continue to haunt our thinking about cinema. The purpose of this article is to begin to challenge the view that film can be profitably studied theoretically by analogizing it to mental processes.[1]

The attempt to develop a theoretically viable approach to cinema by means of film/mind analogies was already in place in the second decade of this century, and it continues to inform much of the most dominant strand of contemporary film theory – that of psychoanalytic semiotics. Readers more familiar with the analytic tradition in aesthetics will recall a variant of the film/mind analogy in Suzanne Langer's conception of film as dream. Perhaps the most elaborate working through of the film/mind analog, with reference to the cognitive-rational aspect of the mind, was developed by Hugo Munsterberg. In this essay, I will be concerned with both the detailed way in which Munsterberg's proj-

ect goes awry and the way that the failure of his attempt may also shed light on the generic shortcomings of any film/mind approach to film theory, including those of our contemporaries.

If Munsterberg is useful in terms of exemplifying a problematic of contemporary film theory, he also illuminates the problematic of early film theory – the film theory of the silent era. Thus, in discussing Munsterberg, it is not only my intent to scrutinize his attempt to forge film/mind analogies, but also to consider his theory critically as illustrative of silent film theory, particularly in virtue of the question of whether and by what means film could be conceived of as an artform.

In early 1915, Hugo Munsterberg, a member of the Harvard Philosophy Department, a leader in the field of applied psychology, and an adviser to the likes of Teddy Roosevelt, Wilson and Carnegie, saw Annette Kellerman in *Neptune's Daughter* and became enthralled with the aesthetic possibilities of the nascent artform, the movies. He spent much of the following summer in nickelodeons and visited the Vitagraph Studios in Brooklyn. Flattered by the attentions of this distinguished academic, a student of Wilhelm Wundt and a protégé of William James, Adolph Zukor made him a contributing editor to the magazine *Paramount Pictograph*. Munsterberg took his role seriously and began to write a great deal about film – this activity culminating in 1916 in his *The Photoplay: A Psychological Study*.

Though by no means the first example of film theory, Munsterberg's text, now called *The Film: A Psychological Study*, was surely the most sustained of the early philosophical explanations and defenses of the film medium as an artform.[2] For many years, however, the book remained forgotten, perhaps because the German-born Munsterberg raised the ire of the popular press due to his strenuous efforts to stop America's entry into the First World War on behalf of the Allies. But when the treatise was reissued in 1970, it seemed almost prophetic, for Munsterberg's attempt to explain the workings of film processes through analogies with mental processes coincided, at least in a very general way, with the efforts of avant-garde filmmakers – like Alain Resnais, Stan Brakhage and Michael Snow – to create works that were said to be modeled on or to objectify consciousness.

Today, Munsterberg's treatise remains interesting for several reasons. On the one hand, it is of exemplary historical value for, despite its early appearance, it manages to set out the underlying aesthetic problematic of silent film with a clarity that was rarely rivaled during the period. But it is also of contemporary interest. For in his use of mental analogies to explain both the particular power and the conventions of film, Munsterberg presages recent psychoanalytic explorations in film theory such as those of Christian Metz and Jean-Louis Baudry. Admittedly, Munsterberg's analogies were to, what might be thought of as, rational mental processes, whereas contemporary film theorists prefer analogs with irrational processes. However, Munsterberg can be seen as the pioneer of the mind/film analogy-approach to film theory, and his writings, therefore, can be discussed within the context of the contemporary debate about whether the mind/film paradigm is a useful one.

The most pressing problem for film theorists of the silent period was to show that film could be an artform, insofar as *art* was the only available cultural category through which the medium could claim serious attention. But, since film was photographic, detractors regarded it as a mere mechanical recording device. Either, it slavishly reproduced slices of reality (the early documentaries of the Lumieres might be thought of as examples here), or, at best, it automatically recorded famous, and not so famous, plays. The point was that film was simply a copying machine, and nothing more. It blandly imitated whatever stood before the camera rather than creatively reconstituting it. In other words, it was presumed that imitation *simpliciter* was not a hallmark of art. And furthermore, since it was assumed that film – as a photographic medium – could do no more than imitate, then film could not be art.

Munsterberg, like other film theorists to come, agreed with the opponents of film that if a medium is to be an artform, it must do more than imitate. And this, in turn, entails that in order to show that film is an art, he must refute the assumption that all the film medium must do (given its photographic nature) is slavishly copy. This, however, involves showing two things: both that film need not necessarily copy reality *and* that films need not be mere mechanical reproductions of theatrical dramas.

Munsterberg pursues these demonstrations through an ingenious discussion of a series of cinematic devices – such as the close-up, parallel editing, flashbacks and flashforwards – that were being refined and popularized during the period from 1908 to 1915. His review of these techniques – which at the time were considered innovations – put him in a position to claim not only that the filmmaker transformed what he photographed but also that he transformed it in a way that was uniquely cinematic (rather than theatrical). Moreover, Munsterberg's explanations of the way in which these devices functioned also enabled him to connect film – specifically, film's peculiar way of transforming the world – with that which Munsterberg, on independent grounds, took to be the purpose of art.

In a nutshell, then, there are three major items on the agenda in *The Photoplay*: first, to show that the film medium, despite its photographic provenance, could imaginatively reconstitute whatever it recorded; second, that the cinematic mode of transforming reality was different from the theatrical mode; and, third, that this mode of transformation implemented the general purposes of art – which purposes could be identified without reference to cinema.

After an "Introduction," in which he sketches the technological development of cinema, and its early stylistic breakthroughs, Munsterberg begins what he calls "The Psychology of the Photoplay." Essentially, this section is an analysis of cinematic devices (or processes of articulation) such as the close-up, parallel editing and so on. This way of beginning – by focussing on characteristic cinematic processes of articulation – reminds one of the procedure of many future film theorists, such as Arnheim, and, in fact, the logical function this section performs also resembles that of opening portions of Arnheim's *Film As Art*. For what is to be shown here is that cinema is not the mere reproduction of anything, neither reality nor theater. (Incidentally, Munsterberg, again like Arnheim, opposes the sound film).

First, Munsterberg examines the impressions of depth and motion in film, noting that in contradistinction with theater, film depth and film motion are, so to speak, *superadditions* that the mind supplies to a series of flat surfaces of still photos. Whereas "theater has both depth and motion, without subjective help," in film "we create the depth and continuity through our mental mechanism."[3]

The contrast with theater and the concern with the relation of cinematic processes to the mind continue throughout Munsterberg's discussion of cinematic devices. For example, in theater attention is directed by means of word and gesture. When an actor points an accusing finger at another character across the stage, my eye follows the line of movement and lands at the appropriate point of interest. But in film, attention can be directed by camera positioning. If you want the audience to attend to the key in *Notorious,* you can show a close-up of it. The close-up selects crucial dramatic elements – objects, faces, hands, etc. – and enlarges them, while eliminating surrounding details. What we do on our own in theater, it might be said,

is done for us automatically in film. The film close-up is somehow equivalent to the psychological process of attention; it is an objectification or externalization of the process.

Wherever our attention becomes focused on a special feature, the surrounding adjusts itself, eliminates everything in which we are not interested, and by the close-up heightens the vividness of that on which our mind is concentrated. It is as if that outer world were woven into our mind and were shaped not through its own laws but by the acts of our attention.[4]

Moreover, this account of the close-up not only purportedly explains its operation but also does so in a way which differentiates such devices from the means available in theater.

This notion of cinematic devices as the objectification of mental processes is central to the claims Munsterberg will make for film as an art. But it should be noted that there is a striking change in the manner of Munsterberg's analysis of cinematic depth and motion, on the one hand, and the analysis of the close-up, on the other. For in the matter of film depth and motion, the psychologist tells us we add something to the visual array, whereas with the close-up, the selecting is something that is done for us. That is, the mental process – attention – that Munsterberg discusses with the respect to the close-up is, roughly speaking, in the film, not in us. A similar shift in direction occurs in the rest of Munsterberg's account of cinematic articulations.

In theater, later moments in a play may call to mind earlier ones; the scenes of Lear's desperation, for example, remind us of his earlier majesty. However, in film this sort of contrast can be literally visualized by means of a flashback. Where theater relies on the spectator's memory, the flashback in film is an analog or functional equivalent to memory. Likewise, when we see that proverbial gun in the first act of a play, we might be thought to imagine its going off in the last;

but, in film, such predictions can be made by a flashforward, as in the case of the funeral barge in *Don't Look Now*. Where the flashback is the analog or objectification of memory, the flashforward correlates with the imagination.

Of course, these comparisons with the mental acts of the theater spectator do not fully characterize the functions of the cinematic devices in question because in film we can have flashbacks to scenes the audience never saw, closeups of details not hitherto shown, and flashforwards to events never imagined. So we are not to think of these devices as substitutes for mental acts the audience would have performed had the action unfolded theatrically. Rather, it seems they must be taken as the operations of an externalized mind in which something is attended, something remembered, and something imagined. Moreover, these devices are modeled on generic acts of human attention, memory and imagination so that the manner in which they work is thought to be explained by analogizing them to mental processes. Perhaps one way of thinking of this modeling is to recall the notion of objectification Suzanne K. Langer has in mind in *Feeling and Form*.

Parallel editing in film – cutting between two events that occur at the same time but in different places and which are generally related dramatically – also differs from standard theatrical procedures where such scenes would be narrated sequentially. For Munsterberg, this is, so to say, a reification of the capacity of the mind to split its attention or to distribute its interest over a number of events at roughly the same time.

Munsterberg also speculates on ways in which cinema might externalize emotional moods – for example, by the use of soft focus, rhythmical editing and camera movement – though he regards his remarks here as tentative because these developments had not yet been fully cultivated by the cinema he knew.

One can read *The Film* primarily as an imaginative explanation of how *then* novel film devices function by means of mentalistic metaphors of the sort that V. I. Pudovkin would later employ to teach narrative film editing in terms of the shifting attention of an ideal spectator. However, Munsterberg himself has a larger project; he wants to use these analyses of film devices to show that the film medium can be an artform. To those who denied film could be art because it merely reproduces what it photographs, Munsterberg points out that a close look at these filmic structures, which constitute basic elements of the medium, shows they transform their photographic materials – specifically, they transform them in such a way that they appear *already* synthesized or molded by the human mind. So if it is a necessary condition for a medium to be art that it transform rather than imitate its referent, then film can be an art. Furthermore, since the mode of cinematic transformation is distinct from that of theater, then, if film is an art, it is an art distinct from theater. That is, for those worried that each art must differentiate itself from every other, film is not a theater clone. But the question remains why transforming reality in such a way that the resulting representation mimes the mind should count as artistic transformation? And to answer that Munsterberg needs to invoke his theory of art.

Munsterberg had worked out his view of art in *The Principles of Art Education* (1905). The fruits of this theorizing are applied to cinema in the second part of *The Film* under the heading of "The Esthetics of the Photoplay." Though many film scholars may find this section of the text disposably archaic, it is absolutely essential to Munsterberg's defense of film as an art. Indeed, since nowadays we take it as given that film is an art, the energies, not to mention the almost florid philosophizing, Munsterberg expends on this issue appear beside the point. And yet we must remember that the question of whether film could be art was *the* question of silent film theory.

Munsterberg's position on the nature of art can best be described as a dePlatonized variant on Schopenhauer. As one would expect, given Munsterberg's German heritage, it is deeply indebted to both rationalist and idealist aesthetics, though under his dispensation these receive a primarily psychological rather than a metaphysical twist. Munsterberg proceeds by drawing a contrast between two modes of thinking: the scientific and scholarly, on the one hand, and the artistic on the other. Sloganized, the difference, in Munsterberg's own words, is "connection is science, but the work of art is isolation."[5] That is, science discusses particular cases in order to connect them within larger systems by means of general laws; science subsumes. Art, on the other hand, places emphasis on the particular. Science yields general knowledge through studying cases. But for art, the particular itself is that which is valuable. Munsterberg, the epitome of the reasonable man, does not place one of these ways of knowing over the other; rather, for him, they are complementary.

The contrast Munsterberg has in mind is not unlike that of his contemporary Henri Bergson. Science is general; art particular. That Munsterberg should defend film by such a formula is particularly interesting in light of the history of film theory. For his fellow emigre, Siegfried Kracauer, will also develop a theory of film based on a contrast between a scientific way of approaching the world, which is generalizing, versus the particularizing mode of film which, for Kracauer, amounts to redeeming physical reality.

The origins of this view are deeply embedded in rationalist aesthetics. Perhaps it is first introduced by Baumgarten who advises that representations be of particulars, albeit ones touched by perfection, as a means of coming to terms with the Leibnizian-Wolffian notion that the objects of sensitive knowledge (Baumgarten's term) are clear but indistinct. The notion that the object of art be particulars is also at least suggested by

Kant's view that that which gives rise to the aesthetic perception of beauty is not subsumable under a concept.

Though the concept of disinterestedness is not so explicit in Munsterberg, he clearly has this Kantian commitment in mind when he writes:

The lover of beauty seeks it in the contemplation of the single object; he isolates it from the world and by that act of isolation it does not come in question any more as means to an effect, as tool for an end, as product of a cause, as a stepping-stone to something else, but merely in its own existence, and, therefore, because it does not suggest anything outside of itself, it brings a rest to the mind of the subject.[6]

If the notion, in this quotation, that the beautiful object lies outside the network of uses recalls the Kantian requirement of a divorce from practicality; the invocation of isolation, particularly of isolation as a means of inducing respite, reminds one of the radical form of Idealist aesthetics propounded by Schopenhauer. For Schopenhauer, aesthetic pleasure, in the main, derives, from the deliverance of knowledge from the service of the will. The realm of the will comprises striving and, thus, is intimately bound up with causality. Beautiful objects present the viewer with objects lifted out of the network of relations of space, time and causality, and afford a kind of objective knowledge not tied to the will and its needful concern with the interrelations of things. For Schopenhauer, this isolation from networks of space, time and causality enables the particular to be viewed in a way that discloses the Platonic Form of the thing.

Echoing Schopenhauer, Munsterberg writes: "The work of art shows us the things and events perfectly complete in themselves, freed from all connections which lead beyond their own limits, that is, in perfect isolation."[7] Unlike Schopenhauer, Munsterberg does not correlate this isolation with the revelation of Platonic Ideas. Rather one finds solace in the particularity of the object abstracted from its relation to everything else. And the nature of this solace is specifically the kind of freedom from striving Schopenhauer emphasizes – the object "brings the desires to rest."[8] Such objects are not only isolated from relations with everything else but are marked by internal perfection, that is to say, they are harmonious wholes; they are unified by traditional organizing features such as plots.

Stated formulaically, Munsterberg holds that: "A work of art, by definition, is (1) a harmonious whole which is (2) divorced from practical interests by means of (3) being isolated from the networks of space, time and causality." Condition (2) states the troublesome but at least well-known requirement of aesthetic disinterest, inherited from such writers as Hutscheson and Kant, while condition (3) specifies that requirement more in the manner of Schopenhauer in terms of isolation from interconnection with everything else. Indeed, Munsterberg's language is even stronger than I have indicated, for he has in mind not only that the artwork is isolated from the rest of the world but that it *overcomes* what he calls the forms of the outer world, namely space, time and causality. And this, in turn, is thought to result in a satisfying freedom from striving on the part of the viewer.

By this point, it may seem that we've drifted quite far from considering film. What can be the relation of film, specifically film as characterized by Munsterberg, and the view that art is the overcoming of forms of the outer world? Speaking of musical tones, Munsterberg says: "They have overcome the outer world and the social world entirely, they unfold our inner life, our mental play, with its feelings and emotions, its memories and fancies, in material tones which are fluttering and fleeting like our own mental states."[9] Here, it is clear that our inner life, our mental states are being contrasted with the outer world, and that something that imitates or in some sense reduplicates those

states *overcomes* the outer world. With this in mind, the relation of Munsterberg's earlier analysis of filmic structures as analogs of mental processes and his theory of film fall in line. He writes "the photoplay tells us a human story by overcoming the forms of the outer world, namely space, time and causality, by adjusting the events to the forms of the inner world, namely, attention, memory, imagination, and emotion." Film, that is, in virtue of constructing its structures as mental analogs, is an instance of art as theorized by Munsterberg.

The requirement that artworks be harmonious wholes can be satisfied by films by means of such features of plotting as unity of action and character, and by such pictorial attributes as balance. In sum, Munsterberg says:

The photoplay shows us a significant conflict of human actions in moving pictures which, freed from the physical forms of space, time and causality, are adjusted to the free play of our mental experiences and which complete isolation from the practical world through the perfect unity of plot and pictorial appearance.[10]

The mention of the free play of the mind and separation from the practical again sound the Kantian chord while Schopenhauer looms in the phrase "freed from the physical forms of space, time and causality."[11] Film is connected with a realm of freedom that has both psychological and metaphysical dimensions. Clearly, what Munsterberg is about here is linking film with existing conceptions of art in order to defend it against its detractors; and the conceptions of art he invokes do not tie the object in any essential way with the imitation of the outer world. Film does not copy the outer world, but rather reconstitutes it in the way that the mind does. This is a defense of the medium of film in general, rather than a defense of any particular film. Munsterberg has shown that film can be an art – under his modified, Idealist conception of art – without being committed to maintaining that the medium had, as yet, produced any masterpieces.

The logical structure of Munsterberg's theory is quite instructive for it is perhaps one of the first appearances of a model that will recur throughout the history of classical film theory.[12] At the general level, it attributes a purpose or role to cinema, here, the production of art. This, in turn, requires a specification of what art is which, for Munsterberg, most notably involves an overcoming of the physical forms of space, time and causality. With this specification of the purpose of film, we are able to zero in on the determinant characteristic of the medium, that is, the characteristic that enables the medium to realize its purpose. For Munsterberg this is identified as the capacity for the medium to objectify the processes of the human mind (which, themselves, must be thought of as overcoming the forms of the outer world). A conception of the determinant feature of the medium, in turn, provides a framework for analyzing the medium's characteristic processes of articulation; specifically, these processes – such as the close-up, parallel editing, the flashback, etc. – are treated as instances of the determinant feature of film. The close-up exemplifies the capacity for the medium to objectify mental processes by being an analog for attention. And so on.

Though the logical structure of Munsterberg's theory is at least clear, neither its premises or presuppositions appear particularly reliable. Perhaps, the premise that film can serve the purposes of art is, by now, incontestable. But the rest of the philosophical superstructure of the theory is shaky. The dependence upon aesthetic disinterestedness is open to all the objections this hotly contested concept invites, and, thus, Munsterberg's theory incurs all the problems associated with what are called aesthetic definitions of art. But these difficulties appear almost minimal when compared to the sorts of pressure that can be brought to bear on the Schopenhauer-derived elements in the theory.

Works of art are said to overcome the outer forms of space, time and causality. What could this possibly mean? One charitable gloss, one which has the virtue of making Munsterberg's view sound true, is that artworks characteristically come with things like frames, proscenium arches, curtains and so on, which are thought of as conventional signs that inform audiences that whatever is enclosed by these devices is, in general, discontinuous with surrounding events and environments. The usher is not part of the play, nor does the red in the painting bear a significant relation to the red of the fire extinguisher that hangs next to it. The artwork, so to speak, has been lifted out of our everyday world. There is a technical sense, which undoubtedly would be tricky to articulate in full, in which for purposes of appreciation, the artwork is to be construed, at least in certain important respects, as outside our space-time continuum. Some may put this extravagantly by saying that the artwork is divorced from the real world and constitutes a world unto itself, where the verbiage here is to be taken as a mix of technical language, metaphor and terms of art.

This interpretation would give us a very concrete way to think of art as a matter of isolation. And clearly Munsterberg has at least this view in mind. But he also means to claim much more, for art is said to *overcome* outer forms of space, time and causality. But to be isolated, in certain very restricted senses, from the existing space-time continuum is not to be divorced from the forms of space, time and causality. The forms of space, time and causality may still have a relevance, in many different ways, to the internal structure of an artwork even if, for example, we regard the world of a fiction as discontinuous from the space, time, cause manifold of the everyday world which we inhabit.

A case in point is plotting, which Munsterberg himself adduces as a unity-making feature in films. Plotting does not overcome the forms of space, time and causality but rather presupposes them. Munsterberg introduces his notion of "overcoming" with reference to music, which, for obvious reason, was the highest form of art for Schopenhauer. And, with a great deal of music, the forms of space and causality, though not of time, may be irrelevant to the internal, artistic structure of the work. But for so many other arts the manipulation of the forms of space, time and causality is integral to their structure. It seems incoherent to speak of artworks as overcoming the forms of space, time and causality since so much art is involved with exploiting these very forms. Moreover, if the value of art is situated in a release from striving, which itself is seen to be engaged by the form of causality, then it is difficult to understand the way in which artforms that involve plots – novels, dramas, and, to Munsterberg's potential embarrassment, film – can liberate us in the appropriate way, since they will be parasitic upon the forms of causality.

It may be thought that this argument against Munsterberg is inadequate for it overlooks the fact that Munsterberg speaks of the overcoming of the *outer* forms of space, time and causality. But this sounds funny. One would have thought that our psychological processes were exactly what connected us to the outer forms of space, time and causality. Indeed, some Kantians would identify these forms with mental forms. But, be that as it may, clearly mental processes do not stand in opposition to the forms of space, time and causality, but are intimately connected to them. And these mental processes, in virtue of their deep connection with space, time and causality, are what make practical activity possible; they do not stand against practical activity, they underlie practical activity. It appears incoherent to suggest that psychological processes overcome space, time and causality since they connect us with these forms. Furthermore, it is incomprehensible that film in virtue of imitating the very psycho-logical processes that link us to space, time, and causality could be thought to liberate us from those self-same forms.

At this point, it might seem that what Munsterberg needs to do to is to drop the Schopenhauer-derived elements in this theory and explicate his notion of isolation solely in terms of the Kantian concept of aesthetic disinterestedness. But, of course, if that is done, then the tight logical connection between his analysis of cinematic devices and his concept of art will be severed.

A disjunction between outer forms of space, time, and causality and mental processes, then, is essential to Munsterberg's theory. But it is hard to see how it is to be drawn. Munsterberg might have something like the following in mind: we can imagine beings with different psychological make-ups than our own. Say that they have no memories, they cannot imagine or predict the future, they have no sense of causal regularities. They are sheer bodily existents and they live in a pure present. They are rather like amoebae; things just happen to them, they forget it, and then something else happens to them. Their psychology restricts them to an experience of the continuum of space, time, and causality on, so to speak, a moment to moment basis; if we had films depicting their experience, they would be long takes of whatever happened in front of the camera followed relentlessly by whatever happened next.

Our psychological processes, however, free us from the kind of pure-present experience of the continuum of space, time, and causality of such sheer bodily entities through our powers of memory, prediction and our ability to focus our attention. And, by extension, our movies, modeled on our psychological processes, might be said to liberate viewers from the mindless realism of sheer bodily filmmakers. So human psychology can be thought of as overcoming the kind of experience of outer forms of space, time and causality that sheer bodily existents would have, and artforms, like film, that mime our psychological processes overcome the realism of baldly sequential, present states.

However, even if sense can be made of this interpretation of the way in which human psychological processes (and, by extrapolation, cinematic devices) can be said to overcome the forms of space, time, and causality, it remains questionable whether this can save Munsterberg's theory. Why? Well the theory has it that art, and film art, somehow release us from our ordinary experience of things with respect to space, time and causality. But we do not ordinarily experience things as sheer bodily existents. So even if there were a contrast between the way we experience things and the way sheer bodily existents experience things, that contrast would appear to have little bearing on the issue. If films replicate our mental processes, then when we view them we will not encounter a contrasting way of seeing the world. That there might be a contrasting way of seeing, such as that of our sheer bodily existents, makes no difference for us when we encounter works of art organized in the ways we already negotiate the outer forms of space, time and causality.

Another potential problem for Munsterberg resides in the contrast he develops between film and theater. For if film becomes an art in virtue of the way it transforms the spatio-temporal continuum of theater, then a question arises about whether theater remains an art. That is, Munsterberg must go on to explain the way in which theater overcomes space, time, and causality if he intends to count theater as an art. As it is, he appears to elevate film to the status of an art at the expense of theater. Undoubtedly, he mistakenly overlooks this problem because he has conflated two independent theoretical issues – the arguments that film is merely a reproduction of reality *and* that film is merely the reproduction of theater. Munsterberg treats these arguments as if they were one, effectively placing theater and reality in the same boat in a way that leaves us wondering how theater can be shown to be an art.

Of course, even if there are problems with the more philosophical aspects of Munsterberg's theory, it might be thought that there still may be something useful in his specific analyses of cinematic devices. That is, though his philosophy of art might leave too much to be desired, nevertheless his explanation of cinematic devices as analogs of mental processes could still be informative. And perhaps one could even go beyond Munsterberg and claim that audiences are able to readily assimilate cinematic conventions exactly because those conventions are modeled on prototypical psychological processes with which we are all already familiar.

However, even Munsterberg's mind/film analogies have come under recent attack.[13] If, for example, we take Munsterberg to be saying that any close-shot is analogous to the way in which one shifts attention, then it becomes crucial to determine what we mean by "way" here. That is, across what specific dimension of correspondence is the analogy being drawn? Mark Wicclair takes the relevant sense of "way" to be phenomenological; he presumes that for Munsterberg's analogs to succeed the appearance of cinematic devices, such as the close-up, must match the ways in which imagery appears to consciousness via the pertinent psychic process.[14] The close-up should have the same characteristics that objects of attention have in consciousness. And on these grounds, Wicclair finds Munsterberg's analogs wanting.

For example, a close-up involves moving in on an object in such a way that the screen size of the object is literally enlarged. This is quite different than attending to an object at a distance since it involves a scale change. Perhaps a more accurate way of miming attention would be to use a diaphanous mask or an iris shot. Likewise, the account of the flashback is subject to obvious disanalogies. If we remember something by means of an image, we entertain two percepts simultaneously, the memory image and the view of whatever is before our eyes. But flashbacks present images sequentially; they are phenomenologically disanalogous with imagistic memory. Perhaps, superimposition is more akin to such memory, though probably this is not quite right either. Similar problems can be generated with each of Munsterberg's analogies.

The upshot of this is that if we construe Munsterberg's analogies phenomenologically, then his account of cinematic structures is flawed. And given some of Munsterberg's descriptions, especially of the correlation of the close-up and attention, it does sound as though Munsterberg has phenomenological analogies in mind. However, the text is ambiguous in a way that might enable us to deflect Wicclair's objections.

Munsterberg, for instance, often speaks of functions. So rather than taking his analogies to be phenomenological, we might take them to be functional. That is, the close-up and attention are functionally analogous in regards to performing the same function – call it selective focussing – in different systems, the cinematic, on the one hand, and the psychological on the other. In a similar vein, we might discriminate between two types of flashbacks – those that repeat earlier scenes, and those that present novel scenes of earlier events in the world of the film. The repetitive flashbacks could be said to perform the same function – i.e., retrieval – in the cinematic system that memory performs in the psychological system while the novel flashbacks that fill in our fictions might be thought to perform the same function – here, postulating – that imagination does in our mental life. And, further functional analogs might be developed between mind and film.

However, despite the fact that we may save Munsterberg's explanations by emphasizing the importance of functional over phenomenological analogies, the real question is whether they are worth saving. For even if the analogies are meant to be functional analogies, it is far from clear that they explain anything about the operation of cinematic devices. For do we really learn anything by being told that the close-up is an analog to the psychological process of attention when we know so little about the way in which the psychological process of attention operates? And analogies to memory and to the imagination are on no firmer standing. Analogies to such processes have no explanatory force where we have so little grasp of the nature and structure of the mind.

The point here is crucial and it applies across the board to any mind/film analogy-approach to the cinema. In order to be instructive theoretically, an analogy must be such that one knows more about the term in the analogy that is supposed to be elucidating than the term that is supposed to be elucidated. That is, we need to know more, for example, about memory than we do about flashbacks if saying flashbacks are analogs to memory is to be informative. This requirement is fundamental to the logic of analogy. However, I am not convinced that this requirement is met by any of Munsterberg's analogies nor, for that matter, by any of the film/mind analogies propounded by film theorists so far.

Indeed, I suspect that the difficulty here is likely to persist into the foreseeable future, that is, for as long as the mind remains mysterious to us. Nor should film theorists be disheartened by this. For, in truth, we probably already know more about the operations of film than we do about the processes of the mind. This may appear to be an outlandish claim to film theorists. But it may be an occupational conceit on their part to envision film to be more unfathomable than it really is. In fact, we understand quite a lot about the way in which films work, about their conventions and their techniques. Far less is understood about the workings of attention, imagination, memory and the emotions. Munsterberg manages to tell us virtually nothing by his analogies between film and the mind.

The way a close-up works is really easily explained; to say it operates like attention actually complicates matters unless we understand how attention works; which, of course, we do not.[15]

These objections to Munsterberg's overall approach has direct bearing on leading tendencies in contemporary film theory. For psychoanalytically inclined film theorists, like Baudry and Metz, have developed elaborate accounts of the working of film by means of mentalistic analogs: in Baudry's case, between the cinematic apparatus and night dream, and in Metz's, between film and daydreams.[16] These theories differ significantly from Munsterberg's insofar as they press analogies between film and irrational mental processes while, for the most part, he relied on analogies with what might be thought of as rational, or at least, not irrational mental processes. Nevertheless, to the extent that these newer theories depend on mind/film analogies, they are susceptible to the same line of criticism just rehearsed with respect to Munsterberg.

One would not, of course, wish to deny that individual films might attempt to mime mental life. Brakhage's *Scenes from under Childhood* and Resnais's *Last Year at Marienbad* are probably best explained critically in terms of the conceptions of the mind that they are meant to illustrate. A critic, that is, may be justified in exploring mind/film analogies where that supplies the most plausible interpretation of why a specific film is structured the way it is. However as a theoretical – as opposed to a critical – project, it is my contention that the mind/film analogy-approach is abjectly uninformative given our present state of knowledge – or, more aptly, lack of knowledge – about the mind, both in its rational and irrational aspects. We learn next to nothing from the claim that films are like daydreams or night dreams when we know so little about dreaming. No one really even knows why we sleep. Dreaming is much more inscrutable than the cinema.

One reason that films are not so obscure to us is that we make them. We make them to work in a certain way and, for the most part, they function in the way they are designed to work. In a very general sense, we tend to understand our own tools and inventions more readily than that which we have not created. I don't mean to say that we understand our creations perfectly, nor that we have no understanding of the physical universe (though that knowledge is derived from experiments which, of course, are the product of our invention). My point is rather the less controversial one that we know a great deal about what we create in virtue of making them to perform the tasks that they successfully perform.

Presently, the computer, a product of human invention, is being exploited by cognitive scientists as a model or analog for the mind. This is an eminently defensible strategy because having designed computers, we know a lot about them, and we can attempt to extrapolate the wealth of information to mental operations. In the past theater, recall Hume's metaphor of the stage, and even film, for example Husserl, provided at least suggestive analogs for the mind, though not ones as powerful as those currently advanced by experts in artificial intelligence. Here my point is not that when all is said and done, the best theories of the mind will be based on analogies with theater, film or even artificial intelligence. But rather these theories have the correct logical structure whereas theories of film based on mentalistic analogs do not. For theater, film and now computers are things that we know much of, for we invented them, whereas the mind is still obscure to us.

Munsterberg developed a very clear version of the mind/film analogy-approach to cinema early on in evolution of film theory. One should not disparage his attempt. But perhaps what is best learned from his effort now is that this line of inquiry should be jettisoned.[17]

Notes

1. For a discussion of the problems of assimilating film to the notion of reality, see the second chapter of my *Philosophical Problems of Classical Film Theory* (Princeton University Press, 1988).
2. Hugo Munsterberg, *The Film: A Psychological Study* (New York: Dover Publications, 1970).
3. Ibid., p. 30.
4. Ibid., p. 39.
5. See Hugo Munsterberg, "Connection in Science and Isolation in Art," in *A Modern Book of Esthetics*, 3d ed., ed. Melvin Rader. (New York: Holt Rinehart and Winston, 1966), pp. 434–442. This is an excerpt from Munsterberg's *The Principles of Art Education*.
6. Ibid.
7. Munsterberg, *The Film*, p. 64.
8. Ibid., p. 66.
9. Ibid., p. 73.
10. Ibid., p. 81.
11. For an exploration of the Kantian aspect of Munsterberg's theory, see Donald Fredericksen, *The Aesthetic of Isolation in Film Theory: Hugo Munsterberg* (New York: Arno Press, 1977).
12. For a more detailed discussion of the structure of this type of film theory, see the introduction to my *Philosophical Problems of Classical Film Theory*.
13. See Mark Wicclair, "Film Theory and Hugo Munsterberg's *The Film: A Psychological Study*," in *The Journal of Aesthetic Education* 12 (July 1979): 33–50.
14. Ibid.
15. Upon hearing this assessment of Munsterberg's *The Film*, Mary Devereaux felt that I had overlooked what was really important about Munsterberg's contribution. She noted that one might take the notion of film as mind not as the basis of a theoretical research program, but as the rhetorical device, a metaphor, one meant to illuminate the new medium for a skeptical audience. Moreover, it was just the right kind of metaphor that the situation called for – one which got people thinking about film in contrast to reality or the slavish recording thereof. I would not want to deny that as such a metaphor the film as mind notion was rhetorically effective. My point is only that it could not be given a literal cash value – neither in Munsterberg's day nor in our own. And this is what renders the approach theoretically dubious, despite whatever might be its heuristic value.
16. For detailed, specific criticism of the theories of Metz and Baudry, see my *Mystifying Movies: Fads and Fallacies of Contemporary Film Theory* (Columbia University Press, 1988).
17. This essay was originally written as part of a series of retrospective reviews that the *Journal of Aesthetics and Art Criticism* planned of books written in this century before its inception. It has been somewhat reworked to be presented as an article independent of that series. This may account for some of its peculiarities; other peculiarities are traceable to me. Versions of this article were read at Vassar and at York University and I have benefitted from the criticisms of the faculties of both those schools, and, as well, particularly from the comments of Donald Fredericksen, Annette Michelson, Jesse Kalin, Mary Devereaux, Evan Cameron, David Bordwell, Peter Kivy, Ian Jarvie and the referees of the *Journal of Aesthetics and Art Criticism*. Paul Guyer supplied especially useful information concerning the intricacies of rationalist-idealist aesthetics.

Hans Richter's *The Struggle for the Film: Towards a socially responsible cinema* (New York: St. Martin's Press, 1986) was written in the late thirties when the late author was in exile from Nazi Germany. Richter's attempts to publish the manuscript abroad and in the United States, where he emigrated in 1941, failed, and the book, in a revised (apparently condensed) version – authorized by Richter himself – did not appear until 1976 in Germany. The text in its reworked form may or may not have benefitted from historical hindsight – the English edition by Althusser-translator Ben Brewster contains some francologisms ("conjuncture," "apparatus"). Nevertheless, *The Struggle for the Film* is still a very interesting, supplementary document which adds to our understanding of film culture in the late twenties and thirties, a period of momentous transitions, such as: from a purist avant garde to a politically engaged one; and from silent film to sound. Opposed both to the ideological role of film under capitalism and to the rise of fascism, *The Struggle for the Film* asks "What is to be done?" of filmmakers at a time that Richter explicitly regards to be one of crisis.

And aside from its historical value, *The Struggle for the Film* may also be of some theoretical use. For in it, Richter is trying to work through a problem that concerns many contemporary independent filmmakers, viz., how to develop a counter-cinema – what Richter calls a progressive cinema – one, that is, capable of posing an effective political challenge to the "official" (Richter's word) commercial film industry. In certain pertinent respects, Richter's situation in writing this book parallels the situation of many avant-garde filmmakers of the last fifteen years or so. As is well known, Richter's earliest film work is of a highly formal sort; his classic *Rhythmus 21* might, for example, be interpreted as a study of the perceptual conditions that give rise to the sense of depth in film. However, by the time Richter writes *The Struggle for the Film,* the political pressures of the times have convinced him that formal experimentation – and its subtending aesthetic allegiance to the autonomy of art – have become historically outmoded. Art in general and film in particular must in the present epoch (i.e., that of mass industrial society) be situated in and engaged with broader social contexts. Richter's movement from avant-garde formalism to a concern with politics and ideology, then, anticipates the shift, over the last two decades, in recent avant-garde concern from the formal experimentation of the minimalist (or "structural") film to, at least nominally, a more politically committed cinema.[1] Thus Richter's thinking about the options for such a cinema, or, as I shall argue, his way of thinking about them, may be instructive for current theory and practice.

Broadly speaking, Richter's philosophical approach in *The Struggle for the Film* is Marxist. That is, Richter's theoretical optic involves what at least appears to be a materialist conception of history. In concrete terms, this means that much of the book takes the form of historical narration, most often concerned with events and figures which appear in virtually every film history. However, it is a narrative that is informed by a theory of history which, in turn, yields a theoretical history of film, one which unearths a problem (a "contradiction") whose solution is also immanent in the historical process.

The Struggle for the Film is divided into two unequal parts: "The cinema as product

305

of the twentieth century," and "Towards a history of the progressive cinema." Part One sketches the history of the film from its origins to the late thirties, and it has a thesis about that process: film initially (and in virtue of materialist/technological predestination) is an art of the masses which became increasingly subject to *embourgeoisement*, a phenomenon which is progressively more apparent after 1925 with the emergence of the Soviet cinema and its overt proletarian allegiance. The *embourgeoisement* of film – which, among other things, results in the passive spectatorship of contentless films – represents a crisis or problem to be overcome (the struggle for the film). Part Two attempts to suggest ways in which engaged filmmakers might productively meet this crisis and contest the influence of the official bourgeois cinema. Richter's primary method here is to look to examples of devices in existing films that thwart the passive spectatorship of official cinema.[2] Richter's criteria for the selection of these specimens of progressive cinema is roughly Brechtian: progressive art encourages participant spectatorship, viewers who interpret what they see in relation to actual social life. Richter finds serviceable strategies in this regard in the avant garde of the early twenties, in what has since been called the art cinema (e.g., Dreyer) and in popular film – especially comedy (Chaplin, as usual, receives lavish commendation) but also drama (e.g., *Viva Villa*). However, at the heart of Richter's program is a commitment to montage as the high road to progressive cinema. When Richter, on occasion, presents original speculations about the way in which progressive cinema might be made (e.g., his view of mechanical acting), he does so essentially as a montagist, and Vertov and Eisenstein have a special pride of place in the text. Like others in the period between the world wars, such as Benjamin,[3] Richter discerns a link between the cognitively stimulating rhetoric of montage and the Brechtian promotion of active spectatorship.[4]

Though it is not clear that they ade-quately support a logically unified theoretical argument, there are a number of key philosophical and factual premises underlying the history of film in Part One. The first is that art is connected to needs. And since needs change as social formations change, art and the appropriate theory of art will alter over time. In point of fact, the modern age has precipitated such a shift: the needs art must satisfy, that is, change with the passage of successive hegemonic classes (the bourgeoisie followed by the proletariat). Corresponding to this transition, there is a putative move from the notion of art as autonomous (e.g., Schopenhauer) and correlative aesthetic theorizing (e.g., Kant) to a conception of art as part and parcel of the social process and to a correlative type of political theorizing (what nowadays is heralded as the end of art theory). The distinctive feature of the modern age is that it is industrial and technological; and in this it is predicated upon serving a mass society even as it requires the masses to serve it. And for Richter the role of art in such a context is to satisfy the needs of the masses.

Film, in this respect, is ideally suited, for in virtue of being the child of its age – it is both technological and industrial – it can serve the masses, just as an assembly line is fitted to produce for a mass market. That is, given its industrial and technological provenance, film is the mass art, an art for and of the age of the masses. What needs do the masses have? For relaxation, spectacle, and knowledge and belief (p. 24), or, alternatively, for entertainment, spectacle, and instruction (p. 39).

With this framework in place, Richter is able to trace the early history of film in terms of the fulfillment, *ab initio,* of the technological/industrial entelechy of this mass art. Richter divides it into three genres – the documentary (which presumably correlates with instruction), the fantastic film (spectacle?), and the fiction film (entertainment with elements of spectacle and perhaps instruction)[5] – each of whose evolution he characterizes, often making sensitive and original observations about films and filmmakers.

The documentary line, which Richter maintains is committed to revealing reality and whose nemesis is cosmetic beautification, begins with the Lumières and is dramatically refined by Flaherty, whom Richter applauds for underscoring the importance of the environment. The tradition finds especially triumphant expression in Vertov, a veritable hero Richter endorses for his concern with rhythm, his aesthetic of the machine (Richter sometimes relies on the dubious associative constellation rhythmical/mechanical/modern), and for making film the tool of some sort of modern perception (one in which invisible processes are made visible; one which shows how things work).

The fantastic line runs through Méliès, Sennett, ciné-dadaists and Chaplin, who shows social reality from the perspective of the impoverished. Like Brecht, and Aristotle and Horace before him, Richter thinks that instruction should be leavened with pleasure – a view too often forgotten by today's politicized avant-gardists.

Richter's account of the evolution of the fictional line of early cinema is largely a review of the development of what is often called the language of film, citing the formal innovations of Griffith and other pioneers, and their augmentation by montagists. Like other early film theorists, Richter spends a great deal of time discussing the significance of the introduction of the close-up and of cinema's spatio-temporal conventions. This formal development nevertheless is seen in a positive political light – as being on the side of history – for it is part of a liberation of thought and vision purportedly comprising, among other things, a fusion of cognition and emotion, and a way of rendering complex, invisible processes concretely intelligible. Film, that is, evolves a new way of seeing – it is both an agent of and an emblem for a new form of modern consciousness.

Early film, then, by Richter's accounting, progressed in a way that began to realize the social mandate inscribed in its material (technological/industrial) base. In certain cases (some documentaries, Chaplin), it introduced new types of content, at times revelatory of social reality, while, in the main, it also constructed a vocabulary of forms which participated in the forging of a new mode of perception for the masses. And, as well, the masses responded eagerly to this new artform. However, the very success of early film provoked a crisis. For the profitability of film turned it into a business, a big business aligned with the interests of the bourgeoisie, not the proletariat.

Richter obviously presupposes that once the medium had developed an emancipatory mode of perception its natural vector of development would be to wed that mode of mass (i.e., appropriate to the mass age) perception to new forms of content, ones socially relevant to the masses. But the takeover of film by bourgeois business concerns stops this process in its tracks. The art of the masses is made to serve the interests of the bourgeois and the rule of capital. The results are the production of films that are: apparently neutral socially, wallowing in sex, adventure, and crime; films of high formal achievement, devoid of social content (*The Student Prince* is his favorite example); plots mired in the problematics of bourgeois individualism. These serve the status quo by suppressing social reality and/or promulgating the bourgeois world view. Richter concludes:

The cinema is in this nonsensical situation: on the one hand, it is one of the most interesting artistic fields of our age, a universal art, an instrument for the abolition of the opposition between thought and feeling; on the other it is a pseudo-art with no correspondence to concrete life, an untruth constantly generating more untruth. This crass opposition reveals the contradictions to be found in cinema, contradictions which are rooted in the age of which cinema is a part. (p. 81)

Richter's own explanation of why the masses acquiesce in this is that the products of the official cinema propose moral daydreams, seductive utopian escape routes from the burdens of everyday life.

Richter's scenario for the crisis of film is underwritten by a materialist theory of history. In brief, this presupposes that the productive base of society determines superstructural elements – ideologies, ways of seeing, and so on. Also, this philosophy of history explains momentous social changes and their attending crises in terms of a conflict between the productive base and other social elements. Specifically, at a certain point of development, the productive capacity of the base outstrips the social forms and ideologies developed in concert with an earlier stage of productive capacity. For example, feudal society fettered the new productive capacities unleashed by the nascent bourgeoisie. This tension between productive capacity and superstructure is thought of as a "contradiction," and such contradictions are not resolved until the superstructure is brought in line with heightened productive capacities, possibly by means of revolution.

In Richter's version of film history, the film medium plays the role of the productive base. Since it is industrial – and since industry, by nature, gravitates towards servicing mass populations – it has the potential of – or even an inherent, historic predisposition towards – serving the masses. Early film tended in this direction. But when film fell under the control of bourgeois business interests, this process was arrested. The means of production were shackled – specifically, the capacity of the productive base to generate, by means of a universal art, a new social content was obstructed. A contradiction (in the Marxist sense) arose between what the base could produce and what was produced and this fettering of productive capacities served the interests of capitalism at large. Also, Richter notes a subsidiary, thematic contradiction. Film, a *mass* art for *mass*

consciousness, becomes an instrument for celebrating bourgeois *individualism* (in contrast, for example, to the possibility of exploring the mass hero of Soviet filmmaking). Such contradictions define the crisis of the film; progressive filmmakers must wrest the means of production from the official cinema.

Official cinema according to Richter has impeded the social evolution of the film. Its contentless narratives (vis-à-vis social reality) – formally stimulating (in the sense of mesmerizing) though empty – and its wish-fulfilling, utopian ("Sunday school") morality stultify the critical capacities of the mass audience. Live social questions are deferred and the passive reception of bourgeois ideology is promoted through entertainment. In this context, the theorist of progressive cinema wants to know:

If the audience are insufficiently receptive – how are they to be made more so?

If they do not learn easily – how can ideas be presented in an easily accessible and forceful way?

If they only respond to primitive stimuli – how can complex contents be clothed in simple stimuli?

If they only see in their own fashion – by what means are their eyes to be opened?

If they would rather be entertained, and even badly entertained than well taught – how can they be taught in an entertaining way? (p. 135)

These are the central questions that preoccupy Part Two of *The Struggle for the Film*. One has the sense that large portions of the text may have been deleted here. Part Two has a fragmentary feel to it and the transitions are often not smooth. In any case, Richter's approach to the preceding questions is not systematic and sometimes not particularly perspicuous. Often, he depends on examples – such as Laughton's acting style in *The Private Lives of Henry VIII* – with little (or only obscure) comment on the methodological principles that enable said examples to implement the aims of progressive cinema – that is, exactly how and why does Laughton's acting style embody an interpretation of Henry in a social perspective rather than only a mere presentation of an individual pathological psychology? With such cases, one might speculate that either Richter thinks the mechanisms underlying his examples are obvious, or, more probably, that it is sufficient to supply fellow progressive filmmakers with paradigms to think about and perhaps imitate.

Where Richter is more programmatic in his recommendations, he is decidedly in favor of a sort of Brechtian-informed montage. Like Brecht, he opposes what he calls unilinear plot and prefers experimentation in the direction of the Soviet mass hero and the essayistic film. On the relation of sound to image, Richter endorses acoustic montage – along with metrical stylization – preferred solutions of theorists like Eisenstein to the problem of sound.[6] Like Arnheim, whom he frequently chastises in asides, Richter conceives of editing as a form of "defamiliarization"; however, in contrast to Arnheim, Richter emphasizes the importance of the "de-naturalized" space-time continuum opened by editing in virtue of the way it allows for the interpretive activity of the spectator rather than that of the filmmaker. Indeed, what seems compelling about montage for Richter is that this style, once embraced, appears to point naturally toward fruition in what Eisenstein called intellectual montage,[7] which, in turn, is a practice ideally modeled for Brechtian spectatorship.

Other of Richter's biases also correspond to those of theorists of the period, especially his penchant for medium specificity. In his discussion of film acting, which he regards as the leading communicative dimension of film, he not only calls, à la Brecht, for interpretation, rather than identificatory portrayal, but urges adoption of a mechanical style of performance – not only because this will secure desired alienation effects, but because it is appropriate to the medium of film.[8] That is, the actor's movements should

be adapted to the movement of the camera machine so that cinema and actor compose an expressive whole – one that is "mechanical." What Richter means here by mechanical is obscure. Perhaps he has in mind something like Meyerhold's bio-mechanical style or Kuleshov's acting exercises. But even if one could get a reliable handle on what constitutes mechanical acting, the essentialist orientation it presupposes strains credulity. It is doubtful that the mechanical structure of the medium dictates the expressive quality of the movement style of acting in it. Does video require *electrical* acting (and what would that be)? Moreover, logically, one suspects that any attempt to link what might be called a *mechanical* style of acting with the *mechanical* action of the film cameras is scarcely more than an equivocation of the term "mechanical."

Of course, the deepest problems with Richter's theory involve his philosophical history of the film. On the most banal level, it is difficult to get clear on its periodizations. When, for example, does the early period of the development of the fiction film end and the era of the official, bourgeois film begin? For the distinguishing mark of the latter is what Richter considers its socially contentless plots, but these go back to the dawn of the fiction film. Also, the distinction Richter makes between fantastic films and fiction films is hard to sustain.

More perplexing, however, is Richter's presupposition that cinema is inherently emancipatory, or, at least, that it has a natural tendency, all things being equal, in that direction. Like Benjamin, Richter, for example, believes that cinema heralds a new form of perception.[9] Richter's own case for the emancipatory nature of cinema appears to derive from his view of technology. Technology and industry are mass forms of production – i.e., they produce for the masses. Cinema is industrial and technological – it is a mass form of production. It is, therefore, an artform (art, here, is the relevant type of production) for the masses.

An artform for the masses has a natural tendency to serve their genuine needs; cinema is such an art.

Clearly, this argument depends on the way "artform for the masses" is interpreted. On the one hand, it could be descriptive – an artform for the masses is one that produces for a mass market. This sense, of course, corresponds to the opening stages of the argument concerned with industry. But there is also a commendatory sense of "artform for the masses," where that means "serves the genuine needs of the masses." And that is the sense of mass artform with which the argument concludes. However, these two senses are not logically connected. A form of production may indeed supply a mass market without serving genuine needs. This is not a logical contradiction.

Is it some other sort of contradiction? If one accepts a certain view of the materialist conception of history, one may be tempted to say that it is a historical law that the forces of production always gravitate toward fulfilling genuine needs, and that production for mass markets that fails in this respect contradicts a historical law. But a law that can be contradicted hardly sounds like a law at all and, in any case, invoking such a law in this context effectively begs the question since what is at stake here is whether film – the form of production at issue – is necessarily emancipatory (destined to fulfill genuine needs), and the purported law does no more than assert that all forces of production, including film, are essentially emancipatory. In short, the conclusion is being presumed from the start. Of course, the basic problem in this discussion is the attribution of a particular *telos* or destiny to technology by the materialist theory of history. Whether a technology serves for good or ill depends on the actual uses to which it is put. Richter, like others, errs in straining to find a *moral* predisposition inherent in the film medium.

As his proclivities toward medium-specificity and his faith in a technologically determined, benevolent *telos* for cinema

indicate, Richter hypostatizes cinema. Indeed, he writes of the struggle for *the* film, as if film as we know it were a single thing rather than a multiplicity of various uses. Instead of speaking as though in the contest with official cinema progressive cinema were the legitimate heir to some throne, Richter should regard both rivals as uses of cinema, and defend the use he advocates in terms of the moral, political, intellectual and aesthetic values it engenders. There is no reason to doubt that a powerful case for a progressive cinema can be made without resorting to notions of materialist destiny.[30]

Since I have criticized the metaphysical foundations of Richter's view of film history, as well as some of his suggestions for a progressive cinema, the question remains as to why I claimed earlier that the book might be of theoretical use. My reasons here have less to do with the substantive claims Richter makes than with aspects of the way he goes about thinking of the prospects for progressive cinema. For some of Richter's ways of thinking about these matters are, I believe, more productive than recent attempts to establish avant-garde and/or progressive film practice on the basis of received post-structural theory.

Three features that might recommend Richter's mode of theorizing to contemporary filmmakers are that it is practical, integrative, and precise. His approach is practical in that it is aimed at bringing about specific outcomes in a concrete situation whose problematic nature is clearly defined. It is theorizing dedicated to figuring out what is to be done within a context where the exigencies are spelt out. It is directed and directive. Thinking is targeted at making films, films which solve certain problems in a given situation with definite needs.

This contrasts sharply with the sort of theorizing available to contemporary avant-gardists from the various popular Althusserian-Lacanian frameworks. These are abstract – descriptive of the conditions of subject constitution in general – and critical – designed to unmask the machinations of ideology (everywhere). Not only does such theorizing fail to supply the filmmaker with a clear-cut sense of what is to be done – since it is critical and descriptive rather than practical. It is also framed in such a general and abstract fashion that any film is likely to fall afoul of its critical categories in one way or another. Taken seriously the metaphysical-critical biases of such theorizing may make any attempt at filmmaking problematical and, in any case, they are hardly instructive, even in a vague way, about what a filmmaker who accepts them might do to contest ideology. Whereas the practical approach to theorizing that Richter illustrates – theory as grappling with contextually situated problems – offers an example of the way in which filmmakers can guide their own activity.

Richter's style of theorizing is also integrative. In searching for solutions to his practical problems, he turns to the historical avant garde and to popular film for suggestions, and he is willing to admit fellow travelers of all sorts to the progressive cinema. Where the tendency in ciné-post-structural theorizing is to find every preceding avant garde, not to mention the history of popular film, complicit in ideology, Richter's perspective is strategic in two senses – he assesses the work of the past in its own strategic context which, in turn, allows him to regard that past as a repository of potential strategies for the present. As a result, historical experience, so to speak, stays open to the progressive filmmaker and can be integrated into contemporary practice.

Richter's theorizing as well has the virtue of being relatively precise as avant-garde theories go. As already quoted, he asks fairly specific questions about the ways in which film spectatorship is to be changed. Some may feel that his answers overestimate the efficacy of montage. But even if one rejects his answers, the relative precision of his questions is salutary. For a large part of theorizing is a matter of getting straight

about what you want to know. Framing clear questions is an integral part of theorizing. The greater the clarity and specificity of one's questions, the greater the likelihood that one can find answers to them. The questions a theoretician poses, particularly where they are well-defined, facilitate research. But even though these remarks are virtually platitudes, they are rarely respected by avant-garde theorists. Too many contemporary filmmakers seem to choose theories because they are edifying worldviews – ones often regurgitated disjunctively in their work. And discussion and debates about avant-garde film theory are generally incomprehensible just because what is at issue is a mystery. Reading *The Struggle for the Film* is tonic, at least in this respect. Contemporary avant-gardists can only profit from the example of Richter's clear questioning.

Notes

1. For a contextualization of the shift away from minimalist cinema, see Noël Carroll, "Film," in the *Postmodern Moment,* ed. by Stanley Trachtenberg (Westport, Ct.: Greenwood Press, 1986).

2. Richter's theory of film takes a classic form. Richter posits a role or value for cinema – a social mandate to serve the needs of the masses. Given his interpretation of this mandate, this enables him to focus upon the characteristic of film that will be determinant in his thinking – the capacity of the medium to engage critical faculties. He then examines various articulatory processes of film – acting, editing, etc – in order to elucidate the ways in which they have been adapted to actualize the determinant characteristic of film. For a discussion of the structure of this type of theorizing, see my *Philosophical Problems of Classical Film Theory* (Princeton: Princeton University Press, 1988).

3. Walter Benjamin, "The Work of Art in the Age of Mechanical Reproduction," in *Illuminations,* edited by Hannah Arendt (New York: Schocken Books, 1969). Though Benjamin is not mentioned by Richter, there are a

number of similarities between the two theorists, as noted by A. L. Rees in the "Forward" to *The Struggle for the Film*.

4. As a result of the popularization of the Bazinian polemic, it is easy to forget that montage was often advocated on the grounds that it promoted a cognitively active audience. Ironically, though putatively opposed aesthetic projects, both Bazinian realism and montage agree in their most fundamental values – the desirability of participant spectators. Their primary debate really seems to be about the means best suited to securing this end.

5. Richter's categories – including the distinctions drawn between spectacle, instruction, and entertainment as well as between the fantastic film and fiction film – are not as tightly crafted as one might wish. Why, for example, is Chaplin included in the fantastic line rather than the fiction line? Similarly, it is difficult to see spectacle and entertainment as discrete categories rather than overlapping ones.

6. Richter's preferences with regard to sound correspond to what I have elsewhere called a silent film use of sound. See my "Lang and Pabst: Paradigms for Early Sound Practice," in *Film Sound: Theory and Practice*, edited by Elisabeth Weis and John Belton (New York: Columbia University Press, 1985).

7. For a recent discussion of intellectual montage see Annette Michelson, "Reading Eisenstein, Reading Capital," in *October*, no. 2 (Summer 1976).

8. On page 159, Richter argues for metrical film dialogue on the grounds that this accords with the mechanical nature of cinema. This seems to involve a specious identification of the metrical and the mechanical.

9. Benjamin, "The Work of Art in the Age of Mechanical Reproduction."

10. Another problem with Richter's approach is that it envisions the program for progressive cinema exclusively in terms of filmmaking strategies, paying no attention to distribution. But surely an advocate of progressive cinema needs not only to be concerned with what is to be seen but also how it is to be seen. Here one must play Adorno to Richter's Benjamin.

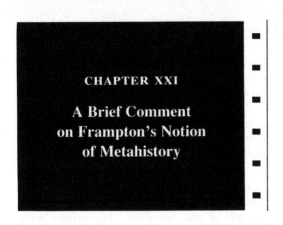

Tonight I would like to speak about certain aspects of Hollis Frampton's film theory, specifically about the contextual factors and logical constraints that I surmise led him to contrive the notion of a metahistory of cinema. My aim is interpretive, rather than critical, which seems appropriate, for unlike that of academic film theorists, such as Arnheim and Metz, Frampton's theorizing was not directed at formulating a general account of the nature of film as it exists, but at an account of what film, particularly his own filmmaking, should be. Loosely speaking, his theory performed primarily a pragmatic rather than a purely cognitive role. In this light, I shall argue that by means of the idea of metahistory, Frampton was attempting to negotiate his way between two theoretical approaches to cinema in such a way that would make it possible for him to continue filmmaking.

Stated broadly, the two theoretical claims that I think Frampton wishes to reconcile can be called the essentialist approach and the historical approach. And in attempting to coordinate these approaches – through the notion of metahistory – Frampton's theorizing parallels, in its own special way, a central struggle or tension within film theory, indeed within art theory and cultural theory, as those have evolved over the past twenty-five years.

Some background clarification is necessary here. It seems to me that over the past twenty-five years there has been a shift from essentialism as the basic form of analysis and, at times, of commendation in film theory and art criticism to an emphasis on history as the privileged discursive framework. For the essentialist, the prime task of the theorist is to identify the nature of an artform and to advocate those styles that appear to exploit best its artistic medium. Bazin, Greenberg, and Brakhage are examples, though hardly compatible ones, of essentialism. By the eighties, however, perhaps as the result of the collapse of Pax Americana and the pervasive uncertainty thereof, faith in essentialism has given way to a preference for history – especially for social and institutional history – as the accepted means for understanding film and the arts. Semiotics, genealogy, reception theory, all putatively sensitive to historical variability, have become favored tools of artworld theorizing, while, in film studies, these developments are also accompanied by the rise of intensive interest in historiography. This change in focus – from essentialism to history – in the study and criticism of film and art is reflective of, if not always synchronous with, the shifts in intellectual ambition between the sixties and the eighties, as witnessed by the current hagiography of the intelligentsia – e.g., Foucault, Rorty, MacIntyre, Ricoeur, Gadamer, late Heidegger, etc. Of course the gross movement of the seismic shift I have in mind here might also be invoked by considering the contrasts between structuralism versus post-structuralism, and modernism versus postmodernism, where the first terms of these oppositions stake out some variant of essentialism to be outflanked by the generally historicizing maneuvers of the second terms.

Now I do not want to suggest that Frampton was directly affiliated with any of the particular figures or bodies of ideas just enumerated. Rather, his own preoccupations roughly shadow the dialectic of essence versus history which sketches, across multiple dimensions, the intellectual movement of the sixties through the seventies into the eighties. The conflict between essentialism and history was apparent in Frampton's film theory by the early seventies, and his way of dealing with the tension between these opposing theoretical options was metahistory. Thus, Frampton's theorizing can be seen as one marker, among *diverse* markers, of a watershed within the course of recent intellectual history.

Throughout Frampton's theorizing, a strong essentialist tendency is evident. In his 1962 conversations with Carl Andre, we find Frampton calling for a critique of photography which will acknowledge that which is special to photography, in contrast to the other fine arts. He writes, "My variables are time, density, slope and so forth, physical values which need not concern a painter."[1] Twelve years later in "The Withering Away of the State of the Art," we find Frampton trying to isolate the differentia between film and video, noting, for example, the special potentials of the latter for optical effects.

In short, film builds upon the straight cut, and the direct collision of images, or 'shots,' extending a perceptual domain whose most noticeable trait we might call successiveness. (In this respect, film resembles history.) But video does not seem to take kindly to the cut. Rather, those inconclusions of video art during which I have come closest to moments of real discovery and *peripeteia,* seem oftenest to exhibit a tropism toward a kind (or many kinds) of metamorphic simultaneity. (In this respect, video resembles Ovidean myth.)

So that it strikes me that video art, which must find its own Muse or else struggle under the tyranny of film, as film did for so long under the tyrannies of drama and prose fiction, might best build its strategies of articulation upon an elasticized notion of what I might call – for lack of a better term – the dissolve.[2]

Of course, this essentialist concern with differentiating media also became a topic of some of Frampton's most significant work. *Poetic Justice,* what might be literally called a *filmed* scenario, contrasts film and literature, while (*nostalgia*) not only forcefully juxtaposes language and photography – i.e., verbal description and pictorial description – but also still photography and motion pictures (as the images begin to incinerate).[3]

At times, as in "Lecture," Frampton took a shot at trying to specify the quintessence of film. Arguing that film is whatever can fit in the projector, Frampton privileges footage as the *sine qua non* of cinema and, in Lessing-like fashion, goes on to declare footage itself to be the appropriate subject matter of the medium. He writes with specious logic but seductive wit that

We *learned* long ago to see our rectangle, to hold all of it in focus simultaneously. If films consist of consecutive frames, we can learn to see *them* also.

Sight itself is learned, a newborn baby not only sees poorly – it sees upside down.

At any rate, in some of our frames we found, as we thought, Lana Turner. Of course, she was but a fleeting shadow – but we had hold of something. She was what the film was *about*.

Perhaps we can agree that the film was about *her* because she appeared oftener than anything else.

Certainly a film must be about whatever appears most often in it.

Now suppose Lana Turner is not *always* on the screen.

Suppose further that we take an instrument and scratch the ribbon of film along its whole length.

Then the scratch is more often visible than Miss Turner, and the film is about the scratch.

Now suppose that we project all films. What are they about, in their great numbers?

At one time and another, we shall have seen, as we think, very many things.

But only one thing has always been in the projector.

Film.

That is what we have seen.

Then that is what all films are about.[4]

But along with his essentialist bias, Frampton also evinced a strong feeling for history. In "For a Metahistory of Film," he regards film art as something that can emerge only at a *specific* historical moment which he identifies as the demise of the

Machine Age (a period signaled by the advent of radar). His reasoning here is based on the premise that film, the *art* of the age of mechanical reproduction, can only enter the ranks of the *authentic* arts when it is obsolete in terms of its value for survival. Frampton's version of the aesthetic disinterestedness thesis, here, however, is less interesting for us than his willingness to connect art theory with history. This sense of historiographic fascination also looms in Frampton's extended ruminations on the origins and proto-histories of artforms. As well, the influence of Pound and Eliot, especially with their emphasis on the ideas of tradition and of a canon, predisposed Frampton to an interest in remaking and reusing the past, which inevitably embroiled him in a vivid sense of the movement of history.

In his writing, Frampton danced between a static essentialism and an inquisitive, animated appreciation of historical processes. This tension, which we might figuratively cast as one between time and timelessness, undoubtedly comes to the fore in some of Frampton's discussions of Eadweard Muybridge's photography. And it appears, as well, to be reflected in some of his films, such as (*nostalgia*), *Surface Tension,* and the central section of *Zorns Lemma,* which rely on the contrast of stillness and formal design on the one hand, versus movement on the other. At the level of theory, this contrast seems transformed into a conflict between viewing film as having a timeless essence, the tendency of artworld aesthetics in the sixties, versus assessing it as an historical process, as something developing over time, a point of view emerging aggressively by the mid-seventies. Frampton's problem, then, was to coordinate these opposing dispositions.

Now the essentialist after Hegel has the wherewithal ready to hand to accommodate a commitment to essences with a commitment to history – viz., the postulation that history unfolds according to a plan, indeed, according to an essential plan. In art theory, one popular version of this tendency is the story that charts the destiny of Cubism through its apotheosis in something like Louis's *Unfurleds,* while in film theory the notion that the essence of photography blossoms in deep-focus cinematography replays the same song with different lyrics. And, of course, one interpretation of *Zorns Lemma* would suggest that Frampton was not always averse to this form of essentialist historicizing: the first part of the film symbolizes a time before film, a time of words without photographs; the second part is a silent film, executed in the preferred style of that period, montage; while the third part, a sound film in the long-take, deep-focus style, ends by blurring the scene into the screen in a gesture pointing toward Minimalist film.[5]

But Frampton, as a creative artist, could not ultimately endorse this type of Hegelian resolution. For his theorizing was designed to serve his *continuing* practice as a filmmaker, whereas an evolutionary theory of history, of the essentialist variety, culminating at a certain moment in the present, or the near present, would entail the end to his practice, or to put things in proper Hegelian idiom, an end to (his, Frampton's) art. That is, the teleological reconciliation of essence and history implies that once the essential destiny of an artform is reached, the form effectively dies (in the sense that there is no reason for anyone practicing in that artform to continue making work in it). The story, so to speak, is finished; the book closed. Thus, ironically, though at one moment essentialism appears to propose a productive strategy for progressive art-making, it can also promote a situation in which the answer to the question "What is to be done?" is "Nothing." This is scarcely a viable *modus operandi* for the working avant-gardist. And Frampton, it seems to me, realized that he could not reconcile history and essentialism by means of a Hegelian-type gambit. Instead, he opted for metahistory as the means to assimilate conflicting theoretical inclinations with his ongoing productivity.

The metahistorian of film, though open to the history of film, does not see film history as converging on the present. The actual history of film is mongrel; there is no destiny inscribed within it. Rather, now, in the present, the metahistorian takes stock of the mess of film history and targets certain conditions of the medium which seem to him to represent its quintessence. For Frampton, these conditions appear to comprise: framing, photographic illusionism and narrative.[6] Now in the actual history of film – the accumulation of footage since Edison – these conditions were not in fact rigorously and self-consciously explored. It becomes the task of the metahistorian to make up for this shortcoming, to, in effect, envision the history of film as it would have been had it been rigorously self-conscious, and to reconstruct it "axiomatically." The metahistorical filmmaker, that is, imagines what the history of film *should* have been (according to his criteria) and then goes on to make it. The crucial consequence of this maneuver is that it places our filmic tradition, oddly enough, in the future. Our tradition, in an admittedly disorienting way of speaking, awaits invention. Commitment to the discovery of the essence or axioms of film does not entail the closure of the development of film but opens onto future developments. Art does not die. Rather, since footage is the subject of film, and since each already exposed piece of footage awaits self-conscious reworking in terms of framing, narrative, and the issue of illusionism, the prospect before the metahistorian is vast, though perhaps not endless (unless, of course, we up the reflexive ante to meta-metahistories and beyond).

In short, the metahistorian of film pro-

poses to create a fictional tradition in the future, oxymoronic as it sounds. Whether this theoretical plunge is philosophically sound and/or whether it could be recast as an allegory revealing certain features of the relation of emerging art to its "tradition" is less important for our understanding of the role the somewhat peculiar notion of metahistory performed in Frampton's program than the recognition that his theoretical sleight-of-hand was artistically generative. It underpins the awesome project of *Magellan,* a work whose ambition, it seems to me, is grounded in the circumstance of an artist/theorist drawn by the allures of both essentialism and the notion of historical tradition but who refused to close down shop because the *zeitgeist* had arrived. Metahistory was a theoretical invention that, for Frampton at least, appeared to carve out a conceptual space in which he could continue to work while simultaneously paying his dues both to essentialism and to his respect for the notion of an historical tradition.

Notes

1. In *12 Dialogues 1962–1963; Carl Andre, Hollis Frampton,* edited and annotated by B. H. D. Buchloh (Halifax/New York: Press of the Nova Scotia College of Art and New York University Press, 1980).
2. Hollis Frampton, from *Circles of Confusion* (Rochester, N.Y.: Visual Studies Workshop Press, 1983), pp. 166–167.
3. For further analysis and contextualization of (*nostalgia*), see Noël Carroll, "Film," in *The Postmodern Moment: A Handbook of Contemporary Innovation in the Arts,* edited with an introduction by Stanley Trachtenberg (Westport, Connecticut 06881: Greenwood Press, 1985). This article is a comprehensive overview of avant-garde film since 1965.
4. See Frampton, "A Lecture," *Circles of Confusion,* p 63.
5. For further elaboration see Carroll, "Film," *The Postmodern Moment.*
6. See Frampton's "A Pentagram for Conjuring the Narrative," in *Circles of Confusion,* p. 63.

7. Though the metahistorian's reorganization of the flow of temporality is nonstandard and somewhat perplexing, it is not unprecedented. In ways quite different from Frampton's, Croce in *History – Its Theory and Practice* and Collingwood in his *The Idea of History* also try to carve out anomalous time warps. This is not to justify the metahistorian but only to say that the relation between past, present, and future has been fiddled with before.

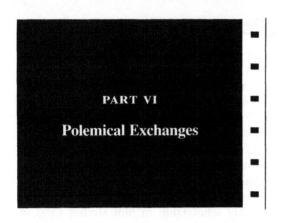

It is my general view that film theorizing should be dialectical. By that I mean that a major way in which film theorizing progresses is by criticizing already existing theory. Some may say that my use of the term "progresses" here is itself suspect. However, I count the elimination of error as progress and that is one potential consequence, it is to be hoped, of dialectical criticism. Of course, an even more salutary consequence might be that in criticizing one theoretical solution to a problem, one may also see one's way to a better solution. Seeing a shortfall in one theory, that is, may alert one to what is to be done and how it might be done (as well as to what is not to be done).

Unfortunately, film theory as it is presently practiced is not noteworthy for this type of dialectical criticism. In place of sustained and detailed criticism of alternatives, it goes in for high-handed ideological debunking, excoriating this or that rival theory with buzz-words like "formalism," or "politically correct" insinuations that rival theories will somehow contribute to the domination of the oppressed. As a result, what we have instead of careful dialectical criticism is academic name-calling.

Thus, the forum in which film theory is "debated" tends to be somewhat harsh and rancorous. It is typically marked by the language of moral superiority – as the self-righteously self-confident defenders of political correctness denounce deviations from their viewpoint. Absent is in-depth analysis of the conceptual, methodological, and em-

pirical problems of competing theories. It is enough to dismiss a rival to say that it supposedly supports Reaganite Republicanism or is inconsistent with the regnant conception of psychoanalytic feminism in the Society for Cinema Studies.

The intolerance of rival views and the studied avoidance of dialectical engagement with criticisms on the part of the Cinema Studies Establishment has obviously influenced that manner in which I have responded to it. I have been more hot-blooded and sarcastic toward contemporary film theorists than I ever am in my debates with my colleagues in philosophy. In philosophy, criticism is the norm. It is expected and it is generally exchanged without bitterness. In cinema studies, politically correct intolerance and avoidance of criticism is the norm. And I confess that this has often inclined me toward anger. Thus, I have called this section "Polemical Exchanges" rather than "Dialectical Exchanges." But, for all that, it is still my hope that one day film theorizing can become a field in which civil, dialectical engagement becomes the standard practice.

As will be evident from the following articles, I take umbrage at the insistent tendency of scholars in cinema studies to dismiss my theorizing as politically reactionary. I am particularly nonplussed by this charge, since I suspect that my voting record on real-world political issues is probably the same as that of most other members of the Society for Cinema Studies. In the sixties and early seventies, I was, like many of my peers, involved in radical politics. And, despite suggestions to the contrary, I remain committed to many of the tenets of sixties' radicalism. For me, sixties' radicalism meant, first and foremost, a radical questioning of authority. Thus, one may read my criticisms of contemporary film theory, especially in its authoritarian aspect, as a continuation of sixties' radicalism. In the sixties, one was convinced that it was appropriate to be skeptical and to challenge dominant beliefs. It was especially appropriate to respond with skepticism to

319

beliefs defended by ideological obscurantism and institutional repression. I have simply applied that skepticism to contemporary film theory. Contemporary film theorists have responded to those criticisms with mystifying vituperation. Hence, the following polemics.

"Cognitivism, Contemporary Film Theory and Method: A Response to Warren Buckland" is a reply to a review that Buckland wrote in *Screen* of my book *Mystifying Movies*. As the introduction to that article indicates, I asked the editors of *Screen* for the opportunity to publish my response to Buckland in their journal. But after they gave me the politically correct run-around with which I was already familiar from other film journals, I was compelled to publish it elsewhere.

Though the essay deals with many of Buckland's specific criticisms of *Mystifying Movies,* it will also be, I hope, of interest to the general reader. For I try to deal with several methodological issues that are larger than the disputes between Buckland and me, and I also attempt to use the essay as an opportunity to clarify my perception of the nature of the debate between psychoanalytic film theory and what is coming to be called cognitivism.

"Cracks in the Acoustic Mirror" is a sustained analysis of the book *The Acoustic Mirror* by Kaja Silverman. I have included it in this anthology because, to my mind, Silverman's book exemplifies a number of the major shortcomings of psychoanalytic feminist film theory in particular and of contemporary film theory in general. It shows little understanding of what is involved in advancing a causal hypothesis. Indeed, it seems so amateurish in these matters as to be almost silly. And it proceeds to speculate about psychosexual development without the empirical foundations of a clinical practice or of research in child psychology. In fact, the empirical and theoretical grounding of this book is so flimsy that I do not think that it could have been published except under the protection of political correctness. People are afraid to criticize it because they fear being labeled antifeminist. Undoubtedly, I will be called an enemy of feminism for demonstrating the flaws in Silverman's book, despite the fact that in an earlier article, included in this volume, I have defended a model – albeit an unfashionable one – of feminist analysis.[1] But even if I will be attacked in this manner, I think that the insults must be borne in order to begin to lift the veil of political correctness that protects shoddy scholarship in film studies (and in literary studies) nowadays.

"A Reply to Heath" is the last installment in my exchange with Stephen Heath in the journal *October*. In the winter of 1982, I published a substantial (at least in terms of size) criticism of Heath's film theory, which I called "Address to the Heathen." Heath responded with a lively, if inconsequential, essay called "Le Père Noël." Both my essay and Heath's are frequently cited in the literature. However, it seems to be generally ignored that I answered Heath's charges in an essay of my own. The field appears to have (conveniently?) forgotten my rebuttals of "Le Père Noël." So, it is worthwhile, I think, to republish them here.

This section concludes with my replies to two criticisms of *Mystifying Movies.* My reply to Jennifer Hammett is admittedly impolite, but I believe that it is appropriate, given the dismissive tone of her rejection of my own positive theories. My exchange with Richard Allen is a different matter. He clearly made the effort to understand my position and his criticisms are reasonably set forth, even if I think they are mistaken. Allen makes his case clearly, carefully, and without invective. I respect that. Allen's article makes me think that genuine dialectical exchange may be becoming possible in film studies.

Notes

1. See "The Image of Women in Film: A Defense of a Paradigm," in Part IV of this volume.

CHAPTER XXII

Cognitivism,
Contemporary Film
Theory and Method:
A Response to
Warren Buckland

Introduction

As its title indicates, my book – Mystifying
Movies: Fads and Fallacies in Contemporary Film Theory *– rejects a great many of
the presuppositions of the cinema studies
establishment in the United States and Britain
today. Moreover, since the British journal*
Screen *was the source of many of those
presuppositions, it is not surprising that it
published a scathing response to* Mystifying
Movies. *That response took the form of a
substantial article by Warren Buckland entitled "Critique of Poor Reason."*

Screen *sent neither me nor my publisher a
copy of this review article. I came across it
over a year after its publication date. I wrote
to* Screen *requesting an author's right to
refute Buckland's charges in an article of
comparable length.* Screen *suggested that I
write a five-page letter to the editor, or, if I
wanted to write an article, that it connect my
dispute with Buckland to larger methodological issues in the debate between psychoanalytic film theory and my view, which is
sometimes called cognitivism. The following
article was my attempt to implement the
second option.*

Screen *rejected the article. Whether* Screen
*rejected it as a result of a judgment that it does
not sufficiently address significant methodological issues or as an attempt to repress
alternative voices in the predictably Stalinist
manner of Lysenko is a question for the
reader to resolve. . . .*

Throughout the eighties, albeit in fits and
starts, there was an attempt, by people like
myself and David Bordwell,[1] to field an
approach to film theory that offers an alternative to the psychoanalytic-Marxist-semiotic
theory which has been disseminated most
notably by *Screen* and which is, especially
when amplified by Lacanian feminism, the
dominant approach to film theory in the
English-speaking world today. This alternative approach has been labeled "cognitivism"
because of the emphasis that it places on the
efficacy of models that exploit the role of
cognitive processes, as opposed to unconscious processes, in the explanation of cinematic communication and understanding.

Cognitivism is not a unified theory in
three senses. First, it is not a single theory,
but a series of small-scale theories, each of
which offers answers to specific questions
about film communication, e.g., how do
audiences assimilate film narratives? Second, it is not a unified theory because
different cognitivist theorists often present
small-scale theories that conceptualize the
phenomena at hand differently and, sometimes, in nonconverging ways. And finally,
cognitivism seems not to be a unified theory
because, partly due to the previous two
considerations, we have no reason to believe
that all the small-scale theories that the
cognitivists have assembled can be organized into a single framework.

On the other hand, though cognitivism is
not a theory, its proponents share certain
convictions, such as: that cognitive models
may provide better answers to many of the
theoretical questions we have about film
than psychoanalytic models do; that film
theory is a mode of rational enquiry and, as
such, is assessable according to our best
standards of reasoning and evidence; and
that theories are evaluated comparatively,
e.g., psychoanalytic theories must be put in
competition with cognitive theories that propose to explain the same data (like narrative
comprehension). Furthermore, Some cogni-

tivists – most notoriously myself – have argued that once the reigning psychoanalytic-Marxist theory is assessed according to canons of rational enquiry and compared to alternative cognitive theories, it appears baroque and vacuous, indeed, altogether an intellectual disaster.

Predictably, cognitivism has evoked the ire of the cinema studies establishment.[2] Not only does cognitivism challenge the foundations of that establishment's paradigm, but it also emerges at a time when it is evident that that paradigm is producing routine, rather than interesting, new results. And it is a commonplace that researchers are apt to abandon a theory when it ceases to provide innovative discoveries. Thus, it should come as no surprise that we are beginning to encounter a number of what might be thought of as "damage control" articles which are dedicated to the refutation of cognitivism and/or to establishing its compatibility with the dominant psychoanalytic model (the new pluralism).

One of the most interesting of these articles – because it is the most sustained as well as the most methodologically ambitious – is Warren Buckland's recent attack, published in *Screen,* of my book *Mystifying Movies.*[3] In what follows, I wish to respond to Buckland's attack in detail. But, more importantly, I would like to address a series of deep methodological issues that his attack raises which are pertinent to any future debates between cognitivism and the ruling psychoanalytic-marxist theory. Thus, though this article is, in part, a reaction to Buckland, it is also an attempt to clarify what I take to be some of the most important methodological issues between cognitivists and psychoanalytic-marxists.

Science Bashing

Buckland, like others, fears that cognitivism, at least under my construal, puts too much faith in scientific method (and analytic philosophy). It is true that I regard scientific method as a useful guide to the sort of rational enquiry that film theorists pursue. But Buckland seems to think that I believe that scientific method and analytic philosophy lead "to an unconditional avoidance of error in order to establish 'the truth.' " (CPR, 81) But let me disabuse him of this. Not only do I never advance such an idea, but I couldn't, since it is evident that talented scientists and philosophers would not be embroiled in defending incompatible theories if they possessed such miraculous methods. I do believe that specific methods (like Mill's) and protocols (like "if one of two competing theories fits the phenomena better, *ceteris paribus*, prefer it to its rival") are truth-tracking; but none so far have guaranteed what Buckland calls the "unconditional avoidance of error." Nor is someone who upholds the value of such methods committed to this view. What I am committed to is that such methods serve as the best (the heretofore most reliable) means for justifying our beliefs. But, of course, I admit that a justified belief can be false.

Buckland likes to chastise science by calling it "imperialistic" – foisting its findings on all comers as the truth. But this is not a shortcoming of science; it is a reflection of Buckland's confusion of the issue of truth with the issue of justification. Scientific method provides us with strong justifications for thing like theories, though, again, a well-warranted theory at time T1 could turn out to be false at time T2. Nevertheless, that a justified theory or belief could be false does not seem to loosen our expectations – of both ourselves and others – that we strive to back up our beliefs with the best justifications available. The psychoanalytic-marxist misrepresents the cognitivist as a "truth-bully." I, for example, don't demand acceptance of my theories as infallibly true, but only as better justified, at this point in the debate, than their competitors.

One way in which Buckland seeks to undercut what for him are the dubious scientific presuppositions of cognitivism is to charge that I think of scientific method as a source of absolute truth and falsity. (CPR, 81) In contrast, Buckland thinks that relativism is the better course, and, in fact, the brand of relativism that he prefers is a variety of social constructivism. But before looking at Buckland's sketch of the social determination of scientific knowledge, we must consider the underlying structure of Buckland's argument.

Buckland confronts us with a dilemma: either one must be an absolutist with respect to scientific knowledge or one must be a relativist; you can't be an absolutist (actually, for the reasons I gave above); therefore, you must be a relativist.

But this argument, though it is often deployed by theorists in the humanities, is too facile. It has not explored all the available options. One can eschew absolutism and relativism at the same time. One can be what is called a fallibilist, which, by the way, is the position the cognitivists, like myself and Bordwell, hold.

The fallibilist admits that she may have to revise her theories in light of future evidence or of theoretical implications of later developments because she realizes that at best her theories are well-warranted, and that a well-warranted theory can be false. There is no claim to a purchase on absolute truth here. But neither is there a concession to relativism in any standard sense of the term. For we are open to revising our theories in accordance with the best available transcultural standards of justification, those shared, for example, by capitalist physicists, Chinese communist physicists, and Vatican physicists.

The fallibilist denies that we could revise all our beliefs, theories, and protocols at once. But any subset thereof is revisable under given circumstances, and, indeed, the entire set might be revised serially. The scientific viewpoint does not commit us to the arrogant presumption that it delivers absolute truth, but only to the more modest claim that there are discernible grades of justification, of which some have proven to

be more reliable than others. All the cognitivist need claim for her theories is that they are more justified, at this juncture in the dialectical debate, than are psycho-analytic-marxist competitors. And she may do this without claiming that none of her theories will ever have to be modified or abandoned.

Of course, Buckland will deny my appeal to transcultural standards of justification because his version of relativism maintains that "the truth values of each theoretical paradigm are predominantly (although not exclusively) relative to the social and historical determinations from which they emerged." (CPR, 81) This is an empirical claim. In order to defend it, a social determinist like Buckland will have to demonstrate that major scientific claims – like the notion that gases expand when heated – have been endorsed by most scientists for reasons that have almost nothing to do with evidence, arguments and observations, and that they have almost everything to do with socio-historical causes.

No one has done this, nor does it seem very likely that it can be done, since it is surely a daunting fact that scientists from very different socio-historical backgrounds (capitalist, marxist, Catholic, Islamic) accept a great many of the same claims (even sometimes across historical epochs). If Buckland were correct and scientists accepted theories not in terms of shared standards of enquiry but in terms of prevailing social agendas in their respective cultures, the fact of recurring strong consensus among scientists over a large number of theories could never be explained. Moreover, with reference to Buckland's bizarre talk about truth values, it is hard to imagine how one would specify the truth conditions for "gases expand when heated" in terms of specific constellations of socio-historical relations: "Gases expand when heated" is true if and only if what? – the relevant socio-historical context is a Protestant capitalist oligarchy!

And, in any case, Buckland's social determinism appears at odds with his attempt to debunk the scientific pretensions of the cognitivist. For he wishes to advance the generalization that in fact all scientific claims are relative to social determinations. But what then is the status of his generalization? Presumably he wants us to regard it as either true, or approximately true, or well justified. But since it is an empirical generalization, his theory must be reflexive, i.e., it must apply to itself. And applied to itself, Buckland's objection reduces predominantly to an expression of the values and aims of the particular socio-historical situation he inhabits. So, either we will have to regard Buckland's view as inexplicably transcending the constraints of social determination (and thereby serving as a self-refutation of the theory), or we will have to regard his view as just as self-deluded as he claims that cognitivism is.

Conceptual relativism, augmented by a social determination thesis, then, is not a promising line of attack for the contemporary film theorist eager to undermine cognitivism. Moreover, the attractiveness of this line for politically-minded film theorists (and literary theorists) has always been mysterious to me. For relativism of this sort turns progressive claims about economic inequality, racial oppression, and sexual bias into the special pleading of certain social formations.

However, in that case, public support of the claims of reformers on the part of persons outside said social formations loses its point. Surely such reformers, a minority in every country in the industrialized West, cannot expect this support unless they can advance their claims as justifiable to people from alien social formations. Since conceptual relativism plus social determinism is so inimicable to the aims of political film theorists, one is tempted to explain its allure for such theorists on the grounds that they think that the theory is probably true. But conceding that much contradicts their allegiance to a social constructivist epistemology.

Buckland presumes that the cognitivist film theorists have not yet absorbed the lessons of post-positivist philosophers of science, viz., that theories should be evaluated pragmatically in a way that is sensitive to the contexts in which they emerge. Usually, these post-positivist insights are fleshed out by noting that competing scientific theories emerge in specific historical contexts (of theoretical debate) in order to answer presiding questions and that these theories are assessed pragmatically in terms of the way they differentially succeed in solving the contextually motivated problems. This mode of assessment is pragmatic (rather than absolutist) because it ranges only over known rival theories (rather than over every conceivable theory that might be brought to bear on the question), and because it focuses particularly on solutions to contextually motivated (theoretical) problems. But if this is the sort of post-positivist view of science that Buckland yearns for, then he fails to note that cognitivist film theory is pragmatic and contextual – with a vengeance.

The entire underlying structure of *Mystifying Movies* is dialectical. The elements of cinema that I have attempted to explain, like perspective and narrative, have been targeted because those are the features that psychoanalytic-marxists have, contextually, isolated as the ones that are in need of explanation. Alternative cognitivist explanations are mounted and explicitly weighed against reigning theories in terms of their comparative justifiability. This approach is not positivist; it is maximally compatible with the sort of pragmatic, contextual sensitivity Buckland advocates, though, ironically, he does not recognize it as such.

Indeed, if *Mystifying Movies* makes any lasting contribution to film theory, I would hope that it would be that it explicitly introduced the dialectical (pragmatic, contextually sensitive) form of argumentation to the field. Moreover, I also believe that I have said enough at this point to block dismissals of cognitivism as a naive version of positivism. In the future, intoning buzz phrases like "absolute knowledge" will not suffice as a way of rejecting cognitivism. If the debate about scientific methodology continues in film theory – as I think it should – then it will be constrained to begin with the understanding that cognitivism is prima facie based on a sophisticated, post-positivist conception of science.

Bashing Analytic Philosophy

For Buckland, not only does my reliance on science as a guide to rational enquiry impose an imperialist, absolutist conception of "truth" on film studies; my commitments to analytic philosophy reinforce this original sin. He writes: "Analytic philosophy presents itself as the only legitimate paradigm based on 'true,' 'objective' knowledge. . . ." (CPR, 81) This is a strange view of analytic philosophy. For analytic philosophy is not a body of knowledge nor is it a paradigm in any strict sense of the term. It is not a paradigm because competing, contradictory theories can be developed under its aegis, which is also why it is not a body of knowledge.

Some analytic philosophers of politics are marxists (or "Analytical Marxists") – like G. A. Cohen – while others are libertarians (e.g., Robert Nozick and Tibor Machen) and still others are liberals (e.g., John Rawls and Ronald Dworkin). And there are distinguished feminists, like Virginia Held, who are analytically inclined. Richard Wollheim advances a psychoanalytic theory of mind while Adolf Grunbaum and Alasdair MacIntyre reject psychoanalysis altogether. Analytic philosophy is a tradition rather than a paradigm or a body of knowledge – a tradition in which different and contradictory theories can be and have been developed. Thus, my allegiance to analytic philosophy in no way begs any questions in my debates with psychoanalytic-marxist film theorists.

There is no reason to suppose that, in principle, someone might not defend some version of a psychoanalytic-marxist approach to film within the context of analytic philosophy. Therefore, there is no justification, methodologically, in complaining that analytic philosophy antecedently stacks the deck against a psychoanalytic-marxist approach in film theory.

Of course, Buckland's reservations about analytic philosophy may spring from an uninformed conflation of analytic philosophy with logical positivism. But by this time in history, logical positivism is a defunct program, due to devastating objections advanced by other analytic philosophers. Moreover, logical positivism has been discredited for several decades. And, indeed, for the reasons stated in the preceding section, my approach to film theory is post-positivist.

Perhaps the strangest feature of Buckland's initial denunciation of the inherent absolutist imperialism of analytic philosophy is that throughout his article he relies heavily on the authority of analytical philosophers both to criticize me and to develop his own recommendations for film theory. Along the way we meet up with Donald Davidson, Hilary Putnam, W. V. Quine, and J. J. Katz, while the theory of relevance that Buckland favors derives from the work of H. P. Grice. But these people are not marginal renegades; they are representatives of the core of the tradition. I cannot see how Buckland can reconcile his rejection of me specifically because of my analytic stance at the same time that he approvingly marshals so many once and future officers of the American Philosophical Association to rebuke me. If ever one were tempted to mobilize psychoanalysis, it might be to explain Buckland's self-contradictory, love-hate relation to analytic philosophy.

The Principle of Charity

A central premise of Buckland's rejection of my arguments against psychoanalytic-marxist film theory is that in interpreting their commitments, I fail to abide by the principle of charity. (CPR, 83–84) The version of the principle of charity that Buckland depends upon is derived primarily from Donald Davidson's article "On the Very Idea of a Conceptual Scheme."[4] Davidson's principle is developed in the context of considering the problem of how one translates from one language to another. His principle of charity advises that in order to maximize the sense of the language that we are translating, we try to optimize agreement between ourselves and our interlocutors. That is, we assume that we share the bulk of our beliefs with the users of the alien language that we are translating. For if we can't formulate most of what x is saying in terms of our own conceptual scheme, we cannot be sure whether or not x is just making random noises.

What Buckland wants to contend, I think, is that insofar as my interpretations of psychoanalytic-marxist film theorists don't respect something like the principle of charity (that pertains to contexts of radical translation between alien languages), my formulations make contemporary film theorists sound pretty silly. Whereas, if I extended the principle of charity to their theories – presuming that what I take to be reasonable corresponds to what they are trying to say – then their theories wouldn't appear as outlandish as I make them out to be.

But I'm not sure, *pace* Buckland's construal of Davidson, that, even if we can provide a convincing version of the principle of charity, we can suppose that it should apply to the interpretation of theories (rather than to the translation of languages) in general or to my interpretation of psychoanalytic-marxist film theory in particular. Wouldn't it be a mistake to interpret Aristotle's physics in terms of contemporary physical beliefs – that is, to attempt to find interpretations of his claims that would make as many of them as possible true by

the lights of modern day science? Surely a principle of interpretation like that would produce a mass of anachronisms.

However advisable a principle of charity might be for translating the ordinary speech ("There's a dog.") of alien languages, it does not follow that the same procedure is appropriate in reconstructing rarefied theoretical idioms, especially those of contesting theories. For such a policy – if carried out completely – would make the best interpretation of two rival theories the one that has them both committed to the same assertions about the relevant phenomena. If I extend the principle of charity to a competing theory my best construal of it necessarily makes it into my theory. If one follows Buckland's advice fully, we wouldn't have rival theories at all. But that's absurd.

For the preceding reasons, I am, in general, reluctant to extrapolate the principle of charity from the context of the radical translation of alien languages to the interpretation of rival theories. But I am also reluctant to accept the principle of charity as a policy governing my interpretation of contemporary film theory for another reason. Contemporary film theory is not an alien language for me.[5] I am a user of the languages in which contemporary film theory is articulated. The context is not one of radical translation.

The contemporary film theorist and I share the same criteria for identifying instances of chairs, tables, dogs, convertibles, perspective and film editing. We already share most of the same beliefs about the world. We may differ about a tiny fraction of the beliefs that make up our highly technical theories. But, at the same time, in virtue of all those beliefs we hold in common, we may be able to surmise with confidence that some of our rival's technical theories not only differ from ours but also actually are silly.

It does not seem to me that Buckland is aware of the incongruities that result from endorsing Davidson's principle of charity as a principle of theory interpretation. Indeed, often it seems to me that Buckland's notion of my lack of charity amounts to his feeling that I am imposing alien (scientific, philosophical) modes of reasoning on contemporary film theory and, thereby, failing to interpret it from the inside. Of course, if that's what I'm doing, am I not charitably extending my beliefs about proof to psychoanalytic-marxist film theorists? But, in any case, I am not convinced that I am employing different forms of reasoning than contemporary film theorists do. For example, I recognize the kinds of arguments and standards of evidence that Buckland uses against me, even if I am not convinced by them.

An example of my lack of interpretive charity, in Buckland's rather than Davidson's sense, which is raised more than once (CPR, 82–83; 89–90), is that I fail to acknowledge that contemporary film theorists stipulate or presuppose that movies engage the unconscious psyches of spectators. That is their starting point. That their theories turn out on my accounting to seem ridiculous is a consequence of my refusal to grant this premise.[6] And undoubtedly psychoanalytic-marxist theory would not seem so ridiculous to me if I accepted this presupposition.

However, I do not believe that a film theorist can stipulate that movies engage people's psyches on an unconscious level (CPR, 83) any more than I believe that an astrologer can be allowed to stipulate that our fates are controlled by the stars. One cannot presuppose whatever one wants; one's presuppositions should be open to discussion and criticism. Film theory is not a formal system. My refusal to accept this stipulation is a substantive issue, not a matter of interpretative protocols.

Indeed, it is my conviction that the most important issue to be confronted in the debate between the psychoanalytic-marxist film theorist and the cognitivist concerns the question of whether and how the premise

that Buckland seems to think can just be stipulated is to be defended. But more on that below.

Misinterpretation I

Due to my putative lack of interpretive charity, Buckland maintains that my arguments against contemporary film theorists miss their mark because I am not confronting their views, but only my own misinterpretations of their positions. By now, given the example of Stephen Heath, misinterpretation is one of the canonical methods of dismissing my objections. Needless to say, I do not believe that my interpretations are as blind as Buckland claims. So I would like quickly to review some of his charges in order to unhorse them. At the same time, I would like to show how very easily Buckland's "new" interpretations can be rejected.

Buckland opens his rebuttal by accusing me of being uncharitable to Baudry's argument in "The Apparatus." (CPR 85–88) The crux of the dispute is this: I take Baudry to be advancing an inductive argument by logical analogy which concludes that the charged experience of cinema is caused by the desire for and regression to primitive narcissism. Baudry reaches this conclusion by adducing eight basic analogies – which sometimes invoke sub-analogies – between film and dream. I try to undermine these analogies – and the various sub-analogies – while also introducing some challenging disanalogies between film and dream. Depending on how you count them, I muster about ten lines of objection to Baudry's argument, though some of these also involve attacking what I've just called Baudry's sub-analogies. Where Buckland believes that I've been uncharitable to Baudry concerns the matter of one of Baudry's sub-analogies. So even if Buckland were right, his worries pertain to roughly 8¼ percent of my arguments.

Baudry claims that dreams and films have

screens and that the so-called dream screen is a figure for the mother's breast. Baudry derives this "insight" from the psychoanalyst Bertram Lewin. I, in turn, challenge the plausibility of the subtending analogy between a screen and a breast, noting:

One must at least question the purported screen/breast association. What is its basis? And how extensive is it? Maybe some white people envision breasts as white and then go on to associate the latter with white screens. But not everyone is white. And I wonder if many whites associate breasts and screens. Certainly it is not an intuitively straightforward association like that between guns and penises. For example, screens are flat; and lactating breasts are not. A screen is, ideally, uniform in color and texture; but a breast has a nipple. (*MM*, 29)

Where did I go wrong? I reject the analogy between screens and breasts because most breasts are not white, breasts are not uniformly colored and textured and because breasts are not flat. Buckland says that I'm unfair here because Lewin says that for a portion of *one* of his patient's dream her putative breast/dream screen was flat. So Baudry could respond to the flatness part of my objection by claiming that within Lewin's theory, one might say that breasts, in the relevant sense, are flat.

Since Baudry never explicitly endorses this claim, I don't see how I can be said to have misinterpreted him. At best, one could say that I overlooked a possible countermove of which Baudry might avail himself upon hearing my objection. Was I uncharitable in failing to rehearse this countermove? Well, I'm not sure. Lewin's claim sounds pretty flimsy. It is not even based on an overt association on the part of his patient but upon an inference that Lewin, rather than the subject, makes regarding her description of her dream. Moreover, as I had already pointed out about the Lewin material (*MM*, 28), the empirical support offered for the hypothesis that all dreams have screens is statistically miniscule as well as being conceptually crude (we are not told

how, in principle, to tell personal, idiosyncratic dream associations and structural elements of dreams, like screens, apart). Given all these problems with Lewin's speculation, it seems to me that I was probably exercising charity in not saddling Baudry with Lewin's flattened breast screens.

Furthermore, if anyone feels that I was remiss in ignoring Lewin's flattened breasts, let me say what was already implicit in the charges I did make. If one patient can, by means of an inference, be said to associate flattened out breasts with screens, that would be scant evidence that all of us have dream screens that we associate with breasts, or even flattened breasts. And anyway, of course, even if Baudry could deflect my flatness argument by invoking Lewin's scarcely motivated and strained speculations, that would still leave over ninety percent of my refutation of Baudry intact.

In criticizing Metz's hypothesis about the role that the Imaginary plays in film reception, I doubted whether the phenomenon of viewing a film sufficiently matched canonical discussions of mirror stage identification. For we do not appear in the film image. Buckland criticizes me for ignoring the fact that authority figures like Metz and Penley assert that it is enough for the film to present an absent "spatial and temporal elsewhere" for the Imaginary to be engaged. (*CPR*, 89)

Well, I know that Metz thinks something like this; but I was asking that the belief be explained and justified. Buckland seems to think that I should accept the pronouncements of his authorities unquestioningly. I, of course, reject such authoritarianism on scientific grounds; I would have thought that it would also be unpalatable on political grounds. But, in any case, the issue is not one of misinterpretation. I don't misrepresent what is being claimed; I only require that the claim be supported by argumentation and explanation.

A crucial aspect of my supposed misinterpretations of Metz is that I don't catch onto Metz's thought that all films are fictional due to their presentation of an absent spatial and temporal elsewhere. (CPR, 89; 91) According to Buckland, this oversight leads me to criticize Metz as if he were writing about the disavowal of conflicting beliefs and disbeliefs with respect to the presence of the profilmic referent of the image; whereas, for Buckland, Metz is discussing the presence of the diegesis. (CPR, 91) Several things need to be said about this.

First, Buckland's inference from fiction in Metz's sense of diegesis is specious. Not all fictions are narrative. Second, Metz's contrast between a chair onstage and a chair on film suggests that he is talking about the play of absence and presence of the profilmic referent.[7] Third, the contrast between the referent and diegesis seems spurious, since narratives refer, even if that reference is fictional. And finally, though I know that Metz thinks that all films are fictional, I have already rejected the plausibility of that claim at length.[8]

Throughout, Buckland shows his tendency to regard my rejection of central premises in the arguments of contemporary film theory to be a matter of misinterpretation, when, in fact, they constitute substantive points in the debate. If someone claims that "the moon is made of green cheese" as a premise in a theory and I dispute this premise, I am not misinterpreting the theory. And, it may go without saying, I regard many of the premises of contemporary film theory as on a par with "the moon is made of green cheese."

For Buckland, it would appear that the interpretation of a theory involves acceptance of the premises of the theory. This hermeneutic principle leaves me dumbfounded. An interpretation undoubtedly involves stating the premises of rival theories. But I see no reason to think that that mandates either believing them or treating them uncritically.

Though Buckland is not willing to advert to my writings other than *Mystifying Movies* when supposedly they show that I am refuting rather than misinterpreting contemporary film theory, he will refer to those writings when putatively they reveal my chronic inability to interpret people correctly. For example, he cites my discussion of certain illusion theories of representation in "Conspiracy Theories of Representation"[9] in order to declare that one of its arguments fails to apply to Metz and Baudry. But why is this a problem, since the article is not about Metz and Baudry?

Certainly Buckland is right in noting (CPR, 90) that both Metz and I agree that film viewers know that they are watching films. However, that is not the issue that is under dispute. Rather the issue is whether or not this needs to be explained in terms of a notion of disavowal. And I, of course, try to argue that commitments to disavowal are extraneous.

In recounting my debate with Stephen Heath on the status of perspective (CPR, 93), Buckland suggests that my emphasis on the biological and perceptual aspects of perspective renderings precludes the fact that perspective has a history and, therefore, a conventionalist status. Of course, I never deny that perspective has a history; people write books about it, and I have read them. But this concession hardly implies that perspective is merely a convention in the sense defended by conventionalists like Goodman and Wartofsky in the philosophical and psychological literature. Indeed, I would even be willing to grant that there are some conventions within the tradition of perspective rendering (e.g., that the most significant elements in the rendering be placed at the vanishing point). But this does not compel me to accept the idea that perspective works solely in virtue of conventions.

Buckland also chides me for my interpretation of contemporary film theory's treatment of perspective because I do not foreground their supposed discovery that perspective is really a representation of a metaphysical position – such as Husserlian Idealism – with religious overtones. (CPR, 92) This is not quite right, for I do dismiss one variation on this theme, viz., Comolli's. (*MM* 137–138) However, Buckland is correct in observing that I do not deal with the version of the thesis propounded in Jean-Louis Baudry's "Ideological Effects of the Basic Cinematographic Apparatus."

The reason that I did not pause to dismiss Baudry's correlation of the cinematic apparatus with Husserlian Idealism was that I thought that the argument was evidently flawed. For Baudry seems to find that the apparatus reflects Husserlian Idealism on the basis of the same features that in his article "The Apparatus" he correlated cinema with Platonism. But Husserlian Idealism and Platonism are incompatible philosophical positions. How can cinema represent two incompatible philosophical positions in virtue of the self-same features? The fact that Baudry discovers that cinema represents Idealism as easily as he discovers that it represents its Platonic antipode suggests to me that the "apparatus" underdetermines what philosophical theories can be associated with it. And this, furthermore, suggests to me that we would be better off dropping the idea that cinema as such is a representation of a specific philosophical or religious position altogether.

Perhaps the most striking aspect of Buckland's accusation of my systematic misinterpretation of contemporary film theory is his explicit refusal to commit himself to the tenets of contemporary film theory once they have been interpreted accurately (i.e., a la Buckland). (CPR, 87) Basically, Buckland seems to be arguing that, though I'm wrong due to my biased interpretations, he, Buckland, is not prepared to say that contemporary film theory, when correctly interpreted, is viable. Moreover, when one realizes that the positive theoretical recommendations that Buckland makes at the end of his article (CPR, 102–103) are basically cognitivist, one begins to suspect that the "Critique of Poor Reason" is "pulling a fast one" on the reader. That is, Buckland really wants to be "more

cognitivist than thou" (or me), and the vociferous complaints about my misinterpretations are camouflage. *Screen* beware: Buckland may be a cognitivist in psychoanalytic clothing.

Misinterpretation II

If Buckland is convinced that I systematically misread contemporary film theory, I am equally sure that Buckland misreads me. I don't think that this is a lack of Davidsonian charity. He simply doesn't take note of the words on my pages.

In reviewing my positive proposals about the nature of our perception of the cinematic image, Buckland complains that I reduce the image to the status of a natural object. (CPR, 97) This just ignores my contention that we should conceptualize picturing (including motion picturing) as cultural inventions. (*MM*, 142–145)

Also, Buckland infers that I am attracted to the hypothesis that pictures are universally recognizable because this entails that pictures have no ideological repercussions. But before this debunking account of my scurrilous motives for embracing the hypothesis is accepted, one should consider all the psychological data I advance in favor of the hypothesis. I'm not championing the view because I have a covert political agenda. I feel drawn to the hypothesis because of the psychological evidence. (*MM*, 139–142)

Buckland also maintains that my theory of cinematic perception is inconsistent. For, on the one hand, I claim that when perceiving a cinematic image we are focally aware of what it is about and subsidiarily aware that it is a representation. But when I offer my characterization of cinematic awareness, Buckland claims that I place "exclusive emphasis upon the focus in which the subsidiaries are marginalised out of the picture (literally!)." (CPR, 97)

This is not so much a misinterpretation as a misreading. It ignores sentences like:

"Human perceptual capacities evolve in such a way that the capacity for pictorial recognition comes, almost naturally, with the capacity for object recognition, and part of that capacity is the ability to differentiate pictures from their referents." (*MM*, 144) This, of course, acknowledges that subsidiary awareness of the picture is part and parcel of all picture perception.

On the other hand, if what worries Buckland is that I think that what he calls the focus commands more of our attention than the subsidiary, he has read me correctly. I do think that the focus generally carries more weight. That's what it means to be the focus rather than the subsidiary. Or, alternatively, what's the problem with marginalizing the subsidiary, since the subsidiary is, by a definition Buckland seems to accept, relatively marginalized?

Buckland criticizes my positive account of cinematic narration on the grounds that it ignores the possibility of the subversion of hypotheses a film induces its audience to formulate. But in my account of what I call a sustaining scene, I, for example, explicitly state: "A scene that begins to answer a narrative question but then frustrates the answer – e.g., a detective following up a wrong clue – is also a sustaining scene." (*MM*, 174–175) Moreover, Buckland's exploration of this supposed lacuna in my view, specifically with reference to horror films, is dealt with more thoroughly in my book *The Philosophy of Horror*.[10]

Buckland thinks that there is a fundamental problem with my positive account of cinematic comprehension: it is what he calls code/semantic rather than pragmatic. (CPR, 100) In contrast, I think Buckland is mistaken in characterizing my theory this way; moreover, I suspect that the origin of Buckland's confusion is that he has taken parts of the theory to be the whole of the theory.

As I understand him, my theory is supposedly a code/semantic theory because it treats cinematic comprehension as if it were "auto-matic." And I suppose that, were cinematic comprehension simply a matter of decoding, one might call it automatic. But two things require emphasis here. First, I do not maintain that film comprehension as a whole is automatic, though I think certain aspects of it may be "virtually automatic," viz., that we are looking where we are looking in a close shot in virtue of the framing, and that we recognize what images are about in virtue of innate perceptual capacities. The latter claim may be controversial, though I think the psychological evidence is on my side, while the former claim is I think incontestable. Moreover, I do not reduce cinematic comprehension to these two processes, but go on to stress the importance of hypothesis formation in my account of erotetic – or question/answer – narration in a way that is more a matter of what Buckland would call a pragmatic theory. Thus, though there are elements of automatism in my theory, the theory as a whole puts a great deal of emphasis on the kind of pragmatic approach Buckland endorses.

Second, even if aspects of my account of cinematic comprehension are automatic, they are not automatic in virtue of some code. That I am looking at the heroine's face in a close shot is not a function of an arbitrarily established code. The perceptual structure of the image, typically, causes one to be looking where one is looking. Similarly, I advance a number of considerations in order to deny that our processing of the cinematic image involves decoding. Thus, not only is my theory as a whole not a semantic/code theory, but even the parts of it that regard some features of cinematic comprehension as "automatic" do not rely on codes. Therefore, I am not a code/semantic theorist. Indeed, throughout my career as a film theorist, I have always explicitly stressed the importance of inference over decoding as a model for many aspects of cinematic comprehension.[11]

Furthermore, once it is clear that I am not a code/semantic theorist, the significance of

Buckland's pragmatic alternative to my approach loses its dialectical force. For the choice between Buckland/Sperber/Wilson and Carroll cannot be decided on the basis of superiority of pragmatic/relevance theories versus semantic/code theories. Moreover, though it is somewhat difficult to make out Buckland's positive recommendations for film theorists – given his clotted, programmatic style of writing – I suspect that my theory of cinematic comprehension is probably compatible with the sort Buckland advocates (that is, if Buckland's view makes sense).

Buckland also bandies about the charge – frequently leveled at cognitivist theorists – that I am a formalist (e.g., CPR, 100). This overlooks the fact that not only do I discuss the use of certain structures in terms of their ideological significance (e.g., *MM*, 158;159) but I explicitly promise that cognitivism can offer piecemeal generalizations about the operation of ideology in film. Similarly, though Bordwell is generally upbraided as a formalist, I can think of few studies as dedicated as his of Ozu to situating his subject so thoroughly in terms of its sociopolitical context.[12]

Of course, Buckland is right in noticing that most of the theories that are proposed in *Mystifying Movies* are what he would call formalist. But that is only to say that I believe that some of our questions of cinema may require what he calls formalist answers. However, I have never precluded the possibility that other questions must confront the issue of ideology. Indeed, in recent papers, I have attempted to extend the cognitivist approach to issues of film ideology.[13] Thus, the real issue is not whether cognitivism is formalist, but whether the contribution that cognitivism can make to what I take to be legitimate questions about film and ideology is productive or not. Specifically, we will need to compare the merits of cognitivist models of film ideology to psychoanalytic models.

Cognitivism is not a fully developed

theory. It is an approach that has guided some theorizing already and which, it is to be hoped, will guide more in the future. I have always agreed that some of this theorizing will pertain to the ideological and political dimension of cinema. In that sense, I have never been a formalist. Moreover, since cognitivist theories of these topics are beginning to be produced, charges of formalism are obsolete. The issue now is whether cognitivist or psychoanalytic theories do a better job answering our questions about ideology. This discussion has barely begun; nevertheless, I welcome it.

Cognitivism, Psychoanalysis and Constraint: The Big Question

Perhaps Buckland's central objection to my approach is that I will only countenance or regard as valid theories of film that are cognitivist. (CPR, 96) In this way, Buckland distinguishes between the good cognitivist cop, Bordwell, and the bad cognitivist cop, me. But, in fact, I have never denied that psychoanalysis might contribute to our understanding of film. I wrote:

Nothing we have said suggests an objection in principle to these more specific questions about aspects of the audience over and above their cognitive faculties. Social conditioning and affective psychology, appropriately constrained, might be introduced to explain the power of given movies or types of movies for target groups. Sociology anthropology, and certain forms of psychoanalysis are likely to be useful in such investigations. (*MM*, 213)

Perhaps these qualifications, and similar ones in my book *The Philosophy of Horror*, have been overlooked by readers because of my protracted, admittedly relentless rejection of one psychoanalytic hypothesis after another. But I have consistently acknowledged that apart from the specific arguments that I have advanced against specific applications of psychoanalytic theories, I have no knock-down argument to show that psychoanalysis is always out of place in film theory. Indeed, as the preceding passage indicates, I explicitly allow that, appropriately constrained, psychoanalysis may add to our understanding of film.

Of course, the sticking point here is whatever is meant by "appropriately constrained." Indeed, I think that the continued debate between cognitivism and psychoanalysis hinges on discussing and debating the kinds of constraints that film theorists should respect when applying psychoanalysis to film. In order to advance this debate, allow me to state my view.

In thinking about when it is appropriate to embrace psychoanalytic explanatory frameworks, it pays to remember that psychoanalysis is a theory that is designed to explain the irrational. Thus, behavior that can be traced without remainder to organic sources, such as brain lesions and chemical imbalances, are not in the domain of psychoanalysis. For they are nonrational causes, not irrational ones. Similarly, behaviors – like certain slips of the tongue of the sorts translators and transcribers make – which can be attributed to limitations of standard cognitive processing are also analyzable in terms of nonrational and not irrational causes, and, therefore, are not proper objects of psychoanalysis. Likewise, behaviors, states, or reactions that are explicable rationally and/or in virtue of normal cognitive processing are not, *prima facie,* appropriate topics for psychoanalysis. Psychoanalysis explains breakdowns in rationality or in normal cognitive processing that are not otherwise explicable in terms of nonrational defects.

Another way to put this is to ask what remains to be explained if we can account for a behavior or a state in terms of rational psychology or in terms of nonrational defects in the organism or processing system. That is, in order to mobilize psychoanalysis, one has to be able to point to some data which are not sufficiently explained by rational (under which rubric I would include

many cultural practices), organic or systemic factors.

Freud himself abides by this methodological constraint in his *Interpretation of Dreams,* where he first, and at great length, disposes of dream theories of the preceding sorts before advancing his own theory. Moreover, I would contend that he was motivated here by more than respect for the niceties of dialectical argumentation. He realized that in order to postulate the operation of repressed unconscious forces he had to demonstrate the failure to accommodate the data of rationalist psychology, standing accounts of cognitive processing, and organic hypotheses. For it is analytical to the very concept of psychoanalysis that its object is the irrational, which domain has as its criterion of identification the inadequacy of rational, cognitive or organic explanations. Put bluntly, there is nothing left for psychoanalysis to explain if the behavior or state in question can be explained organically, rationally or in terms of the normal functioning of our cognitive and perceptual systems.

The relevance of this to the dialectical structure of argumentation in *Mystifying Movies* should be obvious. First I criticize various psychoanalytic explanations of our responses to cinema in terms of their logical and empirical flaws. Then I field a rival hypothesis which I argue is not logically flawed, and which I argue does a better job with the data. In other words, I put theories in competition.

However, there is a feature of this dialectical strategy that is not standard in most other scientific debates. For the theories that I advance in competition to psychoanalysis are all what we call cognitivist. Thus, if they are convincing and if psychoanalytic theory is constrained in the way I argue, then my theories not only challenge psychoanalytic alternatives, but preclude them. For they show that the responses in question are not in the appropriate domain of psychoanalysis.[14]

Of course, I don't suppose that this ends the discussion. Confronted with this strategy, the critic disposed toward psychoanalysis will want to find some aspect of the data that my theories do not explain. But if this is the structure of the debate between cognitivism and psychoanalysis, then it indicates that *Mystifying Movies* has achieved at least one effect. Namely, it has shifted the burden of proof to the defender of psychoanalysis. The underlying purpose of *Mystifying Movies* and of my recent cognitivist account of horror has been to shift the burden of proof to the psychoanalytic film theorist. Indeed, I chose the horror genre as an arena in which to expand cognitivist theorizing just because its traffic with intense emotional states gives it the appearance of being, so to speak, a "natural" target for psychoanalysis. It is now up to the psychoanalyst to show what my theories of horror, cinematic narration, cinematic representation, editing and film music have left out and to show that in order to account for this remainder we must resort to suitably constrained psychoanalytic explanations – rather than cognitivist or biological or sociocultural alternatives.

Again, I have no argument to show that there is nothing left over for psychoanalytic theorists and critics to explain. What I think I have shown is rather: first, that there is less to be explained than is usually presumed, without argument, by contemporary film theorists and, second, that the burden of proof in the debates I have initiated is theirs. Maybe there are aspects of our response to cinema that call for suitably constrained psychoanalytic theorizing. My position is that it is now up to psychoanalytic critics to prove it. They cannot, as Buckland proposes, simply stipulate it.

On the one hand, I am a methodological pluralist in the sense that I favor having a field where there are a lot of theories. For insofar as putting all our available theories into competition delivers results, putting a lot of theories into play is likely to be productive. But I am a robust methodological pluralist since I am not advocating a situation in which everyone just rattles around in their own paradigm. Instead, the available theories should be critically compared in such a way that some may be eliminated, though critical comparison may also reveal that some of these theories are complementary or supplementary or otherwise compatible. Unlike Buckland, I am not ready now to suppose that cognitivism and some form of psychoanalysis are obviously compatible. But neither am I committed to the view that this is an impossible conclusion. At present, my bets are clearly on cognitivism. Yet I have always conceded that only time and critical, reflective debate will settle the issue.

I admit that I know no reason in principle to predict that psycho-analysis will never provide the most satisfactory explanations of some of the data at hand. All we can do is compare the relative strengths and weaknesses of our theories. This, of course, also requires that we interrogate the framework in which we compare our theories. Questions about whether there are constraints to which psychoanalysis is beholden and about what these constraints are constitute the fundamental issue between psychoanalytic film theorists and their cognitivist counterparts today. Let the discussion begin.

Notes

1. E.g., Noël Carroll, *Mystifying Movies* (New York: Columbia University Press, 1988); Noël Carroll, *The Philosophy of Horror* (New York: Routledge, 1990); David Bordwell, *Narration and the Fiction Film* (Madison, Wisc.: University of Wisconsin P, 1985); David Bordwell, *Making Meaning* (Cambridge, Mass.: Harvard University Press, 1989).
2. See, for example, Robert Ray, "The Bordwell Regime and the Stakes of Knowledge," *Strategies*, no. 1, Fall 1988; Dudley Andrew, "The Limits of Delight: Robert Ray's Postmodern Film Studies," *Strategies*, no. 2, 1989; Dudley Andrew, "Cognitivism:

Quests and Questionings," *Iris,* no. 9, Spring 1989; Dudley Andrew, "A Reply to David Bordwell," *Iris,* no. 11, Summer 1990. Also relevant to the debate are: David Bordwell, "A Case for Cognitivism," *Iris,* no. 9, Spring 1989; and David Bordwell, "A Case for Cognitivism: Further Reflection," *Iris,* no. 11, Summer 1990.

3. Warren Buckland, "Critique of Poor Reason," *Screen,* vol. 30, no. 4, Autumn 1989. Henceforth, this will be referred to as CPR in the text where the relevant page references will be cited. My *Mystifying Movies* will be referred to as *MM* with page references also cited in the text. Stephen Heath has also registered prolonged objections to my work in his "Le Père Noël," *October,* Fall 1983. I will not review Heath's attack here because I have already dealt with it in Noël Carroll, "A Reply to Heath," *October,* Winter 1983. Nor will I dwell on the objections made by Robert Lapsley and Michael Westlake in their book *Film Theory* since they did not have access to the theory propounded in *Mystifying Movies.* See Robert Lapsley and Michael Westlake, *Film Theory* (Manchester: Manchester University Press, 1988).

4. In Donald Davidson, *Inquiries Into Truth and Interpretation* (Oxford: Oxford University Press, 1984). It may be of interest to some readers that, ironically, I have used this very article to undermine the post-Saussurean linguistic theory upon which so much contemporary film theory and literary theory depends. See Noël Carroll, "Belsey on Language and Realism," *Philosophy and Literature,* April 1986.

5. This is also a reason to refrain from charging that my approach is incommensurable with respect to marxist-psychoanalytic film theory. For example, the cognitivist and the marxist-psychoanalytic theorist share myriad observation terms, like perspective, convention and film editing.

6. Perhaps Celia Britton has a similar argument in mind when she chastens me for not mentioning that Lacan believes that the unconscious plays a role in determining the behavior of normal people. I, of course, know that Lacan thinks that. My point, however, is that Lacan can't just assert that; he must prove it, preferably by defending his criteria (if he has any) for explaining normal behavior psychoanalytically. See Celia Britton's review of *Mystifying Movies* in *Reviewing Sociology,* vol. 7, no. 1.

7. Christian Metz, "The Imaginary Signifier," *The Imaginary Signifier* (Bloomington: Indiana University Press, 1982), p. 44.

8. See Noël Carroll, "From Real to Reel: Entangled in Nonfiction Film," *Philosophic Exchange,* 1983. This essay is reprinted in this volume.

9. Noël Carroll, "Conspiracy Theories of Representation," *Philosophy of the Social Sciences,* vol. 17, 1987.

10. Noël Carroll, *The Philosophy of Horror,* especially Chapter Three.

11. For example, see Noël Carroll, "Toward A Theory of Film Editing," *Millennium Film Journal,* No. 3, Winter/Spring 1979. This essay is reprinted in this volume.

12. David Bordwell, *Ozu and the Poetics of Cinema* (Princeton: Princeton University Press and the British Film Institute, 1988).

13. See Noël Carroll, "The Image of Women in Film: A Defense of a Paradigm," *The Journal of Aesthetics and Art Criticism,* vol. 84, no. 4, Fall 1990; and Noël Carroll, "Film, Rhetoric and Ideology," *Explanations and Value,* ed. Salim Kemal and I. Gaskell (Cambridge University Press, 1993). These essays are reprinted in the volume.

14. Of course, if you don't accept what I refer to as the constraints on psychoanalysis, you will not agree that the plausibility of my theories neatly removes psychoanalysis from the field. On the other hand, the consequences of this are not devastating for my attack. For my theories are still competing theories which the psychoanalytic theorist must *engage,* one at a time, even if my theories don't have the special advantage claimed for them in the text.

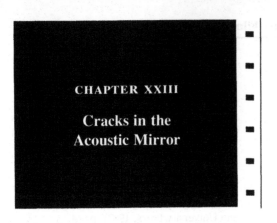

CHAPTER XXIII

Cracks in the
Acoustic Mirror

Recent discussions of sound in film have been influenced by the notion of the acoustic mirror, an amplification, shall we say, of the scenario of psychosexual development espoused by Lacanians. This notion is already subject to diverse formulations, including those of Claudia Gorbman, Mary Ann Doane, and Kaja Silverman. But for purposes of both brevity and clarity, I will focus on only one of these formulations, namely, the one advanced by Kaja Silverman in her recent, influential book *The Acoustic Mirror* (Bloomington: Indiana University Press, 1988). I have chosen this book because I think that it is fair to say that it is the most developed account that we have of the acoustic mirror to date in English. However, I should add that I think that *if* Silverman's accounts of the acoustic mirror – and of related notions like *voice* and the *choric scene* – are the best ones to be had, then perhaps we would be better off without them.

What does Silverman have to say about voice, the choric scene, and the acoustic mirror? What, for example, does she mean by voice? This is very difficult to say. Silverman never really defines it. One can, I think, generally assume that when she speaks of the voice in cinema, she has the *female* voice in mind. However, *voice*, even with this qualification is quite slippery in Silverman's treatment. Sometimes it refers *literally* to the female voice in cinema – i.e., to what a sound recording could record. But at other times, *voice* appears to include the

meaning of what is said and, by even further extension, it refers to processes of communication and discourse that are unspoken. And, metaphorically, *voice* can also apply to the authorial preoccupations of a filmmaker like Cavani. Silverman is aware that at least some of these phenomena are quite different, but she does not seem worried about eliding them under the same rubric. Later, I will suggest why this elision should be worrisome.

Since not even a stipulative definition of *voice* is available in the text, the best way to get at what is signaled by it is to look at the work that it is supposed to do – i.e., to look at the hypotheses and explanations in which it ostensibly figures. Roughly, these hypotheses can be divided into two groups: those that pertain to Hollywood and those that pertain to various alternative cinemas.

Taking what Silverman has to say about Hollywood first, one can say that Silverman claims that the female voice in Hollywood practice is rendered systematically insufficient or is "contained" in order to facilitate the male viewer's own disavowal of his own insufficiency. That is, the insufficiency of the male viewer is purportedly transferred to the voice of female characters in Hollywood narratives. In order to understand this hypothesis, we need to know the nature of the insufficiency that the male viewer disavows, on the one hand, and the way in which that insufficiency is transferred or imposed onto women characters.

There are at least two male disavowals that debilitations of the female voice are said to facilitate. They are

1. The disavowal of the fact that the male viewer is not the enunciator of the film, and, therefore, that he lacks what is called discursive control or mastery. Silverman associates this process of disavowal with the containment of the female voice through several strategies, notably: (a) the sequestering of the female voice in spectacles within the film

(e.g., in song and dance numbers); (b) subjecting the woman's voice to psychoanalysis or to some other form of the "talking cure" within the film itself; (c) deforming or distorting the female voice by imbuing it with a speech impediment or an accent.

2. There is also a second, deeper level of male disavowal here. Putatively, it involves the male's disavowal of the mother's voice as a source of the male's subjectivity or identity and as a source of language. What does this mean?

Both males and females acquire language, in large part, through interaction with the mother, a process Silverman christens as the *choric scene*. The choric scene is the developmental stage when, wrapped in the sonorous envelop of the mother's voice, we learn the names of things. In this choric scene, the mother's voice addresses the child rather in the fashion of voice-over commentary, a metaphor not of my making, but of Silverman's. Indeed, it seems that for Silverman this choric scene is prototypic for voice-over narration in film.

According to the kind of psychoanalytic model to which Silverman subscribes, a sense of subjecthood develops in tandem with this process of language acquisition. In great measure, the mother's voice is a source of that acquisition, providing what Silverman calls an acoustic mirror, which is analogous to the visual mirror of Lacanian psychoanalysis – a mirror in whose reflection the infant male or female shapes its subjectivity.

By hypothesis, the male child eventually tends to deny this dependence on the mother, often by attributing his own helplessness and insufficiency to her. Hollywood cinema repeats and reinforces this disavowal by means of several strategies, including, (a) the lack of voice-over, female narration in Hollywood, which purportedly masks for the male viewers the remembrance of the threatening choric scene (Silverman says the

Letter to Three Wives is the only example she can find of disembodied female narration in Hollywood film), and (b) the second strategy for male disavowal of the choric scene is the putative dedication of the Hollywood cinema to eliciting screams and cries from female characters. Hollywood cinema is said to be a machine for producing female cries – a veritable scream machine. Here Silverman has in mind films like *Sorry Wrong Number,* as well as countless horror and slasher films. Silverman situates the psychic significance of this strategy as a means by which male fantasy transfers, through reversal, the infantile male helplessness, manifested in his childhood crying, to the mother.

As is frequent in a great deal of recent feminist film theory – as exemplified by Laura Mulvey's avant-gardism, on the one hand, and by Teresa de Lauretis's qualified defense of realism, on the other – Silverman's diagnosis of the problems or disavowals of the Hollywood cinema is connected to a prognosis for an alternative cinema. That is, what is denied in the Hollywood cinema is to be secured or restored by feminist film practice.

Of course, what is, according to Silverman, contained, deformed, obscured and, most often, simply banished by Hollywood is the voice of the mother, along with any psychic acknowledgment of the acoustic mirror and the choric scene. In turn, what Silverman regards as a major achievement in feminist cinema is the acknowledgment of the voice of the mother and of the acoustic mirror – not for the purpose of some illusory sense of unity or plenitude, but as a way for women to recognize commonality as daughters (thereby securing a condition for feminist collectivity). This sense of commonality, however, is also said to acknowledge differences as a result of the separation from the mother and the entry into the so-called Lacanian stage of the symbolic, something that Silverman regards as posing the Oedipal issue of castration for men and women alike.

Speaking more concretely and with reference to cinema, Silverman cites a number of avant-garde films that function to implement these ends, including *Riddles of the Sphinx* by Peter Wollen and Laura Mulvey and *Journeys from Berlin/1971* by Yvonne Rainer. In *Riddles of the Sphinx,* the choric scene is reinstituted through the voice-over narration of mothers, like Mary Kelly and the fictional sphinx, as well as through talk between women (thereby establishing a condition for female community, symbolized by the acrobats at the end of the film).

Journeys from Berlin, among other avant-garde films, disembodies the woman's voice and recalls the speech of the mother as the first voice-over. As well, that voice is invested with discursive variety, speaking of matters of theory, sexuality and politics. The female voice that is purportedly contained by Hollywood is thus liberated and empowered, given room to flex its discursive mastery.

Having briefly sketched some of Silverman's central notions, let me now suggest some of the problems that they must confront. I will not now dwell on the philosophical problems raised by Silverman's rather free-style adaptation and use of psychoanalysis – not because there are not estimable difficulties here, but because this is not the right forum for these issues. Instead, allow me to remark primarily on the limitations of these concepts for film theory and criticism.

First – and of central importance from that perspective – is the question of whether, with respect to the Hollywood tradition, these concepts and the processes they denominate fit the facts. I cannot see that they do. If the stability of the male viewer depends on the kinds of containing strategies that Silverman enumerates, then he would have to be unhinged a great deal of the time. Recall what some of these strategies comprise: "sequestering" the female voice within the narrative by means of devices like production numbers; subjecting the female voice to

the talking cure (a strained way of putting it, since persons and not voices are what are typically psychoanalyzed); and, lastly, imposing accents and impediments on the female voice.

Consider these three strategies for a moment. Now substract them from the corpus of Hollywood filmmaking and *notice* that what remains are reels and reels of narrative film in which none of these strategies ever appear. For example, the number of films where women are subjected to the talking cure are statistically infrequent, even miniscule. But the male viewer seems no more unhinged or disturbed by films that fail to employ these strategies than by the films that do. Therefore, it seems vastly improbable that these strategies are performing the causal role that Silverman attributes to them.

Here, as in so much other feminist psychoanalytic film theory – indeed, as in so much other contemporary film theory in general – we see a causal hypothesis advanced without the slightest comprehension of what is involved in making a causal claim. For if the aforesaid strategies were really doing the causal work of containment that Silverman attributes to them, why is that containment still in place when the strategies in question are absent? Nothing can be a cause of x, *ceteris paribus,* if in its absence, x still obtains. Causes and effects co-vary. But Silverman's obliviousness to the need to establish co-variation indicates that she lacks even minimal understanding of the kind of evidence her hypotheses require in order to be intelligible. Her forays into causal analysis are, in effect, virtually ridiculous.

You might think that the way around this allegation is simply to assert that Silverman hasn't told us all the relevant strategies. But I don't think that this will work, unless it can handle another embarrassing bit of contrary data – to wit: all of the extremely powerful female voices Hollywood has given us. Remember Rosalind Russell, Jean Arthur, Claudet Colbert, and Katherine

Hepburn, especially in their screwball comedies, but not only there. If the male viewer really requires "contained" female voices in order to sustain psychic equilibrium, then he should be destabilized by Rosalind Russell's discursive mastery in *His Girl Friday* and Katherine Hepburn's in *Bringing Up Baby*. Has anyone in the history of film exhibited more discursive mastery than Katherine Hepburn in *Bringing Up Baby*? But since the male viewer is not discernibly disturbed by these cases, it seems legitimate to infer that the putatively necessary debilitation of the female voice is not a projectable causal hypothesis. Again, the ill-considered and amateurish causal reasoning here is flabbergasting.

As a side note, it is instructive to observe that Silverman's problem with powerful, active female characters parallels one of the awesome empirical flaws in Laura Mulvey's theory of visual pleasure, notably Mulvey's claim that women are only objects of the gaze and never doers in Hollywood cinema. It is a strange feature of feminist psychoanalytic film theory that it is so inclined to treat women as eternal victims. The evidence available of images of women in film is far more mixed.

Other Hollywood strategies for male disavowal vis-à-vis the female voice are said to involve denying the female voice the position of voice-over-narrator and the putative fact that Hollywood narrative is dedicated to making women characters scream.

As to the claim about the lack of disembodied female narration, I think that it is important to stress that disembodied narration is not a very frequent technique in Hollywood films and that the infrequency of female narration is probably best explained in terms of the infrequency of the technique in general, along with Hollywood's tendency to favor the male viewpoint, rather than in terms of an attempt to repress the mother's voice. Indeed, this latter motive would be difficult to sustain coherently, once one recalls that the male viewers of the classical

Hollywood cinema were able to listen to disembodied female voices on the radio all of the time with no apparent tremors of insufficiency. Moreover, male viewers evince no discernible consternation with embodied female voices in films with respect to *I Remember Momma, Jane Eyre, The Bride of Frankenstein, Naked City, Raw Deal, A Man of Her Own* (the fifties' version), *To Kill a Mockingbird* and so on. What difference should disembodiment make, since the mother in the choric scene is not disembodied? Will Silverman dare to say she knows the child experiences the mother as disembodied? But, in any case, I submit that the technique is so rare, that no one notices that it is absent in films, and even when it is present, as in *Letter to Three Wives,* male viewers, contrary to Silverman's hypothesis, seem unflappable. One begins to wonder if Silverman understands what a *cause* is.

On the other hand, the hypothesis about the Hollywood scream machine faces Silverman with another kind of problem, one that runs through all of her putative Hollywood strategies for manipulating the female voice. If horror films and slasher movies are machines for eliciting screams from female characters, they also do an extremely efficient job of eliciting screams from male characters. Thus, if the helplessness signaled by the screaming female character reassures the male viewer, why doesn't the self-same type of scream, elicited in the same way from the male characters, undermine that assurance?

Similarly, male characters not only also scream, but, remembering Silverman's other strategies, they have accents and impediments "imposed" – if that's the right word for a feature of a fictional character – on their voice, and they are, as well, frequently sequestered, so to speak, in production numbers. And, of course, Gregory Peck was psychoanalyzed by Ingrid Bergman in *Spellbound.* Silverman owes us an explanation of why such examples are not problematic for the male viewer. Until she does, her hypotheses about the causal function of these strategies are, to put it mildly, nonstarters.

As with so much contemporary film theory, one wonders whether Silverman has even a glimmering of understanding about what it takes to advance a causal hypothesis. Of course, she might respond that she is not talking about causal relations. But what could a discussion of containments, the absence of which raise anxieties in males, be if not causal hypotheses?

Perhaps an even more vexing problem with Silverman's speculations about Hollywood filmmaking is her proposal of a connection between the male viewer's hypothesized disposition toward consternation over his lack of discursive mastery, and its displacement in the form of violence done to the voice of female characters. For the male's discursive insufficiency comes down to the fact that he is not narrating the story that is unfolding on the screen. But this narration – whoever or whatever one thinks is doing it – is silent, while the female voices in question need not be involved in story telling. So why does the male viewer recuperate his lack of control of a process of silent narration through the deformation of audible language that is not necessarily narrative. One might try to smuggle a connection in here by describing all narration as *telling* stories, and by presuming that all telling requires a voice, but this involves little more than advancing a pun in place of an analysis.

Thus, there is little profit in Silverman's notions of voice and the acoustic mirror for the theory and criticism of Hollywood film. Are these concepts any more useful when it comes to the avant-garde? Let us consider the examples already mentioned: *Riddles of the Sphinx* and *Journeys from Berlin*. As might be expected, Silverman's psychoanalytic idiom serves the phenomena here better than it did in her account of Hollywood, for the simple reason that, with these avant-garde examples, she is interpreting individual films rather than making

causal generalizations and, importantly, because the individual films that she is interpreting, as a matter of fact, share a great many of Silverman's psychoanalytic allegiances. Therefore, in explicating these films, it is appropriate, hermeneutically speaking, to illuminate their psychoanalytic presuppositions in the same way that it is relevant to advert to Thomas Aquinas when explicating Dante, or to McTaggart's otherwise fanciful theory of time when explicating Eliot.

But even here there are some problems. A key element of Silverman's account is the notion of the acoustic mirror, which she only discovered after the films in question were made. Thus, her invocation of the acoustic mirror with respect to these films cannot be construed as unpacking the presuppositions of the films in question. For if Silverman only just discovered the choric scene, it could not have been presumed by filmmakers at an earlier date.

Perhaps the response here will be that this only shows that the filmmakers could not have consciously presupposed the choric scene. It does not preclude the possibility that unconsciously this developmental stage shaped the filmmaker's choice as a sort of psychic prototype. Of course, this line of defense depends on there actually being a developmental stage of the precise sort Silverman specifies, and Silverman does precious little by way of supplying therapeutic or psychological evidence for it.

There are no summaries of observations of children. And unlike Freud or Lacan, Silverman does not have the empirical background of a clinical practice upon which to base her postulations about psychosexual development. We seem to have little reason to believe that there is an acoustic mirror stage other than Silverman's wish that there be such a stage. That is, the acoustic mirror appears to be completely suppositional with no evidence standing behind it, save perhaps the commonplace that mothers are generally responsible for a great deal of our linguistic education. (Generally, but not always; are male children raised by male caregivers, perhaps gay male caregivers, rattled by disembodied male voice-over narration?)

But maybe the question of whether there is such a stage as that of the acoustic mirror is better left to clinical and child psychologists. A more important question for film critics to consider is if there are choric scenes and acoustic mirrors, can we see their imprint on the details of films like *Riddles of the Sphinx* and *Journeys from Berlin*? And here the problem is that it is very difficult to find strong analogies between the choric scene and the scenes in those films – including the scenes that Silverman brings forth as evidence.

The choric scene/acoustic mirror refers to the mother talking to the child, enveloping it in a sonorous envelop and teaching it the rudiments of language and social intercourse. As mentioned already, Silverman thinks of this as the original voice-over commentary. Now the films in question have voice-over commentary, generally by women and sometimes by mothers (the latter especially in *Riddles of the Sphinx*). However, the content of these voices is like nothing you ever heard on your mother's (or caregiver's) knee. It includes excursii into psychoanalysis and politics, into art history, the reading of dreams, and so forth. That is, none of it is really vaguely like rudimentary language learning or the initiation of the child into social modes of affection. But surely if there is such a thing as the choric scene, it requires more than women speaking, even in voice-over commentary, in order to be mobilized or even for viewers to be mobilized by it. Something very like the original psychic interaction should be replayed. Yet neither of these films supply even moderately exact analogs to the choric scene, and, as a result, Silverman's exegetical references to the mother's voice and to the choric scene appear to be arbitrarily

tacked onto *Riddles of the Sphinx* and *Journeys from Berlin*.

Of course, Silverman is not wrong to observe that the disembodied female voice is important in these films, as well as in other works of the recent feminist avant-garde. That point was well established, if not obvious, long before Silverman wrote *The Acoustic Mirror*. The question is whether the concept of the acoustic mirror, with its subtending psychoanalytic hypotheses about the significance of the mother's voice, adds anything to what is already known critically about these films.

I want to suggest that it does not.

Many feminist filmmakers of the seventies, led by Yvonne Rainer, chose to employ the disembodied female voice, especially a disembodied female voice discoursing on theory, as a powerful symbolic means of asserting their equality and their authority, particularly in the context of the avant-garde film world. The choice of the disembodied voice in this situation was historically very astute and effective for a number of reasons. It undercut what was perceived to be a presiding homology that body/mind : : spectacle/discourse : : female/male. Within this context, the association of the female in film with spectacle and with the role of sex object was subverted and replaced with the voice of theory and reflection, that is, with something that was, among other things, unavailable for ogling. The symbolism of the voice-over female theorist was and still is a means of asserting the equality of women to men as thinkers and speakers with equal access to authority and equal claims to seriousness.

But note that if you are willing to accept this brief indication of the way in which an account of the importance of the disembodied voices in a film like *Journeys from Berlin* might go, then you have little need to resort to psychoanalytic scenarios involving acoustic mirrors. For one can explain why the choice of the disembodied voice was a strategic one given the logic of the art historical situation and the general social context in which Rainer and other feminist filmmakers made their decisions. That is, their choice of this symbolism is fully explicable in terms of their application of what might be called art-practical reasoning in the specific cultural context in which they operated. Complicating this fully rationalistic story by appending references to psychoanalysis, especially with respect to such unsubstantiated processes such as acoustic mirroring, obscures and muddies critical understanding rather than enhancing it.

Thus, it would seem that Silverman's notions of voice, the acoustic mirror and the choric scene are no more helpful in the discussion of the avant-garde than they were in the analysis of Hollywood filmmaking.

So, perhaps, it is better to dispense with them altogether. Or, at least, I hereby so move.

CHAPTER XXIV

A Reply to Heath

Whether, in fact, the hypothetical cabal of Cavell, Danto, and Carroll has been and continues to be more instrumental than Stephen Heath in the professionalization of contemporary cinema studies is a question I leave to informed readers to answer. Heath, at least, says he regards professionalism as reactionary and responds to the epistemological objections propounded in my "Address to the Heathen"[1] by whining that he will not sink to such rank professional preoccupations. It is part of a pernicious conspiracy, Heath would have us believe, to consider epistemology to be the formal inspection and evaluation of theories. Thus, maintaining what he fancies to be his political purity, Heath never addresses the core objections of AH: that suture theory is, strictly speaking, vacuous; that his deployment of psychoanalysis is not properly constrained by consideration of countervailing cognitive-psychological hypotheses; that his analyses of the various mechanics of subject positioning are based on equivocation; that his metaphors are uselessly obscure; that his notion of unity is illicit; that his concept of the cinematic apparatus defies the pragmatic requirements of theory building.

Instead, Heath raises a smokescreen in order to disguise the fact that he is not dealing with issues raised in AH and wastes a great deal of time itemizing my alleged misrepresentations of QC. But surprisingly, nearly half of his complaints – such as his attack of my quotation of Hegel (AH, p. 93) – are extracted from side comments made in my footnotes which are peripheral to the central, still uncontested points made by AH. Perhaps we can explain Heath's footnote fetish by postulating that he takes literally the idea of weighing arguments and that he was unable otherwise to add bulk to the slim PN.

When Heath finally mounts his three sustained counterattacks – concerning perspective, illusion, and interminability – in only one of these, the section on interminability, is he defending himself from objections directed at the core of what is unique to his theory. In the discussions of illusion and perspective he is attacking general introductory points of mine that are not integral to the central epistemological arguments brought against distinctive elements of Heath's theory – such as the apparatus and suture. There is certainly nothing wrong in attacking me. But I am astonished that instead of defending what is unique to his own theory, Heath spends his longest sections rejecting my positions on perspective and illusion in the name of such semioticians as Coleridge. Respecting editorially imposed limitations of space, I shall address only a few of his points.

Misrepresentation: Or, the Author Is Not Dead

The frequent lack of logical and grammatical connectives in QC and its strained use of words often make it difficult to ascertain what is being said. I therefore expected that some questions would arise over my characterizations of its substance, but I could not have anticipated misrepresentation as Heath's main line of defense. Retrospectively, it appears that the turgid style of QC is an evasion tactic. The ambiguity of the formulations in QC allows them to be applied under one interpretation, but they can, when challenged, be defended under another interpretation, one that turns an ostensibly radical hypothesis into a truism. For example, Heath depicted the relation of narrative and perspective in cinema as an interlocking system which overcomes the potential disturbances of film movement in virtue of the narrative's capacity to *center* subjects – a capacity which reinforces what sounds like a functionally equivalent effect of perspective (for example, QC, pp. 36–37). But when this is attacked as equivocation, we are told that all that was claimed by the initially obscure text was the paltry and widely known truth that, historically, one finds that perspective paintings have been used to portray narratives. But why does one need the particular terms "centering" and "positioning" if that is all one wants to say? In PN Heath has undertaken a rereading of QC that represents it as a string of self-evident truths whose rejection implies perversion.

On Point-of-View Editing

In section iv of PN, Heath rejects my characterization of his account of point-of-view editing as a "perspective system" that is somehow geometrically engineered. Yet in his lengthy introduction to the relation of shots in point-of-view editing, we read:

If in the left of the frame an actor in close-up is looking off right, he has an empty space in front of him; if the following shot shows an empty space to the left and an object to the right, then the actor's look appears to cross an *orientated, rectilinear,* and thus *logical* space: it seems to bear with *precision* on the object. One has an eye-line match. The look, that is, joins form of expression – the composition of the images and their disposition in relation to one another – and form of content – the definition of the action of the film in the movement of looks, exchanges, objects seen and so on. Point of view develops on the basis of this joining operation of the look, the camera taking the position of a character in order to show the spectator what he or she sees (QC, p. 46, italics added).

The quotation that initiates the preceding passage is from Mitry. And though Heath goes on to criticize Mitry's account of the "subjective image," he never explicitly parts company with the idea that the relation of the character to what he sees in the point-of-view schema is "rectilinear," "orientated," "logical," and "precise."[2] Since Heath has already told us that point-of-view is "a kind of perspective within the perspective system" (QC, p. 44), what are we to make of these claims about rectilinear space? Heath might claim that he neither endorses nor criticizes Mitry on the issue of rectilinear space, but simply drops the quotation as some sort of historical documentation (whose point remains unspecified). Yet even Heath must know that if one quotes a passage, does not criticize it, and employs it materially in one's exposition, then that counts as an endorsement. Clearly, in the section above, Heath bases the "joining operation" of the point-of-view schema on the model of the eye-line match, which is characterized as a logical, rectilinear – shall we say "geometrically accurate" – organization of space.

The preceding discussion of rectilinear space is couched in "appearance talk." This can be interpreted in at least two ways. Saying the space *appears* rectilinear can mean that it *looks* and *is* rectilinear in its construction, just as when I ask if the dean appeared healthy I am asking for accurate information about his state. Or, saying that the space *appears* rectilinear could mean that the space looks rectilinear but that this is a deceptive illusion. Spectators believe the relationship between shots is geometrically precise, but it is not. In AH, I show that neither of these alternatives is relevant to point-of-view editing. It is unnecessary for the editor to arrange point-of-view schemas by means of the rules of perspective nor do audiences mistakenly believe, nor must they mistakenly believe, that the relation of shots in a point-of-view schema is geometrically precise. I emphasize instead that pragmatic considerations of the narrative context will be of prime importance in the reception of the point-of-view structure. Undoubtedly Heath will say that this is his position, but then why did he include that nonsense about logical, rectilinear space?

In addition, Heath misconstrues my invented *King Kong* example. The problem is that if the space is rectilinear, then the image of Darrow should be taken from a high angle about thirty feet overhead, whereas, I contend, the point-of-view schema will work if the shot is taken at eye-level. Moreover, this incongruity will not be explained by the type of account Heath offers of the Gutman case in *Maltese Falcon* because mine is not an example of subjective marking. It is just a violation of rectilinear mapping. But the spectator would understand the cut despite its failure to match the ostensible geometry of the scene.

Causation

Heath claims that my footnote about his stand on causation is a misrepresentation. I said the analyses in QC are causal (AH, p. 92) because the conception of contradictions – what Heath studies instead of causes – are treated as compelling forces that *produce* states of affairs, because QC explicitly uses the concept of the *causation of the subject* and because the use of metaphors, like those of the cinema machine and the apparatus, strike me as cause-talk. Did Heath deny his analyses are causal? He wrote:

. . . it must be seen that the notion of determination which has proved – or has been made to prove – such a stumbling block for ideological analysis *cannot be conceived of as a problem in cause-and-effect with its answer an explanation from an absolute point of origin* (as though historical materialism were to be, in Engel's words, "easier than the solution of a simple equation in the first degree"). *Analysis will be concerned not with determinations in this mechanistic sense but with contradictions,* it being in the movement of these contradictions that can be grasped the set of determinations – the "structural causality" – focused by a particular social fact, institution or work (QC, pp. 6–7).

I take this as a statement that Heath does not study causation as it is typically understood, but studies something new – "structural causality" – which must be segregated by quotation marks in the manner of a neologism and which is grasped by the movements of contradictions. Heath, of course, refrains from defining any of his terms, but we are left to think that his study is of something other than causality as that is normally conceived.

It seems obvious that the only reason the above passage offers for ideological analyses' not being construed as "a problem in cause and effect" is that cause and effect analysis asserts an "absolute point of origin," a totally obscure formulation that is only given the vaguest explication in terms of some sort of analogy with the facility of solving equations in the first degree. But the ordinary notion of cause and effect is not tied to expression in such restricted mathematical terms. Moreover, I see no reason to think that "structural causality" is at all different from causality *simpliciter* and certainly not in virtue of some demonstrated difference in the symbolic formulations of these concepts.

In PN, Heath parenthetically defines "point of origin" in a new way. Now it indicates that the study of ideology should not be economist. OK. But this still does not show that "structural causality" traffics in "contradictions" that are different from ordinary causes and effects.

In Praise of Lacan

Section vi of PN is devoted to a throwaway remark that I make in a footnote in which I say that Heath congratulates Lacan for the discovery of *lalangue*. In QC (p. 80), Heath asserts that *lalangue* overcomes shortcomings of the *langue/parole* distinction vis-à-vis understanding the subject in language. Given Heath's commitments, isn't this something that recommends *lalangue* to the serious film theorist (even if Heath may want to modify other aspects of Lacan)?

What is so peculiar about this little distraction of Heath's is that he ignores the fact that my footnote is attached to one of the most damning objections I make against suture theory. In order to avoid vacuity, a theory must not only explain why x is the case but also under what circumstances x would not be the case. If I attempted to explain both why a certain flower would live and why it would die by saying "God wills it," my explanation would be vacuous. Similarly, Heath deals with both classical Hollywood films and structuralist-materialist films in terms of suture. There seems to be nothing an avant-garde filmmaker can do to achieve nonsuture; attempts to subvert suture result instead in an intensity of meaning. Thus, by explaining everything, suture explains nothing. Since it is this rather deep issue which preoccupies the page of AH that Heath concerns himself with, why is he wasting space on the question of whether or not he is congratulating Lacan?

Lumière

In PN vii, Heath reproduces two paragraphs from my footnote 32 (AH, p. 115). In one paragraph I present Heath's discussion of Lumière and also something called the "reproduction thesis," while in the other paragraph I comment that Heath *seems* to be arguing that what is wrong with the reproduction thesis is that in saying films reproduce reality it ignores the issue of selection. By using the word "seems," I was signaling that one could not be certain of what Heath was claiming. I thought he was asserting that Lumière's claims about his films were incorrect because the films were not objective insofar as they were representations of "chosen subjects," and that, furthermore, this objection could be extended to the claims of the reproduction thesis. Searching Heath's original passage (QC, p. 4), one

finds *no other reason* given for whatever the problem is with the reproduction thesis except that images are chosen subjects about which we have the right to ask the why and the wherefore of their choice. I spoke of *selection* and Heath uses *choice*. But I do not see how my use of a synonymous characterization of the problem should raise any difficulties.

Heath believes that I misconstrued that which he was identifying as the problem. Whereas I thought the problem concerned objectivity, Heath holds the issue is that the reproduction thesis overlooks that films have ideological contents and usages. And selectivity is offered as the explicit mark of the ideological implication. But then are not films always bound to be ideological? And if they are ideological, doesn't that exclude them from the realm of objectivity? In most usages, to be ideological entails a failure in objectivity. Moreover, Heath himself has said that this section of QC is heavily Althusserian. And does that not imply that if films are ideological, then they at least are not scientifically objective (in the somewhat extended sense of science Althusser employs)? Furthermore, what beyond the fact that images are selected from somewhere for a chosen use is given by Heath as a reason to hold that the images are somehow problematic?

Heath implies that he has some really complex notion of objectivity that would not fall afoul of my simplistic objections. But the burden of producing that account is his; he does not refute me by merely suggesting that he has such an unspecified concept up his sleeve. Also, when he produces this concept of objectivity, we will still have to return to the passage in question to see how the argument there fares in light of this secret definition. Lastly, Heath says I have an entity-view of objectivity. I would have thought that my repeated emphasis on the methodology and practice of rational inquiry would have more than suggested that my notion of objectivity is not an entity-view, but a pragmatic view.

Unity and Production

In PN iii, Heath accuses me of falsely attributing to him the belief that "a coherent narrative film is not really a unity unless it reveals that it is a production – a fictional world constructed by a team of cineastes and by a process of suture" (AH, pp. 151–152). But Heath has wrenched this sentence out of context. In fact, the idea is not attributed to him. It occurs within a series of proleptic arguments by which I attempt to imagine and to refute counterarguments that a "follower of Heath" (AH, p. 151) *might* attempt to concoct in order to deal with my objections to one of Heath's "interminability arguments." I assume that prolepsis is a respectable strategy in rational inquiry. Its purpose is to foreclose certain directions of argument before they are proposed. Heath may not think that this particular line of argument is worth foreclosing, but he cannot claim that I have said he holds the position in question. I am only warning interested parties to steer clear of this option.

Heath thinks the countermove I envision is extremely ill-advised. So do I. For once, Heath and I agree. Our disagreement, I surmise, is that Heath does not believe anyone would try this gambit. But I have heard the claim that this or that film is not unified exactly because its various processes of production (specified according to the *parti pris* of the commentator) are not acknowledged. But, then, it would follow that were the film unified, it would acknowledge its processes of production. Given the dialectics of the filmworld, I believe that such an argument might be mounted, since it is entailed by the strategy that discovers failures of unity on the basis of a work's masking that it is a production. I agree with Heath that it is a confused position, one whose very

manner of implementation is not straightforwardly intelligible. That, of course, was my point.

Unity and Diversity

In PN ii, Heath completely misrepresents the issue. I hold that within the Western tradition of the arts – to which, as a matter of historical fact, narrative film belongs – spectators are instructed to derive aesthetic pleasure from the relations of coherence between the complex and diverse elements that comprise artworks. We learn to attend to patterns of notes, recurring plot motifs, systematic character contrasts, correlations between formal elements and themes, and so on. For this sort of appreciation to occur we must presuppose that the spectator knows that the artwork and/or film is composed of heterogeneous elements and dimensions. That is, I deny that in the tension between unity and heterogeneity there is a point where some totalizing impression of homogeneity dominates the spectator.

I do not deny that at certain stages in his account, Heath does imply that pleasure comes from the play of unity and diversity. But for Heath it appears that an illusion of homogenizing totality always prevails, at least as far as the spectator's experience is concerned. The fiction film works to produce an illusion of homogeneity for the spectator; that is, the spectator fails to recognize that the film is a heterogeneity. But this is what I reject – the idea that there is any point where the spectator is overwhelmed by an impression of homogeneity so compelling that all recognition of heterogeneity disappears.

In AH, I based my contention that spectators are not swept away by illusions of homogeneity on the grounds that artworks and/or films are explicitly disseminated within our tradition as unities-in-diversities rather than as homogeneities per se. In addition, when asked why they think such

347

and such a film is unified, spectators report "because the film's parts hang together" and not because they, the spectators, undergo some ecstatic ALL-IS-ONE experience. And, of course, "unity" is always unity in terms of something – parts, elements, aspects, dimensions, and so on. So to experience unity is to experience the unification of *parts*. There is no homogeneity per se, though QC appears to assert that for the spectator viewing film, there is some overriding illusion of this sort.

Heath muddies the waters by saying that he, as observer and theoretician, knows both that spectator pleasure in films, at certain stages, results in the tension between unity and diversity, and that, again as a theorist, he knows films are heterogeneous. I never disputed that as a theorist he upheld these beliefs. Rather, I question the validity of his theoretical claim that *spectators* are ultimately overwhelmed by the homogeneity effect.[3]

Interpellation

I wrote, "Heath's basic premise is that a prime function of ideology is to construct subjects. (This is also known as positioning or 'interpellating' subjects)" (AH, p. 91). Heath counterposes this to part of a sentence from QC that says, among other things, that interpellation is not the key to ideology. Clearly I made some error, but it is not, I believe, one that has deep repercussions for later criticisms in AH, especially those involving objections to Heath's suture theory.

My primary claim in the preceding quotation is not challenged by Heath, viz., that ideology is concerned to construct subjects. My error is in parenthetically defining "subject construction" by means of "interpellation," whereas interpellation is only an element in subject construction. The subject is not simply positioned by the ideological address but there is also interaction between the subject (subjectivity) and discourse –

the subject sutures or fills in the discourse. Thus, adding part of what is deleted in PN, "interpellation can in no way be the key either to ideology or to subjectivity (the fact of the individual), *the two being held as interdependent*" (QC, p. 103, italics added).

What is the consequence of this? It suggests that my initial account of Heath's program is too Althusserian, but, then, Heath himself admits that he is initially Althusserian. By the time Heath develops the concept of suture and the importance of the subject's part, however, I am explicitly aware that the emphasis has been added to the subject's "filling-in" operation and my criticisms accommodate this (e.g., AH, p. 131). That is, when Heath presents us with his version of suture, which is meant to overcome the simplicities of the initial Althusserian allegiances, my arguments against his position have followed apace and gained in complexity. Specifically, I contest his psychoanalytic account of the subject's suturing of film discourse by means of an alternative cognitive-psychological perspective. That Heath realizes that my initial elision of subject construction and interpellation cannot be traced to my ensuing, detailed attacks on his theory is shown by the fact that he finds the error in no later sections of AH.

Interminability

Heath begins his section "Interminability" by misrepresenting me. In AH (pp. 140–141), I opened with a brief contextualizing remark to the effect that there is a widespread tendency nowadays to regard texts as in some sense infinite. I mentioned two positions within this trend: that each reader has his own meaning, and that since words are interdefined they are claimed to lead to infinite semiosis. Heath vociferously spurns allegiance to these tenets. Why does he bother? I never attributed them to him. I specified that he has his own position which is concerned with ceaseless subject construction.

Another major misinterpretation in this section is the fantasy that my objections to Heath's position are grounded in speech act theory. Admittedly, I attempt to make the enounced/enunciation distinction intelligible to English-speaking readers by stipulatively reframing it as a distinction between a statement and a speech act (AH, p. 148). But no reference is made to the formal machinery of speech-act theory, nor does any argument rely on this theory. If I had meant to employ it, I would have introduced it explicitly as I have done in the past when I have employed it.[4] Instead, all I did was to Anglicize the enounced/enunciation distinction.

In my original attack on Heath's use of the enounced/enunciation distinction I stressed (a) that I did not see how this distinction established a pervasive *split* in the subject, and (b) that I did not see how any such split in the subject in linguistic representations could be extrapolated to cinematic representation. I offered a battery of arguments to show that the mere fact of the distinction did not portend a *split*. And I also searched for an argument from Heath which would demonstrate that the distinction entailed a split subject. In his response, Heath still refrains from supplying an argument, preferring oracular, apodictic pronouncements. He writes, "Carroll refuses the distinction but if by some misfortune he can't get rid of it, then he'd rather be two whole subjects than a split, a subject in process. Still, split there is, of the subject in language which is more than the positions, the representations ceaselessly effected and assumed" (PN, p. 107). Of course, I never said the distinction couldn't be made; I only questioned whether it entailed a split subject. All Heath has done in response is to beg the question by asserting that there is a split.

Heath challenges my dissolution of the supposed subject split in the case of the statement, "When I think what a healthy child I once was" (QC, p. 117). The nature of Heath's rebuttal is a rhetorical question which for some unstated reason he believes I can't answer. He demands to know the criteria by which I count the adult and the sickly child as the same enduring substance. To meet Heath's attack I need only produce the requested criteria. So: A is the same person as B if and only if A and B have the same (i.e., numerically the same) mental states and perform the same (numerically the same) actions. Here the criteria are stated tenselessly. But we can apply this format to the sickly child/adult case in the following way: An adult, A, is the same person as the child, B, if and only if the mental states that A possesses and the actions that A performs are the same actions (numerically) that B will perform and the same mental states (numerically) that B will have.

Heath charges that I have no place for the unconscious in my framework; this is false, since I endorse the concept when employed under the proper constraints (AH, pp. 131–132). Indeed, I even propose the way in which the unconscious will figure in questions of numerical identity (AH, p. 101). Since the unconscious will count as some sort of mental state, then if A and B are the same person, they will have the numerically same unconscious states, motives, intentions, and so forth.

Heath asks whether the kind of thing I identify as a continuing entity is a mind or a body. This, I think, places the question at the wrong level of abstraction. The self-identifiable sickly child/adult persists under the sortal-concept *human being* rather than under that of either mind or body. Heath may be asking what makes something a member of the class human being, but this is logically separate from and not directly relevant to the debate about the metaphysical conditions for numerical individuation. Nor do I believe that the question of what a human being is will be answered by an unqualified vote for mind or body. But again this is a separate matter from that which is at stake: the request for criteria that would be operable for use with questions of numerical identity such as Heath asks in PN footnote 59.[5]

Among the linguistic phenomena to which Heath briefly alludes as evidence of subject splits is the future tense. This is adduced to meet my challenge to him to specify some third-person subject splits insofar as the best evidence Heath offers for subject splits in QC is based on a first person case of the liar paradox. I can almost grasp why someone might imagine that the liar paradox suggests some kind of split. But the future tense can hardly be worked into even such a loose, intuitive suggestion. If I say "That naval officer will be the next King," where is the split subject? There are not two grammatical subjects. Nor are there two ontological subjects, that is, two distinct referents: the naval officer and the King. For the naval officer and the King are the same human being. The only way to derive two subjects would be to attempt to argue that the naval officer is not *now* the King. The entity in question, however, is not standardly individuated under the sortal-concept *naval officer* but under that of *human being*. Furthermore, even if there were split subjects in future-tense, linguistic representations, what would that have to do with film? Film lacks a system of tenses. Moreover, were one metaphorically to extend the idea of tenses to film (e.g., to say that flashbacks were in the past tense), one would still have to admit that the (metaphorically characterized) use of the future tense in film (flashforwards?) is very rare. Hence, if Heath means to base the putative existence of subject splits in film on the idea of a filmic future tense, then he must acknowledge that such splits are infrequent, rather than generic phenomena obtaining in all cinematic representations.

As evidence for subject splits, Heath, omnisciently, writes:

When Carroll brings out his "in a certain patriarchal way of speaking, it is said that a woman is not complete until she has borne a child," we still have an enounced and an enunciation, a statement and the fact of its production, with Carroll

implicated there as a subject. That he projects his distance as ego, proposes himself as subject-master of a simple analogy that in no sense concerns him and is just a term in the pure reason of an argument devoid of any "I," does not stop the discursive act, the reality of the production of the utterance, the involvement of him in that produced utterance quite differently from the projected place of his subject-mastery (PN, pp. 106–107).

Where are we to locate the subject split in my utterance? There are not two grammatical subjects in its main clause. Moreover, the sentence in question does not split the reference of what it identifies as a common mode of speech in our culture. I wrote the sentence, reporting a linguistic practice that I do not indulge in. But for whom does this constitute a split? For the reader? Why? He knows the article was written by me; that I write about others does not split the reader's identity. Nor am I split because I speak of others. Yes, one can make a distinction between me and those I write about. But exactly where is the division or split to be found – that is, in what *ostensible subject*? Heath maliciously charges that I had an immoral intent in writing the given sentence. The theoretical issue, however, should not be obscured by the slander. If x has a motive for uttering a sentence, but the motive is not expressed in the utterance – x says "The apples are delicious" in order to please the neighbor who grew them – neither x himself nor anyone who overhears him is split, though each is numerically distinct from the other. What possible connection could this kind of case have to Heath's other purported evidence of splits in language: the liar paradox and the future tense? You can only lump all this disparate material together by free association if you start out by trying to find something in every case that can equivocatingly be described by some connotation of the word "split." But that is to accept antecedently the notion of a split rather than to demonstrate its acceptability.

In the preceding passage from Heath, the

enounced/enunciation distinction is identified as that between the statement and the fact of its production. If, in certain cases, there is a distinction between the grammatical subject of a statement and the speaker, whom one might call a psychological subject – who, moreover, is distinct from the psychological subjects who hear the statement – how do these admitted distinctions, of which it makes no sense to say that they are masked in ordinary language, portend a split in any of the subjects isolated by our distinctions? The liar paradox might be advertised as "splitting" the grammatical subject in some ill-defined way, but Heath fails, except by way of his unwavering ambiguity concerning the reference of the term "subject," to demonstrate how any psychological subject is split in language or in representation in general.

Heath spends a great deal of energy attacking an analogy that I draw between films and cars. I introduced the analogy to short-circuit an opposition between the film as enounced in the past versus the film as present enunciation, which opposition seems to suggest that the film is in some univocal sense both complete and not complete. Heath writes, "A film is always finished, enounced; and finished, enounced even in its enunciation which is given, fixed, repeated at every 'showing' or 'screening' " (QC, p. 216). And in the next paragraph he adds, "Yet in that fixity, that givenness, there is nevertheless, the making of the film by the spectator." Initially I thought that this was meant to propound a paradox because I thought that the liar paradox was the model for the enounced/enunciation distinction. Now apparently Heath rejects the idea that the distinction entails a paradox, though, as I have shown, this is advanced at the cost of sacrificing what little evidence there is for the idea of subject splits. Even if there is not meant to be an outright paradox in Heath's formulation, however, I still think that the argument that employs the car/film analogy is worth mak-

ing because the apparent opposition Heath still insinuates needs dissolving.

The opposition above appears to be that the film is complete as a production (*yet, nevertheless*) also remains to be completed by spectators, that is, sutured, made coherent, filled in. Notice, first, that we have moved from a relation between a speaker and his production to that of a message and its receiver. But also there is no opposition here. The film is an *embodied* object (not a physical object *simpliciter*) which is complete in terms of its construction *as a numerically distinct* entity before its release, while it is also an object for use that remains to be completed, that is, to *fulfill the purpose for which it was made*. Hence, there is no *univocal* sense in which it is both complete and not complete. It is complete in the sense of having been constructed as an object even if it has yet to be "completed" in the extended sense of fulfilling its purpose. Thus, there is nothing theoretically interesting in the fixity/present enunciation, complete/not complete opposition. Indeed, there is no opposition if we explicate the terms at issue. If there were, we could call every object made for use, like a car, both complete and not complete. But this seems absurd.

Heath challenges this argument by attacking the car/film analogy. Films are different from cars; for example, films communicate, cars transport. But how do these and other disanalogies show that films can be said to be complete and not complete in some univocal sense while cars cannot be?

Illusion

Heath begins "Brecht" with a few self-serving misreadings of "A Brief Digression: The Legacy of Brecht's Errors" (AH, pp. 103–109). In this section I was primarily attacking a tendency of '70s film theory that castigated the visual dimension of mimetic cinema as illusionistic, an idea that film theorists unquestionably associated with Brecht. Heath complains that neither he nor Brecht believes that cases of visual representation prompt illusions.

The case for Brecht is mixed. Some passages (e.g., AH, p. 104) show that Brecht did slip into illusion/delusion talk. On the other hand, I explicitly acknowledge the existence of other writings which suggest that the passages that I quote may not reflect the core of Brecht's thinking (AH, p. 104). I then note, however, that the illusion/delusion thesis, which film scholars thought they got from Brecht, was still worth attacking because of its influence on film studies. Since I make it clear that it is film studies and not Brecht that is under fire, why does Heath waste his energy vindicating Brecht?

Furthermore, I never attributed a simple illusion/delusion model to Heath but refer (AH, pp. 108, 109, 141) to his position as a variation on the Brechtian framework – one that demands an entirely unique set of counter-arguments. Indeed, my attack on the simple illusion/delusion model is called "A Digression" because it *precedes* the attack on QC.

In this section my basic thesis is that the characterization of the relation between film spectators and what they see in terms of illusions is misguided. For anything that is properly called a visual illusion either deceives or is liable to deceive normal percipients in standard viewing conditions. But cinematic images are not illusions in this sense. For example, information derived from binocular and motion parallax in standard conditions quickly reveals that cinematic images are two-dimensional, not three-dimensional stimuli.

In addition, surface irregularities such as scratches, grain, flickers, marks for reel changes, the glow of reflected light, and so on require that the film viewer "see through" the medium to comprehend the represented scene. But to "see through" these irregularities must presuppose that the percipient knows he is viewing a cinematic image. Likewise, many of the institutionalized, appreciative responses to films presup-

pose our knowledge that cinematic images are representations. For example, to commend a film as life*like* entails that the film is being compared knowingly to something *else* – obviously what the film represents. The illusion/delusion theorist, however, holds that the viewer believes the cinematic image is its referent. But if normal practices entail that viewers know they are watching cinematic images, then it follows that the normal viewer believes he is viewing cinematic images and not their referents. That is, combining the illusion/delusion theory with certain ordinary facts about cinema viewing we derive a contradiction – that the viewer both believes and does not believe he is viewing cinematic images.

I suggest that we dissolve this contradiction by abandoning as contrary to fact the proposition that people in any literal sense believe that cinematic images are the referents of said images. Instead, let us say that spectators regard cinematic images as representations of objects and events in virtue of a delimited range of recognizable similarities that obtain visually between the image and what it denotes. This rids us of the idea of illusion which is not only empirically outlandish, but which also affords us no particular explanatory advantages over a recognizability model. That is, we can explain why films are engaging, exciting, enthralling, and so on because people recognize the events the films stand for and viewers are so moved by such events. We learn nothing about movie responses by saying people believe they are in the presence of the actual referents of cinematic images. Indeed, such a theory would have to become very complex to explain why no one flees from Godzilla.

The most dazzling portions of Heath's section on illusion are his attempts to show that my position is self-contradictory. Heath uniformly essays this by taking my original sentences out of context, changing their meaning, and juxtaposing his version of what I say to snippets from other sections of AH.

Heath quotes my "Most plays and films, when seen in standard viewing conditions, don't look like events and locales outside the theater" (AH, p. 106). He interprets this as a blanket statement "denying that plays and films can have relations of looking like events and locales" (PN, p. 94). Heath then notes that this does not correspond to my use of resemblance elsewhere, since I say that mimetic pictures refer by way of resembling objects (AH, p. 113). But tellingly, Heath drops the qualification that I consistently make: that resemblance in mimesis is always in terms of resemblance in certain respects, that is, not exact resemblance.

Heath's refutation hinges on the interpretation one gives to "like" in the original statement (AH, p. 106). It occurs in a paragraph concerned to argue that people don't mistake things such as film images for their referents because of the dissimilarities between film images and what they are images of. In this context, "don't look like" obviously means that film images cannot be taken as having *exactly* the same visual properties as their referents. That "like" can mean having "*exactly* the same qualities" is a perfectly acceptable dictionary sense, and it is obviously the appropriate meaning given my context. Images from *Rio Lobo* don't look exactly like what they represent nor do they look exactly like Wooster Street. Thus, I can keep the three things separate. On the other hand, when I say mimetic pictures resemble their referents, I carefully add that this is resemblance in certain respects. It is not contradictory to assert that cinematic images do not share exactly all the visual qualities of their referents – indeed, they don't share enough to fool people normally – while also maintaining that these images share some recognizable visual characteristics with their referents. My original statement was not a blanket denial of the possibility of *any* similarities, but a denial that cinematic images look exactly like their referents. I neither contradicted myself nor did I foreclose the possibility of the existence

of some recognizable similarities between cinematic images and what they denote.[6]

Heath then abruptly jumps to a different discussion in which he tears a passage of mine out of context, cutting into the argument midway so that no one can tell either what distinctions are being made or why. The section under dispute comes from AH, pp. 115–16. In the broader context, what is at issue here is whether or not we identify the camera image with our own vision. I deny that we do. I claim that if we did, we would phenomenologically experience the image in its entirety as coextensive with our visual field. We would be "inside" the visual field of the camera image as we are "inside" our own sensations and perceptions. But this "insideness" does not characterize our experience of camera images. Most of the time the camera "sees" more than we do; its boundary is wider than ours. Characteristically we can only focus on those portions of the image where there is action. The visual field of the camera affords possibilities of perception. It enables us to scan and to gather new sensations and perceptions from the self-same image as, for example, when a new detail appears in the background of a deep-focus shot.

We look *at* camera images; we don't see-in them, that is, we treat the image (as a whole) as existing independently from our sensations rather than treating the image (as a whole) as a replica of our occurrent perception. We are "outside" the image as a whole rather than experiencing the image (as a whole) as though it were co-extensive with our perception (i.e., as if we were "inside" the projector beam in the way we always feel "inside" the visual boundary of our occurrent perceptions).

What is being compared here as more similar is the experience of looking at cinema images and the experience of looking at reality, and these are analogized in terms of a feeling of the existence of something independent of our perception – a feeling of "outsideness" that accompanies both. I claim that this makes *seeing* a motion picture like seeing a real/nonrepresentational event. But I add that it is only in virtue of this specified comparison that I introduce the Cavellian notion that the *experience* of viewing a film is like our *experience* of viewing the world – that is, we look *at* both. Heath brings forth a contradiction by noting that ten pages earlier I said that most films do not look like events. Well, again, it is not contradictory to say that films do not look *exactly* like the events they denote, but that they do bear similarities to the originals in some respects. Moreover, Heath claims that my stipulation of "outsideness" as the only relevant point of comparison is wrong because there are other points of resemblance. But with this argument Heath misconstrues what it is I am comparing. The screen image is not being compared to the event. At this point, what I am discussing is the comparison of the *experience* of seeing a picture with the *experience* of seeing an event. Here the only pertinent similarity I find is "outsideness." The fact that the image and the event may resemble each other in many more respects is irrelevant to the question of how the experiences *qua* experiences feel similar. What other phenomenological similarities does Heath think obtain between these experiences?

When Heath parodies my denial that we take film images as real in any sense, he is at his most willfully myopic as a reader. Mine is unquestionably a statement made in an argument where what is presupposed as relevant is the standard dichotomy between representations of things and real things in themselves. What I am asserting is that we do not take cinematic representations of things to be the very three-dimensional objects and events they depict. Obviously camera images are also existing objects (both physical and phenomenal). But in the argument in question the dichotomy between real thing and nonexistent thing is never at issue.

Throughout my attack on ciné-Brechtianism I explicitly rely on a strong sense of illusion, a deception sense. I admit that there may be a weaker sense in which any pictorial representation is called an illusion if it shares a specifiable range of recognizable visual similarities with the kind of entity or action it depicts (AH, p. 106). But I explicitly oppose this weaker sense; and I do not believe theorists should use it, including Gibson, White, Hagan, Gombrich, et al., with whom I agree on other matters.

Heath wants to defend the weak sense of illusion. He characterizes film viewing in terms of having "a belief that one is watching *a kind of reality of life*." One reading of this less than luminous notion might be that we see that a given film has certain recognizable similarities to something else, viz., to what it depicts (whether living or *dead* or *inanimate*). But then why connect this to the notion of "illusion?" What is to be gained by formulating the connection as one of illusion rather than one of recognizability? Of course, Heath may have something more in mind by his obscure "kind of reality of life," but until he defines this expression, what he means is anyone's guess, though it does sound like the strong sense of illusion.

If we discard the notion of illusion, we can characterize our emotional, aesthetic, and intellectual responses to films by saying that we know that a given film represents *x* (or, represents *x* as-a-so-and-so), something we find gripping, involving, exciting, boring, funny, historically accurate, anachronistic, engrossing, and so on. Why do I have to feel that I am in India in order to be uplifted by *Gandhi* or to be impressed by its historical details (indeed, how could I be impressed by its *historical* details if I thought I was with Gandhi in India)? Can't I simply recognize that the film depicts the kind of courageous life that excites me and that the film incorporates more period details than many other films I have seen of India? Heath should explain what the weak sense of illusion allows him to account for that another explication in terms of knowledge and recognizable similarities cannot. Instead Heath only recycles old saws such as that of the suspension of disbelief, an unlikely hypothesis that proposes that we are always, contrary to all available phenomenological evidence, thrusting ourselves into a special cognitive state whenever we encounter representations.

Perspective

Heath begins his discussion of perspective by denying that he holds a deception sense of illusion. But in his introduction to the topic of perspective, he quotes his own statement (QC, p. 28) in which he points out that a component element of the account of perspective on which he relies is "deceptive illusion." Heath never rescinds or qualifies this aspect of the operating definition of perspective in his essay. He also refers to Renaissance perspective as a "trap for the look" (QC, p. 70). This is a strange mode of expression for one who does not wish to cast perspective in a pejorative light.

Is Heath a conventionalist as regards perspective? He claims that in painting from the Quattrocentro onwards "there is a real utopianism at work, the construction of a *code* – in every sense a vision – projected onto a reality to be gained in all its hoped-for clarity much more than onto some naturally given reality" (QC, p. 29, italics added). Heath makes clear that he believes that the alleged fidelity of perspective is really a matter of our cultural habituation to this code both in his unqualified quotations of P. Francastel and also in his statement that "For five centuries men and women exist at ease in that space; the Quattrocentro system provides a practical representation of the world which in time appears so natural as to offer its real representation, the immediate translation of reality itself" (QC, pp. 29–30).

Characteristically, Heath sets some red herrings swimming. He points out that there are some very convincing perspective illusions. So what? I never denied that it was possible to construct deceptive visual illusions – consider the Ames experiments.[7] My point throughout was that such rare cases are not the primary data for discussing the standard practices of representation in our culture. Heath wonders why I do not consider the use of perspective apart from pictures. Why should I? Isn't our disagreement about pictorial perspective? Heath insinuates that I wrongly accuse him of claiming that perspective uniquely suits capitalism. But the *footnote* in question (AH, p. 114) makes no mention of Heath and it explicitly cites Brakhage and Berger as proponents of this view. Heath also repeatedly suggests that I correlate perspective and truth despite the fact that I explicitly reject this correlation in favor of the notion of pictorial fidelity (AH, p. 114). Throughout his rebuttal, Heath produces examples of theorists who describe perspective in terms of illusion. In AH (p. 111) I acknowledged that this would be easy to do. My question was whether this traditionalist position was correct. And, of course, I never deny that conventions are involved in representation. Most of my arguments throughout AH emphasize the importance of conventions. I only attack the conventionalist position on *perspective* that Heath and Francastel seem to be proposing.

Heath's frontal attacks on my account of perspective fail dismally. He claims that I say perspective is accurate, but that it is not. It shows railroad tracks converging, but this is false. Yet if he looks at my position, he will note that I say I am dealing with *accuracy as a matter of degree* (AH, p. 112). I say that perspective is *more* accurate than competing mimetic pictorial systems. It is perfectly compatible to hold this while also admitting that the system may contain inaccuracies.

Heath challenges my claim about perspective's relative superiority vis-à-vis spatial accuracy by means of a counterexample: English Ordinance Survey Maps. I do not know whether there is something special about these maps since I have been unable to acquire one. If they are like American road maps, however, then it is clear, that they are not viable counterexamples to my thesis. I claimed that perspective is more accurate in terms of affording spatial information than any other mimetic *pictorial* system. Maps are not pictures. One must be taught to read a map; the mountains on a map are not recognized perceptually as mountains but are coded, often by color. Heath believes that I cannot exclude maps from consideration unless I define mimetic pictorial systems in a circular fashion, using perspective as my species differentia. False. I do not use perspective as a condition for picturing. Rather pictures are, in part, objects that have visually recognizable similarities to their referents such that we can perceptually identify what they refer to. Maps are read, not recognized.

Heath claims that my assertion that perspective is the only mimetic pictorial system grounded in scientific laws is a tautology. Why? The Japanese floating-eye style, the ancient Egyptian frontal-eye style, and what Deregowski calls split-type drawings[8] are all examples of mimetic pictorial systems but they are not grounded in scientific laws. That perspective is and these other systems are not is a fact and not a matter of logic or meaning.

Heath's most important attack on my characterization of perspective is that in using the concept of "appearance" in my account I unwittingly contradict myself. That is, I claim to portray perspective without reference to illusion or to replicas of vision. Yet, purportedly, by speaking of appearance I have covertly smuggled both these elements into my position. I say perspective, compared to other mimetic, pictorial systems, is more accurate in terms of affording spatial information – that is, information about the appearance of the relative disposition of objects in space. Heath interprets this to mean that "perspective gives us accurate information not as to true distance but as to appearance, appear-

ance to the eye" (PN, p. 85). And " 'appearance' in 'Address' shores up a version of the eye/camera analogy" (PN, p. 86).

The word "appearance," however, need not mean "illusion," nor was I using it in that sense. When a policeman questions witnesses about the appearance of a bank robber, the last thing he wants is a report of an illusion. He is requesting a description, a veridical one, of the visible characteristics of the culprit. Except for certain contexts, such as Platonic dialogues, where the operative dichotomy is Appearance versus Reality, an appearance is the outward aspect of any physical thing. There is no reason to suspect that in ordinary language "The milk appears spoiled" means "The milk is not spoiled." Talk about appearances can be talk about how things are, not about illusions.

Also, talk of appearances need not refer to a particular instance of vision, that is, to a specific occurrent visual experience, but may refer to what is visible.[9] That is, a perspective picture described as affording spatial information about appearances is not being characterized as providing a phenomenologically recognizable replica of a specific act or kind of act of vision but as providing information about the structure of ambient light in an optic array which, in turn, is the sort of thing from which humans derive reliable information about the layout of things in space. I used the word "appearance" to signal that the spatial information in perspective paintings is visual. That's not controversial, I hope. But my commitment to perspective paintings affording information about the structure of light in optical arrays hardly commits me to the belief that perspective is a point-perfect replica of the experience of normal seeing. It is not a representation of seeing; it affords spatial information from the optical structure – from the appearance – of the layout of the environment. Moreover, the information afforded by perspective is *more accurate* than that available from any competing, mimetic pictorial system.

Just about the funniest thing that Heath ever read is a claim I make in a footnote (AH, p. 114) that perspective responds to a deep, biologically motivated concern with where things stand in space. I made this point to refute the suggestions of Brakhage and Berger that perspective somehow uniquely suits capitalism. Also, by reference to this biological, evolutionary factor, I think that we can explain the rapid and easy dissemination of perspective across cultures and economic systems. Surely such an explanation seems more plausible than the vision of armed coercion insinuated by Heath's quotation of Francastel: "[W]ith their technical superiority, they [the Europeans] imposed that [Quattrocentro] space over the planet" (QC, p. 29).

Of course, I never say or imply that hunter-gatherers and shipping magnates use perspective drawings in the manner of maps. Nor do I deny that one can write a useful history about a given culture's adoption of perspective. My only point, *contra* Heath, is that biological considerations have some place in our explanations of pictorial representation. Not everything is reducible to social/economic/ideological history.

Heath suggests that I am an extreme empiricist, yet he never defines what he means by *empiricist* except by way of a silly metaphor about stumbling over laws and some mystical gibberish about the world's not containing knowledge of itself. What Heath appears to be accusing me of is believing that we discover scientific laws by looking. If I did in fact believe that discoveries were a simple matter of looking, why would I have stressed the importance of competition between research programs as an indispensable means of endorsing one over the other? Would not Heath's extreme empiricist be able to establish the viability of a single research program by comparing it to what Heath calls the world "out there"? Did I not also emphasize the pragmatic nature of explanation in the concluding section of AH? Perhaps Heath is unable to distinguish between pragmaticism and what he calls extreme empiricism.

Positivism

One of the accusations Heath makes is that I am a "positivist." I'm not sure Heath knows what a positivist, logical or otherwise, really is. I do not subscribe to a verifiability principle in either AH or anything else I've written. Does Heath think I am a positivist because I demand that social scientific theories must be couched in generalizations? Well, I've never said that either. And though I believe there exist social scientific that employ satisfactory generalizations, I do not believe that all such explanations require lawlike generalizations. So I'm not a positivist, or at least not a logical positivist, in the usual sense of that term. Also, I can't be a positivist for the same types of reasons I couldn't be called an extreme empiricist.

Heath says I am a positivist (in his sense) because I only accept biological or cognitive-psychological accounts. This is quite false and can only be the result of a slipshod reading of AH. I accept many different types of explanation and styles of analysis. I constantly refer to institutionalized practices and thus endorse explanations in terms of conventions – so, sociology and social history can fit within my purview. I accept psychoanalytic explanations along with biological, evolutionary, and cognitive-psychological ones. I employ the techniques of analytic philosophy but also take advantage of phenomenology. Nor do I reject the possibility of ideological analysis.[10] Rather, I attempt to find the method which, in competition with other methods, best addresses the phenomena at hand in terms of our specific questions. I do not spurn any approach as a possible source of knowledge on a priori grounds. I am open to any method that will deliver the best explanation in light of the questions we are asking.

As this suggests, I do not believe that

every kind of explanation is equally appropriate to every kind of case. Limitations have to be acknowledged concerning the applicability of various methods. Specifically, I believe that there are some limits to the range of things that can be explained psychoanalytically. This is, of course, where the difference between Heath and me arises. I endorse the use of psychoanalytic explanations, but only under certain constraints, whereas Heath uses them to explain almost everything human, including how we make sense of film editing.

Psychoanalytic theory is designed to explain the *ir*rational. The general paresis and epileptic fits due to injury to Broca's area in the brain are *non*rational and thus not a subject for psychoanalytic enquiry. Similarly, I believe that when an agent does something that is rational, we have no prima facie reason to investigate further into the causes of his actions. That is, a methodological constraint on psyhoanalytic explanation is that it not be mobilized until there is an identifiable breakdown in rationality. Not all beliefs, not all social, aesthetic, emotional, and cognitive responses are candidates for psychoanalytic investigation. Insofar as psychoanalysis is designed to conceptualize irrational behavior, which is only identifiable as a deviation from some norm of rational behavior, there is no work for it to do where the behavior in question is of an *unmistakably* rational sort.

The basic concepts of psychoanalysis are metaphoric extensions of the concepts of the rational – e.g., motive, intention, wish, drive, need, and so on. That is, the concepts are all purposive, ends-seeking. The difference is that these forces are conscious and deliberative in rationalist psychology, but they are metaphorically extended to unconscious forces in psychoanalysis. Psychoanalysis, by examining unconscious intentions and repressed operations, explains actions, purposively characterized, that cannot be explained by conscious or merely tacit intentions, beliefs, and reasonings. But – once

again – where an adequate rationalist explanation is available, we do not require psychoanalysis. Note, however, that unlike the frothing positivist of Heath's reverie, I have no opposition to psychoanalysis properly employed.

Nor am I opposed to ideological analysis. Yet I insist that we must first ascertain that the phenomena we investigate are best approached by seeing them as ideological. If we are investigating a belief (or recommendation) imparted by a film, then we must test to see if it is ideological by establishing that it is false (or unreasonable) *and* that it functions in some system of social domination. If we are concerned to discover whether a symbol system – such as a natural language or a pictorial style – is ideological, then we must establish that it excludes the possibility of the representation of certain facts and interests for the purpose of upholding some practice or institution of social domination. I believe that the technical jargon of certain branches of the law may be relevant examples of this. Thus, I do not oppose ideological analysis per se. I merely disagree with QC in its insistence upon the explanation of all phenomena under discussion in terms of ideology and psychoanalysis. Indeed, I am more of a pluralist and less of a reductionist than Heath is.

1. In what follows, AH refers to my "Address to the Heathen," in *October,* no. 23 (Winter 1982). QC refers to Stephen Heath's *Questions of Cinema,* Bloomington, Indiana, 1981; PN refers to Heath's "Le Père Noel," *October,* no. 26 (Fall 1983).

2. In PN, Heath says that his use of "overlay" indicated that he did not have geometry in mind. Is this supposed nonrelation to geometry part of the dictionary meaning of "overlay," or some well-known jargon usage, or is it a desperate, *ad hoc* invention by Heath?

3. Heath discusses the culminating homogeneity of narrative film in his "simple definition" of film narrative in QC, p. 136. A rereading of this *definition* makes me wonder why Heath believes it inappropriate for me to remind him that opening scenes need not be repeated

at the end of narrative films. For in that definition Heath says that S, which is defined as an initial *state,* leads to S´, which is a return to S.

4. See my "Language and Cinema: Preliminary Notes for a Theory of Verbal Images," in *Millennium Film Journal* nos. 7/8/9. N.B.; I am not now chiding Heath for failing to have read this piece nor can anyone who has read AH *honestly* claim that I reproached Heath for not being familiar with my writing. This essay is reprinted in this volume.

5. Here Heath unleashes a barrage of vague and confusedly connected questions. He challenges the idea of a substance by saying it is a major philosophical topic. But I have no idea of how to respond to such an unfocused observation. What specific inadequacy is this weighty aside supposed to reveal about my position? Also Heath's suspicion that I am talking about bodies when I speak of identifying continuing entities seems to confuse epistemological questions about the public criteria for how we say A is the same as B with metaphysical questions about the criteria for numerically individuating human persons where A = B. Moreover, I do not understand what Heath means in footnote 59, PN, by claiming that the enduring subjects cannot be *reflected* in language. If he means that identity conditions cannot be stated then he will have to demonstrate the failure of the proposal above. If he means that the enounced/enunciation distinction blocks my regarding the sickly child and the adult as ontologically the same person, then he has merely begged the question again. Heath's talk of my supposed commitment to a "pre-anything I" leads me to think that he is confusing empirical questions of genetic psy-chology, on the one hand, with logical, ontological, and linguistic questions of reference. If Heath means to establish the split subject on the basis of maturation, let him bring forward evidence from developmental psychology and not from the philosophy of language.

6. Heath wonders why I employ "Most" in my statement. This was simply to allow for the possibility that there may sometime be some isolated case where the standard viewing condition does provide an exact likeness. I know of no such case, but I did not wish to say that it is absolutely impossible that someone might stage a counterexample that would fool viewers. For the time being, however, we should not build our theories on such far-off possibilities.

7. See, for example, the chair-illusion that is illustrated in R. L. Gregory, *The Intelligent Eye,* New York, McGraw-Hill, 1970, p. 29.

8. Jan B. Deregowski, "Illusion and Culture," in R. L. Gregory and E. H. Gombrich, ed., *Illusion, Nature and Art,* New York, Scribners, 1973, p. 183.

9. I owe the distinction between vision and the visible to John L. Ward, who proposed it to me in a letter dated June 30, 1983. Also, for simplicity's sake, I am dealing throughout this section with cases where the picture is of an existing person, place, or thing. Certain readily available complications must be added to deal with representations of invented entities and events.

10. For example, in AH, despite Heath's misreading, I considered *Fort Apache, The Bronx* to be a candidate for ideological interpretation. I merely asserted that the film's pictorial verisimilitude would not be a significant variable in such an interpretation.

CHAPTER XXV

Replies to Hammett and Allen

I. Response to Jennifer Hammett

From the dialogues of Plato, we learn that there is an ancient quarrel between philosophy and rhetoric. Unhappily, it is still alive and thriving as I learned when reading a review of my book *Mystifying Movies*[1] by Jean Hammett, an orator from Berkeley.[2] Systematically misunderstanding my distinctions and arguments in favor of the sort of bromides a politician would utter if she were running for the presidency of the Society for Cinema Studies, Hammett delivers rhetorical tricks and fashionable slogans where analysis might be more appropriate.

According to Hammett, with respect to the kind of representational imaging that we typically find in the single shot in film – a close-up of Gregory Peck, for example – I am supposedly a realist and I remain committed to the notion of the specificity of the cinematic image. She then goes on to refute my putative realism by asserting that I equate pictorial perception with filmic comprehension and that I proceed as if the whole story of understanding of what she calls the meaning of a cinematic shot were simply a matter of pictorial recognition. Supposedly, I am unaware that context, for example, is important to understanding the meaning of a shot.

Hammett then further imagines that I compound this blunder by claiming that I believe that understanding narratives is also a matter of recognition (pictorial recognition?), and she indicates that I think that

understanding a narrative is tantamount to perceiving narrative structures as if they were physical shapes (p. 91). Here, Hammett alleges that I believe that we perceive narrative structures passively rather than being involved in processes of active participation and construction.

How could one make as many stupid errors as I did? Well, it's not hard when one has Hammett helping you along. Basically, she invents absurd views for me and then she bowls them over with fashionable slogans and prejudices drawn from the reigning doxa. Hammett's fundamental procedure is essentially the rhetorical sleight of hand: misconstrue a reasonable position for a nutty one and then congratulate yourself and your readership for your superior understanding. You could call this technique "refutation *in absentia*."

My position on representational imaging in the single shot is that, as with representational paintings, we realize what the shot represents (e.g., a man, a train, a coronation) by a process that is not involved in reading, decoding, deciphering, or inference. When one looks at a typical picture of a cathedral, one recognizes that it is a representation of cathedral by looking – that is, if one can recognize cathedrals in what we call "real life." We do not have a set of dictionary-like rules that enables us to infer from or to decode lines on a canvas in order to arrive at the proposition "This is a cathedral." We don't read pictures or infer what they are pictures of. We recognize what they are pictures of by looking.[3] Picture-recognition capacities and object-recognition capacities come in tandem, I argue, on the basis of the psychological and anthropological data cited in *Mystifying Movies*.[4]

Here it pays to note that my hypothesis is a rather narrow one about how one realizes that a shot is a shot of *x* – that it is a shot of a rocking horse and not of a persimmon. Against linguistically oriented models that claim that computational processes such as reading, decoding, and inference are involved, I argue that we have many reasons to believe that mediation by such processes ill-suits the data and that a more likely conjecture is that people have an innate recognition capacity for telling what a picture is that develops along with the capacity to recognize objects in real life.

Is this realism of any sort? Well, it is not realism in the ontological sense that people have in mind when they claim that the photographic image is its referent (à la Bazin). I don't postulate any identity relationship between cinematic images and that of which they are images. For me the image and its object are numerically distinct, and they are also qualitatively distinct – they do not pass Leibniz's test for the identity of indiscernibles.

Nor am I a psychological realist. I don't think that audiences take or perceive the shot of x for x itself. Audiences do not experience the shot of x and x to be identical – at least not on my account. I do think that our capacity to recognize what shots of x are shots of and our capacity to recognize x's "in nature" develop together. But, as I stress in *Mystifying Movies,* these capacities evolve in such a way that we are also able to discriminate x's "in nature" from images of x's. We do not confuse them as psychological realists might contend. We don't experience them as identical or equivalent, and I never suggested anything remotely like that. So I am neither an ontological realist nor a psychological realist.

I claim that *some* of the same processes are involved in picture recognition and object recognition.[5] But isn't everyone prepared to concede that much? Such hardly counts as realism. Undoubtedly there will be a dispute about how much of picture perception can be explained by reference to our object-recognition capacities. Since, in contrast to linguistically oriented conventionalists, I think that much (but not all) of our picture-recognition can be explained in terms of hard-wired recognitional capacities (with no

mention of codes and decipherment), it might make sense to call me a naturalist or a nonconventionalist when it comes to picture perception. But it shows a misunderstanding of film theory to call me a realist.

Not only am I not a realist, but I am not a photographic or cinematic realist, despite what Hammett alleges. I reject the notion of the specificity of the cinematic image. For, as should be evident from what I have said so far, I think that the story about perceiving paintings, photographs, and film shots is pretty much of a piece. In each case, the symbols in question activate a recognitional capacity that develops in tandem with our object-recognition capacities. But if the story is the same with respect to paintings, photographs, and film images, then I cannot possibly be committed to the specificity of the cinematic image. For Hammett to insist that I do demonstrates either incredible carelessness, incompetence, or bad faith.

In any case, whether or not I am a realist, Hammett also alleges that the emphasis that I place on recognition (rather than reading or inference) in picture perception is wrong. Why? ". . . Carroll's cognitive theory does not ask what images mean; or perhaps more precisely, Carroll equates meaning with identity. . . . He has made this move, equating comprehension with perception. . ." (p. 88). According to Hammett, understanding an image – understanding what she calls its meaning – involves more than pictorial perception. Images may have different meanings in different contexts. She says of a representation of a tree that "its identity as a tree does not determine which meaning attaches. Thus, 'recognizing' it is a tree would not be the equivalent of understanding its contextual meaning" (p. 88).

Of course. But notice that Hammett has changed the terms of the discussion. I was talking about the best hypothesis for explaining pictorial perception – for explaining how we realize a picture of x is of x rather than of y. In answering this narrow question, I claim that conjecturing a hard-wired process of recognition does a better job than hypothesizing reading and inference.

But Hammett ignores the fact that I am dealing with this narrow issue. Instead, she alleges that I am involved with a problem of her own invention – not how do we realize the shot is a shot of a cow, but how do we comprehend or understand the meaning of the shot? Perhaps the appearance of an image of a cow in a narrative film implies that the locale of the story has shifted from the city to the country. I do not claim that you could surmise that simply by looking. Recognizing that it is a shot of a cow will hardly supply you with a full account of how we take the image to signify something like that. As Hammett says, what I claim about pictorial recognition won't give you an entire theory of filmic comprehension.

But so what? I'm not presenting the discussion of the role of picture perception as a comprehensive theory of what she calls meaning in film. You don't refute a theory about the origin of the Civil War by saying that it fails to be a theory of all war. Hammett rejects what I say about recognition because it can't explain how we understand what she calls the meaning of film *tout court*. But I never claimed that the hypothesis could do that. It is nothing more than a rhetorical bluff to complain that my hypothesis can't deliver the goods when it wasn't designed to convey the particular goods in question to begin with.

Of course, I think that picture perception, understood in terms of recognition, has some explanatory role to play in our understanding or comprehension of the so-called meaning of many (most?) cinematic images. Does Hammett deny that? She says that the meaning of an image of a priest in *Going My Way, 8 1/2,* and *The Silence* differ. Perhaps. But certainly before one identifies each of those putatively differential meanings, one must realize that the images at issue are images of priests, not giraffes. How does one do that? I say by means of our natural recognitional capacities. The images may

have further significances. These will call for further hypotheses in order to be explained, but it does not follow that the recognition hypothesis is not an essential complement to those further hypotheses.

In *Mystifying Movies* I present psychological evidence for the recognition hypothesis. I also point out that the recognition hypothesis squares with our best data about cross-cultural pictorial perception. Hammett never bothers to discuss any of that evidence or argumentation that I adduce. Like the high-school relativist, she seems so assured in her conviction that it's culture all the way down that she is utterly oblivious of her responsibility as a scholar to confront the data as well as the theoretical anomalies that I point out in the conventionalist hypothesis. Instead, she prefers to attack a straw man (straw person) position by asserting again and again that pictorial recognition capacities do not account for every dimension of our understanding of cinematic meaning. Though this may leave the impression with the uninformed reader that something important is being debated here, Hammett's "argumentation" is really nothing but rhetorical smoke and mirrors.

If my account of the perception of the cinematic image was absurd, according to Hammett, my account of narration is even sillier. She writes:

Here as in his account of cinematic images, Carroll equates seeing with comprehending; spectators look and "thereby" comprehend. Oddly, for someone purporting to explain how films appeal to our cognitive abilities, Carroll bypasses spectator cognition altogether propounding something like a "bullet theory" of cinematic meaning. Spectators do not interpret or read films, they receive them (p. 90).[6]

How could I have neglected cognition in favor of looking? Of course, I didn't. In the comment above, Hammett has conveniently repressed mention of the fact that in the preceding chapter I advanced a theory of narrative comprehension in the movies.[7] I claimed that spectators follow movies by identifying the salient questions that the movies under examination raise. The audience then uses these questions to organize the action, tracking details in light of their expectation that answers to the questions posed by the movie will emerge. Thus, on my account, following movies involves cognitive activity, namely, structuring details in terms of questions and answers. It is simply false to say that I characterize following a narrative merely in terms of looking without any higher-order cognitive structuring on the part of the spectator.

I then go on to hypothesize that this cognitive structuring is facilitated and directed by filmmakers through their use of devices like variable framing (camera movement and editing). These devices are typically deployed so that the spectator is looking at – is paying attention to – the elements of the action that are most relevant to her tracking of the presiding system of questions and answers that drive the narrative forward. These devices enable the spectator to follow the narrative perspicuously by guiding the viewer's attention to what is most pertinent to the cognitive structure of questions and answers that she is in the process of evolving. There is no looking and comprehending *simpliciter* in this model. Rather what we see is integrated into an evolving structure of questions and answers. What we see is information that is cognized in terms of a structure that is logically organized around presiding questions and answers. Editing and camera movements in typical movies help us pick out the details that are most relevant to evolving that structure of questions and answers. Would anyone deny that?

I did not concoct some mystical theory of film whereby we look and we know. Rather what we see (and what we are helped and guided to see by variable framing) gets embedded in a cognitive framework of questions and answers by the process of being a spectator. Surely not even Hammett

wants to deny that looking has some role to play in a cognitive account of what it is to follow a narrative film. All I claim about variable framing is that it helps and guides us to look at the details that are most pertinent to the cognitive activity of following the story. Hammett replaces my perhaps pedestrian view of the function of these devices in the service of narrative comprehension with an outlandish view, which she calls the "bullet theory," and then proceeds to "refute" me.

Hammett is disturbed by my "implicit" claim that movies do not require interpretation (p. 90). If by *interpretation* she means cognitive processing, then her allegation that I think that movies do not require interpretation is a remarkable misrepresentation. I think that spectators have to *follow* stories and that this involves cognitive activity in terms of isolating relevant narrative questions and tracking answers. I *explicitly* claim that. Hammett says I believe that a close-up renders an image automatically intelligible. Rather I think that a close-up makes us automatically attend to certain details, typically to the details that are especially relevant to our cognitive activity of following the story.

If, on the other hand, by *interpretation* Hammett is referring to the activity of explaining something that is nonobvious or obscure or puzzling, then it is true that I think that the activity of following the story in a typical movie, as a matter of fact, doesn't typically involve much interpretation, since the story line in most movies (that is, mass-market fictions) is usually not nonobvious or obscure or puzzling. But to deny that interpretation in this sense is always involved in the basic comprehension of movies does not amount to a denial of cognitive activity on the part of the spectator. Following the story is cognitive activity even if it does not involve the cognitive activity of interpretation in the strong sense of penetrating obscurity.

For some strange reason, Hammett treats

my discussion of devices like variable framing – which fall into the category that I call cinematic narration – before she examines my theory of narration. What is especially peculiar in this is that I claim that cinematic narration is hierarchically or functionally subordinated to the purposes of narration, which, on my account, requires the productive activity of spectators. Perhaps by inverting the exposition of my accounts of narration and cinematic narration, Hammett hopes to hide from the reader my claims about the cognitive activity of spectators so as to make persuasive her allegations that I think comprehending films is completely secured by looking. But this is merely a rhetorical shell game.

By the time that Hammett comes to deal with my account of narration, she has convinced herself that I also think that we follow stories by looking. She claims that I treat narrative structures as if they were physical shapes. But this is nothing short of nonsense; I wonder what such physical shapes might look like. But, in any case, the nonsense is not mine. The metaphor of physical shapes is totally Hammett's invention. The narrative structures that I speak of are matters of questions and answers. Thus, they have propositional content. Thus, in a certain sense, *qua* propositional-narrative content, they have nothing essential to do with vision.

Hammett rejects my theory of movie narration, which I call erotetic narration. She says that this is a theory of perceiving narrative and that it must be wrong because one could imagine a case where the question a film raises is about the trajectory of Voyager II and the answer is a complicated equation. Thus, she surmises, erotetic narration cannot simply be a matter of perception. But this putative counterexample is doubly misconceived. First, because I don't think that narrative comprehension is visual rather than propositional and, second, because if I am right about movies (mass-market movies) and their purposes, then it is

highly unlikely that we will encounter movies that answer the questions they pose in such a way that only a handful of physicists can understand the answers.

Hammett also goes after my theory of narration by repeating the allegation that my account of the way in which we follow movie narratives doesn't tell the whole story of how we understand and comprehend the meaning of movies. But recall that the theory in question was only designed to account for how we follow or comprehend movie narratives. Thus, if one's conception of what Hammett calls the "meaning" of a movie is broader than following the basic narrative line then it is true that the theory of erotetic narration does not say how movies make meaning *tout court*. Yet it is no failing in the theory that it doesn't explain what it wasn't designed to explain. There are, I am the first to admit, dimensions of significance in narrative film that have to do with structures beyond setting out the narrative. They are worthy of theorizing. But that does not show an inadequacy in the theory of erotetic narration. In fact, the theory of erotetic narration may be a useful supplement to those additional theories.

Hammett's is obsessed by a global question, How do we understand the meaning of film? As a result, she consistently misconstrues my piecemeal theories about more circumscribed questions such as how do we realize that a single-shot image is an image of x as failed attempts to answer her big question. But I, on the other hand, think that it is more felicitous to partition that big question into a series of smaller ones. So many things might count as what is called "the meaning of film" that it is better to think of it in terms of the activity of diverse mechanisms, functioning to promote diverse purposes (some narrational, some emotional, some allegorical, and so on), which are conducive of diverse effects.

The meaning of film is a rather baggy conception, somewhat loose and vague. There is no reason to believe that one theory or a unified set of theories will comprehensively characterize all the ways of meaning in film. Thus, I suggest that we concentrate on characterizing discrete mechanisms or processes of signification. Hammett fails to see this and consistently criticizes me for not attempting to do something – viz., theorize how film conveys meaning per se – which I think is methodologically ill-advised. Of course, if she ever manages to produce a unified theory of cinematic meaning herself, I will be happy to read it.

Hammett concludes by chiding my overall approach and my conjectures about some of the reasons why movies are such an effective means of mass communication. Her complaint about my overall approach is that it is formalist.[8] Here her objection is based on my emphasis on devices like variable framing and erotetic narration in accounting for the effectiveness of movies. In this, she alleges, I commit the traditional error of film theorists, namely, that of looking at film forms to the exclusion of considering of things like distribution networks and subject matter.

But I go out of my way in *Mystifying Movies* to acknowledge that research into such matters is legitimate and absolutely appropriate in film studies. I say we need to study distribution and subject matter in order to secure a well-rounded understanding of how film operates. I have concentrated on the way in which certain cinematic structures or mechanisms function but am open to and even encourage complementary research programs. That is the definition of the kind of piecemeal theorizing I advocate in this volume and advocated in *Mystifying Movies* as well. To understand film practice, we need theories of movie structure, theories of distribution, theories of advertising, theories of content, and so on. I've concentrated on theories of structure. But I don't deny the advisability of theories of other dimensions of film practice. What's the problem here?

It would seem to me that the only

problem could be that one thinks that we don't need any theories of film structure in addition to those other theories – theories of movie distribution, industry economics, advertising content, and so on. But what could be the justification of a moratorium on theories of film structure? I can't imagine one and, in any case, Hammett doesn't provide one.

Hammett winds up her jeremiad with the requisite charge of political incorrectness. My theory of the power of the movies is naughty because it doesn't acknowledge cultural difference. I'm a big, bad imperialist because when considering the international effectiveness of Hollywood-type filmmaking, I dare to hypothesize that in certain qualified ways, especially at the level of cognition, Hollywood style may address cross-cultural or contingently universal features of humans. But such conjectures are politically incorrect and strictly *verboten*. Hammett writes:

Surely, it is a form of cultural myopia to conclude that because the movies we are familiar with seem readily accessible and because Hollywood has successfully exported all over the world, there is something in the very nature of film that makes them accessible (p. 92).

Am I just ethnocentric? I don't deny that is a speculation worth discussing, only that the conclusion is foregone. There is nothing inherently evil in conjecturing that movies may, in specified respects, address contingently universal features of their audiences.

After all, Hammett herself acknowledges that Hollywood exports films successfully. Certainly it must be legitimate to ask what the basis of that success might be. Especially nowadays in the era of difference, it must be a pressing research question to account for how Hollywood's international success is possible. How can films confected by New Yorkers in Los Angeles be assimilated by receptive audiences in Bali, India, and Lebanon? How can first-time viewers in Africa follow what is called classical editing?

These are unavoidable facts, and they call for theoretical answers. They cannot be banished because they ought not obtain in a politically correct world of difference. There is unavoidable data here about the dissemination of cultural objects, even if the facts offend against the predictions of the politically correct.

Moreover, there are good reasons to hypothesize that certain Hollywood-type structures command worldwide attention because they tap into contingent universal structures of cognition and affect. These reasons have to do with the fact that assimilation occurs where the grounds for adopting cultural diffusion models are not very persuasive inasmuch as hypotheses about cultural diffusion and cultural indoctrination do not fit the data. Hypotheses like mine that account for the successful exportation of Hollywood International by viewing Hollywood-type filmmakers (who may, by the way, live and produce films in Mexico or Japan) as, in certain respects, intuitive psychologists who have discovered some virtually universal effective means of communication may be wrong. But these hypotheses should not be dismissed out of hand as culturally myopic until it is established that such theories are inferior to rival theories that confront the data head-on.

Hammett, on the other hand, doesn't as they say "get it." Why Hong Kong films are popular in South America now can't be explained in terms of Western imperialism or Yankee ethnocentricity. It is a fact (even if for some it is an unpleasant fact) that calls for an explanation. Hong Kong films are successful in places that Hong Kong never colonized, since Hong Kong never colonized anything. Thus, it is at least plausible to mount a rival hypothesis to the imperialism hypothesis, namely, an hypothesis that Hong Kong filmmakers tap into features of cognition and affect that are transculturally shared. To say that such hypotheses are simply not allowed smacks of the Inquisi-

tion. It reminds one of the bishop who refused to look through Galileo's telescope.

II. Response to Richard Allen

When reading pieces like Hammett's "Essentializing Movies," I worry that film theory will never mature beyond rhetorical grandstanding. For if film theory is to become genuinely dialectical inquiry, careful consideration of rival viewpoints will have to replace fashionable sloganeering. But despite my pessimism, perhaps things are beginning to change. Film theory of a more sober and measured bent is starting to appear. One example is Richard Allen's "Representation, Illusion and the Cinema."[9]

The purpose of Allen's article is to develop a theory of illusion in film. The theory he advances is a theory of what he calls "projective illusion." The starting point of his theory is my rejection of the utility of the notion of illusion when speaking of cinematic representations in the single shot. Allen thinks that my rejection of illusion talk is too hasty, and, in contrast, he wants to carve out a meaningful application of the notion of illusion to cinematic representation. Moreover, I thought that in scotching the notion that cinema is illusionistic, we could, so to speak, disavow the relevance of Lacanian theories of disavowal in the explanation of our negotiation of cinematic representation. For if there is no illusion, there is no pressure to postulate unconscious processes like disavowal in order to elucidate how the so-called illusions take hold. But in attempting to reinstate the utility of illusion in characterizing our reception of cinematic representations, Allen also hopes to regain a place for psychoanalysis in the theory of the reception of cinematic representation.

In this brief note, I want to examine Allen's criticisms of me as well as the theory of projective illusion that Allen propounds. I am especially interested in indicating what I believe are some of the shortcomings of

Allen's view which is, of course, a way of dialectically defending my own view against Allen's rival approach. However, before criticizing Allen, I want to acknowledge that I regard his criticisms of me to be respectable and his way of constructing his competing viewpoint methodologically apposite. I readily concede that Allen, unlike Hammett, has studied my arguments thoroughly and that he has gotten them right. There is no misinterpretation or caricature in his objections. Moreover, the way in which he attempts to correct what he takes to be the lacuna in my theory is, in principle, sound. I disagree with his conclusions, for reasons I'll indicate, but I, nevertheless, also think that he has initiated a serious theoretical discussion.

In *Mystifying Movies,* I take an illusion to be something that deceives or is liable to deceive spectators. An illusion is deceptive. The emphasis on deception seems to accord as well with the concerns with illusion in contemporary film theory which emphasizes the way in which so-called cinematic illusions ensnare spectators in epistemically defective states of all sorts, such as misrecognition. In *Mystifying Movies* and in various articles,[10] I rejected the plausibility of attributing illusion, in the sense of epistemic deception, to viewers of pictorial representations, including cinematic images. However, I also conceded that in ordinary language there might also be a sense of the term "illusion" which does not involve deception. One might, for example, call any representational picture an illusion – perhaps in such cases, "illusion" just means pictorial representation. Maybe when people talk about illusionistic painting what they mean, at least some of the time, is simply representational painting. This is not a sense of illusion I'm keen about and if I could legislate linguistic usage, I would, for theoretical reasons, advocate that we get rid of it. But since I can't regiment this usage out of existence, I am willing to at least acknowledge the existence of this usage, while also protesting that it is theoretically useless, if not confusing.

I called this use of illusion benign, since it involved no implication of deception. The notion of the illusion that involves deception and that concerns contemporary film theorists, I called "malign." And I argued that the malignant brand was eminently dispensable theoretically when it comes to explaining how, for example, we assimilate representational images of the single-shot variety. Allen appears to agree that my criticisms of the notion of illusion in the deception sense, which is presumed by contemporary film theorists, hit their mark. But he also is unsatisfied by what I have to say about the benign sense of illusion. He writes: "As it stands, Carroll's distinction between malign and benign senses of illusion is unilluminating, for the definition of an 'epistemically benign' sense of illusion is a trivial one. To the extent that all pictorial representations might be said to look like what they depict, all pictorial representations are illusions" (p. 33). Allen thinks that there is more to be said about illusion in the benign, nondeceptive sense. And, furthermore, he thinks that once we delve into this category, we will come up with at least one irreproachable sense of epistemically benign, cinematic illusion that will show that my dismissal of the notion of illusionism for film theory was premature.

Basically, Allen wants to claim that there is a chink in my argument, namely, that I overlooked a viable sense of nondeceptive cinematic illusion and that as a result I exiled illusion from film theory too quickly. In order to make this objection stick, it is up to Allen to provide an account of the species of nondeceptive, cinematic illusion that I ignored. Allen realizes that this is his burden of proof, and, in order to meet it, he develops a theory of projective illusion, the candidate for nondeceptive, cinematic illusion that I neglected. The crux of Allen's argument against me hinges on his account of projective illusion. How strong is his case?

Characterizing projective illusion, Allen writes:

When you see a zombie in George Romero's *Night of the Living Dead,* you may perceive the image realistically, that is, as the recording of a fictional portrayal of a zombie. It is highly unlikely, but you might perceive the zombie as a reproductive illusion and presume that these creatures were out there in this world, for example if somehow you thought that the film was a documentary. However, there is a third option: you may perceive a world inhabited by zombies. When you see a world inhabited by zombies you do not mistake a staged event for actuality in the manner of a reproductive illusion, rather, you lose awareness of the fact that you are seeing a film. Rather than look through the image "from the outside" at a photographic image of something staged in this world, you perceive the events of the film directly or "from within." You perceive a fully realized, though fictional, world that has all the perceptual presentness or immediacy of our own. I call this form of illusion projective illusion (p. 40).

Allen characterizes the state of projective illusion "as the loss of awareness of the photographic image as image in favor of the experience of a fully realized though fictional world" (p. 43). According to Allen, as we watch a film, we may be aware of the film as medium or aware of the film as fictional world. These states are not simultaneous, but rather may occur sequentially, like the dawning of the duck and, then, the rabbit aspects in Jastrow's "Is it a duck? Is it a rabbit?" Since the state of the film viewer flip-flops between attending the medium aspect and the fiction aspect of the image, the viewer's state cannot be one of deceptive illusion, since in virtue of the episodes of viewing the medium aspect of the image, the viewer does not believe that the image is its referent. But there is still room for nondeceptive illusion in this model, namely, interludes in which the viewer's medium awareness recedes and in

which the viewer perceives the fiction aspect of the image, that is, in which the viewer perceives the fictional world. Moreover, the part of the process that involves the impression of perceiving the fictional world, the projective illusion, may require psychoanalytic explanation.

However, before we call in the shrinks, let's look a little more closely at the notion of projective illusion. It seems to me to be deeply problematic. The analysis presupposes that the viewer moves in and out of states of perceiving the movie as medium versus perceiving a fictional world. This is treated as a matter of aspect perception. But this doesn't seem right. A fictional world, for example, is not an aspect of the variety that Wittgenstein had in mind. For you can't see a fiction. It is not the sort of visible aspect that the aspect-seeing model is designed to handle.

Of course, there are deeper problems here than the inapplicability of the seeing-as model. Even if Allen were to drop that model, he would still be confronted with the metaphysical impossibility of seeing or perceiving a fiction or, even worse, a fictional world. When watching a movie, we don't perceive a fictional world. You can't see a fictional world. When we watch *Night of the Living Dead,* what we see is not a fictional zombie. It can't be done. Rather, we see a pictorial representation that we recognize as a depiction of a rather raggedy, messed-up man or woman, which we imagine, prompted by the narrative, to be a zombie.

Fiction is a matter of imagining or entertaining certain thoughts as the result of our realization that the author intends us to do so on the basis of our apprehension that that is what the author intends us to do. Fiction is a matter of our imagining various thoughts as a result of our insight that that is what the author intends us to do. With visual fictions, what we literally see is not the fiction; rather we see depictive representations whose content we recognize and which we then use to imagine, not see, the fictional circumstances the author has in store for us.[11] We imagine fictional "worlds"; they are not available for sight. What we perceive literally are representations that we use, under the direction of the author or filmmaker, to direct our mandated imaginings. We see an image of what we recognize to be a large reptile and then imagine Godzilla smashing Tokyo to smithereens.

Suppose you don't share my ontological shyness about saying that it is possible to perceive fictions. Allen's theory is still in trouble. He says that we shift between medium awareness and projective illusion. In those interludes of projective illusion, we putatively perceive fictional worlds. This account can't be right. Why? Because it gives us no purchase on our reception of nonfiction films. What can be the projective illusion stage with regard to nonfiction films? It can't be that we are perceiving fictional worlds, or that we think that we are perceiving fictional worlds. Presumably, fictional world talk is inappropriate with nonfiction films. But does our experience of nonfiction films differ at the relevant levels of perception from our experience of fiction films. Surely, we should have a uniform account of our perceptual experience of fictional and nonfictional films and images. But Allen's theory of projective illusion falters in this respect, since with nonfiction films there are no fictional worlds available for projective illusion.[12] Thus, Allen's theory of projective illusion is fatally flawed.

One of the long-standing objections to any illusion theory of pictorial and/or dramatic representation is that spectators don't act as though they believe that images before them are "real." Call this anomaly the behavioral incongruity of illusionism. For example, we don't scramble from the theater when the battleship *Potemkin* lowers its sixteen-inch guns at us. Yet if we are under the illusion that a cannon is pointed at us, would we behave so unaccountably?

How exactly will the theory of projective illusion handle cases like this? If we have suspended our awareness of the movie-as-medium, why don't we get nervous when Eisenstein thrusts that hefty piece of naval artillery in our face? Perhaps, Allen's answer will be that we are not antsy because what we are perceiving, or what we think we are aware of perceiving, is a fiction. But if this is the answer, then we are back to all the problems we've reviewed with the conjecture that we perceive fictions. And if the hypothesis that we perceive fictions is implausible or inadmissible, then it looks like Allen will have to confront the daunting problem of the behavioral incongruity of illusionism rehearsed above.

Maybe Allen could say this. We don't run from the theater because we are flip-flopping between medium-awareness and projective illusion, and those fleeting moments of medium-awareness are sufficient to keep us in our seats. This sounds to me like a variation on a famous theme by Gombrich. But despite its illustrious provenance, I distrust it. On the one hand, I confess that I have never detected this flip-flopping phenomenologically in my own experience of filmgoing. But if such introspective reports carry little or no weight with Allen, there are conceptual considerations as well. This flip-flopping is a perceptual matter on his account. And it can't occur because there is no possible state of perceiving fictions. So half of the flip-flop isn't there; you cannot switch into a nonexistent state. But I repeat myself. At this point, my last argument loops back to my first argument and the ensuing dialectic starts up again.

So, returning to Allen's objection to my theory, my response is that I didn't overlook the possibility of projective illusion because I do not believe that it is a live option theoretically. Moreover, since I am not convinced that there is a mental state of projective illusion, I do not think that we need psychoanalysis to explain it. In short, I still remain unconvinced that illusion is a useful concept for film theory and, in consequence, that we need psychoanalytic mechanisms like disavowal to account for it.

Of course, I do not believe that everything is now settled. I anticipate that Richard Allen will have responses to my objections and, indeed, I would be the first to encourage him to bring them forward. Film theorizing should be dialectical, and Richard Allen has shown me that serious conversation and debate is becoming possible in film studies, despite my frequent and perhaps overly melodramatic laments that "all is lost."

Notes

1. Noël Carroll, *Mystifying Movies: Fads and Fallacies in Contemporary Film Theory* (New York: Columbia University Press, 1988).
2. Jennifer Hammett, "Essentializing Movies: Perceiving Cognitive Film Theory," *Wide Angle* 14, no. 1 (January 1992). References to Hammett's article will be given parenthetically in the text.
3. I leave it to physiological psychologists to discover the biological processes that subtend such recognitional capacities. That is, I don't suppose that recognition is magical, as the phrase "by looking" may suggest to some. Rather, I think that telling the rest of the causal story belongs in the province of biology.
4. Since I first published this hypothesis in my essay "The Power of Movies," a number of similar arguments about pictorial representation have been registered by philosophers and film scholars. The relevant philosophical citations include: Flint Schier, *Deeper into Pictures* (Cambridge University Press, 1986); Christopher Peacocke, "Depiction," *Philosophical Review* 96 (1987); Gregory Currie, "Film, Reality and Illusion," in *Post-Theory: Reconstructing Film Studies,* edited by David Bordwell and Noël Carroll (Madison: University of Wisconsin Press, 1995); Gregory Currie, *Image and Mind: Film, Philosophy and Cognitive Science* (Cambridge University Press, 1995). The relevant cinema studies citations include Stephen Prince, "The Discourse of Pictures: Iconicity and Film Stud-

ies," *Film Quarterly* 47, no. 1 (Fall 1993); and Paul Messaris, *Visual Literacy: Image, Mind and Reality* (Boulder: Westview Press, 1994).
5. N.B.: if I say that *some* of the same processes are involved, I am not claiming that the overall processes are identical.
6. In this quotation, Hammett is alluding to an assertion from page 200 of *Mystifying Movies.* There I claim that as a consequence of variable framing "the spectator is always looking where he or she should be looking, always attending to the right details and thereby comprehending, nearly effortlessly, the ongoing action in the way it is meant to be understood." But notice that by vaguely paraphrasing this sentence, Hammett has effectively taken it out of context. In context, my claim is about how we comprehend shots *nearly effortlessly,* not about how we comprehend shots *simpliciter.* It is a hypothesis about the relative ease of comprehension, not the whole story of comprehension. Charging that the assertion is the whole story of comprehension is a rhetorical trick parallel to Hammett's allegation that I think that pictorial recognition of the single shot gives us the whole story of film comprehension.
7. Here I am using the notion of comprehension in the way David Bordwell does in his book *Making Meaning* (Cambridge, Mass.: Harvard University Press, 1991).
8. Since Hammett charges that I am both a realist and a formalist, one wonders whether she is insinuating that my position is self-contradictory. For formalism and realism are often thought of as opposing positions in film aesthetics. But there is no such contradiction in my theory since I am neither a traditional realist nor a traditional formalist. I am, as I suggested earlier, a naturalist when it comes to the explanation of certain cinematic forms, but there is no contradiction in explaining some cinematic forms naturalistically. Nor am I a traditional formalist, in any case, as I have argued elsewhere throughout this volume.
9. Richard Allen, "Representation, Illusion and the Cinema," *Cinema Journal* 32, no. 2 (Winter 1993). References to Allen's article will be given parenthetically in the text.
10. Including: Noël Carroll, "Address to the

Heathen," *October* 26 (Fall 1983); Noël Carroll, "Conspiracy Theories of Representation," *Philosophy of the Social Sciences* 17 (1987); and Noël Carroll, "Anti-Illusionism in Modern and Postmodern Art," *Leonardo* 21, no. 3 (1988).

11. See Noël Carroll, "A Critical Study of *Mimesis As Make-Believe*," *The Philosophical Quarterly* 45, no. 178 (January 1995).

12. If at this point, one attempts to argue that nonfiction films are really fictions, I would resist this move with the arguments advanced in my article "From Real to Reel," which is included in this volume.

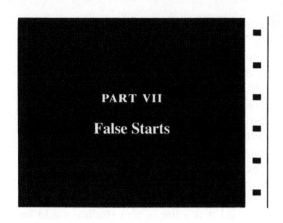

PART VII

False Starts

In this last section of the book, I have chosen to reprint some of my earliest articles in film theory. Originally, I thought to exclude these pieces. But the anonymous reviewers of the manuscript as well as several friends said that they thought that they should be included, since the articles are still referred to sometimes and since they are hard to find. Even very large university libraries tend not to possess the small-circulation journals in which these articles first appeared.

"Film History and Film Theory: An Outline for an Institutional Theory of Film" was an attempt to erect a framework for conducting film theory. It was programmatic. And it was singular – it pretends that *a* theory of film is possible. In that regard, it is not an example of the kind of film theorizing that I recommend now. It is anything but piecemeal. I still think the essay has some strengths. Its plea that film theory be sensitive to film history is still, with certain qualifications, on the right track, and some of the insights about individual films and about film style seem worth preserving. But, on the whole, the essay is flawed.

Perhaps the most egregious error in the essay is its importation of a problem and a framework for solving that problem into film studies from analytic philosophy. In analytic philosophy, a presiding question is "What is art?" This is a question about how to identify a candidate object or performance as an artwork. In writing "Film History and Film Theory," I acted as if there was also a parallel question in film studies. But that seems wrong to me now. Film studies is not concerned with how to establish that a given film is an artwork. If such a question arises with a specific film, I suppose that we would refer it to our best method for identifying art in general. However, in "Film History and Film Theory," I proceeded as though we needed a film theory to solve such questions, whereas now I doubt this.

In this essay, in short, I am doing what I have often chided other film scholars for doing – imposing philosophical concerns and models from another discipline on film studies. I invented a problem for film studies that really didn't emerge from its own practice and, therefore, presented a theory that in many ways is simply beside the point. My enthusiasm about a certain philosophical approach inclined me to ignore its scant relevance to film studies.

I have not given up my enthusiasm for this philosophical problem. But I hope that I have learned to pursue it in the right context. I have written a series of articles for philosophical publications that develop some of the ideas initiated in "Film History and Film Theory."[1] But I have abandoned my conviction of the pressing relevance of this issue for film studies. Indeed, as a result of my own experience of saddling film theory with extraneous philosophical concerns, I have grown suspicious of a similar tendency in other theorists. I think that film theory is an area where practitioners are overly prone to attempt to map theories from other fields on the data with little or no appreciation of the appropriateness of the fit. Can Foucauldian models of epistemes that range over centuries really be applied to film practice, which is itself just a century old? This is not to say that philosophy has no place in film theorizing. We must simply be careful to be sure that it is relevant. In "Film History and Film Theory," I was not. I let my philosophical enthusiasms obscure my judgment.

Though I now freely admit that "Film History and Film Theory" is a step in the wrong direction – a false start – I do not think that the preceding problems with it are the ones that greeted its publication. It was immediately abjured as formalist in an article in the very issue of the very journal that published it. Indeed, it was denounced by one of the editors of that journal. This was my first brush with political correctness in print. Moreover, the journal consistently refused to publish my defense of "Film History and Film Theory." It seems to me that film theorists have been so preoccupied with studying repression that they have become adept at it themselves. I am republishing "Art, Film and Ideology: A Response to Blaine Allan" in this volume to amplify further my resistance to being labeled a formalist.[2]

"Toward a Theory of Film Editing" is my earliest published attempt at film theory. The glaring problem with the article is that its central terms of analysis – inference and interpretation – are simply too vague. That is why it manages to accommodate all the data. Moreover, I wonder whether everything I think of as inference really would continue to qualify under that categorization if inference were really to be perspicuously conceptualized. I think that the article was right in resisting linguistically based or inspired models of film comprehension. But its positive proposals are neither precise nor systematic enough.

On the positive side, I also think that the way in which the article proceeds by thinking about classical narrative editing and avant-garde editing at the same time still has theoretical advantages. And I, of course, remain committed to the cognitivist approach in the essay, even though I think a lot of the details of the theory are too mushy. There are also some interpretive observations about specific shot chains that remain useful.

In fact, looking back at the essay, it now looks to me as though it is really a string of interpretations of various edited arrays more than it is a genuinely unified theory of editing. The vague terms of theoretical analysis allow me to line up a series of critical remarks about examples of film editing. This does not strike me as surprising, given what I know about myself. For when I began in film studies, my interests were primarily critical, not theoretical. Had I thought about it at the time, I probably believed that a life in film studies would be one in which you simply interpreted one film after another. I didn't actually start thinking about theory until semiotics, structuralism, Lacanian psychoanalysis, and the rest arrived on the scene. At that point, given my background in the philosophy of science and aesthetics, I reacted against what I thought and still think is sloppy theorizing. But I also realized that the best defense is an offense, and so I began to attempt to develop an alternative to what I call contemporary film theory. Since my first love was film interpretation, however, it is no wonder that my earliest essays tend to contain much more criticism than my later attempts at film theorizing. I have only become a film theorist gradually. Had there never been Lacanian film theory, I would probably still be turning out long, detailed, loving analyses of Buster Keaton and Harry Smith. I suppose this is one of life's ironies.

Notes

1. See, for example: Noël Carroll, "Art, Practice and Narrative," *The Monist* 71 (1988); Noël Carroll, "Identifying Art," in *Institutions of Art: Reconsiderations of George Dickie's Philosophy*, edited by Robert Yanal (University Parks: Penn State University Press, 1993); and Noël Carroll, "Historical Narratives and the Philosophy of Art," *The Journal of Aesthetics and Art Criticism* 52 (Summer, 1993).
2. I should note that the Leninist conception of ideology employed in this paper is a broader conception of ideology than the one that I favor today.

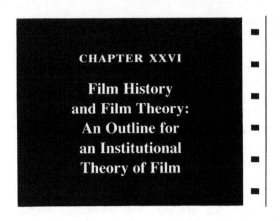

CHAPTER XXVI

Film History and Film Theory: An Outline for an Institutional Theory of Film

I. Introduction

Much of classical film theory is plagued by an imperviousness to film history. In many of the most famous theories, e.g., those of the realists and montagists, we find a tendency to hypostasize one or another aspect of the medium and to evaluate every other aspect in relation to the chosen one. This diathesis for essentialism renders each of the classics, in turn, incapable of dealing with the entire range of achievement that film history offers and that we would expect an adequate theory to account for.

In particular, classical theories are weakest and least persuasive in accommodating new developments in film which postdate the formulation of the theories in question. Montagists are hard put to account for the achievements of film realism; realist theorists have little to offer us about either the resurgence of assertive editing in the sixties or the postwar evolution of film modernism. Of course, both schools can reject developments that don't tally with their sensibilities, though at the cost of sounding rather *ad hoc.*

There are two problems, here, though they are related. The classical theories fail to be *general enough* specifically because film is a social practice and as such it is not a medium whose form is set for all time, but rather has a *developmental dimension.* The failure of classical theory is its failure to recognize that film is social and, therefore, historical. The purpose of this paper is to suggest the outline of a film theory that

would be sensitive to the fact that film, as an object of theoretical study, is a historical process. At the same time, I hope to avoid reducing film theory to film history.

In the attempt to overcome the shortcomings of classical film theories, I will rely quite heavily on what is known in philosophical literature as the Institutional Theory of Art, a position most often associated with George Dickie and Arthur Danto.[1] I realize that in turning to the Anglo-American tradition rather than to European thought, I am writing somewhat against the grain of the dominant academic approach to the inadequacies of classical film theory. In this regard my intent is admittedly polemical, though I do not have space here to even sketch most of my objections to Marxist-Psychoanalytic-Semiology as it is currently practiced. What I will try to supply, somewhat broadly, is a perspective and a research program that is an alternative to the various proliferating European models but I will not always elaborate why I think that this alternative is superior. I ask the reader to weigh this alternative in terms of its internal consistency and its efficacy in dealing with the material. My reservations about contending contemporaries must await future papers.

II. The Structure of Film Theory

It is a methodological cliché that the content of a theory will be influenced by the tasks it sets for itself. But what is the task of making a film theory? To even the casual observer, film theory appears to be an activity directed at answering questions about film of a fairly general sort. But what are these abstract questions?

Generalizing from the history of film theory, there seem to be *at least* three recurrent questions which taxed our forebears. I would like to spend some time looking at these questions because if my proposal is to constitute a theory it should be able to answer them as well.

The question that most strikes one when

reading the classics is "What is the determinant or crucial feature of film?" That is, what is or should be the central factor in our thinking about film? Bazin, for instance, answered this by emphasizing film's capacity to record pro-filmic reality.

Often this question has been answered by invoking the notion of an essence, i.e., in the idiom of an attribute that an object must have if it is to be identified as a film. The idea of the "cinematic," for example, as it is generally used, falls back on some idea of the essential nature of cinema. But the question is broader, I believe, than the essentialist answers. The film theoretician need not presuppose there are such things as essences. The question, as I've stated it, leaves open the possibilities that film may have no essential feature, that it may have more than one and that even if it has one or more essential features, it may not be that this feature (or features) should be determinant in our thinking about cinematic processes. Indeed, in the fifth part of this essay, I will argue that the complexity of the medium is its most significant characteristic, though this is hardly an essential, identifying feature of film.

This question can be answered in either the singular or the plural. For example, the theory defended in Perkins' *Film as Film* fundamentally argues that cinema has two determinant characteristics: the capacities both to reproduce and to reconstitute pro-filmic reality. Also, though the history of film theory leads us to expect a positive answer to this question, a theorist could resolve it by denying that film has any determinant characteristic whatsoever.

Another question that is answered either explicitly or implicitly in the major film theories is "What is the value or role of cinema?" Munsterberg, Arnheim and Balazs, for instance, are all committed to art as the answer. However this problem is solved, the answer is important because it places the theoretician in a particular conceptual position for discussing the determinant feature of film. If one takes art as the value of cinema, then one's characterization of the nature of art can be used to pick out the determinant feature of the medium.

There is a strong relation between the answers to the first and second questions; namely the items listed as determinant features will generally be items that are instrumental in realizing or actualizing or achieving the value or role the theorist names for cinema. For example, Bazin claims that the role of film is to immortalize the past; this commitment enables him to zero in on recording as the determinant factor because it is the most plausible means to the end. Of course, a theoretician may hold that film has more than one value or role; indeed, I suppose that it is logically possible to deny that film has any role though it does seem very unlikely that such a large social institution doesn't have at least some function, even if it is a thoroughly venal or pernicious one.

The last question asked by film theories is really a brace of questions iterated again and again so that they occupy the bulk of the text. It is "What are the processes of articulation in film in relation to the previous two answers?" Dealing with this question usually involves drawing up lists of articulatory processes and relating each process back to the determinant characteristic and the value of cinema. A given theory may include accounts of types of montage or types of spatial disjunctions or types of camera angles or all of these things. Though a theory may not be complete in this regard, this question could be exhaustively answered by considering each dimension of cinematic articulation (e.g., composition, editing, sound, etc.) and by charting the basic variables or structures open to manipulation in each of these dimensions (e.g., the close-up, the long take, parallel editing, jump-cuts, etc.). Film theories are full of available schemas for the presentation of material. However, film theories are not simply lists. They differ from filmmaking guides or manuals which also contain lists because film theories attempt to elucidate each process of articulation in terms of their commitments to a particular determinant feature and value of film.

For instance, Munsterberg holds that film is art, that art is freedom and that the determinant characteristic of film is its capacity to mime certain mental processes that free us from mere physical existence. In treating parallel editing, he analyzes it in terms of how it frees us from an experience of sheer spatio-temporal succession. Munsterberg's theory is probably incoherent, but its form is instructive and can be generalized; *the cinematic variables he itemizes are not only described but analyzed as instances of his proposed determinant characteristic which, in turn, is a means by which film realizes its goal.*[2]

Handbooks tell us some of the structures that are available to filmmakers. They may even offer practical advice like "use flat lighting for comedy." But these lists and suggestions are not theoretical until the items on the lists are related to the questions posed about film's determinant characteristic and role. Film theorists may ask more than these questions, but I think that they must at least have answers to these three if their work is to amount to a theory of film.

It should be noted that by identifying film theory with at least these three questions, the issue of whether it is evaluative or descriptive is left open. This ambiguity enters especially with the disjunction that film theorists speculate on the value *or* role of cinema. A theorist like Eisenstein seems to be recommending a certain practice of cinema whereas the Marxist-Psychoanalytic-Semiologist appears primarily to be reporting the function of cinema in capitalist society. I would not want to deny that either approach is theory, though I am unmoved by both. I believe that the Institutional Theory of Film is descriptive. But I am also fairly certain that we cannot dismiss something as an example of film theory just because it

advocates a certain kind of film. I believe this despite the fact that the theory in question may be wrong just because it is too parochial in its tastes.

Though I derived these questions by generalizing recurrent structures that I found in classical film theory, it should be clear that they are also endemic in current theories. Marxist-Psychoanalytic-Semiology examines a process of articulation like the point-of-view schema within a theoretical context where the role of the dominant cinema is identified as the entrenchment of ideology and where its determinant characteristic is illusionism,[3] which is seen as a means of "naturalizing" ideology. Lacanian psychoanalysis is brought to bear on the POV in order to show how it is an instance of an illusion that propagates ideology.[4] Similarly, I will attempt to set forth answers to these three interrelated questions.[5]

III. Film as Art

Within the short history of film theory, several dominant strategies for answering the basic questions of the discipline have appealed to scholars. These include the consideration of film as language (held with different degrees of rigor by montagists and semiologists), film as dream (espoused by Hoffmansthal, Langer, Sparshott and recently Metz), film as mental process (Munsterberg), film as photographic reality (Bazin, Kracauer and Cavell), and, of course, film as art (held by too many to enumerate). These different perspectives may or may not conflict depending on the interpretation that the theorist gives his or her informing idea. Clearly Bazin used the idea of film as photographic reality in a way which clashed with one idea of film as language, though the same antithesis is not evident in Vertov. Langer connected the idea of film as dream with that of film as art in virtue of her theory that art was the reification of the forms of aspects of our felt emotive life, like dreams. Similarly

Munsterberg argued that film was art just because it mimed certain mental processes.

Adopting one or another of these approaches often dictates specific forms of reasoning in relation to the basic questions of film theory. The film as dream approach involves argument by logical analogy, showing how each, or at least a number, of the processes and structures of representation of film are like the experiences and structures of dream. The determinant characteristic of film will be dreamlikeness while its role or value will be whatever the role or value of dream is, unless like Langer, dreamlikeness is connected to some other quality like art.

I am committed to the film as art approach. This doesn't mean that I hold that all film is art. But rather, that for theoretical purposes, I only want to consider those films which are art. I have chosen this perspective because it seems to me that it is an indisputable fact that it is as art, albeit sometimes qualified as popular art, that film has come to occupy the powerful position it holds in our culture. Film has many uses, but I think that its most significant use in the twentieth century has been to make art. I believe it has, even in its art-making capacity, been used to make other things including not only money but ideology. Nevertheless, I want to stress that the study of film as art logically precedes the study of film as ideology because art, its forms and its traditions, is the filter through which ideology must pass. For instance, a disjunctive cut can only accrue revolutionary significance in virtue of the artistic traditions of continuity editing which such a cut rejects. In order to assess the ideological significance of an articulatory practice (e.g., a style) as radical or reactionary, it is first necessary to locate that practice in relation to a history of styles as, for example, a deviation or a repetition of past styles. The history of stylistic options, i.e., the artistic traditions of the medium, in a manner of speaking, constitute one of the conditions that make both the operation and expression of ideology possible. In short, I believe that the study

of film as a vehicle for ideology is of deep importance and that theorizing about film as art is not incompatible with this task, but rather illuminates the context in which ideological formations, especially in film styles, become comprehensible.

By answering the question of the value of film in terms of art, the stage is conceptually set for answering the other questions since our conception of art can be used to evaluate different candidates for the determinant characteristic. The form our reasoning takes is to hypothesize that the feature of film that is most instrumental in enabling the medium to make art is the determinant characteristic. But what is our conception of art? There are many contenders. Arnheim emphasizes expression; Balazs, self-expression. And formalism presents still further conceptions. Thus, in adopting a film as art stance, we must add another answer to the three basic ones. Specifically we must clarify what we take art to be in order to apply that concept in the rest of our theory.

IV. The Institutional Theory of Art

The Institutional Theory of Art arose in reaction to the dominant attitude toward the idea of art in the philosophical literature of the fifties and sixties. This position, stated in its most widely known version in Morris Weitz's "The Role of Theory in Aesthetics,"[6] claims that art is an open concept. The open concept approach, in turn, was a reaction to what it saw as the fundamental error of all other approaches to the nature of art. To understand the Institutional Theory, a brief account of the open concept notion is necessary.

Proponents of the open concept approach surveyed the history of art theory and found it wanting. Especially with the demise of various imitation theories of art, philosophers and critics attempted to fill the gap with alternative accounts of the nature of art. Expression theories sprang up, like those of Croce and Collingwood, as well as different sorts of formalism, including not only the Russians, but also Bell, Fry, and, in a way, Bergson and Ortega y Gasset. These examples, of course, represent only the tip of the iceberg. Each theory appeared only to be refuted because of a combination of technical difficulties and the inability of any given approach to canvas all the things that were intuitively felt to be in the class of art objects. These theories were especially weak on art that emerged after the theories were proposed. Film theory bears the traces of this activity in aesthetics, since often film theoreticians relied on one or another of the many theories of art that abounded in the first half of the twentieth century, though, of course, in some cases film theoreticians reached back as far as the 18th or 19th century for their ideas.

Looking at this vast disarray, the open concept theory surmised that something must be wrong with the way art theory was being done. Its history was one of failure. This, on its own, didn't prove that art theory, as traditionally practiced, was impossible but it gave the open concept theorists food for thought. They argued that if they could come up with a reason why art theories always failed, they would have grounds for believing that traditional aesthetics rested on an error.

Weitz noted that traditional theories always sought to define the essential characteristic of art. But, following Wittgenstein's analysis of games, he ventured that art might not have any essential feature, the works we think of as art linked only by "family resemblances" rather than by sets of necessary and sufficient conditions. In this sense, art is an open concept; it has no defining characteristic like expressiveness or significant form.

To support this conjecture, the open concept theory noted that intrinsic to our notion of art is a high value placed on innovation, novelty and change. This is not only important in the careers of individual artists, but for the evaluation of art movements, e.g., Classicism is followed by Romanticism which is followed by Realism, etc. Even if a theorist did find a common characteristic for all the art up to a given point in history, say up to the day he or she published their theory, there would still be a question about whether that feature would be the defining feature of works of future art movements given the tropism of successive periods of art toward novelty, especially in terms of challenging and overthrowing the canons of earlier movements. Previous attempts at art theory were wrong because in their search for the definition of art they overlooked the expansionary character of art, attempting to predict, in a way, what art will always be despite the fact that unexpected developments and novelty are among the deepest goals of art.

In their putative refutation of traditional aesthetics, the open concept theorists did not argue that past art theory was without value altogether, but rather without the value past art theorists had assumed. The open concept theorists pointed out that each age and each art movement attempts to define its ideal of art. Unfortunately, this is done in terms of the defining characteristic of art and is misguided as theory. Yet it does serve a salutary polemical and critical function. The traditional theorists, like Bell, actually were involved in calling attention to particular possibilities of art that had been neglected in previous art and criticism. They performed an exemplary critical task, recommending attention to specific features of art that had been barely noticed theretofore. Theorists entered partisan debates about art, especially at points where artists were expanding the boundaries of art, and the theorists elucidated the important features of their beloved objects as well as the subtle family relationships that the art they upheld bore to earlier art. The opening chapters of Perkins' *Film as Film* incisively account for the history of film theory in just this way, arguing that the first generations of film theorists were wrong, but that they operated polemically in specific historical contexts where they illuminated ignored aspects of the medium, enhancing our understanding of film at least temporarily.

The open concept theory regards the theorist as a kind of critic, whose position, whether sympathetic and supportive or hostile and rejecting, develops arm-in-arm with the evolution of art. The theorist, construed as critic, seems to function best when he or she aids the expansion of art's frontiers. In film theory, one of the most effective summaries of the sentiments of the open concept theory comes at the end of Sontag's essay "Film and Theater" when she writes,

For some time, all useful ideas in art have been extremely sophisticated. Like the idea that everything is what it is and not another thing. A painting is a painting. Sculpture is sculpture. A poem is a poem, not prose. Et cetera. And the complementary idea: a painting can be "literary" or sculptural, a poem can be prose, theater can emulate and incorporate cinema, cinema can be theatrical.

We need a new idea. It will probably be very simple. Will we be able to recognize it?[7]

Here, the open frontier of film art is acknowledged and the theorist, if he or she can be called such, is given the responsibility to be on the lookout for the next development in the medium.

Like most philosophical theories, the open concept theory has come in for quite a battering. This is not the place to rehearse all its technical difficulties except for those which are relevant to the formation of the Institutional Theory. The open concept theory presumes that the expansionary nature of art forecloses the possibility of defining art. Its argument against definition is not that past attempts at definition have always failed, but that they have always failed *because art is expansionary*. This argument, however, has an obvious chink in its armor. What if the expansionary character of art can be appropriately accommodated within a definition of art? This is exactly what the Institutional Theory essays, rejecting the basic claim of the open concept theory that art can't be defined.

The clearest statement of the Institutional Theory is George Dickie's. Though flawed, it is a good starting point for developing a stronger version that will be useful for film theory. Dickie defines art in the following way:

A work of art in the classificatory sense is
1) an artifact
2) upon which some person or persons acting in behalf of a certain social institution (the artworld) has conferred the status of candidate for appreciation.[8]

Dickie holds that traditional theory and the open concept theory were both wrong because they assumed that if art had some characteristic feature it would be a manifest property of the object, like Bell's significant form. Dickie's move is to argue that one of the most important characteristic features of art is a non-manifest, relational property, namely belonging to the artworld. He sees the artworld as a social institution, like the law but less formalized, made up of artists, exhibitors, critics and spectators, each of whom plays different roles.[9] Dickie's point is that something becomes art when it is placed in the proper social (institutional) context (like a gallery) in the proper way (established by precedent) by someone – an artist, a curator, a critic – endorsed to do so. These people, so to speak, nominate works as candidates for appreciation; they present works for spectators to judge worthy of attention or interest, though whether the works are appreciated is irrelevant to whether they are works of art. In this sense, Dickie's position is classificatory rather than evaluative.

The Institutional Theory, like the open concept theory, can claim Wittgenstein as its progenitor, though rather than adopting his analysis of games, the Institutional Theory emphasizes his notion of a form of life. Art, it holds, is a society, a form of life, with its own rules and roles. An object is an artwork in virtue of entering that form of life, that social context, in accordance with the rules of conduct of the artworld, understood broadly as an institution like religion or politics. Again, it is not, as traditional theory held, that an object is art in virtue of some manifest, non-relational property, but it is rather in terms of a nonexhibited relational property – its contextual position – that something is art.[10]

Duchamp's *Fountain*, a favorite example for the Institutional Theory, was a simple urinal until Duchamp, operating on behalf of the artworld, placed it in a social context where it became a candidate for appreciation. Indeed, Duchamp, as an artist, can be regarded as one of the key creative proponents of the Institutional Theory insofar as *Fountain* provokes a reflexive meditation on the conditions of art, specifically by foregrounding the importance of the artworld context as a constitutory factor in making an object art.[11]

On the face of it, Dickie's theory is mildly appalling. It relies heavily on Dada-derived pranks as evidence and to many it seems to be saying that something is a work of art just because somebody (albeit working on behalf of the artworld) says it is. Obviously, such a theory can assimilate the expansionary character of art because anything can become a work of art as long as the right somebody says it is. As would be expected, the Institutional Theory has sparked a large literature that plays with the paradoxes that issue from Dickie's formulation through the use of many lively and entertaining counterexamples that bring out the Dadaist in the staidest of philosophers.

Almost every phrase in Dickie's formulation has come under bombardment. I will not present all the objections but merely try to summarize the brunt of the main ones in order to prepare the reader for a reformulation of the central points of the Institutional Theory that I think are significant for film theory.

One objection is that Dickie has not really demonstrated that the artworld is an institution;[12] he presumes that it has a system of rules, but since he does not spell them out, why believe him? Indeed, some of his own examples plus some of the wilder counterexamples make the artworld seem only like an institution in the sense of a madhouse rather than something like the law.

The biggest problems in the theory return to the question of whether or not Dickie can exclude any object from the order of art except for the most arbitrary and *ad hoc* reasons. Are there any limits on who confers the status of candidate for appreciation? Can anyone set themselves up as a bestower of status? Can I declare my bathtub a work of art tomorrow? If not, why not? If so, what's to stop me from declaring everything art? To say the least, that would be an infelicitous consequence for a supposed definition of anything, save perhaps "everything."

Dickie argues that conferring status is like nominating an alderman. But disbelievers have challenged this analogy by reminding us that a candidate for alderman must meet certain criteria before he or she can be nominated, e.g., he or she must be of a certain age.[13] But Dickie has not supplied any criteria for what an artifact must be in order to qualify as a candidate for appreciation. Again the floodgates seem open. Dickie could put some teeth in his theory by admitting that there just are some things that can't be appreciated, but since Dickie (I think mistakenly) seems to think that "to be able to appreciate *x*" means "to be able to like *x* in some respect" he concludes that the things that opponents have cited as "paradigms of things which cannot be appreciated – ordinary thumbtacks, cheap white envelopes and plastic forks – have appreciatable qualities which can be noted if one focuses attention on them."[14] Thus, in terms of "appreciation" Dickie's theory adds no constraints to his definition.

The bulk of the objections to Dickie point

out that he is not restrictive enough.[15] To shore up the approach some criteria for excluding some objects from the artworld must be supplied. It is here that I think that Danto's conception of the artworld, which is more historicist than Dickie's, is relevant. Danto does not give us a definition of art, but he does have an account of the artworld as a society. As one reads his speculations on how a work enters the order of art, one realizes that for Danto since art is a society, it has a history. His examples abundantly show that for him it is the history of art that works as a constraint on what objects can become art at a given time. He invents the case of a tie, painted blue by Picasso, that today we would count as a work of art. He then considers whether the same painted tie would have been art at the time of Poussin or Morandi or Cezanne, concluding that it would not because "there would have been no room in the artworld of Cezanne's time for a painted necktie. Not everything can be an artwork at every time: the artworld must be ready for it. Much as not every line which is witty in a given context can be witty in all."[16]

Danto's point is that art as society means that art has a history, a set of traditions against which a putative object is measured as art or non-art. The artworld is an institution in virtue of these traditions. An object must "fit into" these traditions before it can be an artwork. That is, at every point in the history of art, there is an ensemble of past and present practices and theories; an object must be comprehensible in light of this context if it is to be counted as art. This provides a constraint on what can or cannot be art at a given time because it implies that a putative art object must be interpretable in terms of the traditions, the practices and the theories of the artworld. Danto writes:

The moment something is considered an artwork, it becomes subject to an *interpretation*. It owes its existence as an artwork to this and when its claim is defeated, it loses its interpretation and becomes a mere thing. The interpretation is in some measure a function of the artistic context of the work; it means something different depending upon its art-historical locations, its antecedents and the like.[17]

Though I am not altogether happy with every aspect of this passage,[18] I believe that its stress on the role of interpreting the object in its art-historical context is exactly right. An object can be excluded from the class of art if it cannot be situated by an interpretation in the artistic context of its production. The tradition, the practices and the theories of the artworld at a given time supply the teeth Dickie's theory needed.

Extending Danto's insights while returning to Dickie's attempt to define art, I want to argue that the second clause in Dickie's definition should read that something is a work of art in a classificatory sense only if

2) it can be appreciated as a repetition, amplification or repudiation of prior traditions of the artworld.

I have kept Dickie's concept of appreciation in name only, for unlike him, I am using "appreciate" not to mean "to like" but in the more basic sense, pointed out by Ziff,[19] of "to assess." For an object to be a work of art we must be able to assess it by means of an interpretation that relates it to the traditions of the artworld. I have tried also to flesh out Danto's theory by sketching the three basic modes of interpreting an object in relation to the artistic tradition. It will be under one of these three types of interpretation that an object becomes an artwork. If, at any given point in history, the object cannot be connected with the tradition by means of these kinds of interpretations, it is not art. Moreover, at any point in history, an object may be proffered under an interpretation along one of these three lines and that interpretation may be wrong. For example, it might be logically self-contradictory. In that case, if the object has no other available interpretation, it is not art. Here is solace for the opponent of the Institutional Theory who feared it was too permissive.

If a work is interpretable as a repetition, amplification or repudiation of its antecedents, it is an artwork at the moment of its birth. This doesn't mean that one of its contemporaries must have an interpretation ready to hand, but only that such an interpretation is available within the practices and theories of the artworld at that time. Consider Danto's case of the painted tie; if it were proffered not in Poussin's time, but in the 1920s, it would be art, even if it stupefied every spectator, just because there was enough of the right kind of theory in the air. On the other hand, an object, even accompanied by the right kind of interpretation, can be excluded if the only interpretation it has is ill-founded.

Imagine a film discovered in the Warner Bros. vaults that is made up of the randomly ordered out-takes of a hundred different films of the thirties. Further imagine that this is screened at MOMA, where the program notes declare that this film bares all the codes of the narrative cinema. Here the film is linked with an interpretation that construes it as a modernist repudiation. But the interpretation, in the case as I've outlined it, is implausible. It is at the very least anachronistic to suppose that Warner Bros. in the thirties supplied a context where there were either traditions or practices, let alone theories, that by the wildest stretch of the imagination would enable that film, in that place, at that time to function as a modernist repudiation of narrative filmmaking. We can defeat the interpretation and thus exclude that film from the corpus of art.

We can evaluate interpretations of putative works of art by criteria like accuracy of detail, logical coherence, comprehensiveness of detail, specificity and distinctiveness of interpretation, simplicity in explanation, historicity, etc. Thus, we can exclude some supposed works of art on the grounds that their only interpretations can be defeated because they are implausible when measured against the kinds of criteria we expect from any reasonable interpretation of a work of art. In a manner of speaking, the constraints on adequate interpretations supply a major portion of the "rules of conduct" for designating an object art. Undoubtedly since the criteria for reasonable interpretation of a work of art allow for the possibility of equally strong, even contesting interpretations, there may be some undecidable cases on the boundary between art and non-art, though I think that the number of actual boundary problems will not be great enough to hurt the overall efficacy of the theory. At the same time, the Institutional Theory will be able to exclude many of the more hair-raising cases like our roll of out-takes.

A little more needs to be said about the three modes of interpretation under which an object is classified as art. The most straightforward mode is to establish that a given work is a repetition of past or existing traditions, practices, and theories. A repetition is a modification or variation in the particularities of the content of, for instance, a genre or form. In film, *Gone with the Wind* is a repetition of movies like *Frankenstein*, for though the characters, events, and places have changed, the basic narrative techniques have remained the same. Repetition, in this sense, is not exact duplication. If someone remade *Klute*, shot for shot, so that it was indiscernible from the original, it could only stand as a work of art if it were accompanied by an interpretation that characterized it as a complex repudiation (perhaps involving irony) rather than one that flew under the flag of repetition.[20]

An amplification is a formal modification that expands the means of achieving the goals of a given genre or form. For instance, at a given point in film history parallel editing and the close-up were popularized. The films that sported these new techniques were amplifications of the aim of making film narratives. And, of course, even at the time they were greeted as such; for film, they were appraised as new means for achieving an established end.

Through the concept of amplification, the

Institutional Theory can incorporate aspects of the expansionary character of art which so exercised the open concept theory. But repudiation is even more important in this respect. An artistic repudiation is a rejection of an antecedent style and its associated values. It emphasizes possibilities that are repressed in, or obscured by, the rejected style. For an object to count as a repudiation, it must not merely be different from what has preceded it, it must be interpretable as in some sense opposed or against antecedent artistic traditions.

The disjunctive editing in *Un chien andalou* is a repudiation of the dominant structures of editing, but a similar-looking, mismatched, fragmentary example of film from 1904 would not be, if only because the dominant narrative style had not yet been established. Likewise, Renoir's deep-focus, decentered compositions in *Rules of the Game* repudiate the simple, economic, centrally composed images of the dominant narrative traditions of the twenties and thirties whereas Porter's rather confused, decentered shots, though on occasion similar in effect to Renoir's, are not repudiations of anything, but the common coin of the early days of film.

When a work of art is regarded as a repudiation of a pre-existing tradition, its style stands, in the culture from which it emerges, to what it repudiates somewhat like a logical contrary. At least, it behaves like one. We think this way, for instance, of Classicism versus Romanticism. In film, a similar tension exists between montage and realism. Again a repudiation is not merely different from what has preceded it, but opposed in a way that gives its relation to the past a discernible structure. To interpret an object as a repudiation one must show exactly along what dimensions the object rejects tradition as well as showing that just that sort of rejection was conceivable in the artistic context in which the work appeared. History and tradition, in other words, supply information that constrain what at any given time can function as a plausible repudiation and an expansion of the frontier of art. In the next section, I will attempt to say what the ramifications of adopting this historicist version of the Institutional Theory are for film theory.

V. Notes for an Institutional Theory of Film

The Institutional Theory is attractive for film theory because it is sensitive to the developmental dimension of art forms, a factor notably lacking in most classical film theories. As outlined above, it gives art history an important role to play in aesthetics. At the very least, adopting the Institutional Theory gives the film-as-art theorist a means for deciding what is and is not in his or her field of study. The ability to know what the data is, of course, is important for any theory. But we have traveled a long and winding, almost feckless road if that is the only advantage that the Institutional Theory holds for us.

One thing that the foregoing account tells us is that an art form has the capacity for later works to repudiate earlier ones. This feature seems crucial to me for zeroing in on the determinant feature of film. Historically, film has sponsored, at the very least, one generally acknowledged great debate that involved the opposition of two film styles that were treated as contraries, viz., the contest between montage and deep-focus realism. This is a very complicated issue, and I don't pretend to be able to unravel it completely. But there is one aspect of it that, for our purposes, is especially important. To wit, it was a debate between one style of *composition* in the single shot versus one type of *editing*. In other words, it developed because film is a complex object in the sense that it is made up of a number of discrete channels of articulation. Weighting one channel over another gave film stylists the conceptual space necessary for one type of filmmaking to repudiate another. Perkins has pointed out that film began as a hybrid, the product of the fusion of photography and optical toys like the Zoetrope. Unfortunately he does not explore the full ramifications of this insight, settling as he does on a formula for the cinematic that is meant to reconcile or equilibrate only two capacities of film – its abilities to reproduce and also to reconstitute pro-filmic reality.

Of course, editing and composition are not the only processes of articulation; sound, color, screen size, etc. set up even further possibilities that afford not only opportunities for amplifying existing film styles, but for repudiating past ones. In short, it is the complexity of the medium that is the determinant characteristic in our thinking about film as art.

So far, I have only alluded to complexity in terms of the interplay between the different channels of articulation in film. But even more profoundly, each of the discrete channels of articulation is complex in the sense that each can be manipulated toward very different, often opposing ends.

Alexander Sesonske has pointed out that phenomenologically cinematic space (i.e., the space of a single shot) can be either flat or deep.[21] An individual filmmaker, like Hans Richter in *Rhythmus*, Ernie Gehr in *Serene Velocity* or more conventionally, Busby Berkeley in his production numbers, can play off this tension between the two-dimensional and three-dimensional aspects of cinematic space. But the fact that a filmmaker can emphasize either the flatness of the screen or the depth of the image on the screen opens the possibility, not only that the filmmaker will manipulate the two contrapuntally, but elevate one aspect of cinematic space over another. Proponents of the New American Cinema, who, under the influence of the Greenberg version of modernism, claimed that cinematic space was "really" flat and that the task of the filmmaker was to reveal this basic condition of the medium, made exactly this move in repudiating the deep space of classical narrative cinema. Nor was this just the idle chatter of critics, but an animating idea of a certain form of filmmaking.

My answer to the question about what aspect of film should be central in our thinking about the medium is that its determinant characteristic is its complexity which affords the possibility of individual films entering a developing, historical discourse with other films and other arts. "Discourse," here, is metaphoric. By it I mean that through stylistic manipulation of the complex elements of film, individual films can repeat, amplify or repudiate the concerns and preoccupations of other films and other arts. The phrase "complex elements" refers not only to the fact that film has discrete channels of articulation but that each of those channels is itself complex.

Earlier I claimed that the Institutional Theory suggested a research program for the Institutional Theory of Film. With the specification of the determinant characteristic, the way is clear to see what that research program is. The question in film theory that requires the most voluminous answer is, "What are the processes of articulation of film in relation to its determinant characteristic and value?" The form this answer takes is an analysis of the different processes of articulation and their possible inter-relations as instances of the determinant characteristic. If the Institutional Theory claims a certain type of complexity as the determinant feature of film, then the final, though most crucial, portion of the theory involves a review of the processes of articulation as examples of complex elements that cannot only repeat but amplify and repudiate earlier uses of those elements.

Film theoreticians dwell on the capacities of each aspect of the medium, charting their possible uses, and sometimes adding which uses are legitimate and which not according to the guiding prejudices of the theoreticians. This analysis, whether classificatory or evaluative, is done with an eye to the determinant characteristic and value of film.

Commitments on these issues orient the theoreticians by supplying a framework in which to analyze the articulatory processes. The Institutional Theory seeks to establish how each articulatory element can support the dialectic of repetition, amplification and repudiation.

To a large extent, this essay is a promissory note which I hope to repay with future writing. I cannot now scrutinize every articulatory process in film, but I would like to discuss some aspects of the medium-long shot (henceforth simply "medium shot") in order to provide some idea of how I think that the Institutional Theory would approach the various elements of film articulation.

Composition in the medium shot is one of the basic forms of cinematic articulation. Historically, it was one of the first methods of cinematic representation, seemingly borrowed from theater and painting as a primary format. One might also speculate that this format has a certain phenomenological primacy, that transcends the specific circumstances of film history, and which is due to the fact that our normal experience of people is of whole, identifiable bodies, rather than of parts as we find in the close shot or as specks as we find in long shots. But for whatever reason, composition in the medium shot is a primary process of film articulation and it is the task of my theory to show how it can sustain a reticulum of repetitions, amplifications and repudiations.

Film became linked with storytelling quite early in its history. This gave rise to the problem of how to organize narrative space in the medium shot. Though the saga of early narrative composition is not as well understood and perhaps for that reason not so dramatic as that of early editing, there is a discernible maturation in compositional style between 1900–1920. What became the principles of the dominant style in narrative composition were outlined by the early film theoretician Victor Freeburg, who like many others of our profession, attempted to codify his preferences into a system.[22]

The system he proposed, and which we can easily descry in the bulk of narrative films, is quite commonsensical; probably it is the approach that most of us would naturally opt for when confronted by the problem of organizing narrative space. Neither Freeburg nor the multitude of filmmakers whose practice he theorized named their approach; so for expositional purposes let me call it the economic-psychological method of medium shot composition.

The approach has a hyphenated name because it has two components, one of which is a value and the other which is factual. The value component is that part I call economic. It holds that the task of a director is to lead the audience's attention to the most important elements in the narrative. This attitude is based on an idea of efficiency, and Freeburg's emphasis on this quality reminds us of many of Lev Kuleshov's recommendations about composition. Both, for instance, advocate a simplicity of detail that might be thought of as abstraction in the sense of removing or subtracting distracting objects from the set. The correct composition in Freeburg is that which most efficiently directs the attention of the audience to the key elements of the story; failure in this regard is an error in style. For Freeburg, a good composition is one in which the first item the audience attends to is also the key narrative element in the shot.

How can a filmmaker be assured that he or she has a good composition ahead of time? This is where the theory is factual. Freeburg adduces certain psychological rules of thumb, which modern research could expand, about where the audience is likely to look in a composition. Of course, the value component of the theory tells you to put the key narrative elements in the sectors where the audience is likeliest to look.

The rules of thumb are pretty obvious. The audience is likely to look at stasis in movement or movement in stasis, at the center of the frame, at prominent objects, along continuous lines like diagonals, at light on dark and vice-versa, at geometric figures, etc. Freeburg, like Kuleshov, urges that compositions not be cluttered lest attention be diffused, and he also warns against the use of unusual or unidentifiable objects on the set since they are likely to distract attention from the main action.

Freeburg's analysis is incomplete not only because his list of the manipulable variables for inducing attention is too short, but also because he has not provided us with any account of the comparative strength of the different variables when they are not coordinated to draw attention to one sector of the image. Nevertheless, his speculations are important for film theory in several respects.

First of all he has focused on what might be thought of as the fundamental structures of the medium shot; any medium shot, indeed any shot whether flat or deep, close or long, will guide attention in accordance with certain psychological rules of thumb. Any compositional style begins with these rules of thumb and then goes on to decide how to manipulate them, that is, how the audience will be directed through the image. Freeburg offers one alternative; use the rules of thumb to guarantee that the key narrative element is the first thing the spectator looks at. In this he is articulating the base-line style in medium shot composition not only as it is practiced in film, but in television programs as well. Most medium shot composition is nothing but a repetition of the economic-psychological approach to the narrative image.

Given this base-line, we can begin to chart other possibilities for the use of the medium shot, including what can be designated as amplifications and repudiations. Some of the most famous film directors can, for instance, be understood in terms of repudiating the economic-psychological style. One aspect of that style is focusing attention on a single sector in the image; thus, one clear way to repudiate it is to defocus and simultaneously diffuse attention across many sectors of the image, a phenomenon we find, for instance, in Sternberg, Renoir and Tati.

Consider *Rules of the Game* for a moment. It is as if Renoir had read Freeburg and set out to violate every recommendation in the book. In many shots there is perturbing movement in the background, diverting attention from the central action. In defiance of Freeburg's strictures against distracting objects, we find things obtruding into the frame and on occasion dominating the foreground; the marquis, for instance, argues with his lover while standing next to an arresting oriental statue whose strange, assertive presence, and size command more attention than either of the humans. Important dramatic events are thrust into the background; André sees St. Aubin and Christine while Schumacher's wild chase draws attention to the foreground. The motivation for these, and other similar strategies, in *Rules of the Game* is, of course, well known; they are increments of a style of film realism that attempts to promote in the spectator an encounter with the image that is *more like* the way we experience pro-filmic reality than what we find in a standardly composed film. In terms of the Institutional Theory we can add that this style of realism is also a repudiation of the economic-psychological approach to the medium shot. Here, it is important to note that Renoir is employing the same kinds of psychological rules of thumb as Freeburg discussed; at root, medium shot composition is always a matter of directing attention according to these variables. But where attention will be directed, and why, are matters that are open to invention. And in this light, Renoir can be understood as someone who proffered an opposing viewpoint of the significance of the basic structures of the medium shot.

Lang's *Siegfried* represents another kind of repudiation of the economic-psychological approach. Often objects dwarf the human characters; but even more importantly, an astounding number of shots are composed symmetrically so that the eye is drawn away from individual characters to the overall geometric design of the image. Here the effect is unlike realism; our attention is not diffuse; our eye doesn't circle around and scan the image for detail. Rather we first grasp the entire image as a gestalt. Freeburg noted the eye's proclivity to settle on geometric designs. But in *Siegfried* the recognition of this rule of thumb has not led Lang to employ it for the sake of the narrative. Indeed, the apprehension of geometric designs in the imagery contests and at times supersedes the apprehension of characters and events. But Lang has not bungled the job. He has allowed the physical world and an overriding sense of design to loom over his characters in order to express a theme of fatalism. The composition, as it directs attention to overarching gestalts, literalizes the notion that Siegfried is inescapably trapped in the fatal design of destiny. Lang has made attention to the narrative secondary for expressionistic purposes, repudiating the economic-psychological approach in order to make the individual medium shots function as general symbols, not merely representing their referents, but fate as well.

Keaton's *The General* will serve as my one example of amplification. Like *Rules of the Game*, this film is noted for its use of depth of field. Yet, in contrast to *Rules of the Game* or *Playtime*, one would hardly describe one's attention to its composition as diffuse. Again and again, Keaton uses the uniformly articulated railroad tracks to draw our attention from the foreground to the background. In both sectors of the shot we see objects and activities which are interrelated, often setting the stage for some gag.

For instance, one shot in the film begins with a low angle view of the railway track. The roadbed is quite prominent, indeed, rather large given its proximity to the camera. We note that a portion of the track is missing; it had been removed earlier by the Union hijackers. The rhythmic recession of the line of tracks pulls us into the depth of the shot, past the absent rail and further until finally we see Johnny, played by Buster Keaton, pumping the lever on his handcar, wildly in pursuit of his stolen train. The natural pathway of vision here, as dictated by the formal arrangement of compositional elements, leads the spectator from one crucial element in the situation (the missing rail) to the next (Johnny), preparing us for the predictable gag when Johnny and his handcar go careening onto the roadside.

One way to chart the difference between *The General* and *Rules of the Game* is to see what variables of attention the two films rely on. Here, one might note that Keaton favors the use of continuous lines, like diagonals, to draw our eyes into the background, whereas Renoir favors the use of assertive background movement to catch our attention. This sort of analysis is on a par with pointing out that Tati uses color and sound to tell us where to look in his complex medium shots in *Playtime*. But this analysis doesn't get at the fundamental difference between Renoir and Keaton, namely, in *The General* attention is always directed in a very determinate way; the image is not diffuse and the spectator does not scan it for details. Unlike *Rules of the Game* continued viewings of *The General* are not likely to turn up new discoveries of dramatic situations that you literally did not perceive the first time around. In its use of the depth-of-field medium shot and the long-take, *The General* may be a distant ancestor of Renoir's realist style, but strictly speaking it is still an example of the economic-psychological approach, albeit a sophisticated one. What Keaton has done is to amplify that approach by using the diagonal to tackle narrative events whose elements are far apart in space without taking recourse to the use of editing which would have been the solution of most of his contemporaries, like Lloyd. Keaton has not surrendered the principle that the spectator should first see the key narrative elements; rather, he has mastered the use of continuous, recessive linear compositions, including the use of the diagonal, so that the key narrative elements can be widely dispersed, yet still immediately apparent to the audience.

These examples, of course, are not offered as an exhaustive account of the medium shot, but merely as a sketch of the type of analysis the Institutional Theory involves. Such a theory is inextricably bound to history in a way that theories like Arnheim's or Kracauer's are not because the way in which the possibilities of the medium are charted and elucidated are in terms of repetition, amplification, and repudiation, which are essentially historical categories. It is true that a theoretician may conceive of possibilities of the medium that have not yet been actualized and may even predict the appearance of a new use of one of the processes of articulation. This is compatible with and perhaps somewhat facilitated by the Institutional Theory because despite its historicism the analytic categories it employs are developmental. The only constraints the Institutional Theory urges on such predictions are that the hypothesized possibilities grow from the past as amplifications or repudiations. At the same time, though such predictions are not discouraged by the Institutional Theory, they are not essential to it. Setting out and analyzing the possibilities of the articulatory processes of the medium that have emerged so far is an awesome enough task in itself, which in regard to the future of film will at the very least put us in a better position to recognize and understand new possibilities when and if they develop.

VI. Conclusion

The Institutional Theory of Film envisions film as a society – the filmworld as one of the sprawling suburbs of the artworld. Both the older and the newer neighborhoods are governed by certain established procedures. Individual films enter the filmworld and the artworld by three routes, and at each point of entry they are checked to make sure that their relation to what is already in the filmworld is legitimate in terms of whether or not they can be accompanied by an interpretation that meets certain criteria.

The Institutional Theory of Film, as expounded here, is historicist in two respects. Not only does it use historical categories to elaborate the articulatory processes of the medium, but it also tends to analyze the medium from the inside, accepting as basic certain beliefs that are held by citizens of the filmworld, e.g., that film is art, that art intrinsically values the expansion of its own frontiers, etc. I have attempted to put some of these beliefs in order. But some readers may feel that though the theory avoids the blindness toward history and the developmental dimension of the medium found in classical theory, it blunders into an even deeper sort of error. For in its historicism, the Institutional Theory loses sight of what some claim is the fact that art, even the idea of art, and that of film as art are ideological illusions. In setting out the internal logic, the rules, of the filmworld, the Institutional Theory is engaged in an enterprise akin to counting the bones in the skeleton of a phantom. Or so it might be claimed by those for whom theory should not work at attempting to internally reconstruct the protocol of the filmworld, but should view it externally, from the outside, as a machine for propagating bourgeois ideology that is not even understood as such by the people who run it.

To this I can only answer that though I agree that art and film art are in part conduits of ideology, I do not believe that they are merely epiphenomena of an economic system. The filmworld is unquestionably influenced by its position in a wider culture in relation to an economic history and system, but those influences are minted and circulated in the currency of the filmworld by the structure of that institution. I presuppose that the filmworld is semi-autonomous[23] in relation to the economic base of the broader society, and that for this reason it needs to be studied in its own terms. In this sense, the Institutional Theory of Film, with its emphasis on film art as a social institution, does not preclude studies of the relation of film and ideology but prepares for them.

Notes

1. For a statement of Dickie's version of the Institutional Theory see his *Art and the Aesthetic: An Institutional Analysis* (Ithaca: Cornell, 1974). Danto's views are contained in three important papers: "The Artworld," in *Journal of Philosophy* 6 (1964); "Artworks and Real Things," in *Theoria*, Parts 1–3 (1973); "The Transformation of the Commonplace," in *Journal of Aesthetics and Art Criticism* 33 (1974). The anthology, *Culture and Art* (Nyborg: F. Lokkes Forlag, 1976), edited by Lars Aagaard-Mogensen contains many interesting essays against the Institutional Theory as well as key essays by Dickie, Danto and Joseph Margolis in defense of it. The literature is much larger than this, but this is a start.

2. Though film theorists generally seem to follow Munsterberg in treating the processes of articulation as positive instances of the determinant characteristic, in some cases a given process of articulation can be treated as a negative instance or violation, e.g., Bazin's analysis of montage. But in either case what is significant is that the discussion of the process of articulation is related back to the discussion of the determinant feature.

3. By "illusionism" adherents to this position are referring *both* to techniques of pictorial verisimilitude and to the techniques of classical narration. For example, see Stephen Heath, "Narrative Space," in *Screen* 17 (Autumn 1976). For my own part, I wonder whether or not equating narrative and perspective is involved in a subtle perpetuation of the fallacy of equivocation.

4. E.g., Daniel Dayan, "The Tutor-Code of Classical Cinema," in *Film Quarterly* 28 (Fall 1974).

5. In the introduction to *The Major Film Theories* (New York: Oxford, 1976), J. Dudley Andrew writes "Every question about film falls under at least one of the following headings: raw material, methods and techniques, forms and shapes, purpose or value." This is similar to the characterization of film theory that I am offering but it is important to emphasize that Andrew and I differ not simply on the number and wording of the basic questions of film theory but also because I've not only proposed a list of three issues but I've tried to say how the answers to these issues are systematically interrelated. For me, Andrew has offered a description of what film theories usually contain without a specification of the nature of the conceptual connection between each of the answers a theory proposes. By claiming that the determinant characteristic is related to the role of film as a means to an end, and that the articulatory processes are assessed as instances of the determinant characteristic, I would claim that I have offered an analysis of film theory whereas Andrew has offered a broad description of its elements.

6. Weitz's article, which has been widely anthologized, first appeared in the *Journal of Aesthetics and Art Criticism* 15 (1956). Other related articles include: Paul Ziff, "The Task of Defining a Work of Art," in *Philosophical Review* 62 (1953); W. E. Kennick, "Does Traditional Aesthetics Rest on a Mistake?" in *Mind* 67 (1958); Stuart Hampshire, "Logic and Appreciation," in *The World Review* (Oct. 1952); Morris Weitz "Wittgenstein's Aesthetics," in *Language and Aesthetics*, ed. Benjamin Tilghman (Lawrence: University of Kansas Press, 1973). This is only a sample of the literature; in my exposition I have mostly followed Weitz but aspects of some of the other proponents of the open concept are mixed in as well.

7. In *Film Theory and Criticism*, ed. by G. Mast and M. Cohen (New York: Oxford, 1974), p. 267.

8. Dickie, "A Response to Cohen: The Actuality of Art," in *Aesthetics: A Critical Anthology*, ed. by George Dickie and Richard Sclafani (New York: St. Martin's Press, 1977), pp. 196–97.

9. Though there are different roles, one person can play more than one of them.

10. This property can become quite complex. Later I argue that at the very least it involves

the object entering the artworld at a specific time in one of three specifiable ways.

11. The consistent proponent of the open concept theory might retort by saying that the Institutional Theory is merely another example of a time-bound theory that is really criticism attempting to call attention to the important feature of certain beloved objects, the products of Dada and its heritage.

12. For a detailed attack on Dickie's use of the notion of an institution, see Monroe Beardsley, "Is Art Essentially Institutional," in *Culture and Art*.

13. Ted Cohen attacks the nominating analogy as well as other aspects of Dickie's definition in "A Critique of the Institutional Theory of Art: The Possibility of Art," in *Aesthetics: A Critical Anthology*.

14. Dickie, "A Response to Cohen," p. 200.

15. Dickie's very broad notion of an artifact has also been attacked. But I will not consider those criticisms here because, in this paper, I want to apply the Institutional Theory to film which I think is an artifact in the narrowest, least disputable sense of the word.

16. Danto, "The Last Work of Art: Artworks and Real Things," in *Aesthetics: A Critical Anthology*, p. 557.

17. Danto, p. 561.

18. For example, I think that if the interpretation of the object is wrong, and the object has no other historically plausible interpretation, then the object was never an artwork.

19. Paul Ziff, *Semantic Analysis* (Ithaca: Cornell, 1960), p. 242.

20. It is interesting to consider what the distinction between repetition and duplication might mean for works of art whose aesthetic significance rests solely on their propositional import. Perhaps, if the day after *Fountain* was exhibited, someone else attempted to declare their sink art under the interpretation that he or she was illustrating that "anything can become art," we might be able to dismiss them by charging that they were merely duplicating *Fountain*.

21. In "Cinema Space," in *Explorations in Phenomenology* 4 (The Hague: Marinus Nijhoff, 1973), ed. by David Carr and Edward Casey.

22. See *Pictorial Beauty on the Screen* (New York: Benjamin Blom, 1972). This text was originally published in 1923.

23. By using the term "semi-autonomous" I am *not* promoting an "art for art's sake" position (as some readers of this ms. have assumed). I am rather stressing that each art form has an internal history and structure *as well as* a history in relation to broader social and economic developments. Though I am interested in classification rather than evaluation and though I think the word "law" is too strong, I feel an institutional approach is compatible with the thrust of Trotsky's thinking when he writes "a work of art should, in the first place, be judged by its own law, that is, by the law of art" (in *Literature and Revolution* [Ann Arbor: University of Michigan Press, 1971], p. 178). What I want to say is that first we need a taxonomy of the formal possibilities of the medium as they emerge historically. These can then be correlated to shifts within the broader social and economic base.

The following article is a response to an attack upon the present author which appeared in Film Reader *No. 4. The unusual circumstances of the attack are noted below.* Film Reader, *however, has refused to print an unexpurgated version of Carroll's response to Allan which accounts for its appearance here. The opinions expressed in this rejoinder are those of the author, not* Millennium Film Journal. *The article was written in the Winter of 1980.*

I. Introduction

In *Film Reader* No. 4, an article appeared by Blaine Allan entitled "Up Against the Institutional Wall: A Dissenting View." This was an attack of an article in the same volume by me that expounded what I call an Institutional Theory of Film. What follows is an answer to Allan's charges. But before commenting on the substance of his remarks, I would like to point out the questionable manner in which Allan's article was published.

Allan is an editor of *Film Reader*. Obviously he had no idea of writing an article until mine arrived in the mail. Soon after my article was accepted (Fall 1978), my New York editor informed me that *Film Reader* was contemplating a response to it. I thought that that was fine, as long as I was sent a copy of the response and was given the opportunity to rebut it in the same issue. I made this request at least one year before *Film Reader* No. 4 reached its audience. I

received no reply. And I believed that the idea of a rebuttal had been dropped.

Needless to say, I was quite surprised when I got my copy of No. 4. And outraged. This sort of bushwhacking is not unknown in film "scholarship"; it is a trick we are familiar with from *Screen*. Yet I feel I must object that it is not only cowardly but an abuse of an author's right to assume that his/her manuscript has been accepted in the same spirit it was offered. Since the publication of *Film Reader* is erratic, I have no idea how long Allan will enjoy a free ride at my expense. But no matter. There is a larger issue here.

Film journals, if they are to be scholarly, must stop behaving like high school newspapers. I suppose that Allan felt he could abridge my rights as an author because my article offered a clear and present danger to the revolution. That's ridiculous. It's about time that film scholars disabuse themselves of the fantasy that they are on the barricades. We are a comparatively tiny academic enclave addressing each other, not the proletariat. We are not an appropriate audience for sermonizing or sloganeering. Our remarks – even the most incendiary ones – have no impact outside our community. Therefore, we have no recourse to revolutionary ethics, specifically to abrogating the *prima facie* rights of other researchers.

My response to Allan's attack is divided into two parts – "Skirmishes" and "Insularity?" "Skirmishes" is a detailed review of Allan's objections aimed at revealing his faulty reading and reasoning. Since Allan makes many different kinds of errors, this section is somewhat diffuse. Some readers, not interested in dialectical minutiae, may prefer to jump immediately to "Insularity?" which requires less intimate knowledge of either my original article or Allan's. Here I deal with a point Allan often repeats (but never demonstrates). He charges that my approach is insular and "an endorsement of comparative formalism at its most barren," despite the fact that I claim that my theory *only* asserts that the filmworld is a *semi-autonomous* institution and that my approach is propaedeutic to the study of film and ideology.

Allan does not seem to be of a mind for such distinctions, though Edward Buscombe, in the same volume, notes "Noël Carroll's 'Institutional Theory of Film' certainly seems to be materialist in its implications, if not Marxist." And, of course, Buscombe is right. My approach was designed to be compatible with and even to facilitate ideological studies. Buscombe saw and understood the arguments that Allan either wouldn't or couldn't. Since Allan has no arguments – only monotonous assertions – my only means to answer his charges is to elaborately spell out the position on the relations between artistic traditions and ideology that is already in the original text.

II. Skirmishes

Allan begins his attack with a section called "An Illustration," which I presume is a conceit that is meant to be literary. It involves a kind of parable gleaned from *Ways of Seeing*. Since it has very little to do with my position, I will reserve detailed comment. However, this interlude does introduce us to Allan's peculiar style of reasoning. From his own speculation that the artworld would castigate Berger if he destroyed Botticelli's *Mars and Venus*, Allan concludes that this shows "the art work enters into relations of property and economic value." Now it is true that artworks enter such relations, as I explicitly acknowledge in my essay. But to see that as a *conclusion* of the Berger example is a piece of sky-writing. If the artworld punished Berger in such a case, they might certainly have reasons other than economic ones. Allan has forgotten to close off these alternatives in his "argument." Wouldn't Berger be punished or at least reprimanded for such an act in a communist utopia as well as in a capitalistic society? At best this "argument"

is a monumental enthymeme calling for a lot of hard work to adduce the invisible premises. At worst, it is a bit of complacent, though fashionable, rhetoric.[1]

Allan ends his introduction by suggesting that the artworld is thought of "as a natural body or entity operating on our behalf or for our benefit." What does he mean? Does he mean that the people who follow the artworld and even those who merely watch it from afar don't know that money and power are involved? If so, he's just wrong. If he were correct, how would he explain the fact that it has been quite common for a long time in our culture for someone – either inside or outside the art scene – to describe the latest avant-garde "breakthrough" as a money-making scam or a play for notoriety and power? The idea of the spectator lulled into accepting the artifacts of culture as "natural" is a reflex assumption of much current theory. It should be abandoned because it doesn't fit the facts. It is not the audience that's blind; it's the theorists.[2]

Allan's second section is called "A Parallel." He chides Frank Kermode's theory of interpretation – by dredging up E. D. Hirsch's criticisms of it – and suggests that somehow this has something to do with me. But what? I have my own position on interpretation, published a year before Allan's piece appeared,[3] which is not only antithetical to Kermode's but also not susceptible to the "invisible academy" objection. I have enough holes in my own roof without moving into Kermode's funhouse. How is Kermode's "institution" similar to mine in terms of my view of interpretation? Kermode's construct proffers leaders; mine does not. So why does Allan even bother to bring it up?

Allan next veers into praise of a list of disciplines and schools of thought that he believes help us understand film. His claims about Peirce's influence on fields like psychoanalysis seem strained; and Peirce had much more to say than the few snatches ritualistically repeated by semiologists. For example,

I have yet to read applications of his theory of abduction or of truth in any of the fields Allan mentions. When reading Allan's litany of approaches, however, I was struck by one thing. Lifting a phrase from Buscombe, Allan accuses me of hedging my bets when I readily acknowledge that film and art are parts of larger social structures. But what are we to make of Allan's pluralism – he's covered virtually every horse in the race?

Allan ends "A Parallel" by noting

Critical concern for the cinema has centered throughout its history on the place of film within art. The argument assumes that it can reach a resting point once it achieves this goal of locating a particular form within the sphere of art. Clearly it cannot.

I'm confused about what "argument" refers to here. Does he mean my argument or the film-as-art argument in general? Also, where does "Clearly, it cannot" come from? It is an assertion without argument or evidence, high-sounding but hollow. In any case, if Allan takes it that I hold that the study of film reaches a "resting point" once we situate film within the sphere of art, he just didn't read my article. Later he insinuates a similar charge, suggesting that I think our work is done when we find an interpretation that establishes that a given object is a work of art. I recommend that he re-read section V of my essay.

In "Up Against the Wall" Allan launches his frontal assault. He holds that my distinction between "art" and "non-art" is evaluative, not descriptive. Well, that's for him to prove, which, of course, he doesn't. Is determining whether a group of children is playing the game "football" rather than merely running around, tossing a football to and fro, evaluative or descriptive? To me it seems straightforwardly descriptive even though the criteria for whether an activity is or is not a game of football are matters of institutional fact rather than facts of nature. If Allan wants to say that being an instance of art is not like being a super nova, I agree.

But the categorical distinction between being art or non-art is like the institutional distinction between being married or unmarried. And it is a description of me, not an evaluation, that I am a bachelor.

Allan attempts to impute an evaluative dimension to my position by saying that " 'art' occupies a privileged place as subject of examination. . . ." "Privileged" here is nothing but a tendentious equivocation. Botanists "privilege" vegetables in this sense. Do we take them to be saying "Tomatoes = good; gold = bad"?

Allan further asserts that I *legitimatize* art as the filter through which ideology must pass. Now I do say that in terms of film, ideology is expressed, in large part, via selection of some aesthetic options (rather than others) which, in turn, derive from the history of the evolution of film-as-art. Does that mean that I endorse film art as a conduit for ideology? Of course not. If I say people can only be stabbed with sharp objects I have not legitimatized or endorsed the use of sharp objects to stab people. I've said they can only be stabbed one way (with sharp objects) and not that they should be stabbed. Likewise, ideology in film will generally be expressed in relation to the aesthetic traditions of film; but that doesn't entail my advocacy of propagating ideology.

The arguments that Allan brings against George Dickie, whom he accusingly refers to as my "source," are pure bathos. Dickie uses the idea of nominating an alderman as an analogy for asserting something is a work of art. As I point out in my essay, it is a weak analogy for reasons of logic. But Allan blasts it with bluster by changing Dickie's example and ranting on about bossism. Certainly Dickie has a right to his choice of heuristic analogy – which is based on an ideally functioning electoral process. Allan's response resembles someone who upon hearing that a performance was "as tart as a cherry" remembers that he once had a rotten cherry and then accuses his interlocutor of advocating rotten performances. Allan's free associations concerning electoral processes becloud his comprehension of Dickie's point. Allan also seems to believe that an electoral process *as such* is patriarchal and that, *a fortiori*, so is Dickie's theory. Surely, the artworld and government are male dominated. But it is not obvious that they are necessarily patriarchal. Allan might help us with a demonstration. But the trendy oracle is his specialty.

I was surprised that Allan spends so much effort lambasting Dickie, since, though Dickie is a "source" of my position, he is the one that I part company with quite explicitly. Allan writes as though in attacking Dickie he's attacking me. It is as if I criticized Allan for E. D. Hirsch's "intentionalism" even though Allan denies complete affiliation with his source. But even when Allan admits the difference between Dickie's position and mine, he still tries to hang me with the same wayward charges. He says that my theory is also patriarchal because it emphasizes prior traditions. What does this mean? Tradition = patriarchy? Matriarchies have no traditions? Only men are interested in traditions? A nonsexist society would have no traditions? Allan says that I point to traditions rather than to possibilities. False. All I have claimed is that future developments in film will grow out of past developments. I fail to see how that claim grates against the presuppositions of any of the methods Allan enshrines. Allan also says my theory is "too broadly drawn to be effectively applied." But I do apply it in section V of the essay. Whatever Allan found wanting in that application is never stated. Perhaps he means the theory is not capable of churning out reliable predictions. Of course, he's right. But what film theory can? Indeed, should a film theory even attempt such a feat?

Allan has a high old time with a hypothetical, heuristic example of mine about a work by Picasso that I counterfactually imagine was not understood by his compatriots, but which I claimed, given the case as I outlined it, would still be a work of art. Allan seems to take the case as if it actually occurred and then argues for the same conclusion I proposed. Allan's point here eludes me. He does announce, however, that my position amounts to static essentialism without, of course, addressing my point that my candidate for the determinant characteristic of film is anything but essential. Allan's mode of reasoning appears to be (1) look an argument square in the face, (2) ignore its details, (3) find its conclusion, and (4) assert the opposite. I suppose this is a way of manufacturing copy, but it is hardly scholarly, let alone thoughtful.

Allan also objects that my theory removes "any dynamism from the concept of history." What does "dynamism" mean? My categories of repetition, amplification and repudiation all describe modes of moving from one historical point to another. I derived the idea of amplification from the notion that some artists "solve" the formal problems that beset earlier artists while the concept of repudiation comes from the idea that artistic revolutions overturn past canons. Even if Allan feels my approach is "insular," how can he deny that it pertains to processes of change?

Returning to Dickie's theory, Allan snidely remarks that it appears tautological. But for a philosophical definition to be tautological means that it is true in virtue of its logical form (e.g., "P or not-P" is tautology). Dickie's theory may be wrong but it is not a tautology. Allan seems to prefer Danto's view because it is sensitive to historical contexts and he says that this avoids Dickie's problems with circularity. But Allan has not once shown why Dickie's argument that his position is not viciously circular is unsuccessful. At the end of this breakneck review of Dickie and Danto, Allan elliptically asks "Could there have been an 'artworld' prior to 'art'?" Is he asking this of Dickie, Danto, or me? I take it that this question is designed to stump any institutional theorist, so I'll try and answer it from my point of view.

First, it is important to notice that the question is very vague. It might be suggesting that there were artworks before the modern system of the arts was established in the 18th century by people like Crousaz, Batteux, Harris, Baumgarten, Meier, Mendelssohn, Lessing, etc. That is certainly true, but that does not show that there was not an artworld reaching back into antiquity. The *Ut pictura poesis* of Horace, for example, indicates a classical appreciation of the inter-relatedness and natural affinity of different types of artworks before the refinement of a full blown concept of the aesthetic.

Allan might, alternatively, be asking a "chicken or the egg" question, i.e., "Which came first, the artworks or the artworld?" The answer to this, of course, would have to be highly speculative. But my guess is that art, like science, evolved from religion and magic through a gradual process of specialization until the goals of art became sufficiently distinct from religion that art came to constitute its own realm of value – or, less mystically, its own ballpark (the game metaphor is not a slip of the pen). During that time the ways of making, of seeing and of discussing certain religio-magic artifacts and rituals changed concomitantly so that the first art objects – as opposed to purely religious accessories – appeared just as a community of spectators was prepared to talk about them in terms of their non-religiously significant attributes along with their religious ones. Fixing the exact date – if there was *one* – for this event is a job for historians and archaeologists not theorists. The task of theorists is to show how this institution operates once it is in place – and the discussion of its operation *includes* an account of how it produces ideology.

Before moving to the issue of insularity, I would like to point out that Allan's contrast between my position and Perkins' is based on misunderstanding both of us. I do not claim, as Allan alleges, that the "complexity of the medium" is solely a function of there being discrete channels of articulation in film. Furthermore, I have not excluded the spectator from my approach. The extended discussion of the medium long shot in section V explicitly tries to get at some basic structures of composition by reference to spectators. I suppose I shouldn't be bitter; Perkins is also misread. Allan says Perkins chalks up the "sins of the pioneers" to their exclusion of a consideration of spectators. But as I read Perkins the major problem he finds with classical film theory is its attempt to restrict artistic development by proscriptive rules.[4] As for Allan's throwaway observation about Danto's essay on film (an article I don't have space now to disagree with), all I can say is that if Allan thinks it has anything special to say about spectators, he has misconstrued Danto's examples for Danto's point. Indeed, my essay deals with the spectator more than Danto's does.

III. Insularity?

In the preceding section, I did not deal with the objection Allan repeats again and again, viz., that the approach I advocate is insular, a piece of rank formalism. In my original paper, I claim that the filmworld is a *semi-*autonomous community within a broader society. I never deny that issues and trends of society at large are echoed by the filmworld and by the development of the modes of articulation of film. I simply put forth the observation that the trends and issues of the broader society are not transposed whole cloth from the broader society but are mediated by the forms, history and styles of the filmworld.

For example, a certain type of western became popular in the late sixties and early seventies. Called the "professional western," it was beyond the shadow of a doubt an ideological reflection of the post-WWII cult of professionalism. But how could this be? What do a cadre of dirty cowboys have to do with the Ivy-League, button-down-collar boys at Rand? Nothing, if we restrict our vision to an examination of the overt reference of the narrative and the think-tanks of the power elite.

But, of course, we don't restrict our vision this way. We see that the ideological message is mediated by a form. In this case, it is mediated by a genre with all sorts of subtending conventions. The professional western is seen against the background of conventions; it modifies some of these conventions, putting more emphasis on some than on others, dropping some and subverting others. To understand the ideological operation of the professional western, it is necessary to pinpoint the selections it makes from a gamut of existing alternatives.

In some cases, we do this by isolating the alternatives that a film forgoes; in a certain sense, what isn't in a film can sometimes be as important as what is. And a film can also repudiate given alternatives by introducing an unprecedented *contrary* choice to a given alternative (thereby forging a new alternative).

I don't want to claim that the professional western is involved in repudiating alternatives – e.g., Peckinpah's use of slow-motion is rather a formal amplification of the gunfight-as-spectacle that goes back at least to films like *San Antonio*.[5] But I do think that it is impossible to understand how the particular, ideologically charged message of the professional western is expressed without assessing it within the constraints imposed by or against the spectrum of alternatives afforded not only by the classical cinema but particularly by the classical western.

The research program that I urged under the rubric of the Institutional Theory of Film is concerned with designating the various alternatives available along each dimension of articulation in film. Ideological impulses get articulated via selections (and negations) of the forms that are historically available. As I said in my original paper, we need a taxonomy of the formal possibilities of the medium in order to pith the ideological expressions in a certain film. In this respect, since ideological expression – in fact, any type of expression – is constituted, in large part, through selection from or, at least, reaction to historically formed and sedimented gamuts of alternatives, I claim that specification of said gamuts is a methodologically and logically prior task to ideological analysis *per se*. This doesn't in any way preclude ideological analysis; it facilitates it. That is, you need a clear idea of the loci of alternatives in relation to other possibilities before correlating them to specific ideological movements in the broader culture. In the sense that the ideological impulses of the broader society are mediated, in this way, film and, for me, all the arts are *semi*-autonomous. As I said in the original paper, the influences of the broader society are minted and circulated in the currency of the filmworld, by what I called the structure of that institution. Structure, in the context of the original essay, of course, referred to the gamuts of alternatives available within different articulatory processes which are historically interrelated as repetitions, amplifications and repudiations. To the extent that these elective gamuts have their own internal logic and supply their own constraints, and to the extent that they mold the material they convey, they are *semi*-autonomous.

Allan will have none of this. Unlike Buscombe, Allan is incapable of seeing the necessity of the kind of analysis the Institutional Theory, as I propounded it, encourages. Allan never tires of harping on the anti-formalist refrain. Unfortunately, he offers not a single argument to show that my arguments about *semi*-autonomy or methodological priority are mistaken. He just says they are as if it were obvious – and maybe it is within the clerisy he belongs to. But for the rest of us a proof might be nice. Since Allan has not deigned to supply a refutation, my task is somewhat difficult; I have only a sentiment rather than a position to which to respond. Consequently, in what follows I will have to hypothesize as I go along as to what might be the objections to my position.

I want to propose three arguments in favor of the type of research promoted in my original paper. The arguments are interrelated and are generated from a similar strategy, but they are applied to different cases and to different objections. Their general point is that the type of theorizing I advocate is propaedeutic to ideological analysis whether we are talking about the ideological significance of certain motifs, techniques or entire styles (e.g., the theoretical abstraction called the classical cinema).

Before setting out my first argument, I should say that I am assuming a Leninist conception of ideology rather than one based on, say, Marx, Lukacs, Plamenatz, Althusser, Mannheim, etc. This is not because I agree with Lenin's use of the concept; frankly, I feel the idea becomes rather bloated in his writing. Nevertheless, it does seem to me to capture the sense of "ideology" that is most rampant in film studies. Needless to say, the following arguments might have to be reworked in some of their particulars if different concepts of ideology are assumed. I don't have the space to give variant forms of each argument in order to accommodate each different concept of ideology. But I think I could if called upon to do so.

In examining a given film we may ask about the ideological implications of many of a variety of elements – dialogue, character, cuts, composition, lighting, etc. In *The Farmer's Daughter*, the ideological implications of Mr. Finley's drunken, proto-fascist speech, and of Mrs. Morley's and Joseph's immediate reactions as they listen to it requires little analysis. Mr. Finley's speech is composed of Hollywood trigger-phrases for racialism and the actors who play his listeners select stylized, exaggerated gestures of indignation derived from theater. Perhaps Mrs. Morley's role is a bit more complicated. She must signal indignation to the audience, while pretending to listen to Finley approv-

ingly, while also signaling to us that she is only pretending; difficult as this sounds, it is dramatically pulled off by selecting the theatrical techniques of raised eyebrows and glancings aside. In any case, the message is clear – "true Americans don't brook fascism" and the ideological implication feeds off this – "the people who devote their lives to government are instinctively revolted by bigotry." To understand how this implication gets off the ground, so to speak, we have to see what choices in the style of dialogue and gesture were elected from the gamuts of movie dialogue and acting. That is a necessary condition for explaining its operation. Saying this does not disavow the fact that we will also have to examine the use these choices perform in this film.

This is a comparatively simple case because we are concerned with formal alternatives within a dramatic enactment. However, much current film scholarship seems more concerned with the ideological implications of what might be called the non-character-based forms that organize films – editing, lighting, plotting, screen size, composition, etc. How do we isolate the ideological implications here?

Consider the deep-focus photography, episodic open-ended narrative structures and everyday detail of some Italian Neo-Realism. One could correlate this with the post-WWII triumph of liberalism. That is, these choices each evoke ambiguous associations with freedom, pluralism and egalitarianism which, in turn, can be anchored in the liberal creed of the day. Do deep-focus photography and open-ended narrative structures automatically have this import? Of course not. There are many inept, primitive films with the same features, but their deep-focus photography and open-ended narrative structures do not have the non-manifest relational property of being repudiations of a dominant style of filmmaking that emphasizes closed narrative structures and highly directive photography. It is in virtue of their relation to a gamut of stylistic choices that these Neo-Realist tendencies can be correlated to some rough notion of freedom – i.e., they afford a greater degree of freedom and indeterminacy than alternate choices. And this, in turn, can be associated with liberalism.

In my original paper, my example was disjunctive editing. I wrote "a disjunctive cut can only accrue revolutionary significance in virtue of the artistic traditions of continuity editing such a cut rejects." Whether the ideological implication of a given technique is of the nature of an overt expression or of the nature of a symptom, in other words, its articulation hinges on its being elected from the repertory of historically derived options of the sort the Institutional Theory, I set forth, endeavors to categorize.

The preceding discussion enables me to lay out my first argument somewhat abstractly. I have assumed that when we attempt to divine the ideological implication of a given technique we are searching for what it expresses ideologically. Further, I have argued that expression, ideological or otherwise, in any artform, results, in large part, from selection of a specific technique from a field of alternatives. The selection of one alternative rather than others from a historically sedimented array of electives is a necessary condition for any expression, ideological expressions included, and the elucidation of the place of that alternative within a spectrum (which entails an elucidation of the spectrum itself) is a requisite part of or an assumption of the analysis of what has been expressed. The selection of a technique from such a repertoire, in and of itself, is not a sufficient condition for expression, ideological or otherwise. However, every ideological expression will be generated in part through the selection of an option against the backdrop of the possible moves afforded by the traditions of the medium. The Institutional Theory of Film that I proposed takes the investigation of the elective gamuts of the processes of articula-

tion employed in cinema as its research program, using the historical categories of repetition, amplification and repudiation as its means for structuring the options within each articulatory process. Consequently, the Institutional Theory of Film, if completed, would yield information about the necessary conditions of any ideological expression in film (save perhaps for direct address – e.g., an actor looking at the camera and saying "I'm for the nuclear family because it's good for capitalism. Get it?"). The research program I advocate – or one very much like it – is necessary to the adequate analysis of any sort of expression in film and, therefore, to the sub-category of ideological expression. Therefore, it is methodologically prior to ideological analysis *per se*. At the same time it is not inevitably insular, as Allan charges, because it facilitates ideological analysis. I hasten to add that the sense of priority that I have in mind is not temporal -- i.e., that the research I urge must be completed before ideological analyses – but logical – i.e., ideological research presupposes the information available through the type of research I advocate.

Someone concerned with ideological analysis at this point in the history of the field might sniffle at this argument and condescendingly note that what is at issue is not the ideological significance of this or that technique but the ideological significance of the entire apparatus of cinema as it evolved from Renaissance "illusionism" under the power of the rise of capitalism. Personally, I have little faith in such an enterprise since it ignores the heterogeneity (especially the long-standing institutionalized tradition of anti-realism) within not only fine art and cinema, but even Hollywood. Yet, in any case, a proponent of this line might remain unmoved by my first argument holding that it applies to the analysis of techniques whereas it is the entire ensemble of techniques that requires ideological analysis. But even in this case, the approach I've advocated is methodologically prior. The argument for this is like the first one. Namely we can only identify the ideological significance of the canons of Renaissance representation and their putative extension into the design of the camera and techniques of "invisible editing" because we realize that representational styles could and have been otherwise – e.g., medieval or Chinese art. If there were only one way to represent the world in painting and/or film – culture and period notwithstanding – we would not talk about the ideological implication of our representational practices. If we can carry off an analysis of the ideological significance of the evolution of visual art since the Renaissance, we could only do this by contrasting it to other large-scale representational styles. As I said, I am skeptical about the value or success of this sort of project. But if it can succeed it will still require the type of account I've advocated, showing, for example, how the style emerged through the amplification and/or repudiation of existing options including classic, Byzantine, medieval and oriental art. The type of analysis remains the same but the scale of the alternatives becomes greater. Of course, a research program of this scope would no longer be simply an Institutional Theory of Film but a research program under the banner of my version of the Institutional Theory of Art. What is important, however, is that it is still a study of the institutionalized interplay of the options afforded by the traditions of art.

Lastly, both of these arguments might be rejected on the grounds that they assume that when we talk about the ideological implications of film, we are talking about what is *expressed* that is ideological in nature. Instead, it might be said, we should be talking about the ideological effects of films, that is, the ideological beliefs that films *cause* in spectators. On this matter, I believe that we are well advised in film studies to stick with the idea of expression and eschew causal claims, not only because the problems of designing and defining such a program would be hair-raising, but be-

cause, it seems to me, that the phenomenon we are generally concerned with is not accurately or succinctly described by causal models. However, if someone were determined to analyze the ideological implications of film, construing them as causal effects, I would still argue that the type of approach I recommend would be a necessary, methodologically prior aspect of his/her research.

That is, if we are making causal arguments about the effects of given techniques on audiences, we would have to use some form of inductive proof in making our case. For example, suppose we claim that the ideological effect of a smooth eye-line-match is to instill the belief (or illusion) in the spectator that the event so represented is authorless. To argue this we would have to resort to something like Mill's Method of Difference.[6] We would assert that given a normal dialogue scene, where all the variables are held constant save the editing, when eye-line-matches occur the audience believes the film is authorless but whenever the eye-line-matches are either intentionally or accidentally subverted – e.g., the characters look in the wrong direction – the audience believes the film has an author. From this argument we might go on to postulate the psychological, perhaps unconscious, mechanism that gives rise to this phenomenon. And, we might further claim that we performed this entire analysis without ever taking recourse to the elective gamuts stressed so far in this essay. But have we really?

For inductive arguments like Mill's Methods to be of any use, we need a way of isolating ahead of time the factors we intend to vary in our experiments or the factors whose variations we intend to track in our observations. In the above case, we have to choose the eye-line-match as the pertinent independent variable to consider in relation to its contrary stylistic option. That is, in even a short sequence of film there might be hundreds of possible causes for a given effect. We require a way of ascertaining a limited list of possible conditioning properties to which we can apply Mill's Methods (or some variant form of inductive argument) in order to isolate the cause. The only way to accomplish this is to introduce some criteria of pertinence – i.e., some antecedent induction – to the data which enables us to set up a manageable range of independent variables that are worth considering. I think that it is obvious that we would use what I have called the alternatives within the elective gamuts of the processes of articulation as the prime candidates or possible conditioning factors of the effects we are concerned with. Again, I wish to add that I believe that the degree to which causal analysis is appropriate to answering the leading questions of film theory is severely limited. But if ideological analysis is a species of causal analysis, what I have called the Institutional Theory's research program is still unavoidable because it provides the likeliest means for isolating the variables to be considered as possible causes of given ideological effects.

The above arguments on their own do not incontrovertibly prove that the research program I sponsor is methodologically prior to ideological analysis *per se* since a given theorist may have a concept of ideology, a concept of ideological implication or an idea of the scope of investigation different from the ones canvassed above. My intuition is that the basic strategy of these arguments can be extrapolated to accommodate different ideas about ideology, its means of implication and the scope of ideological research. It is Allan's task to show that these arguments for the necessity of the type of analysis I endorse to ideological analysis are invalid, wrong or beside the point (due to their assumptions about ideology or the nature of ideological implication). Until he does that his charges of barren formalism are themselves barren. Moreover, the accusation of insularity is moot if examining the traditional options of the medium is a prerequisite for "non-insular" research.

Allan found himself up against a wall. He huffed and he puffed but he didn't blow it down. Now, if the wall really belongs to me, I wish he'd stop leaning on it.

Notes

1. Before I become the total villain of this piece I should add the disclaimer that though I am a soft-headed socialist I do not dismiss Marxism *tout à fait*. Who could? Too much brilliant, painstaking research – mostly in fields other than cinema – has occurred under its aegis to reject Marxism out of hand, although these achievements, at the same time, do not compel us to accept it uncritically and without large-scale modification. What I do reject is Allan's sloppiness as well as the current presumption that merely by hawking Marxism – either of the professorial or of the journalistic/cheering squad varieties – one makes a contribution to film studies.

2. This objection extends to many aspects of film studies. Obviously, I cannot argue all its ramifications here. However, when confronted by all the supposed illusions spectators suffer, I feel like The Philosopher (Brecht's voice, I take it) in *Messingkauf Dialogues* when he tells The Dramaturg and The Actor that no one labors under the illusions of their fourth wall theory.

3. Noël Carroll, "Organic Analysis," *The Drama Review*, T79.

4. It is true that Perkins ends "The Sins of the Pioneers" by calling for a "definition of film as it exists for the spectator" but I think it is clear, given the rest of the chapter and the one that follows, that "film as it exists for the spectator" means "film as seen," which Perkins, throughout *Film as Film*, wants to argue can only be appreciated in light of certain hermeneutic principles. In fact, these proposed guidelines are for critics, exegetes and prospective connoisseurs, not the viewer at the level of spectatorship that psychoanalytic film theory purportedly investigates. Also, the appearance of the concept of the spectator at the end of "Sins of the Pioneers" is really a red herring since the point of this chapter and of the next, "Minority Reports," is that the great

problem of film theory is "in imposing obligations on the artist." [*Film as Film* (Harmondsworth: Penguin Books, 1972), p. 26.] As Perkins says of past theories, "Each of these positions presupposes a philosophy, a temperament, a vision – terrain which the theorist should leave open for the film-maker to explore and present" (Perkins, 39).

Perkins does have an entire chapter called "Participant Observers" in which he discusses audience identification in order to dispel the puritanical notion that movies are escapist. He argues that the spectator's emotional response is necessary to completing the effect of a given film. But as you read on you realize that Perkins is not concerned with the type of spectator that Allan wants us to talk about – "the spectator as an individual or even in terms of heterogeneous classes" – but rather with the spectator's response as "a key to meaning" (Perkins, 141). Perkins writes "In order to discuss critically we have to find ways of defining not only images, actions and interpretations but also the nature of our involvement. The precise manner in which any spectator involves himself in the action of a movie, the nuances of his alignment with the actions and aspirations of particular characters, will necessarily be controlled by his personality and experience. But critical judgment depends on demonstrating the validity of a response, on showing that it is inherent in the logic of the presentation and therefore depends on a predictability of dominant responses" (Ibid.).

Now Perkins doesn't give us a method for finding "the logic of the presentation" but he does offer examples from Preminger, Mann, Hitchcock, Fuller, etc. And he does show how certain spectator responses are presupposed if the "meaning" in his examples is to be conveyed. I find nothing wrong, in principle, with what Perkins is doing. But it should be clear that the kind of spectator he is discussing is miles away from Allan's. Perkins' spectator is a theoretical invention or critical construct of the probable responses of someone abiding by Perkins' recommendations for and constraints on interpretation. The spectator embodied in this chapter is an explanatory abstraction supporting Perkins' overall hermeneutic program. Perkins' spectator is already a critic – a critic in Perkins' vein – or perhaps the silent partner of such a critic. If the problem with earlier film theorists is that they excluded *real* spectators, then that is a problem for Perkins as well.

5. This claim about Peckinpah may be too strong. The gunfights at the beginning and end of *The Wild Bunch* could possibly be a repudiation of a certain convention of the classical western which we might call the "one slug/one cut" style of editing gunfights. That is, in most classical westerns a character fires a six-shooter (or Winchester, etc.) and, if there is a cut-away, it generally is to the person hit or just missed. In the classical western, in other words, the editing *often* is structured around keeping track of where the bullets fly. Sometimes this gets obsessive; in *Stagecoach*, I think, a character fires twice and there is a cut to two – not one – Indians falling. *The Wild Bunch* rejects this convention; at points the hail of bullets becomes too thick to figure out who is killing whom, and the editing surely does not disambiguate the mayhem. This possible repudiation, moreover, does seem to be an ideological reflection on the times. If the "one slug/one cut" schema correlates to an American vision of the infantry as marksmen (a tenet of faith through the Korean War), then the editing in *The Wild Bunch*, as a repudiation, correlates to the saturation fire fields of Vietnam. I call this a "possible" repudiation because I have not seen *The Wild Bunch* in years and my "memory" may be my imagination.

6. John Stuart Mill, *System of Logic* (London, 1843), 2 Vols. G. H. Von Wright examines the theoretical foundations of Mill's Methods in *A Treatise on Induction and Probability* (Patterson, N. J.: Littlefield, Adams and Co., 1960). I do not mean to suggest that Mill's Methods could be used as a "logic of discovery" nor as an absolute guarantee or proof of causation, but we would use the methods to establish the adequacy of our hypotheses. Some readers may feel that the considerations raised in my third argument are only relevant to experimental research. However, see Hubert M. Blalock Jr., *Causal Inferences in Nonexperimental Research* (New York: Norton Books, 1961).

CHAPTER XXVIII

Toward a Theory
of Film Editing

The material basis of film editing is the cut, the physical joining of two shots. We can easily account for this process with a little chemistry. Of course, there is also in-camera editing. To discuss this we have to add some mechanics to our story. But editing involves more than chemistry and mechanics. It is a means of communication within the social institution of world cinema. It provides a means of articulation whose practice enables filmmakers to convey stories, metaphors and even theories to spectators.

Because editing is a form of communication, there has been a perennial tendency in the history of film theory to associate editing with that paradigm of communication, language. For instance, Pudovkin writes:

Editing is the language of the film director.
Just as in living speech, so one may say in editing: there is a word – the piece of exposed film, the image a phrase – the combination of these pieces.[1]

Here Pudovkin makes the filmmaker's work in editing linguistic, and implicitly the spectator's work becomes a kind of reading.[2] The film/language analogy, of course, has been taken up by more voices than Pudovkin's and though it is highly suggestive, it is susceptible to some rather straightforward objections. In terms of editing, it is often pointed out that there is no grammar in film. A series of shots, for instance, of a gun firing, a man falling and a woman screaming, can come in any order. There is no correct formula for this scene, and, more

importantly, there is no wrong one either. This is a strong disanalogy with language. Further, a shot generally contains more information than a word, or a phrase, thereby challenging the view that the characteristic shot chain is like a string of words or phrases.

These objections, of course, are motivated by a consideration of the standard practice of cinema. We could redirect our manner of making films in such a way that these objections would be subverted. For instance, we could construct a cinematic dictionary – shots tinted in certain colors would be correlated with specific words. We would only use shots tinted to our specifications in making films. Moreover, we could expropriate a grammar from language as well. For example, shots corresponding to personal pronouns should be in their objective case tints, when following shots corresponding to the prepositions "on," or "between." In other words, we could make film a language, the filmmaker a writer and the spectator a reader. But, save such a momentous decision, shot chains are not characteristically sentences either to be written or read.

To understand editing, we must understand it as a form of communication, without attempting to reduce it to a model of writing and reading. But how does this communication take place? How do ideas and attitudes emerge from the sequential flux of disparate images? Whereas montagists analyze the way editing communicates from the point of view of the filmmaker, my approach to this question is to attempt to characterize editing by examining what the spectator must do when confronted with an array of shots.[3] I will consider a wide range of narrative and non-narrative examples asking in each case *what must the spectator's response be as each new shot is added if he or she is to comprehend it?*

Thinking about traditional, commercial, narrative films first, it is important to note that the average spectator does not respond to the addition of shots as individual shots.

Rather, the new shots add information or imagery to an ongoing story. The alternation from one shot to another is neither experienced nor remembered primarily as a discrete physical event, marked by a splice, but is regarded as an increment of information concerning the progress of the narrative. The spectator responds to new shots as sources of new facts or details of facts about the fictional or documentary environment of the story. Most often, the task of the viewer is to incorporate these new facts into a coherent framework with the earlier information that the film supplies. This task is not analogous to reading. Rather, the task engages the viewer's inductive capacities. The viewer must infer the relation between the new material and antecedent information. Editing does not supply the whole story; the very concept of editing implies that it is only a partial representation. The viewer must fill in the gaps. Usually, he or she does this by supposing an account which makes the new information in the shot chain maximally coherent with what he or she already takes to be the facts of the story. The spectator's role involves inference while the filmmaker's involves implication.

For instance, imagine a shot of a rifle going off, followed by a tight close-up of a woman screaming, followed by a shot of a man lying on the ground. These could be innocent details of a carnival scene – a shooting gallery, followed by an image from an exciting rollercoaster ride, followed by a shot of a tired, homeless drunk. But in the context of a mystery, where previous scenes establish threats against the woman's husband, one interprets the shot chain as a murder. This interpretation need not be necessitated by the details of the shots, but rather is the best hypothesis for making those shots coherent in light of what has gone before. The story progresses by prompting the audience to infer the most coherent account of the relation of earlier material to later details.

By arguing that the audience is involved in induction, I am not holding that the operation must be conscious at all times. In most traditional narrative films, the audience assimilates new information through tacit inference. But this reasoning process can become manifest. For instance, in Chaplin's *The Immigrant*, there is a shot of the Tramp from behind. He is sprawled over the rail of a ship and his shoulders are heaving. This shot appears in the context of a scene where other passengers are seasick. One naturally infers that the Tramp is vomiting over the side of the boat. But after that hypothesis is engendered, the Tramp turns around wrestling with a fish. We realize that he had been fishing, not vomiting; when this is revealed, our original judgment about the shot can be seen as a piece of speculation. A moderately thoughtful viewer might even enjoy reviewing the grounds of the earlier inference.

Hitchcock's celebrated red herrings provide even more dramatic examples of our constant process of inference by contravening the audience's natural hypotheses about the ongoing action. In *Strangers on a Train*, one postulates that Guy Haines' wife is murdered in the tunnel of love. Given the narrative context, when we hear her off-screen screams, we presume she is being strangled, though it turns out that she has merely been flirting raucously. Part of Hitchcock's genius is to reveal to the spectator how much tacit inference from the narrative context shapes our comprehension of the indeterminate visual information on the screen. *Suspicion*, of course, is a spectacular example of this.

In most cases the audience's inferences are based on its knowledge of the particulars of the ongoing story. If a character says he is going to his lawyer's office and this is followed by a shot of an office building the audience infers that the lawyer's office is inside. If characters are concerned that a murder witness will be assassinated and there is a close-up of the barrel of a rifle, the audience presumes that it is aimed at the witness. Subsequent information may prove these hypotheses wrong, though in the traditional narrative film the vast majority of the audience's first impressions will be correct. Here, inference is based on weaving the new information into the already patterned design of previous dialogue and action.

The ways that audiences extrapolate from previous action and dialogue to the significance of new details can involve many different factors. The film may simply predict the next sequence, as in the case of the lawyer's office. Or it may insinuate it, as with the assassination. However, even without overt prediction or insinuation, the audience may still infer that Character A murders Character B when it sees an extremely close shot of a knife being plunged into someone's back without either murderer or victim being identifiable. The audience's justification might be that Character B had just cuckolded A. The audience here would be falling back on a family of related ideas to make this judgment, including ideas about human motivation and action in nonfictional contexts, and, perhaps more importantly, ideas about human psychology in popular media, including not only films and novels, but newspapers as well. That is, these sources suggest that being cuckolded provides a motive for murder. If a killing is introduced it is coordinated most easily with antecedent material as the probable outcome or effect of the preceding social situation. Ideas about human behavior, and about human behavior in popular narratives, supply us with schemas to integrate the new details of the decoupage.

Kirsanov's *Brumes d'Automne* is an example of the importance of such schemas in comprehending editing. It is a silent film. There are no inter-titles. The shots include Nadia Sibirskaya burning letters, shots of chimneys and roofs, of rain splashing in a pond and close shots of a man's legs. One infers that the subject of the film is a memory of a past, perhaps lost, love. We are not able to comprehend this simply through the visual imagery. Rather, we refer what we do see to a well-precedented schema of human action. The woman's doleful appearance, the letters, the unidentified man's ambulating and probably departing legs are assimilated as elements of remembering an old affair. That is, the best account of the details of this film is to relate it to a motivated type of action that we already are familiar with. Our activity is not like reading. We must make a judgment about the significance of the film. We infer that the best account of the juxtaposed details is that they represent an instance of remembering an affair, because the film has more elements in common with such an event than with other types of action that we know.

In some cases, earlier scenes do not predict or even suggest later ones. What factors ground the interpretation of the shot chain of a gun firing, the woman screaming and the man prostrate where there is no previous talk of threats nor available action schemas to adduce? The kinds of factors at the audience's disposal, here, may be quite complex. The audience may have a general idea of the kind of film being viewed. That is, we may believe that it is a mystery film and, for that reason, surmise that the likeliest interpretation is of a murder, just because mystery films usually have murders in them. Before the particulars of the mystery emerge, the audience could form the idea that a film is a mystery in a number of ways. Most simply, the film may be advertised as such. Or the music may be of the sort that is commonly associated with mysteries. A Bernard Herrmann score, for instance, is probably a dead give-away. As the film ensues, the type of lighting may become significant, e.g., shadows, mists, and night are associated with one kind of film and not with others. The general tone of the dialogue, apart from what is said, may also be a clue. I am not saying that there is an invariant set of lighting, vocabulary and musical cues that all mystery films employ.

But there are nevertheless conventional approaches to mystery material that are employed often enough that the viewer can infer that the film involves mystery even before the plot is set out. Of course, the viewer can derive pretty sound foreknowledge of the kind of film he or she is about to see easily enough from newspapers, from reviews, advertisements and friends. But whether from sources external to the film, or through conventions the film employs in its earliest portions, including the titles, a spectator can form an idea of the kind of film being watched. And since the spectator also knows what kinds of events such films generally comprise, he or she can use that information to infer the significance of the new details that editing supplies, even where the story itself does not initially afford a hypothesis.

I am not claiming that the only way a film is understood is through inference. Some individual shots are completely self-explanatory, sometimes through dialogue or commentary, or simply through verisimilitude. In editing, however, the new information of new shots must also be assimilated inferentially either in terms of making the new details coherent with the previous particularities of the story or in terms of a conception of the kind of story we are viewing. Here our knowledge of the kinds of events such films and stories involve can be used to interpret new details. We also employ rather broad notions about human psychology, especially human psychology in popular narratives, to help us. In some cases, of course, we may not have enough previous beliefs to grasp the details of the editing – a film, for example, may begin with a mystifying pretitle sequence. Eikhenbaum dubs this situation "the regressive phrase."[4] In this case, we may wait for later sequences to interpret the action – successive events will elucidate the situation. Here, the audience acts retrodictively. Its posture is still inductive and still involved with postulating the most coherent account

between earlier and later material. However, the direction of thought is reversed, using what comes later to explain what happened earlier.

I do not wish to claim that all of the inductions that a spectator performs when confronted with an edited array are exactly alike. Sometimes the spectator will rely simply on the story to render a new detail intelligible. At other times, the grounds the spectator employs are quite different, using knowledge about the kind of film or story being viewed, as well as notions about familiar types of human action, to evolve an interpretation. In all these cases, the aim is to develop a coherent account of the given, often indeterminate visual material that the editing introduces. This is done in terms of something familiar though, of course, what is adduced as a familiar ground for inference may differ from case to case, at one time relying on the preceding story alone, and, at other times, on our knowledge of the kind of story it is. In many cases, we could reach the same interpretation about the new details of the shot chain by several routes, e.g., by relying on the genre or some invocation of a schema of action. This is not problematic. As with most forms of communication, the narrative film is highly redundant.

So far, though I have mentioned some film conventions, I have not discussed editing conventions as such. Among editing conventions we may begin with two broad categories – conventions of subject matter and conventions of narrative presentation. By conventions of subject matter, I am referring to the fact that for the representation of certain events, for instance train trips, certain elements are typically invoked in the editing, e.g., the wheels and pistons of trains. Such typifications of events are abbreviated representations employing salient elements of the event synecdochically. These devices may appear to require a response more akin to reading than to inferring. Against this idea, I would urge several considerations. Though the content of such passages is conventionalized, they seem to be generally understood because of their place in the narrative and not in virtue of being conventions. Moreover, such sequences have a great deal of visual elasticity; numerically different examples of a train trip, for instance, can differ widely in the amount of shots, angles and screen-time involved. They lack the uniformity of a linguistic symbol, like a word, yet they are still understood. Where the narrative does not supply a hypothesis to understand such a sequence, the audience may still comprehend one, not because it has recognized a symbol, but because it has inferred the whole event from some of its salient parts. The question arises as to whether elements, like train wheels, are salient parts because they are conventionalized representations or whether they are used in conventionalized representations because they are salient parts. Obviously the question is a hard one. Most probably there is a reciprocal relation between the two terms of the argument – elements are selected for conventional representations because they are salient, and their salience is heightened by being conventionalized. But even with this compromise, I, at least, still have the intuition that initially the features that are selected by typical approaches to events are selected because those features are the most salient in the culture.

It could be remarked that the types of action schemas mentioned earlier are often conventions of subject matter. I do not disagree, but I do think that since action schemas are such a statistically large subset of this group that they deserve special attention. I should also remark that, for me, the narrating format called the point-of-view is an action schema. Its ultimate theoretical explanation, I believe, is rather simple, though, of course, it may be used in very sophisticated ways by certain filmmakers.

The POV need not have anything to do with audience identification. In *Empire of the Ants* there is a shot where we see a group of humans multiplied scores of times in an image composed of dozens of irises of the people. Given the storyline, we assume that this is a giant, perhaps hungry ant's viewpoint – the multiple irises representing the structure of the eye of the family Formicidae. We do not understand the shot as a result of empathy, nor need it induce empathy or implicate us in the ant's attempt to conquer the world. The whole story about this POV is that postulating it as what the ant is seeing is the best hypothesis for making that shot coherent with the rest of the narrative.

Nor do POV shots have to be spatially plausible. Even if a filmmaker mismatches the eyelines in a POV structure or cuts an object against a glance that enables a character to see something that would normally be impossible for him/her to see (e.g., Wayne seeing Fonda's death in *Fort Apache*), we still infer the POV structure when it affords the most coherent relation of the shots involved to the rest of the narrative.

As you might expect, I do not see the need for a psychoanalytic interpretation of the POV schema; rather like other types of narrative editing it is premised on eliciting a tacit induction in the spectator to the effect that "character x sees y" is the best explanation of the shot interpolation in relation to the narrative. Of course, a given director may use the POV structure in a way that merits careful critical attention. But from the perspective of theory, as distinct from criticism, the analysis of the POV is similar to that of any other action schema.

The second type of editing convention, which I have called conventions of presentation, comprises the type of editing arrays that film theoreticians have often enumerated, including parallel editing, flashbacks and flashforwards. The first point to be made about these structures, one made for instance by Christian Metz, is that it is generally not the case that the narrative is understood in virtue of these structures, but that these structures are understood in virtue of the narrative.[5] Most often, it is because the story has set out psychological conditions where a memory or fantasy is appropriate that we interpret a flashback as such. We don't need music and elaborate fades to grasp a flashback or a flashforward. Consider Roeg's *Don't Look Now*; the fact that the plot concerns clairvoyance is enough to allow us to infer that the funeral that the major character sees is his own. No formal decoration is required; coherence is our basic criterion. We infer that a shot introduces a memory or a fantasy or a premonition because that is the best explanation that this new material has in light of what has gone before.

Though in the general case conventions of presentation do not play a constitutive role, there are some examples where our knowledge of the existence of these forms does enable us to interpret sequences that cannot be coordinated with previous narrative material. For instance, in *Easy Rider*, a shot of a motorcycle burning is inserted in the middle of the film. No narrative preparation is supplied nor do the surrounding, succeeding shots disambiguate it. Here, the viewer must either disregard the shot as senseless and absurd or he must find a way to make it coherent. Because the viewer knows that structures such as flashforwards are part of the repertoire of devices of narration, he may provisionally infer that the shot is a flashforward. The audience's knowledge of structures of narration, such as parallel development or prolepsis, is derived from many sources, including not only film, but historical narratives, newspaper stories, novels and everyday conversation. The film-maker can exploit the audience's knowledge of the practices of narration by inducing the audience to infer that a practice, like the flashforward, must be in operation if the sequence is to make sense. This kind of inference becomes especially important outside the realm of traditional film, as in the avant-garde works of Markopoulos and some of Brakhage.

Most narrative films will simply repeat the types of editing that have been popular since the early twenties. We are so accustomed to these that we assimilate them as effortlessly as we calculate the sum of ten plus twenty-four. But, as the last series of examples might indicate, some narrative editing will demand extremely conscious rather than tacit activity on the part of the spectator. This is theoretically significant, I think, because it suggests that the forms of narrative editing are not set for all time but are open to development specifically because narrative editing fundamentally involves triggering inductive hypotheses in the audience.

For example, more and more recent Hollywood films are employing what might be called high context editing, e.g., elliptically breaking into scenes *in media res* as in *Close Encounters of the Third Kind*. This demands that the audience work harder at constructing the context and meaning of the new shots through inference. This stylistic deviation from the practice of classical editing serves a specific function in *Close Encounters*, enhancing the mysteriousness of the story (in terms of its subject) by using a style that makes transitions from scene to scene puzzle-like. Thus, intensifying the audience's induction activity becomes a way of amplifying the effectiveness of the narrative.

All narrative editing involves induction; but this example suggests that by making the induction more complex through stylistic departures from established editing practices, the aims of a given narrative can be amplified and the techniques available to narrative editing in general can be enriched. At one point in film history, parallel editing amplified the resources of the narrative in just this way.

Since narrative editing is so deeply involved with inference, heightened ellipticality is an almost natural direction for experimentation for it. Recent commercial films like *Looking for Mr. Goodbar* have taken to using unmarked flashbacks, flashforwards and fantasy cuts at a very pronounced frequency. Here the high context style is being exploited in order to achieve a denser sense of a character's psychology or experience by miming the mind's easy movement from the present to remembrance, anticipation, desire or anxiety. In other words, the narrative film's concern with representing characters is amplified in these cases by the high context ellipticality that demands that without the benefit of elaborate markings (like dissolves) or an established context (like a character's remark "I remember. . . .") the audience infer that the new shots are of different temporal orders or fantasies, in virtue of being a representation of a character's thought process.

This is not to suggest that narrative editing can only develop in terms of psychology, i.e. in terms of miming the mental processes of characters. One rarely explored possibility of amplifying the resources of narrative editing would be to cut from what is (in the context of the narrative) to what might be, or to what ought to be. This need not be motivated in terms of a character thinking, or wishing, or fearing what could or should happen. Here the crosscutting would not be over different times but over different modalities, increasing the power of the filmmaker to draw out the moral significance, the irony, contingency, complexity or generality of his or her story.

For instance, a film might establish that a given character is poor and then cut to a new shot or a sequence of shots where he is well dressed, before returning to a scene where he is again poor. The audience will have to deal with this inferentially; since the narrative confirms his poverty, the shots of the character as well dressed will have to be assimilated by postulating that the director is arguing that the character ought to be better off, or perhaps that he could be better off. That is, the interpolation will be rendered coherent in relation to the rest of the narrative by postulating that the shots of the character as well dressed are of an alternate

or parallel modality, either alethic or deontic, to the facts of the story.

Both Bunuel and Rainer have experimented with juxtaposing scenes where the same character is played by different actresses. The audience grasps this technique by inferring these are two possible ways the character might look. In Rainer's case, this use of alternate modalities serves a thematic purpose, suggesting that, since this character could look like more than one person, her situation can be understood as somewhat generic. As with parallel temporal editing, the use of parallel modal editing can amplify the resources of narration precisely by inducing the audience to infer more complicated explanations of the relation of the new shots or sequences of shots to the details of the ongoing stories.

To summarize briefly, in the narrative film, the audience infers the significance of new shots on the basis of the particularities of the story itself. Where this fails, the basis for inference shifts to the kind of film or the kind of story being presented. Human action schemas or part/whole relationships may also serve as grounds for inferring coherence. As well, the audience may postulate the existence of a narrative structure such as a flashforward or what I have called a parallel modality, if other grounds for explaining the new material fail. In each case, the audience operates inductively, seeking the best explanation of the new material, though the various bases for induction may shift.

So far I have discussed predominantly narrative bases for inference, but even in the traditional narrative film there is nonnarrative editing. Often such editing is predicated on emphasizing a particular sensuous quality of the object, event, or state of affairs represented. The barrenness of a desert could be made salient by a brace of shots showing vast stretches of dry wasteland yawning before the horizon line. Or the speed of an event might be accentuated through its representation by a rapid series of brief shots. Or some plastic feature of an object, like its circularity, could be emphasized by following it with shots of other circular objects.

Within narrative films, emphasis by editing on sensuous characteristics is often subordinated to the overall goals of the story. And, of course, a given shot interpolation may be intelligible both in terms of emphasizing sensuous characteristics and under a narrative interpretation. For instance, in *M* both the gangster chief and the minister of police make the same gesture in successive shots. In the context of the narrative, this is grasped within a framework of the parallel development of the two scenes. However the cut also heightens our sense of the visual similarity of the two meetings. Thus, the relation between shots can be overdetermined. Nevertheless, even within the context of the traditional narrative film, a given shot interpolation may have as its sole aim calling attention to sensuous, including rhythmical, qualities of the objects, states of affairs, and events represented. When this occurs the audience must leave off the kinds of inductive bases previously employed and incorporate the new material in terms of the inductive similarities between the basic sensuous qualities between new shots.

Sometimes, where the similarities between the shots are not ones we customarily think about, the new shots may be experienced as subversions of expectation. The spectator may palpably feel the shift from narrative bases for induction to sensuous ones. This, of course, is an effect sought by certain avant-gardists, such as Leger in *Ballet Mecanique* where the whole film is based on foregrounding the sensuous dimensions of objects. In Leger, we infer that movement as such is the key locus of attention. What is important even in this context is that the spectator's relation to the editing is still inductive, though the basis of induction has shifted from a narrative frame-

work to a search for sometimes complex sensuous regularities.

As the Leger example should indicate, editing predicated on drawing attention to sensuous properties can supply the basis for an entire film. In such cases, the audience must not only infer the particular sensuous qualities being emphasized (on the basis of regularities in one's experience of the work) but also infer the significance in the given film of editing solely in order to emphasize the specific sensuous qualities that are being foregrounded. Leger, for instance, used editing to make the physical rather than the functional properties of objects salient in order to call attention to an aspect of the world that is generally submerged in ordinary film practice. Without making this second inference the audience will not grasp the full thrust of the work, which is contingent not only on its internal unities, but also on the relation of those internal unities to other films.

Analogously Brakhage's *Text of Light* uses editing (as well as other strategies) to draw attention to color as such. At one level the spectator identifies pure chroma as the subject of *Text of Light* by inductively generalizing from what is emphasized in each succeeding, out-of-focus shot – a pattern of light and its vicissitudes. At the same time, this approach to color stands in sharp contrast to more traditional uses of color in film. Brakhage's editing, because it stresses color as such, repudiates the narrative use of color as a means for directing the viewer's eye to key narrative elements or as a means of evoking emotive associations. Brakhage's editing additively underlines the sensuous character of color, a feature repressed in most traditional cinematic practice. In order to comprehend the editing in *Text of Light*, the spectator must inductively identify pure chroma as the subject of the film and must further infer that this is a repudiation of traditional (especially narrative) filmmaking. (A similar point has been made about

Robert Breer's single-frame-editing in *66, 69,* and *70.*)[6]

The sensuous regularities that emerge through editing may sometimes be just that and nothing more. Or they may function as a means of repudiating the practices of narrative film by shifting completely from editing based on causal or chronological categories to ones of a more aesthetic nature. In still other cases, sensuous similarities between shots may portend other similarities of a more thematic nature. Vertov, in *Man with a Movie Camera*, compares the activities of the Soviet filmmaker with various exemplary, everyday work processes. The cameraman cranks his camera in a movement analogous to the way that factory workers manipulate certain of their machines. Here the point is a rhetorical one – to posit the Soviet cameraman as a worker, as a proletarian participating on a par with other workers, doing the same kinds of things in the industrialization of the Soviet Union.

Thematically, similarity may also suggest the unity or identity of disparate events and actions. In Eisenstein's *The General Line*, Martha throws down her plow in anguish. This is intercut with a shot of her speaking in favor of the formation of a cooperative. In the latter shot, she defiantly thrusts her fists downward to emphasize a point. The movement is exactly the same as the one in the shot with the plow, suggesting that her anguish and her defiance are both of a piece, parts of the same revolutionary act.

The use of sensuous similarity – whether in terms of the repetition of visual forms or kinds of movement – may have either a formal or a thematic motivation. The spectator tests both possibilities, opting for the one that fits best. The use of similarity to both these ends is, of course, well-precedented in the practice of music, dance, fine art and poetry and the spectator may often derive a coherent framework for a sequence from his or her knowledge of the various formal and thematic functions of similarity in other art forms.

Related to the use of sensuous similarity is the use of categorical similarity. Here the objects or events edited together need not resemble each other in some manifest way, but belong together in virtue of being members of the same category, usually a very culturally entrenched one. Ruttmann, like most practitioners of the city symphony form, employs this format when, for instance, he organizes separate parts of *Berlin* by editing whole sections in terms of shots on a given topic, like going to work or travel or entertainment. To follow this editing, the audience must infer the category that makes all the disparate kinds of things included in a run of shots fall into one sequence. Actually, in *Berlin*, shifting categorical judgments becomes one of the central pleasures of the film, since Ruttmann is often involved in narrowing or broadening the pertinent framework for organizing the shot chain. At one point, it is lunchtime. Initially, this is set out with many shots of people and animals eating. As you begin to settle into eating as the proper categorical framework, then shots of preparing and serving food are included, though in terms of chronological editing these would have come first; and finally images of cleaning dishes and disposing leftovers appear. At each point, the constituency of what belongs in the category of eating lunch is widened, and the spectator inductively responds by supplying a richer, more detailed framework for organizing the shots.

Contrast, especially in terms of culturally significant oppositions such as up/down, fast/slow, large/small, light/dark, organic/mechanical, circular/angular, etc., can also function both formally and/or thematically, emphasizing sensuous qualities through difference or signaling thematic conflicts. In *Sunrise*, Murnau strongly contrasts the illicit love affair in the swamp with the pure love of mother for child, cutting a darkly lit shot of the former against a brightly lit shot of the latter, using a sensuous cue to heighten a dramatic tension. Likewise, high and low angle shots may be alternated in order to articulate the different social positions of various characters.

Flicker films represent a very interesting use of cutting for the sake of contrast. The editing is predicated on a strong tension between looking focally into the screen or looking at it globally as a square block of color or light. In Vicki Z. Peterson's *Etude in R-Y-B: with Film and Electronic Sound* the tendency toward focal attention is heightened by shots that include a human thumb as well as shots of handwritten notes which draw you into the screen as you attempt to read them letter by letter. But these images are counterposed by color fields whose rate of projection makes you see the screen as such, i.e., as a geometric colored surface resembling a minimalist painting. The spectator notes the regularity of this contrast in his or her experience and postulates it as part of the explanation of the coherence of the work. But to understand the full significance of the flicker film, the spectator must also infer its position within the context of the history of film, observing that by juxtaposing focal attention with an apprehension of the screen surface as a gestalt, the flicker film repudiates the presupposition of narrative film (as well as certain avant-garde forms like Surrealism) that cinematic space is "inside" the frame. The dimensionality of the screen, most often repressed in film, is asserted by the flicker film. Indeed, the flicker film is even more complicated than this in its meditation on film space because it characteristically involves an essential third term that I have not even mentioned, viz., the afterimage which is evoked by the pace of cutting. The afterimage figures in the contrast, using editing to manipulate the spectator into locating the space of the image as "off" the screen, in counterpoint to focal attention which places it "in" the screen, or global attention which identifies it "as" the screen.

To fully comprehend a flicker film the spectator must infer not only this contrastive dialectic but also the way in which it undercuts and repudiates simple traditional views of the cinematic space of the shot by suggesting that it is not only contained "in" the frame but also "on" the screen, and, by way of the afterimage, "in" the mind of the beholder as well.

The use of contrast or similarity as a means to understand a shot interpolation may be motivated by the sensuous qualities of the shot or by the types or categories of the events or situations juxtaposed. Rich versus poor was a type of strong editing contrast, developed very early in film history, appearing in Porter's *Kleptomaniac* and Griffith's *Corner in Wheat*. Recognition of strong contrasts of this sort may be based on the narrative or on the fact that the contrast invoked, such as rich versus poor, is deeply embedded in the culture. Often avant-garde films, such as Baillie's earlier works, call upon the viewer to account for the shot interpolations by postulating extended series of thematic, often tendentious oppositions on the basis of culturally motivated contrasts. The accumulation of similar events from shot to shot may also function in this way – Eisenstein in the Odessa Steps sequence emphasizes the deaths of two mothers, two children and a number of old people to suggest, by repetition, the cruelty of the czarist regime, which employs inordinate force to brutalize those who are traditionally thought of as the weakest members of society.

Whether or not a narrative hypothesis accounts for the linkage of shots in editing, similarity and contrast, used either formally or thematically, can provide further grounds for inferring a means to understand a shot interpolation. In the context of certain narratives, the spectator will have to abandon narrative grounds for dealing with the shot chain and use similarity and contrast as the sole basis for induction. Within a thoroughly, non-narrative context, the spectator will, in all probability, even more quickly shift from narrative bases of induction to contrast and similarity as the grounds for inference. Of course, the similarity or contrast invoked, especially in a non-narrative context, may not be patently obvious, as when in *The Dead*, Brakhage unifies the editing of the film through an inventory of poetic images of death which is not based on sensuous similarities, but on not immediately apparent categorical correspondences.

A spectator may also infer unity in a shot interpolation on the basis of an association of the shot chain with a word, a phrase, or a concept. A very obvious example of this occurs when a filmmaker cuts from an emotionally tense scene to a natural scene, generally some sort of landscape, predominated by physical turmoil. A character is angry or a situation is charged, and there are ensuing shots, for instance, of the sea with waves pounding against the shore. The tempestuous sea, as a personification, is inferred as a correlative to the human event. In everyday language, we analogize human actions to the natural world through innumerable metaphors; for instance we might speak of waves of emotion. The filmmaker, as if playing a charade, can attempt to characterize a human event in light of the metaphors of everyday language. He or she does so by presenting a concatenation of images that will evoke the everyday personification sought after. Consider our hypothetical example. We often speak about turbulent seas. In our case, the filmmaker depicts an appropriately turbulent body of water. This is juxtaposed to an emotionally charged event. We surmise that the charged event is also "turbulent" in light of what appears to be a commonality between a plausible description of such a human event and a description of the juxtaposed natural event. Since language is so deeply implicated in this kind of interpretation, one might be tempted to liken the operation to reading, but reading as such is even less in operation here than it is in charades.[7] From a concatenation of images

of nature, the spectator must infer, not read, a description of the natural event, choosing from a variegated set of everyday personifications, the one most appropriate to the dramatic qualities of the portrayed human events.

The play between language and editing is not always as conventional as the above paragraph may suggest. In *Potemkin*, Eisenstein cuts together a series of still images of lions in order to evoke, in a Breughelesque manner, an old Russian proverb to the effect that public matters arousing great moral indignation can make the very stones roar. Eisenstein follows the Odessa Steps massacre with a series of shots of stone lions in different postures in a way that the still shots of the lions appear animated. A stone lion stands up and roars. This is meant to invoke the proverb in the viewer's mind. Attempts like this are frequent in silent Eisenstein. Recall how Eisenstein cuts from images of Kerensky to a peacock. To understand the interpolation, one must remember the saying "proud as a peacock." In *October*, Eisenstein cuts between shots of a new 75mm cannon being lowered off a factory rack and a soldier, thousands of miles away, crouching in his trench. The downward movement of both shots create the sense that the new cannon is being lowered on the soldier. The cannon seems to be "crushing" him; armament manufacture "oppresses" the soldier.

This type of editing is not idiosyncratic to Eisenstein – in Orson Welles' *The Trial*, K.'s being lost in the legal system is emphasized through spatially inconsistent editing in which the spectator becomes spatially disoriented or "lost."[8] In Pabst's *Secrets of the Soul*, Fellman's impotency is suggested through images of the character falling. Nor is this practice restricted to artistic films. The idea of the gunfighter's skill is often articulated by the fast cut that deletes much of the movement between reaching for the weapon and its hitting its target, thereby projecting a kind of fantasy of speed and precision. Nevertheless, as the frequency and complexity of linguistic references increases in proportion to the more chronologically marked and causally oriented editing of straightforward narration, this type of ideational cutting can come to function as a repudiation of narration, seemingly turning away from the short story, the drama and the realistic novel as the models for film, to certain kinds of poetry or essays as the paradigms for cinema.

Concepts, proverbs, words and metaphors can serve as pretexts for editing. Here, editing is a subclass of the larger practice of pictorial communication that Freud calls dramatization.[9] In our examples, the spectator incorporates the shot chain by inferring its reference in language or in the realm of ideas. This is not like reading; it is more akin to the types of induction practiced in charades. Imagery evokes an idea, a metaphor, a word, a phrase, or even, as in the Gods sequence of *October*, an entire philosophical argument.[10]

Of course, the spectator is not free to make any inference he or she chooses for a given shot interpolation. Rather the induction must be constrained in terms of what is plausible to infer in virtue of the rest of the film and in terms of the cultural context of the film. For instance, it is implausible to explain a shot interpolation in a Harry Langdon film in terms of the way it evokes some Taoist metaphor. Both the film and the cultural context of the film can be brought to bear to judge such a hypothesis incoherent. On the other hand, in the case of Eisenstein, a cut based on an ideogram would be eminently plausible.

Before leaving the topic of editing based on linguistic or conceptual inferences, one general point remains to be made: the significance that the spectator attributes to a shot chain need not be built up atomistically with each shot contributing an original element to the whole conception. For example, in Clair's *Entr'acte*, the entire finale, with its myriad shots, may be subsumed under the notion of a race, which, within the context of the whole film, is yet another pejorative metaphor for Parisian bourgeois society.[11] The spectator does not add up the new information in each shot to reach his conception of the shot chain. Rather shots are assimilated under a general hypothesis, the metaphor of the race, that accounts for the shot chain as a whole. I am not claiming that there are never contexts where the spectator incorporates an interpolation in terms of shot-by-shot articulations. Rather I am emphasizing that the shot-by-shot approach is not always (and I suspect only rarely) in operation. In *Entr'acte*, the abrupt shifts in the final quasi-narrative event are all comprehended under the metaphor of the race. Successive shots are integrated into this overarching metaphor rather than the metaphor being deduced additively from the succession of shots. Early in the shot chain, we infer the metaphor of the race as the best explanation of the sequence and then we assimilate the ensuing juxtapositions into this overall notion. Not every new shot adds to our comprehension, nor does the metaphor of the race simply "fall out" of the shot chain; it must be inferred.

The language used by contemporary French theorists to discuss the problem of how the spectator understands editing is highly psychoanalytic. They ask how a shot chain is "sutured," a striking metaphor for the experience of unity the spectator has of the fragments of the events and states of affairs editing represents.[12] Their approach seems to me to have several liabilities. Because they are dealing within a psychoanalytic framework, they develop accounts of the spectator's understanding that rely on notions of the unconscious and repression. They are forced to postulate many complex and ghostly operations in the spectator's unconscious, which, moreover, are repressed. The repressed nature of these ghostly mechanisms makes them difficult to evaluate and confirm. Furthermore, it seems to me that though spectators are often initially unaware of the tacit operations they perform when assimilating editing, they are not in principle unaware of these operations. The French approach is based on the idea of repression; for the audience to understand a shot chain unconscious, repressed operations must take place. The audience is of necessity unawares. This position seems to me to fly in the face of our normal experience of films. Initially unaware of why we inferred a given sense to a shot chain, we can, without reference to earlier psychosexual stages, reconstruct the conditions that led us to the induction that we performed. In Freudian terms, the position that I hold argues that the operations we perform to assimilate edited arrays occur in the realm of conscious or preconscious thought rather than in the unconscious.[13]

Many of the inferences made by audiences are tacit (or if you prefer, "preconscious"). At the same time, the logic of these tacit inductions can be made apparent *sans* psychoanalysis. The audience has certain strategies available for comprehending a shot chain, not only in virtue of familiarity with films, but also perhaps even more importantly, on the basis of knowledge of a broader culture that employs narrative, simile and metaphor in ways that can be mimed in editing. The audience can infer signification in a shot chain on the basis of the story of the film, on the basis of human action schemas, on the basis of linguistic metaphors, on the basis of similarity and contrast between shots, or via the other strategies of interpretation that I have outlined. These strategies or procedures are a repertory of inference tickets which, when combined with the material of the film and the cultural context of the film, license specific hypotheses about the shot chain. It may be that a given shot chain remains systematically ambiguous between two or more interpretations. Indeed, some filmmakers may intentionally strive after this type of ambiguity. But on my account, such a shot chain is not mysterious. We can reconstruct the basis of

its ambiguity in terms of the way it invites the mobilization of different strategies of interpretation. The picture I have stressed is of a viewer sifting through alternative patterns of explanation to hypothesize the best interpretation of succeeding shots. In some cases, it may be that there is no one best interpretation, insofar as two competing explanations may emerge from different applications of the bases of inference, even in light of the direction of the whole film and its cultural context. This is, of course, not something peculiar to film editing, but a feature of many complex communication practices, and a possible source of aesthetic richness as well as annoyance.

Undoubtedly, some readers will be struck by the general absence so far of any sustained discussion of matching shots. For some, matching may appear to be the real foundation of narrative editing. But for me, matching is more a matter of cutting than of editing. As the sequence involving the discussion of acting in Rainer's *Kristina Talking Pictures* demonstrates, the ability to postulate a coherent unity of action rather than the spatial continuity associated with matching is more fundamental to the flow of the narrative.

At the same time, matching can be used nonnarratively; for instance, in one section of *At Land*, Deren matches the movement of different men walking down the roadside in order to identify them in terms of some sort of anaclitic, psychic significance.

Essentially, matched movement cutting is a means of directing the audience's attention to a certain sector of the frame; it is akin to the use of a compositional device like the use of the diagonal in a medium shot. It engenders a definite pathway of audience attention; for instance, if a character moves from right to left in shot A, then the audience will look to the right side of shot B for his entrance. Using this type of cutting to direct attention, however, may or may not serve narrative purposes. It can function metaphorically or even formally (e.g., by developing a strong sense of a line of movement for its own sake). Matching may or may not be incorporated in a narrative, symbolic, or formal program of editing, being a technique of cutting that only takes on significance in the context of the specific films in which it is used.

I have been presenting a limited number of induction bases for the audience to apply to a shot chain. My sketch suggests that the audience, given a shot interpolation, sifts through its package of templates, searching for the best fit. But what if none of them seems to work? Must the spectator consign the shot chain to senselessness? And if this is so, what of the filmmaker who is striving to introduce a new template? How is such an aspiration to be realized within my approach or am I doing nothing more than briefly enumerating traditional lines of editing?

To deal with innovation in editing, I do not think that it is necessary to change our conception of it as a communication practice that functions by eliciting inferences from spectators. We need only make clearer some of the grounds for inference that we have already alluded to.

Consider the editing in a film like *Last Year at Marienbad*. The editing consistently frustrates interpretation along the narrative lines adumbrated so far. Yet, throughout the film we attempt to apply the narrative repertory of induction bases. The film tempts us. A narrative is constantly suggested though it is impossible to nail down. Here, we postulate the hypothesis that the editing is predicated on revealing our standard presuppositions of coherence in works of art as well as detailing what we generally use as the bases for coherence in narrative films. The editing takes on a meditative, reflexive aspect, illuminating our standard modes of inferring significance by eliciting and then frustrating the success of those inductions. For instance, we see a close shot of the female lead and hear a male voice-over; we assume that it is the narrator speaking to the woman onscreen. Suddenly there is a cut to a broader shot in which we see an unidentified couple carrying on the exchange that we had just attributed to the narrator and the female lead. We realize the error of our earlier hypothesis; the editing reveals our assumptions, making us self-consciously aware of our participation in the process of classical narration.

Postulating this kind of significance to the editing in *Last Year at Marienbad* would, of course, be consonant with the reflexive concerns of modernist art, as well as with the reflexive posture of phenomenology. Since modernism and phenomenology constituted dominant currents of the cultural context from which *Last Year at Marienbad* emerged, we can argue that the editing in the film represents an attempt to articulate, in film, recognizable preoccupations of other cultural spheres.

Last Year at Marienbad may defy interpretation along the traditional narrative lines previously outlined, but we can use the social, cultural, and even political context of the film in order to evolve a hypothesis to account for the organization and manipulation of the editing. Of course, such a hypothesis must be plausibly motivated by the cultural context. One should not postulate that an unintelligible cut in a Broncho Billy Anderson film is an example of modernist reflexivity. That would be historically absurd, although the same claim for a Resnais film is patently plausible. Much of the editing of the films in the New American Cinema can be understood as the attempt to articulate broader cultural themes in film form. At different periods in that movement's history, themes of romanticism, of Jungian psychology, phenomenology, and modernist art forms, such as abstract expressionism and minimalism, served as the grounds for editing. This did not require a qualitative change in the spectator's relation to editing. Rather, it required that the spectator infer the significance of shot chains on the basis of broad cultural preoccupations.

Innovative editing, like innovative art, is

involved in part in repudiating traditional artistic and cultural practices and their associated values. The bases for inferring the significance of innovative editing often depends on inferring the traditional practices and associated assumptions that are being repudiated as well as the new concerns that are being introduced in film form. In *Last Year at Marienbad*, what is repudiated is traditional narration in favor of a reflexive stance toward the processes of diegesis that are rarely bared or interrogated in traditional films. Innovative editing most often foregrounds aspects or possibilities of editing that are generally repressed in more traditional editing. In *Last Year at Marienbad*, self-consciousness is the repressed possibility that is being explored. The task of the spectator in such a case is to compare novel editing with more familiar editing in order to discern the difference between the two in regard to how the novel approach reveals and exploits an aspect or possibility of editing that is repressed by more traditional approaches. In order to do this, the spectator must consider both the traditions of film and the concerns of the broader culture in order to infer the place of an example of innovative editing in larger historical frameworks.

Narrative reflexivity, of course, is not the only form that a repudiation can take. *Un Chien Andalou*, for example, defies the audience's attempts to infer narrative coherence in order to foreground the associative possibilities of editing, eschewing the narrative film's reliance on causality and chronology as the basic ordering structures of cinematic succession in favor of patterns of combination that refer to the processes of irrational thought. Whereas shots in *Last Year at Marienbad* are linked non-rationally in respect to the norms of rationality established by narrativity, the cuts in the Bunuel/Dali film are more specifically irrational, alluding to symbolic processes like condensation, displacement and dramatization, occasioning a return of the repressed both

stylistically and thematically. The editing in the central section of *Zorn's Lemma* emphasizes another possibility of editing. Neither narrative, nor reflective on the nature of narrative, nor associative, *Zorn's Lemma* proposes instead that film editing can be predicated on what can be called its own internal logic, a formal system in the strongest sense of the term which relates neither directly nor obliquely to narrative while also not relying on principles of associative thought. This alphabetical system is completely arbitrary – virtually *sui generis* when compared to traditional practices of editing. The central section of the film forges its own formal pattern and replacement rules which the audience identifies inductively not only to order the great diversity of shots, but also to predict the end of the sequence.

The situation of the spectator in regard to each new example of editing is analogous to the museum curator who must decide whether or not a newly made object can be exhibited as a work of art. Both must take into account the traditions of the art form and the culture as a whole, as well as new developments in art and culture, in order to determine whether or not the new object correlates to some recognizable preoccupation of the culture. In most cases, the new object or new example of editing will simply repeat past concerns and forms. Most editing, for example, will fall back on the kinds of narrative, comparative, and contrastive templates discussed earlier. In the case of innovation, however, the relation to traditional forms may be one of amplification or repudiation, where repudiations also correlate to developments in other spheres of the larger culture. For editing, this is a matter of inferring the place of the new example within the framework of existing cinematic and cultural concerns.

To summarize, editing is a communication practice based on cutting which prompts the spectator to infer the significance of a shot chain in terms of the best available account of the shot chain. The grounds of inference are numerous and varied, including several types of narrative considerations, as well as sensuous and thematic comparisons and contrasts, and linguistic and conceptual evocations. These grounds serve as inductive premises, which, when combined with the particularities of the film itself, and the broader historical context of the film, yield hypotheses about the significance of the shot linkages. The spectator may have to sift through his or her repertory of inductive strategies to unpack a sequence; this search is predicated on postulating the most coherent account of the material of the film. In cases where the editing resists interpretation by means of traditional bases of induction, the spectator will have to note how the shot chain relates to film history as a possible amplification or repudiation of more entrenched practices, as well as turning to his or her experience of the culture to find an explanation for the cutting. The spectator will not read this explanation, but infer it. Where no explanation is forthcoming, the spectator will designate the editing as senseless or as a mistake.

I have offered this account from the perspective of the spectator's terminus in the circuit of communication. On the filmmaker, my characterization places the responsibility for eliciting inferences from spectators by cutting. Of course, most filmmakers will demand an even heavier responsibility. Namely, they are determined to elicit a specific, preordained comprehension of the shot chain from the viewer. I do not believe that it is necessary for an intended meaning to be communicated for a cut to be a successful piece of editing. Some shot interpolations may suggest inferences the filmmaker had not planned. Yet, in most cases, it probably is true that the intended communication is conveyed. How is this possible? In our model, the answer is that the filmmaker and viewer, as members of the same institution of world cinema, share the same bases for induction, and more broadly, the same twentieth-century world culture.

Notes

1. V. I. Pudovkin, *Film Technique and Film Acting*, trans. I. Montague (New York: Evergreen Press, 1970), p. 100.
2. By "reading," I am denoting the practice of getting the meaning from a string of symbols solely in virtue of the established association of those symbols with their referents and their combination via a grammar. Throughout this paper it is this rather technical notion of reading that I am attacking. I have no qualms about metaphoric uses of the term reading where it means "interpretation."
3. In part of what follows some of my proposals will overlap with those of Jean Mitry. However, throughout this paper, I have attempted to treat experimental film both more seriously and more sympathetically than does Mitry.
4. Boris Eikenbaum, "Problems of Film Stylistics," trans. T. Aman, *Screen*, Autumn, 1974, p. 24.
5. Christian Metz, *Film and Language*, trans. M. Taylor (New York: Oxford University Press, 1974), p. 47.
6. Lois Mendelson, *Robert Breer: A Study of his Work in the Context of the Modernist Tradition* (New York: an unpublished doctoral dissertation at New York University, 1978), pp. 23–47.
7. I think that charades may sometimes be more like reading than editing is, because in charades one may break words into syllables and virtually "spell" them out.
8. For further elaboration see my "Welles and Kafka," *The Film Reader*, no. 3.
9. Sigmund Freud, *On Dreams*, trans. J. Strachey, (New York Norton, 1952), pp. 40–50.
10. See my "For God and Country," *Artforum*, Jan. 1973.
11. This interpretation is set out in greater length in my "Entr'acte, Paris and Dada," *Millennium Film Journal*, no. 1.
12. For examples of the suture approach see Jean-Pierre Oudart, "La Suture," I and II in *Cahiers du Cinema*, April 1969 and May 1969, and Daniel Dayan, "The Tutor Code of

Classical Cinema," in *Film Quarterly*, Fall 1974. The Oudart article has been translated with an accompanying interpretation by Stephen Heath in *Screen*, Winter, 1977/78.

13. My complaints in this paragraph reflect a general dissatisfaction with the current use of Lacanian psychoanalysis in film theory. To speak very broadly, I feel that this enterprise is founded on a misconception. It presupposes that a film viewer is somehow under the spell of an illusion that verges on a delusion, i.e., what is on the screen is supposedly taken for reality rather than for the artifact it is. Because this approach begins by postulating a spectator in the complex psychological state of in some sense believing or being deceived into believing the film is real while also obviously aware that it is not, it seems appropriate to psychoanalyze him. That is, it seems reasonable to hypothesize that for the spectator to be in the thrall of such an illusion, some mechanism of repression or regression must be operative. But I want to argue that such an illusion does not characterize the spectator's relation to the screen. The idea of film as reality is an extremely theoretical one. At times it sounds as though proponents of the Lacanian line are assuming that something like Bazin's theory of film is an account of the ordinary presuppositions of filmgoers. This seems to me to be highly dubious. In narrative and representational films, I would

submit, the viewer is aware of participating in something like a game. It is true that most spectators cannot always verbally reproduce all the rules or procedures of this game even though they abide by them. But this is no more a matter of repression than the fact that most speakers of a language can't spell out the grammar of the language. Perhaps if it were true that spectators were in the queer psychological state of believing in the untampered re-presentation of pro-filmic reality while watching a film, we would have to psychoanalyze them, showing how they suture the discontinuities of editing through a panoply of subterranean repressive/regressive operations. But the need for such an approach disappears if we do not attribute such a bizarre delusion to the audience, but instead try to outline the tacitly held rules or procedures that the audience employs in playing the institutionally established game of cinema. This essay is an attempt to outline a number of the procedures that the spectator uses in regard to editing.

Moreover, I do believe that the current expropriation of Lacan has been misguided. (N.B.: The foregoing objections are to the *overall assumptions* of suture theory as applied to film. But the approach also has deep problems in terms of *internal coherence*. For a bracing introduction to some of these, see Barry Salt, "The Last of the Suture?" *Film Quarterly*, Summer, 1978.)

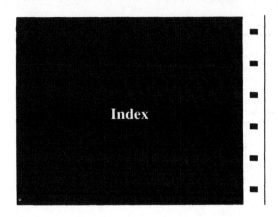

Index

Lightning Source UK Ltd.
Milton Keynes UK
UKOW05f0143100917
308850UK00003B/303/P